The Concept of Equilibrium in Different Economic Traditions

An Historical Investigation

Bert Tieben

SEO Economic Research, Amsterdam, The Netherlands

Edward Elgar
Cheltenham, UK • Northhampton, MA, USA

Figures

Tables

To Pauline

1. Introduction

THE AIM OF THIS BOOK

This book deals with one of the most puzzling concepts of economic science, namely that of economic equilibrium. One may call this concept puzzling, because for what is generally considered a relatively young science it has a remarkably long tradition. The first ideas concerning economic equilibrium can be found in the works of the Ancient Greeks, as will be shown below.

Another puzzling feature of economic equilibrium is its centrality to modern economics. It is said that '[w]herever economics is used or thought about, equilibrium is a central organizing concept' (Hahn 1984, 43). Whether it concerns policy makers or theorists, of the neoclassical, Keynesian or Austrian school, all use some form of equilibrium theory to develop their ideas and support their main theoretical and political claims.

The equilibrium concept has also greatly advanced the mathematization of economics. Mathematical neoclassical general equilibrium theory is considered by many as one of the peak achievements of economics, and finds applications well beyond the domain of economics (for example Rosenberg 1992, 250). Yet no part of economics raises more questions than general equilibrium theory. Philosophers are puzzled by its explanatory role (Hausman 1981a, Rosenberg 1992). General equilibrium theory sets a standard of mathematical sophistication, but its assumptions are in irredeemable conflict with economic reality and the theory is thought by many to have no applications at all (for example Blaug 1992, 161).

For that and other reasons, non neoclassical economists reject this theory as a starting point of economic analysis. They develop alternatives to the neoclassical equilibrium model which are considered more realistic, because they do not rely on the rationality assumption (for example Post Keynesian and Marxist economics) or see equilibrium as a process of never ending change rather than an end-state (Austrian economics and Institutionalists). The equilibrium concept, in other words, is a major cause of controversy between the different schools of economic thought (Caravale 1992 and Lawson 2005).

It is also a very versatile concept. Fritz Machlup (1958) once tried counting the different theoretical manifestations of the equilibrium concept in the economic literature, but ended up complaining about its many meanings. Backhouse (2006, 163) concluded that '[e]quilibrium has become such an extremely elastic notion'. Traditionally, equilibrium is seen as a balance of forces, but it can also be understood as a state of rest or as a tendency towards such a state. In mathematical economics equilibrium is first of all a property of a mathematical model. As a logical concept, it makes no claims about economic reality but solves a system of equations. Others consider equilibrium a metaphor of the harmony or stability of an economic order. It is remarkable that a concept with so many different interpretations could become one of economics' core analytical constructs.

The aim of this book is to clear up some of the puzzles surrounding this concept. Before that task is addressed, it may be worthwhile to have a closer look at some of the points mentioned above; the surprising persistence, centrality and controversial nature of the equilibrium concept.

THE LONG HISTORY OF EQUILIBRIUM THEORY

Equilibrium must be one of the oldest ideas in economics. As early as the sixth century BC Heraclitus of Ephesus (c. 582–507 BC) suggested a circular flow of goods and money, an exchange of 'merchandise for gold, and gold for merchandise' (quoted in Lowry 1974, 434). The idea of circulation between goods and money proved a crucial one and led, amongst others, to the modern formulation of the quantity theory of money.[1] Heraclitus's philosophy is also said to have inspired the idea that the market is a self regulating system (Spiegel 1971, 13). The recognition that a society of self interested individuals need not result in chaos was an important step in the development of economics as a scientific discipline.[2] It suggested that the market society was a separate order which could be explained in terms of a distinct set of laws. Given that order was seen as the profound feature of that society, these explanations took on the form of equilibrium laws.

Another modern equilibrium concept, which has its roots in ancient Greek thought, is that of general economic interdependence. One of the earliest expressions of this idea can be found in the writings of Xenophon (430–354 BC), a student of Socrates. He observed that the price of copper depends on the profitability of the copper trade, suggesting that factor and commodity prices are related through changes in supply (Rothbard 1995, 13). The modern formulation of this idea, mathematical general equilibrium analysis, is considered by many the crowning achievement of economic science.[3]

Further, it is suggested that the idea of equilibrium as stationary prices originates from Aristotle (384–322 BC). He was the first to recognize that traders have a reciprocal benefit from exchange (Lowry 1969). A condition of voluntary exchange is therefore that these benefits are proportional to a certain ratio of, for instance, production expenses.[4] In that case exchange values remain in equilibrium as long as prices cover producers' outlays and so guarantee a continuation of current production levels. This equilibrium concept was the basis of Adam Smith's distinction between natural and market prices (Smith 1937, 55–56).

Centuries later the Scholastics further elaborated upon this idea. Albertus Magnus (1193–1280) was more explicit about the different costs that would determine exchange value. His student Thomas Aquinas (1225–1274) stressed the intensity of human wants as a regulator of value and so brought about the dichotomy of supply and demand theories of price (Ekelund and Hébert 1997, 31). In the sixteenth century, scholastic thinking on economics was carried further by the School of Salamanca. Luis Molina (1535–1600) and Cardinal Juan de Lugo (1583–1660) were two of its key figures. They were responsible for a shift away from the scholastic emphasis on problems of price determination towards a focus on exchange in a supply and demand framework (Rothbard 1995, 101–127).

The French writer Pierre de Boisguilbert (1646–1714) probably introduced the word equilibrium into the economic literature (Spiegel 1975, 614). For him equilibrium signified the hand of God who through his laws had endowed the economy with a specific sense of order (Perrot 1992b). A British contemporary of Boisguilbert, Sir Dudley North (1641–1691), is said to have been one of the first to use the equilibrium concept as an analytical construct. In Cartesian fashion he deduced the equality of the prices of specie and coin money as an equilibrium outcome from the premise that excess demand raises prices while an excess supply tends to reduce them (Letwin 1963).

With the advent of the classical school of economics the deistic overtones of the equilibrium concept gradually disappeared. No longer was equilibrium seen as the product of God's laws, but as a result of the impersonal forces of the market economy. It was recognized that, instead of God's guiding hand, competition would force profit seeking individuals to moderate their selfish greed to a level consistent with a stable economic order. A view common to the classical economic literature was that competition would act like a gravitational force constantly pulling prices to a cost of production level, giving rise to the idea that equilibrium was best seen as a tendency towards that level (for example Smith 1937, 58).

Around this same period the French physician François Quesnay (1694–1774) constructed an arithmetical table of economic relationships – the *Tableau Économique* (1st edition 1758) – showing production and consumption in a condition of perfect balance. The aim of this table was to explain how a unrestricted trade would best guarantee the nation's economic prosperity. With the aid of this table it could be shown that state intervention, for example in the form of taxes or government expenditures, would disturb the precarious balance between consumption and production and cause an inevitable fall of the national product.

Quesnay's Tableau was the basis of Say's law of markets. This law defined an equilibrium condition for the macroeconomy stating that the value of aggregate supply would always equal aggregate demand (Sowell 1972a). This conclusion was contested in the general glut controversy in the early 19th century. Underconsumptionists like Thomas Malthus (1766–1834) and the Swiss historian Simonde de Sismondi (1773–1842) argued that production could well stagnate at a less than full-employment level from a lack of effective demand (Bleaney 1976). Their argument was based on a method of dynamic analysis that we would now call period analysis. This method defined equilibrium in explicit dynamic terms, as a stationary rather than a static state that precludes an analysis of how changes between equilibria take place.

In the meantime, economists struggled to give a satisfactory explanation of market equilibrium because of a failure to distinguish between supply and demand as price-determined and price-determining factors. J.S. Mill (1806–1873) was one of the first to clearly see supply and demand as schedules connecting price and quantities supplied or demanded. Yet for him price theory, a subject he considered by his work 'complete' (Mill 1909, 440), still consisted of three distinct laws of economic value considering the Law of Supply and Demand valid only for goods absolutely limited in supply (ibid., 448). A fully integrated price theory had to await the work of Alfred Marshall (1842–1924) who saw all prices as instances of the same principle of supply and demand. In Marshall's hands, equilibrium theory became a method of dealing with the problem of time in economic analysis. He isolated causes according to their speed of adjustment and analyzed the conditions of market equilibrium in terms of the causes appropriate to the time period under study. He constructed a sequence of equilibria in different time frames each presupposing the attainment of the equilibria of shorter duration. An economy cannot be in a state of long-term equilibrium unless it simultaneously satisfies the conditions of short-term and very short-term market equilibrium.

The introduction of the marginal principle in the second half of the 19th century turned the attention of economists towards a new field of study – microeconomics. From Smith's time onwards, the classical economists had emphasized the problems of the generation and distribution of the national product. Their main concern was the possibility that production would ultimately stagnate in a long-term equilibrium called the stationary state because of a scarcity of natural resources. It was this latter principle – scarcity – which became the heart of the new microeconomics.

For that development to arise, the scarcity principle had to be combined with another principle with a long-standing tradition in economic thought, namely that of rationality. This idea had been part of the hedonistic doctrine which saw human behaviour as the rational pursuit of pleasure and the avoidance of pain (Myers 1983). William Stanley Jevons (1835–1882) translated pleasure and pain into utility terms: goods or activities which give pleasure to people have a positive utility, while pain stands for negative utility (Jevons 1879, 28–33). The scarcity and the rationality principles combined suggest that a rational agent seeks to maximize utility subject to the constraint that his or her resources are limited. A new equilibrium concept had been defined which proved amenable to explicit mathematical treatment. Classical mechanics showed examples of how to solve constrained maximization problems with the use of differential calculus. For Jevons 'the principle of indifference' signifying an equilibrium between choices was a direct analogue of the equilibrium of the lever (ibid., 102–106). Neoclassical economics became the study of making the best use of scarce resources, that is of maximization under constraints. The criterion being maximized and the constraints imposed on the choice would vary from one context to the next: household's consumption and labour supply, firms's production and government policies. But all constrained maximization problems have a common mathematical structure and employ the same equilibrium concept.

Marshall's achievement in the field of price theory was rivalled by that of Léon Walras (1834–1910). Asking if it would be possible for all markets to clear simultaneously, the latter posed a question that would prove crucial to the further development of economic analysis. The emphasis on market interdependencies distinguishes his general equilibrium analysis from Marshall's partial equilibrium approach, which examined the conditions of market clearance for specific markets or industries assuming the behaviour of other markets or industries constant by means of a ceteris paribus clause.

Yet the issue of market interdependencies had been brought up by a host of earlier writers, most notably Boisguilbert, Cantillon, Quesnay, Smith, and Cournot. But the problems raised by the observation that the economic system is a whole – all the parts of which are connected, proved too difficult to solve without the appropriate mathematical techniques. Even Cournot, one of the first to use a differential equation in economics, considered the problem of a general equilibrium of all markets beyond the power of (his) mathematical reasoning (Cournot 1838[1927], 127). The achievement of Walras was that he showed how the problem of general equilibrium could be conceptualized in a system of simultaneous equations. He did not provide a rigorous mathematical solution to the problem of general equilibrium. His 'proofs' consisted in counting the number of known and unknown variables and merely indicate the possibility of providing such a solution.

The existence proof of general economic equilibrium had to await a generation of more able mathematicians and was not found before the 1930s (in Wald 1936). In the meantime in Austria an alternative, non-mathematical formulation of neoclassical economics was developed by Carl Menger (1840–1921) and his students Eugen von Böhm-Bawerk (1851–1914) and Friedrich von Wieser (1851–1926). Menger rejected the notion of an equilibrium state to replace it with the idea that there are structural forces in the market economy continually working to reduce the gap between the quantities demanded and supplied. Out of his concern for the institutions and knowledge conducive to that task grew a subjective variant of the marginal doctrine, analyzing the dynamics of what the orthodox neoclassical would call disequilibrium adjustments. A characteristic of that tradition is the notion that equilibrium theory is a thought experiment allowing one to examine the consequences of real economic forces by comparing their operation to the working of an economy where they are not present, an economy which for that reason cannot be observed in reality and must be considered a utopia. The equilibrium constructs developed by the main Austrian theorists, Schumpeter's circular flow, Mises's evenly rotating economy and Hayek's monetary equilibrium, are what Weber called ideal types.[5]

Yet this Austrian conception of economic equilibrium did not appear so distinct until the 1930s. In 1929 Hayek still saw the equilibrium theory of the Lausanne school as the starting point for all economic explanation (Hayek 1933a, 42n, 86, 95–6). However, by 1933 he started to realize that the perfect competition model underlying this theory was the wrong basis for analyzing the problem of coordination in a decentralized economy. Perfect competition assumes that full coordination has already been obtained and so precludes an analysis of that problem. A proper explanation of the coordination problem requires consideration of the process by which people acquire information and adjust their plans so as to better dovetail their activities. For Hayek equilibrium signified a situation of mutual coordination in which all market participants expect to be able to realize their planned activities (Desai 1994).

The importance of this view was not recognized in a period when the impact of Keynes's economics started to make itself felt. Recent research has shown the problem of coordination to be crucial to Keynes's conception of the economics too (Garretsen 1991). But this point was easily lost in the subsequent (static) neoclassical formulation of his aggregate supply and demand framework, which became the textbook interpretation of the Keynesian model.

In Marshallian fashion, Keynes distinguished between equilibria for different time frames, but emphasized the problems of short-term macroeconomic equilibria, where expectations and output could be assumed constant (Kregel 1976). This choice was not just a matter of convenience. World War I and the Great Depression of the 1930s had caused a feeling that the world economy was inherently unstable and subject to violent shifts. The neoclassical equilibrium construct, stressing the problems of long-term adjustment, overlooked these problems. For that reason Keynes (1936, 3) considered it a 'limiting point of the possible positions of equilibrium'. His aim was to develop a more general notion of economic equilibrium, one which would be able to account for real economic problems such as unemployment. For him unemployment was essentially a problem of the economy as a whole, not a microeconomic problem of market failures.

Yet the choice for the short-term equilibrium construct had also a high pragmatic value. It is suggested that the use of static equilibrium analysis applied to a monetary economy that was out of equilibrium gave Keynes's theory its rigour and simplicity (Kohn 1986). This fact may well explain the quick acceptance of his ideas (Blaug 1991a).

A later generation of Keynesian scholars sought to abandon the concept of equilibrium altogether in order to provide a more rigorous microfoundation for the Keynesian ideas (Leijonhufvud 1968). But their so-called disequilibrium models are better termed 'rationed equilibria' for they employ the technique of constrained optimization (Malinvaud 1977, 5). What distinguishes them from neoclassical equilibrium models is the possibility of trading at non-market clearing prices. But the underlying equilibrium notion is the same: in equilibrium economic agents receive no signals to alter their current choices. Consequently, the economy resides in a position of rest.

The 1970s marked a return to the equilibrium theories of Keynes's classical predecessors. Adopting the hypothesis of rational expectations, Robert Lucas managed to explain aggregate fluctuations of output in terms of an equilibrium model (Kim 1988, Van Zijp 1992). In the new-classical conception of economics markets always clear, even during the phases of the business cycle. Unemployment is a voluntary choice, as market forces keep the labour market at a natural rate of unemployment – a phrase invented by Milton Friedman. To pinpoint the equilibrium the economy is heading for, one only needs to determine this rate.

The introduction of game theoretical concepts helped new-Keynesians explain why individual adjustments are insufficient to clear markets at the macroeconomic level (Cooper and John 1988). The path-breaking work of Arrow and Debreu in the 1950s generated the proof of the existence of general equilibrium, but a similar result is still not found for the issues of stability and uniqueness. The Sonnenschein-Debreu-Mantel results of the 1970s destroyed the initial conjecture of Arrow, Block and Hurwicz (1959) that the tatonnement process was always globally stable. The disappointment caused by these negative results explains the long period of standstill in research in this field (Ingrao and Israel 1990, 343). A parallel development followed a different approach and casted off the straightjacket of tatonnement. This inspired the non-tatonnement process of price adjustment, which allowed for trading at false prices (Fisher 1983).

On a less abstract level, economists prefer the supply and demand framework of Marshall's partial equilibrium approach to causally explain the behaviour of markets (Hausman 1990). Dissenting economists, like the Neo Austrians, criticize these approaches for their mechanical application of mathematical techniques and blind faith in the reliability of econometric testing procedures. But in their turn the dissenters seem unwilling to abandon their version of the equilibrium paradigm (Clark 1987; Vaughn 1992; Caravale 1992, 1997). One may or may not accept Coats's conclusion (1969, 292) that 'economics has been dominated throughout its history by a single paradigm – the theory of economic equilibrium via the market mechanism', but this concept does have a long and continuing history indeed.

THE ALLEGED DOMINANCE OF THE EQUILIBRIUM CONCEPT

Thus the observation that nowadays an economics without the equilibrium concept seems unthinkable, is not surprising. For instance, Hahn (1984, 43) writes that '[w]herever economics is used or thought about, equilibrium is a central organizing idea'. In a similar spirit Klant (1994, 15) says that 'equilibrium, the situation in which supply and demand are equal to each other, is a central concept in economics, and equilibrium analysis the central activity of economists'. What explains the dominance of the equilibrium concept in modern economic theorizing? Hahn argues that equilibrium theory 'make[s] precise the limits of economic analysis' (ibid., 54, 67). In his view, equilibrium theory defines the domain of economics, ruling out disequilibrium as a logical impossibility (Boland 1992, 45). For Hahn, the function of equilibrium theory is to prevent logical errors in economic theorizing and hence the wrong policies that are deduced from them.

The dominance of equilibrium theory in modern economics is reflected in the economic text books. For example, Varian's *Microeconomic Analysis* (1992) explains the workings of the general equilibrium model (henceforth GE model) and its components, even when a general proof of the existence of a general economic equilibrium is considered beyond the scope of the book (Varian 1992, 320). In a likewise manner, modern macroeconomics is an exercise in equilibrium theory. Blanchard and Fischer (1989) adopt a neoclassical benchmark with optimizing agents and competitive markets. A new-Keynesian text such as Romer (1996) may not accept the Walrasian claim that markets clear all the time, but it does proceed from the assumption that aggregate performance has a foundation in optimizing behaviour. Walrasian and non-Walrasian economics alike adopt what Rosenberg (1992) calls an 'extremal strategy'. They are theories expressed in extremal principles according to which the economy's behaviour always minimizes or maximizes the variables reflecting its possible states (Rosenberg 1992, 231). A benefit of a theory based on this principle is that it allows the use of differential calculus to express its leading ideas. Hence, the customary sentence in the preface to most economic textbooks states that a minimal understanding of calculus is required to master its contents. A more substantial consequence of the extremal strategy is that it makes economics an exercise in equilibrium theory. Economic states are explained as the outcomes of optimization procedures which, ceteris paribus, guarantee a continuation of the current situation. According to the GE model, prices remain stationary as long as given conditions, for example technology, preferences and endowments, do not change. In new-Keynesian economics a situation of underemployment will persist as long as real price rigidities prevent workers to allocate available resources between leisure and work differently, and offer more labour at the going wage rate.

The importance of equilibrium theory to contemporary economic research and teaching raises questions about its cognitive status. One can hardly maintain that equilibrium theory is a paradigm case of scientific progress. Yet leading methodologists continue to place the equilibrium concept at the heart of economic science. Hausman (1992) defines the domain of economics in terms of seven fundamental laws which together form its basic equilibrium theory. According to Rosenberg (1992), economics is best viewed as a branch of applied mathematics, which studies the formal conditions of general equilibrium. Like mathematicians, economists emphasize the importance of deductive rigour, and strive to obtain more general proofs of their propositions, without much concern for the usefulness of these results. By best satisfying the demands of deductive rigour GE theory has become 'the most prestigious economics of all and set standards that all economists aspire to reach' (Blaug 1992, 169).

CONTROVERSIES ABOUT EQUILIBRIUM THEORY

However, the example set by GE theory is not appreciated by all economists alike. On the contrary. According to many, GE theory epitomizes much of what is wrong with modern economics. As Blaug observes (ibid.):

> The leading characteristic [of GE theory] has been the endless formalization of purely logical problems without the slightest regard for the production of falsifiable theorems about actual economic behaviour. . . The widespread belief that every economic theory must be fitted into the GE mold if it is to qualify as rigorous science has perhaps been more responsible than any other intellectual force for the purely abstract and nonempirical character of so much of modern economic reasoning.

Similar complaints are voiced by Morishima (1991, 70) who warns that 'GET economists . . . have sunk into excessive mental aestheticism. If this bad habit is not corrected, . . . then the twenty first century will see the degeneration of their subject'. This opinion is shared by another renowned mathematical economist, Maurice Allais, who argues that GE theory has no scientific value and should therefore be rejected, given that it is based on the hypothesis of general convexity of the production fields, 'a hypothesis which is disproved by all the empirical data and leads to absurd consequences' (Allais 1990, 5).

Likewise, in heterodox circles GE theory is an evident target for its lack of empirical support and the unrealism of its assumptions. Neo Austrians consider the neoclassical mainstream a degenerating program, not in the least because of its exclusive emphasis on the analysis of equilibrium states (Rizzo 1996). According to them, 'modern economics is trapped in an ahistorical equilibrium world, unable to render intelligible the purposive action of human beings in the real world' (Boettke, Horwitz and Prychitko 1994, 70). To a large extent Post Keynesians share this Austrian critique of neoclassical equilibrium theory. They also criticize it for its disregard of processes in historical time and point to the importance of uncertainty and institutional change (for example Kaldor 1972, Robinson 1974). But they also reject the notion that market processes move the economy to a predetermined equilibrium, a notion which most Austrians seem to embrace (Clark 1987).

However, the dissenting economists are by no means united in their approach to equilibrium theory. What Coddington (1983) calls 'hydraulic' Keynesians see equilibrium in terms of the stable (statistical) relationships between disembodied and homogenous flows of goods and money in the macroeconomy. A second group of Keynesians wants to dispense with this kind of aggregate analysis and aims to derive Keynesian conclusions from the neoclassical micromodel of rational choice. Their 'reconstituted reductionism' focuses on situations in which prices fail to clear markets, imposing new constraints on individual choice. Finally, focusing on the matters of uncertainty and ignorance, 'fundamentalist' Keynesians reject the aggregate perspective of the former and the mechanical optimizing framework of the latter approach. They go furthest in their rejection of the equilibrium approach, arguing that the economy is inherently unstable or too kaleidic for the equilibrium notion to make sense.

Similarly, Austrian economists are divided about the meaning of the equilibrium concept. Kirzner (1997a and 1997b) embodies a tradition in Austrian economic theory which emphasizes the coordinating function of markets. This function is perceived in dynamic terms, bringing about a greater compatibility of individual plans. Instrumental in this process are the entrepreneurial alertness of economic agents and the dispersion of knowledge through relative price changes. Lachmann (1976a and 1986) and his followers reject the assumption of convergence to a predetermined equilibrium which underlies this view. According to them, there is no reason to expect the equilibrating forces of the market process to dominate the disequilibrating propensity of unexpected changes. What emerges from their reflections is an image of the market as a continuous process without beginning or end, propelled by the interaction between the forces of equilibrium and the forces of change. In Institutionalist circles a similar controversy rages about the applicability of the idea of equilibrium in a world characterized by unpredictable change (Hodgson 1993 and Vromen 1995). This short review of conflicting opinions about the equilibrium concept shows that equilibrium divides the ranks of economists.[6]

THE EQUILIBRIUM CONCEPT IN THE HISTORY OF ECONOMICS

These three aspects of the equilibrium concept – its remarkable persistence in the history of economic thought, the centrality of the equilibrium concept to modern economics, and the fact that many controversies in economics revolve around the concept of economic equilibrium – raise several questions about the history of this concept in economic theory. The most important of these are the following:

1. What is the origin of this concept? The origin of the equilibrium concept in economics is an intriguing question. The ancient Greeks, the earliest writers on economics, were the first to perceive the economy as an equilibrium system. But given that economics as a scientific discipline did not yet exist, it can be asked what led them to view the economy in these terms. Probably, they borrowed an equilibrium concept from philosophy or theology. Concerning the later development of economics, the question arises whether equilibrium as a theoretical tool was developed autonomously, within economics as a science, or whether it was copied from other disciplines such as physics, mathematics, or biology.

2. What does equilibrium mean in economics? The theoretical meanings of the equilibrium concept are manifold. It refers to the equality between quantities supplied and demanded, on specific markets or on a macroeconomic scale. It can be an aspect of the extent to which the expectations of individuals are compatible or of the alertness of entrepreneurs towards unexploited and unrecognized opportunities for profit. In another sense, economic equilibrium reflects a welfare optimum or maximum economic efficiency, but it can also be used to identify a stable (statistical) relationship between aggregate magnitudes. This diversity is reflected in the different backgrounds that equilibrium has as a metaphor. As a physical concept, equilibrium signals a balance between two forces or a position of rest. According to biological metaphors, the economy can be seen as an organism and equilibrium as an aspect of the dynamic relationship between organisms and their environment.
3. What are the methodological functions of equilibrium? As a scientific tool, economic equilibrium performs different methodological functions. In modern economics, equilibrium analysis is a specific form of mathematics which raises questions about its cognitive status. Is it merely an exercise in logic or does it make causal claims about the working of economic forces? Can equilibrium analysis be used to describe certain features of reality or do we need it to support certain normative claims?
4. Did these functions change over time? Needless to say, the function of equilibrium theory and analysis changed over time. The existence of different economic traditions is proof of this fact. Some traditions such as the Austrian school try to revive earlier traditions, while others are based on new developments in equilibrium theory such as the introduction of game theoretic concepts. These traditions or schools of thought adopt the equilibrium concept for different methodological purposes.
5. What explains the persistence of equilibrium concepts? The long tradition of thc cquilibrium concept asks for an explanation: what is the appeal of this concept to economists? There can be scientific reasons such as the idea that equilibrium complies to a scientific criterion, for example that of empirical progressive scientific programs. Another possibility is that equilibrium theory is considered a scientific ideal such as theoretical unification. Normative considerations are a further option explaining the preference for an equilibrium theory.
6. What explains the dominance of equilibrium reasoning in neoclassical theory? Neoclassical theory is considered the pinnacle of equilibrium reasoning. Why are equilibrium concepts so important to this branch of economic science?
7. Why does it arouse such strong criticisms in other schools? The methodology of equilibrium analysis is often a bone of contention between

neoclassical economics and other schools of thought. What explains that combative reputation of non-neoclassical economic traditions in this regard?

These seven questions motivated several studies on the role and development of equilibrium concepts in the history of economic thought.

Milgate's article in the New Palgrave (Milgate 1987) on this subject is an interesting starting point. He attributes the first use of the word equilibrium to James Steuart in 1769 and traces its development to present day equilibrium analysis. The strength of his analysis is that it discusses the changes in the meaning of the concept in economic theory. It contributes little, however, to our understanding of the origin and background of the equilibrium concept. In this regard Lowry (1974) and Spiegel (1975) supplement it by locating the origin of the equilibrium idea in Ancient Greek thought. According to Spiegel, this background has resulted in two separate traditions in GE theory, a 'Platonist' one, stressing the formal aspects of GE theory; and an empiricist tradition, which he calls 'Aristotelian'. The disadvantage of this separation is that it forces the history of the equilibrium concept into these two categories, ignoring those concepts which fall outside their scope.

In this respect, Ingrao and Israel (1990) promise a more general approach. The sub-title of their book *The Invisible Hand* says that it deals with 'economic equilibrium in the history of science'. But this subtitle is misleading, for the subject treated is the history of mathematical GE theory; that is that branch of economics which aims to mathematically prove the existence, stability and uniqueness of a state of general economic equilibrium. Weintraub (1985, 1991) covers the same subject. In his *General Equilibrium Analysis* (1985b) he discusses the development of the existence proof in the GE literature of the period 1930 1954. This case study supports his appraisal of Neo Walrasian economics as a progressive research program in the Lakatosian sense. Surprisingly, this attempt to appraise an economic theory is abandoned in his next book *Stabilizing Dynamics* (1991), where it is argued that 'there is no formula for generating appraisals of work in economics' (Weintraub 1991, 8). What remains is a reconstruction of the literature on equilibrium and dynamics from the 1930s to the present day. These texts, then, are also limited in scope, for their exclusive concern again is the history of mathematical GE theory.

Giocoli (2003) offers an interesting supplement to the history of general equilibrium analysis by discussing the introduction and impact of game theory in economics. He argues that after a delay of 30 years, starting from the second half of the 1970s game theory managed a swift transformation of neoclassical microeconomics. The gist of this turnaround consisted in altering the dominant view on the role of rationality in economic theory. The Nash equilibrium became the embodiment of the idea that economic agents are rational. This formalistic interpretation of the choice theoretic foundation of economics implied an escape from the psychology that occupied earlier neoclassical rationality. But today many economists still find the consequences of this change hard to swallow. As a result, some of them return to the psychological interpretations of rationality of earlier generations. In their view, real human deliberation needs to be the focus of economic theorizing, not some abstract mathematical principle.

Caravale (1992) and Dow (1996) confront different traditions in equilibrium theory. But their analyses focus on contemporary theory and offer no information on the historical development of these traditions. A more historical perspective is provided by Hollander (1987) and Walsh and Gram (1980). Hollander's work on the history of economic thought has but one major theme: to show that classical economics already contained the essential elements of the Walrasian general equilibrium paradigm: the concept of the margin, supply and demand schedules, and a recognition of the relationship between factor and output markets (Hollander 1987, 427–28). Thus a marginalistic revolution never occurred. According to Hollander, the transition to the neoclassical paradigm was gradual, involving a shift of emphasis rather than a sharp break with a past classical tradition. In contrast, Walsh and Gram (1980) argue that such a break did occur. They distinguish between two separate traditions in GE theory, a classical one dealing with the production and distribution of surplus value; and a neoclassical tradition which places the problem of the optimal allocation of scarce resources at the centre of economic analysis.

A thought-provoking contribution to this literature is Clower (1998). In just over 12 pages Clower is able to dissect 'three centuries of demand and supply', as the title of his article runs. Clower's appraisal of the history of economic thought in this field is critical. He denies that three centuries of economic inquiry in terms of supply and demand has given us a better understanding of economic processes. Sarcastically, he notes that there has been 'much growth' in economic theory but 'little development'. What disappoints him most is that economists have systematically ignored the impact of economic institutions and the related logistics of exchange. As a result, they blindly assumed that the economy possesses strong self-adjusting capacities. In particular, markets are assumed to almost always and everywhere work perfectly. Clower investigates the 'diversions' in the history of economic thought that have caused this distorted image of economic reality. In addition, he offers a suggestion to improve our future track record by investigating explicit algorithms for economic exchange in computer simulations. Clower's history of supply and demand theory is clearly one with a message.

Mosini (2006) is a recent addition to the literature on the concept of equilibrium in economics. This book contains essays studying the role of equilibrium in economics from both a historical and philosophical point of view. The historical part focuses on the metaphorical role of equilibrium. This role is assumed to differ between economics and the natural sciences which it is often said to follow (Grattan-Guinness 2006). Further essays in this part concern Smith, Isnard and Cournot. The philosophical part is said to deal with contemporary economics but mainly discusses the methodology of equilibrium economics. In this discussion the question what economists actually do with their equilibrium theories is simply overlooked (for example Lawson 2006 and Backhouse 2006).

Two studies in the Dutch language that must be mentioned in this context are Keesing (1939) and Huussen (1985). Keesing discussed the different conceptions of equilibrium in economics and critically analyzed their function. His general critique was that the use of static concepts of economic equilibrium blocks the progression of scientific knowledge in economics. The reason for this is that, as a static concept, economic equilibrium has paradoxical consequences. This involves the claim that equilibrium theory is both logically consistent in the sense that economic decisions are coordinated and empirically significant because of a supposed real-life tendency towards equilibrium. Keesing advocated a dynamic disequilibrium approach as the best way forward in economics. Huussen analysed the role of the equilibrium concept in economics from a philosophical perspective. His study consists of methodological reflections on its explanatory role in the history of economic thought. He concluded that in a number of specific senses the equilibrium concept plays a pivotal role in economic theory, a role moreover that cannot be replaced by alternative conceptions such as Popper's notion of rationality.

In sum, current texts which deal with the history and meaning of the equilibrium concept address several of the questions listed above. However, the results of these studies are difficult to compare as their focus differs to a large extent. Some focus on a specific tradition in equilibrium theory, for example GE analysis (Kornai 1971; Weintraub 1985b, 1991; Ingrao and Israel 1990), Keynesian theory (Sebastiani 1992; Ertürk 1996), Austrian economics (Rizzo 1979). Others limit the discussion to a specific period, for example the transition from the classical to the neoclassical period (Hollander 1987), or the work of specific economists – for example Adam Smith (Myers 1976) or Léon Walras (van Daal and Jolink 1993). Another feature of these texts is that they define categories of equilibrium analysis which seem mutually exclusive. Spiegel (1975) and Walsh and Gram (1980) are notable examples of this approach. The disadvantage of these definitions is that they artificially constrain the analysis: a concept must fit into one of their categories in order to enter the analysis.

HISTORY OF SCIENCE AND THE SCOPE OF THIS STUDY

Until this point, I have interchangeably used the terms equilibrium concept and equilibrium theory. One may ask if this correspondence is warranted. In my view, concepts and theories are both tools for generating scientific explanations and in that sense not essentially different. Science often makes use of concepts that are themselves the products of theoretical explanation. Nagel (1961, 17) refers to energy and entropy as examples of theoretical concepts that are widely used in scientific explanation, but which lack a direct link with an existing phenomenon.[7] I argue that equilibrium falls in the same category. An equilibrium concept like the balance between supply and demand is an explanatory principle used in many economic theories. Used in this manner, equilibrium is the starting point of theoretical inquiry but often also its end product. For a particular market period, that the quantities supplied S equal the quantities demanded D is a truism, but when we are able to define S and D as functions of the price p, we get the skeleton of a theory. We are now able to state under which conditions price adjustments will be able to bring about the equality of S and D ($S' > 0$ and $D' < 0$ etcetera). Put briefly, one first needs to define the concept ($S = D$) in order to generate a theory which explains it.[8]

How to investigate the historical development of a concept like that of equilibrium (with all its different meanings) in economics? This task must start by recognizing that history is not a value-free science. A history of ideas automatically raises questions about method, because the choice of a subject in a historical analysis is never arbitrary. In the words of Blaug (1975, 234): 'to believe that it is possible to write a history of science "as it actually happened" without in any way revealing our concept of sound economic practice or how good science differs from bad science is to conduct the Inductive Fallacy in the field of intellectual history; by telling the story of past developments one way rather than another we necessarily disclose our view of the nature of scientific explanation.' Put differently, by choosing to deal with one subject rather than another the historian expresses a certain preference of method. Kuhn's warning that all observations are theory-laden applies to historical analysis as well. Just as a prescriptive methodology of science cannot be derived without considering historical facts, the ideal of a value-free, descriptive historiography of science is simply unachievable. As Lakatos (1970, 135) put it, 'Philosophy of science without history of science is empty: history of science without philosophy of science is blind'.

The present study takes this warning seriously. The aim of this book is to investigate the historical development of equilibrium theory in economics as an analytical concept. That means that the focus of the analysis is on the theoretical function of the concepts that in the history of economic thought were addressed as economic equilibrium. In addition, it is asked why in a particular period in history equilibrium theory played the theoretical role it did. Why did Smith believe that market prices would tend towards an equilibrium with natural prices? What was the function of the stationary state in Ricardo's economics? To answer such questions the methodological function of the equilibrium concept must be considered. It then appears, for instance, that Smith used the metaphor of a natural equilibrium because he believed that a free market economy would operate like the parts of a machine working in an orderly fashion. To others, market equilibrium was just an aspect of economic reality that needed explanation.

Methodology in this sense is not what Lakatos meant when he wrote that history of science is 'blind' without the philosophy of science. Lakatos was thinking about the need to express one's methodological convictions as an instrument to guide the selection and analysis of historical topics. In the words of Weintraub (1985b, 55), in order to appraise work in economics 'we first need to say whether it is a theory, a research program or something else entirely'. Here methodology is a meta-theoretical framework consisting of statements about what differentiates good from bad science, what constitutes a progression of knowledge and what not, how to test theories, when to accept or reject them, etcetera.

However, the problem is that economists fundamentally disagree about the nature of economic research and the methodology associated with it. It is therefore impossible to reconstruct the methodology of past economic traditions in terms of a unified framework. This study tries to see the methodology of economic equilibrium theory through the lenses of its original expositors. Inevitably, this approach invokes the aforementioned inductive fallacy. I realize that, in a sense, the history of science and the philosophy of science are both blind because they lack a trustworthy compass. However, I also believe that good history and good philosophy of science ultimately find their audience. Why is Schumpeter's *History of Economic Analysis* still an authoritative text, more than sixty years after its publication? Not because of his philosophical framework, which can be criticized for its excessive faith in the progress of science, but because of Schumpeter's unique blend of economic and historical scholarship that keeps arousing the interest of readers. In similar vein, I hope that historians and economists are persuaded by this narrative that the history and philosophy of science may be blind but that they are not empty.

The lessons that are to be learned from the history and methodology of equilibrium theory in economics are of a diverse nature. In the first place, there is the question of the definitions of economic equilibrium. Chapter 2 explores this issue. Secondly, Chapter 3 studies the nature of neoclassical equilibrium theory – the most dominant branch in modern economics – from a methodological perspective. This chapter shows why there is no unified methodological framework to assess economic theories. But it also argues that the disagreement about the standards of science need not be a problem. Different methodological approaches generate different explanations about the function and importance of neoclassical equilibrium theory, each of which has to be considered on its own merits.

The third topic of this book is the historical development of equilibrium theory in economics which is discussed in the subsequent nine chapters. Chapter 4 addresses the origins of the equilibrium concept in economics. This chapter investigates whether North and Boisguilbert deserve their credits as pioneers of equilibrium analysis. Chapter 5 examines the first graphical model of economic equilibrium, the tableau économique of François Quesnay and the physiocrats. This conception of economic equilibrium is compared to the work of Richard Cantillon who is often considered a predecessor of the physiocrats. However, the analysis will show that his ideas about the nature of economic equilibrium are in some respects the exact opposite of physiocratic analysis. Chapter 6 introduces the work of Adam Smith. He is in popular parlance the founding father of modern economics, but also a perfect example of the many scientific influences that directed the development of economic theory. This inheritance is demonstrated by looking into the natural metaphors that played a role in Smith's analysis of economic equilibrium.

Chapter 7 takes the analysis a step further in time and addresses the statics and dynamics of classical economics. This chapter focuses on the controversy around Say's law of markets in the early nineteenth century. It is argued that this controversy highlights a number of issues surrounding the use of the equilibrium concept in classical economics. Firstly, modern reconstructions of classical economics in terms of a static theory of general economic equilibrium ignore the fact that Ricardo and his followers saw equilibrium as a dynamic tendency towards an equality of aggregate supply and demand. Secondly, the opponents of the Ricardian School in the glut controversy endorsed the view that real economies in those days lacked the capacity to automatically restore an imbalance between aggregate supply and demand. In that sense the glut controversy can be seen as a debate about the nature of economic equilibrium.

Chapters 8 and 9 discuss the relationship between equilibrium theory and mathematical economics. The introduction of mathematics greatly facilitated the development of neoclassical equilibrium economics. However I argue that what I call the mathematical transformation of equilibrium theory also pushed economic analysis into a direction that led to a neglect of typical features of classical economics, such as the notion that equilibrium represents a dynamic tendency of market forces through historical time.

Chapter 10 addresses the subjectivist challenge of the Austrian school, which contributed to neoclassical revolution of the 1870s from a non-mathematical angle. Nowadays, this school is defined in terms of the market process approach, which places the issue of coordination of decentralized decision at the core of its analysis. In this chapter, I shall discuss the roots of this tradition. In particular, I will argue that the founding fathers – Menger, Böhm-Bawerk and Wieser – developed their subjectivist challenge in very diverse directions with profound effects on their conception of equilibrium.

Chapter 11 focusses on the troublesome relationship between equilibrium theory and monetary theory. Due to the influence of the quantity theory, money is generally seen as a veil which can safely be removed to expose the underlying mechanism of real economic equilibrium. It is not for nothing that large parts of economic theory are couched up in real terms and treat nominal changes as transitory effects. This chapter discusses the tensions between the static and dynamic interpretations of the quantity theory in the history of economic thought. It argues that there never was a full victory of real over monetary analysis. Economists have always felt the need to account for the complex dynamics between the monetary and real sectors of the economy, but they have also experienced the theoretical problems of explaining this connection. In those cases, static equilibrium theory often formed a convenient instrument to reduce the complexity of the question to more manageable size. I shall address Keynes's use of this 'short cut' to the analysis of a monetary economy, as well as the attempts of modern theory to integrate money into the framework of general equilibrium analysis.

Chapter 12 investigates the innovating work of the Swedish and Austrian schools in the field of monetary theory. These schools did take the difficult road towards a dynamic analysis of monetary changes. The result was a reformulation of the concept of equilibrium. I shall discuss the theoretical developments linking equilibrium with monetary dynamics in these approaches. I shall also argue that it proved an unsuccessful revolution. The issues addressed were challenging, but the Swedish and Austrian approaches towards monetary dynamics did not gain a wide audience. This chapter explores the reasons of this failure.

The subsequent four chapters investigate the prospects of equilibrium theory through the lense of its negation. If equilibrium theory is considered a troublesome venue, for both theoretical and methodological reasons, then what can economics achieve by putting the analysis of disequilibrium centre stage? I will discuss several traditions in economics, who believe that they are carrying forward economic analysis in this direction. This brings into focus the Post Keynesian school and its call to take seriously the impact of uncertainty in economics (Chapter 13). The Austrian school follows a similar line of argumentation but substitutes a microeconomic point of view for the

Keynesian focus on macroeconomics. The Austrian theory of entrepreneurship as part of their process-oriented approach to economics is the subject of Chapter 14. Chapter 15 then introduces themes that unite several heterodox schools in economics, evolution and institutions. It is here that new ground in uncovered for making disequilibrium a more important concept than equilibrium. Meanwhile in neoclassical economics one does not rest content with the present state of equilibrium theorizing. Chapter 16 discusses the efforts to strengthen the disequilibrium foundations of equilibrium analysis within the neoclassical mainstream.

In spite of these efforts the main finding of these chapters is that the disequilibrium revolution rebounces. Even the harshest critics of equilibrium theory fail to develop an alternative without applying some kind of equilibrium concept. The challenge of disequilibrium theory so paradoxically underlines the centrality of equilibrium to economics.

Chapter 17 concludes this book with the ultimate question: Which way forward in economics: equilibrium of disequilibrium theory? The answer is that a definitive anser cannot be given, but that a horses-for-courses approach is called for, combining the insights of both theories.

NOTES

1. For a history of monetary theory and the development of the quantity theory in particular, see Vickers (1959), Laidler (1991) and Chapter 12.
2. Ekelund and Hébert (1997, 119) consider the perception 'of a natural order to society, existing in the absence of any form of central planning . . . one of the most liberating ideas ever to emerge in the history of economic thought'. An idea, moreover, which 'shunted economic analysis onto a new path'.
3. Schumpeter's unbounded admiration for Walras's general equilibrium economics is well-known. In his *History of Economic Analysis,* he called Walras's work the 'Magna Charta of economic theory' (Schumpeter 1954, 242, 968).
4. It must be stressed that Aristotle was by no means clear about what exactly determined this ratio. For a long time the usual interpretation was that Aristotle used relative labour costs to determine exchange values (Spiegel 1971, 32). More recently, commentators have argued that Aristotle's 'proportional reciprocity' refers to differences in subjective perceptions of utility (Lowry 1969). Finally, Rothbard (1995, 16) maintains that the entire construction is bogus, for Aristotle writes that 'the number of shoes exchanged for a house must . . . correspond to the ratio of builder to shoemaker'. But how can there possibly be a ratio between builders and shoemakers? In what units are we supposed to express such a ratio? Rothbard argues that this ratio has no meaning and that this particular exercise should be dismissed as an unfortunate example of 'Phytagorean quantophrenia' (ibid.).

5. I use this phrase with some hesitation, as Weber's ideal types were part of a specific methodology which in some respects (for example testing ideal types) was in complete contradiction to the approach of the Austrian school. See Klant (1972, 135–143).
6. Caravale (1992, 75) likewise points to the fact that different conceptions of equilibrium are often not made explicit in economic discourse. He remarks that, as a result, equilibrium forms the source of considerable confusion: 'Very frequently theoretical controversies between individual economists and between schools of thought are in fact made more intractable by existing differences in the conceptions of economic equilibrium, which are not clearly spelled out, and in the roles assigned to the notion of economic equilibrium.' See also Lawson (2005) and Lawson (2006).
7. A link of this kind requires additional rules of correspondence, such as experimental procedures for identifying or measuring specific physical properties. See Nagel (1961, 17).
8. Equilibrium is therefore both input and output for scientific explanation, which sometimes breeds confusion. An example is Hausman's (1992) definition of equilibrium theory in terms of seven 'laws' which themselves qualify as equilibrium theory, such as neoclassical consumer choice theory and the theory of the firm. See Hausman (1992, 53) and Chapter 3.

2. What is Equilibrium?

INTRODUCTION

The first question to be addressed in this book is what equilibrium means. This is by no means an easy task, given that economic theory abounds in different conceptions of economic equilibrium. Fritz Machlup (1958) once tried organizing them, but ended up complaining about their many meanings. And this was fifty years ago, long before mathematical economists working in game theory started developing refinements of the Nash equilibrium, which resulted in many new equilibrium concepts. Is there no way to structure this complex heap of different definitions and develop a more workable perspective on equilibrium theory? I believe there is.[1] The purpose of this chapter is to introduce several distinctions concerning the definition of economic equilibrium that I shall use throughout this book and that allow me to present the history of equilibrium theory in economics in a structured manner. One of the key distinctions that plays a role in this history is that between equilibrium as an end-state and equilibrium as a process. I shall explain this distinction and its implications in the next subsection.

Looking at equilibrium theory in this way suggests that the element of time plays a crucial role in our in perception of what equilibrium means. As Rizzo (1979, 2) says, economists do not really have a choice as to whether they will use equilibrium concepts. The notion of equilibrium is an indispensable tool of analysis, because there is no means of studying complex phenomena other than by first abstracting from change altogether. Marshall (1920) was the first to realize the usefulness of equilibrium theory in this sense and to relate the definition of economic equilibrium to the time frame of the question at hand. This suggests a close link between the definition of equilibrium and the statics-dynamics distinction, which I shall discuss further on in this chapter. One of the key notions here is that of equilibrium as a stationary position, which can be seen as a dynamic definition of equilibrium. This chapter aims to clarify the complex relationship between the definition of economic equilibrium and the treatment of time in economic theory.

Finally, I shall elaborate on the implications of these distinctions for the main subject of this book, the history of equilibrium theory. I shall argue that to write this history we need more than a list of possible definitions and their development over time. We need to understand the vision that lurks behind these definitions. I shall explain this point in the closing section of this chapter.

EQUILIBRIUM AS AN END-STATE VERSUS THE PROCESS APPROACH

The basic notion of equilibrium in economics is that of the equality between the quantities supplied and demanded in a particular market. Every economist learns that market equilibrium is represented by the point of intersection of the respective supply and demand curves. Such curves are often of the following shape. Demand Q_d is generally assumed to be a negatively sloped function of price *p*. Hence, the demand function is:

$$Q_d = f(p) \text{ with the first derivative } f'(p)<0.$$

Contrariwise, the quantity supplied Q_s is assumed to be a positively sloped function of price p, or:

$$Q_s = g(p) \text{ with } g'(p)>0.$$

Market equilibrium obtains when:

$$Q_d = Q_s.$$

How should we interpret this equilibrium? We can approach this question by calculating the price which allows the quantities supplied and demanded to become equal. This can be done by a simple mathematical exercise – equating functions *f* and *g* and solving for *p* – which gives us the equilibrium values for price *p* and the quantity traded at this price, *q*. Equilibrium is thus the point (p^*,q^*) in two dimensional space $\mathbb{R}^2$. I mention this point, because it can be generalized to the case of a multimarket economy. Suppose our exchange economy consists of *n* commodities. We have a general equilibrium when supply equals demand on all *n* markets. This means we have to replace the scalars *p* and *q* by vectors representing $\{p_1, p_2, \dots p_n\}$ and $\{q_1, q_2, \dots q_n\}$ respectively. But this does not alter the nature of the equilibrium solution. It still represents a point $(\mathbf{p}^*,\mathbf{q}^*)$, but now in n-dimensional space $\mathbb{R}^n$ with[2]

$$\sum_i f_i(\mathbf{p}) = \sum_i g_i(\mathbf{p}) \forall i \in \{1,2,\cdots n\}$$

This mathematical representation of market or general equilibrium can be used to discuss the difference between equilibrium seen as an end-state and the process approach to equilibrium. The key to this difference is the explanation of price and quantity adjustment that lurks behind the equilibrium solution. Hausman (1990) argues that supply and demand curves in this neoclassical setting are instruments of a causal explanation of price determination. He says that we may speak of causal analysis in this case, because neoclassical price theory distinguishes between causes (anything effecting the shape of supply and demand curves) and effects (prices and quantities traded) even when we abstract from the actual sequence of events in that sequence. According to Hausman, in the background of supply and demand analysis, in both partial and general equilibrium analysis, there is an 'implicit temporal story' about how prices are formed.[3] Is Hausman right? I believe that he misses a crucial point, namely that supply and demand curves do not always give us sufficient information to explain the trajectory from disequilibrium to equilibrium prices. The implicit temporal story that he refers to may have some awkward surprises, which remain hidden if one does not explicate this process. In other words, there is a difference between the process pushing prices towards equilibrium and the equilibrium position that it finally reaches. I shall argue that this difference gives us two conceptions of economic equilibrium, which are of great importance to the history of equilibrium theory.

The Edgeworth box can be used to explain this difference. This box shows the process of recontracting underlying the establishment of equilibrium prices in the two-person economy, but it is also used to give a graphical analysis of Walrasian equilibria (Varian 1992, 316–317). Figure 2.1 represents the Edgeworth box for goods 1 and 2 and agents A and B. Suppose that the total amount of good 1 is $w_1 = w_{1A} + w_{1B}$ and that the total amount of good 2 is $w_2 = w_{2A} + w_{2B}$.[4] The Edgeworth box has a width of w_1 and a height of w_2. A point in the box (x_{1A}, x_{2A}) indicates how much agent A holds of the two goods. At the same time, it indicates the amount that agent B holds of the two goods: $(x_{1B}, x_{2B}) = (w_1{-}x_{1A}, w_2{-}x_{2A})$. In this way, every feasible allocation of the two goods between the agents can be represented by a point in this box.

The line CC in Figure 2.1 represents the contractcurve. This is the set of all tangency points between the indifference curves of agents A and B. The meaning of a tangency point is that for a given initial endowment w_1 and w_2 goods cannot be allocated more efficiently, since neither individual can be made better off without making the other individual worse off. This allocation is an equilibrium in the sense that, once established, at least one of the contracting parties will object against any alternative proposal. The line CC is thus the set of all equilibria.

Suppose X_0 is the initial allocation of goods between agents A and B. It is clear from Figure 2.1 that X_0 is not an efficient allocation and that A and B will try to negotiate a deal that will serve them both better. This process of 'recontracting' may bring them to any point on the line C*C*, which demarcates the set of all efficient allocations that can be reached from the initial allocation through voluntary trade. Note that this 'core' C*C* contains an infinite amount of equilibria. To pinpoint a specific allocation, we need a price ratio. Assuming conditions of perfect competition, we know that the individuals A and B are price takers. They are confronted with the price ratio p_1/p_2 which leads to the establishment of point W as the Walrasian equilibrium inside this core.

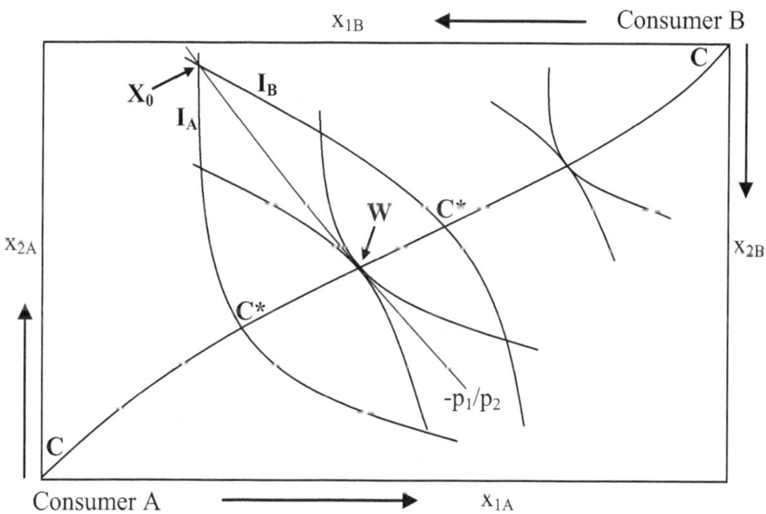

Figure 2.1 Illustration of the core in the two goods exchange case

What do we learn from this exposition? Firstly, it shows that 'mutual consent' or, including the time factor, 'mutual consistency of plans' is a key ingredient of the definition of equilibrium. The equilibrium point W is established, because agents A and B mutually agree that this allocation best satisfies their demands. An improvement for either of them can only be achieved by invoking a conflict with the other, who shall in that case be rationed in his demand. The second lesson is that the problem of price determination is not solved. The derivation of a contractcurve CC and its core C*C* is insufficient to determine the equilibrium solution W. The equilibrium price is established a priori and does not depend on the actions taken by A and B to negotiate an allocation on their contractcurve. In fact, this was also the conclusion drawn by Edgeworth himself in the original exposition of this problem. He showed that under a system of 'recontracting' there will be many solutions, an 'indeterminacy of contract' (Edgeworth 1881, 20).[5]

Now, of course, we may extend our scope of analysis. The price ratio p_1/p_2 is the equilibrium price and in general equilibrium this price is determined. At least, so it seems. The simultaneous equations of the general equilibrium system give the illusionary idea that we are able to explain the price setting process as it occurs in real markets. This is, indeed, an illusion. The conditions under which the general equilibrium system functions are such that they will never be found in any actual market (Kirman 2006). The main problem is that it is unable to handle even the slightest deviation from equilibrium. But, since it is not terribly realistic to assume that the 'Big Bang' produced general equilibrium at the beginning of the universe, we need some account of how the general equilibrium price vector came about. This, however, is something which sixty years of theory development in Walrasian general equilibrium analysis has failed to deliver.[6]

This is not a novel observation. Arrow (1959) already noted that there is a logical gap in the supply and demand explanation of price formation under perfectly competitive conditions. This gap is that each individual participant in the economy is assumed to take prices as given and determine his choices as to purchases and sales accordingly. As such, 'there is no one left over whose job it is to make a decision on price' (Arrow 1959, 56).[7] In other words, the focus in neoclassical general equilibrium analysis is on the determination of the equilibrium price vector as a static position. Blaug (1997) called this notion the end-state conception of economic equilibrium to indicate that the analysis deals with equilibrium as the static outcome of an implicit dynamic process or implicit temporal story, as Hausman termed it.

This conception of equilibrium is closely related to the predominantly mathematical mode of analysis of this type of equilibrium analysis (Blaug 2003). There are other branches of mathematical economic theory like the work of Sraffa (1960) and his followers, which likewise focus on equilibrium as an end-state. Sraffa explicitly ruled out changes in output, so that he could ignore assumptions about the returns to scale. This may have simplified his analysis of the price determining processes in terms of physical input-output relations, but it also firmly locked his analysis within a static framework (Blaug 2008). The simile with Walrasian general equilibrium theory is interesting, because like the Walrasians the Sraffians also have an 'implicit temporal story' to support their static equilibrium theory. This is the gravity model that stood central to the classical economics of Adam Smith and David Ricardo. The key to this model is the assumption that market prices always tend towards a long-run natural price, which therefore operates as a point of gravitation. Similarly, the Sraffians assume as a stylized fact that competition secures a uniform rate of profit in all economic sectors (Kurz and Salvadori 1995, 19–20). But this condition is in fact never relaxed making their theory an explanation of static equilibrium and nothing else. That is, the Sraffians present us with a theory of a long period end-state, but what brings this state into existence remains unknown.[8]

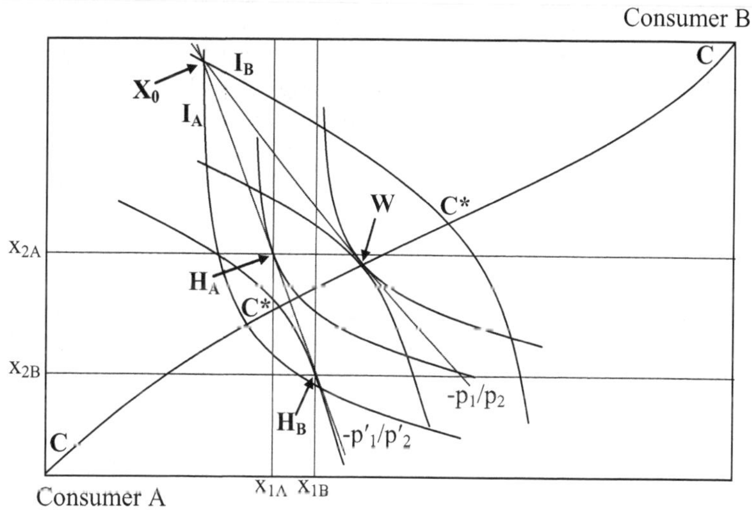

Source: Schinkel (2001, 7)

Figure 2.2 Edgeworth box: trading at false prices

Does it matter that we exclusively focus on equilibrium as an end-state and ignore the process behind it? Representatives of the Austrian school like Cowan and Rizzo (1996) argue that it does. They draw a distinction between what they call the functional mode of explanation and the genetic-causal tradition. Key to the latter approach is that it aims to understand the causes and generative process of economic phenomena like market equilibrium. For Cowan and Rizzo, supply and demand equilibrium, or a comparative static analysis of shifts in this equilibrium position, does not constitute a form of causal analysis. The point is that it overlooks processes which may be of paramount importance to the emergence of equilibrium as an end-state.

Suppose that agents A and B in our example do not know the Walrasian price, but initially face prices p'_1 and p'_2 such that

$$p'_1/p'_2 < p_1/p_2$$

What happens in this case? It can easily be shown that with these prices the plans of A and B do not match: A prefers consumption bundle H_A but agent B will trade up to H_B. There is disequilibrium in the sense that good 1 is in excess supply (the gap between x_{1A} and x_{1B}) while good 2 is in excess demand (the overlap between x_{2A} and x_{2B}). Agents A and B will start a bargaining process, which may bring prices closer to equilibrium but may also result in a widening gap. Crucial is that, once trade takes place at these disequilibrium prices, the core alters and the original Walrasian equilibrium W is no longer among the possible equilibria. The problem is that such trading alters the distribution of wealth, which is assumed given for the derivation of equilibrium.[9] In other words, outside equilibrium, we may have path-dependent effects shifting the position of equilibrium as we move towards (or away from) it.[10] The distinction between equilibrium as an end-state and as a process matters.

But what is a process that equilibrium as an end-state is not? Cowan and Rizzo (1996) describe this difference as follows. They define a genetic connection as a non-deterministic process in time. In this conception, generative causes track a path of changes through time, which cannot be replicated by viewing each point along this trajectory as an equilibrium state. As Joan Robinson (1974, 212) said it, one cannot sequentially compare different equilibrium states, like flipping 'stills through a projector', in order to assemble an image of a process moving through historical time. The reason for this is that these equilibria are linked through dynamic path-dependent effects. This violates the crucial assumption of any comparative static analysis that each equilibrium is independent of the process that is needed to establish it. In this type of equilibrium analysis, the speed of convergence is assumed to be so rapid that potentially disturbing causes have no time to exert their influence (Fisher 1983, 12). However, in historical time a process will exhibit what is called 'dynamic continuity' (Cowan and Rizzo 1996, 296). This means that it links memory, present action and anticipation, which automatically points at the importance of the process of learning and plan revision.

Cowan and Rizzo isolate several genetic causes that play a role in such processes, such as the means-ends framework at the individual level, causes at the market level (competition as rivalry) and the interaction between individual and market (see also Lachmann 1986). The exact nature of these causes can presently be ignored. What matters is that they are on the agenda at all. In the end-state conception of equilibrium, it is assumed that the economy miraculously jumps to this position and no attention is paid to the question how equilibrium comes about. The process conception does pose this question. The economists working in this tradition do not take for granted that competition or other forces move an economic system closer to a position of full coordination as an end-state. They aim to investigate why this should be the case and it is this aim which distinguishes them from their colleagues in the general equilibrium department.

This book shall demonstrate that the process approach to equilibrium has a long tradition in economics. It played a role in the early formulations of the quantity theory of money (Vickers 1959; see also Chapter 11), classical price theory (the notion of competition as a process) and the growth theories of Smith, Ricardo, J.S. Mill and other members of the classical school, which aimed to investigate the tendency of the economy towards a stationary state seen as a process (see Chapters 6 and 7). However, the rise of mathematical economics gave economists the tools to investigate the analytical properties of the equilibrium end-state in far greater detail. The result was a drastic change of the economic landscape. The economics profession became so obsessed with existence proofs of equilibrium states that anyone interested in the process question was automatically pushed to the fringe of economic science. In the words of Blaug (2003, 396), '[t]he Formalist Revolution made the existence and determinacy of equilibrium the be-all and end-all of economic analysis'. Nowadays we find the representatives of the process approach among the members of the heterodox schools of thought, like Post Keynesians, Neo Austrians and Institutional and Evolutionary economists. I shall study in this book what we may learn from these heterodox approaches to economic theory. What do we miss by viewing equilibrium as an end-state and can we improve economic analysis by adopting the process approach? (see Chapters 10, 12 and 13).

To conclude my argument so far, I have argued that the definition of economic equilibrium crucially rests on the compatibility of plans. This is how Hayek perceived the problem of equilibrium when he explored its intertemporal dimension in Hayek (1928), which later became a cornerstone of the general equilibrium literature (see for example Hahn 1973, 2). The importance of Hayek's contribution in this regard is that he recognized that equilibrium does not mean that economic variables remain stationary over time (Lewin 1997). As long as such changes are correctly foreseen, the compatibility of plans may involve the behaviour of variables that are rising or declining. Contrariwise, disequilibrium theory may address the coordination failure of an economy in a stationary position, like Keynes's theory of effective demand in his *General Theory* (Keynes 1936). Following High (1990, 43), I define disequilibrium as a state in which some plans are incompatible. The general task of disequilibrium theory is therefore to explain the process of plan change that results from plans being incompatible, or that causes plans to become incompatible. The term 'process' here refers to the notion of generative causation and dynamic continuity, which I explained above.[11]

How does the Keynesian fixed price literature based on Clower (1965) and Leijonhufvud (1968) fit into this classification? This literature is often addressed as 'disequilibrium' theory, given that it addresses cases where some markets fail to clear. But from the perspective I set out above, it is better seen as a branch of equilibrium theory. Firstly, in the fixed price literature every agent is assumed to maximize his objective function subject to the constraint that certain prices are fixed. This causes demand rationing for certain groups and is the reason why markets fail to clear. The point is that the solution to this set of equations is an equilibrium as far as every individual is concerned. Given the constraints, no one has an incentive to alter his behaviour and remove the excess supply or demand. One might say that the price system fails, but could it do otherwise? Prices are pegged, so we should not be surprised that they prove an unreliable guide to individual action. It is better to define this situation as a 'constrained equilibrium' to indicate that from an individual point of view there is no incompatibility of plans. There is just a set of constraints that no one can possibly alter. As Malinvaud (1977, 5) said: 'most economists think it necessary nowadays to speak of "disequilibrium analysis", meaning an analysis accepting the notion that demands can differ from supplies. ... [I]t is in fact plain equilibrium analysis, but operating within a specific concept of equilibrium.'

Malinvaud added that in this case we are not allowed to speak of dynamic theory, because 'disequilibrium' theory does not consider a process of adjustment. This brings me to the second point. We are dealing here with a clear example of an end-state conception of equilibrium. Solving the system of simultaneous equations determines the quantities traded at this rationed equilibrium. But the theory does not offer an explanation of how the system gets to this point. There is no space for retrospection, prospection, learning or other cognitive acts, which may tie different choices through time. This lack of dynamic continuity is a second reason to disqualify the analysis of constrained fixed price equilibria as disequilibrium theory in the sense as defined above.

The argumentation so far makes it evident that the definition of equilibrium has a strong link with how one views the role of time in economic analysis. This points to the importance of the statics/dynamics distinction, which is the subject of the next section.

STATICS AND DYNAMICS

As a follow-up of his semantic study of the word equilibrium Machlup (1959) turned his attention to the equally notorious words 'statics' and 'dynamics'. The result was just as disappointing. He tried to construct a typology of the statics/dynamics distinction, but encountered so many different meanings that he spoke of 'kaleidoscopic' words. To mention just a few of these meanings, statics and dynamics respectively refer to:

- description of a state of rest versus the explanation of change;
- abstract reasoning about imaginary worlds versus realistic description of observed facts;
- theory of relative prices and output versus theory of accumulation and growth;
- theory abstracting from time versus description of observed sequences in historical time; and
- analysis of equilibrium states versus the analysis of changes towards equilibrium.

In the end, Machlup was so dissatisfied about his semantic cleansing job in this area that he advised to avoid the terms statics and dynamics altogether.

I shall partly follow his advice by not going to deeply into the question how one should define statics and dynamics. I shall offer a few general notions and refer to later chapters when more specific meanings of these terms are at stake.[12]

A basic distinction needed to discriminate between statics and dynamics is that between what Schumpeter called 'stationary' and 'evolutionary' processes (see Schumpeter 1954, 562, 964 and 971). A stationary process refers to a set of state variables the values of which remain constant through time. A well-known example of such a process is the tendency towards the stationary state, which played a key role in classical economics (Brandis 1989). For classical authors like Ricardo and J.S. Mill the stationary state represented the point where economic growth would finally stop allowing the system to reproduce itself year in year out.[13] This stationary position can be contrasted with processes which grow or decline over time. In Schumpeter's terms, these are evolutionary processes.

The reason why Schumpeter distinguished between these two processes is that they give rise to much confusion, because they can both be studied in a static or a dynamic method. Schumpeter's static method uses the definition of equilibrium as an end-state. This method takes advantage of one of the best-known properties of equilibrium, which is that it allows us to ignore the role of time in analysis. With equilibrium as an end-state, we assume the existence of forces to secure a position of equilibrium. We do not know how long it will take these forces to bring the system towards equilibrium, but we believe that convergence will occur swift enough to prevent potentially disturbing causes from exerting their influence. These causes are kept constant in a ceteris paribus clause and need not be worried about. The focus of analysis is entirely on the position of equilibrium itself and, since we know it will be kept at this position, we may as well treat all variables 'as if' they exist at the same point in time. That is, the stationary process that goes on behind the scene of this equilibrium can be ignored. Examples of this type of analysis abound in economics, but the Arrow-Debreu models of general equilibrium are probably the most extreme example. The characteristic of these models is that general equilibrium can be shown to exist, but whether it is unique or stable remains outside our purview. Even the proponents of general equilibrium analysis admit that the Arrow-Debreu model is about equilibrium and nothing else (Kirman 2006, xvi). Outside equilibrium, the Arrow-Debreu model simply cannot function.

However, by studying a sequence of such equilibria we may get a notion of the changes implicit in evolutionary processes. A sequence of this kind can be formed by changing given factors in the ceteris paribus clause, which alters the equilibrium position. Comparing the initial and new equilibrium allows us to study the impact of this change. This is of course the familiar method of comparative statics, which is very popular in economics. Characteristic of comparative statics is that it may be used to form a sequence of equilibria, but that we do not know how much time lapses between the disappearance and emergence of subsequent equilibria. The time factor still plays no role other than the aforementioned implicit temporal story which accompanies any end-state equilibrium.

It is now time to introduce the time factor in a more explicit way. This can be done by including the leads and lags between variables in the analysis of changes over time. This is the defining characteristic of dynamic methods in Schumpeter's sense. Pioneers of this approach can be found early on in the history of economic thought. In 1803 Simonde de Sismondi experimented with an algebraic exploration of difference equations in the analysis of aggregate output (Sowell 1972b). Other early examples are Marx's schemes of simple and expanded reproduction in Chapters 20 and 21 in volume two of *Capital*, which formed the starting point of the macro dynamics of later Marxian economists (Negishi 1989, 200–206). In the 1930s, the sequence approach of the Stockholm school put the analysis of economic changes from one time frame to another at the heart of economic theory (see Chapter 12). The almost Keynesian outlook of the Swedes on the importance of expectations as a driver of temporal changes influenced many in the field of macroeconomics, but in the end failed to have a lasting impact (Laidler

1999). During this same time, Harrod and other members of the Cambridge school like Robinson and Kaldor connected the saving-investment nexus with the issue of capital accumulation (see Chapter 13). This formed the basis of the Keynesian and neoclassical theories of growth, which formed the cutting edge of economics in the 1950s.

All these theories have in common that they pay explicit attention to the fact that economic change is a process which requires time. Their key feature is the aim to include this time factor as an explanatory factor among the *explanans*. This is what Schumpeter defined as the 'dynamic' method and which like the static method can be applied to both stationary and evolutionary processes. Applied to the stationary process, the dynamic method tracks the development of economic variables which do not change in value over time (see also Lindahl 1939, 33). In the evolutionary process, this is not the case because the variables under scrutiny are undergoing constant change. The word 'constant' here is crucial because even a process of change can be regular in some sense. One may think of Harrod's warranted rate of growth or the notion of steady state growth, which allows the state variables to grow at the same pace. The evolutionary process may therefore exhibit an equilibrium feature depending on how one defines it, but it may also be irregular and even explosive, as we know from the problem of bifurcation in nonlinear dynamic systems.

Schumpeter's classification allows us to discuss the role of the equilibrium concept in the statics/dynamics distinction. Habitually, equilibrium is seen as a dividing line between statics and dynamics. This was already the case with J.S. Mill who was one of the first to explicitly introduce these terms into economics. He adopted these, what he called 'mathematical' terms, to divide the subject of his classic text, the *Principles of Political Economy* (1848), into two parts. The statics of political economy are discussed in the first three books of his treatise. The final two books comprise the dynamic part, 'thereby adding a theory of motion to our theory of equilibrium – the Dynamics of political economy to the Statics' (Mill 1909, 695).

In Chapter 7 I shall scrutinize Mill's definitions of statics and dynamics more closely. For the present moment, I want to argue that the relationship between the equilibrium concept and the statics and dynamics distinction is not so straightforward as implied by Mill's words. This is evidently suggested by the main topic of this chapter: which equilibrium concept are we talking about? Equilibrium can be defined as an end-state, but also as a process. Both these options can be combined with Schumpeter's classification of the statics and dynamics distinction, as I have done in Table 2.1.[14] The implication of this table is that depending on how one defines equilibrium, both statics and dynamics can be seen as instances of equilibrium analysis. Equilibrium is certainly not an unambiguous dividing line between statics and dynamics.

Table 2.1 Statics and dynamics

	stationary process	evolutionary process
	assumes equilibrium as....	
static method	end-state	end-state
dynamic method	process	process

The possibility to define dynamics in an equilibrium setting explains much of the confusion surrounding this concept. As Hicks (1965, 15) once said: '[i]n statics equilibrium is fundamental; in dynamics, as we shall find, we cannot do without it; but even in statics it is treacherous, and in dynamics, unless we are very careful, it will trip us completely.' This quotation contains two claims that I shall elaborate on. The first is the point of equilibrium being treacherous. This claim refers to the conclusion stated above that the relationship between either statics and dynamics and the equilibrium concept is not unambiguous. In the case of the static method, it is clear that equilibrium is seen as an end-state, but with regard to the dynamic method its role is not so straightforward. I have shown that the equilibrium concept can be used as part of the dynamic method. But of course one need not do so. In fact, many of the opponents of the equilibrium approach present their disequilibrium theories as a radical dynamic alternative to what they consider as the predominantly static focus of the equilibrium paradigm.

The problem is the role of time in the process approach to equilibrium. Time can be logical or calendar time (Dow 1996). This distinction is crucial, because seen as a logical concept a temporal concept usually leaves no scope for what Knight (1921) called 'fundamental uncertainty'. The key phrase here is 'dynamic continuity' which I have introduced as an ingredient of disequilibrium analysis. The link between memory, present action and anticipation may be so strong that uncertainty is literally ruled out. In economics we encounter this situation in general equilibrium analysis, which assumes that all agents know the exchange rates for the prices at t=0 until infinity.[15] It is evident that with this kind of knowledge actions like learning or the formation of expectations become meaningless. The Walrasian auctioneer secures intertemporal general equilibrium for all times even before trade has started and any incompatibility of plans is ruled out by definition.

However, with calendar time this situation fundamentally changes, introducing uncertainty as a kind of 'risk' which cannot be reduced to a certainty equivalent in probability terms. It is this kind of temporal process which shoulders the dynamics of the so-called heterodox schools of economic thought like Post Keynesians, Neo Austrians and Institutionalists. Their approach differs in a crucial way from the 'process' which I have defined as an equilibrium concept. In calendar time we cannot assume that the process of temporal adjustment tends towards a predestined goal, because there is always the chance of a genuine surprise lurking around the corner, upsetting the process of adjustment we thought would take us closer to equilibrium. When a surprise of this kind occurs, it may even turn out that our first move has widened rather than reduced the distance to this goal. Put differently, the presence of fundamental uncertainty may cause processes to exhibit disequilibrium as a permanent feature involving incessant motion and adjustment. The treacherous aspect is therefore that Table 2.1 contains another dimension in which the term 'process' refers to disequilibrium as I have defined it rather than equilibrium.

This brings me to the second claim, which I distill from Hicks's quotation. This one is almost made casually: in statics equilibrium is fundamental, but also in dynamics *we cannot do without it*. This claim requires an explanation which I postpone to Chapters 13, 14 and 15. In brief, the issue is this. The representatives of the heterodox schools often accuse mainstream neoclassical economics of being shortsighted. In their view, the mainstream engages in a type of dynamic analysis which is not really dynamic, because it ignores the fundamental uncertainty brought about by changes in calender time. Their so-called dynamic theory is equilibrium theory in disguise. Or, to use a favorite image, the mainstream is like the drunk who searches for his lost keys under the lamp post, because that is where the light shines. The heterodox schools argue that the mainstream should venture into what Keynes (1936, 155) appropriately called the 'dark forces of time and ignorance'.

But do the heterodox schools put their money where their mouth is and take this route? I argue that they do not and in general withdraw from the consequences of what they see as proper dynamics. I shall demonstrate this more clearly in Chapters 13, 14 and 15. The main problem is that the heterodox economists fear that a process of ongoing change in historical time will be analytically intractable, making them an easy target for allegations of analytical nihilism. To prevent such accusations they adopt a short cut, which involves the reintroduction of some notion of equilibrium as either an end-state (Sraffians) or a process leading to a predestined outcome (Austrians like Israel Kirzner). It turns out that the escape from equilibrium thinking is not an easy task, which brings me to the 'vision' associated with this term.

THE VISION OF EQUILIBRIUM THEORY

The reason why the equilibrium concept has such a stronghold on economics is that it represents a vision about how the real economy operates. This vision is that economic transactions take place in a relatively harmonious fashion even when decisions about production and exchange are taken at a decentralized level. Put differently, according to this equilibrium vision the economic realm is ruled by a strong sense of order.[16]

Economists have always toyed with metaphors and conceptions to express the innate sense of order in the economy. Adam Smith's 'invisible hand' is probably the most famous example of this practice. The reason why our precursors have been prone to use such metaphors is that they suggested a degree of analytical control. A field governed by equilibrium forces is a field which can be studied with scientific tools like deduction and induction. It offers hope of observing specific regularities which in generalized form may become the foundation of a corpus of theory. The prospect of scientific success in this sense probably explains why economists have always found equilibrium such a comforting thought (McCloskey 1983).[17]

The problem is that such visions easily give way to ideological biases, the main source of many scientific quarrels in economics. Schumpeter (1954) saw them as the ultimate – but by no means the only – source of ideology in economics. For him, a vision literally represented 'seeing' the object of one's study: 'it embodies the picture of things as we see them, and wherever there is a possible motive for wishing to see them in a given rather than another light, the way in which we see things can hardly be distinguished from the way in which we wish to see them.' As a result, 'vision is ideological almost by definition' (Schumpeter 1954, 42).

The question is whether this connection between vision and ideology is such a bad thing. For Schumpeter, all scientific inquiry started with the 'visualization' of a distinct set of coherent phenomena as a worth-while object of analysis.[18] This implied that ideology could have potentially very disruptive effects, since it entered the inquiry at the very start of analysis. Luckily, there are some powerful corrective mechanisms at work. Schumpeter claimed that the rules of procedure that we apply in our analytical work are almost as much exempt from ideological influence as vision is subject to it. The result is that they tend to 'crush out' ideologically conditioned error from the visions from which we start (ibid., 43). Of course this did not imply that the whole of economics was a value-free and purely analytical exercise. The methodological cleansing job called analytical progress faired better in some schools of thought than in others. Schumpeter (1949) referred to Marx's work as the prime case where ideology triumphed over analysis.[19] Likewise, Keynes had a vision which proved more powerful than the analysis of his *General Theory*, modern stagnationism – the notion of a mature capitalist society that tries to save more than its declining opportunities for investment can absorb. But in other cases analytical progress had been thoroughly victorious, like in the Walrasian system in which 'there should be as little danger of ideological vitiation as there is in physics' (ibid., 352).[20]

This process of routing out ideologies is of importance to the subject of this thesis, as Schumpeter more or less made the starting point of economic science dependent on its success. He argued that the history of economic analysis started from the recognition that 'analytic economists have been interested, more or less, in the analysis of the phenomenon that we call competitive price' (Schumpeter 1954, 39). It was the unconcern for this question which characterized what he called 'economic thought' and 'systems of political economy'. To Schumpeter the former did not concern analytical work, but its popular background, 'the sum total of all the opinions concerning economic subjects, especially concerning public policy bearing upon these subjects that, at any given time and place, float in the public mind' (ibid., 38). The latter category was introduced to separate the ideological meaning of economic statements from their analytical content. It concerned systems of economic policies advocated on the basis of certain unifying (normative) principles, such as the principles of economic liberalism, socialism or other political doctrines.

The notion of competitive price was so important to the scientific conception of economics because it suggested a particular domain of inquiry that may be labeled 'economic'. A competitive price suggested that the economy should be conceived as a logically self-contained system where supply and demand together determine exchange values and where markets are interconnected through price changes. It was this conception of a distinct economic order to be investigated by a separate scientific discipline, using its own set of analytical tools, which for Schumpeter marked the start of economic analysis.[21] Blaug (1985, 6) expressed it even clearer:

> The problem that gave rise to economics in the first place, the 'mystery' that fascinated Adam Smith as much as it does a modern economist, is that of market exchange: there is a sense of order in the economic universe, and this order is not imposed from above but is somehow the outcome of the exchange transactions between individuals, each seeking to maximize his own gain.[22]

I have taken some space to explain this reputed relationship between analytical progress and ideology because I shall argue in this book that it is false. There is no point in the history of economic science of which we can say that this is where 'economic thought' or 'systems of political economy' transformed into genuine analysis, thereby marking the birth of economic science. I shall discuss many examples of equilibrium theory which have some analytical qualities, but also embody specific ideological overtones. In fact, I claim that such biases are also present in the field which Schumpeter considered the peak achievement of non-ideological reasoning, namely the Walrasian system. Modern methodologists like Lawson (2005 and 2006) use the differences in ontology to explain the confused state of equilibrium analysis in modern economics. According to him, mainstream and heterodox economists frequently quarrel about the meaning of equilibrium theory, because they do not realize that their perceptions of the underlying economic reality are so different.[23] This example shows that our vision of the nature of economic reality is able to cause significant watersheds in science. And this occurs after 300 years (or more) of 'analytical progress'.[24]

The conclusion is that we need to go beyond the definitions of equilibrium to study the historical development of this branch of theory. I do not find this a handicap. One of my main claims is that there is an important difference in vision which significantly affected the development of equilibrium economics in the eighteenth century. I shall explain this claim in Chapter 4 when I discuss the origins of equilibrium theory in eighteenth century economics. But I first turn to methodology. Why are the procedural rules of science, that Schumpeter referred to, unable to remove ideological biases from equilibrium analysis? And what does methodology teach us about the nature of equilibrium economics as a scientific undertaking? These questions form the core of Chapter 3.

NOTES

1. In the end, Machlup (1958, 9) also offered a definition of equilibrium, which he believed was 'quite clear'.
2. The exact formulation of this condition is as follows. If all goods are desirable and p* is a Walrasian equilibrium, then the aggregate excess demand function z(p) = 0. See Varian (1992, 319). Formally, we are just looking at the subset $\mathbb{R}_+$ representing the set of all positive prices.
3. The work of Walras, the original expositor of the general equilibrium problem, abounds with references to an implicit process of price adjustment. He believed that real markets would 'solve' his mathematical problem of general equilibrium within minutes. He also tried to explicate this process of 'groping' towards the equilibrium price in theoretical terms, but this effort only partially succeeded. See Chapter 9 of this book for a more detailed discussion of Walras's analysis of general equilibrium.
4. It is assumed that indifference curves like IA and IB are convex to the origin.

5. Edgeworth's aim was to demonstrate that Jevons's Law of Indifference was not generally valid, because it implicitly assumed conditions of perfect competition. He argued that two isolated trading agents have no incentive to choose a particular point on their contract curve. They need an outside pressure, which is the market price determined by the forces of competition and the interplay of other suppliers and demanders. See Edgeworth (1881, 109) and Negishi (1989, 332–338).
6. A disequilibrium approach may offer a better scope for success. Weintraub (1979) tried building a disequilibrium model using the Edgeworth box as a starting point. Like Edgeworth (1881), he investigated what would happen with the core if more traders entered the market. Edgeworth claimed that as market conditions approached a situation of perfect competition, the core would shrink as the market price would tend towards an unique equilibrium level. In other word, the indeterminacy of contract would be solved. See also Negishi (1989).
7. See also Koopmans (1957, 179).
8. Kurz and Salvadori (1995, 20) recognize this, but add that an analysis of the dynamics involved in the process of gravitation would 'overburden' the analysis 'with demands that are hard to meet'. I shall further elaborate on this issue in Chapter 13.
9. On this point, see Fisher (1983, 15) and Schinkel (2001, 8–9).
10. Arrow (1959) also realized this. He pointed out that the assumption of perfect knowledge is crucial to the definition of supply and demand equilibrium. Once this condition is relaxed, uncertainty starts playing a role. Suppliers and demanders need to explore the demand and supply curves they respectively face. But while they are doing so, these curves themselves will change due to strategic responses of their competitors. See Arrow (1959, 58–59).
11. High (1990) distinguishes three branches of disequilibrium theory in this sense, which he calls stability theory, market process theory and search theory. However, he constrains his analysis to 'marginal analysis' which brings him to ignore the Marxist and Institutionalist traditions as exponents of the disequilibrium approach. In my discussion of the disequilibrium challenge to equilibrium economics, these traditions are (partly) included. See Chapter 13.
12. This corresponds to another conclusion of Machlup: use more readily understood words like the types of theory statics and dynamics are said to represent. See Machlup (1959, 41).
13. It should be stressed that not all classical economists endorsed the notion of a stationary state. For example, Adam Smith did not believe in the conception of a stationary state as the end point of growth. He argued that 'declining', 'stagnating' and 'advancing' nations would have different long term growth perspectives. See Chapter 6. Also the interpretation of the stationary state differs between authors. For Mill, for example, the end of growth marked a desirable position, because it allowed scope for social improvements, but to others it marked a point of despair, as wages were pushed to their natural (that is existence) level. See Brandis (1989, 76) and Chapter 7.

14. From the explanation given above, it is clear that the static method uses equilibrium as an end-state. The dynamic method refers to the process approach in the sense that it explicitly addresses the leads and lags between variables. A stationary process then concerns the motion of a set of variables whose values are unchanging with the passing of time. The evolutionary process may involve a process moving to a predestined end, such as the stationary state of classical growth analysis, which is a clear example of the process interpretation of equilibrium.
15. This condition is euphemistically referred to as the assumption that the general equilibrium system covers a full set of forward markets.
16. Clower (1998) puts this vision at the core of his historical investigation of three centuries of supply and demand analysis.
17. The essence of the notion of vision as a scientific concept is therefore that it structures a field of study. As Heilbroner (1990, 1112) put it, visions reduce raw perceptions to ordered concepts. 'What is important is to see all visions as expressions of the inescapable need to infuse "meaning" – to discover a comprehensible framework – in the world. Visions thereby structure the social reality to which economics ... addresses its inquiry.'
18. The subsequent steps would involve the 'verbalization' of this vision and its use in the construction of an economic model to be used in analysis. Schumpeter admitted that for practical purposes he assumed a very stylized model of scientific inquiry.
19. The point was that, according to Schumpeter, some elements of Marx's original vision, such as the increasing misery of the masses, were too closely linked to the innermost meaning of his message, too deeply rooted in the very meaning of his life, to be ever discarded.
20. Ironically, modern commentators like Rothbard (1987) and Keizer (1997) consider the Walrasian system Schumpeter's ultimate blind spot. 'For Schumpeter, general equilibrium had to be the overriding reality: the realistic starting point as well as the end-point of his attempt to explain economic change.' See Rothbard (1987, 98).
21. Schumpeter (1954, 241) said that economics discovered its 'fundamental problem' when it started to realize that the economy is a whole all the parts of which somehow hang together – a view he called the 'vision' of equilibrium economics.
22. For a similar statement, see Ekelund and Hébert (1997, 119).
23. Lawson (2005 and 2006) argues that mainstream economics is basically mathematical and adopts equilibrium as a theoretical concept assuming a closed world with atomistic agents. But their heterodox contenders generally focus on equilibrium as an ontic concept, which involves an open system characterized by uncertainty. Mainstream economists are assumed to conflate equilibrium as a theoretical and an ontic concept, which explains why the two camps in economics often talk at cross purposes when the subject of equilibrium theory is raised. I find this thesis challenging, but also believe that Lawson overstates his case. Are mainstream economists really so shortsighted that they conflate equilibrium as a theoretical and an ontic concept? There are certainly examples of this in the history of economic thought, but I can also think of examples to the contrary (for example Léon Walras himself, see Chapter 9).

24. I have already mentioned Clower (1998) as someone who does not share the view that economic theory significantly increased our understanding of economic processes in the past 300 years.

3. Methodological Assessment

INTRODUCTION

In a recent paper Roger Backhouse offered what he called a 'partial' defense of equilibrium economics (Backhouse 2004). He argues that many discussions about equilibrium theory in economics are misdirected because they focus on the wrong item. It has been said more than once in the previous chapters that equilibrium theory comes in many guises. In that sense, it is inevitable that equilibrium proves a continuous 'bone of contention' for economists. According to Backhouse, they should have been wiser. He approaches equilibrium as a method of analysis, which in his view is indispensable, because it allows us to break down complex problems into more manageable pieces. The key word here is abstraction. Any theoretical science abstracts from specific features of reality in order to develop theoretical tools. So, '[t]o criticize it [equilibrium analysis, BT] for abstracting from features of reality such as the irreversibility of historical time is to miss the point. Abstraction is necessary. It may, of course, be the case that the abstractions being made are inappropriate, but this needs to be argued for the specific problem being analyzed. There is no argument to be made in principle about the illegitimacy of equilibrium analysis' (Backhouse 2004, 301).[1]

Is it really this simple? Backhouse should know better. Surely, abstraction is part of the scientific process, but by no means the only one. Backhouse himself refers to Robert Lucas's defense of the equilibrium method and says that we should focus on the substantive points in his argument. The issue is not whether one assumes instant market clearing, like the new classicals do, but how the equilibrium model is used in their method of analysis. Lucas argues that this method involves experimentation to support the theory of microeconomic behaviour, using rationality and optimization as basic components. There is a role for calibration to fit the macroeconomic model onto the data and rationalize the particular method of aggregation. The particular steps in this process need not be repeated here. What matters is the line of thinking, which is geared in terms of defending a particular approach to doing economic research. It should be clear that this approach involves much more than building an abstract equilibrium model.[2]

This raises the question what kind of activity this equilibrium method is. Backhouse (2004) leaves this question unanswered, but he finds himself in good company.[3] The main purpose of this chapter is to argue that economists have been unable to agree on the scientific nature of the theory that many consider central to their science. This gives rise to an interesting paradox. One would expect that the alleged centrality of equilibrium theory at least has a (weak) causal relationship with the scientific success of this theory. After all, economists seem wedded to the rationality postulate and should therefore be wise enough to join in (or mimic) the success of their colleagues. But if we are unsure about the procedural rules of this science, we are confronted with the problem of measuring the steps made forward on the scientific scale. This leaves the question of what explains the dominance of neoclassical equilibrium theory largely unresolved.

I have added the prefix neoclassical to equilibrium theory in the last sentence, to delineate the subject of this chapter.[4] Backhouse correctly observes that economists are sloppy in their use of the terms 'equilibrium theory' and 'equilibrium economics'. They are generally using these terms as shorthand for a specific type of economic theory, namely general equilibrium theory as expounded by Arrow and Debreu. I have defined equilibrium theory in a much wider sense, but for the purpose of this chapter I shall focus on Arrow Debreu general equilibrium theory. It is this branch of contemporary mainstream economics which elicits the most contradictory praises. Some see GE theory as the crowning achievement of economic science, while others reject it as a gross error, reflecting for example the preference of many colleagues for armchair economics rather than an ambition to improve the well-being of people and societies.

Such contradictory praises call for an explanation. In this chapter I shall discuss several different portraits of GE theory as a scientific undertaking. This diversity supports my claim that we are unable to agree on the exact nature of this science. However, the interesting fact of these different images is that they also contain a number of shared observations about economics. These involve the complexity of economic questions, which is invariably said to inhibit empirical testing in economics. More importantly, there is always a role for non scientific arguments like the belief system of the principal actors or the normative implications of GE theory. It is here that Schumpeter's Vision creeps in and seems to play a much more dominating part than Schumpeter had assumed. For one, he argued that scientific progress would in due course reduce the importance of ideology and vision, but current practice suggests otherwise. The uncertainty about the scientific meaning of GE theory seems to strengthen rather than reduce the precognitive beliefs about how the economy actually operates and how its patterns should be studied. This conclusion motivates my search for the relationship between vision and the development of equilibrium theory in the history of economic thought, which I shall undertake in the subsequent chapters.

The present chapter is organized as follows. It first addresses the question why economists disagree about the scientific rules of their discipline, following McCloskey's critique of modernist philosophies of science. Second, four methodological approaches are discussed to answer the leading question of this chapter, what kind of science is GE theory? These concern:

- The notion that GE theory is a form of rhetoric;
- Weintraub's appraisal of GE analysis as a scientific research program in the sense of Lakatos;
- Rosenberg's contention that equilibrium theory is not a science but is best considered a branch of mathematical politics, and finally
- Hausman's analysis of equilibrium economics as an inexact and separate science.

DOES METHODOLOGY MATTER FOR ECONOMICS?

In 1983 Deirdre McCloskey started a crusade against the pretence of what she calls 'modernism' in economics. In a series of articles and books she claimed that economists uncritically adopt an outdated philosophy of science which has long been discarded by philosophers themselves (McCloskey 1983, 486–487).[5] In her view, a consequence of this misplaced adherence to modernism has been that economists make scientific claims they can impossibly justify. For instance, economists still consider predictive success a main criterion of scientific progress, even when the predictive record of economics is weak, to say the least. Another implication is that they unnecessarily constrain their analyses to methods which fit the mold of this modernist philosophy.

A major aim of modernism, as McCloskey defines it, is to strictly separate scientific from non-scientific reasoning. A few characteristics of science are:

- It stresses the observable implications of a theory;
- It aims to test theories by checking these implications in objective, reproducible experiments;
- It adopts Kelvin's dictum: knowledge is expressed in numbers;
- It distinguishes between normative and positive statements and aims to avoid the former.

Theories which do not have these features are classified as non scientific and are therefore best ignored. For example in the modernist view on science information acquired by means of subjective observation (introspection) does not constitute scientific knowledge.

However, economic knowledge is more diverse than the modernist suggests (Caldwell 1982). A main goal of McCloskey's rhetoric has therefore been to advocate a more open-minded approach to economics. Economists are best advised to avoid any methodology that constrains (McCloskey 1983, 490, 511–12). To benefit from the diversity of their discipline they should explore different methods and different aims of science. The uncritical acceptation of a modernist methodology they have no a priori reasons for believing to perform better than alternative approaches, merely harms the goals they may seek to achieve. The function of methodology should be to suggest fruitful ways of doing research, not to proscribe the exploration of other approaches just because they do not fit the precepts of a specific method.

In the final analysis, McCloskey denies that epistemological considerations can justify 'external' cognitive standards. What counts as 'good' scientific practice in economics can only be determined by economists themselves, not by outsiders. At bottom, economics is rhetoric. As all sciences, it uses theories, models, stories and metaphors to persuade an audience of professional colleagues, policy makers, or the lay public. The problem is that modernist claims, as do other 'overblown' methodologies of science, restrict this 'conversation'. So McCloskey seems to support at least one epistemological claim: an open, honest, and tolerant conversation 'improves' science. 'Good' science, in other words, is good conversation and scientific practice is best served by a Sprachethik: 'Don't lie; pay attention; don't sneer; cooperate; don't shout; let other people talk; be open-minded; explain yourself when asked; don't resort to violence or conspiracy in aid of your ideas' (McCloskey 1985, 24, 27).[6] But beyond the advice to conduct an open and honest discourse, no methodology can have anything useful to say about economic science.

Evidently, this conclusion would imply that methodology is useless to our purposes too. If its prescriptions cannot be employed to the benefit of current economic practice, then surely it is equally incapable to assess the scientific quality of past economic theory. However, there are good reasons to question the central contention of McCloskey's post modernist message, the suggestion that cognitive standards external to economics are irrelevant to its scientific practices.

In a sense McCloskey herself prescribes such standards, for what are her conversational norms other than scientific rules borrowed from non-economic disciplines, such as rhetoric, linguistics and literary criticism? So her objections against methodology should apply to rhetoric as well.[7] Can it be that McCloskey is pursuing a self-defeating strategy?

It is unquestionable that the models, theories and other tools economists use are rhetorical devices that are intended to persuade. For that reason it is important to examine the rhetoric of economists, if only to find out which arguments work and for what reason. But the suggestion that economics is a form of rhetoric does not imply that epistemological considerations are irrelevant. On the contrary. McCloskey's rhetorical project shows that it is impossible to make meaningful statements about science without adopting external, general cognitive standards. For, that is the whole point: the study of rhetoric matters because it improves science. Evidently, that conclusion involves a cognitive claim. It says that through McCloskey's writings economics is better able to achieve its goals. By reading her books and articles economists will recognize the dangers of the modernist rhetoric they are using and are therefore able to avoid its pitfalls. Consideration of the rhetoric of their arguments will lead them to conduct a more open and honest conversation improving the quality of their work. Now it is one thing to claim that by considering its rhetoric economics can become a more open and honest conversation. As was said above, it is important to know how economists persuade other economists, policy makers or the public and rhetoric may help us understand the working of their arguments. But it is something else to assert that an open and honest conversation produces better science, for how does one determine this improvement? Should one count citations or references to McCloskey's work to check if economists are beginning to explicitly recognize the importance of the rhetoric of economics?[8] Should one interview economists to see if and how their scientific goals have changed? Are they now using the statistical significance test in a more sensible way? Or have they abandoned the aim of predictive control altogether and are they now striving for better (introspective) understanding of economic processes? The question of scientific progress cannot be answered without bringing in explicit epistemological considerations. In the final analysis, the success of McCloskey's rhetoric proves that she is wrong.

The root of the problem is that value-free statements about science are impossible. As was suggested earlier, descriptions of scientific practice are always methodology laden (Blaug 1980, 33). So part of the rhetorical project was doomed from the start. It is impossible to make meaningful statements about economics by studying the practice of economists alone. Such descriptions will always disclose a preference of method and therefore appeal to meta-scientific standards. In the end epistemology is unavoidable, as indeed some of McCloskey's most adamant opponents have concluded (see for example Rosenberg 1992, 16; Hausman 1992, 269 and Hoover 1995, 733).

Now this conclusion applies to a meta scientific level. It says that the methodologist cannot avoid value-judgements: he or she implicitly assumes a theory of epistemology. But if that is the case, then the same can be said of all scientific activities, as for instance Rosenberg (1992) argues. According to him there is no philosophical reason to distinguish between different sciences. All involve the same type of activity and methodology is just science at a different level of abstraction.

> In the absence of demarcation, philosophy is just very general, very abstract science and has the same kind of prescriptive force for the practice of science as any scientific theory. Because of its generality and abstractness it will have less detailed bearing on day-to-day science than, say, prescriptions about the calibration of pH meters, but it must have the same kind of bearing (Rosenberg 1992, 11).

To Rosenberg the chemist in his laboratory makes the same kind of methodological choices as do philosophers. The former assumes that a pH meter correctly measures ion concentration because it is maintained by a theory of acids and bases. The latter claims that rhetoric works because better conversation leads to better science. Both follow a specific set of rules R for doing research, assuming the correctness of another theory t. This is what Hoover (1995, 720) calls Rosenberg's 'continuity' thesis. It says that the differences between sciences are a matter of degree only, as all sciences adopt a methodology R[t] representing a set of rules constructed in relation to a particular theory. Accordingly, if the methodologist cannot avoid epistemology, then neither can other scientists. In this sense 'all scientists are philosophers of science; or at least all take sides, willy-nilly, on issues in the philosophy of science, and the sides they take influence the direction of their "substantive" work' (Rosenberg 1992, 2). Methodology, then, studies the epistemological considerations of scientists: which ends do they aim for and which methods and rules of research do they employ to achieve them? To cite Hausman (1992, 264), methodological appraisal involves 'investigating empirically how people learn, what sort of methods work best for which sort of problems'. The question that will currently be addressed is: what kind of method is equilibrium theory, and what sort of problems does it address?

THE RHETORIC OF EQUILIBRIUM THEORY

The study of the rhetoric of economic leads McCloskey to criticize the methodology of neoclassical general equilibrium analysis. She considers GEA the most profound example of the negative consequences of what she calls the formalism of economics. Formalism as she sees it is part of the modernist philosophy of science, as described in the previous section, and in this context refers to the use of mathematics in economic reasoning. In particular, it refers to that part of mathematics that treats theory as an axiomatic framework of lemmas and theorems.

McCloskey is not in principle opposed to the use of mathematics in economics, as for example the Austrians are. On the contrary, she believes that '[e]conomics has made progress without mathematics, but has made faster progress with it' (McCloskey 1994, 128). The merit of mathematics is that it increases the transparency of economic arguments and prevents logical blunders. In the eyes of McCloskey, many economic theories would rapidly become muddled without mathematical expression and mathematics therefore has a useful role to play in the process of economic theory development. The problem of formalism in economics is that it is used in the wrong way.

According to McCloskey, economists claim that their formal treatment of economic problems follows the methodology of the physical sciences. First, hypothesis are formulated in terms of formal, mathematical theories. In the second stage of the analysis testing must demonstrate the relevance of a hypothesis and furnish the material to improve upon the original conjecture or reject it. The concentration on pure mathematics in some branches of economics such as GEA is a matter of a division of labour. As Koopmans (1957) writes, economics should have a theoretical and an empirical branch. The theoretical branch should devote itself to the development of theoretical models.

The problem is that this division of labour has gone astray. Due to the focus on the theoretical part, economics has now become more mathematical than the example, physics. McCloskey points to the Sante Fe institute that once brought economists and physicists together in an attempt to improve the scientific culture of economics (ibid., 130). At this instance, the physicists were amazed by the mathematical rigour of mathematical economics. The point is that GEA and other branches of mathematical economics have gone too far in their admiration of the formal approach of physics. They concentrate their efforts on the refinement of their mathematical models and forget that a scientific theory must have something meaningful to say about economic reality. According to McCloskey, physicists are much less mathematically minded. They value the accuracy of their test results more than the mathematical sophistication of their theories. In contrast, economic theories are hardly ever put to the test in an empirical analysis of their consequences. McCloskey concludes that economists have adopted the intellectual values of the wrong subject. Their work belongs to the province of the math department where testing is not an issue. Meanwhile, they mistakenly believe that they are following the scientific example of physics (ibid., 131, 143).

The result is that economics has become a blackboard science. The focus of research is on the mathematical analysis of theorems and lemmas that can be solved without leaving one's armchair. Economists engage in what McCloskey calls 'a fishing expedition in the hyperspace of possible worlds' (ibid., 141). They are exclusively concerned with the solution of existence theorems: find a price vector P such that there exists a competitive general equilibrium E, assuming a production possibilities frontier T and preferences P. However, McCloskey argues that the analysis of existence theorems does not lead to questions that are economically meaningful. What use is there in knowing that a certain theoretical solution to a mathematical problem exists that has no relation to economic reality whatsoever because it is based on highly unrealistic assumptions? It is one thing to derive a theoretical result but the next step should be to investigate how closely real economic affairs correspond to this result. How far is the economy actually removed from being a competitive market system? What is the increase in national income that can be attributed to freer international trade? Such questions are hardly ever explicated. Instead of trying to solve empirical puzzles of this kind economists often rely on the rhetoric of their theoretical arguments and merely assume that they are deriving meaningful statements about real economic problems. What really happens is that they are taking the easy way out. Economic problems are defined so that they fit the mold of tractable mathematical models. McCloskey summarizes the problem as follows. 'The prestige of mathematical argument led economists to believe, contrary to their discipline, that they could get something intellectually for nothing, proving or disproving great social truths by writing on a blackboard' (ibid., 140).

The best theory to address such questions in mathematical terms is general equilibrium analysis. The bend towards social mathematics so explains why GE theory has become dominant in economics. According to McCloskey, this dominance seriously distorts our view on the role of equilibrium theory in the history of economic thought. In her words, 'the first consequence of the unjustified identification of economic theory with mathematical economics and general equilibrium theory is an erroneous history of economic thought. Arrow-Debreu is viewed as a capstone' (ibid., 151). The truth of the matter is that it is a misunderstanding of the heterogeneous character of economic theory before and after Walras and the Lausanne School to claim that the essence of Adam Smith and all other forerunners of modern mathematical economics was an embryonic account of neoclassical general equilibrium analysis.

The second negative consequence of the rhetoric of mathematical economics is that GE theory has become the scientific standard in economics. Some even claim that the pursuit of mathematical existence theorems in GE theory is the only way to generate knowledge in economics. In McCloskey's eyes nothing could be farther from the truth, for the proofs of GE theory

> do not claim to show that an actual existing economy is in equilibrium, or that the equilibrium of an existing economy is desirable. The blackboard problem thus solved derives more or less vaguely from Adam Smith's assertion that capitalism is self-regulating and good. But the proofs of existence do not prove or disprove Smith's assertion. They show that certain equations describing a certain blackboard economy have a solution, but they do not give the actual solution to the blackboard problem, much less to an extant economy' (ibid., 133).

In other words, GE theory fails to the extent that even as a mathematical undertaking it seems a waste of energy because the proofs of GE theory state 'that somewhere in the mathematical universe there exists a solution. Lord knows what it is; we humans only know that it exists'.

EQUILIBRIUM THEORY AS A SCIENTIFIC RESEARCH PROGRAM

The Methodology of Scientific Research Programs

There was a time that the scientific status of GE theory was perceived much less problematic than today. A dominant theory of this kind was seen as the standard case of a paradigm or a scientific research program in the sense of Lakatos (1970). Whatever happened to this methodology and why did it fail to validate the scientific status of GE theory? Well, like other fashions it came and went. This section discusses why.

The attractiveness of Lakatos's methodology of scientific research programs (MSRP) can easily be explained. It allows us to look forward but also backward in time. On the one hand, it provides a structure to investigate scientific practice and to prescribe rules for conducting science the proper way. On the other hand, this methodology can be used to explain the historical development of science by identifying different research programs and tracking their gestation over time.

The crux of both these undertakings is the definition of a research program. This is a structure for doing science defined in terms of a set of so-called 'hard core' propositions, which are uncritically accepted by the scientists working within the program. By following a specific research strategy, comprising a positive and negative heuristic, these propositions are developed into applied theories which form the program's 'protective belt'. In contrast to the hard core propositions, the theories comprising the protective belt are open to empirical scrutiny and should, in case of inadequate empirical support, be rejected. To measure the progress of the program a dual standard is invoked. The program is said to be 'theoretically progressive' if the theories in the belt predict novel facts (Lakatos 1970, 118). The program becomes 'empirically progressive' if these predictions are corroborated in series of tests (ibid.). Note that these standards only apply to the theories in the belt of the program. The hard core propositions are not open to doubt and are consequently not tested. The program as a whole is progressive if it meets the following two requirements. First it must be 'consistently theoretically progressive', that is, 'each successive link ... predicts some new fact' (ibid., 134). Secondly the program must be at least 'intermittently empirically progressive', which means that 'at least now and then the increase in content should be seen to be retrospectively corroborated.' (ibid.). A program that fails to meet these requirements is 'degenerating'. This term indicates that the longer it takes to achieve empirical success the lower the chances that the program will ever become empirical progressive. For that reason, scientists are best advised to abandon degenerating programs in order to join in the success of progressive ones. Consequently, if scientists rationally engineer their careers, progressive research programs will eventually overtake degenerating ones. In the Lakatosian vision, science proceeds as a sequence of rational choices by the scientific community.

By implication, the Lakatosian MSRP allows a rational reconstruction of the historical development of science. This reconstruction identifies competing research programs in order to determine the science's 'best gambits' (Lakatos 1970, 111). This aim follows naturally from the assumption that scientists are rational in the sense that they prefer progressive over degenerating programs. If scientists do not act in this manner, then the history of science should falsify the claims of the MSRP as a meta-methodology. In that sense a rational reconstruction in terms of the MSRP is at the same time a history of science and a test of the MSRP as a methodological program.

It must be emphasized that a rational reconstruction along these lines focuses on what Lakatos (ibid., 91–2) calls 'internal history'. The claim here is that science can be described as a sequence of rational choices made by the scientific community. As such the MSRP concentrates on the internal dynamic of the research program itself. External factors which may influence science, such as the social and political environment, are not accounted for in this reconstruction. Of course a full explanation of scientific changes should include a social history but Lakatos reasons that one can best understand this process by firstly focusing on the internal reasons for theory change first (ibid., 107). 'External' history can later be used to explain any failure of scientists to act according to the MSRP. But in first instance 'internal history' should rationalize that part of science which its practitioners consider its 'best gambits'.

This aim may explain the attraction of the MSRP to economists. The ability to explain the process of theory change as the outcome of a sequence of rational choices must have appealed to economists who consider rationality one of the main assumptions of their own science.[9] Furthermore the MSRP relieved economists of the duty to defend the autonomous character of their science. Indeed for many the development of economics was mainly driven by factors such as class conflict or changes in the socio-political environment (for example Meek 1967a, Spengler 1968). A successful reconstruction of the history of economic thought in terms the MSRP would give economics a more rational, in the sense of scientifically rational, appearance. This ability to raise the scientific status of economics may well explain the appeal of the MSRP to economists (Hands 1985a, 3).

Other reasons for the appeal of the MSRP concern specific features of this methodology. These involve the following considerations:

- The MSRP mitigates the importance of falsification or refutation in demarcating science from other types of activity. The MSRP rationalizes the observation that scientists do not actually attempt to refute their theories. Theories that are maintained in spite of disconfirming evidence either belong to the hard core of a research program or borrow their credibility from related theories in the protective belt that do meet the demand of empirical progress. The MSRP could help to explain the lack of empirical testing in economics.
- The MSRP explicitly recognizes that scientific activity is organized in certain structures. Economic theories are not developed independently but relate in some systematic manner to other theoretical developments. For instance the formation of general equilibrium theory was driven by developments in consumer theory, capital theory and monetary theory. The quantity theory of money led economists to consider the motivations of international trade, inspired a more systematic formulation of supply and demand relations and, through that, even affected the construction of GE theory. The MSRP rationalizes these interdependencies in the history of economic thought. It explains that economists do not choose between specific theories, but organize their activities in an enterprise called the research program.

The controversial scientific status of GE analysis makes it the ultimate litmus test for any rationalizing methodology. In the post war era much intellectual energy has been invested in the development of the GE program, which became a benchmark of deductive rigour and mathematical sophistication that other scientists, even outside economics, aspire to reach. Yet this praise had a price in terms of empirical relevance. Even the most ardent defenders of GE theory concede that it fails to meet any empirical criterion whatsoever (for example Hahn 1984, 45–6). The question therefore arises if economists are justified to consider GE theory as a peak achievement of their science. With what justification can a theory, that so evidently conflicts with reality, be considered one of economics's best gambits? To beg the question is to answer it. One of the most detailed rational reconstructions of economics concerns the history of GE theory, and it is to this topic that I will now turn.

The Neo Walrasian Program

Weintraub (1985b) treated the development of GE theory as a sequence of theories that could be assessed in terms of the MSRP. To that purpose he identified the following set of hard core propositions (Weintraub 1985a, 26; 1985b, 109):

HC1 There exist economic agents.
HC2 Agents have preferences over outcomes.
HC3 Agents independently optimize subject to constraints.
HC4 Choices are made in interrelated markets.
HC5 Agents have full relevant knowledge.
HC6 Observable economic outcomes are coordinated, so they must be discussed with reference to equilibrium states.

These propositions define the essence of what Weintraub called the 'Neo Walrasian research program' (henceforth the NWP). The following positive and negative heuristic (the do's and don't's that guide research in the belt of the program) complement this program:

PH1 Go forth and construct theories in which agents optimize.
PH2 Construct theories that make predictions about changes in equilibrium states.
NH1 Do not construct theories in which irrational behaviour plays any role.
NH2 Do not construct theories in which equilibrium has no meaning.
NH3 Do not test the hard core propositions.

It has to be stressed that Weintraub's formulation of this hard core and heuristic is arbitrary, as the MSRP provides no rules to determine the actual content of these crucial concepts. Accordingly one may easily think of alternative formulations. For example, to account for the different meanings of the term 'equilibrium' in modern economic analysis Backhouse (1991, 405) proposed to replace PH2. with the following:

PH2* Specify the model-specific meanings of equilibrium and disequilibrium and analyze the model in terms of these.

Furthermore Backhouse wants the positive heuristic to reflect the fact that GE theory uses formal models, which leads him to add the following requirement:

PH3 Construct fully-specified, consistent models, simplifying where necessary in order to be able to do this, and draw only those conclusions which can be proved to be implied by the models.

The problem is that the MSRP invites discussion about the meaning and actual contents of the hard core and heuristic of a specific program. What is the actual hard core of this program? Is it constant or does it change over time? Does it identify a unique program or are there several, competing programs? Or are they perhaps different cores within the same program – demi-cores in the terminology of Remenyi (1979)? Such discussions may easily lead to a fruitless hunt for the meaning of terms without greatly improving our understanding of economics' methodological practices.

Weintraub (1985a and 1985b) certainly did not share these doubts. He claimed that his definition of the NWP could be used to rationally reconstruct the history of GE theory. Moreover, he asserted that a reconstruction along these lines demonstrates that GE analysis is indeed one of economics's best gambits and therefore central to most economic theorizing. But to prove this claim he needed to modify the MSRP in one crucial aspect: the two criteria of scientific progress of the MSRP are exclusively empirical. As was explained earlier, these criteria concern the demand for theoretical and empirical progressivity. Further, in spite of the adjective theoretical even the former criterion concerns an empirical requirement, for Lakatos (1970, 118) calls a series of theories theoretically progressive if each new theory 'has some excess empirical content over its predecessor, that is, if it predicts some novel, hitherto unexplained fact'. The emphasis on strictly empirical criteria of progress suggested that a Lakatosian reconstruction of GE theory could never succeed, given that GE theory is first and foremost a program in mathematical economics. It is clear that to explain the internal dynamics of this program an acceptable notion of purely theoretical progress was required, which the MSRP did not provide.[10] Let's see how Weintraub bent the rules a bit to support the scientific credibility of GE theory.

Lakatos's Method of Proofs and Refutations

To escape the conclusion that the MSRP is unsuited to rationally reconstruct the history of GE analysis, Weintraub introduced a dual standard of appraisal into the framework of the MSRP. This standard appraises theories in the protective belt of the program in terms of their theoretical and empirical progressivity, the conventional Lakatosian criteria. But Lakatos had assumed a static hard core and it is this assumption that Weintraub rejected. In his opinion, the history of GE analysis shows that the hard core has its own dynamic and that the MSRP should provide a set of criteria to assess that development. Weintraub found these criteria in Lakatos' method of 'proofs and refutations'. This method was explicitly designed to assess progress in the mathematical sciences and therefore seemed exceptionally appropriate to appraise developments in mathematical economics.

According to Lakatos, progress in mathematical knowledge is driven by the interaction between conjectures and proofs. He suggests that in mathematics a failure to prove a conjecture may lead to a refinement of the original conjecture and in turn to more informative proofs. The process of proofs and refutations results in a sequence of theorems, lemmas and proofs which constitutes an increase in mathematical knowledge. The validity of this thesis was demonstrated in a case study of the history of Euler's theorems on polyhedrons (Lakatos 1976).

Weintraub adopted this method to explain the establishment of the hard core of the NWP. As the hard core of a research program is irrefutable, this formation is not controlled by empirical success or failure. Yet is also clear that 'the actual hard core of a programme does not actually emerge fully armed like Athene from the head of Zeus. It develops slowly, by a long, preliminary process of trial and error' (Lakatos 1970, 48n). Unfortunately, Lakatos does not explain how this process takes place.

Weintraub's solution to that problem is to argue that the interpretation of the terms of the core changes in a process which he calls the 'hardening' of the core (Weintraub 1985b, 141). This means that the propositions of the core remain fixed, but that critical scrutiny fixes the meaning of their terms as the propositions develop into the hard core of a specific research program. For example the hard core the NWP requires clarification of such terms as 'agents', 'markets' and 'equilibrium'. This clarification is a kind of consistency check of the different parts of the hard core. For HC1–HC6 to form the core of a viable research program it should be possible to explain equilibrium while assuming that agents optimize, that markets are interrelated, etc. Should these propositions be inconsistent, then the positive heuristic 'go forth and construct theories with equilibrium outcomes' gives ambiguous advice, to say the least.

Weintraub argued that the search for a mathematical proof of the existence of competitive equilibrium in the GE literature in the period 1930–1954 was inspired by the need to provide a consistency check of this nature. He claimed that at the beginning of this period equilibrium was not considered a problematic notion. It was understood as a balancing of forces which seemed consistent with the predominantly partial equilibrium theories of that period. Consequently the notion of equilibrium raised no questions of analytical importance and economists were not interested in a mathematical proof of its existence. However papers by von Stackelberg and Zeuthen in the early 1930s showed that this view was mistaken. They demonstrated that the equilibrium solution of the GE model developed by Cassel (1927) could not rule out negative prices. Accordingly, this result was inconsistent with the proposition that economic outcomes are coordinated (see HC5). This recognition started a search for an equilibrium solution of the GE model which did exclude such prices and which would be consistent with the other assumptions of the NWP. In this process the notion of equilibrium underwent a series of reinterpretations which were intended to bring about this consistency. The analysis of Robbins (1930) shows that in the early 1930s equilibrium signified stationarity or a balance of forces. But in the late 1930s this interpretation shifted towards the potential reconciliation of individual plans, a notion developed by Hayek (1937) and Hicks (1939). This definition raised a new problem: could expectations be coordinated? Morgenstern (1935) argued that if expectations are endogenous, then adjustment processes may invoke an infinite regress of changes and never reach equilibrium. To circumvent this problem individuals need to know each others' choices beforehand. The only notion of equilibrium consistent with coordinated outcomes is that of an actual pre-reconciliation of plans. This restriction is expressed in the assumption that agents have perfect knowledge (HC5). Only in this manner can the notion of equilibrium as mutual coordination be reconciled with the contention that 'agents have preferences over outcomes', that 'agents optimize subject to constraints' and 'make choices in interrelated markets'.

It was Weintraub's contention that by the early 1950s other key terms of the NWP, 'agents', 'preferences', 'optimize', 'constraint', 'market', had 'hardened' into equally well-defined meanings (Weintraub 1985b, 112–113). As explained above, this process was driven by the need for consistent theoretical reasoning, which forced the GE theorists to abandon conceptions that would not fit the mold of the NWP. The result was a GE model that used

Hicks' conception of households with preferences and optimizing choices, Koopman's production choice theory, and Patinkin's framework of market interrelationships. The hard core of the NWP, then, was not a finished product when Walras published the first part of his *Eléments d'Économie Politique Pure* in 1874. On the contrary, HC1–HC6 were not established as the hard core of that program until in the 1950s Arrow, Debreu and McKenzie showed that the propositions they contained were, by their work, no longer problematic.

Weintraub (1985b) presented this history of GE theory as a positive appraisal of the NWP. He claimed that the hardening of the hard core of that program was a sequence of progressive problem shifts which satisfies the standards of Lakatos's method of proofs and refutations. This means that it produced 'a sequence of interpretations of the terms of the hard core such that (1) each successive interpretation is manifest in a consistent model, (2) each successive interpretation contains the interpretation of the predecessor, and (3) each allows a concept uninterpreted by that predecessor to be interpreted' (ibid., 117). By appraising GE analysis as a mathematical science, Weintraub rationalized the feeling among economists that GE analysis is a peak achievement of their science. In the terminology of the MSRP he managed to reconstruct one of economics's acknowledged best gambits as scientific and his case study therefore corroborates the claims of the MSRP as a meta methodology as well.

Empirical Appraisal of the NWP

But the story does not end with this conclusion. Lakatos's method of proofs and refutations was intended to appraise the non-empirical part of the NWP only. Work in the protective belt of the program should be appraised in terms of the conventional empirical standards of the MSRP, theoretical and empirical progressivity (Weintraub 1985a, 34–35; 1985b, 119–120, 173). One may therefore rightfully ask: is the methodological criticism of the NWP warranted? Is GE analysis indeed empirically empty? Weintraub warned not to confuse this question with the falsifiability of the GE model which after all is part of the hard core and cannot be appraised in empirical terms (ibid., 119). Yet, rather surprisingly, in his 1985 book he did not attempt to determine the empirical progressiveness of the NWP (Rosenberg 1992, 101–102). Nonetheless, he seemed to assume that it satisfies this requirement as well. In a footnote to a discussion of Rosenberg's contention that GE analysis is a branch of applied mathematics that does not have empirical significance, he observed that 'one who claims that general equilibrium analysis leads to no empirical work, or only to retrospective qualitative predictions, makes a serious error' (Weintraub 1985b, 53n).[11] This error involves a denial of the evident fact that partial equilibrium and other applied theories in the protective belt of the NWP are empirically well-supported, applications which are inconceivable without the support of GE analysis (ibid., 13 and 118).

In a subsequent study (1988) Weintraub tried to substantiate the claim that the NWP is empirically progressive. In this case study he reconstructed a theory sequence in applied household economics which is supposed to exemplify the sort of progress characteristic of a successful research program. First, he argued that the sequence involves extensions of the interpretations of the relevant hard core terms. Successor theories extend the hard core in such a way that the predecessor's interpretation is encompassed by the successor's interpretation (Weintraub 1988, 223). Secondly, he then showed that the sequence has excess empirical content: the subsequent theories predict novel facts. This means that in the terms of the MSRP the sequence is theoretically progressive. Thirdly, because these predictions are at least partially corroborated and are certainly falsifiable, the sequence is empirically progressive as well (ibid., 219). On the basis of this evidence he concluded that 'there is, if not justice, at least meaning in the claim that the Neo Walrasian program is progressive in the Lakatosian sense.' (ibid., 224).

In retrospect, it is remarkable that a methodology which stresses empirical criteria of progress did not inspire more empirical appraisals of economic theory.[12] Weintraub (1988) is one of the few detailed case studies of the development of empirical work in GE analysis. Of the studies listed in De Marchi's (1991) summary of applications of the MSRP to economics in the period 1972–1989 just eight concern an explicit empirical assessment of a putative research program. Can a reason for the lack of empirical appraisals of economics be that the separation between empirical and theoretical work in economics is more strict than suggested by the MSRP? Diamond's (1988) citation analysis shows that GE analysis has had a negligible impact on empirical work. In her *History of Econometric Ideas* (1990) Morgan concludes that econometrics failed to realize the ideal of a truly synthetic economics, a union between mathematical and statistical economics. She points out that econometricians have always been concerned with the problem of finding satisfactory empirical models rather than testing economic theories.

These findings confirm Blaug's conviction that it is important to distinguish between economic theories and models. In GE analysis the former study the formal consequences of Walras's suggestion that in equilibrium all markets clear simultaneously. The latter express this belief in a system of simultaneous equations which explain how prices are actually determined in a real-world economy (Blaug 1991b, 506). A failure to show that prices are actually determined simultaneously therefore falsifies the GE model but not the theory. Economists often practice what Blaug calls 'innocuous falsification' (Blaug 1980, 128, 259). They do not test theories but models. This contention suggests that the interaction between the hard core and protective belt of the NWP is limited. Economists hardly reject theories, let alone that a lack of theoretical and empirical progress impinges on the credibility of their formal theories.

Mathematics as a Unique Source of Knowledge

In the final analysis, Weintraub's appraisal of the NWP conveys a normative bias. He considered GE theory a progressive research program, because it uses mathematics as its main tool of analysis and mathematics is, in Weintraub's eyes, a unique source of knowledge.

Recall that in the period 1930–1954 GE analysis 'hardened' into the hard core of a specific research program, the NWP. This process consisted of a sequence of progressive problem shifts in the sense of Lakatos's method of proofs and refutations, which wielded out inconsistent propositions and established an 'unproblematic' well-defined hard core. This observation leads Weintraub to assert that the formation of a genuine research program requires mathematization (ibid., 141, 173). Apparently, he believed that consistent theorizing crucially depends on the ability to formulate mathematical theories. That is why he claimed that 'Neo Walrasian economics is better developed than theory sequences in other social-science disciplines. Its guiding principles, its core propositions, have gone through the hardening process' (ibid.). According to Weintraub, in economics only the NWP has reached a level of formalization which allowed it to develop into a well-defined research program (ibid., 141, 144). But by arguing that it is progressive too, he turned his mathematical standard of appraisal into a compelling strategy of research. In his vision science must be mathematical science (for example Boland 1987).

This standard of appraisal involves a strong cognitive claim: mathematics is a unique source of knowledge. Weintraub identified science with mathematical science because he considered mathematics the purest form of thinking (Weintraub 1985b, 176). According to him, 'knowledge' is not a feature of an independent reality 'out there', but is essentially a product of the mind. Knowledge is generated by a process that likens Lakatos's method of proofs and refutations; ideas are proposed, criticized and refined into new ideas. In this manner the mind systematically organizes sense experiences, a process we call learning. In that sense it seems as if the human mind is 'programmed' to look for structures. As far as learning is a precondition of human survival, one may contend that we necessarily impose structure upon our various sense perceptions. This makes mathematics a unique source of knowledge, for mathematics itself is the study of structures (ibid., 178).

However, this position was not consistently maintained. In another place Weintraub adopted a more moderate point of view, which allowed for other activities to enter the scientific domain. He argued that 'we should be alert to the possibility that a full appraisal may require separate attention to the mathematical work, the theoretical work, the empirical work, and the rhetoric associated with each; each requires evaluation, perhaps by different methods' (ibid., 174). By different methods? It seems that Weintraub underestimated the serious implications of this concession for any appraisal of economics, for how does one combine these different standards into a criterion of scientific status? In this remark one finds the kernel of the problem that would in 1991 force Weintraub to reject methodology altogether. This is the question that, if economists adopt very diverse standards to assess the scientific nature of their work, then how does one know what constitutes scientific knowledge?

Economic Knowledge as a Social Convention

Originally, Weintraub had intended to complement his appraisal of the progressive NWP with a case study of a degenerating program, the stability literature on the dynamics of the GE model. Yet this intent resulted in a rejection of the entire project to reconstruct and appraise economic theory in terms of the methodological framework of the MSRP. What brought him to abandon this project was the understanding that knowledge is a social construction, not something that exists independently of human understanding and interpretation. As was explained above, in his 1985 book Weintraub assumed the existence of a unique, interpersonal source of knowledge, namely mathematics. He argued that mathematics is a very pure form of knowledge which is shared by all people alike. It consists of 'structures [which] do not seem to vary much from person to person or from group of people to group of people' (ibid., 178).

Yet a conference on 'the consequences of rhetoric' caused him to reconsider this opinion. He recognized that certainty is a concept alien to science and that there is no philosophical standard of scientific goodness. All standards must face McCloskey's (1994, 93) probing question, how do you know what constitutes knowledge before it is actually discovered? All normative methodologies commit the fallacy of what she calls 'pre-science': knowing before knowing (ibid.; for a similar comment, see Rosenberg 1992, 108). The problem is that knowledge consists of very heterogenous information which can impossibly be measured in terms of a uniform standard. How does one compare the knowledge that a proof of the uniqueness of a general economic equilibrium requires the assumption of gross substitutability with the estimated value of a Keynesian income multiplier? We must accept that knowledge has many faces and that there exists no single method for discovering it.[13] Accordingly, what constitutes knowledge or not is a matter of social convention. Science is an activity that is carried out by a community of scholars who determine what counts as good scientific practice. Outsiders have only a minor influence on the scientific standards of this community.

Weintraub understood the implication of this view for his historical analysis. If there is no unique standard of appraisal, then a rational reconstruction of economic science merely gives a possible account of its history, not a true description of how it actually developed. History is not something 'out there', a unique and independent piece of information that can be discovered by means of a specific analysis. Every historian writes his own history. What prevents the field from becoming chaos is the necessity to communicate with one's colleagues. Weintraub argued that this requires a shared set of conversational standards which allows a comparison and scrutiny of results. He adopted the terminology of McCloskey's rhetorics project and said that 'conversation' among scholars enforces the adoption of a set of rules, which may become a scientific standard in the community. Accordingly, there is no unique formula for generating appraisals, just as there is no single test for deciding what constitutes 'good' economics and what not. Weintraub now believed that for appraisals of this kind, the history of science is too complex. Indeed, an assessment of that development requires attention to 'the mathematical work, the theoretical work, the empirical work, and the rhetoric associated with each' (ibid., 174). The validity of a historical analysis can only be determined by the relevant community of scholars, that is historians. The primary objective of history is therefore to persuade this community that it performs 'good' science by appealing to its unwritten and probably unconscious conversational rules.[14]

Similarly, Weintraub (1991) tried to persuade his readership that the dynamics literature of the 1950s and 1960s was part of a 'language game' which structured discourse among scholars working in the field of GE analysis. According to Weintraub, conversation stabilizes the meaning of theoretical terms in an agreeable and understandable way (ibid., 124). The result of this language game was a transformation in which economic discourse about dynamics changed into a mathematical discourse about the stability of competitive equilibrium (ibid., 139). This transformation involved a change of scientific practice: the linguistic rules required the analyst to specify a mathematical GE model. But this practice became accepted only because it was accompanied by a stabilization of what Schumpeter would call a particular 'vision'. This was the idea that the economy could be seen as a mechanical entity with a capacity to maintain a position of rest. According to

Weintraub, it was the common acceptance of this view which made the mathematical approach to GE theory and its dynamical problems unproblematic (ibid., 140–142, 146).

This is a striking observation. Instead of routing out ideological bias, we now see that the causality runs in the opposite way. It is scientific progress, however one is inclined to measure it, which enhances a certain vision of how the economy actually functions. Conclusions like this force us to reconsider Schumpeter's claim that in the course of history science helps us to combat the spells of ideology.

The details of this account of the history of GE analysis will not detain us here. The reader is referred to Weintraub's book to determine for him or herself the validity of this particular interpretation. In the present context what matters is that Weintraub himself abandoned the attempt to appraise GE theory in terms of a specific methodological framework, the MSRP, and that his rejection of this approach was inspired by the post modernist criticisms of methodology outlined above. However, also from other corners the MSRP has been attacked as a proper method to appraise the work of economists in general and GE theory in particular.

A Final Word on the MSRP

According to Rosenberg (1992), the attraction of the MSRP to economists was that it offered 'consolation' for a failure to meet more conventional empirical criteria. The MSRP even appraised the most abstract, mathematical work as 'scientific', if it could be shown to form part of the hard core of a progressive research program. However, Rosenberg argued that the comfort, which the MSRP offered, was illusory, for it depended on a false demarcation between science and other activities (Rosenberg 1986, 133; 1992, 100).

The reason for this negative appraisal of Rosenberg was that the notions used to determine scientific progress in Lakatos's sense, 'excess empirical content', 'novel fact', 'corroboration', are ambiguous and impractical (see also Caldwell 1982, 86). For Popper (1963, 243), a novel fact is something which has 'never been thought of before'. Evidently most sciences would fail to satisfy this strict criterion of factual novelty. The failure to specify a more workable sense of empirical content makes the distinction between science and other activities meaningless. All sciences can be made to comply to a poorly defined, ambiguous criterion of scientific status. Rosenberg (1986, 138) therefore called upon economists and philosophers to cooperate in order to uncover more appropriate standards of appraisal. These should improve our understanding of the distinctive aims and claims of economics and its relations to neighbouring enterprises.

Nonetheless, Rosenberg considered the distinction between science and non-science too important to await the outcome of this discussion. For that reason he proposed to adopt a very pragmatic yet 'innocuous' criterion of scientific status, namely predictive success. He argued that what distinguishes true 'science' from other activities is a certain social responsibility. Economics may suggest policy changes which affect the well-being of millions; the laws of physics are relied upon to prevent structures, buildings, and bridges from collapsing; but literary pursuits, music and other arts provide mere entertainment. That is why we demand evidence concerning the safety and effectiveness of the former type of activity. According to Rosenberg (1986, 138; 1992, 18), predictive success at least gives us an estimate of these qualities.

Likewise, Hausman (1992) argued that the MSRP failed as a scientific program because it relied on what he called a form of sophisticated falsificationism. As such, it could never give an explanation for all those typical features and laws of economics which are more or less not borne out by the facts. A falsificationist methodology would eventually remove such laws from our set of hard core propositions. Hausman (1992, 87 and 203) therefore concluded that the MSRP fails as a descriptive methodology. Further, he maintained that applying the MSRP to economics is unenlightening, for it raises questions about such details as the 'true' content of the hard core, or the exact relationship between heuristic and hard core. The MSRP crucially depends on these notions but offers no recipe of how to actually implement them.

The MSRP, then, is uninformative and wrong. A methodology appropriate to economics should explain why economists accept laws they cannot prove to be true. According to Hausman, the proper view of economics is that of an 'inexact and separate' science. It is this view, he asserts, which explains the centrality of equilibrium theory in economics. For that reason we shall return to Hausman's characterization of economics at a later stage.

But the MSRP is more than a prescriptive methodology. It also provides a framework for rationally reconstructing the development of sciences like economics. To appraise the success of this historical task, one may ask if the MSRP satisfies its own criteria. Put differently, to count as a positive appraisal of the MSRP, a rational reconstruction of science in terms of the MSRP must satisfy the criteria of theoretical and empirical progressivity. That is, it must accommodate a novel fact in the history of science which is corroborated in further research. Philosophers agree that by this standard the MSRP is not a good historiography of science.

The De Marchi and Blaug (1991) volume assessing the applications of the MSRP to economics provides an impressive list of developments in economics that the MSRP could not accommodate. These include insights from game theory, the decline of process analysis in econometrics, the literature on the stability analysis in GE theory, the critical work of Sraffa, the anxiety of econometricians to test their hypotheses about equilibrium unemployment, the sociology of the rational expectations revolutions, and a number of other features of the history of economic thought (see McCloskey 1994, 88–89).[15] In these cases theory change in economics could not be modelled as a rational response of the economics community.[16]

To this list Backhouse (1993) added the complaint that the MSRP is too inflexible to give an adequate reconstruction of the history of GE analysis. The MSRP was unsuited to that task because it treats the hard core as a fixed set of propositions, while the role of GE analysis in economics has changed significantly since 1950. In the 1950s GE analysis was fundamental to economic theorizing meaning that most of microeconomic theory was based on the precepts of the GE model or studied its implications. But this role changed in the 1960s, mainly due to the failure to obtain general stability results. In addition new developments, such as game theory, provided an alternative conceptual basis for economics. As a result, GE analysis became peripheral to the NWP. Backhouse argued that its role changed from being fundamental to a large part of the subject, to one where it was fundamental to less and less important subjects. A proper history of GE analysis should account for these changes.

These examples suggest that perhaps 'external' history is more important than was suggested by Lakatos (for example see his 1970, 107) and his followers (for example Blaug 1975a, 257).

The problem is that the description the MSRP gives of theory change in science makes it almost impossible to assess the validity of this account. The unique contribution of the MSRP to the philosophy of science is that it focuses on a series of theories as they develop through time (Caldwell 1982, 96). The central tenet of this view is that theory changes are related in a systematic manner and that methodology should focus on the motives for these changes. According to the criteria of the MSRP, scientists should rationally prefer a progressive over a degenerating research program. However, Lakatos defies 'instant' rationality. 'One must treat budding research programs leniently: programmes may take decades before they get off the ground and become empirically progressive' (Lakatos 1976, 6). Moreover, it cannot be excluded that a degenerating program may in the future become progressive again. From this perspective theory evaluation becomes impossible, for when should one make the final decision to accept a program over its competitors? Indeed scientists could rationally cling indefinitely to a degenerating research program. Is 120 years of theory development enough to conclude that the NWP is not progressive? Ingrao and Israel (1990) conclude that it is. The striking conclusion of their detailed history of the mathematical analysis of GE theory since Canard, Cournot and other predecessors of Walras is that 'there is a contradiction between the theory's aims and the consequences derived from the system of hypotheses constituting its structure . . . The only way out of this situation is to jettison explicitly the programmatic central core, that has been so carefully preserved throughout the many paradigmatic shifts' (Ingrao and Israel 1990, 361–362).[17] Yet Weintraub (1985b) dates the start of the NWP from 1954 when the hard core of program had fully hardened. That would make the NWP a relatively young research program and insulate it from the requirement of empirical progress. Which is right? The MSRP does not permit unambiguous choice.[18]

Conclusion

To wind up the argument of this section, I conclude that the picture of equilibrium theory as a scientific research program in the sense of Lakatos is not convincing. The MSRP offers criteria which would allow us to appraise GE theory as either a successful or a degenerating program, but methodologists simply refuse to take the test. For this the MSRP can be partly blamed, because it calls for patience when a specific program like GE theory fails to predict novel facts and hence does not have excess content. We have just seen that Lakatos advised to treat budding programs leniently, because it may take decades to develop the required tests for empirical progressiveness. How long exactly one is rationally advised to wait no one knows, which virtually robs the MSRP of its explanatory power as a meta theory explaining how science progresses. GE theory may be a scientific research program, but we are not sure.

Weintraub showed what happens when the procedural rules of a scientific methodology start to shift. He amended the rules of the MSRP to validate GE theory as a mathematical research program which could not be expected to meet the criteria of empirical progressiveness. He thus took the easy way out, but the poor mathematical results of stability theory later forced him to acknowledge that the hard core of the NWP was not as hard as he had initially maintained. The result was a complete abandonment of the MSRP. His alternative approach, which treated GE theory as a kind of language game, led to a conclusion which in the rational framework of the MSRP would have been unthinkable. Scientific progress does not reduce the domain of metaphysical claims like ideology in science, but rather in the case of GE theory it tends to strengthen them. We shall see in the subsequent sections that there are others who underline the importance of the particular vision attached to GE theory in the scientific process.

THE DIMINISHING RETURNS OF ECONOMIC SCIENCE

Introduction

Rosenberg (1992) has an outspoken opinion on the object of science and the extent to which economics can be considered a science. According to him, what distinguishes science from other activities is that it aims for predictive success. He maintains that there exists a widespread agreement in the scientific community that (ibid., 17):

- The acquisition of knowledge is the ultimate object of science,[19] and that
- Predictive success is a necessary condition of knowledge.

Rosenberg claims that economists subscribe to this picture of science (ibid., 17 and 56).

> It seems evident that if forced to, most neoclassical economists would endorse an empiricist account of knowledge, which makes the proximate goal of science the successful testing of its claims by experience and, more specifically, by prediction. . . . I share the economists' commitment to predictive success as at least a necessary condition of knowledge.

Concerning the meaning of this criterion, Rosenberg warns that 'what is crucial in science is not the sheer number of confirmed predictions a theory makes, but the proportion of right predictions to wrong ones and the precision of the predictions it makes, along with the amount of surprise generated by its predictions' (ibid., 18). Yet this standard is invoked as being 'the most innocuous epistemological requirement on any science' (ibid., xiv). What inspired him to define a criterion of scientific status in these exclusively empirical terms was not some deep philosophical insight. On the contrary, Rosenberg (1986, 138; 1992, 18–19) holds that contemporary epistemology is unable to define general cognitive standards making a universal and unambiguous demarcation criterion between science and other types of activities impossible. All attempts, then, to distinguish science from non-science are merely conventional and his choice for an empirical standard of scientific status is defended on pragmatic grounds. Not only do economists in general seem to endorse an instrumentalist view on science, Rosenberg says they do so for good reasons. He stresses that the purpose of economic science is to advise policy makers on the right policies to pursue. This aim gives economics a social responsibility many other sciences lack. For example a reader in old English prose need not be concerned about the effects his teachings may have outside the walls of academia. But the economist needs to take such effects into account, for his advice may affect the purchasing power of millions. That is why we require some kind of evidence concerning the reliability of the latter's work. Rosenberg (1986, 138; 1992, 18) claims that predictive success gives at least some estimate of the safety and effectiveness of the policy proposals made by economists.

In his book *Economics – Mathematical Politics or Science of Diminishing Returns?* (1992) Rosenberg uses the criterion of predictive success to assess the scientific status of economics, which to him corresponds to neoclassical economics. The present section will discuss this work in some detail because it has an important bearing on the nature of equilibrium theory. Specifically, Rosenberg is interested in the centrality of GE theory to modern (neoclassical) economics. He considers the cognitive status of this theory one of the most challenging items on the agenda of the philosophy of economics. GE theory raises perplexing questions because of its highly abstract character, its supremely unrealistic assumptions, and the alleged irrelevance of its consequences for real economics. Yet especially economists seem to have a valid reason for their adherence to the equilibrium assumption: equilibrium is what makes economic phenomena predictable (ibid., 193).

Since ancient times scholars have recognized that to explain change one needs to assume something constant. Equilibrium provides this point of reference. Paradoxically, it allows one to explain change by assuming that nothing changes at all, at least not within the time period required for equilibrium to be established. The method of dynamic analysis based on this idea is called comparative statics. It proceeds by comparing equilibria to determine the effect of a change in exogenous variables. Economists are well acquainted with this use of the equilibrium construct. We have seen in chapter two of this book that Marshall was one of the first to recognize that by invoking an appropriate ceteris paribus clause the equilibrium assumption could be employed to examine economic causes of any duration. In his hands the equilibrium assumption became a powerful tool to handle the problem of time in economic analysis. This role may explain the lasting appeal of the equilibrium method to economists. Rosenberg says that the role of equilibrium explanations 'as a stopping-point is the strongest purely intellectual source of the attraction of equilibrium theories in the sciences, both natural and social' (ibid., 205–6). Indeed, the history of science has shown that an idea allowing one to force order upon a disorderly world, is truly irresistible.

The following sections will raise a number of questions about Rosenberg's view of economics. To start with I shall discuss his contention that economics is not, and cannot be, an empirical science. This discussion will be followed by an analysis of the reason why economics fails to comply to the demands of an empirical science. Thirdly it may be asked what function economics has, if it is not a science in Rosenberg's empirical sense. Finally I shall discuss the implications of his contention that economics is best considered a branch of applied mathematics for the nature of equilibrium theory.

Economics is not an Empirical Science

A main theme in Rosenberg's work is that economics is not an empirical science, but is best seen as branch of applied mathematics (Rosenberg 1983) or a form of contractarian philosophy (Rosenberg 1992). To start with the former claim, Rosenberg argues that it is impossible to assess the empirical record of economics. Discussions about the empirical success of economics always take on an unproductive 'yes it does, no it doesn't' character because there is no unambiguous standard to measure empirical progress or predictive success. On the contrary 'the notions of empirical content, novel fact, and corroboration are among the most vexed ones in the philosophy of science' (ibid., 100). But without these notions, the distinction between science and non-science, defined according to some empirical criterion, becomes meaningless.

For that reason Rosenberg's confident assertion that economics is not an (empirical) science seems paradoxical. He tries to escape this paradox by arguing that there is a growing concern within the economics community itself about the lack of predictive success and the unrealisticness of economic theories. At best economics can claim an improvement in generic predictions, but its specific predictions are generally considered inadequate (ibid., 67–70, 103–107, 224–227). Instead of predicting novel facts, the improvement in empirical content it shows typically concern the accommodation of obvious ones. The extensions of Neo Walrasian economics to problems traditionally considered non-economic are a case in point. These applications do not predict or explain novel facts, but rather consist in demonstrating that the actual is possible, that some phenomena whose occurrence is already well-established could have resulted from the operation of rational choices (for some examples, see Hirshleifer 1985).

Furthermore, Rosenberg claims that the ongoing discussion about the scientific nature of economics proves that the empirical success of economics is a matter of serious doubt (Rosenberg 1992, 60, 97, 102, 111). Why else should economists be concerned with intricate methodological questions? Such issues would not arise, if economics could be shown to be a well corroborated and predictively successful science. According to him most economic methodologies are simply defenses of economics' empirically weak record. For example he says that Friedman's instrumentalism was intended to dispel the growing concern about the unrealisticness of economic theories. But this concern arose in the first place because of dissatisfaction with the predictive success of economics (ibid., 60). Likewise Lakatos's MSRP appealed to economists because it justified their emphasis on formal theory building. According to the MSRP testing takes place in the protective belt of a research program only, not in the irrefutable hard core. Rosenberg contends that if economics could be shown to satisfy the conventional empirical standards of appraisal, the need for these elaborate methodological defenses would not arise.

Given the centrality to his work of the claim that economics does not satisfy the criteria of an empirical science, it is remarkable that Rosenberg hardly substantiates it. He rests content with the argument that a unique standard to measure empirical progress does not exist and that it is therefore impossible to make hard claims about the predictive record of economics. Yet he himself specifies a very specific criterion of predictive success, which is the proportion of right predictions to wrong ones (ibid., 18). Rosenberg is forced to be explicit about this standard, otherwise his notion of science would be meaningless. But if one defines such a standard, why not use it to assess the empirical record of economics? Rosenberg does not do so. He simply asserts that economics fails to meet it (Hands 1984, 497; Mäki 1996) and approvingly cites Leontief on the matter. The latter complains that 'in no other field of empirical enquiry has so massive and sophisticated a statistical machinery been used with such indifferent results. Nevertheless theorists continue to turn out model after model and mathematical statisticians to devise complicated procedures one after another' (quoted in Rosenberg 1992, 64). Rosenberg says economics has shown some progress in terms of its generic predictions, but progress of this kind is not considered sufficient. In his opinion a truly progressive science should be able to increase the specificity of generic predictions and it is in this latter regard that economics fails to meet the mark (ibid., 70). As a matter of fact, he argues, it has not progressed significantly beyond the generic predictions made by Adam Smith well over 200 years ago. Now if that does not show that economics is not a progressive empirical science, he asks, then what does?

Complexity and Intentional Psychology

Rosenberg's portrait of economics is not very optimistic. His main thesis is that economics is not and will never become an empirical science. It was argued in the previous section that Rosenberg does not substantiate his claim that economics is not an empirical science, that it is not science at all. Substantially more effort is exerted to validate the related argument that the accuracy of economic predictions cannot improve and that, consequently, economics will never become an empirical science. The main obstacle in the way of empirical success is the familiar problem of the complexity of economic forces. Rosenberg contends that in economics the causes are simply too multifarious for the major ones to be identified (ibid., 116). That is why ceteris paribus clauses are not very helpful in understanding the operation of economic forces and why better economic explanations and predictions are not likely to be had.

The cause of this complexity is the unpredictability of human behaviour. As Rosenberg observes, 'any human behaviour can be the product of an indefinite number of combinations of expectations and preferences' (ibid., 144). Consequently, a causal explanation of economic choice is simply out of the question. Common sense may tell us what motivates people to act in a certain manner, but this common sense explanation cannot be empirically verified. The common sense explanation of human action is that people choose those actions which they believe to be most suited to the attainment of their goals. The problem is, however, that different sets of beliefs and desires may produce the same behaviour. 'Beliefs' and 'desires' are intentional variables that belong to the domain of folk psychology. As such they do not describe natural kinds; that is, 'they do not label types of discrete states that share the same manageably small set of causes and effects and so cannot be brought together in causal generalizations' (ibid., 235).

Yet economists claim to have a causal explanation of economic behaviour. Rational choice theory explains that people choose their actions so as to best satisfy their preferences, given their limited resources and their expectations. But this theory is a straightforward variant on the folk-psychological principle stated above and does, for that reason, not escape the problem that human behaviour is too diverse and erratic for its main causes to be identified. Rational choice theory, then, is patently false. 'The theory of rational choice is inadequate', Rosenberg tells us, 'that is, makes false predictions, because people are irrational' (ibid., 116).[20]

To appreciate the scope of this problem it is necessary to point out that Rosenberg is a methodological reductionist. He denies that macroeconomics is a separate field of study (ibid., 129). For him collective entities have no independent existence, but are aggregates which should be reduced to their fundamental parts, the individual. The success of economic predictions, therefore, crucially depends on the empirical validity of the microtheory of economic behaviour (ibid.). But this theory is false and, more importantly, offers no scope for improvement. Economics, then, is not a science and will never become one.

Economics as Mathematical Politics

This conclusion is of special significance to equilibrium economics, which Rosenberg defines as neoclassical GE theory. It was argued above that an important attraction of equilibrium theory is that systems which tend towards or reside in equilibrium, show predictable behaviour. It is this feature which explains the success of equilibrium theory in physics and evolutionary biology. For example in evolutionary biology equilibrium theory explains the observed stability of gene ratios across populations. But given the degree of complexity of economic forces, it may well be questioned if the economy is stable enough for its behaviour to be predictable in similar terms. The biological systems studied by evolutionary biology are stable because changes in gene frequencies are not self-reinforcing. But people do respond to each other which may cause cumulative price changes. In economics there is no evidence that a stable equilibrium actually exists. Do we really know that prices tend to a stable, equilibrium price level? If this equilibrium does not exist, equilibrium theory is pre-empted. It has no explanatory role because, in contrast to physics and evolutionary biology, in economics there is no actual equilibrium to be explained. The problem of endogenous change suggests that economic equilibrium theory will never enjoy the scientific success of similar approaches in physics and evolutionary biology.

But if economics is not science, what is it? Rosenberg gives two answers. First, he argues that, not only can economics never become an empirical science, economists do not treat it as one. He maintains that the history of their discipline shows that economists are more concerned about the deductive rigour of their theories than about their practical use (ibid., 244). Like mathematicians, they seem unwilling to submit their central theoretical achievements to empirical tests. Indeed, he contends, the development of economics has been insulated from empirical influences. The great depression of the 1930s was an event that temporarily caused economists to lose their faith in the ability of markets to automatically establish equilibrium between supply and demand, but not for very long. When in the 1970s Keynesian economics failed to handle the combination of rising inflation and unemployment rates, economists soon returned to the classical equilibrium theories that Keynes had rejected. For Rosenberg this U-turn shows that in economics lessons from the past have no lasting influence. Together with the relative unconcern for the factual application of economic theory, this observation leads him to suggest that economics is best seen as a branch of applied mathematics (ibid., 220).

Secondly, Rosenberg sees an important role for GE theory as a form of political philosophy. This function is by no means a new one. Economists have long recognized that one of the attractions of equilibrium theory is that it explains why trade between self-interested individuals in a competitive market economy results in coordinated outcomes rather than social chaos. GE theory is the formal explanation of this claim about how the unintended consequences of uncoordinated selfishness results in the most efficient exploitation of scarce resources in the satisfaction of wants. The theory therefore provides a strong argument in favour of a capitalist economic order (ibid., 221). According to Rosenberg, this explains why economists stick to GE theory, in spite of its poor empirical record (ibid., 220). It is ideology, in other words, which explains the centrality or dominance of GE theory, not its scientific track record.

What are the prospects of economics as a branch of applied mathematics? Like other branches of mathematics these prospects are uncertain. The empirical relevance of mathematics stems from the fact that it guides research in other sciences. So even when mathematics itself has no direct empirical applications, it may improve the predictions of other sciences. For example, 19th century non-Euclidian geometry failed to give a logically consistent explanation of the structure of space. But it had an unsuspected pay off when it proved essential in the theory of relativity, and so aided empirical progress in physics. Likewise, the predictions of GE theory are not borne out by the facts. But shorn of its original economic interpretation the theory finds unsuspected applications in other fields. For example evolutionary biology uses the formalism and results of GE theory to explain balance and competition in the evolution of the biosphere (ibid., 250). This was a pay-off that no GE theorist could have expected. As a form of mathematics, economics need not be, what Rosenberg calls, a science of diminishing returns.

THE INEXACT AND SEPARATE SCIENCE OF ECONOMICS

Introduction

Like Rosenberg, Hausman is concerned with the role of GE analysis in economic theory. In earlier publications (1981a, 1981b) he explained that abstract GE theory has no explanatory role. In these studies he argues that, contrary to a common view (for example Debreu 1959, Malinvaud 1972), GE models do not explain prices because they contain illegitimate simplifying assumptions (Hausman 1981a, 144). In his opinion their main function is heuristic: they are useful in the development of empirical economic theories. Also the insights from GE theory prevent us from committing logical errors. GE theory shows that most arguments in favour of a competitive economic system are based on rash speculation rather than coherent reasoning. Such reasoning would show that the beneficial operation of the invisible hand is an illusion, because even the sufficient conditions for GE cannot be satisfied. In contrast to the assumptions of GE theory, in reality agents do not possess full relevant knowledge, a full range of future markets does not actually exist, etc., which renders the theory inapplicable to real economies. Yet in spite of this conclusion Hausman does not consider the further development of these theories a waste of intellectual energy. The success of the existence proofs of GE theory makes him confident that GE theory has the potential of becoming an explanatory theory (ibid., 155).

> Such models show that equilibrium theory is capable of examining at least some sorts of complicated economic equilibria, and thus they give theorists reason to believe that they are on the track of an adequate general economic theory . . . By weakening and complicating the stipulations needed to demonstrate the existence of more complex equilibria, theorists can come closer to being able to apply the models to real economies.

Equilibrium Theories and Equilibrium Models

Hausman further elaborates on the role of equilibrium theory in his book *The Inexact and Separate Science of Economics* (1992). To explain this role he distinguishes between the meanings of models and theories in economics. He asserts that for economists models are definitions of predicates (Hausman 1992, Chapter 5). That explains why, in general, economists theorists are not concerned with the practical use of their models, nor try to test them. Models are sets of assumptions which make no claims about reality. They are trivially true and therefore untestable. Their main function is conceptual exploration, not to make statements about economic reality. Accordingly, they may be assessed mathematically, not by empirical tests. In contrast, theories do make claims about reality. Theories, Hausman argues, are sets of connected lawlike assertions. The validity of these assertions can be established in empirical tests. Theories, then, are true or false.

This interpretation of theories and models in economics is contrasted with the logician's notion of this distinction. According to the logical positivist, scientific theories are sets of sentences which are closed under logical deduction. These sentences are expressed in a formal language, say the first order predicate calculus, and have the advantage that they are syntactic objects whose identity is independent of their interpretation. Accordingly, by focusing on the sentences of which a theory is composed, one can investigate the deductive consequences of these sentences without semantic distraction. The interpretation of these sentences follows in a next step of the analysis and gives rise to the meaning of a model. In logic an interpretation is said to constitute a model of the theory if and only if it makes all the sentences come out true (Hausman 1992, 71).[21]

Hausman's distinction between models and theories partly explains why economists are relatively unconcerned about the practical use or realism of their theories. This unconcern is not an act of ignorance, but, to the contrary, results from a sensible division of tasks. Like for other sciences, the progress of economics depends on the conceptual exploration of new theories. These explorations are the aim of GE models. As was explained above, the validity of these models is a matter of mathematical assessment only. A proper GE model must obey the rules of logic or satisfy other criteria of the mathematical sciences. To demand that these models satisfy empirical criteria as well is meaningless, for models make no claims about economic reality. Insofar as one is working with a model one can dismiss any questions about the realism of the assumptions one makes. Empirical tests can only be performed on theories, which are developed in a next stage of the analysis. A model becomes a theory when it is supplemented by a general theoretical hypothesis asserting that the assumptions of the model are true of some portion of the world. But, to repeat, this step must be clearly separated from the exploration of new concepts by means of GE models.

It has to be observed that this use of the term equilibrium model deviates from the common meaning of this term in economics. An example of this practice is Blaug (1991b, 506) who uses the term GE theory to refer to the set of formal conditions which define GE. For him the GE model is an application of this theory, a conjunction of a system of simultaneous equations and the initial conditions required to explain a set of actual prices. Weintraub (1985b) also considers GE models applications, but wants to avoid the term GE theory. The problem of this latter term is that it often refers to both elements of the hard core of the NWP and some of the models in the protective belt of that program. So to avoid confusion it is better to restrict the use of the adjective 'general equilibrium' to (1) models (that is applications in the belt of the NWP), and (2) approaches, which are a set of rules and research strategies to generate models (Weintraub 1985b, 121–22).

Fundamental Economic Theory and the Laws of Economics

Hausman considers GE models augmentations of a fundamental theory which he calls 'equilibrium theory'. GE models are not the only possible augmentation of this theory. Partial equilibrium models (or microeconomics in Hausman's terminology) are another.[22] What makes equilibrium theory fundamental to economics is the fact that it consists of a set of laws which most economists would agree to being essential to economic theorizing.

These laws concern generalizations about consumer behaviour, firm behaviour and economic equilibrium. Hausman isolates seven fundamental laws of economics. These are:

1. The law of rationality. This law presupposes that individuals have complete, transitive, and continuous preferences and do not prefer any available option to the one they choose (ibid., 30).
2. The law of consumerism. This law says that people typically want more of all commodities and services. It implies self interest and non satiation (ibid.).
3. The law of diminishing marginal rates of substitution. This law is a more precise formulation of the intuitive notion that the utility generated by the consumption of a unit of a specific commodity or service diminishes with the total number of units consumed (ibid., 30, 32).
4. The law of diminishing returns in production (ibid., 43).
5. The law of constant returns to scale (ibid.).
6. The law of profit maximization (ibid.).
7. The law of economic equilibrium: markets clear or come quickly to equilibrium (ibid., 51).

The first three laws make up neoclassical consumer choice theory. Laws 4–6 form the theory of the firm. Together these theories form what Hausman calls the 'basic equilibrium model' and explain that equilibrium is attained (ibid., 53).[23] The claim central to Hausman's book is that most economic theories employ some subset of the laws which make up this model. Hausman defines economics, not in terms of a specific domain of inquiry, but in terms of the causal factors with which it is concerned (ibid., 90–91). The centrality of equilibrium theory to economics derives from the fact that it defines the causal factors which form its subject of study.

There is some ambiguity in the use of the term equilibrium model here. Given Hausman's clear distinction between economic theories and models, how can something be both an equilibrium model, which makes no claims about economic reality, and an equilibrium theory, which consists of a set of lawlike assertions? It is evident that the neoclassical models of consumer choice, the firm and economic equilibrium are definitions of predicates. For example, the consumer model assumes the completeness, transitivity and continuity of preferences, which are nothing but definitions of a consumer's preference ordering. The mystery is why we should consider these assumptions generalizations about people's actual tastes. They have meaning in a mathematical model only. Hausman says that 'the "laws" that make up the theory of consumer choice show themselves in mathematical disguise' (ibid., 36). Apparently economists are making causal claims without realizing it (ibid., 28; see also Hausman 1990). Hausman seems to suggest that for economics to make sense as a scientific enterprise economists must be making causal claims. 'Despite what they sometimes say, economists do not treat equilibrium theory as merely a fundamental model, to which no empirical commitments pertain. For economists believe that they can predict and explain economic phenomena in terms of equilibrium theory.' (ibid., 273). So what Hausman calls an equilibrium model, economists treat as a theory consisting of actual laws. Apparently, that is why he speaks of the fundamental equilibrium theory and the basic equilibrium model interchangeably.

The key to Hausman's view of economics as a science is the peculiarity of what he calls the laws of economics. Although they are said to form the heart of the basic equilibrium model, sometimes economists employ contraries to some of these fundamental laws. For example, 'constant returns to scale' is one of Hausman's laws that make up the theory of the firm. But there are also equilibrium theories which assume increasing or decreasing returns to scale. This odd fact leads Hausman to assert that the laws of equilibrium theory do not have the same status as fundamental natural laws (ibid., 52; but see Hausman 1981b, 114). A physicist is not likely to assume that force is proportional to acceleration in one model, but to content that force is proportional to acceleration squared in another. The reason for the different status of fundamental laws in economics is that they are inexact. They are not precise explanations, but serve as useful first approximations. This gives the theorist scope to supersede or reject them in particular investigations. We shall return to the nature of economic laws below.

So why isolate these factors as crucial to all economic explanation in the first place? After all some of them are universally recognized to be false generalizations. People have other economic motives besides profit and utility maximization. The law of constant returns to scale does not apply to so-called natural monopolies. These important exceptions to the laws said to be fundamental to economics point to the following questions. What leads us to consider the generalizations listed above as laws? What explains the appeal of the laws of equilibrium theory to economists? To answer that question we need to consider the vison and strategy of economics.

Vision: The Inexact and Separate Science of Economics

According to Hausman, the reason for the centrality of equilibrium theory to contemporary economics is to be found in the vision inherent in this theory, which is that of an inexact and separate science. This typification is based on J.S. Mill's views on the nature of economics (Hausman 1981c). Crucial to the idea of an inexact science is the distinction between major and minor causes.

'Major' causes are called that way because they affect the phenomena to be explained in all cases. In contrast, 'minor' causes exert their influence only in some cases. For example it is asserted that in economic affairs people are always motivated by their self-interest. For that reason rationality can be considered as a major cause of economics. However, the dominance of this cause does not preclude that other incentives or feelings affect economic decisions as well. Hate or vengeance may cause an entrepreneur to start a price war when he fears losing part of his market share to new competitors. But, evidently, economic agents are not always motivated by hatred, which makes it difficult to detect such minor causes.

A science is called inexact when it explains only part of the causes affecting the explanandum (Hausman 1981c; 1992, Chapter 8). Probably all sciences are inexact in this sense, as it seems impossible for any science to account for all causal factors working in all cases. Most sciences concentrate on the main forces at work and temporarily assume other causes constant. Generally scientific laws concern an 'explanation-in-principle'. They show what the effect of a specific cause would be, assuming that disturbing or minor causes are not present. The latter condition is called a 'ceteris paribus' (CP) clause. Inexact laws, then, are qualified laws because they carry with them, explicit or implicit, ceteris paribus clauses.

Hausman (1992, 136–37) maintains that by specifying a CP clause an inexact law may become exact. After all, a CP clause is composed of causal factors. Hence, in order to correctly specify a CP clause all the relevant causes must be known, which would suggest exactness. Inexactness, then, implies vagueness. A CP clause is invoked but, since the content of this clause is not precisely known, it is best considered vague. According to Hausman, the laws of economics are typically of this form. They are inexact because they do not fully explain all economic events: they focus on their main causes only. The minor causes of economics are contained in CP clauses. However, given the complexity of the causes operating in the economic realm, a full account of these causes is impossible. Many of these causes depend on the context of the problem at hand, which implies that their effect cannot be known before the event. In economics, then, CP clauses are unavoidably vague.

Now the claim of Hausman is that equilibrium theory or the basic equilibrium model captures the main forces of economics. That is why one may consider it fundamental to economics. Furthermore, these causes explain a specific domain of economic events. It is well known that in the social sciences causes are generally intertwined or complex, which makes it difficult to attribute effects to specific causes. Yet what makes economics a separate science is the ability to distinguish a distinct domain of events which can be accounted for by the causal factors we have labeled economic

(Hausman 1981c, 376–77; 1992, 90–95). This separate economic realm, then, concerns the effects of the rational choices of utility maximizing consumers and profit maximizing firms. Or, as Hausman puts it, '*economics studies the consequences of rational greed*' (ibid., 95, emphasis in the original). The laws that govern this separate economic realm are the subject of equilibrium theory.[24]

For two reasons the vision of a separate economic science has important implications for the methodological practice of economists. In the first place the vision of a separate science asserts that economics is an unified science (Hausman 1981c, 376; 1992, 93). Since economic causal factors predominate in the economic domain, the scope of economic theory is the entire economic domain. Put differently, the theory provides a unified account of all economic phenomena. Secondly, the belief that economics is a separate science suggests that economics is, within its own domain, complete. It is clear that economics cannot fully explain economic events. Disturbing factors always cause a degree of inexactness in economic theory. But to the extent that economic events are the result of major causes, economic theory claims to be complete. At a high level of abstraction economics provides the whole truth about the economic domain.

Equilibrium theory, then, gives a complete and unified explanation of economic events. It is unified because its scope is the entire domain of economic phenomena. It is complete because it claims to explain the major causes governing this domain. These two features of equilibrium theory may explain why (neoclassical) economists are unwilling to consider alternatives to this theory. Theories which threaten the explanatory unit of equilibrium also theory threaten the ideal of a separate economic science. To retain this ideal, the following methodological rules are invoked (ibid., 95–6):

1. Generalizations about choice or other economic phenomena are ad hoc and should be avoided unless they are derivable from equilibrium theory and further legitimate generalizations about preferences, beliefs and non-economic constraints on choices.
2. Further generalizations about preferences, beliefs, and constraints are legitimate and may be incorporated only if they do not threaten the central place of rational greed, the possibility of equilibrium, or the universal scope of economics.

Strategy: The Inexact Method A Priori

The above discussion suggests that the structure of economics implies a specific strategy for doing research. Equilibrium theory concentrates on equilibrium outcomes and advises economists to explain these events as the consequences of the rational choices of economic agents. It so sets an agenda for economic research. But prescription of one method implies a prohibition to pursue others. By suggesting that economics should comply to the ideal of a complete and unified science, equilibrium theory also limits the problems economists address and the methods they consider fit for solving them. In other words, a separate science may well become a dogmatic science.

Now in all sciences a certain degree of dogmatism is warranted, if a specific approach proves to be successful. In fact a dogmatic attitude may well be a necessary condition of scientific progress. It may take a stubborn scientist to convince other scholars of the benefits of a new approach, as confirmations of predictions are easily nor quickly obtained and often prove controversial. However, this excuse cannot be invoked in the case of equilibrium theory, which, Hausman suggests, is a dominant theory in economics. So, to invoke the former excuse, is the separate science of economics successful?

To answer that question a theory of assessment is needed. Which criteria do we need to apply to measure the success of economics? Hausman maintains that the proper method to assess the performance of an inexact and separate science is that of Mill's deductive method. The appropriateness of this method follows from the property of inexactness. For example, economic events can never be fully explained because economic causes are complex and often context-dependent. The complexity of causes and the singularity of certain events make the inductivist approach unsuited to economics. One can never infer from the observation of economic events alone that certain causes operate in the economic realm. A specific event may well have several causes which are complexly intertwined, or have a unique cause which for that reason cannot be detected in repeated tests (Hausman 1981c, 373, 378).

According to Mill, the best method to handle this complexity is a deductive one (see Hausman 1981c; 1992, Chapters 8 and 12). However, it must be noted that for Mill induction and deduction are not opposites. On the contrary, Mill's deductive method requires induction to provide the laws whose deductive consequences are verified in empirical tests. This method, then, consists of three stages. In the first, one establishes certain laws by induction, which for Mill need not involve experimentation. For example, the psychological laws of economics are inductively established by means of introspection. In the second stage the consequences of these laws are deduced by employing the rules of logic. These are then, thirdly, verified in empirical tests. This final step is not intended to test the lawlike statements of the first stage. They are borrowed from other sciences and appear already well-established. Verification is required to determine the reliability of the laws deduced in step two (Hausman 1981c, 380–81; 1992, 142–148).

Hausman claims that economists employ this deductive method with one minor alteration. Economics is an inexact science, which means that verification may not be sufficient to establish the reliability of economic laws. In economics empirical evidence is uncertain because causes are complexly intertwined and often context-dependent. Consequently, economists may choose to ignore disconfirmations, if they consider other properties of a theory more important. So in the fourth step of what Hausman (1992, 148, 222) calls the 'inexact method a priori' economists compare alternative accounts of a falsified theory on the basis of explanatory success, empirical progress and pragmatic usefulness. The inexact method a priori can now be summarized as follows (Hausman 1992, 222):

- Formulate credible (ceteris paribus) and pragmatically convenient generalizations concerning the operation of relevant causal factors.
- Deduce from these generalizations, and statements of initial conditions, simplifications, etc., predictions concerning relevant phenomena.
- Test the predictions.
- If the predictions are correct, then regard the whole amalgam as confirmed. If the predictions are not correct, then compare alternative accounts of the failure on the basis of explanatory success, empirical progress and pragmatic usefulness.

It is this method which is appropriate to an inexact science like economics. Moreover, Hausman claims, this method gives an accurate description of how economists actually assess the validity of their theories. For that reason he calls it the 'economists' deductive method' (ibid., 221–223).

Still, to make this method work in an inexact science an important assumption is required. Economic causes are often complexly intertwined and it may therefore be asked how one is to ascertain their separate effects. Mill believed that the deductive method can be employed in economics because social phenomena are governed by 'mechanical' laws. In contrast to what he calls 'chemical laws' mechanical laws are composed of independent causes (Hausman 1992, 137). The deductive method handles the complexity of causes by separately investigating their effects. For example, in his *Principles of Political Economy* (1848) Mill studied the effect of a falling profit rate on the rate of economic growth, whilst assuming constant technology and no population growth (Mill 1909, 710). The effects of these latter causes are individually assessed in two subsequent studies, which assume a constant profit rate and no population growth or a constant technology respectively. The path of economic development is then explained by adding the separate effects of these causes. Mills asserted that this compounding of causes is only possible in mechanical sciences. Evidently, if the effects of the individual causes on the rate of economic growth change with the operation of additional ones, it becomes impossible to attribute a specific effect to changes in the profit rate, technology or population size. In a chemical science the effect of the simultaneous operation of causes will differ from the sum of their individual effects. Accordingly, the explanatory task of a complex science like economics crucially depends on the possibility to isolate and individually analyze separate causes.

So to assess the success of equilibrium theory by means of the deductive or a priori method, one needs to assume the independence of the seven laws which make up this theory. Indeed: 'Even if the basic generalizations of equilibrium theory are qualified laws, they will not help us understand real economies with their inevitable disturbing causes, unless economic phenomena are mechanical phenomena' (Hausman 1992, 138). The example mentioned above shows that Mill simply assumed that economic causes satisfy this condition. Yet the only justification for this assumption is explanatory success. Are the laws of equilibrium theory independent, and will the deductive method therefore work to explain the causes of this separate science? It is to this crucial question that we must now turn.

Is Equilibrium Theory an Inexact Science?

The problem of justifying the laws of economics is that they are inexact. The laws of economics are generalizations about consumer and firm behaviour and the attainment of economic equilibrium. But these laws do not fully explain the economic domain, as there are always factors which interfere with their operation. To rule out the effect of these interferences a ceteris paribus clause is invoked.

However in economics a CP clause is unavoidably vague. Due to the complexity or singularity of causes, the CP clause does not give a full account of all the interfering causes.[25] But then, what kind of 'laws' are generalizations qualified with vague ceteris paribus conditions? In other words, what allows us to speak of economics laws? Are they empirical regularities? Evidently not, for an inexact law does not fully explain the events under study. Fundamental economic theory is true only under various, not fully specified, conditions. According to Hausman, a generalization qualified with a vague CP clause is a law only if it satisfies the following four conditions (Hausman 1981b, 131-33; 1992, 140–41).

- The statement must be lawlike. This condition says that, if true, the statement would be a law.
- The ceteris paribus law must be reliable. Reliability is a statistical requirement. It means that, even when the CP clause is ignored, for some class of cases observations rarely disconfirm the law.

- A qualified claim must be refinable. If one adds specific qualifications, the generalization should become more reliable, or reliable in a larger domain.
- One is not justified in regarding a statement with a CP clause as a law unless it is excusable. This condition says that one should not invoke CP clauses blindly. CP clauses are invoked to rule out the inferences of specific causes. They should be used as an excuse only, if one has a notion of the effect of these interfering causes.

These conditions must prevent the scientist from invoking a CP clause to explain away apparent disconfirmations. So, do the laws of equilibrium theory satisfy these four conditions, or are they an illegitimate excuse for a lack of empirical confirmation?

Hausman confidently asserts that equilibrium theory satisfies the above conditions (ibid., 149). Yet he does not substantiate this claim, for, he says, that would require an in-depth analysis of the particular applications of equilibrium theory, which he considers beyond the scope of his book. He does point out that the problem of the laws of equilibrium theory lies in condition four. Economists often show little concern to explain the empirical anomalies they face, and invoke the CP clause as an excuse (see also Hausman 1981a, 135). However, Hausman considers this practice justified because it is not based on an act of ignorance, nor does it involve a methodological defence. Instead, he maintains, economists have rational reasons for disregarding this evidence in order to maintain the vaguely qualified laws of equilibrium theory.

What makes the choice to retain equilibrium theory in the face of disconfirming evidence rational is the uncertainty of empirical evidence in economics. In a complex science like economics hard tests of theories are simply impossible. Tests can never account for all the causes working and disturbing factors are easily invoked to explain away a negative result. Economists are therefore advised to approach disconfirmations with caution, especially if they have good reasons to believe the theory tested to be a priori true. Hausman claims that economists face this dilemma in the case of equilibrium theory.

An important attraction of the laws of equilibrium theory is their credibility. The propositions about consumer and firm behaviour are easily checked by means of introspection. Everyday experience tells us that the laws they suggest are reasonable approximations of actual economic and market behaviour. To paraphrase Robert Lucas, everybody knows why there are no 50 dollar bills on the sidewalk. Common sense supports the notion of economics as a science of what Hausman calls ‘rational greed’. The propositions about economic equilibrium are plausible, because we know introspectively that there is a real causation between the failure of the Brazilian coffee harvest and the rise of the price of coffee. Yet there is no doubt that in a strict sense the laws of equilibrium theory are false. People are not always rational profit seekers; one may observe a fall of the coffee price in spite of a harvest failure. What characterizes the laws of equilibrium theory is that they are only valid at a high level of abstraction. In Hausman's words '[w]ithout qualifications and a margin of error they are false, but with these, they seem true; and economists have good reason to be committed to them' (ibid., 210).

But there are more reasons for the appeal of equilibrium theory. The laws of equilibrium theory, such as diminishing returns to scale in production and diminishing marginal rates of substitution, permit determinate mathematical formulations of economic theory. Clearly, firms have other objectives besides profit. But the assumption of profit maximization allows us to construct a tractable model of firm behaviour, which is elegant and can be used to study the consequences of different assumptions about the production possibilities firms face. The recent history of economic thought has shown that neoclassical economists are hesitant to sacrifice the simplicity and coherence of their mathematical models to gain a more accurate explanation of economic behaviour.[26]

Another pragmatic benefit of equilibrium theory is the ease with which it can be employed in welfare theoretical analyses. More specifically, supplemented with a seemingly harmless normative principle the theory can be shown to support the moral superiority of a capitalist economic order. The plausibility of this argument derives from the definition of rationality, which is crucial to the basic equilibrium model. The neoclassical consumer model identifies individual welfare with the satisfaction of preferences. Further, most economists accept what Hausman calls 'the moral principle of minimal benevolence' (Hausman 1992, 66). This principle states that it is a morally good thing if people are better off. So, according to this principle, it is, ceteris paribus, a morally good thing to satisfy an individual's preferences. It then follows that Pareto improvements are moral improvements and Pareto optima are morally desirable. This conclusion has normative implications for the model of competitive equilibrium, for the first welfare theorem says that perfectly competitive equilibria are Pareto efficient (Varian 1992, 326–329). Accordingly, it can be concluded that, ceteris paribus, perfectly competitive equilibria are morally desirable and market failures are morally undesirable. What makes this argument so attractive is that it relies on the least controversial of moral premises: who would not agree that it is morally good to make people better off? In Hausman's view the ease with which these welfare theoretical conclusions can be drawn from equilibrium theory partly explains why it is 'absolutely central' to contemporary 'orthodox' economics (Hausman 1992, 69).

But why should one let the pragmatic and empirical reasons for accepting equilibrium theory prevail over the apparent disconfirmations of the theory? Hausman says that we should have greater confidence in the a priori reasons for believing the theory to be true than in the conclusions of questionable empirical tests. Equilibrium theory is the result of a long process of conceptual development and refinement and is supported by our intuitive beliefs and everyday experience. In contrast, in economics test results are always controversial because of the complexity of economic causes. Economists probably act rational when they disregard this evidence and retain equilibrium theory (ibid., 207–209, 253).

In sum, the centrality of equilibrium theory in economics is not the result of a dogmatic or false methodology. The inexact method a priori advises economists to empirically verify deduced results, not to resist testing. The problem is that in a complex science like economics test results are an unreliable source of knowledge. Faced with poor data economists are forced to invoke additional criteria to assess the usefulness of their theories. Additional virtues of theories may be pragmatic and concern, for example, mathematical tractability or rely on alternative sources of knowledge, such as introspection and common sense experience. So even when equilibrium theory appears to fail the excusability condition, it can still be an inexact science.

Dogmatism in Economics

But there is an important qualification to this conclusion, for it wrongly suggests that economics is on the right track to becoming an inexact science in Mill's sense with all the pragmatic, mathematical and empirical virtues of equilibrium theory discussed above. Hausman seriously doubts that economics moves in this direction. He believes that '[t]he obstacles in the path of empirical success in economics are so profound and the costs of empirical research so high that standards of excellence in economics, such as mathematical prowess, can persist indefinitely regardless of whether they contribute to or hinder progress in the discipline' (ibid., 262). McCloskey (1994) thinks economics has already reached this stage. According to her, economists have adopted the scientific standards of the wrong discipline, namely those of the mathematics department. Although Hausman is highly critical of her rhetoric project, he does share her conclusion that economics 'is in need of a major overhaul' (Hausman 1992, 263).

His problem is that ultimately the validity of equilibrium theory is an empirical question. The inexact method a priori forbids economists to rest content with the current state of economic science. It is one thing to temporarily ignore questionable empirical evidence to safeguard the mathematical consistency and other pragmatic virtues of contemporary economic theory. It is something else to abandon the attempt to improve the empirical record of economics altogether. Hausman believes that economics fails in this latter respect. He thinks economists should put more effort in acquiring better empirical techniques and more detailed knowledge. To that purpose they should take more advantage of new developments in experimental economics. They should be willing to make use of observational data of all kinds (Why ignore the information provided by surveys and field reports?) and show a more active engagement in the process of data gathering (ibid., 253–54). Unfortunately, the reward structure of economics discourages such initiatives. A remarkable feature of economic science is the high esteem of mathematical theoretical work, which leads to an unwarranted neglect of developments in empirical economics (Leontief 1971). As Mayer (1993) observes, economists continue to strengthen the already strongest link of their science, the elegance and precision of their mathematical theories. The low esteem for empirical work in economics suggests that economists are too easily discouraged by the complexity of the empirical problems they face. To the extent that they do not try to overcome these problems, one may conclude that the centrality of equilibrium theory and the emphasis on the development of mathematical theories in economics is indeed a form of dogmatism.

In the final analysis the ideal of a separate science of economics has an important drawback. A separate science relies on a limited number of major causes to explain most events in the domain under study. A science with this characteristic has the obvious aesthetic appeal of a unified and coherent theory. For economists equilibrium theory embodies this ideal. 'The methodological commitment to a separate science leads to the view that equilibrium theory is (at a suitable level of abstraction and approximation) the whole theoretical truth about economics' (Hausman 1992, 274). Put differently, equilibrium theory promises to explain all economic events in a single theory (ibid., 95, 225) and with some justice, economists find this prospect hard to resist. But the suggestion that economics may one day become a 'one-theory' science also has a cost: it may well lead to a disregard of alternatives to equilibrium theory; alternatives, that is, which do not share the vision of a separate science (ibid., 95–6, 274).[27]

Furthermore, equilibrium theory emphasizes 'rational greed' as a main motive of economic decisions. The importance of rationality to the neoclassical formulation of equilibrium theory gives it an undeniable normative appeal. It was explained above that on the basis of the plausible assumption of 'minimal benevolence' equilibrium theory suggests that perfectly competitive equilibria are morally desirable. Challenges to individual rationality and equilibrium theory undermine this moral claim and may, for that reason, be ignored by defenders of a liberal market order (ibid., 274, 278).

Towards a More Eclectic Economic Science

In earlier studies Hausman (1981a, 1981b) defended equilibrium theory on the grounds that it offered theoretical assurance that a more accurate explanation of economic events could be developed. He argued that the success of the existence proofs of GE theory showed that the theory held the promise of becoming explanatory at a level of abstraction which would render it applicable to real economies (Hausman 1981b, 155). In his 1992 book Hausman is less optimistic about the prospects of equilibrium theory. Abstract GE theory (the equilibrium model) makes no empirical claims and is for that reason not applicable to real economies. In his view, the function of equilibrium models is conceptual exploration.[28] Equilibrium theory, on the other hand, is explanatory, but only at a high level of abstraction. The problem facing the future of economics is that it offers little scope for improvement. The laws of economics are inexact and as long as equilibrium theory remains central to economics there is little hope that they can be developed into more exact explanations of economic events.

This problem, we have seen, is partly caused by the difficulty of testing economic predictions in a complex environment. This problem should motivate economists to explore ways of getting better data, or to consider alternative styles of theorizing, such as that exemplified by the institutionalists. But Hausman's assessment of economics shows that contemporary economists are unwilling to proceed this way. Instead of trying to strengthen the weakest link of their science, the poor predictive record of economics, they invoke the mathematical coherence and pragmatic use of their theories as excuses to maintain the status quo ante. Hausman rationalizes this apparent dogmatism with an appeal to the inexact method a priori. However, this excuse cannot justify the neglect of theories just because they adopt a non-equilibrium perspective to economic problems. There is no methodological justification for the demand that science should aim at explaining events in terms of a limited number of causes. It is one thing to assert that economic causes allow us to separate a domain of economic events from other social phenomena. It is something else to claim that one should explain this separate domain in terms of a single unified theory. Are the seven laws of equilibrium theory all there is to economic explanation? One can hardly imagine that there are no other vaguely qualified laws in economics which would satisfy the lawlikeness, reliability, refinability, and excusability conditions. What sets the laws of equilibrium theory apart from other generalizations in economics is the ability to combine them in a single coherent economic theory. Until now alternative accounts of economics have not shown the same degree of theoretical consistency as neoclassical economics.[29] But if they satisfy the conditions of an inexact science, there is no methodological reason why they should not ultimately replace an equilibrium theory which continues to fail the test of predictive accuracy. The truth of the matter is simply this: 'If it leaves out important causes, then no mathematical expertise or elegance in modelling will make equilibrium theory into a good theory' (ibid., 1992, 280). One may add, no matter how convincing the moral claims of equilibrium theory are, they will not make it a good theory. To safeguard the future of their discipline, Hausman calls upon economists to be more open-minded: 'to be more eclectic, more opportunistic, more willing to gather data, more willing to work with generalizations with narrow scope, and more willing to collaborate with other social scientists' (ibid.).

CONCLUSION

Joan Robinson (1962b, 21) once likened scientific method to a 'kind of elephant – something which exists and can be described, not defined'. This chapter brings me to a similar position. I have discussed several scientific portraits of GE theory, but in the final analysis I am still unable to define the nature of GE theory as a scientific activity. This failure also makes it impossible to explain the centrality of GE theory in economics. Without a framework to measure scientific progress, there is no way of telling whether economists have been rational or foolish by adopting GE theory as part of their tool kit. This leaves the second main question of this chapter unanswered.

It appears that economic methodology is a multifarious undertaking, which is able to generate very different images of the same branch of economic theory. The conclusions of these different portraits are not in full agreement, to say the least. What is striking is that the overall assessment of GE theory is generally negative. Whichever perspective one takes, it seems that GE theory is certainly not the scientific success that some take it to be. But the degree to which GE theory fails to live up to its reputation differs significantly. We have seen that McCloskey is downright cynical in this regard. Rosenberg is only slightly more positive and stresses that the only positive scientific contribution of GE theory is to be expected in fields not belonging to the domain of economics, like evolutionary biology. Hausman once belonged to the camp of the hopeful, but has now joined sides with those disappointed in the excessive formalism and lack of scientific progress in GE theory. Weintraub is clearly the least critical voice, partly because he abandoned his attempts to appraise GE theory in terms of a prescriptive methodology like the MSRP. His current interests concern a more narrative historical exegesis of the development of science. But this aim does not bring him to extrapolate general lessons for current practice. He defines his role as that of a historian, a role which one should sharply distinguish from that of an economist who wishes to argue with other economists about current economic analysis and practice. His goal as a historian is 'to produce a richly narrative integration of economic, social and political history; economic and social policy; economic theory; the natural and social sciences; the rhetoric of economics; and the history and philosophy of economic thought', which is quite a mouthful (Weintraub 2002, 7).

The interesting aspect of Weintraub's historical approach is that it allows him to include the soft aspects of science, like the belief systems of economists. We have seen that he argues that the current focus on the mathematical aspects of GE theory tends to strengthen the vision underlying this theory, which is that of a laissez faire capitalist economic order. In the more rational approaches to scientific methodology, one would aspect such factors to play a very minor role, if at all. One of the lessons of this chapter is that this suggestion – once promoted by Schumpeter – is at odds with the current practice in the philosophy of economics. In every case study scrutinized in this chapter, we have seen that metaphysical aspects like vision and ideology are pivotal. Rosenberg explains the centrality of GE theory in terms of its welfare theoretic implications. Hausman offers a highly detailed account of the procedural rules appropriate to inexact sciences like economics, but the upshot of his argument is that metaphysics literally plays a role at every stage of theory development. The very starting point of his approach is the vision of economics as an inexact and separate science, which entails a claim about how economic forces are structured in major and minor causes. We have no clue whether economic forces are actually inexact in this way, which makes this vision a classic example of Schumpeter's precognitive acts structuring our field of study before we commence scientific inquiry. Hausman also shows what the consequences are of such visions. They generate a scientific ideal which theories must live up to. In the case of economics, this is that theoretical explanation must strive to generate a unified explanation of economic events, focusing on a limited number of major causes. Hausman's seven laws of equilibrium theory are assumed to best approach this ideal, which is why they are considered central to economic theory.

If vision and ideology seem so important to scientific practice, it is surprising that they receive so little attention. This is the other conclusion that

I draw from this chapter. I find the literature on the methodology of economics lacking, if we want to understand what economists are actually doing. With the exception of McCloskey and related rhetorical approaches, the general approach is to appraise economics in terms of meta-scientific criteria taken from the philosophy of science. I find it utterly mystifying why methodologists fail to the apply the criteria, which they themselves advocate as the standards of science. The examples in this chapter are telling enough. The MSRP calls upon us to examine the empirical progressiveness of research programs like GE theory. But, with the exception of a few studies like Weintraub (1988), this hardly occurs. Rosenberg claims that predictive success is the minimal requirement one can ask from any science. But does he try to establish what his principal object of study, GE theory, achieves in terms of this criteria? No. He merely assumes that a mathematical theory like GE theory is unable to generate empirical applications, thereby bypassing entire branches of this theory, like that of computable general equilibrium models, which I shall discuss in Chapter 16. Hausman develops sophisticated arguments to explain the lawlike character of generalizations in inexact sciences like equilibrium theory. But does he investigate whether equilibrium theory actually meets these criteria? No. He simply considers the in-depth analysis of the particular applications of equilibrium theory beyond the scope of his work. Needless to say, this ignorance does not prevent him from asserting that economists generally show too little concern for the empirical anomalies of their equilibrium theories. Methodologists commit the very error which they believe applies to GE theory: they focus on theoretical arguments alone and deplore the muddy empirical work of checking whether their theories correspond to empirical reality.

To make matters worse methodologists adopt escape clauses when they find that their object of study fails to meet the requirements of their meta-economic framework. The best known of these clauses is the one used by Lakatos. Be patient. Do not discard degenerating scientific research programs too quickly, because the losers of today may well become the winners of tomorrow. We have seen others like Weintraub and Hausman defend equilibrium theory on similar grounds, without explicating the duration of this trial period. In my opinion, such unqualified statements are the final nail in the coffin of economic methodology, because they can be used to explain away any discomforting observation.

The case studies presented in this chapter constitute my database for drawing these conclusions. Other cases can be added and would perhaps give a more positive twist to my view on economic methodology. I support Lawrence Boland's enduring efforts to criticize neoclassical equilibrium economics from within as part of his aim to develop a methodology for a new microeconomics (Boland 1986 and 1992), but I have ignored his work in this chapter. I have also completely side-stepped critical realist approaches to economics like the work of Tony Lawson (1997 and 2003). Lawson criticizes mainstream equilibrium economics for its excessive focus on mathematical-deductivist methods, which in his opinion are being applied in conditions for which they are not appropriate. Apparently, the ontology which they assume is not that of the real world. But how do we know that Lawson's alternative, which he calls social ontology, is more appropriate? As far as I can see, social ontology entails nothing more than the dual claim that social entities cannot always be reduced to atomistic individuals and that we cannot exactly foretell the future, because economic change concerns an open process in a historical sense. But does social ontology permit us to build better economic theories? Lawson certainly claims so, but his evidence is disappointingly meagre. In his 1997 book *Economics and Reality* he states his intention as not just being critical but also constructive, to sketch the structure of a more sustainable, fruitful, alternative approach. However, this constructive part is literally relegated to the final two pages of his book.

The methodological investigation of economic practice should have a higher pay off than this. The least I expect from economic methodology is that the profession practices what it preaches. Also its focus should be more on improving economic practice, rather than combatting with one's colleagues about the meaning of terms like 'hard core', 'explanation', 'causation', 'ontology', 'model', and other philosophical subtleties. The conclusions of economic methodology should not consist of vague generalizations. Take the following lessons that can be seen as the common assessment of equilibrium theory by all four portraits discussed in this chapter:

- Equilibrium theory has its faults and is certainly too mathematical, but this does not make it meaningless. The value of the mathematical approach is conceptual exploration. (So, what are the lessons that we draw from conceptual exploration?)
- Testing in economics is difficult due to the complexity of economic forces. To overcome this hurdle, more efforts should be put in generating better empirical tests. (This is begging the question. How do we overcome the complexity issue in empirical economics?)
- Mainstream equilibrium theory is too narrow-minded due to its focus on equilibrium theory. A more eclectic approach would enrich and improve economic theory. (Which non-mainstream theories would be suitable for this task and in what way would they improve economic practice?)

I have put my comments to these lessons within parentheses. The fact that economic methodology does not (yet) answer these question does not make it a futile undertaking. I agree with Hausman's argument that we need to study how people learn, which sort of methods they employ to solve which kind of problems (Hausman 1992, 264, 268). Studies of this kind may perhaps learn us how to better employ these methods, or how to prevent errors that people are prone to make. This purpose motivated my investigation into the methodological practices of economists.

NOTES

1. The point about the irreversibility of historical time is not accidental. The main point of Backhouse's article is to argue that Joan Robinson's (1974) challenge of history versus equilibrium is misconceived.
2. In defense of Robinson, I would like to point out that she once called equilibrium 'indispensable' because it furthered economic analysis (Robinson 1962b, 81). She was certainly not an opponent of abstract theory per se, but aimed to frame this kind of theory in a historical context to create an open, historical model. Backhouse (2004) ignores this subtlety and turns Robinson's position on equilibrium theory into a strawman. See Cohen (1993) for a more accurate interpretation.
3. Backhouse (2006) delves deeper into this question. Now equilibrium is being said to form a method for problem-solving. 'Different concepts of equilibrium are used to solve different problems' (Backhouse 2006, 151). What the added value of equilibrium is as a problem solver remains unknown. 'Different types of model are constructed for different purposes, resulting in enormous variety' (ibid., 155). Equilibrium has become such an 'elastic notion' (ibid., 163) that apparently we can say virtually nothing about its role.
4. In Chapter 1 I have defined the equilibrium concept as an explanatory principle. Hence, one may pose the more general question what kind of explanatory principle the equilibrium concept is. Nagel (1961, 20–26) lists four types of explanation in science, which he calls deductive, probabilistic, teleological and genetic. I argue that equilibrium theory fits all categories, depending on its formulation. See for example Sober (1983) and Huussen (1985).
5. Three of her main publications are *The Rhetoric of Economics* (1985), *If You're So Smart: the narrative of economic expertise* (1990), *Knowledge and Persuasion in Economics* (1994).
6. The reader may wonder why these terms are put between quotation marks. The problem is that McCloskey not only writes about the rhetoric of economists, but also uses rhetoric to make her point that rhetoric matters. For example, to stress the follies of modernist philosophy of science she calls it Methodology with a capital M. But as she rejects all epistemological claims of Methodology, it becomes unclear what she means when she claims that 'good' science is good conversation or that honest discourse leads to 'better'

science. In what sense can one say that science is 'improved'? How can one establish this 'progress'? Do these statements involve cognitive claims? If so, McCloskey needs to make them explicit. Since she has not done so, it seems best to place words which carry this philosophical baggage between quotation marks.

7. For a criticism of the rhetorical project along this line, see Hoover (1995). Of course McCloskey would reject this reading. She would argue that all science is the same type of activity, namely conversation. Accordingly, her conversational norms are not external to science, but are shared by all sciences alike. They are '[f]ar above method with a small m, at the peak of the scholarly enterprise' (McCloskey 1985, 24). These words suggest that McCloskey is a methodological monist. Indeed her puzzling contention that 'Economics is a collection of literary forms, not a science. Indeed science is a collection of literary forms, not a science. And literary forms are scientific' (ibid., 55), seems to support that suggestion.

8. This should not be misread as a derogatory remark. It is based on the observation that the aim of McCloskey's rhetoric is largely pragmatic. She lists a number of practices that result from a modernist view on science and that economists are therefore best advised to avoid. Among the modernist vices of economists are (1) a wrong use of statistical significance tests, (2) the false idea that theoretical models suggest solutions to real economic problems, and (3) a misplaced trust in the ideal of social engineering (McCloskey 1997). If reading McCloskey helps economists to recognize and avoid these fallacies, the spread of her ideas may indicate a turn to the better in economics. An example of a citation analysis to determine scientific progress in a specific field of economic theory is Diamond (1988). He counts references to Debreu's work in GE analysis to check the empirical progressivity of the GE program in economics. His conclusion is that GE theory lacks empirical support because most empirical studies in economics are not based on Debreu's formal work in GE theory.

9. Indeed, following Blaug (1975a, 257), one may question if economists would be so irrational to abandon internally consistent, well corroborated, fruitful and powerful scientific ideas because of specific external reasons. As Blaug contends, the history of economic thought does not suggest they do. However a skeptic might answer that economics has never produced internally consistent, well corroborated, fruitful and powerful scientific ideas, and that scientific rationality is therefore an empty notion in economics.

10. For a similar observation, see Wade Hands (1985a, 13).

11. And in a related manner: 'One who claims that general equilibrium analysis is not explanatory, or that the analysis is not empirical, is simply a prisoner of textbook presentations. It is almost a scandal that philosophers of economics do not seem to understand the role of applied economics, and the work that has been done in applied econometrics' (Weintraub 1985a, 27n).

12. Mäki (2008, 413) reviews the ups and downs of Lakatos's MSRP in economics in the period 1976–2008 and observes that numerous applications of the Lakatosian framework

have been published, but that few of these studies did what the framework recommended doing, namely comparing rival research programmes for their relative progressiveness.

13. Surprisingly, even Rosenberg (1986, 138) accepted this criticism. 'The same problem that Lakatos's methodology falls afoul of shows that the whole question of appraising economics according to some general standard common and peculiar to science rests on a mistake.' Yet Rosenberg (1992) adopted empirical progressiveness as a general criterion of scientific status, because he considered prediction a commonly accepted goal of science. Indeed empirical progress is considered 'the most innocuous epistemological requirement on any science' (ibid., xiv). In the light of his earlier comment that nothing constructive can be said about empirical progress, this is a peculiar position. For a comment on Rosenberg's portrait of science along this line, see Mäki (1996).
14. Accordingly, here 'good' is defined simply in terms of satisfying these criteria.
15. One of the few positive appraisals in the volume is Backhouse (1991). He modified Weintraub's formulation of the NWP to account for the development of mainstream macroeconomics since Keynes. This version of the NWP is considered both theoretically and empirically progressive. It predicts 'novel facts'; for example the Friedman–Phelps prediction of the consequences of sustained high aggregate demand in the 1960s, which were corroborated by actual events; in 1970–1971 rising unemployment was needed to stop inflation from rising still further. According to Backhouse these examples show that the MSRP can be fruitfully employed to explain the history of macroeconomics since 1945. For a critical comment on his reconstruction, see Janssen (1991).
16. According to the MSRP, economists abandon degenerating research programs in favour of progressive ones.
17. This programmatic core consists of the three questions of the existence, stability and uniqueness of general economic equilibrium (Ingrao and Israel 1990, 3 and 360).
18. In similar vein, Mäki (2008, 412) concludes that 'Lakatos was unable to solve the difficult problem of setting rules for determining the conditions under which refutation and replacement should happen'. Hence, he left unexplained for how long a research program is permitted to degenerate.
19. '[A]ll scientists at least pay lip service to the doctrine that the goal of science is knowledge . . . for surely it is undeniable that all sciences have for their ultimate goal knowledge' (Rosenberg 1992, 7 and 15).
20. Again Rosenberg makes a bold claim for which he provides no evidence. How do we know that people are irrational if testing in economics is impossible? That is the real problem of the complexity of economic causes. If economic forces cannot be isolated, then the predictions of economic theory are meaningless. Indeed Rosenberg concedes that 'the theory of rational choice is condemned to predictive sterility' (ibid., 128). But in that case he has no basis for saying that the theory of rational choice makes false predictions. The real problem is not the falsity of rational choice theory, but the impossibility to give a causal explanation of human choice.
21. This interpretation of the theory–model distinction has been formalized in the structuralist approach to scientific theories. This approach examines if a theory has intended

applications, which make the sentences constituting the theory come out true. Because set–theoretic axiomatization is a fundamental part of this program, the structuralist approach has thus far been restricted to fairly mathematical scientific theories. In economics one has attempted to reconstruct GE theory in structuralist terms. This approach will not be discussed in this chapter, but for an example see Hands (1985b).

22. So microeconomics (partial equilibrium models) and GE models share the same theoretical vision: both employ the assumptions of the basic equilibrium model. They differ in the extent of the interdependencies among markets they consider. Generally, microeconomics studies problems involving a small number of agents and commodities, whilst GE theories place no limitations on the interdependence of markets. Another difference concerns the theoretical aims of these approaches. Microeconomics is practical and may serve predictive purposes. Supply and demand schedules allow us to give a causal explanation of the effect on the oil price of the discovery of a new oil well in the North sea. In contrast GE models serve no clear explanatory or predictive purposes. The conditions they assume (for example agents have complete and accurate knowledge concerning the availability and prices of commodities both in the present and in the future) render the model inapplicable to real economies. The claims of the GE model, in other words, are impossible to test (Hausman 1981a; 1981b, 145; 1992, 52n, 55–6).

23. For a graphical representation of the basic equilibrium model, see Hausman (1992, 53 and 271).

24. The properties of inexactness and separateness are not independent. A separate science can be distinguished from other sciences because the events that constitute its domain can be traced to a unified set of causes. Separateness therefore presupposes inexactness (Hausman 1981c, 381, and see Mäki 1996, 26), not the other way around, as Hoover (1995, 724) seems to suggest.

25. A cause can be said to be singular when it operates in a single case or a in limited number of cases only. This makes it difficult to analyze the effect of such causes.

26. On the other hand mathematical flexibility may also be a reason why neoclassical economics was able to retain its predominantly mathematical mode of theorizing. The neoclassical models are easily adaptable to new circumstances and a small change in the assumptions of the theory often suffices to accommodate an apparently disconfirming observation. The ability to handle empirical anomalies in this way may explain why neoclassicals never felt the need to overturn what can be considered the theory's main assumptions: the rationality of economic agents, stable preferences and instant or swift market clearance (see for example Heijdra and Löwenberg 1988). The relationship between the role of mathematics in economics and the realism of economic theory is critically discussed in for example Boland (1992), Mayer (1993), Clower (1995) and Lawson (1997).

27. In other words, it is this ideal which is responsible for the dogmatism of economics, not the method of theory appraisal economists endorse, the inexact method a priori (Hausman 1992, 275). This, clearly, is one of the main theses of Hausman's book. It is therefore important to point out an important problem of this contention, for how can one separate

the structure and strategy of economics involving the commitment to economics as a separate science and their method of theory appraisal respectively? The problem is that the commitment to a separate economic science is both an ideal and a characteristic of economics. As a characteristic of economics, separateness describes a property of existing economic theories, namely that they involve a limited number of causes which delineate a specific domain of events. But as an ideal to be strived for, separateness prescribes a specific rule of theory appraisal, which says that an acceptable theory should satisfy the criterion of theoretical unification. So, to the extent that economists maintain the ideal of separateness, Hausman's contention that the dogmatism of economics is not a problem of theory appraisal is incorrect (see also Mäki 1996, 26–7).

28. Hausman considers this function 'an absolutely crucial part of the scientific enterprise' as it facilitates a sensible division of tasks in economics (ibid., 79). He suggests that science may benefit from a separation of questions concerning the exploration of new concepts and models from questions concerning the extent to which these models apply to the world. In similar terms Weintraub (1985b, 118) claims that the distinction between a hard core and a protective belt in GE analysis constitutes a sensible division of research activities. In GE analysis theoretical work established a well–defined set of propositions about GE, a process Weintraub calls the 'hardening of the hard core'. Applications of GE models in the belt of the NWP were intended to show that the program was empirically progressive as well. However, Hausman seems to doubt that the distinction between hard core and protective belt constitutes a sensible division of tasks. He argues that 'the consistency of the "hard core" propositions . . . can be established in simple models and does not require the sophisticated mathematical work of the past four decades' (Hausman 1992, 100). But his comment misses the mark, for Weintraub's conclusion applies to the period 1930–1954. Indeed, it is to be seriously doubted if he would consider the developments in GE theory of the past four decades progressive at all (see Weintraub 1991 and Weintraub 2002).

29. Weintraub would say, besides the NWP, other approaches in economics have not gone through the 'hardening' process and have, consequently, not reached a degree of conceptual clarity and theoretical consistency that one requires of a research program in the sense of Lakatos' MSRP. The two programs he considered most likely to ultimately reach this stage are Simon's behavioral program and the evolutionary program of Nelson and Winter (Weintraub 1985b, 142). In his opinion, other approaches (for example Neo Austrian or Post Keynesian economics) have very low chances of developing into genuine research programs, mainly because they prefer non-mathematical methods of economic research.

4. The Origins of Economic Equilibrium

INTRODUCTION

How to start the historical investigation of a concept so elusive as equilibrium? We have already seen that with some good will, we are able to trace the roots of equilibrium thinking as far back as ancient Greek economic thought. It is not my intention to review the history of economic thought of the past 2300 years. For the purpose of this book, I shall locate the origins of equilibrium economics somewhere around the start of the eighteenth century.

My reasons for doing so are partly pragmatic and for another part inspired by the desire to restrict attention to scientific conceptions of economic equilibrium. But what does scientific mean in this regard? The word science may have a specific methodological meaning in the sense of experimental science, but it also has the broader and more general connotation of a systematic inquiry. This notion is often used to pinpoint the start of a specific science like economics. An example is the focus of Schumpeter (1954) on the history of economic analysis, which he sharply distinguished from 'economic thought' and the 'systems of political economy'. However, I shall argue in the next section that 'analysis' as Schumpeter used it placed emphasis on the object of inquiry rather than its method. Nonetheless, there is merit in the demarcation proposed by Schumpeter and I shall use it to motivate the starting point of this inquiry.

This starting point concerns the analysis of supply and demand equilibrium in the work of two preclassical economists, Sir Dudley North (1641–1691) and Pierre de Boisguilbert (1646–1714). I could have selected an earlier period. For example, in the sixteenth century the School of Salamanca was responsible for a shift away from scholastic thinking on problems of price determination towards a focus on exchange in a supply and demand framework.[1] I also could have selected other contemporary writers like Sir William Petty (1623–1687) or John Locke (1632–1704). The reason to focus on North and Boisguilbert is that more than the aforementioned authors they treated the economy as a relatively self-regulating system, ruled by the laws of equilibrium. This is where North and Boisguilbert cover common ground. However, I shall also argue that we see in their work the start of two different visions on the nature of this self regulating system, one focusing on the stability of this order and the other stressing the disrupting effects of changes away from equilibrium. These visions supported the development of two different traditions in the history of equilibrium theory, one in eighteenth century Britain and one across the Channel in Continental Europe. The distinction between these traditions is not often recognized, which makes it a suitable subject for this chapter.[2]

The organization of this chapter is as follows. I shall first elaborate on the meaning of the term 'economic analysis' and discuss the reasons to select North and Boisguilbert as the principal subjects of this chapter. The subsequent sections investigate the supply and demand analyses of North and Boisguilbert respectively in conjunction with their visions on the self regulating nature of the economy. The final section draws conclusions.

THE START OF EQUILIBRIUM THEORY

In the history of economic thought North and Boisguilbert are both known as early anticipators of economic liberalism, transitional figures in the period between mercantilism and economic liberalism. Yet both are also referred to as early anticipators of modern equilibrium analysis. In his article on the history of the equilibrium concept in economics Spiegel (1975, 614) says that Boisguilbert introduced the term 'equilibrium' into the economic nomenclature. He claims that '[w]ith Boisguilbert the equilibrium concept appears in the economic literature and from this time on this concept was never to disappear from it' (ibid.). Chalk (1951, 323n) also mentions him as the first economist to use the equilibrium concept as an analytical tool. More nuance is shown by Schumpeter (1954, 216) who introduces him as 'one more of those authors who saw the economic organism as an equilibrium system of interrelated magnitudes'.

But no claim of priority in science or it is contested and the 'discovery' of equilibrium economics is no exception to that rule. North's *Discourses upon Trade* (1691) is also considered the 'first full equilibrium analysis in the history of economic theory' (Letwin 1963, 198). Choksy (1995, 489) even surpasses Letwin in his estimation of North's analytical achievements and recognizes in his system the outlines of a mathematical general equilibrium framework of interrelated commodity and factor markets.

These praises indicate that North and Boisguilbert are two plausible suspects when it concerns the origins of equilibrium economics. The question remains why exactly. The quotations given above are not unanimous on the criteria used to establish someone as the first to have used a specific theoretical concept like equilibrium. On one side of the spectrum authors like Spiegel are simply looking for the first use of the word equilibrium in an economic text. But this does not really seem satisfying, as equilibrium has several meanings and one would like to have some notion of its substance as a theoretical concept.[3] On the other side of the spectrum there are people like Choksy who are searching for nothing less than an embryonic account of a specific equilibrium theory like GE theory. In my opinion, this is not a sensible undertaking when it concerns texts from the end of the seventeenth century. The outlook and theoretical acumen of a merchant and pamphleteer such as Dudley North was simply too far removed from someone like Walras with a principle interest in turning economics into a mathematical science. To cite just one difference: I have typified GE theory as a prime example of an end-state conception of equilibrium, but North's ideas are nothing of the sort. We shall shortly see that his rudimentary supply and demand analysis typically discusses equilibrium as a tendency and nothing more.

The best option is to look for equilibrium thinking in economics as a form of systematic inquiry, as economic analysis in a scientific sense. Schumpeter (1954) seemed to do so when he distinguished economic analysis from what he called 'economic thought' and 'systems of political economy'. To Schumpeter the former did not concern analytical work, but its popular background: 'the sum total of all the opinions concerning economic subjects, especially concerning public policy bearing upon these subjects that, at any given time and place, float in the public mind' (ibid., 38). The latter category is introduced to separate the ideological meaning of economic statements from their analytical content. It concerns systems of economic policies advocated on the basis of certain unifying (normative) principles, such as the principles of economic liberalism, socialism or other political doctrines.

This separation between ideology from analytical content can of course only succeed partially, because we have already seen that Schumpeter argued that vision and therefore ideology plays a crucial role in the formation of a new science. Thus, with regard to the start of the history of economic analysis, he argued that the crucial treshold was that 'analytic economists have been interested, more or less, in the analysis of the phenomenon that we call competitive price' (Schumpeter 1954, 39). In a similar sense, Blaug (1985, 6) stated that:[4]

> The problem that gave rise to economics in the first place, the 'mystery' that fascinated Adam Smith as much as it does the modern economist, is that of market exchange: there is a sense of order in the economic universe, and this order is not imposed from above but is somehow the outcome of the exchange transaction of individuals, each seeking to maximize their own gain.

I have cited these sources to indicate that what mattered most to the start of economic analysis was not the development of a specific method of analysis, but the perception of a sense of order in the economic universe which allowed organized thinking about the problems associated with this universe. Put differently, vision may have been a stronger impetus to the start of economic science than analysis per se.

I stress this point because it has an obvious relationship with the start of equilibrium theory in economics. The notion of order strongly suggests that the causal laws governing this field of study must maintain some kind of balance or equilibrium. It therefore seems logical that the first scientists investigating this order used metaphors, images or theoretical concepts expressing equilibrium to organize their ideas about this new field of study. This is where we should locate the origins of equilibrium economics. I claim that equilibrium theory in this sense did not exist prior to the eighteenth century, mainly because the writers in the early periods in the history of economic thought lacked the notion of order underlying it. This notion is more than a vision of harmony. It actually consists of several elements, all contributing to the establishment of order. These elements are:

- Focus on the pursuit of profit as a main economic motive.
- The notion that exchange of goods or services is not a zero sum game, so that a free market society can be conducive to general economic welfare.
- The idea that the process of exchange between profit driven individuals is a self-regulating order. It does not require the guiding hand of an outside force like the ruling authority to proceed in a harmonious way.
- On a more technical level, there is the vision that the economy is a system of markets, which are interconnected though price and income changes. Supply and demand are used as forces to explain how these changes come about.[5]

This is a complex set of ideas which did not exist prior to the eighteenth century. There is no doubt that, for example, the Greek and Scholastic thinkers anticipated parts of this equilibrium vision, but not all of them. First, they lacked the idea that the economy is a self regulating or self organizing system of exchange and production relationships. Second, economic writings prior to the High Middle Ages seldom addressed what are now considered economic questions. Generally they are an amalgam of ethical, theological, political and economic arguments, which makes it difficult to assess their contribution to the development of an economic conception of equilibrium. In short, they are not what Schumpeter would call economic analysis.

Ekelund and Hébert (1997) observe that in Greek times competitive markets were still a largely unkown phenomenon. Trade was often bilateral, while wealth and privileges were distributed in large measure by custom, tradition and government directives. This facet of Greek society may explain the emphasis in Greek economic thought on the problems of two party exchange and distributive justice. More importantly, trade was condemned as unnatural if it was done with the aim to make a profit. It is clear that the Greeks considered competition a disruptive force in society and not a means which would bring about a harmonious organization of economic exchange.

Moreover, in Greek economic literature the problem of exchange value was generally approached from an ethical point of view (Lowry 1979). It was recognized that prices depend on the costs of production, but the latter had to reflect, for instance, the social status of the producer in question. What the Greeks called a just price had to compensate a nobleman for the costs of his higher living standard.

Similarly, in scholastic thought economic problems were of minor importance compared to ethical considerations. To be sure, the Schoolmen had a firm grasp of the different supply and demand factors affecting price formation (Hamouda and Price 1997). They considered several supply side factors entailed in a merchant's bringing wares to the market: abundance or scarcity, transport, storage and risk. On the side of demand they isolated need or utility as a price determining factor. Yet in medieval times the discussion of price formation was never considered as just an abstract issue. Instead, it focused on the ethical problems of a scarcity economy. Hamouda and Price point to the fact that a basic characteristic of the medieval economic situation was a lack of production and supply, making the medieval markets sellers' markets. The Schoolmen recognized that excess demand would raise market prices, leading them to ask what a just compensation for productive efforts would be. The scarcity problem also pointed to the issue of an unequal income distribution. In the poverty stricken medieval economy the majority of the population was barely able to feed itself. With regard to this subsistence economy it could well be asked if market prices were 'just' in relation to the needs of people. Was it just that people perished in poverty, while a small minority enjoyed splendour and luxury? The immense income inequalities of the medieval subsistence economy inevitably infused scholastic discussions of price formation with moral considerations concerning the issues of commutative and distributive justice. Indeed 'there seem to be strong grounds for asserting they [the Schoolmen, BT] were nowhere near as concerned about the theoretical determination per se of these prices as about the ethical implications of price formation on sellers and buyers' (Hamouda and Price 1997, 193). Moreover, the scarcity economy made it difficult to focus on seller's competition as a factor in maintaining an orderly process of market transactions.

Yet gradually in the mercantilist period there emerged one idea that was to be of decisive importance for the economic thought of later generations. This was the idea that the individual pursuit of profit may have an unsuspected consequence, namely economic order (Letwin 1963). A reason for the emergence of this idea was that it could be used to sanction the newly acquired wealth of an emerging commercial class. Traditionally, this class had been considered with a degree of moral suspicion. According to the Greeks, profits in exchange violated the demands of commutative justice because they could only come about at the cost of someone else's loss. Consequently, they considered trade a vulgar occupation beneath the dignity of citizens. In the late 16th century some authors recognized that a notion of economic order could be used to boost the social status of the mercantile class. Contrary to popular belief, these authors maintained that profits in trade did not harm the commercial interests of others. Instead, trade allowed both parties to an exchange to better satisfy their desires and could therefore be considered mutually advantageous. That conclusion implied that trade did not necessarily violate the demands of commutative justice and could be used to sanction the profit motive and trade as proper elements of human conduct.

The moral vindication of the profit motive as an economic incentive was an important stepping stone towards economic liberalism and its underlying notion of economic order. The idea that trade was mutually advantageous suggested that private and social interests were identical. Motivated by their desire for profit people engage in trade and thereby offer others an opportunity to exchange goods and better satisfy their wishes. In that sense individual economic action could be said to promote the general well-being as well. The implications of this view were far reaching. First, it was recognized that freedom to exchange was conducive to economic prosperity. The call for economic liberalism so became the natural corollary of the profit motive (Chalk 1951). Second, the identity of private and social interests could be said to constitute a form of economic order. Hobbes had argued that only an absolute ruler could prevent a society of self interested individuals, which would collapse in a chaotic struggle for goods. The only guarantee of social harmony was a social contract in which such a ruler was appointed. Economic liberalism constituted a break with this line of thinking because it suggested that social order would come about automatically and unintentionally, the result of the actions of innumerous individuals all trying to better their own position. In a free economic system, their tendency to economically gain at the expense of others is checked, not by the political or military force of an absolute ruler, but by the force of competition. Competition means that buyers and sellers have alternatives open to them if they are faced with unreasonable demands in the market place. The risk to lose customers or a buying opportunity due to competition will moderate the demands of sellers and buyers respectively and allows transactions to proceed in a relatively orderly fashion. It was the contribution of 18th century economic thought that we distinguish supply and demand as the two economic forces that bring about this order and analytically demonstrate how their interaction could stabilize prices and establish an equilibrium of quantities bought and sold.

It will be my task in the next two sections to demonstrate that we find the four constituent elements of what I have called the equilibrium vision in the writings of North and Boisguilbert. However, I also intend to show that the theoretical development based on this vision shows an important difference, which would affect the subsequent formation of economic doctrines in the eighteenth century. This difference is the focus of the analysis of a self regulating market order. We shall discover in North the roots of the typical Anglo-Saxon focus on the forces that will give this order stability. The work of Boisguilbert, however, is of a different nature. Influenced by the French social and economic conditions during the reign of Louis XIV, he feared most that state intervention would upset the economic order. His principal aim was to explain what would be the dire consequences of this meddling with the economy. This led to a focus on the movements away of equilibrium, a line of thinking which later French economists found hard to shed.

SIR DUDLEY NORTH: A PIONEER IN ECONOMIC THEORY

Scientific Method and Political Objectivity

Letwin considers North's notion of equilibrium as an example of equilibrium analysis because it is the result of strictly deductive reasoning. He claims that 'North was the first economic writer to construct a cogent analysis, founded on a few broad, general principles of axiomatic simplicity, which enable[d] him to provide a mechanistic explanation of an economic process, and to reach policy conclusions that are deducible strictly from the premises' (Letwin 1963, 198; see also Choksy 1992). That North opted for what Letwin considers a scientific mode of inquiry is remarkable, for he certainly was not a scholar. His biographer records that he had neither taste nor talent for study (Letwin 1963, 184). He left school at an early age to learn a practical trade. As a merchant he made a fortune in the Levant trade and lived in Turkey for a period of twenty years. When he returned to England in 1681 'he looked a barbarian, and was not more cultured than one'.[6] And this is the man that we are told to consider as a forerunner of Walras and later exponents of general equilibrium analysis?

I find this claim hard, if not impossible, to swallow. I do agree that North's *Discourse upon Trade* from 1691 contains an interesting notion of a price equilibrium derived in terms of supply and demand, which is why North figures in this chapter. But the claims concerning its scientific character are exaggerated and the assertion that he must be seen as an anticipator of mathematical general equilibrium analysis is simply a joke. There is not a trace of mathematical reasoning in this pamphlet and one must look very hard to find evidence of the idea that markets are interconnected through prices and incomes. What North offered was a form of partial equilibrium analysis of price formation in the money market, which pointed forward – and no more than that – to the specie-flow mechanism that later and more able theoreticians like David Hume would develop.

It is time to discuss Letwin's argument for considering Dudley North a pioneer of equilibrium analysis. Letwin (1963) claimed that North introduced a scientific conception of equilibrium analysis in his work as a means to safeguard the objectivity of his political statement. This requires some explanation. North was elected to the British parlement in 1685, but he also had extended commercial interests as a major shareholder in the Levant and African trading companies. This combination of these interests made it difficult for him to maintain that he was serving the people's interests in Parliament. A merchant of his standing was quickly accused of special pleading. This is evident from the preface to his *Discourse upon Trade* (North 1691[1907]), where the writer is said to seek only

> the Publick Good, and . . . to rely wholly upon Truth and Justice . . . He seems to be of a Temper different from most, who have meddled with this Subject in Publick; for it is manifest, his Knowledge and Experience of Trade is considerable, which could not be attained, unless he were a Trader himself; and yet it is not to be collected from anything he says, of what Nature his dealing hath been; for he only speaks impartially of Trade in general, without warping to the Favour of any particular Interest (ibid., 7, 10).

This of course nothing more than an appeal to trust the blue eyes of the author of this pamphlet, but North offered an additional argument. He referred to his method of investigation as a guarantee of the objectivity of the author. This was an interesting innovation. In the mercantile period, it was quite common to start an economic discourse with a disclaimer of some kind, as most pamphleteers were public officials and businessmen with obvious political or commercial interests (Spiegel 1971, 97). But not many took the trouble to defend their honour in terms of a philosophical argument. North did. He said that his analysis consisted in logical deductions from self evident truths, a method he associated with the 'new' philosophy of Descartes (ibid.,

11). The fact that the axioms were self evident truths and that one could follow the logical deductions step by step was supposed to guarantee the objectivity of the argument. Moreover, was it not evident that from true premises followed true conclusions? Letwin concludes that North's adoption of a deductive method was a rhetorical trick to avoid the suggestion that his writings were intended to further the commercial interests of a specific group. By coincidence 'this method of guaranteeing objectivity is also the method par excellence of scientific theory'. Thus '[i]n the search for a way of dispelling the problem of special pleading, a scientific method was hit on' (Letwin 1963, 97).

This may be true, but what has this deductive method to do with the analysis of economic equilibrium? Letwin treated equilibrium as a logical extension of the deductive method, because he believed it to be an amoral and objective argument par excellence. He used to following, interesting simile to support this suggestion (Letwin 1963, 199).

> A guillotine blade is in equilibrium once it has come to rest at the bottom of the guides; whether that equilibrium is desirable or not depends on whose head has rolled. Machines that tend toward equilibrium will be given free scope only by those men who believe that the position at equilibrium is in some degree desirable.

In other words, do not blame the equilibrium mechanism for killing people. However, I do not find this metaphor very helpful when discussing the role of equilibrium in economic affairs. I just argued at length that in economics the concept of equilibrium generally rests on moral, ideological and other metaphysical preconceptions that are not deducible from first principles. This applies all the more so to a science in its infant stage, like economics was in the days of North and mercantilism. I therefore find it especially inappropriate that Letwin attributed to North an amoral conception of equilibrium. If anything, I would have expected from North an equilibrium concept with a moral overtone, representing some kind of vision about the desired functioning of the economy.

Moreover, in my opinion, this is exactly what is at stake in North's *Discourse upon trade*. This pamphlet was his contribution to the parliamentary debates on the Recoinage question. Recoinage involved the answer to the fear of an inadequate money supply due to clipping and other illegal activities. To maintain Britain's money supply, in 1690 several Bills were proposed to forbid the exportation of bullion and to reduce the interest rate from 6 percent to 4 percent. In the Parliamentary debates concerning the Recoinage question North opposed the usury laws and other proposals to restrict the money trade. His argument was that the markets for money and loans did not require state control to prevent a shortage of money. On the contrary, he argued that the proposed Bills were likely to prevent market forces from automatically determining an optimal supply of coin and bullion. That is, North promoted a thorough laissez faire approach and can in fact be considered one of the first coherent British laissez faire thinkers in this period (Schumpeter 1954, 369).

In my opinion, this is the proper background to discuss North's introduction of a rudimentary form of equilibrium analysis in a supply and demand framework. His pamphlet represents a vision about the orderly outcome of market exchange when the state abstains from active interference. His equilibrium analysis was intended to support this outlook on the nature of a liberal economic order and can certainly not be detached from this political view. In this case, as in many others in the early stages of the history of economic thought, vision and analysis go hand in hand.

Supply and Demand as a 'Universal Maxime'

The basis of North's equilibrium involves the claim that supply and demand drive market prices to a stable level. He defended this notion in terms of a well-known metaphor, that of a balance. He said that in equilibrium prices are stable, like a balance between two buckets of equal weight (North 1691[1907], 36). The forces bringing about this equilibrium are those of supply and demand. He argued that excess supply would tend to lower prices, whereas an excess of demand over supply would raise them. His formulation of this principle is a clear example of what has been called the proportion theory of supply and demand (Bowley 1973, Chapter 3). The focus of this analysis is on the proportion or ratio between the quantities supplied and demanded at a given market price. If for this price the quantity supplied proves insufficient to satisfy demand, the competition between buyers will tend to raise it. In the reverse case, as sellers compile unsold stock of commodities, they will try to undersell each other and market prices are likely to fall. The ratio between supply and demand, then, determines the direction of changes in the market price. In the words of North (1691[1907], 21) 'as more Buyers than Sellers raiseth the Price of a Commodity', so the 'Plenty of any thing makes it cheap' (ibid., 34, see also p. 18). This principle is what he called the 'Universal Maxime' of his price analysis.

This type of analysis must be distinguished from modern supply and demand analysis in terms of schedules, connecting prices and quantitities supplied and demanded. For North the ratio between supply and demand indicates the direction in which market prices can be expected to change. In modern analysis supply and demand are mathematical functions, showing the quantities people are willing to supply and demand at different prices. This mathematical interpretation underpins the end-state conception of equilibrium in modern analysis. This end-state is nothing but the equilibrium solution to the equation of the supply and demand functions. Try deriving this solution when you do not have a proper notion of a mathematical function between dependent and independent variables.

Of course, Dudley North did not possess this knowledge, nor did any contemporary economist. In economics, J.S. Mill was one of the first to understand that a proportions theory of value conflates the causes and effects of price changes. Do supply and demand determine prices, or are they themselves quantities determined by prices? In the proportions theory of Mill's precursors, supply and demand inequalities cause prices to change, yet in turn supply and demand themselves also depend on the current price level. The root of this error is a conflation of changes along and changes of supply and demand curves. To distinguish between price-determined and price-determining influences, a clear conception of supply and demand as functional relationships is required. In the words of Mill (1909, 448, emphasis in the original)

> the idea of a ratio, as between demand and supply, is out of place, and has no concern in the matter: the proper mathematical analogy is that of equation. Demand and supply, the quantity demanded and the quantity supplied, will be made equal. If unequal at any moment, competition equalizes them, and the manner in which this is done is by an adjustment of the value . . . [T]he value which a commodity will bring in any market, is no other than the value which, in that market, gives a demand just sufficient to carry off the existing or expected supply.

Prior to Mill only a few economists understood that, properly seen, supply and demand should be ex ante magnitudes. North certainly did not conceive of supply and demand in these terms and it is therefore nonsense to attribute to him an embryonic mathematical theory of equilibrium price determination. His price theory is an early example of a process theory, discussing the causes behind the tendency of prices towards a stable level. It is this aspect of his work which makes him a pioneer of equilibrium economics.[7]

Underlying this supply and demand analysis, there was an important suggestion which formed an important contribution to the development of a more consistent price theory. North rivalled the insight of John Locke, made around this same time, that supply and demand are truly universal forces: all prices are determined by supply and demand (Vaughn 1980, 45). This was a provoking thought at a time when gold and silver were still considered the ultimate sources of economic value. For North (1691[1907], 26) gold and silver were commodities like any other, with an exchange value determined by supply and demand. This insight led him to reject the mercantile view that a nation grows rich by accumulating gold and silver. In his perception the source of a nation's wealth was a thriving industry and prosperous trade, not its stock of gold and silver (ibid., 25–26, 34, 37). Locke followed a similar line and used the supply and demand framework to put the quantity theory of money on a much firmer foundation (Negishi 1989, 31–40).[8]

North did not venture into this terrain. He used the supply and demand framework to investigate the forces determining the supply of money. After all, it was the fear of an inadequate money supply which had caused the Recoinage question in British parliament. But could a shortage of money actually occur? North argued that this would not happen if only the state would not interfere by raising interest rates by decree, nor forbid the exportation of bullion. He underpinned this claim by demonstrating that supply and demand would maintain a price equilibrium between coin and bullion. Money was supplied by the Mint, which suggested that the prices of coin and bullion should tend to equalize. For North, it was evident that a price differential between them could never be sustained for long. As coin paid a premium over bullion, people had a strong incentive to mint money. They thereby increased the supply of coin and lowered its price relative to that of bullion. In the reverse case, as bullion received a premium over money, coins could easily be melted and sold as bullion. The resulting fall in the price of bullion would tend to reduce the excess demand for bullion which had caused the price differential in the first place. In this manner 'the buckets work alternately, when Money is scarce, Bullion is coyn'd; when Bullion is scarce, Money is melted' (ibid., 36). North recognized that ultimately the buckets must balance, as the prices of coin and bullion adjust to bring their supply and demand into closer conformity.[9]

Equilibrium Vision and Economic Liberalism

The use of supply and demand to explain prices was not really a novelty in the late seventeenth century. I have already referred to the members of the School of Salamanca as early practitioners of a scarcity theory of value which included a role for supply and demand. Likewise, in the framework of the quantity theory it was actually quite common to discuss the changes of the money supply in terms of supply and demand. However, all these early progenitors lacked what I have called the equilibrium vision, which includes, besides a supply and demand 'theory' of price formation, a focus on the pursuit of profit as a main economic motive, the notion that free market exchange is conducive to general economic welfare and the idea that the process of exchange between profit driven individuals is a self regulating order. I shall briefly show that in North's *Discours upon Trade* we find all these elements.

To start with the latter point, the debates on the Recoinage question clearly show that North promoted the self regulating capacity of economic forces. He used the result of his 'bucket' analysis to argue against the promulgation of laws which would obstruct the free operation of the price mechanism. Concerning the specie controls, he argued that the fear of a shortage of money was unwarranted. His analysis showed that a freely operating market would always supply the necessary amount of coin, suggesting that there was no need for the state to regulate its supply by means of legislation or direct intervention.[10] On the contrary, 'This ebbing and flowing of Money, supplies and accommodates itself, without any aid of Politicians' (ibid.). Likewise, in the case of the usury laws he rejected the proposal to reduce the rate of interest by law. He maintained that the interest rate is determined by the supply and demand for loans and cannot be controlled by the state (ibid., 21; see also Letwin 1963, 194). In *A Discourse of the Poor*, a tract published in 1753 under the name of North's brother Roger, supply and demand analysis is used to discuss the economic effects of the Poor and the Settlement laws (Choksy 1992). Again, North proposed to abandon these laws because they merely harmed the goal they sought to achieve. The Poor and Settlement Laws hindered the geographic mobility of workers and so prevented the migration of labour to regions with better employment opportunities. In other words, they prevented the price mechanism from bringing about a more efficient allocation of labour resources and so aggravated the problems of unemployment and poverty, rather than solving them.

These cases show that North consistently pursued a laissez faire policy based upon the results of his equilibrium analysis. For him a society free of state intervention was a better society, because it gave people the freedom to pursue their own goals. That freedom would also allow prices to play their coordinating role and bring markets nearer to equilibrium. With Choksy (1995, 488) one may conclude that North's policy recommendations reveal his firm belief that a free market economy can be an entirely self regulating system.

It is therefore not surprising to find that North anticipated Smith's invisible hand, the idea that order is brought about spontaneously by profit seeking individuals. Like Smith, North stressed that greed is a main economic motive. He observed that '[t]he main spur to Trade, or rather to Industry and Ingenuity, is the exorbitant Appetites of Men, which they will take pains to gratifie, and so be disposed to work, when nothing else will incline them to it' (North 1691[1907], 27). But even when greed is a selfish motive par excellence, other people may be expected to benefit from the activities motivated thereby. As North put it:

> The Glutton works hard to purchase Delicacies, wherewith to gorge himself; the Gamester, for money to venture at Play; the Miser to hoard; and so others. Now in their pursuit of those Appetites, other Men less exhorbitant are benefitted; and tho' it may be thought few profit by the Miser, yet it will be found otherwise, if we consider, that besides the humour of every Generation, to dissipate what another had collected, there is benefit from the very Person of a covetous Man; for if he labours with his own hands, his Labour is very beneficial to them who imploy him; if he doth not work, but profit by the work of others, then those he sets on work have benefit by their being employed (ibid.).

North here suggested that by striving to satisfy their personal wants, people unintentionally help others to satisfy theirs. This argument closely resembles Smith's classic statement of the invisible hand in the *Theory of Moral Sentiments* (1759) where a similar example is found (Smith 1759[1976], 184–85). The logical result of this view is that free trade furthers the economic well-being in general, or as North put it, 'there can be no Trade unprofitable to the Publick; for if any prove so, men leave it off; and wherever the Traders thrive, the Publick, of which they are part, thrives also' (North 1691[1907], vii). A point not yet recognized in North's formulation of the invisible hand argument is that it is competition which forces individuals to moderate their selfish demands and allow economic transactions to proceed in a relatively orderly fashion. Still, the essence of the argument is there: by seeking their own interest, individuals advance a goal that was no part of their original concerns, the general well-being.[11] Of course, to an economic liberal the idea that private and social interests are compatible is crucial, for it suggests that a nation's economic prosperity is best served by giving individuals sufficient freedom to pursue their own goals. State intervention is likely to constrain people in this endeavour and is therefore best avoided. The quotation cited above appears in a section where North defends the case of 'Free Commerce' and is clearly intended to support his laissez faire policies.

The focus on the benefits of free trade and the self-regulating nature of market exchange demonstrates that with Dudley North and contemporary liberal writers the transition began from mercantilism and its interventionist policies to the liberalism of the classical economic school. North contributed to this transition by developing a rudimentary supply and demand analysis as the foundation of his laissez faire approach to economic policy. In this section we have seen that this analysis focused on supply and demand as two forces that would not fail to bring prices to a stable level, as long as the state would abstain from intervention. It is this aspect of his work which makes him a pioneer of equilibrium economics.

PIERRE DE BOISGUILBERT: EQUILIBRIUM AS A LAW OF NATURE

Introduction

In France the opposition against mercantilism, exemplified by Colbert's economic policies, also grew stronger towards the end of the 17th century. One of the first to promote the cause of laissez faire liberalism in France, and probably the one who introduced the term 'laisser faire' into the economic literature, was the magistrate Pierre de Boisguilbert (1646–1714). I shall compare his ideas on the equilibrium mechanism with North's and conclude that there is an interesting difference in focus. For Boisguilbert, economic analysis was first and foremost an instrument to unmask the disastrous consequences of active state involvement with the economy. This focus led him to underline, not the stability of the economic order, but the risk of a cumulative change away from equilibrium, once it got disturbed by outside forces like the government. In his work economic equilibrium can be seen as a law of nature that is easily toppled over due to human interference.

It is this latter aspect which will stand central in this section. Boisguilbert almost literally believed that like nature, the economy was predominated by balance or equilibrium. Van Dyke Roberts (1935, Chapter 10) said that it was this belief which guided him in his theoretical analysis. His notion of the economy as a natural order is therefore a clear example of a vision guiding theoretical research. For his policy lessons it is important to note that Boisguilbert believed nature played a harsh game with the lives of human beings. It could maintain a harmony of forces but this harmony was at times disrupted by destabilizing forces. This notion returns in Boisguilbert's definition of economic equilibrium and sets him apart from Dudley North and the Anglo–Saxon focus on stability as the all important characteristic of equilibrium.

Welfare and Stagnation

Pierre de Boisguilbert was a magistrate in his native city of Rouen. In that position he was responsible for law and order, supervised the food supply and the collection of taxes.[12] As an economist, he is best known for his tax reforms and his free trade policies. His appeals for lower tax rates and a freer trade make him one of the first French reformers (Bast 1935; 1966) and a forerunner of the economic liberalism of Adam Smith and the classical school of economics (Van Dyke Roberts 1935).

One of Boisguilbert's achievements in the field of economics was that of developing a notion of underconsumption: the idea that economic stagnation is due to insufficient aggregate purchasing power (McDonald 1954). His stress on underconsumption and stagnation strongly reflected the economic conditions of the society and period he lived in. In the closing years of the 17th and early years of the 18th century, the French economy had been weakened by a number of factors. Firstly, France was engaged in a series of wars which placed a tremendous burden on the French treasury, ultimately producing large budget deficits, debasement of the currency and oppressive taxation.[13] Secondly, the French economy experienced a considerable loss of wealth and human capital when the revocation of the Edict of Nantes in 1685 led to the persecution and emigration of the Huguenots. Thirdly, a number of severe famines occured in a relatively short time span (1693, 1694, 1698 and 1709). Boisguilbert estimated that as a result of these problems the national income in France had fallen by one-half since 1660 (Boisguilbert 1695[1966], 583; 1707b[1966], 885).[14] It was this secular stagnation of income and production which he sought to explain and which led him to develop a specific conception of economic equilibrium.

To Boisguilbert economic equilibrium was synonymous with a state of opulence, while disequilibrium meant stagnation, decline, and misery (Hébert 1987, 189). He believed that there existed a kind of equilibrium in the economy which would make all French citizens better off. The problem was that the state had created obstacles which prevented the economy from reaching this state of opulence. These obstacles took the form of trade regulations and high tax rates. To finance Louis XIV's extravagant lifestyle and costly wars, trade in the French kingdom had been subjected to countless tolls and tariffs. Often transportation of food from one region to another was not worth the effort because the tolls caused long delays and made the journey unprofitable. The other main income sources of the French state were sales and income taxes. One of the most hated taxes was the *aide*, an excise on wine and other beverages. Boisguilbert observed that the *aide* had raised the price of wine enough to curb consumption. As a result of lower sales, vineyards were being destroyed and three out of four Frenchmen had to drink water (Boisguilbert 1695[1966], 603, 609). The *taille* was an income tax based on the yield of property. Since most noble, rich and powerful men were exempted, the tax was highly regressive. Moreover, it could only be collected at high cost. As the yield of property had to be estimated, people delayed payment as long as possible. Prompt payment of the *taille* suggested affluence, which naturally raised one's assessment. Owing to the hostility of taxpayers, collection could take months. Meanwhile, fields and workshops were abandoned and population and income declined. In this manner, Boisguilbert asserted, high and unequal taxes ruined the nation (ibid., 593–599).

To restore the economy these obstacles had to be removed. The essence of Boisguilbert's analysis of the French economic situation was his belief that once the tax system had been reformed and trade regulations had been abandoned, the economy would naturally regain its 'equilibrium'. His reformist contemporaries shared his analysis of France's depressed economy. However, they did not share his belief that simple corrective measures would swiftly restore prosperity, in part because they did not conceive of the French economy in terms of a resilient economic order. What separates Boisguilbert from his immediate contemporaries is his awareness of a relatively autonomous economic order, capable of effecting such changes (Spengler 1984, 73). It is this awareness which lies at the root of his equilibrium analysis and which also influenced his fiscal and free trade policies.

Nature's Order and Economic Well-being

The core assumption of Boisguilbert's work is that he believed that society is ruled by what is called a natural order. The notion of a natural order is part of natural law philosophy which affected many thinkers in the Enlightenment period (Gay 1969). The emerging economics profession did not escape this influence and we shall encounter the concept of a natural order many times in the next few chapters when I discuss the equilibrium vision of, amongst others, the physiocrats and Adam Smith. The notion of a natural order gave an enormous push to the natural sciences, as it suggested that there was set of natural laws 'out there' to be discovered by scientific inquiry, and they were actually found. In the 18th century Newton's physics was the most important example, portraying the universe as a mechanical system governed by natural laws. We shall later see that such scientific conceptions of natural law philosophy were of great importance to economists like Adam Smith. I shall here demonstrate that for Boisguilbert another part of the natural order mattered more, namely its origin. If nature is structured so beautifully, the question naturally arises who or what is responsible for this order. At the end of the 17th century, the answer to this question would unequivocally point to devine providence and it was this line of thinking that mattered most to Boisguilbert.[15] He marvelled at the sense of order endowed by God in nature and he argued that an order with similar qualities operated in the economic realm. It is this influence which pushed him towards equilibrium thinking in economic affairs.

Having been educated by the Jesuits at Rouen and later as a student at the Jansenist college at Port Royal, Boisguilbert must have been acquainted with theological discourses along these lines (Van Dyke Roberts 1935, 12–13, 19). His interest in natural law and related philosophies is clearly indicated by the references to Seneca in his work (Perrot 1992a). His biographer Van

Dyke Roberts maintains that Boisguilbert's religious convictions significantly affected his economic work. Discussing his conception of economic equilibrium, she states that '[t]he Bible became the point of departure for his theory.' (Van Dyke Roberts 1935, 240). Another influence may have been Fontenelle's popular *Pluralité des Mondes*, published in 1686, in which nature is compared to a machine, operated by 'wheels' and 'counter-weights' (Spengler 1984, 73). Boisguilbert described the economy in similar terms, stating that its parts function together like the 'machine' of a watch (letter of 20 July 1704, in INED 1966, vol. I, 320–21).

To Boisguilbert nature set an example of how the economy could operate as a comparatively autonomous, self regulating system. In his writings he often referred to Nature as a guardian of economic equilibrium (Boisguilbert 1707c[1966], 992):

> La nature donc, ou la Providence . . . établissent d'abord une égale nécessité de vendre et d'acheter dans toutes sortes de trafics, de façon que le seul désir de profit soit l'âme de tous les marchés, tant dans le vendeur que dans le acheteur; c'est à l'aide de cet équilibre et de cette balance que l'un et l'autre sont également forcés d'entendre raison et de s'y soumettre.

In other cases nature provided examples of how forces would ultimately balance. One such example was the Lake of Geneva, which provided a reservoir for the stabilization of the water level of the river Rhône flowing through it (Boisguilbert 1707b[1966], 870). Similarly, he considered trade a natural channel to dampen price fluctuations.

Natural equilibrium in this sense was considered beneficial: it signified an ideal world of general affluence and well-being.[16] In equilibrium, people profit from all opportunities nature offers and consequently 'l'opulence est portée au plus haut où elle puisse être' (Boisguilbert 1707c[1966], 987). In this sense equilibrium is considered the 'unique conservateur de l'opulence générale', a phrase which returns several times (ibid. 993, 995, 996). But if mankind acts against the natural laws of the economy, for instance by trying to control economic life, this 'happy situation' (ibid. 993) ceases to exist. According to Boisguilbert, it was nature alone that could maintain economic order; all human attempts to do so were destined to fail. In his words, '[C]'est à la nature seule à y mettre cet ordre et à entretenir la paix; toute autre autorité gâte tout en voulant s'en mêler, quelque bien intentionnée qu'elle soit' (ibid., 992). From such attempts there could be no other result than a cessation of trade and a destruction of capital goods. To Boisguilbert economic disequilibrium was synonymous to economic decline and human misery.[17]

If nature was the ultimate reason or final cause of economic wealth, it was man's desire of profit which was the efficient cause of economic order. Like North, Boisguilbert understood that in economic affairs people pursue nothing but their own, personal interests; 'parce que l'ardeur de gagner était si naturelle qu'il ne fallait point d'autre motifs que l'intérêt personnel pour les faire agir' (Boisguilbert 1705[1966], 795). It was profit alone which constituted the 'spirit' of all trades (Boisguilbert 1707c[1966], 992). Yet also like North he recognized that the profit motive can be a public virtue as well, as 'All are occupied night and day with their own particular interests, but, at the same time, *although that is what they care about least,* they are contributing to the general good' (Boisguilbert 1707c[1966], 991, transl. Irwin 1996, 65, emphasis added).[18] Clearly, Boisguilbert fits a line of writers that understood that economic order is an unintended consequence of self-interested behaviour long before Adam Smith used the metaphor of the invisible hand to describe this feature of a free market economy.[19]

However, what characterized Boisguilbert's vision of economic order was its emphasis on the final cause of the order, namely nature's inherent goodness. This sets him apart from authors like Adam Smith who would later stress competition as an efficient cause, bringing about a tendency of prices to move in the direction of cost levels. As a result of competition, suppliers are unable to earn profits above the normal or equilibrium rate for long periods. In contrast, Boisguilbert assumed that nature curbs abuse of self-interest and brings about equilibrium.[20] According to him, 'Authority is necessary in order to have peace and the laws of men observed among a large number of men, who seek only to destroy them and to deceive and circumvent one another from morning to night, and who aspire continually to establish their wealth on the ruin of their neighbours' (ibid., 992). Yet the role of government in providing this authority was secondary. Probably based on his own experiences as a magistrate, Boisguilbert was highly suspicious of the intentions of civil servants and contended that 'it is nature alone which can create order and maintain peace among them' (ibid.). The state's best policy was to abstain from intervention in the economy and to 'laisse faire la nature' (ibid., 993; and 644, 795, 873, 897), one of the earliest recorded statements of this kind in the economic literature (Oncken 1886). Behind his advice to deregulate the economy and reform the tax system, there is the belief that the economy is part of a self regulating order of natural laws in which economic prosperity is the unintended result of the production and exchange activities of self interested people.

The Unstable Properties of Economic Equilibrium

The role of nature in Boisguilbert's equilibrium theories of the economy is that of a peacemaker, establishing harmony between the potentially conflicting intentions of economic agents. In the case of bilateral exchange this harmony refers to the condition of commutative justice: both parties exchange the same quantity of value. However, that does not imply that no gains are made in trade. Boisguilbert stressed the fact that people's subjective perceptions of these values differ and that consequently all parties gain by the exchange: trade allowed them to obtain those goods they lacked in exchange for those of which they had a surplus (Boisguilbert 1707b[1966], 891, 895–6). He stated that 'trade is nothing but reciprocal utility; and all parties, buyers and seller, must have an equal interest or necessity to buy or sell.' (ibid., 876–77). To him this reciprocal benefit explained why trade was so important to economic prosperity and why the state should abstain from regulating it.

Boisguilbert used the condition of commutative justice as a starting point of his analysis of market exchange. This condition lead him to argue that equilibrium prevailed when supply equalled demand. Morever, he called the equilibrium price 'proportional', because it could be assumed to cover at least the costs of production (Van Dyke Roberts 1935, 223; Kubota 1966, 80). Interestingly, this condition is generalized to all markets: prices are proportional if they permit all goods sold to cover the costs of production. This becomes clear from the following statement (Boisguilbert 1707c[1966], 993).

> On a dit, et on le repète encore, qu'afin que cette heureuse situation subsiste ['qu'on laisse faire la nature', BT], il faut que toutes choses et toutes les denrées soient continuellement dans un équilibre, et conservent un prix de proportion par rapport entre elles et aux frais qu'il a fallu pour les établir.

It appears that Boisguilbert's equilibrium theory of market exchange has two characteristics: First, it refers to the condition that prices equal costs and, second, it assumes that in equilibrium all markets clear (Billoret 1989, 67).

Boisguilbert's use of supply and demand to explain prices is clearest in his consideration of the price of grain.[21] He assumed the demand for grain to be inelastic, as grain was the main foodstuff and could not be missed (Boisguilbert 1707a[1966], 868–869). Concerning the determinants of the supply price, he referred to wages, the maintenance of the capital used (land, utensils and implements), rent to the landlord and a profit to the entrepreneur as the main cost factors (Van Dyke Roberts 1935, 241; Kubota 1966, 80). The market is said to be in equilibrium when supply equals demand, 'like a balance suspended in equilibrium because the weight is equal in each of the two scales' (quoted in Van Dyke Roberts 1935, 228; Boisguilbert 1707a[1966], 859). The analysis even foreshadows marginal theory. Boisguilbert recognized that there cannot be two different prices for the same product in the same market. 'Thus, for example, if there are two sacks of wheat beyond what is necessary for the usual consumption, which the dealer is obliged to sell at whatever they will bring, this will lower the price for all the grain sold in the market' (ibid., 227). In other words that portion of the product which is offered at the lowest price determines the price at which the rest will sell.

Billoret (1989, 72) points out an important difference between the Anglo-Saxon and French economic traditions in the 18th century. The British economists in this period were convinced of the stability of the position of equilibrium and based their studies on this assumption. In contrast, the French adopted a more pessimistic view. They were concerned about the instability of economic equilibrium and studied the consequences of its disruption. Boisguilbert exemplifies this approach. He was eager to clarify the cause of extreme variations in the price of grain and feared that a disruption of the equilibrium price of grain would have far reaching consequences for the economic well-being of France. To explain the price swings of grain he isolated two causes, the inelasticity of its demand and the speculative behaviour of merchants. He observed that on rumour of a shortage in the crop the buyers who ordinarily buy their supplies from week to week or month to month, hasten in panic to supply their needs for the entire year. However, in the hope that the problem will increase sellers will refrain from making their ordinary sales, using every means to get their creditors to wait for payment. These two factors cause violent changes in the price of grain when the equilibrium between its supply and demand is disturbed. Boisguilbert illustrated this point with the use of a metaphor, that of the balance (Boisguilbert 1707a[1966], 859; quoted in Van Dyke Roberts 1935, 228–229).

> It is like a balance suspended in equilibrium because the weight is equal in each of the two scales. A hundred pounds of any material whatever cannot receive an increase of even two pounds in one of the two scales without destroying the equilibrium. This, then, is precisely what takes place with regard to the price of grain. An increase or a diminution of twenty sacks at the market or staple house above or below the ordinary supply of five hundred sacks offered every week, destroys the balance, and makes it fall immediately on one side.

This quotation shows that, in contrast to North, Boisguilbert used the metaphor of the balance to illustrate, not the stability of the market price, but, on the contrary, the manner in which relatively small changes in supply lead to wide price swings that do not tend towards equilibrium. Given the reactions of buyers and sellers set out above, a shortage of grain became a self-fulfilling prophecy, as changes in supply caused cumulative price changes. Yet in spite of this conclusion Boisguilbert believed that essentially even the price of grain was a stable one. The problem was the fragility of the equilibrium price. Maintenance of equilibrium required obeisance to the laws of nature and in the case of the grain trade the state had violated these laws. It had attempted to control this trade by means of export duties and other regulations. In the opinion of Boisguilbert interferences of this kind obstructed the operation of natural forces that would otherwise stabilize the grain price and maintain market equilibrium.

To support this conclusion, he introduced a natural analogy, that of the flow of rivers. Rivers provided a vital life force, water, but also occasionally threatened the lives of people in the form of floods and droughts. According to Boisguilbert, these fluctuations in a river's water level were stabilized, not by means of manmade constructions like dykes and dams, but by natural reservoirs, lakes, which the river flows through (Boisguilbert 1707a[1966], 870). Similarly, trade stabilized market prices by providing a vent for surpluses.[22] However, in the French grain trade duties and other regulations obstructed the flow of grain between the market and its natural reservoirs, supplies from other regions and even foreign countries, and so aggravated the effect of a change in the grain supply on its price. Therefore, to dampen excessive variations in the grain price one had to abandon the regulations obstructing its trade. Boisguilbert was highly optimistic about the effect this would have on the stability of the grain price. He observed that the sight of a ship carrying grain would suffice to allay the fears of a grain shortage and re-establish balance in the grain market (ibid., 863). To him it was beyond doubt that free domestic and foreign trade worked to produce equilibrium in the grain market: 'pour résumer le tout, il est incontestable que la sortie ou l'arrivée des blés en France ne produit point d'autre effet que de redresser la balance lorsqu'elle déroge trop à l'équilibre' (ibid. 864).[23] As he believed this tendency towards equilibrium to result from the operation of natural forces and to only occur if one obeyed the laws of nature, one can say that to him economic liberalism literally implied 'laisser agir la nature' (ibid., 870).

Boisguilbert did not restrict his equilibrium analysis to the grain market. He extended his analysis by considering the relationships between different economic sectors and activities (Molinier 1959). He understood that the grain trade was not an isolated market, but that its price changes had effects upon other markets as well. In his analysis these changes are propagated through income changes. He isolated about three hundred different professions in France and described the interconnections between them as a 'chain of opulence'. He reasoned that division of labour would induce people to specialize in one trade and exchange surplus production with others. Accordingly, sellers in one market would be buyers in another. This suggested that losses in the grain trade would depress demand for other products as well. In other words, income changes cause disequilibrium to spread to other markets. Interconnections like this lead Boisguilbert to argue that equilibrium is only attained, if all markets are in equilibrium simultaneously. It requires 'all things and all products to be continually in equilibrium to each other and to the expenses necessary to produce them' (quoted in Van Dyke Roberts 1935, 241; Boisguilbert 1707c[1966], 993).[24] Again the instability he attributed to this equilibrium is remarkable. He argued that disequilibrium in a single market would suffice to break this 'chain of opulence'. It would contaminate other markets, cause a decline in general purchasing power and lead to a cumulative contraction of economic activity. In Boisguilbert's opinion, a chain reaction of this kind had caused the fall in French national income since 1660. To redress the situation the economy needed reform: abandonment of trade regulations and a less oppressive tax system. Only free trade would revive the natural forces of the economy and boost economic activity and national income in a matter of weeks. Confidently he announced in the introduction of his *Factum de la France* (1707) that the proposals for reform contained therein would boost French national income with 80 million livres in just one month and required no more than two hours work from the nation's ministers.

To conclude this section it is useful to repeat Boisguilbert's vision of equilibrium as the 'unique conservateur de l'opulence générale'. In the economic realm, this vision was given substance by defining equilibrium in terms of the following two conditions: (1) prices cover the costs of production, and (2) supply equals demand in all markets. A violation of one of these conditions would mean a loss of purchasing power somewhere in the economic system. Such loss would not remain isolated, but lead to a chain reaction of price changes and a collapse of aggregate demand. In the eyes of Boisguilbert, equilibrium was a highly desirable affair, but also an extremely fragile one. For him, general economic equilibrium referred to an ideal society, governed by wise legislators that obeyed the laws of nature. In reality economic regulations, levies and taxes, upset the operation of a system that would naturally govern economic life. To illustrate the fragility of this natural system he used the image of a watch. In the economic process 'tous les sujets sont autant de pièces d'horloge qui concourent au commun mouvement de la machine, le dérangement d'une seule suffisant pour l'arrêter entièrement' (letter of July 1704, in INED 1966, vol. I, 320). To avoid disruption of the economic machine, it had to be deregulated. In the absence of state controls, like oppressive taxes and trade regulations, the economy would quickly regain equilibrium and function like the natural order it essentially was.

CONCLUSION

This chapter underlines the importance of vision for the development of economic theory. I have found Schumpeter's notion of a vision, guiding the analytical efforts of a budding science, of particular use, because it means that we do not need to search for the roots of a specific scientific conception of equilibrium theory. We have seen that such efforts led some commentators to 'discover' embryonic mathematical general equilibrium theories in the work of authors who were probably unable to spell the word mathematics. I reject this kind of precursoritis and believe that we need to assess the work of past authors on their own merits.

Concerning the origins of equilibrium economics, I have tried to do so by tracing the elements of a particular equilibrium vision. This vision included several elements such as the focus on the profit motive as a main economic incentive, a recognition of supply and demand as forces guiding a self-regulating economic order and, finally, the idea that self-regulation or free trade is benefiting general well-being. I have demonstrated that we find all these elements in the works of Dudley North and Pierre de Boisguilbert, which is why I believe that we may rightfully call them pioneers of equilibrium economics.

However, I have also taken considerable pains to argue that there is a subtle but important difference in the focus of their equilibrium theories. A self-regulating order is a system which sustains itself within specific boundaries. But what happens when the system moves beyond these limits? North would stress the correcting influence of supply and demand changes, nudging the system back to equilibrium. But for Boisguilbert, the focus of analysis would be different. He would first of all argue that such boundaries threatening economic stability are easily transgressed and that in this next zone one lacks self-correcting forces. He was interested in the question of how one could create the right institutional conditions to enliven or strengthen such self-correcting forces, to move the outer boundaries of the self-regulating order as it were. In the next chapter I shall argue that the opposition of these two equilibrium visions was not an accident, but shaped different economic doctrines in the century that was to follow.

NOTES

1. Luis Molina (1535–1600) and Cardinal Juan de Lugo (1583–1660) were two key figures in the School of Salamanca. See Rothbard (1995, 101–127).
2. An exception is Billoret (1989).
3. Another problem with this approach is that one may easily overlook a still earlier utterance of the word equilibrium. This happened to Milgate's (1987) historical review of the equilibrium concept. He attributed the first use of the word equilibrium to James Steuart in 1767, but it should become clear from this chapter that he missed other important equilibrium theorists, who published their work much earlier.
4. To provide a third example, Ekelund and Hébert (1997, 119) say that '[t]he idea of a self-regulating economy operating within a market economy was a new one in the mid-eighteenth century'. Moreover, they claim that '[t]his perception of a natural order to society, existing in the absence of any form of central planning, was one of the most liberating ideas ever to emerge in the history of economic thought', for '[i]t shunted economic analysis onto a new path'. See also Hébert (1987).
5. Schumpeter (1954, 241) says that economics discovered its 'fundamental problem' when it started to realize that the economy is a whole all the parts of which somehow hang together – a view he calls the 'vision' of equilibrium economics.
6. For these and other details of North's life and career, see Letwin (1963, 183–189).
7. The focus on the process aspect of market exchange, explains that some Austrians have claimed North as a precursor of their economic doctrine. For example, Rothbard (1995, 324) argues that North pioneered in a method which Mises in the 20th century would call 'praxeology'. This is a method for understanding economic action by deducing the logical consequences of a set of self-evident axioms. But, just as North did not anticipate a mathematical GE theory, this Austrian claim asks too much from this 17th century author. Mises (1949) grounded praxeology in a specific theory of human action, which is completely lacking in North. What remains is an intuitive apprehension of a market process approach, based on a loosely formulated supply and demand analysis.
8. I shall discuss Locke's contribution to the development of the quantity theory of money in more detail in Chapter 11.
9. The actual recoinage of the British money stock took place on 4 May 1696 when hammered silver money was officially demonetized. All the hammered silver coins were subsequently melted down and manufactured into so-called milled money, bearing a serrated edge to prevent clipping. What then happened in the money market was exactly what North had predicted. When around 1695 the rumour recoinage spread, people feared the loss of value of their silver coins and started swapping them for gold coins, which at this time had no officially-declared value. This increased the price of gold by almost 50 percent, leading to a dramatic rise in importation of gold to profit from the large difference between national and foreign prices. In other words, the supply and demand mechanism sprang in action to restore the par between gold and bullion. See Kleer (2003).

10. One step further and North would have hit on the specie-flow mechanism concerning the par between national and international price levels. Unfortunately, he lacked the proper knowledge of the quantity theory of money to draw this inference. Fifty years later Cantillon, and especially Hume, would develop the specie-flow mechanism as an instrument to demonstrate the futility of state controlled money supply management. See further Chapter 11.
11. For the famous passage in the *Wealth of Nations*, see Smith (1937, 423).
12. For a detailed account of Boisguilbert's life, see Van Dyke Roberts (1935) and Hecht (1966).
13. For example the nine years' war with the League of Augsburg (1689–1697) and the War of the Spanish Succession (1701–1713) which pitted France against Great Britain, Austria, Holland and parts of Spain.
14. Hamilton (1969, 135) argues that this is a gross exaggeration of the real extent of France's economic problems in this period. He concludes that the French economy was probably stagnant from about 1689 through about 1716. Yet in spite of the misfortunes mentioned above in 1716 France was certainly the richest and most powerful nation in the world.
15. There is even a religion founded on this notion, Deism. This religion uses the idea of a natural order to widen the distance between God and every day, personal affairs. In Deism, God is seen as the creator or clockwinder, who created the mechanism of the universe and its self-subsistent natural laws and then retired from the scene. Some therefore call it the rational god. See Gerson (1990). In the Enlightenment Deism was used to protect rationalistic arguments about society and its rulers as being atheistic, a condemnation which in these days could easily lead to prosecution and imprisonment (Gay 1966).
16. See Spengler (1984, 75): 'For this system [the economic order, BT], together with the natural and providential laws regulating it, was good. These laws, if conformed to, assured prosperity in the form of proportional prices and balance between buyers and sellers at prices satisfactory to each.' On the beneficial nature of Boisguilbert's equilibrium, see also Billoret (1989) and Perrot (1992a).
17. Hamilton (1969, 128) says that Boisguilbert 'seemed to feel that even a moderate disturbance of equilibrium would inevitable lead to a depression'.
18. I shall occasionally give translations of certain passages as a way of clarifying their meaning. Most translations are by Van Dyke Roberts, but I have here used the translation by Irwin because I consider it more accurate. In all cases, I give the reference to the French original.
19. See Perrot (1992b) for a discussion of authors that anticipated Smith in this regard.
20. As Kubota (1966, 81) puts it, 'sa philosophie de la solidarité sociale, sous-jacente dans toutes ses études, lui interdit de voir dans cet état de concurrence une simple compétition'.
21. See his *Traité de la nature, culture, commerce et intérêt des grains*, a tract first published in 1704–1705 (Boisguilbert 1707a[1966]). In this period the price of grain was at the

centre stage of economic and political debate. In a timespan of twenty years France suffered four famines because of a shortage of grain. But even in times of normal harvests, the price of grain was accustomed to undergo great variations because of wars, taxes and trade regulations.

22. 'Il faut des réservoirs, mais c'est à la nature à les faire, et non pas à l'autorité et à la violence. Et pour reprendre l'exemple des sources, les étangs et les lacs qu'elles forment naturellement, et sans aucun ministère étranger, causent un très grand utilité, sans aucun des fâcheux accidents marqués ci-dessus; témoin le lac de Genève: loin de tarir la source du Rhône, lorsequ'il y est entré ou qu'il l'a formé, il en ressort plus auguste et plus majestueux qu'il n'était auparavant. Il en va de même des réservoirs des blés fait par la nature' (Boisguilbert 1707a[1966], 870).

23. This quotation shows that Boisguilbert advocated an unrestricted, free grain trade, including both exportation and importation. This is a marked difference with the Physiocrats, who in the mid 18th century carried the banner of economic liberalism to the French royal court. Although passionate defenders of free trade, they showed little zeal for the freedom of importation of grain. They feared that importation would depress domestic grain prices and thereby lower agricultural production, in the Physiocrat's perception the unique source of the nation's economic wealth and its engine of growth. See further Chapter 5.

24. Some commentators argue that Boisguilbert anticipated Say's law of markets, the idea that the value of aggregate production equals that of aggregate demand. McDonald (1954) was one of the first to point out that in Boisguilbert national income (*revenue*) is determined by the value of consumption. Evidence of this claim is found in the following statement: 'on établit pour principe que consommation et revenue sont une seule et même chose, et que la ruine de la consommation est la ruine du revenue' (Boisguilbert 1695[1966], 602). Boisguilbert never explained the meaning of Say's law (that excess aggregate demand for goods means an excess supply of money and vice versa). Yet he did point out that on an aggregate level supply and demand are connected simply because markets are connected. As suppliers in one market are buyers in another, demand changes are likely to propagate through the economic system and may even affect general purchasing power (Billoret 1989, 69).

5. The Circular Flow of Goods and Money

INTRODUCTION

This chapter takes this historical investigation of equilibrium theory into the 18th century. I shall sidestep many interesting authors and focus on the work of two men who are often mentioned in the same breath of air, the Irish banker Richard Cantillon (ca.1680–1734) and the French physician François Quesnay (1694–1774).

Cantillon is praised as the first 'modern' economist (Spengler 1954). This praise is mainly due to the analytical quality of his one known published work, the *Essai sur la nature du commerce en général*, published posthumously in 1755. Crucial to this work is the conception of the market economy as a self-regulating mechanism which tends towards equilibrium (Hébert 1987). The theoretical apparatus behind this equilibrium tendency was highly innovative for its time and included uncertainty, entrepreneurship and a clear conception of a bargaining theory of price determination. It is not surprising that today Cantillon is seen as a precursors of the process approach to equilibrium theory (Vickers 1959 and Rothbard 1995).

Yet Cantillon did more than explain the working of the price mechanism. A second important element of his work was the circular flow of money and income. Very likely, Cantillon was indebted to Boisguilbert on certain aspects of this concept (Groenewegen 1987). In turn he influenced Quesnay and his band of followers, known as the physiocrats. As Schumpeter (1954, 218) argued, the fundamental features of Quesnay's analytical set up are foreshadowed in Cantillon's work. In particular, this concerns the *tableau économique*, the diagram showing the flows of money and goods between different economic groups. Schumpeter (1954, 243) even called this 'Cantillon-Quesnay *tableau*' the 'first method ever devised in order to convey an *explicit* conception of the nature of economic equilibrium'. All the more reason to critically assess the contributions of these two men to the development of equilibrium theory and investigate whether we are doctrinally right to consider them the expositors of the same conception of economic equilibrium.

Given my conclusion to the previous chapter, it should come as no surprise that I believe this view to be erroneous. In very broad lines I shall argue that Cantillon possessed a theoretical tool which the physiocrats lacked, while vice versa the physiocrats developed a tool which Cantillon ignored. They would have benefitted from a joint effort, but of course the fickleness of time made that impossible: Cantillon passed away long before Quesnay even started to think about economic questions. As it stands, their theories contain some important differences concerning the conception of economic equilibrium. I therefore call for a de-homogenization of these two fathers of the classical economic tradition.

The difference that I shall discus is the familiar one of a stable versus an unstable economic order. There seems to be doctrinal kinship, not running along the line Cantillon-Quesnay, but along the lines North-Cantillon versus Boisguilbert-Quesnay. To support this claim I shall first discuss Cantillon's conception of economic equilibrium as a self-regulating system. Next I compare this conception with Quesnay's *Tableau économique*. In the process I shall discuss the possibility of a missing link between these economic traditions in the person of A.R.J. Turgot. In the literature, he is often described as a follower of the physiocrats, but closer inspection reveals that he has much more in common with Cantillon. Finally, the closing section compares the methods of these different traditions and draws conclusions.

CANTILLON AND THE SELF-REGULATING NATURE OF THE MARKET ECONOMY

Introduction

Cantillon was a key figure in the development of 18th century economics. In spite of the fact that the *Essai* was published twenty years after Cantillon's death, it greatly influenced the work of contemporary economists on both sides of the Channel. In France the physiocrats owed him their main theoretical idea, the circular flow of money and income. In fact there is a direct connection between the *Essai* and the rise of the physiocratic doctrine in the mid-1750s. Victor de Riqueti, marquis de Mirabeau, Quesnay's closest associate, had the manuscript of the *Essai* in his possession for 16 years before its publication in 1755. He greatly praised the work in his own *L'Ami des Hommes* (1760). The first edition of this work was in 1756 a first attempt to build an economic system on the basis of Cantillon's analytical framework.[1] In this aim Quesnay succeeded much better. In 1758 he published the schedule of the *Tableau économique*, the work that became the 'bible' of the physiocratic movement.

But Cantillon's influence stretched beyond France. Malachy Postlewayt plagiarized large parts of the *Essai* in his *Universal Dictionary of Trade and Commerce* which was published between 1751 and 1755. This means that he must have had a copy of the English original (Spengler 1954). Cantillon is also likely to have influenced Hume's monetary ideas, especially his conception of the specie-flow mechanism. But most importantly, Smith's *Wealth of Nations* bears the marks of Cantillon's influence. Although Smith only referred to him once, it is evident that his economics was shaped in several crucial aspects by the *Essai.* In particular Cantillon showed him that the distinction between natural and market prices could be used to account for the relative harmonious nature of economic exchange. It is this aspect of Cantillon's work that will be discussed next.

Intrinsic Value and Market Prices

One of the key features of Cantillon's economics is that it treats the economy as an organized system which tends towards a state of equilibrium. As Spengler (1954, 424) writes, 'Cantillon was the first writer to describe at so great length the supposedly self-adjusting and essentially autonomous character of the economic system. [...] His most important contribution to the theory of self-adjustment was his account of the workings of the price mechanism'.

This mechanism was based on a distinction between intrinsic value and market price. Intrinsic value is a cost price and is defined as follows: 'Price or intrinsic value of a thing is the measure of the quantity of land and of the labour entering into its production, having regard to the fertility or produce of the land and to the quality of the labour' (Cantillon 1755[1931], 29). Cantillon used what can be called a land theory of value (Brewer 1988). He believed that value ultimately depends on the only factor of production that cannot be reproduced, land. In contrast, the other cost factor, labour, can be reproduced indefinitely, as people are said to 'breed like mice in a barn, if they have unlimited means of subsistence' (Cantillon 1755[1931], 83). Consequently, population pressure kept wages at a minimum subsistence level, which, according to Cantillon, was socially determined and could therefore differ between regions. The fact that labour supply was perfectly elastic at the minimum wage rate meant that labour costs could be reduced to quantities of land as well. Cantillon calculated that workers needed about double the produce of the land which was required to maintain them (ibid., 33). This 'par' between land and labour allowed him to reduce labour costs to quantities of land and to express intrinsic value in terms of land alone.

The advantage of expressing value in terms of land was its stability. Cantillon maintained that intrinsic values would never vary, whereas market prices would change under the influence of demand. According to him:

> [t]here is never a variation in intrinsic values, but the impossibility of proportioning the production of merchandise and produce in a state to their consumption causes a daily variation and a perpetual ebb and flow in market prices. However, in well organized societies the market prices of articles whose consumption is tolerably constant and uniform do not vary much from the intrinsic value (ibid., 31, see also p. 119).

The important question is of course how market prices come into line with intrinsic values. The keyword here is competition.

Cantillon took over the view of earlier writers like North and Locke that market price is determined by the proportion of quantities demanded and supplied. In his words '[i]t is clear that the quantity of produce or merchandise offered for sale, in proportion to the demand or number of buyers, is the basis on which is fixed . . . the actual market prices' (ibid., 119). According to this proportions theory, demand determines market price for a fixed supply of commodities. If demand is greater than the quantity offered for sale, market price must rise above intrinsic value. In the reverse case, if there are more sellers than buyers, market price will fall below intrinsic value (ibid., 30–31).

However, in one crucial respect Cantillon surpassed the analysis of his predecessors; he explained the process of price formation in terms of a market demand schedule. It was already explained that intrinsic value is a cost price expressed in quantities of land. Market price or the actual exchange value of goods was arrived at through a process of bargaining. Referring to the price of beef in terms of silver, Cantillon says that '[t]his proportion is come at by bargaining. The butcher keeps up his price according to the number of buyers he sees; the buyers on their side, offer less according as they think the butcher will have less sale' (ibid., 119). Now Cantillon realized that bargaining can only explain exchange rates in a situation of bilateral exchange, while market prices are set in an atomistic market with many buyers and sellers. He tried to deal with this problem by constructing a kind of demand schedule. To demonstrate how prices are set in a situation of multilateral exchange, he used the example of the market for green peas in Paris (ibid., 119).

> Several maîtres d'hôtels have been told to buy green peas when they first come in. One master has ordered the purchase of 10 quarts for 60 livres, another 10 quarts for 50 livres, a third 10 for 40 and a fourth 10 for 30 livres. If these orders are to be

carried out there must be 40 quarts. Suppose there are only 20. The vendors, seeing many buyers, will keep up their prices and the buyers will come up to the prices prescribed to them: so that those who offer 60 livres for 10 quarts will be the first served. The sellers, seeing later that no one will go above 50, will let the other 10 quarts go at that price. Those who had orders not to exceed 40 and 30 livres will go away empty.

Cantillon's demand schedule is discrete, but clearly suggests a negative relationship between quantity demanded and market price. The example cited assumes a sellers's market: sellers are are able to extract from each buyer the highest price they are willing to pay. Cantillon also discussed what will happen in a market with many buyers and sellers, if instead of 40 the extent of the market were 400 quarts. In that case the maîtres d'hôtels would get the new peas 'much below the sums laid down for them'[2] while sellers 'in order to be preferred one to the other by the few buyers will lower their new peas almost to their intrinsic values' (ibid.). In other words, in a competitive market, price will be forced in the direction of intrinsic value.

According to the proportions theory, on a given market day demand will determine price, because supply is a fixed quantity. However, over a more extended period supply is a variable also and the question arises how supply adjusts so as to bring market price into conformity with intrinsic values. In Cantillon's explanation of this process entrepreneurial behaviour plays a central role.

Cantillon divided society into two classes, dependent and independent people. Almost all of society belonged to the dependent class, because for their economic well-being most people depended on the purchasing power of others. In that regard only 'the Prince and the proprietors of land' could be said to be truly independent because they owned the only scarce factor of production, land (ibid., 55). In turn, dependent people were divided into two classes, undertakers and hired people. What separated these classes was the fact that hired people earned a fixed income, like the 'general who has his pay and the courtier his pension'. In contrast, undertakers ('entrepreneurs' in the French original) are faced with an uncertain income. They have to incur costs in order to produce goods or services, while their proceeds depend on a highly unpredictable factor, market price. To illustrate the unpredictability of demand, Cantillon exclaimed:

> Who can foresee the number of births and deaths of the people in a state in the course of a year? Who can foresee the increase or reduction of expense which may come about in the families? And yet the price of the farmer's produce depends naturally upon these unforeseen circumstances and consequently he conducts the enterprise of his farm at an uncertainty' (ibid., 49).

This example refers to agriculture, but the argument applies to all who conduct an enterprise with capital or are undertakers of their own labour. Cantillon was one of the first to show that the essence of entrepreneurship is the accommodation of uncertainty (Hébert 1987, 196).

The importance of Cantillon's description of entrepreneurship is that it explains the mechanism of supply adjustment. Entrepreneurs will be attracted to a line of business which they expect to be profitable. By the same token, they will be driven out of a market where they incur losses. The result is that over an extended period, supply will accommodate itself to the demand for products. Or as Cantillon puts it:

> Undertakers . . . proportion themselves in a state to the customers or consumption. If there are too many hatters in a city or in a street for the number of people who buy hats there, some who are least patronised must become bankrupt: if they be too few it will be a profitable undertaking which will encourage new hatters to open shops there and so it is that the undertakers of all kinds adjust themselves to risks in a state' (ibid., 53).

With Rothbard (1995, 359) one may conclude that Cantillon's entrepreneurs are the 'equilibrators' of the economy.

Now the idea that profit-seeking agents govern production was by no means a new one. In the field of monetary theory, earlier writers like North used the profit motive to argue that the prices of bullion and coin would find an equilibrium level. What distinguishes Cantillon from this type of analysis is that he understood that the function of the price system is to allocate scarce resources. By way of contrast, in the 17th century value and price theory generally focused on practical problems of commercial policy (Bowley 1973, 69). Not surprisingly, in the mercantilistic literature the most important of these problems was to stop the outflow of precious metals. North and others (for example Mun and Misselden) showed that the notions of supply and demand could be used to argue that money supply would find its optimal level automatically and that the foreign exchange market should therefore be free of control. As Bowley argues, to support this claim it was sufficient to show that profits attracted merchants, whereas losses would drive them out of business (ibid., 81). To solve the problem of money supply did not require analysis of the influences affecting supply and demand or of the function of the price system in the allocation of productive resources.

In contrast, Cantillon treated relative prices as signals to adjust resource use. He cited the example of farmers who reduce their flock of sheep in order to free resources to increase the grain supply. This leads to higher wool prices, while grain is in excess supply. Consequently:

> Farmers will take care the following year to have less grain and more wool, for farmers always seek to use their land for the production of those things that they think will bring the highest market price. But if the next year they have too much wool and too little grain for the demand, they will not fail to change from year to year the use of the land until they have adjusted their production more or less to the consumption of the inhabitants. So a farmer who has adjusted more or less his output to the demand, will have part of his farm in grass, for hay, another part in grain, another in wool, and so on, and he will not change his plan unless he sees some considerable change in demand (Cantillon 1755[1931], 60–62).

No writer before Cantillon had so clearly explained the allocative function of the price mechanism. By seeking profitable ventures, entrepreneurs promote the efficient use of resources. In the process, supply and demand are brought into closer conformity. Or in the words of Murphy (1986, 6), Cantillon's entrepreneur is 'the highly visible hand' that ensures that markets work and move towards equilibrium.

But we have to do proper credit to the views of Cantillon concerning the self-adjusting capacity of the free trade economy. It is by no means true that he had a blind faith in the healing powers of the supply and demand mechanism. This becomes apparent in the field of international trade where Cantillon developed the first contours of the specie-flow mechanism (Vickers 1959). The essence of this mechanism is the interaction between international price differences and the balance of trade. Cantillon observed that an increase of the money stock would not just raise the national price level, it would also worsen the terms of trade for a nation and thus cause a balance of trade deficit. This implies that part of the increase in the money stock will be exported until the balance of trade has again reached an equilibrium level.

However, Cantillon himself never reached the conclusion that the specie-flow mechanism would push national price levels to an international equilibrium level that eradicates any trade imbalances between countries. He observed all kind of endogenous changes and frictions that in reality made international monetary equilibrium an improbable affair. In other words, he did not think of the world economy as tending firmly to equilibrium. Vickers (1959, 189) and Rothbard (1995, 359) are therefore quite correct in calling him a 'semi-equilibrium' theorist when it comes to explaining price formation in the field of international monetary relations.

A Circular Flow Model of the Economy

Cantillon is often placed in the line Petty-Quesnay, the writers that developed the conception of surplus output and used that concept to analyze the circular flow of money and income. For example, Schumpeter (1954, 218) argues that 'few sequences in the history of economic analysis are so important . . . as is the sequence Petty-Cantillon-Quesnay'. In particular 'Cantillon was the first to make this circular flow concrete and explicit, to give us a bird's-eye view of economic life. In other words, he was the first to draw a *tableau économique*. And barring differences . . . this *tableau* is the same as Quesnay's' (ibid., 222). Likewise Walsh and Gram (1980) consider Cantillon a founder of classical equilibrium theory, which in their conception is the theory of the accumulation and allocation of surplus output.

I shall argue in this section that this is incorrect. Cantillon did indeed develop a circular flow model explaining how incomes and goods circulate among the classes of society, just as in the *Tableau économique.* But he left out an important detail which greatly affects its operation. There is no capital and hence no time element (Brewer 1988, 3). Cantillon did not assume that someone saved a part of his income, and in his framework food appears to be the only input into production. This 'capital' is used up in one period, but has no effect on productive capacity in subsequent periods, which is a key notion of capital. Quesnay and the physiocrats neither paid full attention to the saving-investment nexus, but their treatment of capital is certainly more complete. For one, Quesnay recognized the effect of capital investment on productivity and developed a model of capital accumulation with dynamic income-generating effects. Such effects are lacking in Cantillon's circular flow, which is not surprising given the failure to include a time interval between inputs and outputs.

With this limitation in mind, I shall discuss the three elements which make Cantillon's conception of the circular flow work. First, agricultural output is the starting point of the circular flow of income, because: '[a]ll the produce of the country comes directly or indirectly from the hands of the farmers . . . The three rents of the farmer must be considered as the principal sources or so to speak the mainspring of circulation in the state' (ibid., 123). The second element is closely related to this ultimate source of production and concerns the notion of surplus income. He referred to rent income as surplus output: 'the overplus of the land is at the disposition of the owner' (Cantillon 1755[1931], 7). In third place, the flow of income is made possible by the activities of entrepreneurs. They have an intermediary role and ensure that when the output of the farmers arrives in the city it is circulated amongst the various groupings: 'Circulation in the cities is carried out by entrepreneurs and always correspond directly or indirectly to the subsistence of menservants, workmen, etc.' (ibid., 145). This circulation is possible because there is reciprocity in exchange, demand for a good involves the supply of another and vice versa: 'All these undertakers become consumers and customers one in regard to the other, the draper of the wine merchant and vice versa' (ibid., 53). Thus Cantillon envisaged a circular process whereby income, output and expenditure are interrelated in the economy.

As said, the starting point of the circular flow is agricultural output. Cantillon assumed that the proceeds of agricultural production are divided into three equal shares or rents. Two thirds are used respectively to pay the landowner's rent and to cover production costs (wages of farming assistants, maintenance costs). The remaining third constitutes the farmer's profit (ibid., 43). Interestingly, Cantillon assumed that no money is saved. He stated that farmers spend their third rent 'on living more comfortably instead of saving it' (ibid., 123). In this manner he prevented leakages out of the expenditure circuit, as landlords did not save either. Further, the circulation model included two types of goods, agricultural products and 'city' goods, commodities that are manufactured in the city. From these assumptions followed the following picture of the circulation process.

Landlords were assumed to spend all the income they derived from the first rent in the city. Farmers spent more than one half of their profit income (that is one sixth of agricultural income) on urban commodities. This meant that more than one half of agricultural income was destined for expenditure in the cities. The remaining half was retained within the agricultural community. It consisted of payments in kind, as country folk could be assumed to be able to satisfy their own demand for the basic necessities of life, food, cloths and lodging.

> The farmer may brew his beer or make his wine without spending cash, he can make his bread, kill the oxen, sheep, pigs, etc. that are eaten in the country: he can pay in corn, meat and drink most of his assistants . . . If coarse linen and cloths are made there [in the country, BT], if houses are built there, as is often done, the labour for all this may be paid in barter by valuation without cash being needed (ibid., 123–25).

Further, Cantillon assumed that half of the population lived in the cities and that consequently the citizens consumed more than half of the produce of the land. Thus the farmers exported more than half of the agricultural output to the cities and with the income so earned paid the landlord's rent and bought urban commodities equivalent to one sixth of the agricultural output. The expenditure of the landlords and the farmers generated income for the urban community which allowed them to purchase agricultural commodities. With this information the following input-output table can be constructed (in terms of agricultural output).

Table 5.1 shows that each sector's output or income is entirely exhausted by the sector's total payments to other sectors.[3] Given the technical coefficients of production of this input-output table, the process of production and consumption, of income and expenditure may go on year after year. The circular flow continues indefinitely (Cantillon 1755[1931], 137).

Table 5.1 Input-output table of Cantillon's circular flow model

	Purchasing sector			
	Farmers	Landowners	Artisans (city)	Output
Producing sector				
Farmers	1/2	. . .	1/2^{m}	1
Landowners	1/3^{m}	. . .	. . .	1/3
Artisans (city)	1/6^{m}	1/3^{m}	?	1/2
Expenditures	1	1/3	1/2	1 5/6

Note: ^{m} payment in money

The Method of Imaginary Constructions

How should we interpret this circular flow model from the perspective of equilibrium theory? Murphy (1986, 261) says that we should see it as a piece of static theory, because it was used by Cantillon to solve a static problem, namely to determine the (stock) demand for money and its counterpart, the equilibrium money supply.

Murphy's diagnosis is right, but his conclusion is not. There is no doubt that Cantillon used the circular flow model to investigate a static problem. He first described this model in Chapter 3 of Part II of the *Essay*, 'Of the circulation of money' and it was intended to give a quantitative estimate of the demand for money. The table above shows that money was only needed to conduct exchanges between country and city. Cash was needed to pay the landlords' rent, which they used to buy urban commodities. Farmers used one sixth of their income to the same purpose. Consequently, '[t]he cash circulating in the country must therefore be equal to at least one half of the produce of the land, by which means the other half or somewhat less may be consumed in the country without need of cash' (ibid., 125). In other words, the demand for money amounts to half the value of agricultural output. Subsequently, Cantillon discussed how the rapidity of circulation influences this demand. He observed that the need for cash will be smaller (bigger), the higher (lower) the rapidity of circulation. Taking account of this rapidity, brought him to conclude that 'the money circulating in a country is equal in value to the ninth part of all the produce of the soil' (ibid., 131).

But is Cantillon's equilibrium model thereby the product of a static theory? This would be a surprising conclusion for someone who is widely praised for his process analysis of monetary changes (Vickers 1959, 187;

Rothbard 1995, 355). Key to his interpretation of the quantity theory was that money enters the economy in a step-by-step process and does not simply increase prices in a homogenous aggregate. Today his name is even attached to the effect which traces the microeconomic distortions following a change in the money supply, that is the Cantillon effect (Blaug 1985, 164–165). And this man is portrayed as someone who developed a static equilibrium model as his principal theoretical tool? This at least suggests a contradiction which needs explaining.

The explanation which I offer is the following. Cantillon pioneered in a method which would later be known as the method of imaginary constructions. The essence of this method is the use of a deliberately fictitious equilibrium model with static properties as a benchmark for the analysis of real economic problems. The advantage of a comparison between the static benchmark and the real situation is that it highlights the impact of certain aspects of reality associated with dynamic change, such as entrepreneurship, uncertainty, money et cetera (Moss 1997). Thus Wieser (1927) introduced a benevolent dictator model to study the effect of market exchange in a decentralized economy. Hayek (1941) adopted a similar trick, but now the benevolent dictator defined the opposite of an economy with dispersed information. As a final example, I refer to Mises (1949) and his Evenly Rotating Economy, a stationary equilibrium model that served no purpose but to investigate how entrepreneurship and human action would push this economy off its evenly course.

I am not saying that Cantillon should be seen as an Austrian *avant la lettre*, but the similarities in research strategy are noteworthy. Firstly, there is the method of analysis which stresses reasoning in terms of logical deduction aimed to investigate the chain of causes and effects operating behind the scene of observable reality. He used this method to challenge the empirical investigations of William Petty in his *Political Arithmetick* (1690). Cantillon made a mockery of this work, calling it 'fanciful and remote from natural laws, because he [Petty, BT] has attached himself not to causes and principles, but only to effects, as mr. Locke, mr. Davenant and all the other English authors who have written on this subject have done after him' (ibid., 43). It seems that statistical investigation simply was not the province of Cantillon. A bit later in his *Essay* he said that '[t]here is no branch of knowledge in which one is more subject to error than Statistics when they are left to imagination, and none more demonstrable when they are based upon detailed facts' (ibid., Part II, Chapter 3, 21). To delve deeper, one needed a deductive method investigating the train of events set in motion by certain first principles like entrepreneurial activity.

This is exactly what Cantillon did and which makes it hard to interpret his theory of the circular flow as a static theory. In my opinion, it was used to understand the effects of entrepreneurial activity in a decentralized economy. There is a remarkable chapter in the *Essay* which assumes that the circular flow is generated by a single person, a clear example of a benevolent dictator model (ibid., Part I, Chapter 14). This single person is the landowner, who runs the economy like a large estate. Naturally, this landowner controls all the means of production and employs them in such a manner that the resulting production best suits his wishes. He grows corn to feed his labourers, which costs him one third of the total produce. He also employs artisans and overseers and also pays them for their services in corn. In other words, orders are made and carried out according to the 'grand' economic plan drawn out by the landlord, which leads to a circular flow of payments (in kind).

In the next step of the analysis, the owner becomes weary of running this large estate and longs for his pension. He decides to farm out his land to his overseers and likewise hires managers to govern the task of the artisans. Thus, he loses direct control over production in return for a payment of rent. The effect of this retreat is that the overseers become a new economic class; they start to act as undertakers. Cantillon argued that in this case the same mix of production comes about. The estate operates as before, when the owner was still in full control. The reason for this is that former landlord did not change his demand and has the money to make his demand effective. The lesson of this benevolent dictator model is that entrepreneurial activity ensures that the composition of supply matches the demand for goods and services. One could draw up a flow diagram following the stream of payments between the actors and, with the addition of the element of rent, the result would match the diagram of the monopoly state with money taking the place of the payments in kind. This thought experiment thus teaches us what decentralized decision making can achieve, when people are motivated by entrepreneurial incentives.[4]

What is also interesting about this example, is that it demonstrates how Cantillon interpreted the circular flow, namely as a process. He concluded his analysis of the benevolent dictator example by performing a kind of stability analysis. He raised the question what would happen to the circular flow when the undertakers would not copy the mix of products demanded by the landlord in the monopoly case. Suppose, for example, that some farmers reduce their flock of sheep in order to free resources for a larger harvest of corn. Cantillon showed that this causes an excess demand for mouton and an excess supply of corn, providing a potential for gain that the profit-seeking farmers will try to exploit in the next production cycle. In other words, all the independent decision nodes are motivated to follow the changes in demand as closely as possible. In the process, they push market prices towards their intrinsic values. I conclude that the circular flow describes the end result of what in essence constitutes a dynamic process.

THE TABLEAU ÉCONOMIQUE

François Quesnay and the Physiocrats

Unlike Cantillon, François Quesnay was not an economist by profession. To the contrary, he was the personal physician of Louis XV and his mistress Madame de Pompadour and did not publish anything on economics before the age of 60. His position as court physician brought him into contact with Victor Riqueti, marquis de Mirabeau (1715–1789). It was Mirabeau who claimed that he had the manuscript of Cantillon's *Essay* in his possession for 16 years before it was published in 1755. He also used parts of Cantillon's economic system in his own *L'Ami des Hommes* (1760), which was first published in 1756. Together Quesnay and Mirabeau founded the first school in economics (Fox-Genovese 1976). They called themselves 'les économistes' to stress the scientific nature of their writings, but later became know as 'the physiocrats', after their prime politico-economical principle: physio-cracy, which means 'rule of nature'.

In political economy the physiocrats were among the first laissez faire thinkers. They called for complete internal and external free enterprise and free trade, unfettered by monopoly privileges or restrictions. Other characteristic features of their 'rule of nature' are the claim that agriculture was the only productive economic undertaking and their plea for an *impôt unique*, a single tax to be paid by landowners. They are included in this chapter because their leader Quesnay formalized Cantillon's conception of a circular flow in a diagram, the *Tableau économique* (1758–1759). Schumpeter (1954, 243) refers to this 'Cantillon-Quesnay *tableau*' as the 'first method ever devised in order to convey an *explicit* conception of the nature of economic equilibrium'. Purpose of this section is to examine this conception of equilibrium which, according to Schumpeter, is an equilibrium of social aggregates. In particular, it will be argued that its main function was to study the economy in disequilibrium. Like Boisguilbert, the physiocrats associated disequilibrium with economic decline and misery, whereas equilibrium signified economic prosperity. The aim of their 'disequilibrium analysis' was policy-oriented. It demonstrated the need for specific measures to keep the economy in equilibrium. Not surprisingly, these measures required the introduction of typical physiocratic policies, free trade and a single tax on rent income.

The Equilibrium Properties of the *Tableau Économique*

The fundamental propositions of physiocracy can be summarized as follows. First, society consists of three classes; farmers, landlords and artisans. Of these, only the farming class is considered productive because it produces a surplus or 'net product' over costs. The industrial sector is unable to produce a similar surplus and is for that reason called 'sterile'. Landlords do not produce at all. Their sole function is to spend the rent income they receive from the farming class.

Second, production requires capital. Quesnay was one of the first to distinguish between fixed and variable capital. More specifically, he regarded capital as consisting of a series of 'advances'. Fixed capital or 'original advances' were livestock, buildings and implements. Fixed capital also included the 'landlord's advances' – drainage, fencing and other permanent land improvements. Variable capital or 'annual advances' comprised all the expenses incurred during the period of production, for example wages and raw materials (Quesnay 1766, 310, n.1). Quesnay assumed that a more capital-intensive method of production in agriculture would produce a larger surplus, both absolute and relative to the quantity of capital. All this was a step forward, when we compare it with Cantillon's treatment of capital.

Third, production takes place in cycles. The definition of capital suggests that Quesnay acknowledged a time interval between inputs and outputs, although analytically this played no role in the circular flow mechanism of the *Tableau économique*. Typically, in his *tableaux* this time interval is one year, very likely the average harvest period in 18th century France. The cycle starts with the purchase of variable capital, which allows production to take place. At the end of the cycle the sale of products recompenses the producer for his costs and provides him with the means to invest again at the start of the next cycle.

Fourth, the growth of national income critically depends on how demand is distributed between industrial and agricultural goods. A diversion of demand in favour of industrial goods, will reduce agricultural investment. Consequently, the economy's net product will fall.

Fifth, the money circuit is closed. In the equilibrium of the *Tableau* all three classes exactly match their expenditures and receipts during the cycle of production. As a result, the physiocrats believed that hoarding money would be detrimental to economic growth. They argued that hoards constitute a reduction in consumption expenditures and therefore of the funds available for re-investment. That in turn reduces the surplus and the rate of economic growth.[5]

All these elements are combined in the *Tableau économique* which shows the exchange of money and goods between the three classes. Quesnay and his associate Mirabeau published several versions of the *Tableau* between 1758 and 1766. The differences between these versions have inspired a lively debate among scholars concerning their relationship and meaning (Meek 1963, Negishi 1989, Herlitz 1996). This debate will not concern us here. To examine its equilibrium nature, it suffices to explain the final version of the *Tableau* called the *Analyse* and comment briefly on some of the earlier versions.

Much of the fame of the *Tableau économique* rests on the fact that it is a diagram. The different versions of the *Tableau* have in common that they graphically show the exchange of money between the three classes. This gives the *Tableau* the feature of a model: it is an abstract representation of the operation of the economy as a whole. In a time when mathematical models were not yet used by economists, Quesnay's graphics formed a new tool of abstract reasoning applied to the macroeconomy. That may explain the physiocrats' belief that Quesnay had invented a new science, one based on arithmetic which therefore allowed of exact calculation (Quesnay 1764[1972], xl). The admiration of some of Quesnay's followers for this invention was boundless. His closest associate Mirabeau considered it one of the three greatest inventions of mankind, alongside the invention of money and writing.

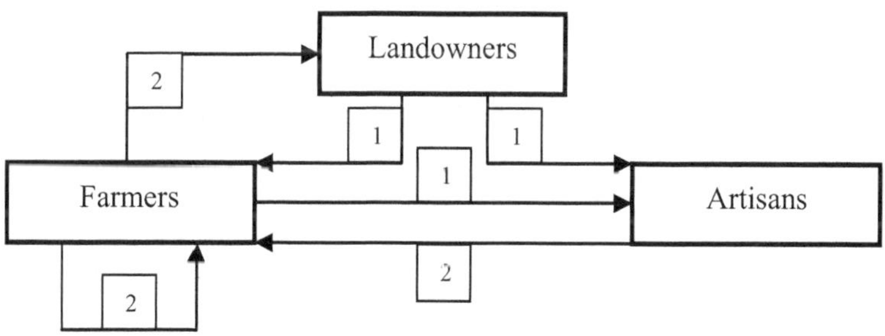

Figure 5.1 Money flows in the Tableau économique

In the *Analyse du Tableau Économique* (1766) the process of circulation is as follows. At the start of the cycle the productive class (farmers) owns the entire stock of money, which is five billion francs. Two fifths of this amount is reserved for working capital. They are necessary for the upkeep of the productive class and its livestock during the year. These are represented in Figure 5.1 as payments from the farm sector to the farm sector and do not circulate between classes. Another billion is used to buy manufactured goods from the sterile class. These are necessary to replace worn-out fixed capital. That makes total production costs in agriculture three billion francs. The remaining two billion represent the 'net product', a surplus that is not necessary to maintain production at the same level. This sum goes to landlowners as rent. They in turn spend their income on food and manufacture (both one billion). The circuit is completed when the sterile class spends its income on agricultural products, one billion on food and one billion on raw materials. Thus the three billion originally spent by the farming class returns to them, one billion coming from the proprietors and two billion from the manufacturing class. In this manner the process may continue indefinitely.

The same process can also be conceived of in real terms. Gross value added by agriculture is five billion, three billion of which constitute costs of production incurred in cultivation. During the cycle the farming class consumes two fifths of its own output as working capital. One fifth is sold to the sterile class in exchange for fixed capital, manufactured goods and services. The remaining output is paid as rent to the landowners. They exchange half of this income for manufactured articles. The sterile class now owns two billion of agricultural commodities and no further exchanges take place.[6] Note that the allocation of commodities at this stage allows the reproduction of the original gross output in both the productive and the sterile class. Farmers have two billion units of food for consumption and one billion units of manufactured goods. These are used to produce five billion units of agricultural commodities during the cycle. Artisans have two billion units of agricultural goods which they use to produce two billion units of manufactured goods. If it is assumed that rents are payment for land services, the total production equals nine billions units of goods. Again an input-output table can be constructed to show the mutual interdependence between the three classes.

Table 5.2 Input-output table of Quesnay's Analyse du Tableau économique*

	Purchasing sector			
	Farmers	Landowners	Artisans	Total Output
Producing sector				
Farmers	2	1	2	5
Landowners	2	...	...	2
Artisans	1	1	...	2
Total expenditures	5	2	2	9

Note: * in billion units of commodity

The three equilibrium conditions of the *Tableau économique* can now be explained as follows. First, Figure 5.1 shows that expenditures and receipts are balanced for all classes. In equilibrium each class receives just enough money to meet its financial requirements. Second, from the input-output table it can be inferred that also in real terms supply equals demand in each class. Third, taking account of the time element, it appears that the *Tableau* describes an economy in a stationary equilibrium. At the end of the production period, both the productive and the sterile class have just sufficient capital to reproduce the same gross output in the next period. Real production, therefore, continues over time at the same level.[7]

The Step Towards Disequilibrium Analysis

Although the *Tableau* is a tool of abstract reasoning, it can be said to describe the economy in a state of bliss. It assumed an economy that was fully cultivated by the best possible methods. In this state, agricultural production reached a maximum, as is suggested by Quesnay in the following discussion: 'Dans l'état de prosperité d'un royaume dont le territoire serait porté à son plus haut degré possible de culture, de liberté et de facilité de commerce, et ou par conséquent le revenu des propriétaires ne pourrait plus s'accroître, ceux-ci pourraient en dépenser la moitié en achats à la classe sterile' (Quesnay 1766, 318). However, this did not imply that he imagined that the economy would develop into a stationary state. He suggested that this state could be improved upon by further increases in productivity in the future (Meek 1963, 274). The main function of the *Tableau* was to demonstrate that deviations from a state of maximum prosperity could come about and to analyze their causes. In other words, in a specific sense it was a tool of dynamic welfare analysis (Eltis 1975a and Eltis 1996).

The interesting aspect of this analysis is that it focused on the behaviour of the *Tableau* in a situation of disequilibrium. The typical argument would run as follows. Quesnay would explain the working of the *Tableau* and the way in which it reproduced the same value of goods year after year and then change one of the assumptions underlying his analysis. For instance, a change in market prices could affect the value of the agricultural surplus and upset the landlords' spending pattern. The consequence of this would be a loss of equilibrium, because it proved impossible to reproduce the same value of commodities. This could be shown by drawing a new *Tableau*, one showing the economy in disequilibrium. As Mirabeau (1760, 67) put it, '[d]ans la nouvelle planche que je présente, le Tableau a perdu son équilibre. Il s'agit de voir et d'expliquer les causes et les effets de ce dérangement'.

This type of disequilibrium analysis is found in several of the physiocratic writings. The *Philosophie rurale* (1764), a co-product of Quesnay and Mirabeau, contains about forty *tableaux* most of which show an economy in disequilibrium (Eltis 1996). These studies best show the function of the *Tableau* as a tool of policy analysis. They are designed to compare the effects of different economic policies. As Quesnay described the purpose of his models, they enable a clear estimation of the 'organization and disorganization' which government policy could bring about (quoted in Meek 1963, 273). Needless to say, these exercises focused on the core issues of the physiocratic doctrine, free trade and tax reform.

There are three causes of disequilibrium which Quesnay and Mirabeau considered particularly important.

First, a change in tastes may cause the propensity to consume agricultural products to deviate from its equilibrium value of one-half.[8] Suppose, for example, that the proprietors suddenly increase their expenditure on the products of the sterile class by one-fifth and that the productive class and the sterile class follow their example. In part six of Mirabeau's *L'Ami des Hommes* (1760) Quesnay calculated what will happen in this case. He showed that the net product will fall from 2000 to 1684 *livres* because the productive class lacks working capital to reproduce the same value of output.[9] This means that proprietors will have less revenue to spend in the next cycle and the net product will fall still further.

Second, a change in the methods of taxation may affect the rate of return that farmers actually receive on their advances with consequent growth or decline in these. A key factor of the physiocratic doctrine was the claim that only the net product should be taxed. This was their proposal for an *impôt unique*, a single tax. Their argument was that rent income was 'disposable'. It was a surplus over necessary costs, which meant that reduction of it would not affect the economy's capacity to reproduce the same value of output in the next year. The 'disorganization' caused by a different taxation policy could be shown by means of the *Tableau*. For example, a personal tax of 25 *livres* on the income of the sterile and productive classes reduced total output by more than 50 (Meek 1963, 290).

Third, the reduction of market controls (freer food markets both at home and overseas) would boost the rate of return in agriculture. Here Quesnay assumed a positive relationship between the price of grain and the net product. That explained the rise in total value output when the opening up of markets allowed farmers to get better prices for their products (Eltis 1996, 29).

Characteristic of the changes brought about by these causes is the lack of stabilizing forces to return the economy to its former equilibrium level.[10] The *Tableau économique* is an input-output model with fixed coefficients of production. It is either in equilibrium or an a dynamic path away from it. One is tempted to compare it to Harrod's famous 'knife edge'. Quesnay simply lacked the means to model of the process of capital accumulation with stable properties. He did not explain the relationship between saving and investing, which could have provided a balancing mechanism through the interest rate.

There is no marginal productivity theory to link variable factor inputs to their prices. In general, there is no role for price formation whatsoever. One should therefore not be surprised that the *Tableau économique* lacked stabilizing forces (Meek 1963, 292). Although, it has to be said that in some cases Quesnay did envision a kind of stable end point to the dynamic disequilibrium process, but clearly at a sub optimal level, as is shown in the following quotation (Quesnay 1764, quoted in Eltis 1996, 25):

> I believe it is necessary to represent here and to provide calculations which describe in summary form, the fixed state of a nation, where through defects in cultivation, productive advances yield a revenue which is less than in a state of prosperity, on which the calculations of the Tableau are based. Such a state of poor cultivation can persist for some time without continual deterioration, because the two active classes refund the cost of their upkeep to each other, and so this state of weakness and depopulation could even stabilize at a fixed point, if the Nation were subject to absolutely no external shocks; but one will see what enormous degradation this state of economic stagnation causes to the mass of wealth of the Nation, and in consequence what reduction in its vigour, its power, its population, and indeed its physical and political existence, will result from the slightest errors in a subject where so few people yet wish to understand the consequences.

How the economy could regain its equilibrium from being in this depressed state, was something which the physiocrats did not explain through the dynamics of the *Tableau*. After all, this required the intervention of a powerful outside force, the king himself. He was the one who had to adopt the physiocratic principles of free trade and a single tax, which was needed to 'reboot' the economic mechanism and give the parameters of the circular flow their proper equilibrium values (Eltis 1975b).

Turgot and the Missing Link

In a specific sense, the *Tableau économique* is a general equilibrium model. It describes the interdependencies between the different sectors of an economy in stationary equilibrium. Moreover, it was argued above that for this situation to prevail it is necessary to assume that supply equals demand in each sector. However, an important difference with modern neoclassical models of general equilibrium is that it ignores the function prices have in the process of resource allocation. Quesnay did not explain price formation in terms of supply and demand and consequently lacked a mechanism of resource allocation.

In Quesnay's writings there are few references to the process of price formation. In the article *Taxation* (1757) he discussed the difference between the prices of manufacturing and farming. The prices of manufactured goods are said to only reflect material and wage goods. These prices can not include a profit because competition will reduce earnings to the level of production expenses. 'Thus this, or restitution of expenses, is not like the revenue of landed property, an original form of wealth representing a pure profit' (Quesnay 1757[1963], 105). From this statement, it can be inferred that the prices of agricultural products did include a profit. This was the net product which was paid to landlords as rent. But Quesnay failed to explain why in agriculture competition did not push prices to cost levels. Or, as Meek (1963, 387) phrases the question: 'if competition causes manufacture to be sterile, why does it leave agriculture productive?' Meek concludes that the cause of the problem was that the physiocrats treated the net product as a physical surplus of output over input; it was literally a gift of nature. Although they do seem to have assumed the existence of a kind of permanent excess of demand over supply in the case of agricultural produce, in general they ignored the problem of rent as a value surplus. They simply assumed the existence of a net product and did not inquire into the economic forces which permitted it to emerge and persist in a competitive economy. In the words of Hollander (1987, 48), '[t]he phyiocratic notion that agricultural activity alone yields a surplus is thus based upon a serious analytical error, since it neglects the economic principle of scarcity, or pricing in terms of demand and supply'.

Evidently, this neglect has consequences for the allocative function of prices. For instance, it explains why the notion of a uniform profit rate is absent in Quesnay's writings. In spite of the fact that profits differ between agriculture and manufacturing, there is no tendency of capital to move between these sectors. As a result, there is no equilibration of economic activities on an economy-wide scale in Quesnay's economic system.

In this respect, Quesnay was surpassed by A.R.J. Turgot (1727–1781). Turgot is generally considered a 'fellow-traveller' of the physiocrats. Like them, he called for a single tax on the net product of land and was a staunch defender of the free trade doctrine.[11] But concerning his theoretical economics, there are good reasons to distinguish Turgot as an original thinker.[12] In particular, Turgot explicitly addressed the question of market exchange and used a concept of economic equilibrium that sharply contrasts with the physiocrats's use of this concept. Could Turgot have provided the missing link to the *Tableau économique*?

Turgot's treatment of market exchange was based on a careful distinction between three different kinds of value. First, there is what he called 'esteem value'. This is the purely subjective perception of the value of a commodity by an individual. Perceptions of this kind are based on the usefulness of a commodity to satisfy a particular want as well as on its relative scarcity. Second, in market exchange, esteem values give rise to a 'current' or 'mean' value, which is determined by supply and demand. As such, it is assumed to reflect an average of the subjective value-perceptions of market participants. However, a second determining factor of current value is the 'fundamental value', the third concept of value distinguished by Turgot. Fundamental value is defined as a cost price. It is 'what the thing costs to him who sells it, that is, the raw material costs, the wages of his labor, and the profits of his stock' (quoted in Groenewegen 1970, 181). Under the pressure of competition current value will be brought into conformity with fundamental value. It is evident that this construction closely resembles Cantillon's distinction between intrinsic and market value.

These three concepts of value are combined in a discussion of market exchange. Groenewegen (1970) distinguishes no fewer than six different exchange situations in Turgot's writings.

1. Exchange between two individuals of two commodities which have zero esteem value at the margin;
2. Isolated exchange proper: two individuals, two commodities;
3. Isolated exchange: four individuals and two commodities;
4. Multiple exchange: many individuals, two commodities;
5. Multiple exchange: many individuals, many commodities;
6. Intertemporal exchange: present against future goods.

The interesting aspect of this sequence is that it shows that by increasing the complexity of the exchange situation Turgot explained the process of price formation. Here, like in Cantillon's treatment of market exchange, the key factor is bargaining. For instance, in the case of isolated exchange proper two persons A and B try to determine an exchange rate for corn and firewood (Turgot 1769[1844], 85). To simplify matters, it is assumed that A owns the sole supply of corn, while B is the sole supplier of firewood. The exchange will come about on the basis of the subjective estimation of value which A and B place on their respective commodities. Turgot assumed that A values 3 units of corn at 9 units of firewood, while B estimates the value of 6 units of wood at 9 units of corn. To determine a price '[s]lowly each of them will increase his offers and reduce his demand, until they finally agree to give a certain quantity of corn for a certain quantity of wood' (ibid., 86, translation Groenewegen 1970, 188). Turgot tried to make this price precise by arguing that it would lie exactly midway between the esteem values. In that sense, he literally considered the current price an equivalent of the average esteem value (ibid., 189).

In the case of multiple exchange essentially the same process takes place. If there is competition between various sellers of two commodities, the current price will be determined through a series of offers and counteroffers.

Also in this case 'the price midway between the different offers and the different demands will become the current price, whereto all the buyers and sellers will conform in their exchanges' (ibid., 191). In the short term, this outcome may deviate from the fundamental value or cost price. But in a competitive market, such deviations will not last for long:

> for as soon as a commodity can only be sold at a loss, its production is discontinued until the resulting scarcity has again raised it to a price above its fundamental value. The price can similarly not be much above the fundamental value for any length of time, for the high price, implying high profits, would call forth the commodity and generate lively competition among the sellers. Now the natural effect of this competition would be to lower the price until it again approaches the fundamental value (ibid., 182).

From the above, it becomes clear that Turgot saw equilibrium as a tendency of price towards a stable level determined by costs. This use of the equilibrium construct is even more clearly expressed in Turgot's capital theory (Turgot 1766[1844]). To a large extent this theory was based on Quesnay's treatment of capital. But Quesnay was only concerned with agricultural production, whereas Turgot applied the analysis of capital to all productive sectors of the economy (Groenewegen 1971, 338). Consequently, he saw a role for the price mechanism in the allocation of productive resources. Profit differentials would cause entrepreneurs to reallocate capital to a more profitable sector. The result of such adjustments would be a tendency towards an uniform profit rate, an equilibrium tendency which is illustrated in terms of the following mechanical analogy (Turgot 1766[1844], 57–58).

> Les différents emplois des capitaux rapportent donc des produits très inégaux; mais cette inégalité n'empêche pas qu'ils n'influent réciproquement les uns sur les autres, et qu'il ne s'établisse entre eux une espèce d'équilibre, comme entre deux liqueurs inégalement pesantes, et qui communiqueraient ensemble par le bas d'un siphon renversé, dont elles occuperaient les deux branches; elles ne seraient pas de niveau, mais la hauteur de l'une ne pourrait augmenter sans que l'autre ne montât aussi dans la branche opposée.

What is more, Turgot found the key to the equilibrium mechanism in the money market. Unlike the physiocrats he did not denounce saving as a leaking away of expenditures, but recognized that saving is crucial as a way to 'advance' or loan capital to the factors of production. Turgot stressed that hoards will always find some profitable outlet. They will either be used to buy land, to be invested as advances to workers and other factors, or to be loaned out at interest. All these uses of savings return money to the circular flow.[13] He even investigated the role of the interest rate in maintaining the balance between the supply and demand for capital (Rothbard 1995, 397–398).

This brief examination of Turgot's ideas on price formation and capital accumulation indicates that, indeed, he found the missing link of the *Tableau économique*. Whereas Quesnay ignored the role of supply and demand in price formation and focused on a rather unstable process of capital reproduction, Turgot's writings are riddled with mechanisms which give the economic process stability. In this sense, it is indeed wrong to associate him with the physiocrats. If only Quesnay and his followers had paid better attention to what Turgot had to say. One can only surmise about what a joint effort would have produced. Perhaps a *Tableau économique* with stable properties. However, the followers of Quesnay believed that Turgot strayed off the right path too much and took measures to bring his work more in line with that of the master.[14] It should be clear that such measures do not testify of a very warm relationship between Turgot and the physiocrats. For economics this is to be regretted. He could have helped Quesnay to explain the step-by-step process which takes the capital-producing economy from disequilibrium to equilibrium. A full explanation of this kind had to await the pioneering work of Knut Wicksell more than a century later.

TWO METHODS OF ECONOMIC ANALYSIS

The resemblance between the work of Cantillon and Turgot is by no means coincidental. Turgot was a student of Vincent de Gournay (1712–1759), an avid advocate of Cantillon's work in the late 1750s (Schumpeter 1954, 244 n1). The physiocrats were also well acquainted with Cantillon's work. Quesnay explicitly refers to him in his article *Grains* (1757), while Mirabeau even knew his *Essai* long before it was published. Moreover, they adopted his division of society in three classes and like him stressed the role of the landowning class to maintain the circular flow of expenditures. But the question remains why Quesnay and the physiocrats had such a different outlook on the nature of economic dynamics than Cantillon and Turgot in this period. Was it just a matter of theoretical brilliance, which gave the latter two a better insight in the workings of the system? Or was there also a difference in vision?

I believe that both factors played a role. Above I have given several theoretical arguments for the difference in focus. In addition, there existed a difference in method which was closely related to the conception of the economy as a natural order, just as we have seen in the case of Boisguilbert.

Turgot and Cantillon occasionally adopted the common phrases of natural law philosophy like 'natural law' and 'natural right', but the metaphysics associated with these terms does not seem to have affected their ideas to a great extent. In their works, the prefix natural appears a mere literally embellishment rather than a guiding theoretical concept. But in the physiocratic doctrine, meaning after all 'rule of nature', this is very different. One of the best known statements of the physiocratic doctrine appeared in a book with the title *L'Ordre naturel et essentiel des sociétiés politiques* (Le Mercier de la Rivière 1767[1910]). Quesnay himself was profoundly influenced by natural law philosophy, as is shown by his article on 'Le droit naturel' (1765).

However, I want to stress in this closing section that his interpretation of the natural order and natural law philosophy differed from earlier authors like Boisguilbert. In the spirit of the Enlightenment, Quesnay was captivated by a sense of scientific progress, which also permeates his notion of natural law. In 'Le droit naturel' he distinguished between two groups of natural laws, one physical and the other moral; 'les lois naturelles physiques' versus 'les lois naturelles morales'. Physical natural laws referred to the harmony and regularity of natural events and were intended to show how the laws of nature would benefit mankind. They are said to be 'the laws of the trains of events as favorable as possible to the happiness of all sentient beings'. Even a rainstorm cannot but benefit man, because while it may inconvenience the traveler and cause destruction, it also waters the field (Quesnay 1765[1888], 735). Moral natural laws have the same aim, but refer to human actions and the resulting train of events in human societies.

For Quesnay, a key feature of natural laws was that they are discoverable. He stated that mankind possessed a special faculty to recognize and understand natural laws, namely intelligence. This faculty, which other living creatures lacked, allowed man to learn from nature by observing regularities in sequences of events. From these regularities, lawlike statements could be deduced by means of reason. In this manner, he argued that the laws of nature could be learned which allowed mankind to take maximum advantage of their benefits (ibid., 736).

Moral natural laws was a special category which concerned the operation of human societies. They taught mankind how to best organize their mutual relationships in order to maximize the welfare of all members of society. Three things need to be explained about this aim of moral natural laws. First, the organization of human society is achieved through a legal system, the most essential element of which is the right to own property. This is made clear by Le Mercier de la Rivière (1767[1910], 23):

> L'ordre essentiel à toutes les sociétiés est l'ordre sans lequel aucune société ne pourrait ni se perpétuer ni remplir l'objet de son institution. La base fondamental de cet ordre est évidemment le droit de propriété, parce que sans le droit de propriété la société, n'auroit aucune consistence, et ne seroit d'aucune utilité à l'abondance des productions.

This quotation also suggest that, second, welfare is interpreted in material terms: the maximum satisfaction of wants depends on the availability of goods. Thus (ibid., 21, italics in the original):

> L'ordre essentiel à toutes les sociétiés particulieres est donc l'*ordre des devoirs et des droits réciproques dont l'établissement est essentiellement nécessaires à la plus grande multiplication possible des productions, afin de procurer au genre humain la plus grande somme possible de bonheur.*

Third, to protect the right of property and to enable the undisturbed production of goods authority is needed (ibid., 14). This is surprising, because we have seen in the previous chapter that for Boisguilbert natural law was closely related to the war cry of economic liberalism, 'laissez faire, laissez passer'. But the physiocrats reasoned differently. They claimed that the authority of an absolute monarch best quaranteed that protection was offered equally to all people. This explains their call for what has been called a 'legal despot', albeit it one that was educated in natural law philosophy (Fox-Genovese 1976).

The *Tableau économique* neatly complied to these rules of the natural order. It assumed a system of property rights and a king that would protect these rights. In order to fulfill this role, the king was entitled to raise taxes. Furthermore, the burden of taxation was best placed on the net product, the revenu of the soil, because a reduction of this revenu would not upset the reproduction of goods. Finally, this process of reproduction could be shown to maintain output at the highest level possible, if freedom of trade and enterprise prevailed. In this sense the *Tableau économique* and its stationary equilibrium can be said to represent an ideal situation, namely one that complied to the laws of the natural order (Meek 1963, 378). An equilibrium of this kind could come into being if the French king adopted the rules of physiocracy, dropped all taxes in favour of a single tax on the net product and allowed free trade, so that the economy could proceed according to its natural laws.

But this was not a blind faith in the workings of the natural order. I have called it a scientific conception, because it urged the *philosophes* to empirically investigate the nature of this order. You may call this the physical side of the natural laws underpinning the *Tableau.* It is interesting to observe how Quesnay tried to uncover these laws. One may consider the calculations of the different versions of the tableau as pure arbitrarily, but they are not. It is not well-know that he did extensive statistical research to give them an empirical base. This base is found in the two articles, *Grains* (1756) and *Fermiers* (1757), which preceded the publication of the *Tableau*. These articles analyze the state of agriculture in France and the possibility of economic growth in this sector. The problem of agriculture in France was that it used old-fashioned cultivation techniques, which resulted in what Quesnay considered a low annual growth rate of 35 percent.[15] In contrast in England the rate of growth in agriculture was at least 100 percent, which was the result of a capitalist method of production on large-scale farms. In the *Philosophie Rurale* the *Tableaux* of these two countries are compared to show the possible gains from economic development.[16] One is almost tempted to see this analysis as a kind of comparative static investigation of the tools needed to promote economic progress. But it is clear that we are not allowed to do so, because the mechanism of the *Tableau* lacks a crucial assumption. Comparative statics critically depends on the assumption that equilibrium is self-correcting, but in Quesnay's work and that of his physiocratic followers this is certainly not the case. When the economy topples over, there is nothing to prevent its fall.

NOTES

1. It is highly uncertain whether Mirabeau wrote this book himself. Probably large parts of it were written by Quesnay, who is nowadays often listed as a co-author of *L'Ami des Hommes*.
2. The French original reads 'des sommes qui leur étoient prescrites', which much clearer indicates that competition pushes market price below the demand price of individual buyers.
3. Note the agricultural bias in this table. Cantillon completely ignored the possibility of exchanges between artisans. Apparently, they just consume foodstuffs and other produce from the land.
4. An evident difference between Cantillon's thought experiment and the Austrian theory of economic planning is that in the Austrian conception central planning is impossible in principle and practice, because without markets there are no prices, and without prices the allocation of scarce resources cannot take place. See further Chapter 10.
5. This stress on the continuity of consumption suggests a notion of Say's law of markets (Spengler 1945). The physiocrats recognized that supply and demand are related because buyers of a good are sellers of another and vice versa. This view is best expressed by Le Mercier de la Rivière who wrote that '*La consummation est la mesure de la reproduction*, car des productions qui resteraient sans consommation, dégéneraient en superflu sans

utilité, sans valeur; et dès lors on cesserait de faire les avances de leur culture . . . Ainsi en considerant le commerce comme une multitude de ventes et d'achats faits en argent, *personne n'est acheteur qu'autant qu'il est vendeur;* et comme acheter c'est payer, *personne ne peut acheter qu'en rasison de ce qu'il vend*, parce que ce n'est qu'en vendant qu'il se procure l'argent pour payer ce qu'il achete' (Mercier de la Rivière 1767[1910], 254, 258, italics in the original).

6. For sake of simplicity, it is assumed that the sterile class does not consume manufactures itself. This question has proved one of the main issues in the literature on the *Tableau*: if the sterile class produces two units of manufactured goods and exchanges these for food and raw materials, where does the sterile class gets its own manufactured goods from? One solution is to assume that they export half a unit of food in exchange for manufactures. As Meek (1963, 282–83) has shown, the number of people in the sterile class is one-half that in the productive class, so that the total personal consumption of the sterile class must be one-half that of the productive class. Now in the *Analyse* it is assumed that the productive class has two units of food, one unit of which is used as fodder. That leaves one unit for personal consumption. If the sterile class has the same per capita consumption, their total personal consumption of food is half a unit. That leaves half a unit of food for exports. For a critical comment on this explanation, see Negishi (1989).

7. These three conditions are not valid for all versions of the *Tableau*. Herlitz (1996) shows how Quesnay developed them by changing the properties of the subsequent *Tableaux*. A defect of the earlier versions was that they violated the conditions of monetary equilibrium, that is the circular flow of money was incomplete (for example Spengler 1945, 200; Meek 1963, 276). This was the result of the fact that they traced each individual money transaction, assuming that both the productive and sterile class would spent half of each money unit they received buying goods from the other class. That resulted in an intricate pattern of expenditures and receipts, which gave these *Tableaux* their name, the 'zig-zag'. However, the zig-zags did not include enough transactions to complete the annual circulation. At the end of the year the sterile class possessed 1 billion of unwanted money, while the productive class still needed 1 billion to pay the proprietors. This problem was discovered and circumvented when Quesnay replaced the zig-zags by an abbreviated *Tableau* that just showed the end result of these individual transactions. Hence the name *Précis* of this *Tableau* (in Quesnay 1764[1972]).

8. The propensity to consume agricultural products is a crucial value in the working of the *Tableau*. Barna (1975) shows that to obtain stationary equilibrium the propensity to consume must have a value of one-half. In that sense, Quesnay can be said to have chosen 'coefficients and ratios for his model which satisfy the equilibrium conditions' (ibid., 492). That does not mean that production can not be raised by changing the propensity to consume. In fact, Herlitz (1996) calculates that the revenu reaches its maximum when the propensity to consume is 0.72. However, the effect of this increase will be temporary. If this propensity is maintained, future production will decline again and fall well below the original starting position.

9. The unit of the *Tableau* changed dramatically between editions. In the first editions (1758) it was 200 *livres*. From that point onwards, it rose to 300 *livres* (1759–1760), 525 *livres* (1760), to 1000 *livres* (1764) which became 1 billion *livres* in the final edition (1766).
10. For more detailed discussions of the disequilibrium dynamics of the *Tableau*, the reader is referred to Eagly (1969), Eltis (1975b), Barna (1976) and Eltis (1996).
11. In contrast to the physiocrats, Turgot got a chance to carry out these ideas. In 1774 Louis XVI appointed him as minister of finance and commerce. Two of his reforms concerned the establishment of internal free trade in grains and the abolishment of the craft guilds. However, the opposition against these reforms proved strong and Turgot was forced to resign in 1776. His ministry had lasted only twenty months.
12. For an assessment of Turgot's place in the history of economics, see Groenewegen (1983).
13. It is clear that such notions ultimately led to the formulation of Say's law of markets.
14. This should be taken literally. Turgot's best known work, *Réflexions sur la formation et la distribution des richesses* appeared in 1769–1770 in the *Ephémérides du citoyen* the journal of one of Quesnay's disciples, Dupont de Nemours. Dupont, however, made various alterations in the text, in order to bring it more into accordance with Quesnay's doctrines.
15. Quesnay described this agricultural system as 'la petite culture'. It involved cultivation on small farms, ploughing with oxes, no crop rotation, etc. In contrast 'la grande culture' involved specialization of crops, crop rotation, production on large farms, ploughing with horses, etc.
16. These *Tableaux* are reproduced in Eltis (1996).

6. Adam Smith's Love of System

INTRODUCTION

In the ranking order of modern sciences economics is often classified as a natural science. This means that the regularities that form the basis of economic analysis are not the product of social forces, but of natural ones, like the human psyche, the availability of natural resources or the current state of technology. Hence modern economists speak of the natural mechanism of the market, the natural rate of economic growth and a host of other natural economic variables.

This chapter will trace the idea of economics as a natural science to its earliest beginnings, as it is closely related to the development of equilibrium economics. In fact the term 'equilibrium' itself is a natural metaphor, as was argued in the previous two chapters. In the work of early liberal writers like Boisguilbert and the Physiocrats 'equilibrium' signified the search for the natural laws of the economy. But the great popularizer of the idea of economics as a natural science was Adam Smith.[1]

Today Smith is considered the father of economics because he was above all a system builder. He was the first to build a coherent economic system to examine 'the nature and causes of the wealth of nations'. In this book, which made him famous during his own lifetime, Smith frequently used the prefix 'natural' or 'naturally'. He spoke of a 'natural course of things' or a 'natural order of things' determining capital investment. The rate of profit is said to be 'naturally low in rich, and high in poor countries'. Prices gravitate around a 'natural price', while one of the main topics of the book is the 'natural progress of opulence' due to increased division of labour, expanding population and the accumulation of capital. Of course Smith used the word in different meanings. 'Naturally' often means merely 'spontaneously' or 'ordinarily'. Also he associated 'natural' with liberty and the absence of state regulation. But these semantic ambiguities cannot conceal the fact that Smith's economics involved the analysis of natural magnitudes (for example Clark 1992).

This chapter will argue that Smith's ideas on economic equilibrium were influenced by what may be called his natural outlook or vision. The nature of this relationship has been the subject of a long debate in economics. For a long time commentators assumed a direct connection between Smith's natural outlook and his exposition of an equilibrium system. Put simply, they reasoned that because (a) Smith believed in the existence of a divine natural order, (b) a natural order assumes an equilibrium of natural forces and (c) Smith's belief in a natural order shaped his economic thought, it can be assumed that (d) Smith's conception of economic equilibrium possesses the features of a natural order. A main representative of this view was Alexander Gray (quoted in Lindgren 1969, p. 897):

> Herein lies the a priori element in Adam Smith; there is a natural order, appointed by a wise Providence in which self-interest will supply the necessary drive to make the machine go, and will also act to produce equilibrium between contending forces.

But in the wake of positivism it was argued that Smith's use of the vocabulary of natural law philosophy was mere rhetoric and did not affect his scientific ideas. Bittermann (1940) was one of the first to defend this view. He classified both Smith's economics and his moral theory as scientific on the grounds that they used an empirical method. Accordingly, the order of nature played no significant part in Smith's science and contained no implications of specific standards or policies (Bittermann 1940, 718, 719):

> While Smith believed in some natural order, he stated his theories in a form such that its main conclusions could be accepted or rejected irrespective of the implied theological sanction . . . Smith's arguments in these instances would be as correct or as incorrect if the 'invisible hand' were struck out and some quite empirical phrase, say 'self-interest' substituted.

Bittermann concluded that in all of Smith's works the word 'natural' had an empirical content, devoid of ethical meaning (ibid., 705).

This controversy about Smith's naturalism is of paramount importance for the interpretation of Smith's conception of economic equilibrium. If Gray is right, this concept is part of Smith's scientific vision and therefore an a priori concept. But if Bittermann is right, there is nothing metaphysical about Smith's concept of equilibrium. Like all other natural magnitudes in Smith's analysis it must be considered an empirical concept and nothing else.

In this chapter, I shall argue that the truth lies somewhere in the middle. In my opinion, there is a third way, a view between these two extreme positions. It will be argued that nature plays two different parts in Smith's economic analysis.[2] In the first place, Smith saw nature as a machine. He often compared nature to the operation of a machine and used this analogy to structure his ideas about nature's laws. Smith's second concept of nature is that of 'process'. As it is essentially timeless, the mechanical view of nature cannot account for the historical development of society and its economic structure. Smith addressed this issue by approaching it as a process in historical time.

In other words, there is a dichotomy in Smith's method of science: he used different methods to study different problems. Universal economic laws, such as the laws of market exchange, could be studied as natural science based on mechanical analogies. Here the idea of order was an important guide to scientific investigation. But Smith was too much aware of historical contingencies to analyze the process of economic development in similar terms. History was the domain of a conjectural method that lacked the mechanical vision of order and adopted a process-type approach leaving more scope for historical contingencies.

As a corollary Smith's conception of equilibrium also has different meanings. According to the machine metaphor, equilibrium must be seen as a balance of natural forces. Characteristic of these forces is that they are universal; they apply to all times and places. But also part of the natural order are certain ethical preconceptions. The idea of a machine suggests a machine-maker. This was god who had created the universe for the benefit of mankind. Accordingly a balance of economic forces served the welfare of society. Economic equilibrium was considered 'just' because it satisfied the demands of commutative justice.

In contrast the process-approach lacked these ethical overtones. Here equilibrium took the shape of a tendency that always seemed present, but never quite reached its ultimate goal. The steps of this process concerned the socio-historical conditions of societies in a specific phase of economic development. Economies could come to a standstill, while others simultaneously experienced periods of rapid growth or decline. Equilibrium, then, was not a natural law in the sense that it applied to all times and places. To the contrary, as a process equilibrium was determined by the fickleness of time.

This chapter first addresses Smith's method of science and then discusses the role of equilibrium in his moral and economic theory respectively.

SMITH'S LOVE OF SYSTEM

The reason to examine Smith's conception of science is Gray's contention that this method a priori assumes equilibrium. As Mirowski (1989, 198) puts it, '[f]or Smith, the essence of science was the evocation of order'. This view of science was prompted by Smith's belief in the existence of a natural order. He believed that the universe was the creation of a benevolent deity. As a divine creation, the laws of this universe exhibited two main features, harmony and universality. Being synonymous with 'goodness', god could not be considered to promote conflict. Thus god's laws were assumed to be essentially harmonious. The idea of equilibrium as a balance of contending forces can be seen as an aspect of this divine harmony. Further, god's laws were universal. God did not intervene to control the operation of nature's laws. The creation of these laws was an unique affair. Once in place, they governed the course of nature and could therefore be assumed to apply to all times and places.

This view of Smith's science is contested by those who stress the empirical nature of his method of inquiry. For example, Campbell (1971) contends that the references to nature in semi-religious fashion in Smith's work are mere window-dressing. According to him, these references can be removed from the analysis without doing harm to its scientific value. In his words, 'it is possible to remove the theological terminology and Smith's reflections about a benevolent Deity and not affect the empirical content of his work' (Campbell 1971, 61). Equilibrium is therefore an empirical proposition, not an a priori assumption. Likewise, the ethical characteristics of equilibrium must have an empirical source and cannot be the result of a priori reasoning. Thus, if there is a belief in god immanent in Smith's work, this belief is a consequence and not a cause of his study of nature. 'It is admiration, the emotion which *follows* on a scientific explanation that prompts belief in God . . . Belief in a god, even when based on the argument from design, is certainly an extra-empirical faith, but of all the arguments for God's existence, that from design is most dependent on the assessment of empirical evidence' (ibid., 60. Italics in the original). In other words, Smith's faith never coloured his view of the world. Belief in god was subject to empirical scrutiny, like any cognitive claim.

In view of these two interpretations of Smith's conception of science, the question to be answered in this section is: what was the source of Smith's belief that nature's laws promoted equilibrium between contending forces?

Natural Theology and Natural Philosophy

To study this question a distinction must be made between natural theology and natural philosophy.

Natural theology addresses the ultimate cause of nature. Greek philosophers called this cause the 'unmoved mover' and identified it with god. The Stoics gave this idea a decisive twist and argued that, as god was the creator of the universe, the living cosmos could be considered the manifestation of god. They reasoned that theology was part of physics and knowledge of nature's laws would give man knowledge of god. This knowledge had two specific qualities.[3] First, the study of nature would show that god's laws were universal and regular. God did not create chaos, but had constructed the universe as an orderly arrangement of laws that produced a regular pattern of events through time. Hence the Greek use of the word *archē* as god. In classical Greek, *archē* signifies a beginning or starting point, but it also is the principle of any orderly arrangement (Gerson 1990, 5). Second, the Stoics assumed that nature was purposeful. The idea that nature was of divine origin suggested that the laws of nature served a common goal which expressed god's intention on earth. This goal was the happiness of mankind. Knowledge of the laws of nature would therefore teach man how to improve the welfare of society. But the purposiveness of nature also suggested that nature was a source of morality. God's intention could only be realized by following nature's laws. Thus, the rules of proper human conduct could be derived from nature.[4]

In natural law philosophy the distinction between the forces which give nature meaning and govern its the operation respectively, is described in terms of final and efficient causes. Final causes refer to the ultimate purpose of nature, the metaphysical force which is responsible for its existence. Efficient causes, on the other hand, are the laws of nature as they manifest themselves in the movement of natural objects, like the orbits of planets, the growth of plants and trees and the behaviour of humans and animals. The explanation of the causes behind these events is the domain of natural philosophy. Or as Smith put it, natural philosophy is the study of the 'connecting principles of nature' (Smith 1795a[1980], 45).

The reason to distinguish between natural theology and natural philosophy is that they are two cornerstones of Smith's scientific method.[5] We know from Dugald Stewart, Smith's first biographer, that natural theology was part of the lectures which Smith delivered at the university of Glasgow. The subject of these lectures is said to be 'the proofs of the being and the attributes of God, and those principles of the human mind upon which religion is founded' (Stewart 1793[1980], 274). Unfortunately, Smith's ideas about natural theology were never published and no copies of his lectures on this subject remain.[6] Smith's natural philosophy is better documented. The *Theory of Moral Sentiments* (1759) contains many references to his method of inquiry. But even better, he wrote three essays about 'the principles which lead and direct philosophical enquiries'. The case studies which he choose to examine these principles are the *History of Ancient Physics*, the *History of Ancient Logics and Metaphysics* and the *History of Astronomy*. The latter essay gives the most detailed discussion of the science of natural philosophy and the role of the concept of order in that science.

Standards of Judgment in Natural Philosophy

The concept of order can be said to be the central organizing principle of Smith's method of inquiry. The problem was that nature was too complex to be explained in terms of a constant conjunction of events.[7] Only in some cases, such as the eclipses of sun and moon, was it possible to directly observe the connecting chain between cause and effect.[8] However, if the connection between cause and effect was not so obvious, creative guesswork was called for and it is in this connection that the assumption of order becomes crucial to Smith's method of explanation.

If two events are not connected in a straightforward fashion, the philosopher will posit 'a chain of intermediate, though invisible, events . . . [to] link together those two disjointed appearances' (ibid., 42). However, the choice of this intermediate chain must possess certain qualities if it will succeed in bridging the gap between cause and effect. The key demand for this chain is that it must be familiar. It consists of events 'which succeed each other in a train similar to that in which the imagination has been accustomed to move' (ibid.).[9] Only if this demand is satisfied, can the mind move 'smoothly and easily' between cause and effect and will its 'wonder' about an unusual succession of events be stopped. Philosophy, then, addresses itself to the imagination. It is inspired by the sentiments of surprise and wonder; surprise because of the singularity of a 'succession of objects which follow one another in an uncommon train or order' and wonder 'how it came there' (ibid., 40). The task of philosophy is to reduce the feelings provoked by these sentiments to an agreeable level (ibid., 45–46):

> Philosophy, by representing the invisible chains which bind together all these disjointed objects, endeavours to introduce order into this chaos of jarring and discordant appearances, to allay this tumult of the imagination, and to restore it, when it surveys the great revolutions of the universe, to that tone and tranquillity and composure, which is both most agreeable in itself, and most suitable to its nature.

The historical essays are intended to examine the constituent parts of the familiarity principle. What explains the success of the astronomical systems of the past? What, in other words, makes people accept one system of cosmology over another?

The criteria that explain the scientific success of theories are simplicity, coherence, empirical accuracy and beauty. Simplicity refers to the number of connecting principles that are necessary to explain events. Since the task of philosophy is to reduce the complexity of observed events, it is evident that the 'intermediate chain' between cause and effect should be as short as possible. For example, the theory of concentric spheres required seventy-two spheres to account for the movement of the heavens. According to Smith, this complex construction explained why the theory lost attraction when Copernicus made the earth move round the sun and constructed a much simpler picture of the solar system without additional spheres.[10]

The second criterion is that of coherence. Coherence refers to the ability to account for a great number of observed events. Copernicus not only constructed a simpler astronomical system, he also was able to explain more events than previous theories. In turn, his system was replaced by Newton's which proved superior in terms of simplicity and coherence, as it required just a single principle to account for the movements of the planets, gravitation. But theoretical elegance is not enough to explain the superiority of a theoretical system. Newton himself had stressed the need for empirical verification, as a check on the validity of theories.[11] Likewise Smith required of theoretical systems that they accurately described observed events. Not surprisingly, Smith considered this an outstanding feature of Newton's system (ibid., 104):

> It [the system of Sir Isaac Newton, BT] is every where the most precise and particular that can be imagined and ascertains the time, the place, and the quantity, the duration of each individual phenomenon, to be exactly such as, by observation, they have been determined.

In the end, simplicity, coherence and empirical accuracy explain why Newton's system 'prevails over all opposition' and why it must be considered 'as the greatest discovery that ever was made by man, the discovery of an immense chain of the most important and sublime truths, all closely connected together, by one capital fact, of the reality of which we have daily experience' (ibid., 105).

The Aesthetic Element in Smith's Standard of Judgment

At least, these three requirements should rationally explain why Newton's system prevailed over others. The surprising fact of Smith's epistemology is that emotional factors play an equally important role. As Thomson (1965, 219) remarks:

> It is a striking feature of Smith's system of science that he more frequently refers to his own standards of judgment as *aesthetic* than as strictly *rational*, and that as his final criterion of truth he is willing to accept neither the rational test of consistency nor the empirical standard of correspondence with the observed facts (italics in the original).

However, the extent to which Smith allowed aesthetic factors to play a role is disputed. Thus Campbell (1971, 41) maintains 'however well a theory satisfies imaginative and therefore aesthetic criteria, it is rejected if it does not fit the observed facts'. Yet there are reasons to question Campbell's conviction that ultimately empirical accuracy will decide the race between competing theories.

The reason for this doubt is Smith's strong belief that the 'connecting principles of nature' are too complex to be directly observed. Even the principle of gravity is a mere invention of the mind. Although the principle seems familiar – one experiences falling objects everyday – we cannot be certain that it really exists, because the force itself is not visible. In the words of Smith (ibid., 105):

> We have been endeavouring to represent all philosophical systems as mere inventions of the imagination, to connect together the otherwise disjointed and discordant phenomena of nature . . . to make use of language expressing the connecting principles of this one as if they were the real chains which Nature makes use of to bind together her several operations.

Now if the connecting principles themselves cannot be known with certainty, the best option is to describe them in terms of something which we do have direct knowledge of. According to Smith, the analogy of something familiar may help to understand the working of a causal mechanism that is concealed behind the complexities of nature. So if we cannot peek behind the scenes of nature, we invent our own stage. For Smith the analogy that would best serve this function in natural philosophy was that of the machine.[12] Frequently the astronomical systems are compared to machines. In fact, the term system itself suggests a mechanical analogy. In the *History of Ancient Physics* Smith remarks that people started to conceive of the universe as a machine after the first machines had been invented by mankind. Moreover, the idea of a machine suggested the existence of a machine maker and thus it was science which gave rise to theistic religions (Smith 1795b,[1980], 113–114):

> As soon as the universe was regarded as a complete machine, . . . the resemblance which it bore to those machines which are produced by human art, necessarily impressed those sages with a belief that in the original formation of the world there must have been employed an art resembling the human art, but as much superior to it, as the world is superior to the machines which that art produces. The unity of the system, which, according to this ancient philosophy, is most perfect, suggested the idea of the unity of that principle, by whose art it was formed; and thus, as ignorance begot superstition, science gave birth to the first theism.

But Smith did not restrict the machine analogy to the analysis of religious and astronomical systems. Likewise, society is described in terms of this metaphor. 'Human society, when we contemplate it in a certain abstract and philosophical light, appears like a great and immense machine, whose regular and harmonious movements produce a thousand agreeable effects' (Smith 1759[1976], 316). This comparison was not some literary embellishment. It formed one of the main pillars of Smith's moral theory and strongly affected his perception of society for the following reason: the metaphor of the machine suggests the most perfect adjustment of means to ends. For that reason it appeals to people's sense of beauty and facilitates the acceptance of the image that society operates like a machine. As Smith continued: 'As in any other beautiful and noble machine that was the production of human art, whatever tended to render its movements more smooth and easy, would derive a beauty from this effect'. It is this beauty which pleases the senses and it makes it on that account a criterion which explains why people accept certain theories and reject others.[13]

The consequence of this line of reasoning is far-reaching. The development of theories which describe society as a machine-like mechanism, governed by regular and harmonious laws, becomes an aim of science in itself. Thus, in the *Theory of Moral Sentiments* the invisible hand has nothing to do with the way societies in reality operate. It is a metaphor to describe the beautiful adjustment of means to ends in a society which runs like a machine. Driven by their self interest landlords

> are led by an invisible hand to make nearly the same distribution of the necessaries of life, which would have been made, had the earth been divided in equal portions among all its inhabitants, and thus without intending it, without knowing it, advance the interest of society and afford the means to the multiplication of the species (ibid., 184–185).

Now it is not the satisfaction derived from goods and services which brings the landlord to act in this way. On the contrary, the passage was intended as a criticism of Hume's utility theory, which stated that utility corresponds to the convenience suggested by commodities and services. Surprisingly, Smith – the father of capitalism – argued that when viewed alone, the pleasures of 'wealth and greatness' must be considered as vain (ibid., 182–83):

> Power and riches appear . . . to be . . . enormous and operose machines contrived to produce a few trifling conveniences to the body, consisting of springs the most nice and delicate, which must be kept in order with the most anxious attention, and

> which in spite of all our care are ready every moment to burst into pieces and to crush in their ruins their unfortunate possessor.

Smith argued that people labour night and day to obtain 'wealth and greatness', but in retrospect their efforts are not worth the trouble.

> He studies to distinguish himself in some laborious profession . . . with equal assiduity solicits every opportunity of employment . . . and . . . serves those whom he hates. [But] in the extremity of old age . . . in the last dregs of life, his body wasted with toil and diseases . . . he begins at last to find that wealth and greatness are mere trinkets of frivolous utility . . . If we consider the real satisfaction which all these things are capable of affording . . . it will always appear in the highest degree contemptible and trifling (ibid., 181–83).

In other words, it is not richness which constitutes the real happiness of human life. 'In ease of body and peace of mind, all the different ranks of life are nearly upon a level and the beggar, who suns himself by the side of the highway, possesses that security which kings are fighting for' (ibid., 185).

But if wealth turns out to be a deception, why pursue wealth anyway? The reason is that the pursuit of wealth is part of the orderly arrangement of society. It is self interest which 'rouses and keeps in continual motion the industry of mankind'. Moreover, by pursuing their self interest, people unintentionally promote the social welfare as well. In other words, on a meta-level society appears to work like a perfect machine. People are motivated by an impulse which makes them work night and day and which at the same time furthers the general interest. This adjustment of means to ends gives the social arrangement an aesthetic quality. At the end of the analysis, 'the *love of system*, the same regard to the beauty of order . . . serves to recommend those institutions which tend to promote the public welfare' (ibid., italics added). That in reality the pursuit of wealth will not bring people what they expect from it is irrelevant.[14] What counts is the beauty of the explanation.

Smith's Love of System and the Principle of Order

At the end of this section I return to my original question. Is the assumption of order in Smith an empirical proposition or is it an extra-empirical element of Smith's science? Supporters of the former position argue that the principle of order was indeed part of Smith's scientific outlook, but that it did not affect the scientific content of his theories. Ultimately, empirical verification was the decisive test for theories. Extra-empirical elements such as religious beliefs fell outside the scope of what Smith would call science. Metaphysics (natural religion) was the domain of final causes, while efficient causes were the proper subject of scientific inquiry (natural philosophy) because they are liable to empirical testing. Smith was always careful to distinguish between efficient and final causes and it is therefore unlikely that the concept of order would have affected the scope of his theories, unless it could be proven to have empirical relevance.

The point is, did Smith have such proof? I argue that the answer to that question is negative. Indeed the empirical success of Newton's physics underlined the orderliness of nature. But Smith never showed that the laws of moral and economic behaviour, his main fields of study, similarly conformed to a pattern of order. In economics and moral theory the assumption of order was not the result of empirical study. On the contrary, the principle of order was in itself a standard of verification. According to Smith, theories had to conform to the aesthetic standard of beauty. Part of the explanation of Newton's success was the fact that his astronomical system could be shown to function like a machine. The use of this mechanical analogy made people accept a theory the real causal mechanism of which they were unable to observe. Smith employed the same strategy in the field of social studies. In his moral theory and his economics, sympathy and self interest respectively are to society what gravitation is to physics. Both are aspects of the mechanical analogy applied to these fields and bring out the orderly arrangement of means to ends in society. So one may conclude with Worland (1976, 604) that 'the basis of Smith's economics is a "mechanical analogy" borrowed from Newton, which analogy leads one to conceive of the economic system as a "machine" the parts of which interact to produce coherence, equilibrium, and system stability'.[15] The difference with Newton's physics is that this arrangement is not supported by empirical evidence.[16] It merely conforms to an aesthetic quality of the analogy which Smith choose to describe the causal mechanism inherent in society. Whether this analogy was borrowed from Newton, as Worland contends, or was inspired by Smith's own religious beliefs is besides the matter. The point is that as a scientific concept the idea of natural order in Smith's moral theory and economics is metaphysical and does not refer to aspects of reality.

THE PRINCIPLE OF GRAVITATION: SYMPATHY AND SELF INTEREST

Final Causes in Smith's Moral Theory

The conclusion of the previous section is that Smith was well aware of the distinction between final and efficient causes and explicitly sought not to confuse them in the study of natural events (Smith [1759]1980, 87):

> In every part of the universe we observe means adjusted with the nicest artifice to the ends which they are intended to produce; and in the mechanism of a plant or animal body, admire how every thing is contrived for advancing the two great purposes of nature, the support of the individual and the propagation of the species. But in these and in all such objects we still distinguish the efficient from the final cause of their several motions and organizations . . . The wheels of the watch are all admirably adjusted to the end for which it was made, the pointing of the hour. All their various motions conspire in the nicest manner to produce this effect. If they were endowed with a desire and intention to produce it, they could not do it better. Yet we never ascribe any such desire or intention to them, but to the watchmaker, and we know that they are put into motion by a spring, which intends the effect it produce as little as they do.

The problem is, Smith continued, that when it comes to the affairs of the mind the 'watchmaker' is often ascribed a role in the explanation of efficient causes. For example, it is argued that people uphold the laws of justice, because they know that society's survival depends on justice, not because they fear punishment. Smith tried to avoid this mistake. The final cause of society was the 'wisdom of God' (ibid.) and not the proper object of study of natural philosophy. Likewise, moral philosophy studied moral judgments as efficient causes that aimed to realize the final cause of society, but were not motivated by it (Campbell 1971, Myers 1983).

The *Theory of Moral Sentiments* (1759) is Smith's study of these efficient causes as they relate to moral decision-making. In essence, this theory addresses the question of how people judge their own behaviour and that of others, but it also tries to explain the development of rules that people use to make these moral judgments (Heath 1995). At least, it professes to be the study of the efficient causes controlling these judgments. The point is that in spite of Smith's intention to avoid teleological explanation in terms of final causes, such causes do play a role in the theory of moral sentiments. Moreover, this role is not of minor importance. Final causes in Smith's moral and economic schemes are the safeguards of social order.

Smith's moral theory can be described as 'conventionalist' because it treats the standards of moral assessment as the conventions of a specific community (Bittermann 1940, Lindgren 1973). According to Smith, people learn to make moral judgements by observing how other people choose between right and wrong.[17] He believed that people have a strong incentive to conform to established rules of judgment. Rejection of these rules would command the disapproval of a large part of the community and for that reason causes pain. In the reverse case, acts would be in line with the community's ideas about right and wrong and one would experience a feeling of pleasure. Smith described this feeling as the pleasure of 'mutual sympathy' to stress the fact that moral behaviour was a shared feeling between community members. Attracted by the pleasure of mutual sympathy and repelled by the pain of social disapproval, people would be inclined to do the right thing and act in accordance with the moral rules of the community.[18]

The hand of Newton is clearly visible in this construction. Sympathy acts as a kind of gravitational force working upon the moral sentiments. Social pressure forces people to reduce their sentiments to a level that is agreeable to the group.[19] This applies to all sentiments, social and selfish. Even social passions like benevolence or justice can be considered inappropriate, if they do not fit the situation. For example, consider the politician who tries to benefit from a national disaster by publicly showing his compassion with the victims. Citizens instinctively recognize this act of benevolence as insincere and therefore inappropriate to the situation. The politician is merely looking for a cheap way to gain the public's attention and promote his own political goals. The right way to act in this situation is to show restraint and to reduce one's compassion to a level that is acceptable to the public. Smith's claim is that politicians will indeed be induced to show this restraint. Like others, they seek the sympathetic approval of the public and this requires that their emotional reactions are fitting and appropriate to their causes. Sympathy thus brings about an equilibrium between the four cardinal virtues; justice, benevolence, prudence and self-command.[20]

The function of this equilibrium is evident: common standards of moral assessment guarantee social order.[21] The question is, what brings about this equilibrium? Myers (1976) stresses the fact that Smith was looking for the efficient causes of this process to counter arguments of earlier writers who discussed the 'balance of the passions' in terms of final causes.[22] The inductive nature of the learning process involved seems to support this view. The moral faculties of people are not implanted in mankind by some unknown force. In the words of Smith, they are the result of 'experience and induction'.[23] For that reason, Raphael (1975, 97) describes Smith's moral theory as an exercise in empirical psychology which can stand comparison with the 'best known of modern psychological explanations of conscience, Freud's account of the super-ego'.[24]

However, there are good reasons to argue that Smith's moral theory does depend on the operation of final causes. To start with, sympathy, the central force controlling human emotions, is not an empirical fact. Like the force of gravity, it is a theoretical assumption that underlies his analysis of the moral sentiments. Yet the effects of sympathy are far-reaching because it motivates people to maintain their social bonds. In that respect, Smith's moral theory may appear similar to Newton's physics which explains cosmic harmony. But there is a difference. Newton's explanation of the regular pattern of the heavens is corroborated by the facts. In contrast, Smith's rosy picture of the harmonious character of social intercourse is in stark conflict with the course of human history. A wealth of illustrations and examples enlivens the *Theory of Moral Sentiments*, but none of them deals with the human appetite for war. It seems that the scholar Smith was blinded by the scientific and economic progress of his time and ignored the harsh facts of life that contradicted his positive outlook on the affairs of the human race.[25]

Furthermore, Kleer (1995) analyzes ten cases in the *Theory of Moral Sentiments* which require the intervention of something more powerful than efficient causes. Some of these cases involve crucial elements of the social order, such as the distinction of ranks by which political order is maintained and the restraint of self-interest within the bounds suited to the maintenance of societal relations. Kleer shows that the explanation of this type of behaviour involves human motivations which are not just the result of social pressures. Specifically, they are based on forms of instinctive behaviour that are not learned, but are somehow part of mankind's mental luggage.

The most obvious of these is the belief that people will receive their due rewards or punishments in afterlife. Smith ([1759]1980, 163) writes that the fear of violating general moral rules, as also the pleasure of observing them, are strengthened by the common belief that such rules 'are the commands and laws of the Deity, who will finally reward the obedient and punish the transgressors of their duty'. Thus the 'terrors of religion' enforce the natural sense of duty and force people to obey the rules of society.[26]

Concerning the distinction of ranks, the instincts of mankind are directed towards the respect and admiration accorded to the aristocracy and the natural aversion of injuring them in any way, by which they are able to retain power without challenge. This admiration is not the result of calculated self-interest. For the benefits conferred by the wealthy are few, while the respect which they command is quite general. The admiration of the rich betrays a very pragmatic approach of nature to secure social harmony. Smith argued that the common people are too stupid to understand that leadership should come from the wise and virtuous. To remedy this defect, nature has implanted in them the instinct to subordinate to the higher classes because differences in wealth are easier to understand than differences in skill and wisdom. Ironically, in this case the invisible hand of nature requires highly visible instruments (Smith[1759]1976, 226):

> Nature has wisely judged that the distinction of the ranks, the peace and order of society, would rest more securely upon the plain and palpable difference of birth and fortune, than upon the invisible and often uncertain difference of wisdom and virtue. The undistinguishing eyes of the great mob of mankind can well enough perceive the former: it is with difficulty that the nice discernment of the wise and

virtuous can sometimes distinguish the latter. In the order of all these recommendations, the benevolent wisdom of nature is equally evident.

These examples suffice to show that final causes play an important role in Smith's conception of moral equilibrium. Moreover, this equilibrium strongly resembles the cosmic harmony that Newton discovered in the heavens. Like the planets, people's moral decisions are governed by a central force. Only, in the field of moral theory this force is called sympathy, not gravitation. But their effects are the same; they bring about equilibrium.

Final Causes in Smith's Economic Theory

The impact of Smith's natural outlook on his economic theory can best be analyzed by examining his theory of value. This theory is based on a distinction between market and natural prices. Natural prices are determined by cost of production and consist of wages, rents and profits.[27] Market prices are current prices and are determined by the quantities actually demanded and supplied on the market.[28] Consequently, supply or demand may cause market prices to deviate from their natural level. In case market prices rise above this level, extra gains will be made and resources flow into this particular industry. Conversely, if the market price is lower than the natural level, the resulting losses will drive resources out of this industry. In both cases, shifts in supply result in a tendency of market prices to restore equilibrium with the natural price level. In the words of Smith, '[t]he natural price, therefore, is, as it were, the central price to which the prices of all commodities are continually gravitating' (Smith 1937, 58).

This is clearly a model of what may be called social physics (Clark 1992, 69). Prices are social phenomena, yet they are treated as being regulated and determined by laws and forces which are similar to those of the physical sciences. Smith even adopts the language of Newton's physics. Prices 'gravitate' towards an equilibrium level, as competition pushes resources to their most profitable employment.

But the influence of the natural or physical model goes further than the use of a particular metaphor to discuss the dynamics of price adjustment. Unlike gravitation, competition is not an impersonal force. The equilibrium it establishes carries a normative meaning that cannot be attributed to the equilibrium of planetary movements. Of course, the reason for this difference is that economic exchange involves human decision making, while the orbits of planets are not under the spell of human influence. Smith tried to bridge this difference by invoking the metaphor of the invisible hand. Personal economic decisions ultimately result in better economic conditions for all, but this result was not intended when the decision was made. In that sense market equilibrium can still be seen as a natural outcome that is unaffected by the wishes and decisions of people. Economic order is the result of human action, but not of human design.[29]

However, the traces of the designer's hand are more visible than intended by Smith. This can be seen by looking at the process by which exchange ratios are established. Smith claimed that economic exchange is the exclusive domain of self interest because '[i]t is not from the benevolence of the butcher, the brewer of the baker, that we expect our dinner, but from their regard to their own interest' (Smith 1937, 14). Smith seems to suggest that economic behaviour is incompatible with altruistic motivations. But on closer inspection, this distinction between egoism and altruism is drawn too sharp.

Recall that in the *Theory of Moral Sentiments* Smith had argued that people have a strong desire to gain the sympathy of their fellow citizens. This principle can be used to explain why in economic traffic people may pursue their personal interests and yet maintain social harmony.[30] The key to this explanation is the difference between between what Smith called 'selflove' and 'self interest'. Selflove is unmitigated greed and will never gain the sympathy of anyone but oneself. Self interest, on the other hand, is selflove attuned to a level that can carry the moral approval of others.[31] From this point of view, it can be argued that social pressures will constrain people's egoistic motivations, even in the marketplace.[32] People will not maximize their gains at any price, but try to make bargains that are acceptable to the community. This requires that the price agreed upon is a fair price. It must be a voluntary agreement between parties and not entail fraud or deceit. In that sense a natural price can be said to be a 'consensus' price because it will not cause injury to any party (Young 1986, 375). Likewise, natural factor prices reflect the community's standards of justice and propriety. For example, the natural wage rate would reflect the levels of compensation that the community believes are fair and reasonable. In other words, when paid their natural rates, the suppliers of resources are justly compensated for their efforts, just as a natural price can be said to constitute a just exchange rate because it is fair and does not inflict harm upon anyone (Oswald 1995, 463).

Equilibrium prices, then, entail more than a mechanical balance of forces. They are also standards of fairness based upon a society's generally accepted standards of right and wrong. The natural forces that govern prices are scarcity and people's natural desires.[33] But these forces do not operate in isolation. Specifically, they are conditioned by the moral forces which bind the community.[34] One of these forces commands people to abstain from injuring others and to voluntarily do 'whatever we can with propriety be forced to do' (Smith[1759]1976, 269).[35] This principle of commutative justice underlies Smith's conception of market exchange and makes his equilibrium prices just prices at the same time.[36]

CONJECTURAL HISTORY AND NATURE AS A PROCESS

Is There a Dichotomy in Smith?

The great works of economics vary in many respects but have one common characteristic: they create an industry of followers trying to figure out what the master really meant. Adam Smith proves that this process may last centuries and that apparently each generation feels the impulse to discover anew the importance of his work. In Smith's case the main issue at stake concerns the relationship between his two published books, the *Theory of Moral Sentiments* (1759) and the *Wealth of Nations* (1776). These books created a flood of literature devoted to the question of what has become known as the Adam Smith problem: the relationship between Smith's moral and economic theories.[37] A problem related to this issue is the role of historical analysis in Smith's view of science. Smith belonged to a group of scholars which developed a specific form of historical analysis and has become known as the Scottish Historical School.[38] Characteristic of this analysis was its link with economic development and social organisation, many examples of which are found in the *Wealth of Nations*.[39] For example, book three of the *Wealth of Nations* is devoted to 'the different progress of opulence in different nations' and discusses the economic history of Europe from the Roman Empire onwards. Likewise, book four compares competing 'systems of political economy' by analyzing the historical development of the countries which adopted them. This historical point of view raised another question of consistency. Natural science explains observed events in terms of universal laws. These are causal relationships that are assumed to be operative in all times and places and therefore independent of historical circumstances. It therefore appears that Smith used two methods in the *Wealth of Nations*, a historical one which took notice of historical contingencies and the method of natural science which involved universal laws.

Several commentators have stressed the natural law/historical dichotomy in Smith. Skinner (1965, 18) remarks that 'Adam Smith as an *economist* is too often regarded in this light [as a moral philosopher, BT] rather than as the founder of an essentially *historical* movement' (emphasis in the original). Evensky (1987) discusses the 'two voices' of Smith, the moral philosopher and social critic. This second viewpoint is that of 'historian, contemporary observer and social critic, and from it he sees that the real world is not the Design of his ideal vision' (Evensky 1987, 447–48).[40] The suggestion that Smith pursued two different research programs is worked out by Clark (1992). According to him, the core of these programs are, respectively, a search for natural laws and the natural order and a historical and institutional investigation of existing social phenomena, each of which give a distinct vision of society.

A way to characterize these programs is to examine their dominant metaphors. In the previous section it was shown that the metaphor of nature as a machine guided Smith's scientific investigations into the natural laws of moral and economic behaviour. Like nature, society was seen as a rational order that would automatically find its balance. In this world of order there was little scope for change in a historical sense. Changes from the regular patterns of events that form nature's laws were seen as deviations caused by temporary interventions. Thus God was held responsible for comets, earthquakes and other unexplained events in the physical universe. Likewise, interventions in the social universe would be explained by non-natural human institutions. But in the long run nature's forces would regain their regular course and order would be re-established. A system that sees nature as a machine has no room for growth and development. Yet this view was in stark contrast with the fast developments that were taking place at the end of the 18th century. The economy started to feel the impact of mechanization and large scale production, in fact science was seen as the engine of progress, and the political landscape was on the brink of irreversible changes. With reason it could be argued that instead of the unalterable order of nature, change, growth and development were fastly becoming the norm.

This led to the rise of a different conception of nature; nature as a process. The meaning of this metaphor was that nature could be conceived as a sequence of changes in historical time. Was this, then, a random process, lacking a guiding principle such as gravitation? No, there was certainly structure in this process and it also had a conception of equilibrium. One may compare this conception to the one used in evolutionary biology. Darwin gave the idea that changes in nature are irreversible a decisive push, but before him the members of the Scottish Historical School applied the notion of evolution to the analysis of the historical development of society (Hodgson 1993). As a member of this school, Smith adopted this method and partly used it in his economic analysis. He also incorporated the metaphor of nature as an evolutionary process. The equilibrium notion involved in this process is that of a tendency, a combination of forces continuously pulling the development of society in a certain direction. But in contrast to the end-state conception of equilibrium, what matters here is the road travelled and not the final destination. Moreover, a journey along this road is affected by the time element. It is an open process in the sense that the outcome of the journey may be affected by the historical events during the trip. Thus, the laws of the development of society are not universally valid, but they do possess structure. This structure stood central in the studies of Scottish Historical School by means of a method known as conjectural history.

The Stages Theory of Historical Development

The Scottish Historical School approached the study of history as a scientific discipline. Smith and his colleagues believed that everything in society and history was bound together by a succession of causes and effects. The study of this process was considered scientific, because it aimed to discover the regular pattern of historical developments. But description was not enough. Processes had to be explained in terms of natural causes like people's natural propensities or a nation's natural resources. In other words, the Scottish historians saw history as a branch of *natural* science, which could be studied with the aid of the new scientific methodology which had already proved so fruitful in other spheres of inquiry.

The main force behind the historical development of society was people's natural desire to improve the material conditions of life. According to the Scottish historians, it was an empirical fact that self interest and the drive for improvement of economic well-being were determining factors of social behaviour in the history of mankind. This observation made these factors the ideal principles upon which to found an examination of the laws of history.

But if the study of history was based on the assumption of constant principles of human nature, how could history analyze the changing structure of human society? The relationship between the uniform causes of history and the variable nature of social changes was established as follows. The Scottish Historical School adopted a method that is now known as invisible hand explanation (Petsoulas 2001).[41] In attempting to explain the process of change in civil society, it was assumed that man, by following his natural propensities, inevitably produced results well beyond his original intention. The unintended consequences of human behavior caused society to develop blindly in the sense that its course in history was the result of human action, but not of human design. Still, the School believed that by studying the unintended consequences of human behaviour from the perspective of certain empirically established natural propensities of human conduct, the regular pattern of cause and effect in the history of mankind could be discovered.[42]

The basic propositions of the laws of history discovered by the School are threefold. In the first place, it was argued that the mode of subsistence is the main force behind the process of socio-economic development. In particular, the mode of subsistence determined the way in which people organize the process of production. People's growing desire for grains led to the formation of the first human settlements in order to cultivate the land and take up agriculture as an economic activity. Likewise, the introduction of large-scale production in factories towards the end of the 18th century accomodated a higher demand for consumption articles and allowed people to enjoy a higher standard of economic well-being. But a hundred years before Marx, the

Scottish historians perceived that in turn the organization of the economic process would affect the social structure. The appropriation of land during the agricultural stage of history generated an inequality of fortune and made property a basis of social subordination. In the industrial era the factory system suggested a class distinction between workers and capitalists and exploitation of the labour force. Thus, historical analysis of social and political problems found its root in the dynamics of economic development.

The second basic proposition behind the laws of history is the causal connection between property relationships and the form of government (Meek 1967a, 38). The School observed that institutions like centralized forms of government first appeared in the history of mankind when people started to develop a sense of ownership concerning objects, land and people. The function of government in this early phase of history was to protect the right of property against theft and other forms of intrusion.[43]

The third basic proposition is that society develops in distinct historical phases. Smith distinguished four of those phases; hunting, pasturage, agriculture and commerce. These stages are defined in terms of the two other basic propositions. The drive to improve the material conditions of life led people to first domesticate animals in the stage of pasturage, and later to cultivate the land and commence agriculture as a productive activity. In the subsequent stage of commerce, trade becomes the dominant means to generate wealth. Linked to the changing mode of subsistence is the development of institutions like property and government. In the first stage, hunting, there exists no government at all because there is virtually no private property. Life is maintained by the spontaneous fruits of the earth. Property in the form of flocks and herds is first introduced in the second stage, pasturage. According to Smith, it is only then that government comes into being. The functions of government are further developed in the stage of agriculture because now land itself comes to be divided between private individuals. Smith also considered defence a typical task of government. The need for this task arises during the commercial stage, as free trade takes commerce across borders and makes security a national issue.

Note the endogenous character of the forces controlling the movement of society through these stages. The natural desire for better living conditions starts the process and keeps it going, but this force is facilitated by the introduction of institutions that arise as an unintended result during the process. Thus, the introduction of property allows wealth to be accumulated and gives the desire for wealth an extra impetus. But the strengthening of one force calls forth the development of another to control its effects. Government provides a check on people's uncontrolled greed by protecting accumulated fortunes against the envy of the less well-to-do. In similar vein, the force of social subordination performs a controlling function. According to Smith, the peace and order of society rests upon the distinction of ranks and it is interesting to note how the social relations that underlie this distinction change during the process of economic development.[44] Personal qualities such as physical strength or age determine social subordination in the primitive stages of society.[45] But qualities of this kind are less likely to command authority in groups of larger sizes and in communities where property becomes a power factor. Thus, the source of the distinction of ranks shifts from personal leadership to differences in fortune and birth when societies evolve through the stages of agriculture and commerce.[46]

Equilibrium as a Process

Smith's famous metaphor of the invisible hand is often identified with the force of competition. As Brown (1994, 166) remarks, 'the analysis of WN is still largely characterised in terms of a system of competitive markets which efficiently allocate economic resources . . . a linchpin figuratively illustrated by the metaphor of the invisible hand'. In that regard one would expect this metaphor to appear in chapter 7 of book 1 of the *Wealth of Nations*, 'Of the natural and market price of commodities'. But here one looks in vain for a description of the invisible hand. The sole reference to it is in chapter 2 of book 4, 'Of the restraints upon the importation from foreign countries of such goods as can be produced at home'. The topic of this book is not the process of resource allocation, but the 'systems of political economy'. It discusses and compares the mercantile and agricultural systems in order to establish the superiority of the system of natural liberty. This theme and the manner in which it is pursued suggests that the metaphor of the invisible hand and consequently Smith's second conception of economic equilibrium is based on a different paradigm than his analysis of the price mechanism. Above I argued that the analogy of the machine determined Smith's ideas about the working of markets. However, changes in historical time are impossible to describe in terms of a mechanistic metaphor and it is for that reason that Smith's theory of economic growth relies on a different natural metaphor, that of nature and hence equilibrium as a process.

Under the pressure of competition producers and suppliers bring about a cost-efficient allocation of scarce resources and push the economy towards maximum rates of economic growth. This is the classic argument in favour of a system of free competition and it is often argued that Smith was the first to systematically explore this economic rationale of a free market society. For instance, Hollander (1987) considers the historical parts of the *Wealth of Nations* a 'digression' from its main theme, the analysis of the competitive capitalist exchange system. This analysis is said to stand on its feet 'independently of the Scottish procedures and the broad overview of progress and the origins of institutions . . . Smith based his reform programme on a model of development involving principles of allocation theory in a dynamic context – a perfect example of a hypothetico-deductive system crying out for mathematical formulation' (Hollander 1987, 312). This view is rejected by Brown (1994) who argues that the importance of Smith's mechanistic model of competitive equilibrium is grossly overstated. According to her, Smith's analysis of the dynamics of economic development had nothing to do with his theory of the market mechanism. Instead, it was based on a theory about the superiority of investment opportunities in the different stages of economic development. In contrast to the mechanistic theory of market exchange, this theory takes account of the changing historical circumstances of society and can be considered an example of conjectural history in the tradition of the Scottish Historical School.[47]

The conjecture defended by Smith was an ideal path of economic development against which actual British and European progress could be measured. A comparison of this kind could be used to demonstrate the adverse affects on economic development of interventionist government policies and archaic institutions like the British university system or the Christian church. In this manner the optimum pattern provided a benchmark to isolate policies and institutions that had a favourable effect on growth and formed the basis of Smith's reform program.

To make a comparison between different paths of economic development a standard of comparison is required. In the language of natural law philosophy this standard was the 'happiness of mankind'. But in Smith's economics the standard of human well-being takes on a specific economic meaning. In the *Wealth of Nations* economic well-being is measured in terms of money. It is the sum of the yearly revenues of the three income groups, labourers, capitalists and landowners. Their rewards, respectively wages, profits and rents, are the constituent parts of price. They are the 'three original sources of all revenue as well as of all exchangeable value. All other revenue is ultimately derived from some one or other of these' (Smith 1937, 52). This means that the annual product of a country can be decomposed into the three income categories of wages, profits and rents. It is identical to the annual revenue taken as the sum of all wages, profits and rents.[48] Throughout the *Wealth of Nations* the terms 'annual produce', 'exchangeable value of the annual produce' and 'annual revenue' are used synonymously to refer to the wealth of a nation. Put differently, economic welfare in terms of money provided a benchmark against which the progress of a country's development could be assessed (Brown 1994, 169).

Smith's analysis of the 'natural progress of opulence' in book three of the *Wealth of Nations* is based on a hierarchy of sectoral activities. From a macroeconomic point of view, the opportunity costs of a particular investment can be evaluated in terms of the annual product. This allows different investments to be ranked according to their contribution to the annual revenue of society. On the basis of this criterion Smith ranked investment in agriculture first because it contributes to all three forms of revenue, wages, rents and profits.[49] Manufacturing is placed second. It generates wages and profits but not rents because it lacks the helping hand of nature.[50] In third place is wholesaling, which produces mainly profits and a small amount of wages derived from transporting the goods.[51] Last in the line of investment priorities is retailing because it contributes to profits only.

This hierarchy of investment opportunities sets out the best order of historical development for any country. In the words of Smith (1937, 360):

> According to the natural course of things, therefore, the greater part of the capital of every growing society is, first, directed to agriculture, afterwards to manufactures, and last of all to foreign commerce. This order of things is so very natural, that in every society that had any territory, it has always, I believe, been in some degree observed. Some of their lands must have been cultivated before any considerable towns could be established, and some sort of coarse industry of the manufacturing kind must have been carried on in those towns, before they could well think of employing themselves in foreign commerce.

Thus the order of a country's historical development that will generate the greatest annual revenue is one where capital is first directed to agriculture, then to manufactures, and then to the wholesaling and retailing trades (Brown 1994, 174).[52]

This quotation clearly shows the connection between Smith's treatment of economic development and his historical analysis. In the first place, there is the link with his account of the stadial development of society through the four stages of hunting, pasturage, agriculture and commerce. The development of towns is said to depend on the availability of agriculture, a clear example of the mutual dependence between the mode of subsistence and the changing social structure. Secondly, the rules of economic development are portrayed as historical laws in the sense that they are founded upon the past experience of growing nations. Smith mentions the American colonies. Their rapid progress is attributed to the fact that 'almost their whole capitals have hitherto been employed in agriculture' (ibid., 347). Further examples are ancient nations like China, Egypt and Indostan. 'Even those three countries, the wealthiest that ever were in the world, are chiefly renowned for their superiority in agriculture and manufactures. They do not appear to have been eminent for foreign trade' (ibid., 348). But the laws of history are also forward-looking (this is the conjecture involved) and thus all nations now, or in the future, must follow this pattern of investment. The abundance of fertile grounds will assure that in the early stages of development investment in agriculture is the most lucrative business. Driven by the 'natural inclination' for economic gain, mankind thus adopts the investment strategy that is set out by nature to generate maximum economic growth.

That in reality most nations fail to comply to this ideal strategy is a different matter. Books three and four of the *Wealth of Nations* are devoted to the question of why the 'police' of Europe favoured foreign trade and the commerce of the town instead of agriculture and the economy of the countryside. As a consequence of this policy, growth was retarded in most European countries and reached a level well below the rate that could have been achieved under the optimal scheme set out above. The culprits were the mercantile and agricultural systems of political economy. The mercantile system wrongly favoured investment in manufactures for exportation and tried to achieve this goal by repressing the prices of agricultural products, thus discouraging investment in this sector. The fault of the agricultural system was that it focused exclusively on agriculture. This led to overinvestment in this sector, to the neglect of manufactures and foreign trade. As a result, it likewise upset the optimum pattern of investment and economic development. The best policy was to refrain from intervention and let the 'natural progress of opulence' take her course. Competition and free market entry would ensure that people take up investment opportunities in the correct order of agriculture, manufactures, wholesaling and retailing trade which would result in the largest annual revenue. Thus Smith combined historical analysis with the insights from his theory of investment priorities to demonstrate the superiority of the system of natural liberty over alternative systems of political economy.

Brown (1994) uses this result to argue that the model of competitive equilibrium plays no part whatsoever in Smith's defence of a free market society. This inference can be criticized, for instance on the grounds that investors respond to differences in relative prices, which makes the process of resource allocation instrumental to the realization of the optimum intertemporal pattern of investment (Hollander 1987, 171). But this issue will not detain us here. Smith's examination of the natural progress of opulence in terms of a hierarchy of capitals suffices to show that his defense of the system of natural liberty is multifaceted. The mechanistic model of competitive equilibrium plays a part in this argument, because it explains why scarce productive resources move between industries in response to profit differentials and establish an efficient allocation of resources over alternative uses. This maximizes the long run earnings of the three productive groups, labourers, capitalists and landowners, which implies that the annual revenue is maximized as well.

The theory of the hierarchy of capitals at least establishes that an alternative explanation of the superiority of a free market system is available. This explanation does not run in terms of a mechanical analogy, but adopts a different metaphor. This metaphor has a biological connotation and sees nature as a process. That this metaphor affected Smith's notion of economic equilibrium is shown by the fact that in the *Wealth of Nations* the term 'natural balance' does not appear in the context of market balance, but refers to the sectoral balance of industry.[53] The equilibrium suggested by this balance is that of an optimal pattern of changes as society goes through its stages of development. The forces that control this historical development are uniform and endogenous to the process, as was shown above. But the uniformity of causes does not imply that all nations follow the same pattern of development. The steps of this process may be similar, but the timing and manifestation of the different stages are not. Unlike the mechanistic explanation of growth, the process approach takes account of historical contingencies that affect the trajectory of development.

The traces of this approach are clearly discernable in Smith's growth theory. This theory has parameters which depend on sociological, legal and institutional factors.[54] These factors exerted their influence through either the rate of capital accumulation or the rate of population growth.[55] The relative ratio of these rates would determine whether a country would be advancing, stationary or declining. Ricardo later reformulated this theory in a deterministic manner, which foresaw the end of growth in a stationary state. But this mechanistic interpretation of growth was anathema to Smith who saw the process of economic development as a secular trend. According to Smith, the growth process of different nations was controlled by the same type of forces, but these forces did not have uniform effects. What these forces did achieve, however, was to demonstrate the non-chaotic nature of the process of economic development. Societies could be advancing, stationary or declining, but as long as they adhered to the system of natural liberty, the process of capitalist reproduction would proceed in a relative orderly fashion.

CONCLUSION

Adam Smith was a man of many talents. In line with the humanist tradition of the Enlightenment he studied the topics of classical learning, cosmology, natural theology, moral philosophy, rhetoric and logic. His scientific interests brought him to write on what would now be called the philosophy of science. He followed recent developments in physics, was well acquainted with the economic and political history of Europe, delivered lectures on jurisprudence and, lest one forget it, wrote a treatise on economics. It is therefore not surprising that his work has many faces.

A few of these viewpoints have been studied in this chapter. A key feature of his scientific outlook was his love of system. This outlook may have been inspired by his religious beliefs or his admiration for Newton's physics, but whatever its source it led him to construct natural science as a theory of equilibrium. In the planetary system this equilibrium pointed to the regular pattern of movements of the planets controlled by the force of gravitation. In the field of social studies he isolated equilibrating forces with similar effects. Thus his theory of moral sentiments assumes a balance of the passions governed by the central force of sympathy. His economics, likewise, contains a gravitating force in the shape of people's self-interest, facilitating a process of competition which explains why market prices always tend towards an equilibrium with natural prices. These theories are all instances of Smith's conception of natural science which revolved around the analogy of nature as a machine.

In physics the adoption of this analogy was relatively harmless. In the physical world efficient and final causes are easily separated because of the possibility to empirically verify the effects of specific causes. Concerning the working of the mind, such checks are impossible, and consequently the application of physical analogies is not without danger. Smith's moral theory shows how easily teleological reasoning affects the content of theories. Smith was not able to explain social subordination in terms of his moral theory. As a result, he ascribed the distinction of ranks to people's natural propensity to admire the rich and noble (in the sense of aristocratic). Similarly, Smith's natural outlook imputes meaning onto the equilibrium of economic forces. The meaning implicit in the equality of supply and demand is that people refrain from hurting each other and maintain social order. In this manner price equilibrium satisfies a standard of fairness and can be considered 'just' from a moral point of view.

But nature takes on many guises and Smith did not confine himself to a single natural metaphor. The second metaphor that plays a part in his economics is that of nature as a process. In contrast to the mechanistic explanation of market equilibrium, the process approach fostered a conception of equilibrium which allowed change in a historical sense. The nature of this equilibrium was endogenous and explained the optimum pattern of economic development through the different stages of history. Unlike the mechanical balance of forces, this equilibrium was not necessarily stable. Two of the five books of the *Wealth of Nations* are devoted to the question why the nations of Europe failed to comply to the natural progress of opulence and were forced into an 'unnatural and retrograde order' (Smith 1937, 360).[56]

Often the reason of these disturbances was the adoption of interventionist policies which dictated the mercantile and agricultural systems of political economy. Smith's historical analysis demonstrated that a free market society was the best guarantee against instabilities of this kind. But Ricardo and his followers removed historical explanations in the tradition of the Scottish Historical School from the domain of political economy and seemed to have focussed on a more mechanical adjustment of economic forces in the short and in the long run. Whether this is true or not is discussed in the next chapter.

NOTES

1. Mirowski (1982) attributes Smith's fame as the founding father of economics to the fact that he approached economics as a natural science. '[I]t seems that the predominant value of our science is this faith in the "natural" mechanism of the market and the "natural progress" in the economic affairs of the race. It is this "vision" of Smith that . . . places him in the hallowed position he occupies in the history of economic thought' (Mirowski 1982, 198). In similar vein, see Viner (1927, 306).
2. This argument follows the lead of Macfie (1971) who says that 'Smith's central endeavour throughout all his writings was indeed to explore and build into his system of thought the inclusive scope and manifold interrelations of this system of Nature'. But the way in which this was done resulted in very different conceptions of for example the Invisible Hand metaphor.
3. See Fitzgibbons (1995, 33). 'The Stoics had believed that God as Nature had conceived of a regularity of structure and form and that God as Providence provided for the well-being, not necessarily of every individual, but of the human race.'
4. For a detailed study of the history of natural theology in Greek philosophy, see Gerson (1990). The classic study of the idea that nature has purpose and is the creation of a divine being is Lovejoy (1936).
5. Later it will be argued that conjectural history is the third pillar of Smith's science.
6. Note that Smith approached this subject as a scientific issue. The matter of his own religious convictions is likewise unresolved. On Smith's own religion, see Campbell (1971), Lindgren (1973) and more recently Pack (1995) and Evensky (1998).
7. Smith seems to have adopted Hume's idea that causality refers to a constant conjunction of events, as can be inferred from the following passage. 'When two objects, however unlike, have often been observed to follow each other, and have consequently presented themselves to the sense in that order, they come to be so connected in the fancy, that the idea of the one seems, of its own accord, to call up and introduce that of the other' (Smith 1795a[1980], 40).

8. In the words of Smith: 'In the Wonders of nature, however, it rarely happens that we can discover so clearly this connecting chain. With regard to a few even of them, indeed, we seem to have been really admitted behind the scenes' (ibid., 43).
9. Smith writes that 'no system [of astronomy, BT], how well soever in other respects supported, has ever been able to gain any credit on the world, whose connecting principles were not such as were familiar to all mankind' (ibid., 46). This leads Lindgren (1973) to argue that Smith's standards of scientific judgement are conventionalist because acceptance of a theory depends on the values of a specific community. On Smith's familiarity principle, see also Campbell (1971).
10. Ptolemy's epicycles simply begged the question of the connection between them. Thus his system could not account for the movement of the solar system as a whole. 'The system of Copernicus afforded this easily, and like a more simple machine, without the assistance of Epicycles, connected together, by fewer movements, the complex appearances of the heavens' (ibid., 73).
11. Hence Newton's fourth 'rule of reasoning in philosophy': 'In experimental philosophy we are to look upon propositions inferred by general induction from phenomena as accurately or very nearly true' (quoted in Redman 1993, 213).
12. See Campbell (1971, 40–41). 'For Smith a new theory is explanatory only if it is based on an analogy with a familiar mechanism . . . [A] theory which is to be acceptable to the imagination must suggest a simple hypothesis of a type which is *familiar*; the invisible chains which it uses to bind events together must be of a sort which have common visible counterparts. In practice this is a demand that all scientific theories must suggest some mechanical analogy, an invisible *machine* behind the scenes whose workings result in the motions of visible objects' (italics in the original).
13. 'For Smith a proposition is more likely to be valid if it exhibits beauty' (Oswald 1995, 458). On this aesthetic standard, see also Thomson (1965).
14. Indeed 'people are induced to promote social welfare by the pursuit of objects of illusory pleasure' (Davis 1990, 347). To a certain extent they are 'misled' by the invisible hand. On this element of deception of the invisible hand, see also Macfie (1959) and (1961).
15. In similar vein, see Thomson (1965, 226) and Skinner (1972, 471).
16. For example, see Macfie (1961, 307). 'If one reads the *Moral Sentiments* alone, surprise may be felt that Smith puts such weight on this "beauty of the well-contrived machine", yet states it merely dogmatically. He never demonstrates this "derivation"'.
17. 'Our continual observation upon the conduct of others, insensibly lead us to form to ourselves certain general rules concerning what is fit and proper either to be done or to be avoided . . . It is thus that the general rules of morality are formed. They are ultimately founded upon experience of what in particular instances our moral faculties, our natural sense of merit and propriety, approve or disapprove of' (Smith [1759]1980, 159).
18. See also Kleer (1995, 283). 'It is the pleasure of mutual sympathy which attracts all persons to the performance of "moral" acts (that is acts of which others will approve) and the pain of absent sympathy which repels them from "immoral" actions'.

19. Indeed, the pleasure and pain caused by the presence and absence of sympathy respectively can be said to constitute metaphors for social pressure. 'Social pressures set the standards by which each person judges and then adjusts his own feelings. Society is a psychological mirror in which we discern the propriety or impropriety of our own passions' (Myers 1976, 563).
20. On Smith's moral equilibrium, see Anspach (1972, 181), Myers (1976, 561–563), Evensky (1987, 451–452) and Heath (1995, 466).
21. In the words of Smith, the sentiments will have 'such a correspondence with one another, as is sufficient for the harmony of society' (Smith [1759]1980, 22).
22. Myers (1983) gives an extensive review of these theories. He distinguishes two kinds of explanations of the balance between the passions. First, there is a class of theories which attributes a natural balance to the mind. Second, self-interest is seen as the moral equivalent of the force of gravity in nature. In both cases, god or the architect of nature can be considered the final cause of this moral equilibrium. Myers argues that the unique contribution of Smith was that he was able to remove final causes from the picture. His explanation of the classic problem of self-interest and public welfare ran in terms of efficient causes, like the division of labour. The discussion in the present section suggests that this conclusion is not valid for Smith's moral theory, which belongs to the second class mentioned by Myers. See also Myers (1972).
23. 'The general maxims of morality are formed, like all other general maxims, from experience and induction. We observe in a great variety of particular cases what pleases or displeases our moral faculties, what these approve or disapprove of, and by induction from this experience, we establish those general rules' (Smith [1759]1980, 319).
24. For similar views, see Campbell (1971) and Lindgren (1973).
25. This view is supported by the reports that Smith was 'shocked' by the events of the French revolution in 1789 (Raphael and Macfie 1976, 19).
26. The instinctive nature of this belief is clearly expressed by Smith in the following passage. 'When we thus despair of finding any force upon earth which can check the triumph of injustice, we naturally appeal to heaven, and hope that the great Author of our nature will himself execute hereafter, what all the principle which he has given us for the direction of our conduct, prompt us to attempt even here' (Smith [1759]1980, 169).
27. 'When the price of any commodity is neither more nor less than what is sufficient to pay the rent of the land, the wages of the labour, and the profits of the stock employed in raising, preparing, and bringing it to the market, according to their natural rates, the commodity is then sold for what may be called its natural price' (Smith 1937, 55).
28. 'The market price of every particular commodity is regulated by the proportion between the quantity which is actually brought to market and the demand of those who are willing to pay the natural price of the commodity' (ibid., 56).
29. This description of the idea of spontaneous order was first introduced by Adam Ferguson, contemporary of Smith and fellow-Scotsman. See Hayek (1967b).
30. Smith never mentioned the principle of sympathy in the *Wealth of Nations*, but there are indications that he applied this principle to economic problems. For example, in Smith's

Lectures on Jurisprudence the principle of sympathy is used to explain why people respect property rights and trade goods rather than rob each other. For a more detailed discussion, see Young (1986).

31. Fitzgibbons (1995) stresses the fact that in the *Wealth of Nations* Smith hardly used the term 'self interest', but mostly speaks about 'selflove'. See also Nieli (1986).

32. Heilbroner (1982) speaks of the 'socialization' of the individual. The idea is that commerce has a 'civilizing' influence on people. In the primitive stages of society, trade is virtually impossible because people do not respect property rights and in general lack the trust that is required to drive trade with strangers. But as people experience the benefits of trade and the division of labour it facilitates, they learn to respect the laws of justice and the reigning political order; that is they develop the moral qualities necessary to make a commercial society work. See also Young (1986).

33. In this respect, 'natural' can literally mean that motives are implanted by nature in man. For example, about people's natural propensity to better their condition Smith says that it 'comes with us from the womb, and never leaves us till we go into the grave' (Smith 1937, 324).

34. Some of these bonds are personal checks that may not work in a free market society. Macfie (1967) mentions friendship, neighbourliness, patriotism, public opinion and individual conscience. Macfie discusses the interesting thesis that Smith believed that free trade policy would be inadequate because he feared that the threat of competition would be insufficient to replace the loss of personal ethical controls on human selfishness. For that reason, he built in a final check, the invisible hand, as an extra safeguard to control the unwanted side-effects of people's selflove. In that regard, the invisible hand is not a metaphor for competition, as is often maintained, but must be considered a complement of competition, a means to assure that social order will be maintained, even in those cases where competition fails to constrain people's desire for economic gain.

35. Of the four cardinal virtues, self-command, benevolence, justice and prudence, the latter two can be said to operate in the economic sphere. Justice is of importance to economic activities because it provides a set of rules that aim to constrain people's self interest. Prudence, on the other hand, motivates people to improve their position, not just in terms of fortune, but also in terms of health, rank and reputation. Brown (1994) classifies justice and prudence as virtues of the second order because they do not involve moral decision-making. In matters of justice compulsion is provided by the law itself and there is no need for moral imperatives, while prudence only commands 'cold esteem' and is not particularly valued for its moral quality (Brown 1994, 49–52). For that reason, Brown contends that there is no place for moral discourse in the *Wealth of Nations*. She calls Smith's economics essentially amoral (ibid., 46). I support Kleer (1993) who rejected this conclusion and argued that Brown exaggerates her argument. Justice and prudence may command a lower moral esteem than the benevolent passions, but that does not mean that they fall outside the scope of Smith's moral scale. They are still moral sentiments, albeit of a lower intensity than the benevolent passions.

36. For a similar conclusion, see Young (1986, 375), Clark (1992, 69), Fitzgibbons (1995, 176) and Oswald (1995, 463).
37. The 'Adam Smith problem' was first raised by Oncken (1897). He asked whether Smith's two great works are consistent in the sense that they can be considered as parts of a larger, encompassing theoretical framework. The alternative is to view them as independent works which may even, at points, contradict each other. Fitzgibbons (1995) is a strong supporter of the former view and gives a comprehensive review of Smith's system of politics, economics and moral theory. Brown (1994) rejects this view and stresses the differences between Smith's moral and economic discourses. For other contributions to this debate, see Viner (1927), Morrow (1927), Macfie (1959), Skinner (1970), Anspach (1972), Nieli (1986), Young (1986), Evensky (1987) and (1998), Pack (1995) and Oswald (1995).
38. Members of this group were Adam Ferguson, Henry Home (Lord Kames), William Robertson, John Millar and Dugald Stewart, while David Hume may be considered a forerunner. See Skinner (1965) and Meek (1967a).
39. Indeed, the Scottish Enlightenment also fostered the 'father' of social theory, Adam Ferguson. See Verburg (1991).
40. For a textual analysis of Smith's different voices, see Brown (1994). She argues that Smith's moral work is written in a dialogic form characterized by multivocity. This literary style is particularly suited for moral discourses dealing with issues regarding people's conscience. Smith's economic work, on the other hand, adopts the monologic form, where a single unitary voice of authority or tradition is at work. Brown claims that the theoretical core of Smith's economics was not the equilibrative mechanism of competitive markets. According to her, the focus of the *Wealth of Nations* is a theory which aims to explain the process of economic growth and takes account of the changing historical circumstances of society (Brown 1994, 167 and 170).
41. On the role of this type of explanation in economics, see Nozick (1994).
42. From this point of view, it is wrong to identify the invisible hand with the market order. Petsoulas (2001) argues that Smith applied the metaphor of the invisble hand to *all* stages of history, not just to the stage of commercial society, which is commonly associated with the invisible hand.
43. Smith wrote that 'Till there be property there can be no government, the very end of which is to secure wealth and to defend the rich from the poor' (Smith 1759, 20). See also Smith (1937, 674).
44. The endogenous nature of government and social subordination is underlined in the following statement. 'But as the necessity of civil government gradually grows with the acquisition of valuable property, so the principal causes which naturally introduce subordination gradually grow up with the growth of that valuable property' (Smith 1937, 670).
45. 'The first period of society, that of hunters, admits of no such inequality [of fortune, BT]. Universal poverty establishes there universal equality, and the superiority, either of age or

of personal qualities, are the feeble, but the sole foundations of authority and subordination' (ibid., 672).

46. In sum, Smith distinguished four causes of social subordination; superiority of personal qualifications, age, fortune and birth. Of these, birth and fortune are considered the most powerful causes of subordination. 'They are the two great sources of personal distinction and are therefore the principal causes which naturally establish authority and subordination among men' (ibid., 673). Personal qualifications like strength and wisdom are deemed a feeble source of social distinction on the ground that they are 'invisible qualities; always disputable and generally disputed' (ibid., 671). Age is a stronger foundation of social distinction because it is 'a plain and palpable quality which admits of no dispute' (ibid.).

47. In turn, Brown can be accused of exaggeration. She denies that the importance of the distinction between market and natural prices lies in the model of resource allocation (Brown 1994, 170). Partly, this is true because differences in the natural rates of rents, wages and profits are used by Smith to discuss the economic dynamics of advancing, stagnating and declining nations (chapters eight through eleven of book one). But market and natural prices are also used to explain why economic agents shift resources from one industry to another in response to changes in the market rates of rent, wages and profits. Clearly, the mechanics of these equilibrium adjustments involve the issue of resource allocation. In defence of Brown, it must be observed that there is a certain ambiguity in Smith's ideas about price formation. Schumpeter (1954, 557–58) points out that the chapter on market and natural prices seems to suggest a factor productivity theory of distribution. However, this line is lost in chapter six of book one which discusses the component parts of price. Here it is argued that labour is the sole productive factor, while the revenues of land and capital are deductions from the total product that is in its entirety the product of labour.

48. 'The whole annual produce of the land and labour of every country, or what comes to the same thing, the whole price of that annual produce, naturally divides itself . . . into three parts; the rent of land, the wages of labour, and the profits of stock; and constitutes a revenue to three different order of people; to those who live by rent, to those who live by wages, and to those who live by profit' (Smith 1937, 248).

49. 'The labourers and labouring cattle, therefore, employed in agriculture, not only occassion, like the workmen in manufactures, the reproduction of a value equal to their own consumption, or to the capital which employs them, together with its owners profits; but of a much greater value. Over and above the capital of the farmer and all its profits, they regularly occassion, the reproduction of the rent of the landlord' (Smith 1937, 344).

50. According to Smith, rent is the 'work of nature which remains after deducting or compensating everything which can be regarded the work of man'. As a consequence, investment in manufactures reproduces less capital than agriculture. 'No equal quantity of productive labour employed in manufactures can ever occassion so great a reproduction [as in agriculture, BT]. In them nature does nothing; man does all' (ibid., 345).

51. Wholesale trade is further subdivided in three different activities; the home trade, the foreign trade of consumption and the carrying trade (ibid., 348). Of these activities the home trade is ranked first on the grounds that its rate of turnover is much higher than capital employed in the foreign trade. Note that this argument of the advantage of quick returns is not applied to the ranking order of investment opportunities set out bove. As Cannan argues, it might have made 'havoc' of the argument as to the superiority of agriculture (in Smith 1937, 349n6).
52. Since such arguments lead to the conclusion that growth progresses at a rate which is neither uniform over time nor uniform across sectors of the economy, Reid (1987) describes Smith's theory of accumulation as a disequilibrium model. In his mathematical reconstruction, disequilibrium may be an adequate term, depending on how one defines equilibrium, but given that Smith never used a mathematical model and focussed on a historical study of growth, I prefer the term 'process approach' to explain the nature of this theory.
53. 'The monopoly of the colony trade besides, by forcing towards it a much greater proportion of the capital of Great Britain than that would naturally have gone to it, seems to have broken altogether that natural balance which would otherwise have taken place among all different branches of British industry' (Smith 1937, 570).
54. Smith's growth theory will be discussed in more detail in the next chapter.
55. For an example, see Smith (1937, 70–74).
56. Recall that according to Smith the optimum path of economic development started with agricultural investment. Yet towards the end of book two he observed that in most nations of Europe agriculture was still underdeveloped which suggested a suboptimal pattern of development. He then concluded the book with the remark that '[w]hat circumstances in the policy of Europe have given the trades which are carried on in towns so great an advantage over that which is carried on in the country, that private persons frequently find it more for their advantage to employ their capitals in the most distant carrying trades of Asia and America, than in the improvement and cultivation of the most fertile fields in their own neighbourhood, I shall endeavour to explain at full length in the two following books' (Smith 1937, 355).

7. Statics and Dynamics in Classical Economics

INTRODUCTION

There is an uneasy tension between equilibrium analysis and the concept of time in economics. On the one hand, equilibrium theories are the economist's main tool to distinguish between economic effects of different duration. This is done by means of the familiar method of comparative statics, which assumes that supply and demand constantly work to bring markets closer to equilibrium. As causal factors can be assumed to affect market equilibrium over different time periods, the distinction between equilibrium of different duration (for example short term versus long term) allows one to isolate and analyze the causal forces of the time period in question. But, on the other hand, the theory that is used to deal with the element of time in this manner is timeless. How long does it take to establish equilibrium in the transition phase between the old and the new position? Supply and demand analysis usually does not address this question, but simply assumes that market equilibrium re-emerges after a disruption. This recognition brings Diamond (1994, 7) to argue that neoclassical equilibrium theory is not about equilibrium at all, but about the working of forces.

The roots of the static conception of market equilibrium are said to lie in the work of Adam Smith and his classical successors. For instance, Hollander (1987) argues that Smith's discussion of natural and market prices contains an 'embryonic' account of neoclassical general equilibrium theory, involving such concepts as supply and demand schedules and the concept of the margin. Smith's theory can therefore not have focussed on the process of market adjustment, as trading at non-equilibrium prices is precluded (Hollander 1987, 68). In a similar sense, Ricardo's treatment of economic development is restated in terms of long-run equilibrium growth theories that fail to explain changes out of equilibrium. As Blaug (1985, 143) puts it: 'At one time, Ricardo was regarded as the virtual inventor of the method of comparative statics and certainly the prime example of the age-old tendency of economists to emphasize long-run equilibrium values at the expense of any consideration of short-run, disequilibrium adjustments.'

The previous chapter showed that Smith attributed different meanings to the nature of causes in the social sphere. On the one hand, he saw nature as a mechanism, which would point to a static interpretation of his market theory in line with Hollander (1987). However, it was argued that his science of history was based on a different conception of nature, that of an ongoing process of changes, and this approach is often taken as a lead to stress the dynamic nature of Smith's economic work. Meek (1973, 255) called the orientation of Smith's value analysis 'dynamic rather than static' on the grounds that it leaves scope for the influence of physical, social and institutional factors. Walsh and Gram (1980) and Groenewegen (1987) placed him in the tradition of 'surplus' theories of value. In contrast to neoclassical marginal analysis, which explains market prices in terms of given schedules of supply and demand, this tradition focusses on the accumulation and allocation of surplus output. As time plays a crucial role in this analysis – will the corn produced this year be enough to provide the necessary inputs for next year's production? – it may be called 'dynamic' in comparison to neoclassical marginal analysis which takes the production process as a given and concentrates on the 'static' problem of the allocation of given resources among alternative uses.

The statics-dynamics controversy also plagued classical macroeconomics. Say's introduction of the 'law of markets' in 1803 provoked severe criticism from the so-called 'glut theorists' (Spence, Lauderdale, Chalmers, Malthus and Simonde de Sismondi) who believed that an aggregate excess supply, causing a stagnation of production, was a real possibility. Ricardo, Say, James Mill and other members of the Ricardian school rejected this conclusion on the grounds that price adjustments would be quick enough to always maintain equilibrium between aggregate supply and demand. As a result, growth would never stagnate from a lack of demand.

Some see this controversy as a failure to appreciate the difference between static and dynamic analysis. As Ricardo once wrote to Malthus (letter of 24 January 1817 in Ricardo 1951–1955, VII: 120):

> It appears to me that one great cause of our difference in opinion, on the subjects which we have so often discussed, is that you have always in your mind the immediate and temporary effects of particular changes – whereas I put these immediate and temporary effects quite aside, and fix my whole attention on the permanent state of things which will result from them.

This would suggest that Ricardo used Say's law in a framework of comparative static analysis. However, Sowell (1972a) denied that the glut controversy revolved around the long-term growth feature of Say's law. He maintained that the cause of the controversy was Ricardo's failure to understand the particular type of dynamic analysis which was used by Malthus and Simonde de Sismondi to attack Say's law. This analysis was based on a theory of equilibrium aggregate income, which explicitly draws attention to the role of time in the circular flow between expenditures and incomes.

This chapter aims to unravel some of the confusion surrounding the role of statics and dynamics in classical economics. It will be argued that a clarification of this role will aid our understanding of the problematic relationship between time and equilibrium analysis. More in particular, it will be shown that:

- Classical analysis as developed by Smith, Ricardo and J.S. Mill was based on a particular static method, investigating the nature of market change as an evolutionary process. Table 2.1 in Chapter 2 classified this method as static, because it does not explicate the temporal process. But it is clear that equilibrium in this approach is seen as a process, because of all the variables under scrutiny are undergoing constant change. Familiar examples are Smith's definition of natural prices as a point of gravitation and the use of the mythical stationary state as the stopping point of economic growth in the works of the Ricardians. The point is that the classical economists failed to specify the time required to bring about this equilibrium. That is why it belongs to the category of the static methods, even though it has an evolutionary process as its main object of investigation;
- This particular approach of the classical economists proved a source of confusion, when questions emerged which required a more explicit account of the temporal aspects of economic changes. I shall argue that this happened in the general glut debate, which revolved around Say's law of markets. For the Ricardians, the issue at stake was simple: nothing could stop the process of growth before the arrival of the stationary state, and this conclusion applied with special force to a general glut of markets. But as they had no idea how long it would take for this day to finally arrive, a highly confusing debate emerged with the defenders of the glut thesis. In particular, Malthus and Simonde de Sismondi, belonging to the latter camp, developed a kind of period analysis showing that a difference between aggregate supply and demand could persist and stagnate production for a while. In terms of Table 2.1, this approach classifies as a dynamic method, albeit it one handling equilibrium as an end-state. Therefore, the glut controversy involved a classical example of economists talking at cross purposes, because they failed to appreciate the differences between their static and dynamic methods.

These lessons are explicated as follows. First I will explain what I mean when I typify the classical approach as a static method, using J.S. Mill's definition of the statics and dynamics distinction. Next I focus on the process interpretation of equilibrium, underlying the price theory of classical economics. The final subject of this chapter is the glut controversy and the different viewpoints on statics and dynamics it involves.

THE ELUSIVE MEANING OF STATICS AND DYNAMICS

My classification of the method of classical economics as being static seems to involve a contradiction. How can a static method involve the explanation of equilibrium seen as a process? The term process evokes images of something typically dynamic, so why call the method investigating this process static? I have explained the reasons for doing so earlier, in Chapter 2. The characteristic of a static method is that it fails to include the leads and lags of economic changes in its explanatory framework. A method of this kind nonetheless can be used to causally investigate processes of a dynamic nature with the restriction that the temporal relationship between causes and effects remains unknown. In this section, I intend to show that this is exactly how the classical economists belonging to the Ricardian school approached their science. I shall support my claim by studying the method of J.S. Mill, who was the first of the classicals to give an explicit definition of the statics and dynamics distinction. This definition is highly interesting as a benchmark of the approach *not* taken by Mill. In spite of what he claimed to offer, the dynamic theories of Mill do not adopt a temporal framework, but implicitly assume that their subject matter evolves over time. They are a fine example of a static approach to causal analyses and we can prove this point by using Mill's own definition of the statics and dynamics distinction.

J.S. Mill introduced 'equilibrium theory' as a dividing line between statics and dynamics. He adopted these, what he called 'mathematical' terms, to divide the subject of his classic text, the *Principles of Political Economy* (first published 1848), into two parts. The statics of political economy are discussed in the first three books of his treatise. The final two books comprise the dynamic part, 'thereby adding a theory of motion to our theory of equilibrium – the Dynamics of political economy to the Statics' (Mill 1909, 695).

The distinction of these terms was intended to clarify the role of time in economic analysis. The domain of statics was restricted to those economic events which did not need consideration of changes through time. Mill's theory of equilibrium is said to deal with 'the economical laws of a stationary and unchanging society'. This involved analysis of the 'economical phenomena of society, considered as existing simultaneously'. Mill's dynamics, on the other hand, saw 'the economical condition of mankind as liable to change'. It was in a literal sense a theory of motion and aimed to establish the laws that govern these changes and their 'ultimate tendencies'. (ibid.). Note, however, that Mill's definition of static analysis was not intended to dispense with the element of time altogether. It merely gave time a different and less important role. In equilibrium, economic variables would remain unchanged which implied that motion through time could be ignored. In this situation, magnitudes could be treated as if they existed at the same point in time.

This description suggests that Mill defined his dynamics as a form of period analysis. Recall from Table 2.1 that this method takes account of the leads and lags between economic variables at different points in time and describes how they are causally connected. Moreover, according to Mill, this method should be considered unrelated to equilibrium theory, which is seen as the principal theory of static analysis.

This impression is confirmed by his discussion of the difference between statics and dynamics as empirical laws in his *System of Logic* (1844). Here he stated that 'some are uniformities of co-existence, some of succession. According as the science is occupied in ascertaining and verifying the former sort of uniformities or the latter, M. Comte gives it the title of Social Statics, or of Social Dynamics; conformably to the distinction in mechanics between the conditions of equilibrium and movement' (Mill 1974, 917). The reference to Auguste Comte, the French positivist philosopher, suggests that Mill borrowed the distinction from him. Comte had seen the nature of the temporal sequences studied as the fundamental difference between statics and dynamics. He defined statics as the method of studying the relationships between phenomena existing at the same point in time. His dynamics concerned analysis of the leads and lags existing between events at different points in time (Comte 1975, 230).[1] Note that this distinction corresponds to the definitions of statics and dynamics used in Table 2.1.

However, Mill's economics did not practice what his methodology preached. His examination of the progress of society in the *Principles* did not constitute dynamic analysis as defined above. Indeed, as W.J. Ashley notes in his introduction to Mill (1909), in the *Principles* the distinction between statics and dynamics becomes something very different from what Comte had intended (ibid., xx). Likewise, Schumpeter (1954, 563) points to the fact that Mill did not carry through his definition of statics and dynamics. Instead of addressing the temporal leads and lags of economic changes, his dynamics constitutes a static method which assumes that equilibrium is a centre of gravitation. He stressed that market prices fluctuate around a natural level, as 'demand and supply always rush to an equilibrium' (Mill 1909, 456) and compared the economy to the sea which 'everywhere tends to a level; but it never is at an exact level' (ibid., 453). About the stationary state he said that it was impossible to ultimately avoid it; 'that we are always on the verge of it, and that if we have not reached it long ago, it is because the goal itself flies before us'. Put differently, for Mill the principal meaning of equilibrium was not that of an end-state, as the economy never actually reaches this state, but that of a process. This is clearly shown by the fact that he approached the study of economic dynamics as an investigation of economic change in terms of tendencies.

The classical economists spoke of 'tendencies' instead of 'forces' because they realized that the mutual interaction of forces obfuscates the causal relationship between specific forces and their effects. This margin of error is expressed by the term 'tendency': the precise effect of a cause may not be known but it may *tend* to bring about this effect. Whether or not the tendency ultimately results in the predicted effect, depends on the relative strength of counteracting forces. This process of interacting tendencies can be investigated by isolating them one at a time by means of what Marshall called the *Caeteris Paribus* clause: 'The study of some group of tendencies is isolated by the assumption *other things being equal*: the existence of other tendencies is not denied, but their disturbing effect is neglected for a time' (Marshall, 1920, 366). Mill adopted this method to investigate the tendential laws of the progress of society. According to him, three major tendencies controlled this progress: the tendency to increase of respectively population, the stock of capital and the 'arts of production'. The first one, population growth, caused a 'tendency of profits to a minimum', which would eventually stall production growth in a stationary state. This tendency and therefore the establishment of a stationary state was counteracted by the other two tendencies. To ascertain their individual effects Mill investigated them one by one, assuming that the other tendencies would remain 'stationary'. He established their combined effect on the rate of growth by adding up these effects. In this manner, he unraveled the complex question of dynamic forces and the economic changes they bring about.

The point is that tendency laws cannot account for the temporal leads and lags of these changes: they are not what Comte would call 'laws of succession'. Tendencies refer to the expectation that a certain effect will occur, but the realization of this expectation crucially depends on the assumption that disturbing causes remain constant. In other words, tendencies are conditional statements which require a precise specification of the ceteris paribus clause. Only then can the predicted tendency be verified and may time play a meaningful role in the analysis.[2] However, the classical economists are renowned for their neglect of precisely this factor. The time period required for dynamic effects to materialize was rarely specified, and

Mill was certainly no exception to this rule (Brandis 1989). What did it mean to be always on the verge of a stationary state, as Mill claimed? How long would it take the profit rate to reach its minimum level? Mill, nor his classical colleagues, never explained such questions. Their dynamic analysis constituted generalizations of historical changes without a time horizon. As a result, they were not able to describe the sequence of events in time that is necessary to establish laws of succession and give time its proper place in the dynamic analysis of economic changes.

This conclusion drives home my point that Mill's dynamics is a kind of static analysis, even by his own standards. It is hard to find a better example of Hicks's observation that the statics-dynamics distinction is 'treacherous', and that 'unless we are very careful, it will trip us completely' (Hicks 1965, 15). In the next sections, I shall substantiate my related claim that the classical economists approached equilibrium as a process rather than an end-state. I will do so by differentiating between microeconomic issues, related to the development of price theory, and the macroeconomic questions of economic growth and the distribution of the national income.

EQUILIBRIUM AS A PROCESS IN PRICE THEORY

Introduction

I have attributed to classical economics a process interpretation of equilibrium, meaning that it stresses the causes pushing the economy towards a stable level rather than the analysis of the ultimate end-state itself. This is a position that is not shared by all commentators in the history of economic thought. There is an important branch in our science which stresses the continuity between classical and neoclassical economics. The practical implication of this view is that it attributes to classical economics many of the features of modern neoclassical theories, such as an end-state conception of equilibrium. An example of this approach is Hollander (1987, 65) who claims that Smith described 'an embryonic account of general equilibrium theory', including the full use of the supply and demand mechanism seen as functional relationships. Similarly, Rankin (1980, 631–32) asserts that 'there is little doubt that by the beginning of the nineteenth century classical economists were explaining short-run market prices in terms of a market-clearing model which assumes implicitly an inverse functional relationship between price and quantity demanded'. But with these tools comes an implicit assumption, namely that equilibrium is determined at the point of intersection between the functions of supply and demand. As such, it seems as if the classical economists were merely addressing equilibrium as an end-state conception.

This suggestion is strengthened by the work of the followers of Sraffa (1960), who interpret classical economics from a different doctrinal corner. They believe that supply and demand played no role whatsoever in classical value theory. Their main argument in favour of this claim is Ricardo's labour theory of value which explains relative prices in terms of relative labour-input requirements. Such prices are a clear case of long-run prices and require that competition ensures a uniform wage rate (or profit rate) in all employments. Under these conditions, it can be shown that prices are determined irrespective of the pattern of demand. The Sraffians argue that what matters most to economics is not the disruptions of market supply and demand, which have a temporary duration, but the effect of permanent forces like population growth and capital accumulation. These control the movement of the economic system towards what Garegnani (1976) called the 'long period position'.

This focus places the classical tradition once again under the dominion of a theoretical framework seeing equilibrium as an end-state (Blaug 2008). It is this view which I aim to dismantle in this section.

What Does the Pull of Natural Prices Mean for Supply and Demand?

The best place to start this exercise is Smith's distinction between market and natural prices. The latter is described as 'the central price, to which the prices of all commodities are continually gravitating' (Smith 1937, 58). They are defined as a cost price which covers the payments made for rent, wages and profits. At this price, 'the commodity is then sold precisely for what it is worth, or for what it really costs the person who brings it to market' (ibid., 55). On the other hand:

> [The market price] is regulated by the proportion between the quantity which is actually brought to market and the demand of those who are willing to pay the natural price of the commodity, or the whole value of the rent, labour, and profit, which must be paid in order to bring it thither. Such people may be called effectual demanders, and their demand the effectual demand; since it may be sufficient to effectuate the bringing of the commodity to the market (ibid., 56).

Prices may therefore deviate from their natural levels, as there is disequilibrium between supply and demand. However, Smith realized that a disequilibrium of this kind will not last for long. The fact that there is a difference between market and natural prices means that there are profit differentials between alternative employments. These induce a shift in production to the most profitable market, thereby restoring the equality between supply and demand. 'The whole quantity of industry annually employed in order to bring any commodity to market, naturally suits itself in this manner to the effectual demand. It naturally aims at bringing always that precise quantity thither which may be sufficient to supply, and no more than supply, that demand' (ibid., p. 58). Given that Smith here speaks about the *whole* quantity of industry, leads some people argue that he was not just speaking about the behaviour of particular industries, but that he considered the force of competition powerful enough to maintain equilibrium simultaneously in all markets (Hollander 1987, 65).

What role do supply and demand play in this gravitational process? It is quite easy to translate the pull of natural prices upon market prices in terms of the modern schedules of supply and demand. Just assume that Smith's market price is determined in the short run by changes *along* given supply and demand curves. The determination of the natural price can then be seen as a matter of long run changes towards a perfectly elastic long run supply curve. In this construction, disequilibrium emerges when the market price deviates from this long run supply price, calling forth competitive pressure to shift the short term supply curve in order to restore the equality between these prices (Skinner 1970, 91–93).

But is it accurate to attribute this modern interpretation of supply and demand schedules to Adam Smith? I do not believe that the evidence is very convincing, but I shall refrain from debunking the arguments in favour of this neoclassical translation of Smith. What I find more important is that the very spirit of his price theory and the uses to which he put it are so uncongenial to modern supply and demand analysis that I find it hard to take such claims very seriously.

For example, one of the more notorious assumptions underlying the neoclassical model of perfect competition is that everyone is a price taker. Are we to believe that Smith's gravitational theory of price formation constitutes an embryonic account of this model? In modern theory, market participants are assumed to be price takers, because they come in very large numbers and are therefore individually unable to significantly affect the ratio of exchange. But Smith never explained the working of market exchange in terms of the number of buyers and sellers. For him competition was essentially a behavioural activity, a race between different individuals to dispose of excess supply or to obtain goods in limited quantities (Blaug 2001, 38). This race was facilitated by the ease with which contestants to the battle could leave or enter the market. The measure of competitive intensity was therefore not the number of sellers in the market, but the tightness of restraints into industries and occupations. In the 'simple system of natural liberty' which Smith promoted, such restraints would be minimal, facilitating the competitive process. In a monopoly, the situation would be the opposite, blocking the entry of new contestants to the market and chocking off the competitive process. In other words, for Smith a very competitive market could be one with a limited number of sellers, provided it possessed a high degree of factor mobility.

In modern price theory, the focus is diverted from the flow of traders in and out of industries, because it assumes that all trading activity stops once prices reside in equilibrium. At this price, suppliers and demanders conduct their business to everyone's satisfaction and then retire to consume the fruits of their competitive efforts. This latter part is, of course, never told, but it illustrates the nature of market equilibrium as an end-state. It is literally a state, a point frozen in time where nothing ever happens. This was certainly not how Smith saw the price setting process. The focus of his gravitational theory is on the direction of price changes, rather than on some frozen state representing the perfect balance between supply and demand.

Just see how he used the concept of effectual demand to explain the pull of natural prices (Bowley 1973, 124). As was explained above, the effectual demand is the quantity people are willing to buy at the natural price. This demand plays a crucial role in Smith's price mechanism, because it is the ratio between the quantity actually offered at the market and the effectual demand which determines the change in market price. Smith simply jumped from market to natural prices and completely sidestepped the careful distinction between shifts *of* and shifts *along* supply and demand curves that we find in modern price theory. The theory of effectual demand constitutes a tendential law, just as we have seen in our previous discussion of Mill. It states that market prices always have a tendency to nudge in the direction of natural prices. But whether the equality of these prices is ever actually attained, is highly uncertain.[3] In the real economy, counteracting tendencies may easily forestall the attainment of equilibrium for a while. What results is a view of the competitive process as a path of past transactions, while the functional interpretation of supply and demand rests on them being ex ante concepts.

We have earlier discussed that a comparative static exercise in terms of supply and demand functions requires a ceteris paribus clause to isolate disturbing causes. I have also stressed that this approach ignores the actual process of convergence towards equilibrium, let alone the speed with which convergence is attained (Fisher 1983, 12). But Smith put such matters at the centre stage of price theory. Speed of convergence was the defining characteristic of the system of natural liberty, because anything blocking the shift of resources between industries hindered the pull of market prices towards their natural level. This explains the interest of Smith in factors effecting this speed of convergence, such as the vagaries of harvests, the various restrictions on freedom of entry to different occupations, freedom of access to technical knowledge and inventions, privileges and the natural limitations on the supply of particular types of natural resources (Bowley 1973, 125). For Smith, competition was a process operating in calendar time, whose quickness could therefore be actually measured and related to causes with an observable impact.

As the capstone to my argument, I would like to point to Smith's interpretation of natural prices. Ricardo is renowned in the history of economic thought for his quest to find an invariable yardstick of economic value, suggesting a unique measure of natural prices. But Adam Smith treated natural prices very differently and argued that they depend on specific economic and social conditions, a connection that is wholly anathema to the abstract theories representing the modern, mathematical explanation of prices.

I explained in the previous chapter that Smith had been a leading member of the Scottish Historical School, which developed a specific form of historical analysis explaining change in terms of evolutionary stages. The aim of this type of inquiry was to explain the transition of one phase of economic development to the other in terms of uniform causes. This historical approach also affected Smith's value theory. In particular, the notions of growth and decline are important to this theory.

To Smith supply and demand were manifestations of the long-run forces which govern the economic development of advancing, stationary and declining nations. The point was that economic values would oscillate around natural price levels, but that these equilibrium points themselves would change as a result of economic growth or decline.[4] The interesting fact is that Smith used the supply and demand framework to explain these changes. He argued that in a fast growing economy like North America natural wages were rising, because the rate of capital accumulation was higher than population growth. In spite of the high birth rate and the 'continual importation of new inhabitants', the supply of labour was unable to satisfy the demand with rising natural wages as a result (Smith 1937, 71). But in a stationary economy like China wages would remain at the minimum subsistence level. Here there was no scarcity of hands, 'the number of hands employed every year could easily supply . . . the number wanted the next year', which meant that 'the competition of the labourers and the interest of the masters would soon reduce them [the wages of labour, BT] to this lowest rate which is consistent with common humanity' (ibid.). Finally, in a declining nation economic activity was falling which meant that 'every year the demand for servants and labourers would in all the different classes of employments be less than it had been the year before'. 'Want, famine, and mortality' were the result and would reduce the number of workers until 'the number of inhabitants in the country was reduced to what could easily be maintained by the revenue and stock which remained in it'. Smith cited Bengal and some other of the English settlements in the East Indies as examples of declining nations in this sense (ibid., 73).

Smith's natural prices were, therefore, anything but a fancy abstraction such as the natural rate of unemployment or the natural rate of interest in modern economics. They described actual features of actual nations going through their distinctive phases of economic development.

Ricardo's Cost of Production Theory of Value

Later proponents of the classical doctrine saw the notion of gravitation as the central organizing concept of the classical analysis of value and distribution (for example Garegnani 1976). According to them, the long-period position allowed them to explain the level of output in the long run as a function of the surplus of revenue over costs. Surplus output also determined the distribution of income between land, labour and capital while the costs of production explained relative prices and controlled the process of resource allocation. Moreover, Garegnani (1976) argues that explanation of these processes did not require the introduction of supply and demand as opposite forces.[5] What mattered was not the influence of supply and demand, which produced temporary effects, but the effect of permanent forces like population growth and capital accumulation. These controlled the movement of the economic system towards, what Garegnani calls, the 'long period position'.

Ricardo is considered the prime exponent of this type of analysis. He rejected Smith's analysis of price changes in terms of a ratio of supply and demand on the grounds that the effect of a change in this ratio 'will be only of temporary duration' (Ricardo 1951–1955: I, 374). According to Ricardo '[i]t is the cost of production which must ultimately regulate the price of commodities, and not, as has often been said, the proportion between the supply and demand' (ibid.). He concentrated on the effects of permanent changes and used the principle of gravitation as an organizing concept to differentiate between the tendencies of the 'long period position'.

The key to his cost of production theory of value is a stylized one-factor model of production. When cost of production determines price, it should be equal to the average input requirement of that factor per unit of output multiplied by its nominal price. Suppose there are two goods, X and Y. Then the cost of production equations for long run prices are:

$$p_X = w_X a_X$$

$$p_y = w_y a_y$$

Assuming homogenous labour and perfect competition, ensures that $w_x = w_y$. As a result, relative prices are entirely determined by relative labour-input requirements, irrespective of the pattern of demand:

$$\frac{p_x}{p_y} = \frac{a_x}{a_y}$$

This theory was later seen as a labour theory of value, due to its emphasis on labour as the sole factor of production. However, Stigler (1958) has aptly shown that Ricardo had no intention of ignoring other factors of production. Stigler stressed that the confusion is about the difference between the labour theory of value seen as an analytical proposition and the same theory stated as an empirical proposition. Ricardo never adopted the former one, but did work out the second option because he believed that the quantity of labour employed in production was by far the most important cause of the changes in relative prices.

How should we interpret this cost of production theory? In the current literature on Ricardo, there is a controversy about what is called the 'new view' which attacks the traditional interpretation of Ricardo's long run prices as a point of gravitation (Peach 2007). According to this traditional view, Ricardo had treated the natural or subsistence wage as a persistent centre of gravity for market wages in an unrestricted historical domain. But for the new-view proponents, the natural wage is the attraction point for wages only in some far distant stationary state in which economic growth has ceased. The key notion of this view is that market wages may remain above their natural level in the more primitive stages of society. The pulling force of the natural wage becomes a dominant factor in the more advanced stages of economic development due to the impact of diminishing agricultural returns.

I shall not deal with this issue in a detailed manner. In my opinion, the differences between the two views are overstated. Both sides acknowledge that Ricardo's writings are complex and that evidence for both views can be found (Peach 2007, 305). For the purpose of this chapter what matters most is the interpretation of the natural price level in Ricardo's cost of production theory. Should we consider it an end-state conception or is the process-interpretation more appropriate? Modern classical economists like Sraffa and Garegnani stress the end-state conception, but I believe that they are wrong in this regard.

Whether old view or new view, I argue that the tendency of market prices towards their natural level in Ricardo suggests a process taking place in historical rather than logical time. The end-state conception of equilibrium is typical of the formalistic, mathematical approach to economics, because in this framework it is difficult to reconcile the dynamic adjustment path with its static outcome.[6] Ricardo's theoretical skill and the deductive quality of his work are often praised, but that does not mean that like Sraffa he was aiming to solve a difficult mathematical problem. Ricardo was very much a product of his time. He was first and foremost a political economist in the traditional sense of that word. As Dixon (2008) argues, his notion of order was politically inspired. His long-run perspective was not just an analytical fiction, it was also necessary to promote his political agenda, which was to show how the economic system could be self-regulated without the immediate hand of powerful short run interests. In Dixon's words, Ricardo's views 'suggest a consistent vision of political order for which the market was as much a political as an economic arrangement' (Dixon 2008, 236).[7]

It is for this reason historically inaccurate to attribute to him a problem which emerges in modern, mathematical formulations of his price theory. As Meek (1967a, 5) said, the very concept of a distinction between static and dynamic analysis was quite alien to Smith and Ricardo. Blaug (1958) reasoned in similar terms. He observed that '[n]o doubt the Ricardian system makes implicit use of a stationary state as a methodological fiction. It combines this, however, with the notion of an actual stationary state toward which the economic system is tending, and superimposes on both a host of quasi-dynamical pieces of analysis' (Blaug 1958, 31–32).

I shall ignore a whole range of issues related to this problem, such as the invariable measure of value, to focus on the different meanings of the natural wage in Ricardo. It is at this point that we encounter what Blaug above calls the combination of the stationary state with an actual stationary state and its related 'quasi-dynamical' analysis. It also allows us to demonstrate the legacy of Adam Smith to Ricardo's thinking on this point, as Stirati (1995) has argued.

We have seen above that to Smith supply and demand were manifestations of the long run forces which govern the economic development of advancing, stationary and declining nations. He argued that economic values would oscillate around natural price levels, but that these equilibrium points themselves would change as a result of economic growth or decline. In part, we find the similar construction in Ricardo, which is best shown in Chapter 5 'On wages' of his *Principles of Political Economy and Taxation* (first published 1817).

Adam Smith developed a bargaining theory to explain the 'common wages of labour'. This theory rested on the assumption that wages are the outcome of a contract between two parties with opposing interests, namely labourers and capitalists (Smith 1937, 66). Smith noted that the bargaining positions of these two contracting parties are affected by the ruling economic circumstances. This fact led him to argue that the natural wage of labour will not always equate the subsistence wage. Smith defined natural rates in terms of the ordinary and average rates in a given period and neighbourhood. Put differently, for him natural prices, which act as a point of gravitation in his theory of value, are historically determined. His theory of wages constitutes a clear example. Smith's theory of wage bargaining explains that in advancing economic conditions labourers are in a position to demand natural wages far above the subsistence level. It is only in a stationary or declining nation that they are forced to accept wages at the subsistence level, due to their weak bargaining position (Stirati 1995, 114).

Please note that we are speaking here about the determination of the *natural* wage level. Smith offered a supply and demand theory of the secular changes in the wage level. During the changes taking place in this transition, it could well be that, due to all kind of disruptions, the market wage would deviate from its natural level. In this case, the competitive mechanism would simply pull it back to the natural rate.

Ricardo substituted the population mechanism for Smith's bargaining theory of the natural wage rate. The population mechanism is the explanation associated with the iron wage law which says that wages reside at the minimal subsistence level, because any deviation from this level will call forth an increased population growth that outruns the availability of food supplies. In other words, it is the immanent pressure of population growth on scarce agricultural resources which keeps the market wage at its natural level, which is at the same time the minimum subsistence level.

The point is that Ricardo did not consistently adhere to this theory. There are several places in his *Principles* where he offered a different explanation of natural wages. In these cases, we find a theory which much resembles Smith's bargaining theory and assumes a historically determined natural wage. Ricardo noted that '[i]t is not to be understood that the natural price of labour, estimated even in food and necessaries, is absolutely fixed and constant. It varies at different times in the same country, and very materially differs in different countries. It essentially depends on the habits and customs of the people' (Ricardo 1951–1955: I, 96–97). Like Smith, he offered an explanation of the changes in the natural wage in terms of the proportion of the supply and demand for labour. Hence, the 'different stages of society' would produce different natural wages, due to the different growth rates of the factors determining the supply and demand for labour. On the demand side, this concerned the accumulation of capital, which was the means of employing labour. Ricardo wrote that 'the productive powers of labour are generally greatest when there is an abundance of fertile land: at such periods accumulation is often so rapid, that labourers cannot be supplied with the same rapidity as capital' (ibid., 98). But in the more developed nations, the law of decreasing returns starts to kick in, producing lower rates of capital accumulation and hence a lower demand for labour. Eventually, population increases faster than the funds required for its support, leading to the familiar iron law of wages. The point is that this law is not universal in the sense that it applies to all places and all times. On the background, there is a story of historical development which explains that '[i]n the natural advance of society, the wages of labour will have a tendency to fall, as far as they are regulated by supply and demand; for the supply of labourers will continue to increase at the same rate, whilst the demand for them will increase at a slower rate'. I conclude that, following the example of Smith, Ricardo is here speaking about the development of the natural wage, indicating that to a certain extent his definition of the natural wage reflected historical conditions and supported a theory of supply and demand adjustment taking place in historical time.

Towards a Mathematical Theory of Prices

Ricardo's cost of production theory later gave rise to the view that the classical economists had ignored the role of demand. In the long run, supply conditions determine the costs of production and therefore relative prices, while demand changes only cause temporary deviations of the market price from its natural equilibrium level. Jevons was among the first to argue that this approach to the problem of economic value was fundamentally wrong. He argued that '*value depends entirely upon utility*' (Jevons 1879, 1, emphasis in the original), and forcefully contended that Ricardo had 'shunted the car of Economic science on to a wrong line' (ibid., li). In his view, cost of production can only affect value by changing supply, and hence the final degree of utility. The result was a different conception of economic equilibrium. In contrast to his classical forerunners, Jevons saw equilibrium as a mathematical condition, not as an organizing concept of long term economic changes. According to him, '[e]quilibrium of exchange of goods resembles in mathematical conditions the equilibrium of weights upon a lever of the first order' (quoted in Schabas 1990, p. 91). This made mathematics the preferred language to discuss the statics and dynamics of value theory.

In similar terms, J.S. Mill argued that his forerunners had adopted the wrong approach to value theory and that the problem of economic value should be addressed in mathematical terms. Like Ricardo, he claimed that the idea of a *ratio* between supply and demand was wrong but for very different reasons. He recognized that Smith had compared two different things, supply as the quantity actually supplied and effectual demand, which was defined as the willingness to buy. But:

What ratio can there be between a quantity and a desire, or even a desire combined with a power? A ratio between demand and supply is only intelligible if by demand we mean the quantity demanded, and if the ratio intended is that between the quantity demanded and the quantity supplied (Mill 1909, 446).

Moreover, this error showed that Smith failed to comprehend the distinction between price-induced changes and the role of price as a dependent variable. In modern terms, he had confused movements along and the shifts of supply and demand curves. Of course, this error was inevitable, as Smith had never defined supply and demand as functional relationships between price and quantity supplied or demanded. This point was correctly recognized by Mill who argued that the equilibrium between supply and demand should be addressed in mathematical terms. He stated that:

The idea of a ratio, as between demand and supply, is out of place, and has no concern in the matter: the proper mathematical analogy is that of equation. Demand and supply, the quantity demanded and the quantity supplied, will be made equal. If unequal at any moment, competition equalizes them, and the manner in which this is done is by an adjustment of the value . . . the value which a commodity will bring in any market, is no other than the value which, in that market, gives a demand just sufficient to carry off the existing or expected supply. (ibid., 448, emphasis in the original).

Mill's words lead to the logical conclusion that market equilibrium requires the solution of a mathematical equation and is therefore of a different nature than the gravitation of economic forces towards a long term equilibrium. It is an end-state conception rather than a process-oriented one, the concept that stood central in the classical economic tradition.

Should we conclude from this observation that with Mill, and the introduction of a more mathematically inspired theory of price formation, the process-approach of the classical economists disappeared from the scene? I argue that this certainly did not occur as a result of Mill's careful definition of supply and demand functions. In spite of his suggestion that we should deal with price theory in terms of a mathematical theory, for the main part he retained the theoretical structure of the classical doctrine with its focus on cost of production as a point of attraction. The distinction between three different 'Laws of Value' betrays his classical bend of mind. According to Mill, the Law of Supply and Demand was only valid for goods which are absolutely limited in supply (ibid., 448, 455, 456). A much larger and more significant class concerned goods which could be multiplied without restriction. In classical fashion, Mill argued that the value of the commodities belonging to this category were determined by the costs of production, which comprised his second Law of value. Here supply and demand played no role but had only a transient effect on the level of prices (ibid., 455). In addition a third Law of Value applied to commodities which are produced under conditions of decreasing returns to scale (ibid., 444–45).

The synthesis of the utility and cost of production theories of value had to await the work of Marshall. He contested Jevons's claim to have started a 'revolution' in economics and argued that he had misunderstood or ignored that in Ricardo value referred to long-run relative prices. Jevons's attempt to disprove a theory which analyzed 'the ultimate tendencies, the causes of causes, the *causea causantes*, of the relations between costs of production and value, by means of arguments based on the causes of temporary changes, and short-period fluctuations of value' could never substantiate his claim to have discovered 'a new doctrine of value in sharp contrast to the old' (Marshall 1920, 676). He correctly perceived that supply and demand form a general theoretical framework for the explanation of prices, but that the exact conditions of market equilibrium depend on the time period in question. In the short period, long term changes may be assumed constant, while in the reverse case short term fluctuations of price probably cancel each other out and are for that reason irrelevant to the analysis. 'Thus, as a general rule, the shorter the period which we are considering, the greater must be the share of attention which is given to the influence of demand on value; and the longer the period, the more important will be the influence of cost of production on value' (ibid., 349). Marshall's method of partial equilibrium analysis brought price theory one step further on the road to a rigorous mathematical formulation of the laws of economic value in both the short run and the long run.

However, Marshall never considered economics as a mathematical science. He used mathematics as an instrument to check the logical rigour of his theoretical deductions. To him economic statics was a first step towards the solution of more complex, dynamical questions. But the solution of these questions required a different set of tools. In the long term economic changes obtain the characteristic of a historical process. Over a period of years firms, markets and even industries grow and decline in response to changed supply and demand conditions. But unlike the swings of a mechanical balance, these economic changes of the long term are not reversible and are therefore of a different nature. 'In the earlier stages of economics we think of demand and supply as crude forces pressing against one another, and tending towards a mechanical equilibrium; but in the later stages the balance or equilibrium is conceived not as between crude mechanical forces, but as between the organic forces of life and decay' (Marshall 1898, 318). Hence, the study of economic changes required a language which could account for the different stages of the economic life-cycle. Marshall found this language in the realm of biology and concluded that when it comes to the study of economic growth '[t]he Mecca of the economist is economic biology rather than economic dynamics' (ibid.). So, Marshall never saw economics as a static science, in spite of the fact that he put supply and demand at the centre of economic analysis and was able to formulate supply-and-demand equilibrium as a mathematical equation, using the tools of marginal analysis. On the contrary, he recognized that in economics the point of gravitation is shifting as a result of long term forces and introduced the term evolution as a metaphor of this process. In this regard, Marshall was the last of the great classical economists of the 19th century.

DID THE GLUT CONTROVERSY PROMOTE A DIFFERENT TYPE OF DYNAMICS?

The Different Meanings of Say's Law

Ricardo's stress on the relevance of long-term forces to the study of economic forces was certainly not shared by every writer of the classical period. Especially during the glut controversy, voices were raised against the assumption of a self-correcting economic mechanism. This controversy dealt with the law of markets, nowadays associated with the name of Jean-Baptiste Say, which states that the value of aggregate supply should equal the value of aggregate demand. However, the interpretation of this debate is hindered by the fact that Say's law has different meanings and that it is not clear which version of the law was at stake in the controversy. This section will not solve this problem. My main interest is that the glut controversy points to the different approaches of statics and dynamics in classical theory.

The essence of Say's law is that aggregate supply and demand are not independent. It formalizes the insight that on an economy-wide scale firms cannot expand output without raising demand at the same time, because their aggregate production costs must equal factor incomes. This means that, given that hoarding is precluded, an increase in aggregate supply will raise aggregate demand with an equal amount. This version of the 'law of markets' is known as Say's identity. The weaker version of the 'law' is known as Say's equality. According to this version, the general price level adjusts so as to ensure that aggregate supply and demand tend towards equality. In this situation an excess supply (demand) of commodities is reflected in an excess demand (supply) for money. Say's identity rules out the possibility of macroeconomic disequilibrium in this sense.[8]

In modern economics, the meaning of Say's law as a macroeconomic proposition is clear, but the surprising fact is that the historical meaning of the law continues to cause disagreement (Baumol 1999). The root of this problem is that in the history of economic thought the law of markets is not a unique law but really a complex of ideas. The following propositions were a part of this complex:

- Real income determines real demand, so money is only an intermediary;
- Leakages out of the circular flow of income are impossible. In other words, there is no need to worry about hoarding;
- Saving is essential if the economy is to expand. Therefore, it must be seen as productive consumption in contrast to the unproductive consumption of luxuries;
- Partial overproduction is possible, but in a competitive market economy the mistakes which cause disequilibrium are quickly rectified. Hence, a general excess of production over aggregate demand will not occur;
- Oversaving, that is a surplus of aggregate income over aggregate demand, is impossible, because savings always find a productive employment, that is investment;
- As a consequence, failure of effective demand cannot be a cause of recessions and unemployment.

The latter proposition formed the main point of disagreement in the early 19th century between the proponents of Say's law and the so-called 'glut theorists'. To place this controversy in the proper context, it is important to note that in this period no one denied the possibility of recession and unemployment. The Napoleonic wars had shown that the economy could experience prolonged periods of economic slowdown. The point was whether aggregate overproduction or 'underconsumption' was the cause of this stagnation. This question divided the ranks of economic writers. On the one hand, Ricardo and his followers maintained that a general glut of markets could not arise as a permanent feature of the economic system.[9] They saw recession and unemployment as the manifestations of extraordinary circumstances such as the wars with France, which hindered the free flow of international trade. As such, the Ricardians believed 'gluts' to be temporary disturbances that would automatically disappear once trade was able to regain its normal course. On the other hand, the glut theorists maintained that general excess production was possible and that the stagnation of growth was caused by forces endogenous to the economic process.[10] In particular, they pointed to forces which caused aggregate demand to fall behind the growth of aggregate production. That is, in their view underconsumption was the cause of recession and unemployment.[11]

Given the disagreement about the meaning of Say's law, it is not surprising that modern commentators argue about the correct interpretation of the glut controversy. According to Blaug (1958, 1985), the controversy dealt with the long-term, secular growth feature of Say's law.[12] In this view, Say's law implied that capital would always find a profitable employment, smoothly moving the economy in the direction of a stationary state without disruptions caused by a lack of demand. Saving, or 'parsimony' as Smith called it, was thus seen as the best means to promote economic growth. The glut theorists contested this conclusion. They denied that saving would automatically find a productive outlet in investment and argued that saving would reduce the nation's purchasing power. This would cause a fall in the profit rate and a stagnation of growth. Since the capitalist economy lacked an automatic mechanism to restore the equality between aggregate supply and demand, this stagnation would be permanent.

The conclusion that the glut controversy dealt with the possibility of a secular stagnation of growth is rejected by Sowell (1972a and 1974).[13] He claimed that the controversy was a debate about short-term frictions preventing a timely restoration of the equality between aggregate supply and demand. According to him, the glut theorists never denied that in the long run capital accumulation could proceed unimpeded until a falling profit rate would bring it to a final stop. The issue disputed, then, was that aggregate supply would always equal aggregate demand, even in the short run. In his view, Malthus and Simonde de Sismondi demonstrated that a capitalist economy could produce an universal glut of markets, while the Ricardians denied that this was possible at all. With an appeal to Say's law they argued that over-production could arise in specific markets only, but not on an economy-wide scale.

Which version of Say's law was at stake in the glut controversy? I intend to show that a single answer to this question cannot be given. The participants to this controversy were not consistent in their use of the law of markets. The antagonists adopted different versions of the law and varied its meaning as it suited their purposes. This is an important explanation of why they were talking at cross purposes.

The debates do emphasize the different attitudes towards equilibrium theory and are for that reason an important source of information about the role of statics and dynamics in classical economics. As Dow (1996, 53) puts it:

> The expression of Say's law within Ricardo's comparative static framework supported the notion that there was no unique equilibrium level of output (or employment); at all levels of output, demand would accommodate supply. Among non-Ricardian Classicists like Malthus and Simonde de Sismondi, however, Say's

law was employed within a dynamic framework of analysis which suggested that there was an equilibrium level of output to which the economy gravitated over time.

I shall argue that Dow's summing up of the glut controversy is wrong on two accounts. In the first place, the focus on the comparative static framework ignores to process-oriented nature of the Ricardian approach. In my terminology, Ricardian growth theory adopts a *static* method because it does not give us an explicit account of temporal leads and lags in the process of change (see Table 2.1). But its object of research is a clear example of an evolutionary process. Malthus and Simonde de Sismondi, on the other hand, never believed in gravitation as a dominant economic force. Their conception of equilibrium is stationary, an end-state as I have termed it in Table 2.1. However, their analysis of this stationary positions suggests a form of *dynamic* analysis, which a century later would be called period or sequence analysis, due to its focus on the leads and lags of economic change. Therefore, the glut controversy gives us insight into the development of two different forms of analysis, supporting different conceptions of economic equilibrium.

Ricardo's Growth Theory in Static Dress

For the purpose of clarifying the static nature of classical growth theory, I shall now discuss what in a certain sense forms a caricature of this theory. This caricature involves an analytical construct which treats the growth process as being wholly atemporal; that is, the leads and lags between variables play no role whatsoever in this account of the growth process. As should be clear by now, I do not believe that the classical theorists handled growth theory by ignoring time in this sense. But it does highlight their tendency to deal with temporal changes in a rather vague manner. What I have to tell in this section is therefore just half of the full scope of classical growth theory. I shall briefly explain the main elements of Ricardo's theory of growth, treating it as a typical case of static analysis. I shall subsequently use it as a benchmark to argue that the real interest of the classicals lay with the growth process seen as a process, handling growth as a secular trend of the economy.

It is not very difficult to give a static interpretation of classical growth theory. In a sense, it forms a continuation of the problem we have discussed in the past few chapters. Forerunners of the classical doctrine, such as Cantillon, Quesnay and the other physiocrats likewise explained the process of capital reproduction, but failed to do so adequately due to their inability to understand the fundamental nature of the saving-investment relationship.

Investment means that current purchasing power is employed, not for current consumption, but for consumption at some future date. This forward looking character of capital investment forms the chain which links subsequent production periods through time. We have seen that the preclassicals generally ignored this intertemporal aspect of the investment cycle and it is this trick that is employed to explain the classical account of growth in static dress.

Hicks (1965, 36–42) provided an example of how this can be done. He explained Smith's theory of capital accumulation in terms of a single-period model. This single-period is analytically self-contained through the assumption that there is only one capital good, which is a circulating capital good. Hicks assumed that corn forms this one capital good and that the single period is the agricultural year. During this period the harvest of one year is transformed into that of the next. This reproduction requires two productive aids, a natural one as the soil manages to grow a new harvest of corn every year, and a human one in terms of the manpower needed to cultivate the land. As corn is assumed to be the labourer's diet, corn is both input and output of the production process and the capital stock is thus a wage fund. Under these conditions the growth rate of the economy will be a constant which depends on labour productivity and the wage rate.[14]

Hicks (1965) claimed that this 'is the model that was in Smith's mind'. I do not agree with this conclusion, but I shall for the present ignore the question what Smith 'really' meant. I find the Hicks model useful, because it provides a simple link between classical growth theory and Say's law. The crux of this relationship concerns the assumption of capital homogeneity, which allows this model to function as a self-contained period. Relaxation of this condition would introduce the possibility of a choice between different capital goods. This would give expectations a role and connects the periods through time; 'before' and 'after' would become meaningful terms. If there is just one homogenous capital good, there is nothing to do with our savings but to invest them in this capital. As a consequence, there can be no problem of *mal*investment. The only possible problem is *over*saving – savings going to waste because they are not invested but hoarded. This explains why oversaving or underconsumption was the pinnacle of the controversy about the possibility of a general glut of markets.

Since Sraffa's introduction to the collected works of Ricardo (1951–1955), the latter's ideas about economic growth have become the prime example of a corn model with homogenous capital. The essential difference with the work of Smith is that Ricardo saw land as a scarce factor. As Blaug (1958, 13) put it, Ricardo viewed economic growth as having an inherent land using bias. Hence, the process of capital accumulation would need an increasingly growing supply of corn to replace the wage fund. This raised a problem, because the scarcity of land set a limit on the expansion of agriculture. The natural result would therefore be rising prices of corn, rising nominal wages and a fall in the profit rate. This rate would of course tend towards zero which marked the arrival of the stationary state. One may see this state as an equilibrium based on the condition that population growth and investment growth are both reduced to zero.

The explanation of this slowdown is ingenious and has three crucial components. The first component is Ricardo's theory of rent. Ricardo was one of the first economists to apply the concept of the margin to productivity analysis. He assumed that the marginal productivity of labour in agriculture would fall with the expansion of output because both a more intensive cultivation of a given quantity of land (intensive margin) and the expansion of cultivation to less fertile land (extensive margin) required more labour to produce the same quantity of corn. It can now be shown that rent is a payment for the higher productivity of intramarginal land. In Ricardo's words, 'rent is always the difference between the produce obtained by the employment of two equal quantities of capital and labour' (Ricardo 1951–1955: I, p. 71). By focussing on the process of price formation at the margin of cultivation, Ricardo was able to get rid of the rent factor as a constituent element of the cost price.

This brings me to the second ingredient of Ricardo's theory of growth. With rents out of the way and corn being the only capital, Ricardo could focus on the quantity of labour as the main component of costs of production and therefore of prices. This labour cost of production theory explained that the expansion of output, requiring the use of increasingly less fertile fields, would lead to higher nominal prices of corn – the wage good – because the production of an unit of corn would require an increasing quantity of labour. This ingredient was combined with the third factor, which is the Malthusian population mechanism. Ricardo was able to treat the real wage as a constant, assuming that population pressure would always maintain wages at the minimum subsistence level. This implied that the changes in nominal wages could directly be tied to the profit rate in agriculture, which in its turn set a standard for profit in every economic sector.

This nexus between the nominal wage rate and the profit rate is in fact the key to unlocking the secrets of Ricardo's growth theory. I shall therefore explain it by using the following example.

Suppose that in the initial situation the price of corn is €1 per unit. In this economy 4 workers produce 120 units of corn. Their wage rate is 20 units of corn which means that the wage bill is 80 units in real terms and €80 in terms of money. Further, it is assumed that the annual depreciation per unit of capital is €5. This leaves a residue of €20 which is paid as profits (see Table 7.1).

With the progress of population and capital, cultivation must be extended to less fertile lands. This is shown in Table 7.1 where the expansion of production leads to a fall of the total product on the new land. The next four workers produce 100 units of corn which raises the price of corn to €1.2 (=120/100 x €1). Money wages rise as result of this increase but real wages remain constant, given that population growth keeps wages at the subsistence level in the long run. Also a rent of €24 (=120x€1.2 – 100x€1.2) is paid, which is the difference between the produce of labour in the successive stages. The result is that profits fall to €4 as higher nominal wage rates and increasing rents place a two-way squeeze on profits.

Table 7.1 Calculation of profits in the Ricardian system

	Original situation			Expansion of output		
Value of product	120x€1	=	€120	120x€1.2	=	€144
Wage rate	20x€1	=	20	20x€1.2	=	24
Wage bill	4x€20	=	80	4x€24	=	96
Depreciation	4x€5	=	20	4x€5	=	20
Profits	€120–80–20	=	20	€144–96–20–24	=	4
Rent	. . .	=	0	€144–120	=	24

In the Ricardian system, economic growth inevitably causes this fall. Output growth results in investment growth which in turn leads to a higher demand for labour and therefore higher wages. But high wages induce population growth and the consequent pressure on the food supply pushes cultivation to less fertile fields and lowers the productivity of capital. As a result, the costs of production increase and profits fall. Falling profits reduce the rate of investment until production growth stops which marks the arrival of the stationary state.

Seen in this way, the stationary state is a perfect example of an end-state conception of equilibrium. Given the assumptions and the initial conditions (for example fixed quantity of fertile land, limited or no technological progress in agriculture), there is no escape from the conclusion that the economy must halt in a stationary state. The modern followers of Ricardo like Sraffa, Pasinetti and Garegnani have pushed this line of thinking to its logical conclusion. They adopt a long period perspective on the issues of pricing, growth and distribution and ignore the temporary disruptions that may affect the economy on its route to this position (Pasinetti 1960).

Marx's Extensions: Simple and Expanded Reproduction

Karl Marx was probably the classical economist who most succeeded in developing this single-period model into a more sophisticated theory of growth. Marx recognized that we should make a distinction between different types of goods in the process of capital accumulation, namely capital goods and consumer goods. This distinction was the basis of his reproduction schema in volume II of *Capital*, involving simple and expanded reproduction.

The production of consumer and capital goods took place in what he called different departments. Both these departments required variable capital *v* and constant capital, marked *c*. Variable capital consisted of the 'labour-power in action' and its value was assumed by Marx to match its labour-embodied value. Constant capital consisted of fixed capital and circulating constant capital, such as raw materials, semi-finished products et cetera.

This capital produces a total output in both departments taken together with the value c + v + s. The factor *c* represents the labour value of constant capital used up in production and thereby transferred unto the new products. Then there is another portion which is used to replace the variable capital *v* and an excess over and above it, which forms the surplus value *s*. This latter part emerges because fixed capital also embodies labour time and this return constitutes an unearned profit to the owners of the means of production.

In Marx's formulation of simple reproduction, total output will furnish the required means to carry a new round of production at the same level of output. In other words, the whole output of department I (capital goods) must be able to replace the capital used up in both departments:

$$c_1 + v_1 + s_1 = c_1 + c_2$$

Secondly, the whole output of department II (consumer goods) must match the wages bill plus the unearned income which is assumed to be spend unproductively:

$$c_2 + v_2 + s_2 = (v_1 + v_2) + (s_1 + s_2)$$

Both equations state the same condition, namely:

$$v_1 + s_1 = c_2$$

This condition says that the net output of department I must be sufficient to replace the worn-out capital in department II. This shows that Marx's single reproduction defines the condition of stationary production and leaves no room for net investment.

The formulation of expanded reproduction investigates the conditions for a growing economy with growth taking place at a constant rate. This leads to an adjustment of the condition stated above in the sense that the net output of department I must grow with the increase in gross investment expenditures in department II. Behind the scenes, there should be a balancing mechanism ensuring that the growth in savings matches this increase in net investment, but this was not spelled out by Marx. In his opinion, excess-consumption, reflecting a lack of funding for investment, ran counter to the spirit of the capitalist system. He called this possibility 'an illusion . . . for it takes for granted that the aim and compelling motive of capitalist production is consumption, and not the snatching of surplus value and its capitalisation, that is, accumulation' (Marx 1997a, 503). The reverse case of oversaving would likewise not pose a problem, if credit money was introduced into the system or if capital could be exported (Blaug 1985, 251).

What Ricardo and the Classicals Really Meant

In Marx, like in Ricardo, there is a focus on long-run prices, but this focus does not place them in the general equilibrium camp. Contrary to the end-state conception of equilibrium, the work of Ricardo and Marx bristles with notions suggesting a process-approach that is so typical of the classical economic tradition. They both see competition as a force tending to equalize the profit rate in different employments. Ricardo stressed that 'a fall in the general rate of profits is by no means incompatible with a partial rise of profits in particular employments. It is through the inequality of profits, that capital is moved from one employment to another.' (Ricardo 1951–1955: I, 119). Marx stated that 'capital withdraws from a sphere with a low rate of profit and invades others, which yield a higher profit. Through this incessant outflow and influx . . . it creates such a ratio of supply to demand that the average profit in the various spheres of production becomes the same' (Marx 1997b, 194).

It is clear that gravitation towards an uniform price level is the core equilibrium concept in Ricardo and Marx, and one may add, every other classical economist belonging to the Ricardian school. We should interpret this use of the equilibrium construct in the same manner, as we have done in the case of J.S. Mill above. It forms part of a method to investigate the causes of economic change in terms of tendencies. Ricardo (1951–1955: I, 120). thus spoke of:

> the natural tendency of profits to fall; for in the progress of society and wealth, the additional quantity of food required is obtained by the sacrifice of more and more labour. This tendency, this gravitation as it where of profits, is happily checked at

> repeated intervals by the improvements in machinery, connected with the production of necessaries, as well by discoveries in the science of agriculture which enable us to relinquish a portion of labour before required, and therefore to lower the price of the prime necessary of the labourer.

De Marchi (1970) has shown that this process of tendencies and counteracting tendencies can be a confusing one, if one does not keep the distinction in mind between analytical propositions and historical generalizations. De Marchi argued that both notions play a role in Ricardo's use of the tendency-statement. We have seen in this chapter that the Ricardian system is a framework for analyzing the forces which play upon the profit rate. Accordingly, the actual outcome of the growth process may well be a rising profit rate if the tendency of wages to rise is countered by another force, for example technological progress. Ricardo saw such improvements as an important cause of the rise in the profit rate in the period 1793–1813 (Hollander 1977, 8). It is therefore wrong to infer that he exclusively adopted a constant wage model which assumed that technological progress would not take place. That view is the result of a confusion of the analytical idea that the profit rate tends to fall as a result of rising wages only, assuming that other causal factors remain constant, and the view that the profit rate actually declines as a result of this complex of forces. There are several examples where we see Ricardo approaching tendency statements in the latter sense, which forced him to fill in some of the blanks required to support such predictions. Thus, he seemed to have supported a very short-run period of about 5 years and a short-run period of about 25 years (De Marchi 1970, 222). This latter period referred to the short term deviation of the profit rate as a result of a sudden flourishing of technological innovations (Ricardo 1951–1955: I, 94–95 and 98). He also said that wages may depart from their natural level for periods at least as long as this. There is even the suggestion of a period of disequilibrium lasting 'indefinitely' (ibid., 95).[15] What other evidence does one need to reject the idea that Ricardo endorsed an end-state conception of equilibrium?

In the case of Marx one should draw the same conclusion. His treatment of the falling profit rate as a tendency statement is well-known (Reuten 2004). He further aimed to determine the profit rate and the relative prices in what has been called a 'successivist' approach (Kurz and Salvadori 1995, 12–13). In the first step of this approach, Marx specified the rate of profit as the ratio between the labour value of the economy's surplus product, denoted as s, and the labour value of the capital stock C, consisting of constant capital c and variable capital v. This results in the formula:

$$\rho = \frac{s}{C} = \frac{s}{c+v}$$

In the second step of the analysis this profit rate is used to calculate prices, starting from cost prices measured in terms of labour values. This is the famous transformation problem that shall not occupy us here any further. What matters is the stepwise approach in which variables are determined in succession over time, not simultaneously. As Mongiovi (2002) argues, this approach has characteristics of intertemporal general equilibrium analysis, showing the dynamic nature of his general methodology. This method can be opposed to the theory of value of Sraffa (1960) which leans heavily on the determination of the profit rate and relative prices in a system of simultaneous equations (assuming the wage rate given). But it can also be contrasted with the approach taken by the strict non-equilibrium Marxists, who believe that the most essential phenomena of a market economy cannot be understood in an equilibrium framework (Freeman and Carchedi 1996, xviii). Marx's own approach seems to have rested somewhere in the middle, making use of the pull of equilibrium forces but also taking account of the historical setting required to make the system work and finally break with the demise of capitalism (Dow 1996, 127).[16]

Supporting Say's Law of Markets

The importance of classical growth theory for the interpretation of Say's law is the focus on long run prices, which seems to leave no room whatsoever for deviations or disruptions of shorter duration. Ricardo said it himself, when he tried to describe in a letter to Malthus their most important disagreement (letter of 24 January 1817 in Ricardo 1951–1955, VII: 120):

> It appears to me that one great cause of our difference in opinion, on the subjects which we have so often discussed, is that you have always in your mind the immediate and temporary effects of particular changes – whereas I put these immediate and temporary effects quite aside, and fix my whole attention on the permanent state of things which will result from them.

His growth theory showed that there was no risk of oversaving or underconsumption stalling the process of capital accumulation. There was only one factor which could stop growth and that was the diminishing returns to scale in agriculture, which was the ultimate cause of the stationary state. But Ricardo emphasized that a stationary state should not be confused with secular stagnation. In a stationary state, prices are equilibrium prices which guarantees that supply equals demand in all markets. Accordingly:

> All that is produced will be at its fair relative prices and will be freely exchanged. Surely the word stagnation is improperly applied to such a state of things, for there

> will not be a general glut, nor will any particular commodity be necessarily produced in greater abundance than the demand shall warrant (Ricardo 1951–1955, IX: 25).

Indeed, as Peach (1988, 107 and 113) argues, Ricardo stressed the inverse relationship between wages and profits to such an extent that he seemed to have ruled out any account of short-term macroeconomic disequilibrium. It this type of reasoning in terms of long-term positions which Sowell (1972a) takes as evidence that Ricardo adopted the identity version of Say's law.

There is sufficient textual evidence to support this conclusion. Ricardo never became tired of explaining that a sluggish adjustment of consumer demand would not cause a general overproduction of commodities. Time and again he explained that specific markets could glut because people did not desire the particular goods on sale, but such gluts were partial.[17] On an aggregate level relative price changes would induce producers to supply the right product mix (Ricardo 1951–1955, I: 292–293; II: 306; III: 108). Accordingly, only disposable income could limit aggregate demand, not the satiation of human wants (ibid, VI: 108). But this was of course impossible, due to Say's law. This suggests that Ricardo saw no possibility for an excess supply of commodities, because under competitive conditions investment would always generate sufficient demand. Indeed, even Hollander considers Ricardo's use of Say's law 'rigid and unqualified' (Hollander 1977, 2).

In this judgment, Hollander is probably right. Ricardo's use of Say's law was rigid and unqualified. Pressed by Malthus on this matter, Ricardo conceded one case in which excess aggregate production could emerge. This concerns the case of an economy which produces necessaries only and is clearly an exception. Ricardo argued that for such an economy, if capitalists simply reinvest their entire profit income, they produce a supply of food in excess of its demand. Or: 'If every man were to forego the use of luxuries, and be intent only on accumulation, a quantity of necessaries might be produced for which there could not be any immediate consumption. Of commodities so limited in number there might undoubtedly be a universal glut' (Ricardo 1951–1973, I: 293). It needs no explanation that, for Ricardo, this example did not impugn the general principle. He argued that in contrast to commodities in general, the desire for food was limited by the physical necessity to survive. Approvingly, he quoted Smith 'that the desire of food is limited in every man by the narrow capacity of the human stomach, but the desire of the conveniences and ornaments of building, dress, equipage, and household furniture, seems to have no limit or certain boundary' (ibid.).

Rigid or not, Ricardo did not adopt Say's law as an identity, as Sowell claims. The citations given above clearly indicate that Ricardo placed full emphasis on the analysis of long-term price and output trends. It was the price mechanism which would ensure that markets offered the right product mix to meet the demand from consumers. This shows that it was the long-run equality between aggregate supply and demand which was the relevant version of the law of markets to him, not their short-run identity (Blaug 1958, 90; Hollander 1979, 504; 1987, 248).

We may call upon Jean-Baptiste Say himself to support this interpretation. Say attacked Ricardo for what he considered a rigid interpretation of the law of markets. Explaining his point, it becomes clear that Say referred to the possibility of a glut of markets as a secular trend, not something that is caused by a temporary shortfall of aggregate demand (Say 1821, 49n.).

> Mr. Ricardo insists that, notwithstanding taxes and other charges, there is always as much industry as capital employed; and that all capital saved is always employed, because the interest is not suffered to be lost. On the contrary, many savings are not invested, when it is difficult to find employment for them, and many which are employed are dissipated in ill-calculated undertakings. Besides, Mr. Ricardo is completely refuted, not only by what happened to us in 1813, when the errors of Government ruined all commerce, and when the interest of money fell very low, for want of good opportunities of employing it; but by our present circumstances, when capitals are quietly sleeping in the coffers of their proprietors.

So, there can be a problem of 'excess' hoarding, but we should see this problem as an effect, not as a cause of a glut of markets. The real cause of the unstable balance between production and consumption is government interference, as taxes and government spending distorted the normal pattern of demand. In other words, Say referred to a supply-side effect working on the perceived profitability of investment. As 'production [did] not keep pace with consumption' some producers would face unexpected revenue losses (Say 1880, 140). It was this cause which led entrepreneurs to keep their capitals in their coffers with the aforementioned 'ruin of all commerce' as a result. According to Say, the loss of business confidence in general would have far-reaching implications, such as discouraged investments, stagnating production and wide-spread unemployment (ibid., 140).[18]

> Because the sources of profit are dried up . . . [t]he labouring classes experience a want of work; families before in tolerable circumstances, are more cramped and confined; and those before in difficulties are left altogether destitute. Depopulation, misery, and returning barbarism, occupy the place of abundance and happiness.

In modern eyes, such consequences do not seem typical of the economic problems caused by a temporary shortfall of aggregate demand. The critique of Say therefore underlines that what mattered to the classical economists was the possibility of a general glut of markets seen as a secular trend, that is as a long run inequality between aggregate supply and demand. This conclusion contradicts the opinion of Sowell that the glut controversy focused on the relevance of Say's identity and the likelihood of short-term imbalances in the macroeconomic sphere.

Let me offer one final piece of evidence in support of this conclusion. J.S. Mill once again proved the one with the clearest insight into the crux of the matter. Reviewing the glut controversy, he gave an exceptionally clear expression of what is now known as Say's equality. Mill emphatically rejected the glut theorists's explanation of economic stagnation. He argued that 'what [they][19] termed a commercial crisis . . . is really an excess of all commodities above money demand: in other words, there is an under-supply of money' (Mill 1909, 561). And look what he did with this insight. He used it to develop a business cycle theory, explaining the cyclical fluctuations of output around a secular trend (Blaug 1958, 99; Hollander 1987, 260). In other words, he employed Say's law to construct a theory of macroeconomic disequilibrium, which in this case clearly refers to long-term changes in output. The demand for money played a key part in this theory, as the demand for money reflected the changing moods of investors. An increase in the demand for money implied a growing concern among investors that their outlays would not yield sufficient returns. The result was a contraction of aggregate output as the excess demand for money matched the excess supply for goods. The spread of a bullish mood could vice versa cause an expansion of output. Put differently, Mill's theory of the business cycle revolved around the expectations of speculators who cause a periodic pattern of expansion and contraction in aggregate output (Hollander 1985, 513ff; 1987, 560ff; Forget 1990, Skaggs 1994).

The secular trend in question of course referred to the path towards the stationary state, as predicted by Ricardo's growth model. This was a secular trend of a falling profit rate that could not be stalled by a lack of effective demand. Mill's theory made explicit what other classical economists of the Ricardian school only vaguely stated: Say's law of markets was an equality, asserting that an excess demand for money or an excess supply of commodities tends to be self-correcting.

There are some passages in which Ricardo played with similar notions and hinted at the interest rate mechanism operating as a balancing force between the aggregate supply and demand for money and goods respectively. For instance, he argued that changes in the money supply would have a temporary effect on the interest rate (Ricardo 1951–1955, I: 297; III: 91, 118; for a formal representation see Akhtar 1975 and Caminati 1981). He conceded that for these brief intervals, the money values of commodities supplied and demanded do not correspond. Put differently, in this case Ricardo allowed for a temporary excess demand for money.

Why did he not follow through the logic of these initial steps? He certainly possessed the deductive skills to have arrived at the result that Say's law logically involves the connection between the money market and the real economy. We cannot look inside his head, but a plausible explanation concerns the focus of his interests. In contrast to Say and Mill, he did not consider an excess demand for money a relevant factor for his discussion of the contemporary crises (Hollander 1979, 536). His principal interest was the explanation of the trend of output rather than the swings around this trend.

To understand this position we need to return to his political agenda, which I briefly discussed at the start of this section. When Ricardo published the first edition of his *Principles* in 1817, he had completely withdrawn from an active involvement in business life and devoted all his energy to his tasks as a member of Parliament (Dixon 2008). We should not underestimate the effect this had on his economic writings. He clearly used is economic analysis an instrument to further his political goals. Free trade and protective measures like the Corn laws were among the main topics of the day. In Parliament, Ricardo plead for a gradual removal of the Corn laws and economic theory provided the arguments why. 'I contend for free trade in corn, on the ground that while trade is free, and corn is cheap, profits will not fall however great be the accumulation of capital' (Ricardo 1951–1955, II: 208). Hence, the prediction of a stationary state proved an useful device to scare-off the friends of protection. Cheap corn meant that money wages could be kept low, preventing the profit rate to fall. With Ricardo's fundamental theorem of distribution, the connection between free trade and the corn price on the one hand and the prospects for economic growth and wealth on the other hand, could easily be established. It turns out that Ricardo's pessimism with regard to the limits to economic growth were political and not economic in character (Blaug 1958, 32).[20]

Malthus's Rejection of Say's Law: Underconsumption

The reason why Sowell (1972a) tried to interpret the glut controversy in terms of a debate about the relevance of Say's identity is that he believed that the glut theorists developed the contours of a pre-Keynesian theory of an equilibrium aggregate income, which dispelled this notion of Says' law. I do not find the evidence in favour of this reading very compelling. There are certainly suggestions in the work of Malthus and Simonde de Sismondi, as the principal glut theorists, which point in the direction of such a theory. But these suggestions are poorly worked out and generally fail to capture the essence of a truly dynamic theory of equilibrium income, which is the difference in timing between saving and investing.

The defining characteristic of underconsumption theories is that they differentiate between a demand for consumption and investment goods (Bleaney 1976, 18). In these theories, underconsumption is explained as the result of an apparent contradiction. This is that saving reduces the demand for consumption goods while at the same time it finances an expansion of the capacity to produce those commodities. This suggests that saving leads to a lack of demand which may stall production through its effect on the profit rate.

Malthus developed the paradigm case of the underconsumption theories which regard oversaving as the threat immanent in capitalist production (Schumpeter 1954, 740n). To Malthus, saving implied a concomitant act of investment. Like most authors of this time, he considered the demand for hoards insignificant and assumed that savings are at all times immediately invested (Blaug 1958, 86). It must be noted that in these theories over-saving does not refer to a lack of aggregate demand caused by a difference between ex ante saving and investment.[21] Instead, Malthus was concerned about the effect savings have on profits and the rate of capital accumulation. He feared that 'the principle of saving, pushed to excess, [will] destroy the motive to production' (Malthus in Ricardo 1951–1955, II: 7–8).

Malthus promoted two main arguments for his proposition that there can be excessive accumulation. In the first place, he criticized Ricardo's argument that the wants of mankind cannot arrest the process of capital accumulation. We have seen that in Ricardo's view only the diminishing returns in agriculture would be capable of doing so (ibid., VI: 318). Malthus denied that aggregate supply and demand are always and automatically equal, because people may not have the will to purchase (ibid., VI: 132).[22] He claimed that 'the tastes and habits of a large body of people are extremely slow in changing; and in the mean time the application of capital in larger quantities than was suited to the progress of the change, would certainly fail to yield such profits as would encourage its continued accumulation and application in the same way' (ibid., 347–348). According to Malthus, consumer preferences adjust very slowly, causing aggregate demand to lag behind aggregate supply when an increase in the capital stock results in higher production rates. The excess supply of commodities lowers profits and temporarily stalls production. This is what Malthus referred to as a universal glut of markets (ibid., II: 308).

Secondly, Malthus argued that labour cannot occasion the demand for the commodities it produces with the new capital invested. To explain this point, it should be noted that Malthus did not include profits in the costs of production. He treated profits as a surplus which remains after labour costs have been deducted from the sale proceeds. By doing so, he created a difference between the exchangeable value of a commodity and the costs of production in terms of labour. In order to pay the capitalists a profit, the labour-commanded value of the commodity should be higher than its labour-embodied value. This means that labour does not receive in wages the value of the commodities it produces. For this reason the demand from productive labourers cannot guarantee the profitable continuation of production. Or: 'To justify the employment of capital, there must be a demand for the produce of it, beyond that which may be created by the demand of the workmen employed (ibid., II: 300–301). Only the purchasing power of the unproductive labourers can furnish this demand. But the capitalists and landowners must reduce their consumption in order to save and realize the expansion of the capital stock (ibid., II: 302–303, 308). By paying labour less than the value of its production, the mechanism of capitalist production creates its own trap: Capital accumulation must lead to a lower profit rate through a lack of demand. In line with this view, Malthus claimed that savings reduce the demand for consumption goods, while at the same time they increase the capacity to produce and supply these goods. He therefore concluded that the demand for these products would not be able to keep up with the pace of production. This was a second argument which led him to reject Say's law (ibid., II: 306–308).

Malthus's argument suggests a sequence analysis of the temporal leads and lags involved in the investment process. Closer inspection reveals that it fails to fulfil this promise. Underconsumption in Malthus' theory arises when there is an excess supply of consumers' goods. This suggests that there is a difference between investment and consumers' goods and therefore a dynamic relationship between saving and investing. Investment goods increase the future capacity to produce consumption goods and provide a link between different production periods. By saving, an individual curtails his current consumption in order to increase the quantity of goods available for consumption at a future date. Saving and investing refer to different time periods and a theory based on their relationship analyses a sequence of production periods. But Malthus failed to appreciate this dynamic aspect of the investment process. In his theory, there is no lag between the act of investment and the increase in production resulting from it. He assumed that investment leads to an immediate increase in production. In his theory savings reduce consumer demand and increase supply in the same period, so creating the impression that they cause overproduction. He completely ignored the fact that investment involves a demand for wage goods to be advanced in this period, while the increased production occurs in a later period.

So, Malthus's analytical basis for contending that growth would stagnate because of a lack of effective demand is extremely flawed. In fact, it rests on a confusion of the temporal relationships involved in the saving-investment relationship. But since he never explained how long a 'temporary' stagnation would last, his controversy with Ricardo ended in a meaningless quarrel about the meaning of such words as 'temporary' and 'permanent'. As Blaug (1958, 93) concludes, the failure to define the time period necessary for changes to take place 'reduced most of the gluts controversy to a battle over the strength of historical forces working to develop new tastes and wants'.

Simonde de Sismondi: Class Conflict and Market Frictions

The Genevese historian and economist J.-C.-L. Simonde de Sismondi was more explicit about the lag involved in the saving-investment relationship. In his *New Principles of Political Economy* (1819) he developed a dynamic argument based on the view that this year's consumption demand is financed out of last year's revenues (Simonde de Sismondi 1991, 104). This is the foundation of a definition of economic equilibrium in terms of the balance between consumption and production (Dome 1989). Simonde de Sismondi was concerned about the level of aggregate income which guarantees the continued production of the same volume of output in succeeding periods. In an earlier book, *De la Richesse Commerciale* (1803), he had even stated this problem in algebraic terms (Sowell 1972b). Clearly, consumption and production here referred to quantities existing at different points in time.

Sowell elaborately claimed that this was the starting point of Simonde de Sismondi's development of a theory of equilibrium aggregate income. But just as with Malthus, the time dimension of this theory is poorly worked out. Simonde de Sismondi was probably more interested in explaining the effects of class conflict than in using effective demand to underpin his claim of a stagnating economy. Hence, he appears to me more a Marxian *avant la lettre* than an early Keynesian. Moreover, he was not consistent in his rejection of Say's law. He often committed the fallacy of composition and offered the observation of particular non-clearing markets as evidence of a general glut of markets.

The vital aspect of Simonde de Sismondi's underconsumption theory is the distinction between two social classes, workers and capitalists. In Marxian fashion, he assumed that capitalists own the means of production and force the working class into a state of dependence (Simonde de Sismondi 1991, 82). This economic power compels the workers to accept wages which, in terms of labour time, are valued lower than their products (ibid., 83). The result is an unequal distribution of income which causes economic growth to stagnate (Schumpeter 1954, 740; Bleaney 1976, 73). Capitalists are assumed to impede the process of growth by consuming part of the funds which can be used for reproduction (Simonde de Sismondi 1991, 274). In Simonde de Sismondi's theory, then, the problem of underconsumption is caused by the poverty of workers. This is what distinguishes him theoretically from Malthus. We have seen that the latter's theory was based on the possibility of an excess degree of saving. Malthus assumed that workers do not save. In his reading of the glut problem, they could therefore not be expected to cause a general excess of production and were not important for an explanation of this situation.

The interesting aspect of Simonde de Sismondi's underconsumption theory is the relationship it posits between revenue, consumption and reproduction. Did he investigate the temporal relationship between saving and investing in a proper way? His start was promising. He stated that '[i]t is the income of the past year which must pay for the output of this year' (Simonde de Sismondi 1991, 104). Simonde de Sismondi here referred to the income of the workers whose wages are advanced by the capitalist. He observed that 'investments' in the wage fund cause a lag between expenditures and income. Producers demand wage goods in order to employ labour, but these advances do not generate output until a later period. This implies that aggregate income depends on the revenue of the goods produced in a previous period. In order to continue the same level of production, it is necessary that this income should be sufficient to pay for the current output. Simonde de Sismondi referred to this condition for equilibrium as the 'mutual balance' between the 'national income and the yearly product'. (ibid., 93). In case of a disruption of this balance, '[i]f the annual income did not buy the total annual product, a part of that product would remain unsold, it would glut the warehouses of the producers, immobilize their capital, and production would stop' (ibid.).

The start was good, but the outcome was not a theory of effective demand. Like Malthus, Simonde de Sismondi was mainly concerned with explaining a supply-side effect. He stressed that aggregate demand would be insufficient to repay the expenses of production. As a consequence the rate of profit would fall, lowering the rate of capital accumulation and causing the economy to stagnate. In other words, ultimately what mattered here was the effect that a lack of demand would have on the profit rate.

In addition, Simonde de Sismondi was not very clear about the exact relationship between revenue, consumption and reproduction. He referred to the 'mutual proportion subsisting among them' and their 'equilibrium' (ibid., 105), but it remains unclear how these quantities influence each other. For certain, the equilibrium between spending and production is a delicate one. Simonde de Sismondi suggested that:

nations fall into ruin equally by spending too much, and by spending too little. A nation spends too much whenever it exceeds its revenue, because it cannot do so except by encroaching on its capital, and thus diminishing future production . . . A nation spends too little, whenever, being destitute of foreign commerce, it does not consume the excess of its production above its exportation' (ibid., 105).

The profits of capital are defined as 'the difference between the sum of advanced wages and the buying price to the ultimate consumer' (ibid., 117). If the producers consume an income beyond their yearly profits, they destroy a part of their capital and thereby a part of the future labour income. On the other hand, if they curtail consumption in favour of investment they cause a fall in aggregate demand below the value of the supply forthcoming. Since they depend on decisions taken in different periods, it is concluded that aggregate supply and demand need not always and automatically equal each other.

This suggests a form of sequence analysis, based on the analytical distinction of separate periods of production, but this suggestion is not made explicit. The least one would expect of such a theory is an explanation of how the different magnitudes are causally related trough time. But these leads and lags are not worked out. Like Malthus, Simonde de Sismondi rested content with the suggestion that it is the lag between income and expenditures which creates the possibility of a disequilibrium between them.

But there is more. There is a distinctive Marxian twist to his rejection of Says' law. This is how a Sismondian attack on the Ricardians would typically run. First, he would criticize Ricardo and Say for asserting that production is unlimited (ibid., 74). We have seen that they generally claimed that there was no limit to the demand for goods and therefore no limit to the employment of capital (Ricardo 1951 1955, I: 296, VI: 131). In their view, an increase in production would always generate a demand sufficient to sell the entire supply at cost-covering prices. By reversing the dependence between production and consumption, Simonde de Sismondi tried to dispel this conclusion of Ricardian analysis. He treated consumption demand as a fixed quantity on the grounds that labour income depends on the revenues of a previous period (Simonde de Sismondi 1991, 104). Since labour income is fixed, the profitability of production in each period depends on a given factor, the demand for consumption goods. For this reason, he asserted that '[a]ggregate consumption determines an equal or greater reproduction' (ibid., 104). And: '[A] consumption increase may alone determine an increase in reproduction, and that on its part consumption can *only* be determined by the income of the consumers' (ibid., 107; emphasis added). Here lies the root of the problem of underconsumption in a capitalist economy. Reproduction depends on the amount of consumption demand sustaining it. But the income of the class which most effectively promotes this demand is rationed by the economic power of the capital-owning class: Capitalists pay workers less than the (labour) value of their products. So, the capacity of the economy to reproduce itself decreases as industrial society produces an ever more unequal distribution of income. In Simonde de Sismondi's theory, the prediction of underconsumption is linked to the development of property relations in an industrial society.

But there is a second line of reasoning in Simonde de Sismondi's criticism of Ricardo's formulation of Say's law (Meek 1963, 330; Bleaney 1976, 76). He tried to disprove the conclusions of this doctrine by questioning the reality of the assumption that competition tends to secure a long-term equilibrium between economic sectors in terms of a uniform rate of profit (Simonde de Sismondi 1991, 228, 257, 618). Simonde de Sismondi noted that an equilibrium rate of profit is never actually observed in real economies. On the contrary, prolonged differences in profit rates between economic activities seem the rule rather than the exception (ibid., 257). He did not accept that production would smoothly adjust to changes in demand and sketched a vision of an invisible hand struggling to clear markets. He stated that in reality market failures are frequent and arise as a result of many frictions impeding adjustment (ibid., 277, 624). In other words, in this case, his dismissal of Say's law involved a fallacy of composition.

His investigation of these frictions is nonetheless not without interest. He stressed the link between persistent dislocations and the presence of fixed capital, both human and physical (Bleaney 1976, 76; Dome 1989). Simonde de Sismondi argued that capital and labour are not easily transferred between alternative employments. He observed that in industrial economies production operates with fixed capital, which cannot be quickly amortized without incurring great costs (Simonde de Sismondi 1991, 256, 257, 624). Similarly, labour skills represent a kind of fixed capital. They are employment-specific and costly to acquire. Workers invest time to learn the tricks of their trade and generally lack the financial means to acquire the skills of another (ibid., 124, 228, 257, 624). These rigidities prevent a timely transfer of productive resources between declining and progressing industries.

The illegitimate step from frictions to the macroeconomy was then made as follows. Simonde de Sismondi (ibid., 277–78) maintained that there was abundant proof:

> of that superabundance of production which exceeds consumption; of a manufacture that does not proportion itself at all to demand . . . No other fact appears to us in more places, under more guises, than the disproportion between the means for consumption and those of production; the inability of producers to

> leave one industry when it declines, and the certainty that their ranks will be thinned by bankruptcies. How is it that the philosophers do not want to see what everywhere springs to the eyes of the common man?

Simonde de Sismondi regarded these dislocations as evidence of a universal glut of markets. The error of the philosophers in question, Ricardo and Say, was that they made 'the annual output . . . the same thing as the income'. However, '[w]ith this principle it becomes absolutely impossible to understand or explain the best demonstrated fact in the whole history of commerce: the satiation of markets' (ibid., 278). To Simonde de Sismondi, stagnation was a fact of life. But his assertion that a general excess of production could in fact occur was based on the observation of satiation in particular markets. Of course the fallacy of composition makes this an invalid inference.

This conclusion illustrates that Simonde de Sismondi's criticism of the law of markets was not always the product of well-reasoned argument on the basis of a specific dynamic theory. In many instances, he discussed frictions which would prevent markets to adjust to changes. Theoretically, such microeconomic arguments cannot dispel the validity of Say's law which is a macroeconomic proposition. But Simonde de Sismondi's work does show that concern for the role of time in economic analysis raised questions about the validity of the concept of economic equilibrium as a scientific tool. After all, in his view markets failed to clear because the adjustment of production took considerable time and was expensive in terms of money and human suffering. He wrote that unemployed workers could die from deprivation because they lost their working skills (ibid., 256). Moreover, the education of a new workforce could take as long as a generation (ibid., 624). It is clear that to Simonde de Sismondi the tendency of supply and demand towards equilibrium was not a theoretical issue which could be abstracted from. Instead the forces which prevented the alignment of supply and demand were real and important enough to warrant the attention of the economic profession.

CONCLUSION

There is a crucial relationship between time and the concept of equilibrium in economics, but this connection is certainly not easy to explain. This is one of the lessons of this chapter. We have seen that J.S. Mill gave an accurate definition of the distinction between statics and dynamics, but subsequently failed to carry through this definition in his own work. The reason for this mishap was the force of tradition. I have argued extensively in this chapter that, contrary to modern translations, classical economics was deeply involved in the analysis of processes taking place in historical time. It was a tradition focussed on the analysis of secular changes which naturally points to the meaning of equilibrium as a process. I have discussed how this process approach operated in both the microeconomic and macroeconomic domain. I have also argued that this approach differs from modern interpretations of the classical doctrine which focus on equilibrium as an end-state.

This distinction is important if we consider the meaning of the glut controversy. This was certainly a confusing debate with parties talking at cross purposes. But I have argued that we can at least distinguish one common thread and that is the focus on Say's law seen as an equality. The interpretation of the debate in terms of Say's identity misdirects our attention to the analysis of short-term rather than long-term effects of macroeconomic disturbances.

I have also argued that the debate brought us several perspectives on a theory in which the time element between saving and investment was more fully worked out. This raised expectations about a truly dynamic theory by our standards, a theory that could be used to explain economic stagnation as an equilibrium with all the proper leads and lags in place. But more than a promise this never became. In general, the classical authors, like their preclassical forerunners, did not have a proper notion of capital, or at least could not model it in an appropriate way. This line of dynamic analysis had to await the arrival of more able theorists, such as Eugen von Böhm-Bawerk and Knut Wicksell. But before we reach this turn in theory, I shall first investigate the impact of the developing mathematical method on the definition of equilibrium in 19th century economics.

NOTES

1. To illustrate that both statics and dynamic involve processes in time, Comte also spoke of the difference between 'uniform motion' and 'varied motion' (ibid., p. 123, 125).
2. See Blaug (1980, 69): 'A *tendency statement* in economics may be regarded ... as a promissory note that is only redeemed when the *ceteris paribus* clause has been spelled out and taken into account, preferably in quantitative terms.' See also de Marchi (1970, 220).
3. Myers (1976) argues that this element of uncertainty was a deliberate choice of Smith, which explains why he never formulated the conditions for market equilibrium in mathematical terms. Smith evidently was unwilling to abandon the rich and vast variety of social life, with its many fascinating complexities, in order to emphasize an abstraction. Myers says that his treatment of equilibrium was incomplete, tentative, and contingent, and he probably intended it this way.

4. The opening remark of chapter 7 of the WN 'Of the natural and market price of commodities' is that natural prices are regulated 'partly by the general circumstances of the society, their riches or poverty, their advancing, stationary or declining conditions; and partly by the particular nature of each employment' (Smith 1937, 55).
5. Hence, he argues that the word equilibrium does not seem appropriate to describe the position of the economic system characterized by natural prices, wages and profits (Garegnani 1976, 26 n.2). That is why he uses the term 'long period position' instead of 'long period equilibrium'.
6. It is not for nothing that Sraffa (1960) based his reinstatement of classical value theory on the assumption of a fixed quantity of output. The possibility of changes in output would have necessitated additional assumptions concerning the economies of scale, which would have complicated his analysis to a great extent. See also Kurz and Salvadori (1995, 19–20).
7. The short run interests in question pointed to the efforts of British merchants to use the parliament to defend their own, particular commercial interests. The Corn laws of 1815 form a well-known example. See also Blaug (1958, 5–10).
8. The classic statement of the distinction between Say's identity and Say's equality is Baumol and Becker (1952). The history of Say's law is discussed in Lambert (1956), Skinner (1967), Sowell (1972a) and Schoorl (1980).
9. Members of the circle around Ricardo were James Mill and John Ramsey McCulloch. For a review of the troops and the rise and decline of Ricardian economics, see Schumpeter (1954, 469–480) and Fetter (1969).
10. In contrast to the Ricardians, the glut theorist cannot be said to represent a genuine 'school'. The group lacked a leading spokesman and therefore an unified doctrine. 'Members' of the group were Spence, Lauderdale, Chalmers, Malthus and Simonde de Sismondi. On their theories, see Sowell (1972a) and (1974).
11. For a review of underconsumption theories in the history of economic thought, see Bleaney (1976).
12. This view is supported by for example Baumol (1977) and Hollander (1979, 1987).
13. For a sympathetic reading of Sowell's interpretation, see for example Rashid (1977).
14. If p represents labour productivity and w the wage rate, the growth rate equals $(p/w)-1$.
15. This latter possibility concerns the case of an 'improving society' which I have discussed earlier.
16. On first sight, it is odd to regard crisis as the equilibrium outcome of capitalistic development, but on the other hand it is the final result of several tendencies working over the very long run, such as the tendency of unemployment to rise, for industry to become more concentrated, for the profit rate to fall, and so on.
17. These lessons were specifically directed to Malthus, who saw the satiation of human wants as a main cause of economic stagnation and his most important point of disagreement with Ricardo. In June 1817 he wrote to Ricardo 'But to come to a still more specific and fundamental cause of our difference, I think it is this. You seem to think that the wants and tastes of mankind are always ready for the supply; while I am most

decidedly of the opinion that few things are more difficult, than to inspire new tastes and wants, particularly out of old materials' (letter of 26 June 1817 in Ricardo 1951–1955, VII: 122).

18. Viewed in this way, the difference between Say and Ricardo was certainly not so great as suggested by Say. See chapter XIX 'On sudden changes in the channels of trade' in Ricardo's *Principles*, in Ricardo (1951–1955, I: 263–281).
19. Malthus, Simonde de Sismondi and Chalmers are referred to.
20. The literature suggests several other items, linking Ricardo's political views and his stance on Say's law. For example, Meek (1967b, 64) pointed to the risk that viewing stagnating aggregate production as a cause of recession could place the capitalist method of production in a bad political light. It suggested that crisis was the endogenous outcome of capitalism, while Ricardo believed that industry was the future of England's economy. Secondly, the recognition of an excess demand for money as an important cause of the depression could have inspired an inflationary policy (Hollander 1979, 539). If an increase in the money supply was an adequate remedy against depressed economic conditions in the short term, then it could be argued that a persistent inflationary policy would be effective in the long run also.
21. It can therefore be questioned whether Malthus defined an equilibrium aggregate income in terms of the equality of ex ante aggregate supply and demand. Of course Keynes's (1933) interpretation of Malthus's work suggests that he had such a theory (see Sowell 1972a, Rashid 1977). But given that an increase in savings was assumed to operate through the profit rate it seems more likely that he had in mind a supply-side effect (Blaug 1958, Hollander 1987, Negishi 1989, Chapter 4).
22. See Rashid (1977) for an interpretation of Malthus's theory of gluts along these lines.

8. Mathematical Revolution

INTRODUCTION

One of the outstanding features of modern economic theory is the use of mathematical models. Moreover, this is a feature that is closely associated with the use of equilibrium concepts, especially in the neoclassical branches of economic theory. That is the reason why the mathematical formulation of economic equilibrium is often seen as a key development in the history of equilibrium economics, to the extent that this history is taken as the story of how economics became a mathematical science. As Ingrao and Israel (1990, 1) put it in their book *The Invisible Hand: Economic Equilibrium in the History of Science*: 'From the outset it has been the aim of the theory whose historical development, main achievements, and state of art are chronicled in this book to use mathematics as its basic tool in describing and analyzing economic reality.'

The previous chapters showed that the history of equilibrium economics is much more than a development which pushed economic science towards mathematical theory. Still, the dominance of mathematical theories of economic equilibrium in modern economics raises some important questions about the connections between the historical development of, on the one hand, equilibrium economics and on the other hand mathematical economics. A first question is why economists turned towards mathematics as a tool of research. Was this the result of forces extraneous to economics? It has been argued that successful mathematical sciences, like physics and astronomy, set an example which economists tried to follow (Mirowski 1989). Or are the causes internal: economists abandoned a degenerating scientific paradigm to develop a new one which proved more successful than its competitors? A second question concerns the consequences of the mathematical method in economics. Did mathematical equilibrium theory shunt economics onto a track – to paraphrase Jevons – that generations of economists were unable to leave? This is a question of path-dependency that can be compared to the problem of why today everybody uses the QWERTY-keyboard while faster alternatives are available.

This chapter addresses this question by looking at the marginalistic revolution of the 1870s. Around this time, three writers simultaneously, and independently of each other, introduced a new price theory which differed from the classical approach, because it put utility and demand at the core of the analysis rather than supply and the costs of production. These writers were Carl Menger, Léon Walras and William Stanley Jevons. The latter two saw their theories as radical departures from the past because they offered a mathematical explanation of prices. Walras considered economics a mathematical science 'on a par with mechanics and astronomy' (Walras 1909, transl. Mirowski and Cook 1990, 213) while Jevons believed mathematical economics 'to be the only basis upon which an ultimate reform of the science of political economy can be founded and a solution to many difficult problems effected' (Letter to Walras, 30 May 1874, in Jaffé 1965 vol. I, 402).

The main question for Chapter 8 and Chapter 9 concerns the impact of the shift towards mathematics as a prime tool of economic analysis. Did mathematics cause a transformation of equilibrium theory in economics? Blaug (1997) claims that Cournot in his *Mathematical principles of the theory of wealth* (1838) was the first to fully substitute the end-state conception of market-clearing equilibria for that of the process conception of competition. Did this also occur with the other pioneers in mathematical economics, like Jevons and Walras? And if so, why did this transformation occur? I shall argue that the end-state conception of equilibrium was not just the result of a mathematical formulation of the problem, but was also associated with a specific vision of economic reality.

This chapter focuses on the contribution of William Stanley Jevons to the development of a mathematical theory of equilibrium in economics. Schabas (1990) speaks of a 'Jevonian revolution' to indicate that due to Jevons's work the mathematical method really took hold in economics. I question the nature of this revolution. The purpose of this chapter is to show that it was not the mathematical method per se which determined the revolutionary character of Jevons's contribution to the development of mathematical economics. In fact, mathematical reasoning only played a minor part in his economics. It was his explanation of why mathematics was important to economics that influenced subsequent developments in economics to a great extent. This explanation was that economics essentially should be seen as a quantitative science. It deals with measurable objects like prices, incomes, quantities traded et cetera, which implies that it was thoroughly empirical in nature and therefore in method. It was this message which caused a break with the prevailing classical methodology in economics.

I shall argue that this quantitative method introduced specific assumptions into economics which led Jevons to exclude dynamic questions from its domain. In Jevons's view, the theory of static equilibrium formed the heart of this quantitative economic science. Moreover, static equilibrium was not just a theoretical concept. For him it formed in a literal sense the nature of economic reality.

One question can be answered from the outset. Jevons is rightfully seen as one of the pioneers of mathematical economics, but he was by no means the first to introduce mathematics into economics. I shall first discuss a few of his predecessors.

EARLY WORK IN MATHEMATICAL ECONOMICS

Both Walras and Jevons stressed the novelty of their mathematical approach to economic theory and were genuinely surprised to find that they had been preceded by others. Jevons published his *Theory of Political Economy* in 1871, Walras followed suit in 1874 with the first part of his *Élements d'économie politique pure*. But they soon learned that many had gone before them.

In 1878 Jevons was forced to concede that '[t]here are, in fact, a whole series of books, hitherto quite unknown, even on the Continent in which the principal ideas of my theory have been foreshadowed' and eventually concluded that the 'mathematical method is as old as the science of Economics itself' (letters to his brother Tom respectively Henry Sidgwick, quoted in Schabas 1990, 27 and 28). In time, he came to see this legacy as support for his theory rather than as a threat to his claim of originality and appended to the second edition of his *Theory* a bibliography of works on mathematical economics since the early 18th century.

Walras learned of Jevons's existence in 1874, just before the publication of his *Elements*, and had to concede his priority with regard to the development of a mathematical theory of economic value and exchange on the basis of the principle of marginal utility.[1] He also paid tribute to Heinrich Hermann Gossen (for the discovery of 'utility curves'), Augustin Cournot (for the application of mathematical functions to economics) and his father Auguste Walras who had endeavoured to explain economic value in terms of both scarcity and utility.[2]

However, the history of mathematical economics goes back further than these names. The physiocrats were probably among the first to explicitly use mathematical calculation in economic theory. As was explained in Chapter 5, the *Tableau économique* graphically showed how the rate of economic growth depended on the agricultural surplus (the *net produit*) and how the division of the national product took place between the three income classes, the land-owning class, agriculture and the sterile class (husbandry, etc.). The physiocrats assigned numerical values to the variables of their *Tableaux*, such as inputs and outputs and the division of incomes. In this manner the *Tableau économique* was used as an instrument to calculate the effect of different tax schemes and other policy measures on economic welfare. François Quesnay, the founding father of the school, formulated the physiocratic vision on the role of mathematics in economics as follows (Quesnay 1764, xlii):

> La science économique est appronfondie & développée par l'examen & par la raisonnement; mais sans les calculs, elle seroit toujours une science indéterminée, confuse & livrée par-tout à l'erreur & au préjugé.

However, it was the content rather than the method of the physiocratic doctrine that inspired the next steps in the field of mathematical economics. The physiocrats made the strong claim that agriculture is the only source of economic value, but they never explained why. Quesnay's *Tableaux* simply assumed that the rate of reproduction of a given input is higher in agriculture than in other economic sectors. Also, they never dealt with the problem of economic value or price at a more disaggregated level. There was in their work no systematic analysis of the relationship between prices and the quantities demanded and supplied.

This omission provoked a response by two, now almost forgotten, forerunners of the mathematical method in economics, Achylle-Nicolas Isnard (1749–1803) and Nicolas-François Canard (1750–1833). Both rejected the physiocratic assumption that all net product derives from agriculture and tried to demonstrate that other economic activities generate a surplus of revenue over costs as well. In the process, they developed some interesting mathematical notions of economic equilibrium.

Isnard's *Traité des Richesses* (1781) was a first step in this direction. The key to this book is an equation of exchange which relates relative values to the quantities traded in the market. According to Isnard, the proportion between the (absolute) values of the commodities M and M' must be equal to the inverse of the ratio of their respective quantities exchanged. Or:

$$M/M' = b/a$$

In this formula a represents the quantity exchanged of commodity M and b indicates the quantity exchanged of commodity M'.

Isnard clearly saw a and b as equilibrium quantities (there is no unsatisfied demand), but also treated them as constants. There was no notion that it is a process of price adjustment which causes the equality between supply and demand. This leads Ingrao and Israel (1990, 66) to content that Isnard failed to develop a notion of economic equilibrium because his equation of exchange does not represent a balance of forces. However, Isnard was not unfamiliar with this notion. For example, he argued that the profit rate of the use of capital in industry, commerce and agriculture would tend to a uniform level. This tendency was a matter of supply and demand pressures in the sense that production moves to better earning places:

> Cette uniformité à lieu & l'équilibre établit, parce que les fonds se rendent & affluent dans les lieux où l'interèt est le plus fort . . . lorseque les choses sont plus payées dans un lieu que dan un autre, elles y affluent & l'équilibre se rétablit (Isnard 1781, 49).

This equilibrium mechanism underpins Isnard's capital theory and can be seen as a background to his equation of exchange.

The best proof of the analytical quality of Isnard's work is the extension of his equation of exchange to the multi-good case (ibid., 19–21). Isnard demonstrated that the ratios of values between three goods can be determined in a multi-equational system. The condition for solving this system is to ascertain that the number of equations equals the number of goods exchanged. Until the 1930s, the counting of equations and unknowns remained the only procedure to check the existence of an equilibrium price vector in a general equilibrium system.

But there was more. Isnard also reduced the number of unknowns by expressing values in terms of an arbitrary standard commodity (ibid., 22). Innovations like these fuel the claim of Jaffé (1969) that Isnard's work had a direct influence on Walras's formulation and treatment of the general equilibrium system. According to Jaffé, 'nearly the whole of the formal apparatus of Walras's theory of exchange, apart from the utility maximization engine, was ready at hand in Isnard's *Traité des Richesses* for Walras to use' (ibid., 29). Moreover, he claims that a detailed comparison of their theories shows that Walras followed this example closely and worked out the mathematical framework of his general equilibrium theory with Isnard's *Traité* 'at his elbow' (ibid., 42).[3]

This conclusion may be exaggerated (and in any case, hard to prove) but the work of Isnard surely suggests a French line of economic thought which runs from the physiocrats to Walras and the school of Lausanne. The key characteristic of this tradition is that it placed economic equilibrium at the core of the analysis (albeit in different meanings) and used mathematics as a convenient tool in the process of economic reasoning.

Canard is a representative of this tradition. Like Isnard, he developed a mathematical notion of economic equilibrium which grew out of his criticism of the physiocratic focus on land as the sole producer of economic wealth. Canard identified labour as the source of all wealth, but did accept the physiocratic notion of economic equilibrium as the reproduction of the national product. Stronger even, he considered it the basis of political economy: 'L'équilibre des trois sources de rentes est la base de l'économie politique; c'est à ce principe que se ramènent toutes la questions de cette science importante' (Canard 1801, 15).[4] This equilibrium is established because each individual chooses for himself the most advantageous combination of the three types of income. If one type of income is more attractive than another, competition will shift in its favour until a new equilibrium level is reached. The flow of money and goods through the channels of trade is subsequently compared to the circulation of blood, just like the physiocrats had done. There is even an echo of Boisguilbert's 'chain of opulence' in the suggestion that 'all channels of general circulation communicate with all the others in such a way that the world of trade becomes a single whole that participates in the law of equilibrium'.[5] The force behind this equilibrium is 'the tendency of all individuals to seek always their greatest advantage'.

All this was not new when Canard published his *Principes d'économie politique* in 1801. The novelty of his work lies in the analysis of the problem of price determination. It is here that he gives a mathematical definition of economic equilibrium and even applies a kind of marginal analysis to solve for the equilibrium price.

Canard's explanation was based on the assumption that the intensity of supply and demand is determined by the sellers' need (b) and their competition (n), respectively the buyers's need (B) and competition (N). Initially, buyers and sellers bid different prices (buyers higher than sellers) and the difference between their offers L (from Latitude) is the starting point of the analysis. Canard argued that the strength of supply and demand determines the actual price which is x above the minimum price and $(\mathrm{L} - x)$ below the maximum price. The buyers' strength, which is represented by the product of B and N, tends to raise x, while the product of b and n (sellers' strength) has the effect of raising $(\mathrm{L} - x)$.[6] Canard thought of the products BN and bn in terms of forces. Multiplied by respectively $(\mathrm{L} - x)$ and x they expressed the determination of the contractors. Hence, the contractors agree when $\mathrm{BN}(\mathrm{L} - x) = bnx$. Canard called this equilibrium condition, the equation of determination (ibid., 30 and 31, italics in the original text).

> Cette équation, que j'appellerai *équation des déterminations*, exprime l'égalité *des momens de deux forces opposées*, qui se fond équilibre. C'est au principe de l'équilibre de ces deux forces que se rapporte toute la theorie économique, comme c'est au principe de l'équilibre de lévier que se rapporte toute la statique.

Sixty years before Jevons, one finds here an explicit reference to the parallel between an equation of exchange and the equilibrium of the lever.

The first half of the 18th century saw relatively few contributions to mathematical economics. In France, the school of J.B. Say put its mark on the young economic science with its distrust and dislike of mathematical formalization (Ingrao and Israel 1990, 89). It is therefore not surprising that the two notable exceptions came from other scientific circles, in this case that of the engineers. Both Antoine-Augustin Cournot (1801–1877) and Jules Dupuit (1804–1866) were products of the French *grandes écoles*. Cournot attended the École Normale while Dupuit graduated from the École des Ponts et Chaussées. This schooling gave them a firm knowledge of mathematics and applied mechanics, which they subsequently used in their studies of economic problems. Their efforts in the field of economics led to the first mathematical investigations of the law of demand.

Dupuit was not just an engineer. As the inspector-general of civil engineering he was one of the most distinguished engineers in France at the time. His economic interests were inspired by his involvement in the construction of public works. In addition to the engineering aspects of public works like roads, bridges and water works, he wanted to know the social value of these works. Was public investment a profitable undertaking from the viewpoint of society as a whole? This question pointed to the meaning and measurement of public utility.

Dupuit approached utility as a microeconomic question. He defined it as the greatest sacrifice each consumer is willing to make in order to obtain a certain quantity of a good.[7] This definition suggests a subjective interpretation of utility and indeed Dupuit averred that each consumer attaches a different utility to the same object according to his or her wishes and desires (Dupuit 1849, 16). The marginal utility of some particular good diminishes with increases in quantity, because subsequent units are used to satisfy less pressing needs. Dupuit thus explained the rationale of the law of diminishing marginal utility, which he illustrated with practical examples like the value of an increase in the supply of drinking water to individual consumers.

To Dupuit this law was not an abstract relation, suitable only to theoretical investigation. As an engineer, he sought practical solutions and aimed to ground theory in fact. Accordingly, the utility curve was made into an instrument of applied economic analysis by means of the assumption that utility has a pecuniary expression (ibid., 22). Consumers's sacrifice in terms of money declines as their consumption of subsequent units of a good satisfies the less pressing needs. On the basis of this assumption, Dupuit constructed a demand curve which states a negative relation between price and quantity consumed (ibid., 25):

> Écrire dans deux colonnes la loi de consommation de ce produit, c'est-à-dire la quantité d'objets consommés correspondant à chaque prix, depuis zéro jusqu'aux prix qui fait disparaître toute consommation, en faisant croître ce prix par légères différences; prendre les diminutions successives de la consommation amenées par l'augmentation de prix, et les multiplier par le prix correspondant à cette dimunition.

Note that this 'curve of consumption' makes no distinction between price and marginal utility, because the utility of a commodity is measured as a demand price. Dupuit also provided a geometrical and graphical analysis of the demand curve (Dupuit 1844[1934], 62–65 and 208).

But, as was noted above, the demand curve was nothing more than an instrument. Dupuit's real interest was welfare analysis: what was the effect of tolls and transport charges? Or, what was the optimum provision of public goods from a welfare perspective? Dupuit's answer to these questions is a powerful display of equilibrium analysis. The starting point of this analysis was the recognition that total utility, the surface under the utility curve, is divided into three parts: consumer surplus, producer surplus and lost utility. This division allowed him to assess the effects of monopoly pricing and price discrimination. Also, it was the basis on which he established a general rule for the provision of public goods. This rule was that the government should provide these goods, if a pricing scheme could be devised such that the revenue covered the total annual cost, while producing some 'net utility'. In other words, the marginal annual receipts of an enterprise should cover the marginal costs to be amortized annually over a specific number of years (Ekelund and Hébert 1997, 279).

Probably the most important predecessor of Walras and Jevons was Antoin-Augustin Cournot. Both acknowledged him as a forerunner and praised the qualities of his *Recherches sur les principes mathématiques de la théorie des richesses* (1838). Cournot was a professional mathematician (his teachers were Lagrange, Laplace and Poisson) and therefore in a better position to apply mathematics to economics than most contemporary economists. He criticized the economics profession for their focus on numerical calculation. According to him, the value of mathematics to applied sciences like economics was that it constituted a convenient tool for expressing complex ideas. It could perform this role because it could describe relations between variables in terms of functions even when these variables concerned magnitudes which could not be estimated numerically.

Given this view, it is not surprising that Cournot was able to solve a problem which had troubled the classical economists to such an extent, the relation between market price and the quantity consumed (see Chapter 7). Cournot called the proportions theory of price determination 'devoid of meaning' (Cournot 1838[1960], 45). He correctly defined the law of demand as a mathematical function which treats the quantity demanded as the dependent variable and price as the independent variable, or D = F(p).

The problem of most classical economists was that they were unable to separate the relationship between dependent and independent variables from the influence of other causal factors. Or, they were insufficiently aware of the importance of a ceteris paribus clause. Cournot perfectly understood the value of the assumption of 'other things equal'. He was well aware of the fact that demand depends on many factors like 'the habits and customs of the people, on the average wealth and on the scale on which wealth is distributed' (ibid., 47). But the demand curve is drawn up under the condition that 'all these conditions relative to demand remain the same'.

This does not mean that to Cournot the demand curve was an apriori concept. He believed that mathematics provided a tool for theoretical reasoning but in the end theory had to correspond to empirical reality. In the case of the demand curve, market price p is defined as the average annual price with F(p) the quantity sold annually in the market under consideration (ibid., 51). In other words, Cournot's demand function 'is a curve connecting time-series data on sales and the prices at which these prices are realized' (Ekelund and Hébert 1997, 262).

However, Cournot's empiricism did not restrict the domain of theoretical analysis. On the contrary, he was one of the first to consistently apply marginal analysis to the investigation of the market mechanism. He mathematically derived a rule for profit maximization which stated that marginal revenue should equal marginal cost. As Cournot put it: 'Whatever may be the abundance of the source of production, the producer will always stop when the increase in expense exceeds the increase in receipts' (Cournot 1838[1960], 59). He used this rule to give a clear statement of the simple competitive model which he called 'unlimited competition' (ibid., 90–98), but he was also able to deal with situations of imperfect competition like monopoly. Famous is his treatment of duopoly theory in terms of a reaction curve which laid the groundwork for many other ideas of importance to economics, such as game theory. The idea that the output decisions of entrepreneurs depend on what they expect their competitors to supply, also led him to analyze the stability of various equilibrium situations (ibid., 99–116).

These studies are all exercises in partial equilibrium analysis. Concerning general economic equilibrium, Cournot was pessimistic that the mathematical method would bring analytical progress. He realized that 'for a complete and rigorous solution of the problems relative to some parts of the economic system [it is] indispensable to take the entire system into consideration'. But Cournot believed that this would 'surpass the powers of mathematical analysis and of our practical methods of calculation' (Cournot 1838[1960], 127). For this reason, Schumpeter (1954, 960) concludes that he had no more 'than a vague and nonoperational idea of general equilibrium'.

This short review may suggest that France was the only country where prior to the marginal revolution of the 1870s mathematics was applied to economic problems. This impression is wrong. Important developments in the field of mathematical economics originated in the German economic tradition which, due to the famous *Methodenstreit* between Menger and Schmoller, is now mainly known for its historical and anti-theoretical approach of science. According to Streissler (1990a, 55), one may even speak of a proto-neoclassical school in Germany which in the period 1825 to 1875 already used 'partial equilibrium analysis of demand and supply par excellence'. The key notions of this school were:

- The explanation of commodity prices and factor prices in terms of both supply and demand;
- The deduction of supply and demand to their underlying causes, respectively costs of production and utility;
- The use of marginal concepts to discuss the effect of utility on demand and to root supply in the production decisions of entrepreneurs.

One of the founding fathers of this tradition was Karl Heinrich Rau (1792–1870), the author of a popular textbook which had the same title as Carl Menger's: *Grundsätze der Volkswirthschaftlehre* (first edition 1826). From the fourth edition (1841) onwards, this book contained a supply and demand schedule diagram with the equilibrium price at the intersection of the schedules (Streissler 1990a, 51). Likewise, Hans von Mangoldt (1824–1868) in his *Grundriß der Volkswirthschaftslehre* (1863) presented a graphical analysis of price in terms of supply and demand schedules. But in addition he provided a mathematical analysis of market equilibrium in the case where the supply of the good in question depends on the prices of substitutes or complements (Mosselmans 2000).[8]

Several authors of this German protoneoclassical tradition discussed demand in terms of marginal utility. The best known of these is Hermann Heinrich Gossen (1810–1858). He formulated the principle of diminishing marginal utility and gave it graphical and mathematical expression. His 'Gesetz der Abnahme der Größe des Genusses' depends on two factors: marginal utility tends to fall with (1) the time duration of the 'pleasure' experience, and (2) the repetition of the pleasure experience, that is the consumption of an extra unit (Gossen 1854[1967], 4–5).[9] Also he recognized that for maximum welfare, a given quantity of a good should be divided among alternative uses in such a manner that the marginal utilities are equal in all uses (ibid., 11).

Concerning the marginal analysis of production and distribution, Johann Heinrich von Thünen (1783–1850) is a name that must be mentioned. Von Thünen developed a marginal productivity analysis of wages, but is best known for his economic theory of location (Ekelund and Hébert 2002). Like Ricardo, he recognized that differences in the cost of production of producing agricultural products result from utilization of land of different quality and location. The latter effect (differences in location) is analyzed in a hypothetical economy of circular form and uniform fertility. The marketplace is located at the center of this economy which means that transportation costs determine the extensive margin of production. As transportation costs differ between products, resources should be allocated up to the point where the cost of producing one product equals the cost of producing any reasonable substitute, a clear illustration of the principle of equimarginal allocation.

But there is more. Schumpeter (1954, 466) says that von Thünen was 'the first to use the calculus as a form of economic reasoning'. Also he used numerical data to support his generalizations which made him 'one of the patron saints of econometrics'. Other achievements to his credit constitute his vision of the general interdependence of all economic quantities and the necessity of representing this 'cosmos' by a system of equations.

JEVONS'S CONCEPTION OF SCIENCE

To economists Jevons is mainly known as the author of the *Theory of Political Economy* (1870), first published in 1871, and a number of applied economic studies like *A Serious Fall in the Value of Gold* (1863) and *The Coal Question* (1865). But the range of his academic pursuits was much broader than economics. He was initially trained to become a chemist, a discipline which introduced him to the natural sciences and related fields like logic and mathematics. Philosophy was another of his passions and one which brought him to study the nature of human knowledge (that is psychology). A five year stay in Australia prompted a study of meteorology (he was the first to systematically collect weather data in Australia) and one of his more outlandish scientific endeavours was music theory (Mosselmans 1999). Given this range of interests, it is not surprising that he considered his *Principles of Science* (1874) his most important book.

The crucial aspect of Jevons's conception of science was that he was an empiricist through and through. According to Jevons, in science 'the investigator begins with facts and ends with them' (Jevons 1877[1958], 509). In essence, his conception of science was very simple. He believed that observational experience is the only source of knowledge. He said that 'it is quite impossible to make any real additions to the contents of our knowledge except through new impressions upon the senses' (ibid., 218). In other words, for Jevons induction was the prime tool of scientific analysis.

This position may seem strange for one who was an avid advocate of the use of mathematics in science, but from Jevons's point of view the preference for induction was perfectly logical. He believed that induction was the inverse operation of deduction and could only be performed by the use of deduction (Jevons 1879, 17). In that sense, the empirical method and the use of mathematics were closely related.

Moreover, in Jevons's view mathematics presumed the existence of quantitative notions in science. These were not just numerical values but any variable which was measurable in principle. As Jevons put it, 'if [a] thing may be greater or less, or the event may happen sooner or later, nearer or farther, then quantitative notions enter, and the science must be mathematical in nature, by whatever name we call it' (ibid., 7). From this point of view, it can be argued that to Jevons quantity and mathematics were one and the same (Schabas 1990, 75). He stressed that every science as it progresses will become gradually more and more quantitative. And, as soon as the quantitative character of a sciences emerges, it becomes a mathematical science.

So what was this inductive method which could be said to be the inverse of deduction? Jevons called it the 'complete method' to indicate that it combines observation, deduction and induction 'in the most complete and perfect way' (Jevons 1879[1957], 17). According to this method, observation is the first step of science. The facts of experience are the basis on which to 'frame an hypothesis as to the laws governing those facts'. Then 'we reason from the hypothesis deductively to the results to be expected'. Finally, verification must show that predicted results are in accordance with reality. '[W]e then examine these results in connection with the facts in question; coincidence confirms the whole reasoning; conflict obliges us either to seek for disturbing causes or else to abandon our hypothesis' (ibid.).

However, the process of hypothesis formation was more demanding than the blind accumulation of facts. Jevons observed that many sciences had developed successful theories before consulting the facts. For example, '[h]ad physicists waited until their data were perfectly precise before they brought in the aid of mathematics, we should still have been in the age of Galileo' (Jevons 1879[1957], 6). In light of the experience of the physical sciences, Jevons advised scientists to be creative, to develop bold hypotheses. For inspiration they could draw on the theoretical framework of more advanced sciences. In a sense, the use of analogies was nothing but the application of the principle of induction to the sciences themselves. As

Jevons put it, '[i]t is the proper course of reasoning to proceed from the known to the unknown . . . The physical sciences may therefore be properly made the practise-ground of the reasoning powers, because they furnish us with a great body of precise and successful investigation' (Jevons 1877[1958], vii–viii). The result was that in Jevons's writings the physical sciences often figure not only as an example of how science should proceed but also as an example of how theories should be built. This method of working had important implications for the place of equilibrium theory in economics, as will be shown below.

The advice to develop bold hypotheses did not prevent that ultimately empirical reality determined the borders of the theoretical domain. 'I hold that in all cases of inductive inference we must invent hypotheses, until we fall upon some hypothesis which yields deductive results in accordance with experience' (ibid., 228). In the final analysis, science was to Jevons solely an empirical matter. He was careful to point out that mathematics could never increase the degree of certainty of a scientific theory. Mathematics greatly facilitated the logical rigour of the deductive process but 'agreement with fact [was] the sole and sufficient test of a true hypothesis' (ibid., 511).

It has to be stressed that the inductive method as formulated by Jevons was by no means a new methodology in the middle of the 19th century. J.S. Mill had already described it as the Concrete Deductive Method in his *System of Logic* (1844) and it had in fact become the standard view in the philosophy of science in this period (Blaug 1980, 2). Jevons did not hide this fact. He said that Mill was 'substantially correct in considering our science a case of what he calls the Concrete Deductive Method' (Jevons 1879[1957], 6). The point was that Mill saw it as one of several possible inductive methods, while Jevons considered it 'induction in its essential form'. Moreover, from his words we may infer that he considered it the only relevant method as 'it is found to be the method of all the inductive sciences' (ibid., 8).

But induction is a road with many obstacles. Jevons understood that the human eye was denied direct access to the laws of nature. Concerning the operation of nature, 'we are in the position of spectators who witness the productions of a complicated machine, but are not allowed to examine its intimate structure' (Jevons 1877[1958], 222). Luckily, the spectators do observe something which may lift a tip of the veil. Some events appear in regular patterns and this observation feeds our suspicion that there is a causal mechanism at work. In his own words, 'when we find two phenomena which do proceed, time after time, through changes of the same period, there is much probability that they are connected' (ibid., 451). In this view, causation was nothing but the correlation of events through time. The best one could say of a cause was that it preceded its effect in time and indeed Jevons seems to have upheld this notion of causation (MacLennan 1972, 59–60; Peart

1993, 443). This result put probability theory at the heart of Jevons's epistemology. According to him, the nature of scientific knowledge was probabilistic as the appearance of natural events was governed by the laws of chance. The following quotation succinctly summarizes this view (Jevons 1877[1958], 150).

> Nature is to us like an infinite ballot box, the contents of which are being continually drawn ball after ball and exhibited to us. Science is but the careful observation of the succession in which balls of various character present themselves; we register the combinations, notice those which seem to be excluded from occurrence, and from the proportional frequency of those which appear we infer the probable character of future drawings.

Jevons realized that the 'infinite ballot-box of nature' could never be fully explained. Repeated observation of the same pattern of events would raise one's confidence in the postulated correlation between two or more variables but a rational expectation of this kind could never become absolutely certain. The obstacle here is Hume's induction problem: one cannot make general statements about an infinite number of events (that is the future) on the basis of a limited number of observations (Schabas 1990, 69). Therefore, our use of inductive inference proceeds under the assumption that nature's probability distributions will be constant through time (Jevons 1877[1958], 239 and 150).

> Even when by the theory of probabilities we succeed in forming some notion of the comparative confidence with which we should receive inductive results, it yet appears that we must make an assumption. Events come out like balls from the vast ballot-box of nature, and close observation will enable us to form some notion . . . of the contents of that ballot-box. But we must still assume that, between the time of an observation and that to which our inference relate, no change in the ballot-box has been made.

Jevons was in other words well aware of the limitations of scientific knowledge and on several occasions warned against the pretensions of science. Given that nature would always remain a black box, no claim to knowledge would withstand the test of time. Especially, he feared that the establishment of a standard of orthodoxy would stifle the freedom of scientific inquiry that he considered so important to the advancement of science. This was the case in economics where the teachings of the Ricardian school dominated scientific discourse and left no room for new developments. Jevons had experienced this resistance at first hand. As a student of political economy, he paid dearly for his unwillingness to respect the views of his professor, Jacob Waley (Schabas 1990, 20). A few years later in 1862 he presented his first sketch of a 'general mathematical theory of Economy' to section F of the British Association, but the paper was received 'without a word of interest or belief' (quoted in ibid.).[10] It is therefore not surprising that he somewhat sarcastically concluded that 'in the republic of the sciences sedition and even anarchy are [more] beneficial in the long run' (quoted in ibid., 82).

In turn, Jevons had his own blind spot and appeared at times a not very subtle philosopher of science. Without explanation he assumed that one method would serve all sciences, whether moral or natural. Moreover, this method leaned heavily on the ability to generate testable predictions. Schabas (1990, 55) concludes that Jevons was 'first and foremost the practical scientist with little patience for philosophical problems that might impede the task at hand'. Black (1972) says that Jevons's scientific training and his experiences with meteorological research in Australia had shown him the scientific use of data collecting and statistics. This may explain why he valued the natural sciences to such an extent and saw them as the prime example for other sciences like economics.

The cost of this empirical approach came in two forms. First, Jevons had an excessive belief in the law-like character of nature. In contrast to his careful remarks about the probabilistic character of theories, he saw nature as deterministic: all appearances and events are governed by law. He could not accept the idea that events are random or not subject to law because that would rob science of its only instrument of inquiry, induction. Second, he literally believed that nature was 'a world ruled by number' (Schabas 1990). Understanding the laws of nature meant the estimation of a numerical relationship. In many cases, one lacked the statistical instruments to make the necessary calculations, but in principle the manifestations of nature were measurable magnitudes. Both effects had their impact on how Jevons saw the nature of the economy and, consequently, his view on the role of equilibrium theory as a mode of explanation in economics.

THE INTRODUCTION OF MARGINAL UTILITY

A good way to characterize the role of Jevons in the marginalistic revolution is to repeat the words of Terence Hutchison who once said that what was most important about marginal utility was 'the adjective rather than the noun' (Hutchison 1953). The aim of Jevons's *Theory of Political Economy* was to correct the erroneous view that labour is the origin of value. According to him, 'value depends entirely upon utility' (Jevons 1879[1957], 1). He called this 'a somewhat novel opinion' because he was aware that utility per se was by no means a new concept in economics. On the contrary, the roots of the idea that utility considerations play a part in the determination of market prices goes back to Greek and Roman times. What was novel was his explanation of the way in which utility governs economic choices and thereby the determination of prices. Prices depend on marginal, not total utility and by explaining this difference Jevons earned his title as father of the marginalistic revolution.

The basis of Jevons's concept of utility was Jeremy Bentham's theory of pleasure and pain. According to this theory, all human feelings have two dimensions, the attraction of pleasure and the fear of pain. By looking at the circumstances associated with these feelings, Bentham tried to estimate the extent of pleasure and pain in different feelings. Jevons used two of these circumstances – the intensity of a feeling and its duration – to go a step further and explain pleasure and pain as quantities. He argued that the quantity of a feeling would increase with its intensity and its duration and demonstrated in a diagram how these relationships could be represented geometrically.

In Jevons's *Theory of Political Economy* the introduction of the feelings of pleasure and pain served two purposes. In the first place, the notion that pleasure and pain were quantities supported the claim of Jevons that economics was a quantitative science and thereby a mathematical science. Secondly, he used the feelings of pleasure and pain to define the notion of utility. In Jevons's representation of the economic world, all people are driven by pleasure and pain which makes them calculators *pur sang*. Their main goals are to minimize pain and to maximize pleasure and the explanation of these calculations was, in the words of Jevons, 'the problem of economics'. The step from feelings to economic choices was taken by looking at the sources of pleasure and pain. Jevons saw labour as the most common manifestation of 'economic' pain. By contrast the sources of pleasure were the products of labour, goods like food, clothing, buildings, utensils etcetera. The sum of the quantities of pleasure and pain generated by production and consumption could be said to form 'an addition to a person's happiness' and it was this quantity which Jevons called 'utility'; '[i]t is a convenient name for the aggregate of the favourable balance of feeling produced – the sum of the pleasure created and the pain prevented' (ibid., 45).

Jevons stressed that as defined in this manner utility was not an intrinsic quality of a thing. A persons's enjoyment of a given commodity may differ depending upon his preferences and circumstances. The example cited by Jevons was that of water. A given quantity of this commodity may save a person from dying. Evidently, its utility in this situation will be high. But in circumstances where water is abundant the use of the same quantity of water is 'a matter of comparative indifference'. In other words, utility is an 'abstract quality' of the relationship between a person and a commodity and not an inherent property of any one thing (ibid., 38 and 44).

This line of reasoning suggests that there is an important difference between total and marginal utility or 'the degree of utility', as Jevons called it. He argued that the utility of a given quantity of food would decline with the total quantity of food consumed and demonstrated this relationship in a diagram. In his view, utility could be represented in a mathematical way as a function of x, the quantity consumed. Using this representation, he mathematically derived the equation of the degree of utility which is 'the differential coefficient of u considered as a function of x' (ibid., 51). Total utility is then the area under the utility curve and marginal utility is the addition to this quantity produced by the consumption of an infinitesimal quantity of x. With these concepts properly defined, Jevons was able to give an accurate statement of the 'general law of the variation of the final degree of utility'; '*the degree of utility varies with the quantity of commodity, and ultimately decreases as that quantity increases*' (emphasis in the original, ibid., 53). Today this law is commonly known as Gossen's first law.

The careful exposition of utility theory was necessary to clear up for once and for all the confusion surrounding the word value. The popular use of this word was 'value in use' which was the same as total utility in Jevons's terminology. Another meaning of the word value was 'esteem' or 'urgency of desire'. This meaning could now be distinguished as the final degree of utility. Finally, the word value signified the price or market value of a commodity. According to Jevons, the meaning of value in this sense was not a quantity but a ratio: the quantity of commodity x exchanged for one unit of another good. Thus the market value of a commodity was best called 'the ratio of exchange' in order to prevent confusion with the other meanings of the 'dangerous' word value (ibid., 79).

Jevons's theory of exchange explained this ratio as follows: '*The ratio of exchange of any two commodities will be the reciprocal of the ratio of the final degrees of utility of the quantities of commodity available for consumption after the exchange is completed*' (ibid., emphasis in the original, 95). This is the famous equation of exchange, the centrepiece of Jevons's mathematical economic analysis. The equation of exchange is an equilibrium condition because it determines the price at which both participants to the exchange are able to maximize their utility. In the words of Jevons, '[t]his point of equilibrium will be known by the criterion that an infinitely small amount of commodity exchanged in addition, at the same rate, will bring neither gain nor loss of utility' (ibid., 96). The intuition behind this condition is that the price of a commodity represents a cost (in terms of utility foregone) which must be balanced with the gain produced by the consumption of an extra unit of the commodity in question. If cost and gain are not equal, the exchange will continue because people will find it beneficial to buy or sell an extra unit. 'Exchange will thus go on until each party has obtained all the benefit that is possible, and loss of utility would result if more were exchanged. Both parties, then, rest in satisfaction and equilibrium, and the degrees of utility have come to their level, as it were' (ibid.).

The main aim of Jevons was to give a mathematical explanation of the equation of exchange as an optimality condition but he only partly succeeded in this aim. His main achievement was the formulation of the equation of exchange in terms of functional relationships. But he did not determine the equilibrium price by deriving the first order conditions of the individual's optimization problem, that is he did not attempt to find the maximum point on the utility curve. Instead his proof consisted in the equation of the quantities exchanged between two market agents, given their supplies. In equilibrium the loss of utility (marginal utility times the quantity supplied) should equal the gain of utility (marginal utility times the quantity demanded). By substitution, this equation can be reworked into the equation of exchange. Of course this is not a mathematical proof but an equality: the equation simply defines equilibrium. The equilibrium derived in this way cannot be shown to be a maximum point in the sense that it represents the price at which the two market participant maximize their respective utilities.[11]

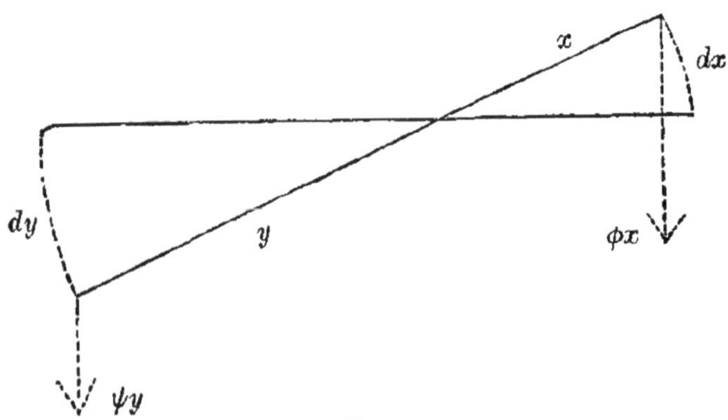

FIG. 6.

Source: Jevons (1879[1957], 133)

Figure 8.1 Equilibrium of the lever

This failure may explain why Jevons found it necessary to use an analogy in order to demonstrate the equilibrium character of his equation of exchange. This analogy was the theory of the lever. Jevons found it remarkable that 'when we take the theory of the lever . . . we get equations exactly similar in form as those of the theory of value as established above' (ibid., 104). This similarity occurred because the theory was based on the principle of virtual velocities. If a lever in equilibrium is disturbed by an infinitesimal small displacement, another displacement will occur which exactly balances the force of the original disturbance. According to Jevons, the mechanism of this equilibrium could be translated into the terms of his theory of exchange. Here marginal utility took the place of force working upon the arms of the lever. The displacements of the arms were the infinitesimal quantities exchanged, *d*x and *d*y. Finally, the total supply of x and y represented the length of the arms. In order to make the analogy even more explicit, Jevons included a diagram which showed the working of this equilibrium of exchange (φx and ψy are the symbols of marginal utility).

> The reader will not fail to notice the remarkable analogy between this theory and that of the equilibrium of two forces regarded according to the principle of virtual velocities. A rigid lever will remain in equilibrium under the action of two forces, provided that the algebraic sum of the two forces, each multiplied by its infinitely small displacement, be zero. Substitute for force degree of utility, positive or negative, and for infinitely small displacements infinitely small quantities of commodity exchanged, and the principles are identical (Jevons 1879[1957], 133).

The great achievement of Jevons was that he defined a new concept of economic equilibrium which used the mathematical notion of a maximum point. In his eyes, economic equilibrium was a set of prices and quantities which allowed the trading partners to maximize their respective utilities. Moreover, he was able to state this definition in terms of a single equation, the equation of exchange. But the extent of his mathematical analysis did not go much further than the description of the problem of exchange. Jevons was not able to prove that the balance of the forces of supply and demand in a two-party exchange constitutes a maximum solution. As Schabas (1990, 52) concludes, for Jevons mathematics was first and foremost a heuristic device: 'The calculus guided him toward the marginal analysis of prices and cost as well as the equimarginal principle.' But in his theory of exchange '[t]here are neither formal proofs nor a systematic recognition of all the various underlying assumptions'.

THE TRANSFORMATION OF EQUILIBRIUM

Jevons's theory of exchange changed the classical conception of economic equilibrium in a crucial respect. The classical economists had seen the concept of equilibrium as a characteristic of the dynamic movement of economic changes. To them equilibrium was the point of attraction, the equality of supply and demand to which economic forces always tend after a disturbance. In this view, economic changes were a tendency controlled by the laws of economic equilibrium. With Jevons this notion of equilibrium as the end point of a process of change disappeared. He also observed that changes take time and that markets are not always in a supply and demand equilibrium, but in his economic theory the concept of equilibrium is completely static.

This static conception had its roots in Jevons's working method. As argued above he was a scientific monist who based his methodology on the example of the natural sciences. His 'complete method' prescribed that science should start and end with empirical facts. Peart (1993) refers to this method as 'inductive quantification' because its aim was to describe the laws of nature in terms of quantitative equations. Observation was just the first step of this process. The main challenge of Jevons's inductive method was to develop quantitative (by which he meant mathematical) hypotheses on the basis of observed facts. These had to be compared with specific experience. Confirmation rendered the hypothesis more probable while falsification was an indication that the theory had to be abandoned. In this manner, theories could be improved upon in a manner which bears resemblance to Popper's notion of verisimilitude: inductive quantification eliminates erroneous hypotheses and renders corroborated theories more precise, moving the researcher closer to the true theory, or in Jevons's case, the true function (Peart 1993, 447).

Perhaps surprisingly, given Jevons's empirical approach to science, the *Theory of Political Economy* was mainly concerned with the stage of theory development. His explanation of the theoretical nature of this work was that 'before we attempt any investigation of facts, we must have correct theoretical notions'. This was the reason why he made 'hardly any attempt to employ statistics in this work' (Jevons 1879[1957], 22).

But, according to his scientific method, theory was by no means an artificial construction. On the contrary, the building blocks of one's theory had to be derived from the observation and description of actual events. Jevons performed this task by means of the well known strategy of simplification. His theory of exchange is what after Weber is called an 'ideal representation' of reality (Mosselmans 1999, 177). It describes certain aspects of reality that are considered vital to the problem at hand and ignores other 'disturbing' influences.

Jevons's theory of exchange depends on a theoretical concept of the market which greatly resembles our modern notion of perfect competition. He called his market 'theoretically perfect' when the following conditions were satisfied: 'when all traders have perfect knowledge of the conditions of supply and demand, and the consequent ratio of exchange.' In this market 'there can only be one ratio of exchange of one uniform commodity at any moment' (Jevons 1879[1957], 87). Further, in a perfect market there are no transaction costs (ibid., 106 and 115) and a large number of traders must be assumed, so that any one small trader 'will not appreciably affect the ratio of exchange' (ibid., 112). Of course, not every market functions in this manner but in Jevons's view it was this 'theoretical conception of a perfect market [that] is more or less completely carried out in practice' (ibid., 86).

With this definition of a theoretical market an attempt could be made to explain the process of price formation. Here Jevons encountered the problem that exchange is essentially a dynamic process; even for a given supply people bargain in order to reach agreement about the price. Jevons argued that this process of bargaining could be abstracted from and assumed that trading only takes place at the equilibrium price. In his words, '[h]olders of commodities will be regarded not as continuously passing on these commodities in streams of trade, but as possessing certain fixed amounts which they exchange until they come to equilibrium' (ibid., 93–94). Note the difference with the classical focus on competition as a process. In Jevons's focus on market-clearing equilibria as static positions, there is no room for the classical rivalry between buyers and sellers or the flows of traders into and out of markets and industries.

To explain this focus on a situation of exchange equilibrium, he again referred to an example of the science of mechanics. This science showed that the assumption of equilibrium could be used to simplify more difficult dynamical questions. Take the case of the pendulum (ibid., 94):

> It is much more easy to determine the point at which a pendulum will come to rest than to calculate the velocity at which it will move when displaced from that point of rest. Just so, it is a far more easy task to lay down the conditions under which trade is completed and interchange ceases, than to attempt to ascertain at what rate trade will go on when equilibrium is not attained.

It is for this reason that Jevons treated 'the action of exchange' as a 'purely statical problem'.

However, at the same time he realized that the 'real condition of industry is one of perpetual motion and exchange' (ibid., 93). This remark suggests that Jevons considered the equilibrium theory of exchange just a first step in a process of theoretical development that should lead to an explanation of exchange in dynamic terms (method of successive approximations). But this suggestion is illusory and is not followed through. One looks in vain for steps towards more dynamic theories and encounters instead a defence of the equilibrium theory. By and large, he believed that his static theory offered an adequate explanation of the ratio of exchange that is agreed to by suppliers and demanders. The surprising fact is that this conclusion was not based on a rigorous empirical test of the theory, as his own conception of science demanded. Instead, he suggested that such proof could easily be obtained and maintained his theory even in the face of conflicting evidence. In his own words, 'the Theory of Exchange may seem of a somewhat abstract and perplexing character; but it is not difficult to find practical illustrations which will show how it is verified in the actual working of a great market' (ibid., 108).

One comes to the conclusion that Jevons made a distinction between theory and the application of theory. According to him, it is in the field of practical problems that important deviations from the static theory of exchange are encountered. Indeed, '[i]n practice, no market ever long fulfills the theoretical conditions of equilibrium, because, from the various accidents of life and business, there are sure to be people every day compelled to sell, or having a sudden inducement to buy. There is nearly always, again, the influence of prospective supply or demand, depending upon the political intelligence of the moment' (ibid., 111). But disequilibria of this kind belonged to the domain of applied theory and could for that reason not be considered falsifications of the more fundamental static theory. As he continued the passage quoted above, '[w]e shall never have a Science of Economics unless we learn to discern the operation of law even among the most perplexing complications and apparent interruptions'.

He discussed a number of these complications, such as a varying number of buyers and sellers, forms of imperfect competition, indivisible goods and the problem of substitutes. Jevons had no perfect solutions for these problems but he did indicate how the equations of his equilibrium theory could be adjusted so as to account for them. In this manner, he was able to support his claim that his equilibrium explanation of economic exchange could be used to analyze a great number of practical cases, even when these cases seemed to conflict with the abstract nature of the theory.

WHY DID JEVONS BELIEVE IN STATIC EQUILIBRIUM?

The extent of Jevons's faith in the power of the equilibrium assumption is perplexing. In the *Theory of Political Economy* there is hardly any reference to the disequilibrium adjustments that so occupied Jevons's classical predecessors. There is no movement to a stationary state, nor does one find a supply and demand analysis of market dynamics. Especially, this latter fact is surprising. Why did Jevons not draw supply and demand functions to show that profit-seeking suppliers and demanders would end up trading at the equilibrium price?

There are two possible answers to this question. In the first place, Jevons can be accused of a methodological inconsistency, as White (1989) has done. A second explanation is that he did not possess the mathematical skills to address more complex cases of his theory.

Methodological Inconsistency

To start with the former point, White stresses that Jevons's ideal representation of exchange equilibrium depends on many unrealistic assumptions, such as the requirement of prefect knowledge among traders. This theory of exchange was the theoretical foundation of what he regarded as the laws of supply and demand, which means that these laws are theory-dependent. They are conditional upon the fact that real markets satisfy the conditions underlying his ideal conception of a market and the subsequent exchange equilibrium. However, according to White, Jevons's applied economics treated supply and demand as observational statements, devoid of any theoretical content. He simply focussed on the observed correlations of properties, such as a regular pattern of price changes and the quantity traded. But what does a statistical law of this kind mean? Without a clear statement of the conditions under which the law is valid, it is impossible to say if the correlations concern changes *along* or changes *of* supply and demand curves. Unfortunately, Jevons never specified such conditions and merely stated that they were 'unquestionable truths . . . founded upon facts [which] cannot be shaken by any theory' (Jevons 1879[1957], vi).

Jevons was extremely optimistic about the availability of numerical data in economics. In a well-known statement he declared that:

> The very abundance of our data is perplexing. There is not a clerk nor book-keeper in the country who is not engaged in recording numerical facts for the economist. The private-account books, the great ledgers of merchants and bankers and public offices, the share lists, price lists, bank returns, monetary intelligence, Custom-house and other Government returns, are all full of the kind of numerical data

> required to render Economics an exact mathematical science. Thousands of folio volumes of statistical, parliamentary or other publications await the labour of the investigator (ibid., 10–11).

But in spite of this optimism, there are only a few examples where he tried to estimate a demand or supply curve. In the *Theory of Political Economy* he discussed the numerical determination of a demand schedule of corn (Jevons 1879[1957], 155–157). This example was based on the famous statistical tables of Gregory King and Charles Davenant. Their tables showed that the relationship between the price of corn and the quantity of corn brought to the market was not proportional but quadratic. Jevons reached this conclusion by showing that a function of the form $Pc = \{A/(Qc-B)^n\}$ could be used to emulate the price series, where A, B and n were parameters to be estimated. Inspection of the data convinced him that the exponential parameter n was approximately 2; his estimates of A and B were, A=0.824 and B=0.12.

This example shows that his statistical method was to describe a time series of correlated data in terms of a very general (polynomial) function. It should be added that Jevons considered this relation probabilistic. He assumed that the prices and quantities in the King-Davenant tables were averages in a binomial distribution (White 1989, 436). In effect, this assumption implied that disturbing causes would cancel out. Jevons understood that there were many factors which complicated the estimation of a demand law. To start with, people had different preferences. Other complications were income and substitution effects. A rise in the price of corn would seriously lower the income of people because corn was a means of subsistence. Consequently, they would probably lower their consumption of other commodities as well. As a result, Jevons doubted that a valid estimation could be made of the demand function of commodities which formed 'the main elements of expenditure' (Jevons 1879[1957], 148).[12]

However, this wise lesson was forgotten when he made the estimation of the King-Davenant demand law. In this case, he came to the conclusion that in spite of all complications his formula 'was not far from the truth' (ibid., 158). In Jevons's conception this meant that the demand law could be considered a numerical estimation of the underlying cause of demand, marginal utility.

> The price of a commodity is the only test we have of the utility of the commodity to the purchaser; and if we could tell exactly how much people reduce their consumption of each important article when the price rises, we could determine, at least approximately, the variation of the final degree of utility – the all important element in Economics (ibid., 147).

Apparently, the fundamental character of this cause, utility, meant that other causes effecting the price of a good could be classified as temporary. On average, they would cancel out and not disturb the pattern of price and quantity changes described by the estimated demand law.

This working method is a fine example of Jevons's methodological rule that in science one has to make assumptions about the behaviour of causes in time (Peart 1993). His main concern was that natural causes were too complex in order to connect cause and effect in a determinate way. He dealt with this problem by assuming that a causal law is a probabilistic relationship between cause and effect under the assumption that 'other things remain equal'. In his opinion, the repeated correlation of cause and effect increased the likelihood that disturbing forces would on average not effect the causal relationship in question.

Peart (1993) has shown that this assumption played an important role in several of his applied economic studies. One of the best-known examples is *A Serious Fall in the Value of Gold* (1863). This study aimed to prove the validity of the quantity theory of money by showing that the permanent purchasing power of gold had fallen as a result of a large supply influx. To this purpose, he described the development of 39 different prices in the period 1841–1862 in terms of an index number (the average price in 1841–1845). According to Jevons, the strong correlation of the observed changes (a 10 percent increase between 1845–1850 and again between 1860–1862) proved that the changes in these prices had a common cause, the influx of gold. Of course, temporary forces affected prices due to varying demand and the conditions for investment and supply, but such price alterations could be assumed to cancel out in drawing the average price (Peart 1993, 453).

As Peart points out, this approach caused a breach with the method of classical economists like J.S. Mill. Mill tried to deal with the problem of multiple causation by isolating tendencies (see also Chapter 7). The task of the applied economist was to seek out 'disturbing causes' which were analyzed in terms of their comparative static effect. A disturbing cause would upset equilibrium and bring about a tendency towards a new equilibrium situation. The effect of the change could then be ascertained by comparing the two equilibrium situations. With Jevons, disturbing causes never got a chance to upset equilibrium in the first place because their effect was always assumed on average to be absent. His focus on the probabilistic connection between fundamental forces meant that the idea of equilibrium as a tendency lost its meaning in the work of the applied economist.

Mathematical Skills

The second reason why Jevons ignored disequilibrium effects is that he was unable to handle such effects in the static framework of his equation of exchange. He was well aware of the impact of trading at disequilibrium prices on the final outcome of the exchange process. This issue had been one of the main points of controversy in his debate with Fleeming Jenkin. Jenkin had been one of the first in England to discuss the process of price formation in a geometrical analysis of supply and demand diagrams. From that point of view, it was not surprising that he criticized Jevons for his neglect of the process of bargaining between traders. This criticism touched the heart of Jevons's equilibrium explanation of exchange, namely that market participants are price takers and that there is at any one moment only one price so that there is no room for arbitrage.

The dispute was never settled, partly because Jenkin rejected utility theory as a theoretical foundation of supply and demand analysis and partly because Jevons believed the criticism was unjustified.[13] As Figure 8.1 illustrates, he saw utility theory as an adequate explanation of the forces behind the price setting process. But this explanation is insufficient because Jevons was unable to establish the link between marginal utility and the buyer's demand curve (Blaug 1985, 312 and 327). Moreover, he saw no fundamental distinction between individual and market demand curves. In his view, market demand was a mere aggregate in the sense that 'total demand is the sum of individual demands' (quoted in Schabas 1990, 43). He had defined the transactors of his theory of exchange as 'trading bodies' with the implication that the laws of exchange are the same. Whether trade takes place between individuals or nations, in both cases a ratio of exchange is established that satisfies the equilibrium condition of the equation of exchange. 'The principles of exchange are the same in nature, however wide or narrow may be the market considered. Every trading body is either an individual or an aggregate of individuals, and the law, in the case of the aggregate, must depend upon the fulfilment of law in the individuals' (Jevons 1879[1957], 89).

But, of course, there is a fundamental difference between isolated and competitive exchange. The approach of Jevons means that the functions of marginal utility in the equation of exchange represent the collective marginal utility of the trading body. This step is only possible if one assumes that one can add up the utility of individuals, a possibility explicitly rejected by Jevons.[14]

At another instance, he praised the ability of his mathematical theory to handle more complex cases of exchange. His equation of exchange concerned the case of a two-party exchange but could easily be extended to include 'more numerous bodies'. The trick was to realize that at the individual level supply and demand are simply two sides of the same coin, which implied that 'exchanges in the most complicated case may thus always be decomposed into simple exchanges, and every exchange will give rise to two equations sufficient to determine the quantities involved' (ibid., 116–117).

However, in his *Principles of Science* (1877), published a few years after the *Theory of Political Economy*, Jevons was far more negative about the scientific prospects of his mathematical theory. There he claimed that the complexity of economic relations seriously limited the scope for theoretical advancement in the direction of a general equilibrium analysis of exchange. Speaking about the scientific nature of economics, he said that:

> If a science at all, it must be a mathematical science because it deals with quantities of commodities. But as soon as we attempt to draw out the equations expressing the laws of demand and supply, we discover that they have a complexity entirely surpassing our powers of mathematical treatment. We may lay down the general form of the equations, expressing the demand and supply for two or three commodities among two or three trading bodies, but all the functions involved are so complicated in character that there is not much fear of scientific method making rapid progress in this direction (Jevons, 1877[1958], 759–760).

The difference between these two statements is remarkable. It almost seems as if Jevons had in a matter of years radically changed his opinion about the usefulness of a mathematical approach. Steedman (1997) says that he lacked the mathematical skills to develop his intuition of the general equilibrium nature of economics. Another explanation may be that in the *Theory* Jevons overstated his case for rhetorical purposes. In the 1870s the general attitude towards a mathematical approach of economics problems was still very hostile and it took a lot of persuasion by some of the ablest men to change that. Whatever the reason, the fact remains that, in spite of many fruitful suggestions, he never went beyond his first mathematical result: the static analysis of bilateral exchange.

A REVOLUTION THAT WENT ASTRAY

With Jevons the notion of economic equilibrium underwent an important transformation. His focus on static equilibrium explained in terms of marginal utility theory classified dynamic changes in the market environment as disturbing causes. In his scheme such disturbing causes could be ignored while they had been the centre of attention in classical economics. This transformed the equilibrium concept from a tendency statement about the dynamic working of economic forces into a static proposition about the relationship between the ratio of marginal utilities and the relative price of two commodities.

The surprising fact is that this outcome was not the logical outcome of Jevons's mathematical method. I have described this method as thoroughly empirical, as a form of inductive quantification. According to the rules of this doctrine, the critical test of a scientific theory was the verification of empirical propositions made on the basis of this theory. Jevons stated that a theory had to be abandoned in case of repeated failure to pass this test. Hence why the focus on a static equilibrium solution?

It is here that Jevons's mathematical revolution went astray. He failed to use his scientific method to critically test his equilibrium theory of economic exchange. This constitutes a clear case of what Popper has called an 'immunizing stratagem': the effort to save a theory from rejection by adopting auxiliary hypotheses that make it impossible to refute its conclusions. The immunizing stratagem of Jevons was the assumption that disequilibrium movements are always disturbing causes that can be ignored. With regard to a market with free competition, he believed that prices and quantities would always tend towards their equilibrium level so that one could concentrate the mathematical analysis on the static position of supply and demand equilibrium and ignore the dynamic changes that establish equilibrium. Also, he believed that his statistical studies of the time series of prices and quantities (of for instance corn) corroborated the theoretical laws of supply and demand. Without proof he concluded that data points, which did not fit the statistical pattern of the supply and demand law, could be ignored because they could be assumed to cancel out in a large sample of observations. For Jevons, the step from economic equilibrium as an analytical ideal to a statistical regularity was just a small one.

NOTES

1. See the preface to the *Elements* (Walras 1954, 36) and the letter of 23 May 1874 to William Stanley Jevons (in Jaffé 1965 vol. I, 397).
2. It was Jevons who brought Gossen to the attention of Walras. On 15 September 1878 he wrote Walras about the discovery of a book 'which contains many of the chief points of our theory clearly reasoned out. It is by Hermann Heinrich Gossen and is entitled somewhat as follows – Entwickelung der Gesetze der Menslichen Verkehr (??)'. In Jaffé (1965 vol. I, 581).
3. More indirect proof points to the fact that Walras knew the book early in his career as an analytical economist and had the book in his private library. Also he placed Isnard at the

head of his bibliography of early works in mathematical economics with the words that it 'correctly states in algebraic symbols [the ratios of values] as equal to the inverse ratios of the quantities of commodities exchanged' (quoted in Jaffé 1969, 25). See also the letter to Jevons of July 13, 1878 in Jaffé 1965 vol. I, 570).

4. The three types of income are landed income, industrial income (the result of 'learned' income), and income on movable property resulting from trade or interest on money.
5. 'Le circuit du travail circule dans tous les canaux de ce système de ramifications, comme un fluide, en ce mettant par-tout en équilibre. Chaque vaisseau qui fait circuler le produit de travail est accompagnié d'un vaisseau analogue, qui fait circuler l'argent dans un sens contraire; et le système de la circulation de l'argent et du travail, pris dans leur ensemble, ressemble à la circulation du sang' (Canard 1801, 231).
6. Note that a rise in (L – x) means a greater difference between the actual and the maximum price.
7. 'See Dupuit (1849, 13): 'L'économie politique doit prendre pour mesure de l'utilité d'un objet le sacrifice maximum que chaque consommateur serait disposé à faire pour se le procurer.'
8. His analysis probably had little effect on the development of German economic thought, due to the fact that von Mangoldt's *Grundriß* was republished after his death in 1868, carefully purged of all his mathematical formulations. The argument of the editor for abandoning the mathematics was that he did not believe that the equations could lead to a quantitative estimation of supply and demand, which meant that they had no practical value. On the details of this curious fate of von Mangoldt's mathematics, see Mosselmans (2000).
9. Mirowski (1989, 213) ignores this second aspect of Gossen's law of diminishing marginal utility. He contends that Gossen failed to develop a notion of *marginal* utility because he related the 'pleasure' of consumption to the time during which the pleasure was experienced and not to the quantity consumed. This conclusion is wrong because Gossen took both factors into account.
10. In search of an academic position, the young scientist Jevons perceived this cold reception as a tremendous blow. However, Schabas (1990, 118) concludes that in retrospect Jevons met with far less resistance than has commonly been described. Schabas here refers to the fact that in England mathematical economics took hold relative quickly in the 1880s.
11. See also Schabas (1990, 52). Speaking about the equation of exchange, she says that 'rather than apply the differential calculus to the functions he [Jevons, BT] posits, he simply equates ratios of infinitesimals. As an example of applied mathematics, the *Theory* is sketchy and incomplete'.
12. He also understood that income and substitution effects meant that the equation of exchange was no longer valid because it could not be assumed that the marginal utility of money was zero.
13. For a more detailed analysis of the Jenkin-Jevons debate, see White (1989).

14. About the measurement of feelings, Jevons (1879[1957], 14) said that one cannot 'compare the amount of feeling in one mind with that in another'. See also Schabas (1990, 34).

9. The Dreamland of Léon Walras

INTRODUCTION

The man responsible for the vision that the economy can be seen as a vast system of interrelated markets that must be studied in terms of a system of mathematical equations was Léon Walras. Walras tried many professions (novelist, journalist, bank employee) before he followed in the footsteps of his father Auguste Walras and became an economist. His scientific career started when in 1870 he was finally named to a professorship in the faculty of law of what was later to become the university of Lausanne in Switzerland.

The main ingredients of Walras's vision on economic science are fourfold:

- Economics is a mathematical science;
- Marginal utility explains the determination of market prices;
- In a system of free competition all markets simultaneously tend to a situation of economic equilibrium (supply equals demand), and
- General economic equilibrium is a relative welfare maximum.

These were the main points of his *Elements of Pure Economics* (EPE) which was first published in two parts in 1874 and 1877. A month before the publication of the first part of the book Walras discovered that Jevons in 1871 had published a mathematical analysis of exchange which was also based on the notion of marginal utility. He readily conceded Jevons's priority concerning this point in the preface of the EPE but also retained his right to claim originality for 'certain important deductions' of his own (Walras 1954, 36). This modest phrase hides that there are important differences between the mathematical theories of Walras and Jevons. The most important one is that Walras step by step construed a mathematical general equilibrium theory of exchange, production, capital and money, while Jevons only touched upon the general equilibrium nature of economic problems subjects in an intuitive manner.

The praise for the technical superiority of Walras's EPE is therefore not surprising. Famous is Schumpeter's (1954, 242) judgement of EPE as the 'Magna Carta of economic theory' because of Walras's formulation of equilibrium in a system of interdependent quantities in terms of a mathematical system of equations. Schumpeter believed that '[t]he history of economic analysis or, at any rate of its "pure" kernel, from Child to Walras might be written in terms of this conception's gradual emergence into the light of consciousness'.

However, Schumpeter was unclear about the purpose of his theoretical efforts. Did Walras purport to explain existing economic conditions or did he have a normative goal in mind? Schumpeter was so fascinated by the mathematical aspects of general equilibrium theory that he failed to address this more embracing question. Why should we have a general equilibrium theory?[1]

Today this question divides the ranks of the students of Walras's legacy. Towards the end of his career, William Jaffé the translator of EPE and editor of Walras's collected correspondence came to the conclusion that the meaning of Walras's general equilibrium theory was normative (Jaffé 1977 and 1981). According to Jaffé, it is the scientific answer to his lifelong involvement with the 'social question'. This was the issue of creating a just social order in the context of an economy where profound changes take place.[2] Jaffé maintains that Walras' general equilibrium theory was a blueprint of an economic system that, if allowed to function in reality, would produce a social welfare maximum, given certain conditions of justice. In other words, the imperfect practical situation could be adjusted to conform to the perfect ideal of the general equilibrium model. For that reason, he called it a 'realistic utopia'.[3]

Walker (1984 and 1988), Morishima (1977) and others rejected this conclusion arguing that it violates one of the central elements of Walras's economic system and that was the strict distinction between pure, applied and social economics. In Walras's scheme questions concerning right and wrong belonged to the domain of social economics and were therefore excluded from the domain of pure theory. The aim of pure theory was to explain natural laws which were defined as causal relationships between events that stood outside the reach of human control. In that sense, general equilibrium theory as pure economics was intended to explain the operation of real economies. It was an abstract account of reality, not a utopian dream.

The reply of Jaffé (1980, 340) was that Walras's preoccupation with the problem of social justice was so great that his pure economics became imbued with a distinctive moral content and was given a normative direction. 'By osmosis, as it were, this paramount preoccupation passed through the partition Walras himself erected to separate his normative economics from his pure economics.' Moreover, he concluded that Walras's theory of tatonnement in both the exchange and production case was utterly unrealistic because it was static.

Walker conceded that the so-called pledges model of the fourth and final edition of the EPE is a static explanation of general economic equilibrium, but he did not believe that this model is representative of Walras's thought. His stated intention was to give an abstract explanation of real economic processes and the pledges model does not fit this aim. Walker believed that the earlier editions of the EPE contain the elements of a dynamic theory of general equilibrium which should be considered the 'true' Walrasian model. In a long series of papers Walker tried to piece together the elements of what he called Walras's 'disequilibrium production' model.

This chapter argues that there is a third possibility. Following Koppl (1995), it may be argued that Walras was too sophisticated to confuse science with normative arguments and ignore his own carefully constructed partition of the sciences. The problem is mainly one of language. Koppl argues that the modern distinction between positive and normative arguments does not correspond to Walras's distinction between pure and moral sciences. For Walras, all scientific reasoning, whether pure, applied or moral, had the character of what we now call normative science. As a result, his pure theory of general economic equilibrium concerned an ideal perfection with great analytical qualities but also with a distinctive normative content. In that sense, it was most aptly described by Schumpeter as a 'dreamland of equilibrium'.

WALRAS'S ATTITUDE TOWARDS MATHEMATICS

There is a certain tension in Walras's attitude towards the use of mathematics in economics. On the one hand, he seemed strongly normative in his defence of the mathematical method and suggested that mathematics would turn economics into a science 'on a par with mechanics and astronomy' (Walras 1909, in Mirowski and Cook 1990, 213). On the other hand, he advocated the use of mathematics on very practical grounds, for instance because certain analytical problems could not be solved without the help of calculus.

To begin with the latter, in the preface to the fourth edition of EPE Walras summarized the general equilibrium approach of his pure economic theory. He ended this description with the words that '[t]his whole theory is mathematical' (Walras 1954, 43). The explanation of this conclusion is that the theory can be described in ordinary language as well but that the proof of the theory must be given mathematically. There are two aspects of the theory in particular that demand a mathematical explanation. The first is the proposition that equilibrium in exchange requires that each party to the exchange is able to attain maximum utility. Secondly, there is the suggestion that without mathematics it is impossible to explain how a general economic equilibrium is established. Walras here referred to the problem of 'groping', the process by which price changes ensure that supply equals demand in all markets.[4]

What in these cases does mathematics achieve that verbal language apparently cannot? Walras had in mind very specific tasks. First, in order to explain market equilibrium it was necessary to deduce offer and demand curves. This required the technique of optimization, as consumers were assumed to choose the optimal point on their utility curve, given their income. Second, by showing that the number of equations is exactly equal to the number of unknowns, it could be demonstrated in a mathematical theory that the problem of general equilibrium in exchange, production, capital and money was a determinate problem.

The question of the meaning of mathematics to economic science was a lifelong obsession to Walras. He first demonstrated the mathematical problem of utility maximization in exchange in 1873 in a paper presented to the 'Académie des sciences morales et politiques' in Paris. The cold reception from the Academy frustrated Walras the rest of his life. Ingrao and Israel (1990) show how in the course of his career he adamantly tried to gain scientific credit for his general equilibrium theory. When the economics profession in France denounced his theory, he turned to those whom he rated much higher on his scientific standard, the physics and mathematics community.[5] He believed to have reached a breakthrough when the great French mathematician Henri Poincaré responded favourably to his request to give his opinion about the mathematics of EPE. Poincaré's answer was careful. On the one hand, he supported the definition of marginal utility in mathematical terms and said that the use of calculus was a legitimate instrument to study the results of economic equilibrium in a system of simultaneous equations. On the other hand, he warned that the functions of the system were arbitrary as long as the main hypotheses of the theory lacked specification in terms of empirical relevance. For instance, mechanics had to justify why friction could be ignored and bodies be could assumed as infinitely smooth. In similar vein, Walras needed to explain why he believed that men were 'infinitely selfish and infinitely farsighted' (Poincaré, letter to Walras of 30 September 1901 in Jaffé 1965 vol. III, 165; see also Ingrao and Israel 1990, 158–159).

Walras failed to see that Poincaré had raised a fundamental objection. Without the assumption of unlimited foresight, the assumption of general economic equilibrium in Walras's system becomes untenable. But Walras ignored this objection and believed that he had won the support of one of France's greatest mathematicians.[6] In his reply to Poincaré he said that 'you have given me complete security as regards the starting point of my theory' (Walras, letter to Poincaré of 3 October 1901 in Jaffé 1965 vol. III, 167) and wrote to many of his friends and correspondents that Poincaré now supported his theory. He considered this so important that he published the letter as an appendix to the last article he wrote in his life. This was the article 'Économique et Méchanique' which appeared in 1909 and contains Walras's final word on the role of mathematics in economics.

The article shows that he considered this issue a fundamental one because it touched upon the very nature of economic science. He agreed with Jevons, whom he cited in this regard, that economics is a mathematical science because it deals with quantities which can be described in terms of greater or less. However, he made a distinction between quantities that are exterior and interior to the human will. The former are those 'which take place in Nature's theatre where we play no active role' (Walras 1909[1990], 206). Walras referred to them as 'physical' facts that are the objects of the 'physico-mathematical' sciences. By contrast, interior facts are controlled by our own moral and rational faculties and are for that reason considered 'psychic' facts. They are the objects of what he called the 'psycho-mathematical' sciences. In other words, the mathematical sciences were not all alike. According to Walras, astronomy and mechanics were clear examples of the physico-mathematical sciences, while economics belonged to the other class, the psycho mathematical sciences.

This distinction was meant to counter the criticism Walras frequently encountered that he tried to measure human feelings, like people's satisfaction of goods and services. He stated that exterior facts can be measured in an objective way because they appear to everyone in the same way. But interior facts are psychic and therefore remain subjective and individual. In other words, he had been well aware of the subjective nature of economic facts, but that did not diminish the fact that they were mathematical. They were quantities just like physical facts with the restriction that their magnitude could only be established by the person experiencing their sensation.[7]

At this point in the article, Walras made a surprising move. Instead of elaborating on the methodological role of mathematics – what is the function of mathematical reasoning in the two sciences and how does it relate to other methodological functions like induction and empirical verification? – he reverted to a much more superficial level. He wanted to show that the mathematical formalisms of the two sciences are similar. To that purpose he compared, firstly, the equilibrium in exchange (theory of maximum satisfaction) with the equilibrium of a balance (theory of maximum energy) and, secondly, the general equilibrium of the market to that of the universal equilibrium of celestial bodies. It is unclear what this cumbersome comparison should achieve.[8] Walras claimed that the theories are close analogies but he remained silent on the meaning of this conclusion. He ended with his earlier observation that the *only* difference between the two mechanical theories on the one hand and the two economic theories on the other hand, is the objective appearance of the mechanical phenomena and the unperceived internal character of economic phenomena.[9] This led him to conclude that both theories are by the nature of the phenomena they study, mathematical theories.

What was Walras trying to achieve? It is clear that he wanted to defend his mathematical approach of economics. But he supported his cause in a conspicuous manner: he reasoned from theory to subject matter. The analogies suggested that the mathematical structure of economics and mechanics was similar and this was taken as evidence by Walras that their domain of inquiry was identical in terms of its quantitative character. But this had been his argument to advocate a mathematical approach in the first place. He was running in circles and without an empirical justification of his mathematical general equilibrium theory, he was unable to break through it.

What rests is a normative stance. Ingrao and Israel (1990, 160) conclude that Walras transformed a descriptive problem into a normative one. He was not interested in the question of how abstract (mathematical) theoretical notions related to the real magnitudes they were supposed to describe in an abstract fashion. Instead he tried to adjust reality to the conditions of his mathematical equilibrium theories. 'The problem was not longer that of the abstract removal of "friction" but its *elimination from the real world*' (ibid., their emphasis). In other words, he did not want to relax the unrealistic assumptions underlying his theory, but to educate people so that their behaviour would better correspond to the demand of the model. As he wrote to Poincaré, '[i]n fact, there is friction in the economic mechanism; and men are neither perfectly selfish nor perfectly farsighted. The applied theory of the production of wealth must therefore take care to indicate this friction and work towards removing it completely as possible with a view to obtaining a maximum of utility as approximate as possible' (Walras, letter of 3 October 1901 in Jaffé 1965 vol. III, 167; translation Ingrao and Israel 1990, 160). Mathematics was Walras's tool of social reform.

CLASSIFICATION OF THE SCIENCES

To better understand the purpose of Walras's general equilibrium theory, it is necessary to explain his classification of the sciences. In his scheme, general equilibrium theory belonged to the domain of the pure sciences. Pure science was contrasted with moral science on the ground that events could be classified in two domains. Walras (1954, 61) distinguished between natural events and human phenomena. The key characteristic of natural events was that they 'result from the play of the blind and ineluctable forces of nature' (ibid.) and therefore remained outside the scope of human control. In contrast, human phenomena found their motive force in the deliberations of the human mind. This was the basis of the classification of the sciences. Pure science studied the forces of nature while moral science addressed the products of the human will. The former could also be called 'science proper' because it aimed to observe, describe and explain the forces of nature. But in the domain of human events there was also the possibility of controlling events and that classified moral science as 'art or ethics' because it 'advises, prescribes and directs' (ibid., 61–62).

The idea that natural forces cannot be controlled by human willpower led Walras to distinguish between *things* and *persons*. Things lack consciousness, a property which characterizes persons. According to him, this meant that a fundamental distinction must be drawn in the realm of human phenomena. On the one hand, there are phenomena which are manifestations of human actions in respect to natural forces. This is a relation between persons and things. On the other hand, people interact with each other and this category comprises the relations between persons and persons. He called the first category 'applied science' or 'art' and the second class 'moral science' or 'ethics' (ibid., 63).

What kind of science was economics? To answer this question Walras investigated the functions performed by people in the economic realm. The general aim of economics was to study social wealth, as indicated in the subtitle of EPE.[10] According to Walras, the essence of wealth was that people wanted to possess or appropriate the object providing wealth. This first function followed almost automatically from the definition of social wealth, because useless things are not in demand from anyone and there is no need to appropriate useful objects that are available in unlimited quantities. Secondly, the moment things can be called someone's property they can be exchanged as well. In other words, they become valuable because they stand in a certain relationship to each other: their ratio of exchange constitutes a price one must pay in order to possess the good. Thirdly, valuable things are things that can be produced and multiplied by industry. In sum, value in exchange, industry and property are the three generic phenomena that form the domain of economic inquiry.

Walras then classified economics according to the nature of these three generic phenomena. He stated that *value in exchange* constitutes a natural phenomenon and is therefore the object of the pure branch of economics. At first sight, this seems a curious classification because exchange takes place between people. But Walras argued that prices are formed without the directing will of the human intellect. In a rather confusing passage, he stated that for a given price the seller cannot sell at a higher price because the commodity in question 'is not worth any more' and the buyer cannot buy at a lower price because the good 'is not worth any less' (ibid., 69). This suggests a tautology, values explain prices and vice versa. In the context of his theory of market equilibrium it becomes clear that he assumed a system of free competition and that all buyers and sellers should be seen as price takers.

Industry belongs to the domain of applied science. Here the idea is that persons subordinate things to the purpose of persons. For example, agriculture increases the number of plants and animals which are used for food and clothing. In the manufacturing industry all kind of raw materials are processed to make capital and consumer goods. In other words, the production of social wealth constitutes an activity between persons and things and that makes it the object of applied science (ibid., 73–76). Finally, *property* is an agreement between persons to respect what is 'mine and thine'. It involves the concept of justice and as such concerns relations between persons. That means that the distribution of social wealth is a moral issue and belongs to the domain of social economics (ibid., 76–79).[11]

The classification of the three branches of economics in terms of the relations between things and persons also gives distinct criteria to judge the scientific merit of pure, applied and social theories. The theory of exchange is a pure science and addresses the laws of nature. That means that 'truth' is its scientific criterion. The object of industry is to produce material welfare; goods and services that are scarce and useful. Here utility is the appropriate yardstick. Then lastly, in the case of property, the demand for an equitable distribution of wealth is the measuring rod and that means that justice is the basic scientific premise.[12] Table 9.1 summarizes Walras's classification of the sciences and its application to economics.

Table 9.1 Walras's classification of the sciences[13]

General science			Economic science		
science	*addresses...*	*in terms of...*	*this activity...*	*belongs to...*	*goal*
pure	natural events	things–things	exchange	pure econ	truth
arts	human events	things–person	industry	applied econ	utility
ethics	human events	person–person	appropriation	social econ	justice

This table shows that Walras's pure economics cannot be considered in isolation (Jolink 1991, Bürgenmeier 1994). In the preface to EPE Walras stated that it was his intention to publish a treatise of political and social economy which would consist of three books. The first one was EPE. The other two parts were intended to cover respectively the *Elements of applied economics* (or the theory of the production of wealth) and the *Elements of social economics* (or the theory of the distribution of wealth via property and taxation). But he failed to carry out this task and the 'elements' were replaced by 'etudes', his collected essays on the subject.[14]

SCIENTIFIC METHOD

It is curious that Walras's careful classification of the sciences is not carried through to the level of the method of these sciences. He only hinted at a difference in method between pure science ('observes, describes and explains') and the arts ('advises, prescribes and directs'), but he never elaborated on this point.[15]

In the realm of economics, he suggested a ranking order in the sense that pure theory must precede applied theory which in its turn, one may add, is a prerequisite of social theory.[16] But the exact nature of this order remains unclear. One may surmise that applied and social theories were in a sense both applications of pure economics; studies devoted to practical questions which were based on the findings of the more abstract pure theory. In that sense, they could even be seen as a test of the empirical validity of pure economics. But unfortunately, such an interpretation does not correspond to Walras's own practice. He greatly valued abstraction as a means to build theories, but he never explained how the empirical validity of these theories should be checked. His standard phrase was that the mathematical solution of supply and demand equilibrium 'is the selfsame problem that is solved empirically on the market by the mechanism of free competition' (Walras 1954, 162–163, 169, 241–242, 282, 318, 380). But why this is the case, was not explained.[17] He probably never intended the confrontation with practice as a test of pure theory but rather as a means of applying it (Jolink 1991, 57).

This view corresponds to his remark that the mathematical method is not an 'experimental method' but a 'rational method' (Walras 1954, 71). He made this remark with regard to the method of pure theory in the case of economic exchange. Here he again referred to the example of mechanics and hydrodynamics and claimed that 'the theory of value in exchange is really a branch of mathematics which mathematicians have hitherto neglected and left undeveloped' (ibid., 70). The rational element of mathematical science consisted in the fact that they 'go beyond experience' in the sense that its theoretical concepts are not intended as realistic descriptions of observed phenomena.

> From real-type concepts, these sciences abstract ideal-type concepts which they define, and then on the basis of these definitions they construct a priori the whole framework of their theorems and proofs. After that they go back to experience *not to confirm but to apply their conclusions* (ibid., 71, my emphasis).

According to Walras, this was standard practice in mathematics and he referred to the example of geometry. He claimed that the proofs and theorems of geometry would only hold in ideal circumstances that in reality could at best be approximated. Yet reality admitted of very wide and fruitful applications of these propositions.

Walras believed that the same would hold true in pure economics. The theoretical concepts of pure economics should be based on abstract terms that were derived from experience. In other words, pure theory worked with what he called 'ideal-type concepts' which were abstractions from 'real-type concepts' like those of exchange, supply, demand, market etcetera. The result was an ideal market with ideal prices which stand in an exact relation to an ideal supply and demand. To Walras 'the return to reality' was not a matter of assessing whether the ideal represented reality in a correct manner. He stated that his only aim was to generate practical applications. So, like in geometry, one should ask, 'do these pure truths [ideal demand and supply, BT] find frequent application?' (ibid., 71). Walras himself was convinced that after reading EPE one would reach a positive answer to this question.

The presence of practical applications as an implicit test of pure science gives the notion of an ideal theory an added quality. The ideal stood for an aspect of a perfect construction like a perfect circle, but to Walras it also signified an end or a goal for action. According to Koppl (1995), Walras derived his distinction between the notions of real and ideal from Vacherot's *La métaphysique et la science* (1858).[18] Vacherot had defined science as the 'idealization of reality' and art as the 'realization of the ideal'. The ideal symbolized perfection and was derived as an abstraction by means of extrapolation from the imperfect. But given that art was aimed at the realization of the ideal, it is clear that Vacherot's conception of the ideal was not objective in the sense of value-free. Vacherot wrote in the context of the 'secular religions' and his notion of the ideal had the added flourish of deification (Koppl 1995, 48). In Walras's general equilibrium analysis this religious background was removed but another hidden agenda took its place, namely that of scientific socialism.

Below this matter will be further explored. The point to stress here is that science as the 'idealization of reality' was developed with a specific task in mind. As a result, even Walras's pure science had what we now consider a normative character.

MARKET EQUILIBRIUM

To Walras, the analogy of a frictionless machine in economics was the assumption of perfect competition. He argued that buyers and sellers in competition determine the price of commodities because they try to outbid each other. Therefore, 'the more perfectly competition functions, the more rigorous is the manner of arriving at value in exchange' (ibid., 84).

His pure theory of market equilibrium was therefore based on what he referred to as the 'hypothetical regime of perfectly free competition' (ibid., 40).[19] This theory assumed a given supply of goods to indicate that demand was the leading force in the process of price determination. The condition of equilibrium was therefore that supply equaled demand; at this point the market price would remain stable.

This conception of market equilibrium was by no means new but on several accounts Walras's treatment of the problem constitutes a case of analytical progress. Also his interpretation of economic equilibrium differed from the meaning of this concept in the work of both his classical predecessors and his co-fathers of the neoclassical revolution, Jevons and Menger.

Perfect Competition

To start with the last point, in line with his conception of pure economics Walras saw economic equilibrium as an ideal situation. It used ideal-type concepts like ideal supply and demand and an ideal market which were based on what he termed real-type concepts. Surprisingly, he elaborated only vaguely on what in the case of market equilibrium these real-type concepts had been. He mentioned a number of markets that could be said to function more or less like a perfect market such as the stock exchange, grain markets and fish markets. These examples were chosen to illustrate that *competition* was the essence of the market mechanism. For that reason even the city streets with their stores and shops of all kind could be said to form markets because, although poorly organized, they possessed a reasonable degree of competition. The ideal market was therefore one in which competition was perfect. However, the meaning of this mechanism was not defined but explained in terms of a metaphor. To Walras, the ideal-type market underpinning his analysis of economic equilibrium was a perfectly competitive market, 'just as in pure mechanics we suppose, to start with, that machines are perfectly frictionless' (ibid., 84).

But like a machine competition cannot function blindly. Walras realized that it is a process governed by rules. He referred to the stock exchange of large investment centres like Paris and London as an example of how competition works in a well-organized market. This was the real-type example of the ideal markt with perfect competition that figures in Walras's pure economics (Kregel 1995). He explained how prices were established on the Paris stock exchange. This market was what he termed a 'call market'. For a given price, buyers and sellers were invited to call the quantities they wanted to buy and respectively sell at this price. These calls were then quoted on the official list of the exchange. When the quantities demanded equaled the quantities supplied, the price was a market-clearing price and the orders to buy or sell were executed. In case of a disequilibrium, new prices were proposed until the market-clearing price was discovered. Walras stressed the fact that trading was suspended until this moment; exchange at disequilibrium prices was not allowed. Excess-demand meant that in the next round a higher price would be listed on the board. The response to excess supply was the reverse and in this manner the market would grope towards the equilibrium price. Since all orders to buy or sell were publicly exhibited during the auction, there was perfect information in this market.

As Kregel (1995) points out, the stock market has a number of features that are relevant to the interpretation of Walras's market model. First, the market has a physical dimension. In order to find the equilibrium price buyers and sellers need to be able to observe the quoted price and that means they will have to conduct their business in a meeting place like the Bourse. Second, the market requires a clearing institution that sets an opening price, collects bids and offers and if necessary readjusts the price in order to establish the equilibrium price. This function is necessary to prevent that traders make bilateral deals which would violate the condition of perfect information and the law of one price. The fact that offers and bids can only be effectuated through an official of the bourse ensures that all relevant information about supply and demand is spread throughout the market. Therefore, perfect information is the third feature of the stock market as a model of market exchange.

But such features are not common of markets in which purchases and sales are not made by auction. In the street and corner shops that Walras mentioned, there is no central clearing institution that ensures the establishment of a single equilibrium price. Trade is therefore often effectuated at what from an aggregate point of view must be seen as a disequilibrium price. Furthermore the stock market is able to operate as a call market because the number of traders is limited. But in the real world the number of potential buyers and sellers is virtually unlimited. As a result, Walras's theory of economic exchange is not applicable to a market economy and is in that sense unrealistic.

The point is that Walras never intended it to be realistic. He was aware that securities are a 'very special kind of commodity' (ibid., 86). He cited the example of the stock market in order to give an introductory idea of the phenomenon of exchange and the mechanism of competition. Yet his pure theory of market exchange, based on this example, was not an accurate description of how equilibrium is reached on real markets. On the contrary. Walras compared his mathematical explanation of economic equilibrium and the real market process in terms of their end result. He claimed that the mechanism of market competition is the 'practical solution, reached through a rise or fall in prices' of the same problem of exchange 'to which we have just given a theoretical and mathematical solution' (ibid., 106). But the processes by which these solutions are reached are different and one may add, incomparable. According to Walras:

> The rapidity and reliability of the practical solution leave no room for improvement. It is a matter of daily experience that even in big markets where there are neither brokers or auctioneers, the current equilibrium price is determined within a few minutes and considerable quantities of merchandise are exchanged at that price within half or three quarters of an hour.

In the timeless dimension of the mathematical theory of exchange this process feature is simply absent with the result that 'the theoretical solution would be absolutely impracticable in almost every case' (ibid.).

This was a new approach in economic theory. In the past, the classical economists had believed that their market theories gave an accurate account of the process of competition as it takes place in the absence of disturbing causes. This view on the nature of economic theory was essentially taken over by Carl Menger and the Austrian School. They saw economic coordination – the process by which markets tend towards equilibrium – as the core problem of economics and tried to explain the causal forces behind this process. Walras abandoned this approach. The process type of analysis that formed the core of the classical doctrine was hard to reconcile with Walras's mathematical formulation of equilibrium theory which put the end-state conception of equilibrium centre stage. I therefore conclude that realism was the first victim of the mathematical transformation of equilibrium economics.

It is important to note that this conclusion also partly applies to Jevons who seems to occupy a midway position. Like Walras Jevons aimed to transform economics into a mathematical science but he did so halfheartedly. We have seen above that Jevons considered his theory of exchange an ideal representation of real economic processes and that he referred to the example of classical mechanics to support his mathematical analysis of the problem. The result was a static theory that showed little resemblance to the working of real markets. But Jevons believed that static theory was just a first step towards a dynamic theory which could explain market behaviour in terms of more realistic details. He never succeeded in providing this dynamic extension but that is not the issue here. It is the aim that counts. Walras believed that unrealistic pure theories could be useful in their right which explains why the unrealism of the perfect competition model never concerned him. To be more precise, both Jevons and the Austrians followed the method of successive approximations to bring their ideal theories into closer conformity with reality. Walras followed a different modelling strategy. His idea of analytical progress was to extend the partial explanation of market equilibrium to the problem of a general equilibrium of markets. This framework was subsequently developed into a general theory of exchange, production, capital accumulation and money. Walras believed that by covering more markets the mathematical solution of his general equilibrium theory obtained a more universal status. This is why Walras's analysis remained within the static framework of his general equilibrium theory.[20] The realism of assumption and in its wake process analysis firmly remained outside the purview of his general equilibrium theory.

Graphical and Mathematical Analysis

Walras's partial explanation of market equilibrium concerned the case of the exchange of two goods. He aimed directly at the analysis of market exchange instead of isolated exchange by assuming that individual demand curves were additive so that aggregate and therefore market demand curves could be constructed. An interesting feature of Walras's graphical and mathematical analysis of this problem is that it abstains from the use of the utility concept. His starting point was two decreasing demand functions:

$$D_a = F_a(p_a) \text{ and } D_b = F_b(p_b)$$

The analysis consisted in the derivation of the offer curves of A and B which could then be used to determine the equilibrium quantities of A and B. It was not until a later chapter that Walras argued that consumers were driven by the desire to maximize their utility and established the mathematical relationship between utility and demand curves.

In the demand equations, D_a denotes the total quantity of good A demanded by the group of individuals that are holders of B, the other good. The price p_a is defined as the reciprocal of the quantities exchanged which means that $p_a p_b = 1$. Also the offer or supply of B will be equal to the exchange value of the demand for A, or $O_b = D_a p_a$. The offer curve of B can then be construed from the demand curve of A by plotting all points O_b for different points p_a (which by definition also gives p_b) as is done in Figure 9.1 (see ibid., 98–103).

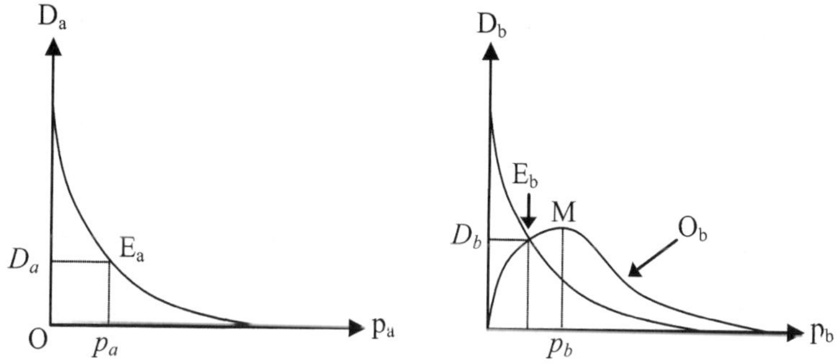

Figure 9.1 Walras's offer and demand curves

The result is the curve O_b which has a maximum at M. This is the price of B which corresponds to the maximum area of the rectangle formed by the two points D_a and p_a under the demand curve D_a.

In the example of Figure 9.1, the quantity M is greater than the quantity exchanged at the equilibrium price E_b which means that the offer curve O_b cuts the demand curve D_b from below. Walras argued that in this case the equilibrium would be stable. For $p_b < E_b$, demand is greater than the offer which provides an incentive to suppliers of B to raise their price and close the gap between p_b and E_b. To the right of E_b ($p_b > E_b$) market forces likewise move price p_b closer to its equilibrium level.[21] Walras called the result of this graphical analysis 'the law of effective offer and effective demand or the law of the establishment of equilibrium prices' (ibid., 105, emphasis in original):

> *Given two commodities, for the market to be in equilibrium with respect to these commodities, or for the price of either commodity to be stationary in terms of the other, it is necessary and sufficient that the effective demand will be equal to the effective offer of each commodity. Where this equality does not obtain, in order to reach equilibrium price, the commodity having an effective demand greater than its effective offer must rise in price, and the commodity having an effective offer greater than its effective demand must fall in price.*

In EPE this law is subsequently amended to include cases of a more general nature, such as the exchange of more than two commodities and the possibility of production and capital accumulation. But the case of two-commodity exchange offers an insight that is not present in the more complicated cases. This is the dynamic analysis of the stability conditions.

The graphical exposition prompted Walras to change the shape of the offer curve and study the nature of equilibrium for different cases (see ibid., 108–113). First, he observed that the offer curve may have no intersection with the demand curve at all. In this case, the bids and offers are such that no transactions take place and that equilibrium is therefore impossible. Second, and more interestingly, the offer curve may have several points of intersection and this leads to the possibility of multiple equilibria. Figure 9.2 replicates Walras's discussion. He observed that the equilibrium points E_1 and E_3 are similar in character in that the offer curve cuts the demand curve from below, as in Figure 9.2. Here, market equilibrium is stable. But at E_2 the offer curve cuts the demand curve from above and that means that market forces will tend to widen the gap between the current price and the equilibrium price E_2. In other words, this equilibrium is unstable.[22]

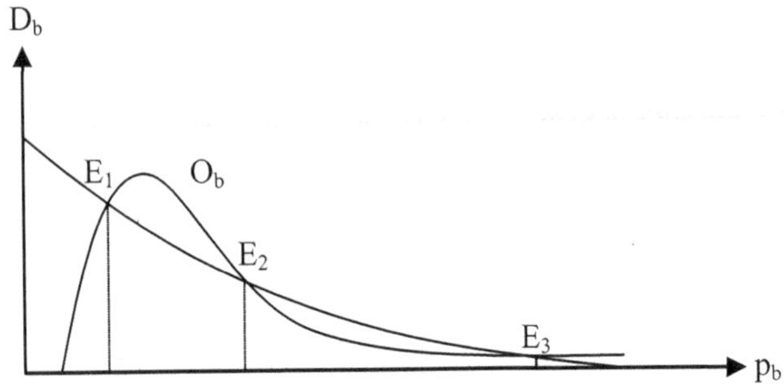

Figure 9.2 Multiple equilibria in Walras's market analysis

Theorem of Maximum Utility

The study of the properties of supply and demand curves in the simple case of a two-person barter economy proceeded without the notion of utility. Walras made an important step forward by showing that individual demand functions are determined by utility maximization.

To this purpose he defined the marginal utility of a goods, or 'rareté' in his terms, as the 'intensity of the last want satisfied'. Unlike Jevons, Walras was not very interested in the psychological roots of this notion. His prime concern was the mathematical properties of what he called the utility or want curve. He believed that marginal utility would always diminish from the first unit consumed to the last. The utility curve was the geometrical expression of this belief. This function described the relationship between utility on the x-axis and the quantity consumed on the y-axis. Rareté was the derivative of this function, while the term effective utility designated the sum total of wants satisfied by any given quantity consumed of a commodity. In other words, effective or total utility could be represented by the area under the utility curve. The algebraic representations of these functions are as follows (see ibid., 120):

$u = \Phi(q) = \int_0^q \phi(q)dq$ for total or effective utility, and

$r = \Phi'(q) = \phi(q)$ for marginal utility or rareté

In this formula q denotes the quantity consumed.

The definition of utility theory in these mathematical terms gave Walras the instruments to derive his first important result: the theorem of maximum utility. In his words, this theorem states that (Walras 1954, 125, emphasis in the original):

> *Given two commodities in a market, each holder attains maximum satisfaction of wants or maximum effective utility, when the ratio of the intensities of the last wants, or the ratio of their raretés, is equal to the price.*

To their mutual surprise, Walras and Jevons discovered in the spring of 1874 that they had both developed the equimarginal principle in very similar terms.[23] Jevons had read Walras's article 'Principes d'une théorie mathématique de l'échange' in the *Journal des Economistes* of April 1874. Walras, on his turn, was told by the Dutch economist D'Aulnis de Bourouill that his work showed great similarity to Jevons's *Theory of Political Economy*, which inspired him to write to Jevons.[24]

The rest is history, one is tempted to say. The almost simultaneous discovery by Walras and Jevons (and although he is not mentioned here, Menger) that prices could be seen as a ratio of marginal utilities started a development that later became known as the neoclassical revolution in economics. Unfortunately, as Jaffé (1976) shows in his classic article, the label father of the neoclassical revolution wrongly suggests that Walras, Jevons and Menger developed the same theory. Indeed, the theoretical differences between their works are important.

The point to be mentioned here is that Menger fundamentally objected the use of mathematics in economics while Walras and Jevons saw the use of mathematics as the innovation that would steer economics towards a more scientific course. But they in their turn lacked the knowledge to provide the emerging neoclassical theory with a solid mathematical foundation. As was shown earlier, Jevons never provided a mathematical proof for his equation of exchange, as I argue above. Walras fared much better in this regard, but his geometrical and algebraic proofs lack originality.

The collected papers and letters of Walras provide a fascinating account of the manner in which he constructed the mathematical building blocks of his general equilibrium theories. Specifically, it appears that he profited greatly from the correspondence with several scientists (economists and others) who were better versed in mathematics than he was himself. He wrote to professional mathematicians about his most pressing mathematical problems and asked them to provide solutions and to check his theorems and proofs. Some of them patiently explained to him the principles of the mathematics he was engaged in, others politely declined. The same strategy was followed with regard to fellow economists with an interest in mathematics and other readers of his works.

The first one to give Walras a crucial push in the right direction was Paul Piccard, engineer and professor of mechanics at the Academy of Lausanne. Jaffé says that it was Piccard who opened the eyes of Walras to the technique of maximization and its use in the derivation of individual demand curves from utility curves (Jaffé 1965 vol. I, 308–311; see also Walker 1983, 6). Jaffé discovered in the archives at Lausanne an expository note of Piccard to Walras which, according to Jaffé, was written in the autumn of 1872. The importance of this note is underlined by the fact that before this date there was no sign of a theory of utility maximization in the work and papers of Walras. Piccard explained to Walras step by step the proof of the theorem of utility maximization in the case of two-commodity exchange and the manner in which the demand curve can be derived from the utility curve. This was the basis of Walras's theorem of maximum utility in EPE.

Piccard started by drawing the utility curves for commodities A and B and stated that the problem involved the maximization of the sum of the areas under these curves. He then showed that the mathematical solution of this problem requires the use of infinitesimal calculus. Given incomes and the exchange ratio, the optimum choice between A and B is the point where the gain of an extra unit of B times its price matches the loss of a unit of A. If this condition is not met, the consumer can increase its total utility by exchanging A for B (or vice versa depending on the sign of the inequality). Thus Piccard presented to Walras the mathematical formula of the theorem of maximum utility: $MU_a/MU_b = p$. In addition, he showed him how to derive the demand curve of A as a function of p by taking account of the budget constraint.

It is always difficult to determine the genesis of original ideas, but Piccard's note strongly suggests that one of the fundamental theorems of EPE was not Walras's own invention. A matter which supports this conclusion is the surprising fact that in the first three editions of EPE Walras did not give an algebraic proof of the equimarginal principle. His proof consisted in a cumbersome analysis of the geometrical properties of two utility curves A and B in order to show that the optimum condition would indeed maximize the sum of the area under the curves. It was the Russian economist L. von Bortkiewicz who showed Walras how to differentiate the function of total utility with regard to A and B in order to derive the first and second order conditions of the maximization problem.[25] In the fourth edition of EPE Walras adopted this solution almost to the letter (see Jaffé 1974[1983], 90).

It appears that Walras had only an elementary knowledge of the branch of mathematics he so eagerly advocated, differential calculus. Why did he not use the method of constrained optimization to derive the theorem of maximum utility? This method was explained to him as early as 1877 by Hermann Amstein, a professor of mathematics at the University of Lausanne.[26] Walras had posed him a question about his equations of production and in reply got a formal statement of Lagrange's method to maximize or minimize an objective function subject to a constraint. Pencilled notations added to Amstein's letter show that Walras kept it for years, but failed to exploit his suggestions until after 1900 when the fourth and definitive edition of EPE had already been published (see Jaffé 1965, vol. I, 519).

GENERAL EQUILIBRIUM

The field where Walras broke new ground was the definition of general equilibrium. He was the first to formulate general equilibrium as a mathematical problem and to investigate the conditions of general equilibrium in a system of simultaneous equations. Much can be said about the mathematical shortcomings of his analysis, but the fact remains that he created an ingenious system which started with the case of exchange and then gradually complicated the analysis by subsequently introducing production, capital and money. Given the state of art of economic science in the late 19th-century, this was a major achievement.

Exchange

Walras's analysis of general equilibrium in exchange rests on three pillars:

- *A more general formulation of the demand function*: the demand for commodity A is a function of the prices of all other commodities available, whereas in the two-commodity case it just depends on the price of A and B.
- *The assumption that supply equals demand in all markets*. In the two-commodity case, market equilibrium prevails when $D_{a,b} = D_{b,a}p_{b,a}$ and

$D_{b,a} = D_{a,b}p_{a,b}$. In the GE-system this condition is adjusted in order to account for the fact that the total demand for A is a function of the exchange of A for B plus the exchange of A for C plus A for D etc.

- *The law of one price*. In the context of the GE-system this law means that the price ratios of indirect as compared to direct exchange are equal. Arbitrage ensures that the price ratio of the exchange of A for B is the same as the sum of the exchanges A for C and C for B.

The starting point of Walras's GE-analysis was the introduction of m(m–1) demand functions to describe the exchange relations between m commodities, assuming a given quantity of supply. He realized that in the case of barter the demand for commodity A depends on the exchange ratio between A and each of the other (m–1) commodities. Therefore:

$$D_a = \sum_{i=b}^{m} F_{i,a}(p_{b,a}, p_{c,a}, p_{d,a} \cdots)$$

Here $p_{a,b}$ denotes the price of commodity A measured in B.

The second step in the GE-argument was to realize that in general equilibrium supply equals demand in all markets. As there are m commodities, the number of equilibrium equations must also be m:

$$D_{a,b} + D_{a,c} + D_{a,d} + \cdots = p_{b,a}D_{b,a} + p_{c,a}D_{c,a} + p_{d,a}D_{d,a} + \ldots$$
$$D_{b,a} + D_{b,c} + D_{b,d} + \cdots = p_{a,b}D_{a,b} + p_{c,b}D_{c,b} + p_{d,b}D_{d,b} + \ldots$$

However, Walras selected commodity A as the numéraire of his system and that means that one of these equations is superfluous: if (m–1) markets are in supply and demand equilibrium, then by definition the m-th one is also, given that prices are expressed in terms of the standard commodity.

Finally, the possibility of arbitrage has to be ruled out. In the multi-commodity economy, arbritrage is possible if for example:

$$p_{a,b} \neq p_{c,a}/p_{b,c}$$

Therefore, general equilibrium requires:

$$p_{x,y} = p_{y,z}/p_{z,x} \quad \text{for } x, y, z \in \{a, b, c, \ldots m\} \text{ and } x \neq y \neq z.$$

These price ratios add another (m–1)(m–1) equations to the system. Therefore, the total number of equations in Walras's system – the demand functions plus the equations of exchange plus the price ratios – is 2m(m–1) for precisely 2m(m–1) unknown variables (the m(m–1) equilibrium prices and quantities).

Walras completed the proof of general equilibrium in exchange by showing that the demand functions can be derived from the condition that each individual maximizes his or her utility. This relationship can easily be established because in equilibrium for each commodity the ratio of marginal utility should be equal to the price. To arrive at a 'mathematical solution' of the general equilibrium problem thus required three conditions (ibid., 169):

> first that each and every party to the exchange obtain the maximum satisfaction of his wants, the ratio of his *raretés* then being equal to the prices; second that each and every party give up quantities that stand in a definite ratio to the quantities received and vice versa, there being only one price in terms of the *numéraire* for each commodity, namely the price at which total effective demand equals total effective offer; and third that there be no occasion for arbitrage transactions.

This set of conditions supported what Walras called the 'mathematical' or 'scientific' solution of general equilibrium. The next step was to show that this solution corresponded to the 'empirical' market solution, the set of prices arrived at in the market by the mechanism of free competition. In spite of the adjective empirical, this was not a description of the actual functioning of markets but an ideal representation of price adjustment through 'tâtonnement' or 'groping'. The misleading label 'empirical' refers to the Paris stock exchange, which served as the (real-type) example on the basis of which the ideal model of price adjustment was constructed.

The theory of tâtonnement explains how prices approach equilibrium through successive correction. Like on the *Bourse*, prices are cried at random and adjusted according to the following rule: excess-demand results in a new price which is higher than the first one, while in the case of excess-supply a lower price will be quoted. This process continues until supply equals demand, which is the moment when the suppliers and demanders are allowed to actually conduct the exchange.

In a single-commodity market 'groping' according to this rule works in a straightforward way, but in a multi-commodity market adjustment is complicated by the fact that prices are interdependent. Walras solved this problem by assuming that prices are adjusted one by one while other prices remain constant. For example, at the initial price vector **p'** aggregate supply and demand for commodity B are in disequilibrium. In Walras's formulation:

$$\Delta_b(p'_b, p'_c, p'_d \ \ldots) \neq \Omega_b(p'_b, p'_c, p'_d \ \ldots)$$

Where Δ_b is the demand function and Ω_b is the supply function. Walras assumed that prices p'_c, p'_d . . . et cetera have been previously determined so that p_b alone needs to be determined. The adjustment of this price takes place according to the price rule mentioned above: excess-demand raises prices while an excess-supply tends to lower them, given that prices other than p_b remain constant. The result is a new price vector which clears the market for this good:

$$F_b(p''_b, p'_c, p'_d \dots) = \Delta_b(p''_b, p'_c, p'_d \dots) - \Omega_b(p''_b, p'_c, p'_d \dots) = 0$$

Once this operation has been carried out, the price of commodity C can be adjusted in order to establish equilibrium for this commodity as well. This turns the inequality

$$F_c(p''_b, p'_c, p'_d \dots) \neq 0$$

into the equality

$$F_c(p''_b, p''_c, p'_d \dots) = 0$$

Walras argued that this procedure, subsequently applied to all remaining commodities, ultimately generates a general equilibrium price vector **p''**.

The problem ignored until this stage is the interdependence of markets, the defining characteristic of a general equilibrium system. Walras did not neglect the feedback effects of price changes, but argued that they could be abstracted from. He realized that the equilibrium prices already established will not remain unaltered when the other prices still need to be adjusted. Nevertheless, he assumed that the resulting new inequalities would probably be more closer to zero than the initial inequality. The reason for this convergence was the fact that the price-elasticity of the commodity in question is higher (that is the effect of a change in the price of B on the demand for B) than the cross-price elasticities. As Walras put it, a change in the price of good B has a direct effect on the excess-demand for this commodity which brings it closer to zero. But the changes in the prices of other goods only have an indirect effect on this excess-demand, some bringing it closer to equality, other working in the opposite direction. According to him, the result was that these changes 'up to a certain point cancelled each other out. Hence, the new system of prices . . . is closer to equilibrium than the old system of prices . . . and it is only necessary to continue this process along the same lines for the system to move closer to equilibrium' (ibid., 172).

Production

The extension of Walras's general equilibrium model to the case of production introduced a new kind of commodity, the capital good. Walras defined capital goods as all forms of social wealth that are not used up after their first use. The notion of capital thus involved a time dimension because it takes several time periods to consume a capital good. For that reason, Walras distinguished between the capital goods themselves and their services. In the general equilibrium model with production, he assumed that the quantity of capital goods remains constant; there is no investment and therefore no economic growth. The capital goods proper produce services that are consumed during a single production period. In this manner, the time dimension could be abstracted from. The theoretical problem now became to find a new set of equations to determine equilibrium simultaneously on the markets of products and of productive services.

Walras approached this task by carefully describing the different kinds of productive services and their functions. This analysis will not be repeated here. It suffices to mention that Walras distinguished between three types of fixed capital: land, human capital and capital proper. The services of these capital goods were offered by their owners (land owners, labourers and capitalists) on the respective markets for these services. Walras was able to draw up the supply and demand equations for these markets by assuming that there was an intermediary figure who demanded services on the service markets and offered newly produced goods on the product market. This figure was the entrepreneur who purchased productive services and combined them to activate the processes of production. The entrepreneur was motivated by the aim to maximize profits and this posed a problem to Walras. After all, his profit is made up of the difference of the value of the product sold and the costs of the services and products used in the productive process. But in competitive equilibrium such profits are reduced to zero which leaves the entrepreneur without a motive to act and an income to live on.

Walras solved this dilemma by treating the entrepreneur as an idealization; as an economic function rather than the activity of a concrete person or institution (Ingrao and Israel 1990, 107 and Van Daal and Jolink 1993, 48).[27] This explains why he reasoned that '[a]ssuming equilibrium, we may even go so far as to abstract from entrepreneurs' (Walras 1954, 225). Equilibrium was an end-state, which no longer required their services. They had reduced profits to zero and in the process brought about an equality of supply and demand on the markets of products and productive services. The conditions of general equilibrium in the case of production were therefore as follows. They consisted in the eyes of Walras of the two conditions of general equilibrium in the case of exchange plus the condition that 'the selling prices of the products equal the costs of the productive services that enter into them' (ibid., 224).

Marginal Productivity

The mechanism of production brought Walras to consider an important analytical innovation which, however, he was unable to integrate into his general equilibrium theory. This was the question of the prices of the factors of production in relation to their function as inputs in the productive process, or marginal productivity theory. Walras introduced the term 'coefficients of production' to designate the quantities of the respective productive services that enter into the production of one unit of each of the products (ibid., 240). He stated that these coefficients are variables determined by the condition that the costs of production of the products be minimal. He also suggested that it would be easy to include the necessary equations into the system of general equilibrium but 'in the interest of greater simplicity' he assumed the coefficients to be constants. This is all there was of Walras's marginal productivity theory in the first two editions of EPE.

Again, it appears that Walras's poor mathematical education blocked the development of his economic theories. Jaffé (1974) argues that Walras could have completed his marginal productivity theory in 1877 had he been able to understand the mathematical formulation provided to him in that year by Hermann Amstein. Amstein had demonstrated him in a letter how Langrangean multipliers could be used to solve the minimization problem of the costs of production. Jaffé's analysis shows that it took Walras 17 years before he began to grasp the mathematics involved. He was helped in this matter by Enrico Barone who had sent him his (unpublished) Italian translation of Wicksteed's *Essay on the Co-ordination of the Laws of Distribution* (1894). In this essay Wicksteed showed that cost minimization implies that each production factor is paid its marginal product and that the sum of the shares earned by the factors will exactly exhaust the whole production. Wicksteed's essay induced Walras to add an appendix to the third edition of EPE in which he explained his own version of the marginal productivity theory. He introduced a production equation and a function for the cost of production and summarized his findings as follows (Walras 1954, 385, emphasis in original):[28]

> *1. Free competition brings the cost of production down to a minimum. 2. In state of equilibrium, when the cost of production and selling price are equal, the prices of the services are proportional to their marginal productivities, that is to the partial derivatives of the production equation.*

However, the remarkable fact is that in his general equilibrium analysis he retained the assumption of fixed coefficients of production; he never used marginal productivity theory to support this analysis.[29]

Groping in the Case of Production

Walras was aware that the assumption of static equilibrium would pose more problems in the case of production than it had in the pure exchange model. The kernel of the problem was that production takes time which means that it is unrealistic to assume that changes in production plans are effectuated instantaneously. Walras tried to deal with this problem by assuming that production is postponed until the equilibrium prices are established. He assumed that entrepreneurs make their offers known to consumers by means of 'tickets' which represent the quantities they intend to supply at the current price. Price adjustment takes place according to the model of the auction market that was used to explain groping in the case of exchange. Different prices are 'cried' in order to invite offers and bids and a market maker adjusts the quoted price so as to establish equilibrium between them. At this stage the order can be given to actually carry out the production orders represented by the tickets.

Walras assumed that landowners, labourers and capitalists also offered their services in terms of tickets. In this manner, he could claim that production is adjusted in order to establish equality between the selling price and the cost of production without introducing a time element that would force him to address the dynamics of this adjustment. Thus his 'law of the establishment of equilibrium prices in the case of production' consisted of two elements. First, in order to establish supply and demand equilibrium for products and productive services, it is necessary to raise (lower) the price of those products and services who are in excess-demand (supply). Second, in order to establish that the selling price of products be equal to the costs of the services employed in making them, it is necessary to increase (decrease) the output of those products with a selling price which is greater (lower) than the cost of production.

However, unlike his analysis of the manner in which price adjustment tends towards an equilibrium level in the case of exchange, Walras did not investigate the details of groping in the case of production. He was therefore unable to show that price adjustments according to the aforementioned 'law of the establishment of equilibrium in the case of production' actually bring prices closer to their equilibrium level.

Existence, Stability and Uniqueness of General Equilibrium

Schumpeter (1954, 1001–1002) strongly praised Walras's consistent approach of the different models comprising his general equilibrium theory. Specifically, he pointed out that in each of the four models (exchange, production, capital formation and money) Walras first addressed the existence problem of general equilibrium and then attempted to show that this equilibrium is the one that market forces under conditions of free competition tend to establish; an exercise that Schumpeter saw as a formal proof of the stability of the equilibrium solution. He stated that even the proof of uniqueness has a place in his general equilibrium system and referred in this respect to Walras's argument that in the case of the exchange of an arbitrary number of commodities equilibrium will in general be unique, given that the number of commodities in the market is very large (see Walras 1954, 200).

As was shown above, the issues of the existence of and the tendency towards general equilibrium figure prominently in the different steps of Walras's general equilibrium analysis. But one may doubt that they have the analytical quality that Schumpeter attributed to them.

In the first place, Schumpeter (1954, 1002) himself admitted that much of the analysis concerning the adjustment towards equilibrium is based on very restrictive assumptions, or as he called it 'heroic theorizing'. The best example of this lack of realism concerns the use of tickets to arrest actual production activity while the equilibrium prices are being established. Also Walras was very selective in his choice of price mechanism. The only price rule he used was the very obvious one that an excess-demand leads to a price increase and an excess-supply to a price decrease.

Secondly, Schumpeter misleadingly suggested that Walras had a preconceived plan to systematically investigate the existence, stability and uniqueness of general equilibrium in the four cases concerning exchange, production, capital and money. Nothing could be further from the truth. Indeed, in all these cases he aimed to establish that an equilibrium solution is possible, but the so-called proof of the stability of this solution had little to do with mathematical reasoning. It is only in the case of exchange that he tried to explain the mechanism by which prices are supposed to move closer to their equilibrium level. In the other cases, he merely gave an intuitive explanation of what he called the 'laws of the establishment of price equilibrium'. Let alone that he seriously addressed the question of uniqueness. Walras broached this question once and that was in the passage Schumpeter referred to. There he argued that whereas partial equilibrium analysis had to consider the possibility of multiple equilibria, in general equilibrium analysis this possibility was precluded, assuming that the number of commodities in the market was very large. But he merely stated this conclusion without an explanation. Hardly what one would call an example of rigorous mathematical analysis. One may conclude with Ingrao and Israel (1990, 112) that 'none of the three analytical problems raised by general equilibrium theory – existence, uniqueness and stability – received either solution or clear definition in the *Eléments*'.[30]

GENERAL EQUILIBRIUM: IDEAL OR REAL?

The question that remains to be answered concerns the goal of Walras's general equilibrium analysis. It is clear that he saw general equilibrium theory as form of pure science which addresses the laws of nature. In terms of his classification of the sciences, discussed above, such laws are to be studied in terms of ideal-type theories which have an indirect relationship with reality because they are based on real-type concepts. However, their aim is not to describe events as they go on in the real world but to explain laws that are valid for all times and places, which of necessity gives them a highly abstract character. Pure science in this sense generates the instruments to study questions at the applied level. This branch of science stands closer to reality because it addresses questions in terms of their utility rather than their truth content. The point is: did Walras's general equilibrium analysis stay within the boundaries of pure science or did he also aim to describe and explain the working of market economies as they function in reality?

This issue emerges most clearly in the context of typical dynamic questions such as the movement of market prices towards equilibrium and the process of capital accumulation and economic growth. In EPE dynamic questions of this kind are consistently explained in terms of static theories.

The best example of the static framework of EPE is the theory of groping that explains the establishment of supply and demand equilibrium in a multi-commodity economy in a sequence of steps. This theory was not intended to describe the sequence of price adjustments as they really take place on markets, but rather to break down the process of price adjustment in different steps for analytical purposes. As Jaffé (1981[1983], 252) contends, Walras's theory groping is a theory of 'virtually timeless, simultaneous and mechanical adjustment operation which [Walras] broke down into its constituent parts for purposes of exposition and analysis'.

Secondly, the assumption of trading with tickets in the case of the production model was likewise intended to suppress the complications of dynamic analysis. It was argued earlier that Walras introduced this assumption to prevent that actual production could take place before prices had reached their equilibrium level. Also he assumed that the quantity of capital goods would remain constant and that only the productive services of capital goods are used up during a given production period.

Finally, in the theory of capital formation a similar trick is used. This theory introduces the market where savings and new capital goods are exchanged. But the equilibrium in capital formation reached on this market is a notional concept because it only expresses intentions. Walras assumed that the new capital goods are not actually delivered in the period under scrutiny. They enter the market in a subsequent period in order to retain the static assumption that the quantity of capital goods is constant even when the economy is assumed to be growing at a positive rate. It is worth quoting Walras in full on his matter (Walras 1954, 282 and 283, emphasis in the original text):

> We shall resolve the further difficulty apropos the lapse of time required in the production of new capital goods in the same way that we resolved it in the case of final products, by assuming production to be instantaneous. Thus equilibrium in capital formation will first be established *in principle*. Then it will be established *effectively* by the reciprocal exchange between savings to be accumulated and new capital goods to be supplied *within a given period of time*, during which *no change in the data is allowed*. Although the economy is becoming *progressive*, it remains for the time being *static* because of the fact that the new capital goods play no part in the economy until a later period subsequent to the one under consideration.

It may be asked why Walras went to such great lengths to preserve the static framework of his general equilibrium theories. The answer is that he gave priority to the analytical consistency of his pure economics. Ingrao and Israel (1990, 103) say that Walras followed the method of successive approximations. According to this method, general equilibrium analysis would proceed in steps from static to dynamic analysis as a means to gradually incorporate into the system increasingly complete and complex elements of real markets. Indeed the succession of the models of general equilibrium (exchange, production, capital formation and money) in EPE seems to support such an approach. But the treatment of dynamic questions points in another direction. Walras was not interested in going from an ideal description of economic exchange and production towards an increasingly more realistic explanation of these same phenomena.[31] His aim was to develop an equilibrium theory that was increasingly more general in the sense that it incorporated more markets. In the process he introduced more and more unrealistic assumptions in order to maintain the analytical consistency of this framework. The ideal and static characteristics of his general equilibrium theories are in that sense two sides of the same coin.

By far the most persistent and convincing advocate of the opposite thesis is Donald Walker. He claims that Walras aimed to give a realistic description and explanation of existing economic systems and institutions. His conclusions are to a large extent based on a careful analysis of the different editions of EPE. He argues that the equilibrium theories developed in the first three editions of EPE are more representative of Walras's thought than the fourth and definitive edition. Moreover, the earlier theories are profoundly dynamic and show his intentions to give an accurate explanation of real economic processes.

To start with, Walker (1987, 360) argues that the common element in all five editions of EPE is a theory of market behaviour that was based on the example of how real competitive markets function. Walker points to the fact that the static part of this theory concerned the conditions of equilibrium and the dynamic part the 'the attainment of equilibrium through the play of the raising and lowering of prices until the supply and demand quantities are made equal' (ibid., 763). Walras referred to this dynamic theory of price adjustment as the empirical counterpart of the mathematical solution of his system of equations. In Walker's opinion, this suggests that Walras intended to give a realistic description of the exchange tatonnement process.

In the field of production, Walras was less consistent. One of Walker's main arguments is that in the first three editions of the EPE Walras developed what he calls a 'disequilibrium-production model' (ibid., 761). The basis of this model was the recognition that in real economies production occurs while prices are still seeking their equilibrium level. That made it a much more realistic theory than its successor in the fourth edition of EPE. In this edition Walras introduced the use of tickets, or pledges as Walker calls them, in order to abstract from actual production activity during the disequilibrium adjustment process. Walker considers this theory a mistake, an 'incomplete afterthought'. It was intended to solve an analytical problem, namely that actual production violates the condition that all the data are constant while equilibrium prices and quantities are being established. Walker claims that in due time Walras became aware that production would transform his fixed equilibrium solution into a moving equilibrium that invalidated his mathematical solution in terms of a static system of simultaneous equations. To remedy this problem, he assumed in the fourth edition of EPE that production was instantaneous, just as exchange was instantaneous and conditional upon the establishment of equilibrium prices and quantities. The result was a theory that was consistent with the mathematical conditions of equilibrium, but at what price? Walker considers the pledges model 'extremely unrealistic' and in flagrant contradiction with Walras's earlier dynamic equilibrium theories of production.

The question then is, which theory is the right one in the sense that it represents Walras's true intentions? Walker has a clear answer to that question. He claims that the disequilibrium-production model was a basic part of Walras's general-equilibrium theory for almost his entire career. In contrast, he introduced the pledges model in 1900 at the very end of the period in which he made theoretical contributions. This theory 'by its characteristics revealed the weakening of his creative powers'. The true intention of Walras was therefore to describe and explain existing economic phenomena and not to portray the economy in terms of an ideal model on moral grounds.

The problem with Walker's interpretation and others who support similar conclusions (for example Morishima 1977 and Ménard 1990) is that they are unable to explain the division in Walras's thought. Why did Walras abandon the realistic disequilibrium-production model in favour of an abstract model that stood so far from reality? Walker's explanation that Walras was too old to do serious theoretical work does no credit to his scholarship of Walras and is in fact too simple to be believed.

The surprising fact is that Walker does not refer to Walras's methodology of theory formation. As I discussed above, Walras saw all theories in the domain of pure science as ideal constructions in the sense that they used real-type concepts in order to derive ideal-type concepts that could be used as the building blocks of theoretical reasoning. He used the example of the stock exchange to construct a model of perfect competition that formed the foundation of his equilibrium explanation of exchange. This model of perfect competition contained many elements that were evidently unrealistic, such as the assumption that the numbers of buyers and sellers is unlimited and that every market participant has perfect information about the supply and demand conditions. Ideal constructions of this kind drove a wedge between Walras's theories and observable reality, not only in the fourth edition in 1900 but from the start in 1874 when the first edition of EPE was published.

Walras explained why he called his theories ideal constructions but he was extremely vague about the aim of these theories in relation to reality. How did one choose between true and false theories? Was logic the only criterion or was there also an empirical test involved? Walras never addressed this matter. In EPE, the only clue is his frequent statement that the mathematical solution of economic equilibrium coincides with the 'practical' or 'empirical' solution reached by the process of groping in competitive market economies. Walker takes this statement as evidence that Walras's ultimate aim was to describe the working of real market processes. But this conclusion overlooks the fact that Walras compared practice and theory in terms of their end result. He believed that real markets and his ideal representation of perfect competition generated the same outcome, namely economic equilibrium. But he considered the process by which they reach this outcome as almost incomparable. That is why with regard to the mathematical theory of exchange, he stated that 'the theoretical solution would be absolutely impracticable in almost every case'.

It appears that Walras was not at all interested in the realistic description of actual processes of change. He proved an instrumentalist *avant la lettre*. The implicit test of his ideal theories was the presence of useful applications and that was not a matter of realism. He pointed to the example of geometry, a highly abstract science that was only valid under ideal circumstances that are hardly ever observed in reality. Yet reality admitted of very wide and fruitful applications of its propositions. Likewise, the relevant test of pure economics was 'do these pure truths find frequent application?'. Walras was convinced that in the case of his general equilibrium theories the answer to this question would be affirmative, even when the theories contained assumptions, terms and processes that had little relation with reality.[32]

Stated in these terms, there was no conflict between the aim of Walras's general equilibrium theories prior to and after 1900. The introduction of tickets in the fourth edition of EPE strengthened the mathematical foundation of the general equilibrium model. From the point of view of pure science, that was a desirable improvement and the fourth edition of EPE was in that sense a logical step in Walras's development of the general equilibrium model, rather than a sudden break.[33] The price of analytical progress was an increasing number of unrealistic assumptions but that was not an objection in the eyes of Walras. On the contrary, he must have considered it a recommendation. After all, 'the scholar has a right to pursue science for its own sake, just as the geometer has the right to study the most singular properties of geometric figures, however fantastic, if he finds that they arouse his curiosity' (Walras 1954, 71 and 72). To paraphrase Walras in this regard, in the realm of pure economics, anything was possible as long as it aided the development of a logically consistent mathematical theory of general equilibrium.

THE MORAL DIMENSION

To develop an ideal representation of a market economy is one thing, to claim that this theory has a moral dimension is another. Jaffé says that Walras's preoccupation with the social question passed through his strict partition of pure, applied and social economics with the result that his general equilibrium theories became imbued with a distinctive moral content. Walker (1984, 451) rejects this argument saying that there is no place in any of Walras's writings where he states that his theory of general equilibrium has a normative purpose and there are many places where he stated that it does not. Who should we believe, Walras or the modern interpreter of his work (in this case Jaffé)?

Jaffé (1977, 330–331) says that the assumption of perfect competition represented for Walras not only an analytical ideal but an ethical ideal as well, because he considered it an indispensable pillar of social justice. 'He counted on free competition in an ideally perfect market to perform automatically the moral function of stamping out profits that are something for nothing, unearned, the fruit of guile and antisocial conspiracy and therefore unjust.'

I explained above that Walras carefully classified the different sciences and their goals and used this distinction as a framework for the three works that were intended to form his complete economics: the *Elements of pure economics* (or the theory of social wealth), the *Elements of applied economics* (or the theory of the production of wealth) and the *Elements of social economics* (or the theory of the distribution of wealth via property and taxation). Given this framework, it is odd to assume that Walras used his pure economics to secretly convey a normative scheme, as Jaffé maintains, while he could have discussed such matters more effectively and above all openly in the context of his social economics.

The reason why there is a moral dimension to Walras's general equilibrium theory has to do with the triad pure science, applied science and social science. Following Vacherot, he described science as the 'idealization of reality' and art as the 'realization of the ideal'. This division of tasks placed the development of ideal theories in the domain of pure science in a specific context. To Walras the justification of pure science was, first, the ability to investigate the economy in terms of its perfect qualities and, second, its suitability as an end or goal for action (Koppl 1995). Jaffé (1977[1983], 340) describes this 'latent purpose' as 'to demonstrate the possibility of formulating axiomatically a rationally consistent economic system that would satisfy the demands of social justice without overstepping the bounds imposed by the natural exigencies of the real world'. Koppl (1995) argues that scientific socialism was the hidden agenda of Walras's general equilibrium theory. General equilibrium theory could be used to this purpose, because it described an ideal economic system which allowed all market participants to maximize utility.[34] The task that remained to be done was to ensure that reality conformed itself to this ideal. Walras realized that this was a matter of institutional reform. In this role, he used general economic equilibrium as a benchmark to investigate policies for reform. Obviously, this would lead to the conclusion that the conditions for a free competitive economy should be installed where needed, but Walras was not a follower of laissez-faire policies. He recognized the shortcomings of the market mechanism and believed for instance that the provision of public services could not be entrusted to private parties. Such goods needed a different allocation mechanism and a guiding role of the government.[35] But all these matters could be studied within the context of the general equilibrium model, which described an ideal that with the proper conditions in place would be automatically produced by real economic forces. This aspect constitutes the normative characteristic of Walras's general equilibrium theory.

Jaffé considers this normative bias a unscientific aspect of Walras's pure economics. However, the normative aspect of his general equilibrium theory can better be compared to what Schumpeter (1954, 41) has called a scientist's 'vision'. According to him, the first step of scientific activity is to visualize a distinct set of coherent phenomena as a worth-while object of our analysis. Vision in this sense comprises several aspects of the scientific process such as instruments, goals and beliefs. The vision of Walras is made up of the choice to use mathematics as the preferred language of scientific inquiry and to study the economy as a system of interrelated markets, but also of his determination to find an answer to the social question in combination with his liberal moral values. This vision structured Walras's pure economics in the sense that it gave it direction (study the properties of exchange and production under the hypothesis of perfect competition) and meaning (show that an economic order which complies to the conditions of general economic equilibrium is a welfare improvement compared to existing conditions). In this sense, Walras's hidden agenda and his pure theory of general economic equilibrium are not incompatible (see also Koppl 1995, 51). His general equilibrium model was a dreamland in two senses: it embodied the ideal of the frictionless economy and also contained a blueprint of a society that would improve the economic well-being of many people.

THE FUNCTION OF THE EQUILIBRIUM CONCEPT

The conclusion of this section is that the concept of equilibrium played a pivotal role in all three parts of Walras's economics.

First in pure economics the role of the equilibrium concept was technical and involved the optimization of individual choices and the calculation of a vector of prices and quantities so that supply would equal demand simultaneously on all markets. This is the prime example of the equilibrium concept seen as an end-state.

Second in the field of applied economics Walras used the concept of equilibrium in the classical notion of point of gravitation. He was for instance an advocate of comparative statics to address applied questions. He argued that one could interview consumers directly in order to determine the cause of an economic disturbance.[36] This could be a change in the quantity possessed or a shift of someone's utility curve. The essence of the analysis was that a new equilibrium would established, so that the effect of the disturbance could be assessed by comparing the two equilibrium situations. Like in classical analysis, the main driver behind the process of adjustment towards a new equilibrium was the entrepreneur. He responded to profit opportunities by entering a new market or expanding output while losses prompted him to leave a market or curtail production. In this manner, Walras (1954, 224) explained why 'equilibrium is the normal state, in the sense that it is the state towards which thing spontaneously tend under a regime of free competition in exchange and in production'.

Third in social economics the assumption of equilibrium made it possible to argue that an ideal economic order could serve as a blueprint for actual economic changes and therefore as a basis for economic policy. Walras believed that under the right conditions (free competition et cetera) economic agents would voluntarily converge towards the equilibrium situation of the ideal design. This is only possible if one strongly believes that the processes of change in real economic situations are controlled by the forces of equilibrium. Walras expressed this belief in terms of a metaphor. He argued that in order to come 'more closely to reality' we must drop the assumption of a fixed market period and adopt the hypothesis of a continuous market. In this market it is no longer possible to postpone production in order to await the establishment of equilibrium prices and thus we pass, in Walras's words, 'from the static to the dynamic state'.

In the dynamic state a flurry of production activity takes place; consumer goods, capital goods and raw materials 'are like so many shoots that are continually being pruned at one end while they are constantly growing at the other. Every hour, nay, every minute, portions of these different classes of circulating capital are disappearing and reappearing'. Given that all stocks of commodities undergo this process of renewal and destruction, and each commodity in a different time cycle (Walras 1954, 380):

> [T]he continuous market is perpetually tending towards equilibrium without ever attaining it, because the market has no other way of approaching equilibrium except by groping and before the goal is reached it has to renew its efforts and start over again, all the basic data of the problem, for example the initial quantities possessed, the utilities of goods and services, the technical coefficients etc., having changed in the meantime. Viewed in this manner, the market is like a lake agitated by the wind, where the water is incessantly seeking its level without ever reaching it.

The importance of this statement is that it shows the extent of Walras's faith in the self-correcting nature of economic forces, but also that in his social economics he substitutes the process conception of equilibrium for that of the end-state conception. Even if we consider that the basic data of the general equilibrium model are in reality variables to be determined by the economic process itself (that is endogenous variables), then there are still powerful forces that control the process of change and steer it towards an equilibrium level. According to Walras, it is the task of social economics to study the nature of these forces and to use them in order to improve the economic destiny of mankind. It is a pity that in the history of economic thought Walras's pure economics overwhelmed his achievements in the field of social economics. Greater concern for the latter could have been an antidote to the transformation of equilibrium into an end-state conception that emerged in the mathematical inquiry of general economic equilibrium.

THE DIFFICULT ROAD FOR MATHEMATICAL ECONOMICS

Chapter 8 and Chapter 9 have shown that the mathematical method gradually made its entrance into the domain of economics. This was not a sudden revolution in the sense that Jevons and Walras introduced a form of analysis that was new to economics. Their zeal to promote the cause of mathematical economics greatly facilitated the development of this branch of economics, but this contribution cannot hide the fact that many elements of their mathematical theories had been anticipated by others who were less effective in the marketing of their ideas.

The use of the equilibrium concept in mathematical economics opened a new field of study such as the analysis of consumer behaviour in terms of marginal utility and the analysis of firm behaviour in terms of marginal productivity theory. These theories constituted a break with classical economics in the sense that they used different concepts (marginal utility and productivity), different analytical tools (mathematics and statistics) and followed a different agenda for research (the allocation of a given quantity of scarce resources was the main problem rather than issues related to reproduction and distribution).

These changes were the core elements of an emerging new paradigm, neoclassical economics. Jevons and Walras were pioneers in this field but their break with the past was not so abrupt as suggested by the phrase 'marginal revolution'. In their work the innovation of a mathematical equilibrium theory was combined with features that one would qualify as typical classical. For example, Walras tried to extend his general equilibrium analysis to an investigation of the continuous market that involved the reproduction of the different classes of capital goods. Jevons's rhetoric suggested a radical departure from the doctrine of Ricardo and his followers but his famous catena shows that his utility theory is better seen as a complement to the classical analysis of market prices (Jevons 1879, 179):

> Cost of production determines supply.
> Supply determines final degree of utility.
> Final degree of utility determines value.

The point at which the break with the classical past became best visible was the notion that the mathematical concept of economic equilibrium is seen as an ideal concept rather than as an aspect of reality. Chapter 7 argued that classical economists generally placed the analysis of production and distribution in the context of historical forces. Consequently equilibrium was seen as a tendency, a process of adjustment through historical time. This was an element that vanished in the work of Jevons and Walras. They saw equilibrium theory as an ideal construction which abstracted from complicating factors and introduced unrealistic assumptions in order to enable a mathematical treatment of economic problems. The result of this approach was a diminishing interest in the study of dynamics effects and the gradual replacement of the equilibrium concept as an end-state by the process-oriented approach. This is what I have called the transformation of equilibrium theory.

This strategy was partly based on the example of successful mathematical theories such as physics. These examples showed that it was not necessary to develop theories that accurately described aspects of reality in order to achieve scientific progress. On the contrary, theory development could be aided by bold hypotheses and unrealistic assumptions, provided that it supported the logical consistency of theories and generated useful applications.

This latter conclusion is of special importance because it was at this point that Walras and Jevons were forced to look beyond the mathematical properties of their equilibrium theories. It appears that both men upheld an uncritical belief that the outcomes of their abstract models were in close conformity with actual economic processes.

Chapter 8 demonstrated that Jevons unjustly assumed that the step from economic equilibrium as an analytical ideal to a statistical regularity was just a small one. As a result his mathematical revolution went astray.

Walras in his turn habitually claimed that the mathematical results of his general equilibrium models corresponded to the empirical outcome of the operation of a free market economy. He saw this claim as the starting point of a new round of theoretical research, namely to investigate the process of the establishment of equilibrium prices, not as an agenda for empirical research. The result was an innovative mathematical theory of price adjustment, his theory of groping that, however, required some very unrealistic assumptions such as the condition that prices are adjusted sequentially rather than simultaneously and the use of tickets to prevent actual production activity from taking place during the adjustment process. Yet in the scientific framework of Walras this was not a handicap. He was not interested in the realism of the assumptions, underlying his general equilibrium analysis. As an instrumentalist *avant la lettre*, the only relevant test was the possibility of practical applications. He argued that the pure theory of economic equilibrium was a useful instrument for questions in the field of applied and social economics because economic changes had a dominant tendency to move towards equilibrium. The result was that he rested content with the static formulation of general equilibrium theories. In his vision, it was not the task of the theorist to adjust his theoretical models to the demands of reality. On the contrary, he believed that economic reality would converge upon the ideal of general equilibrium, if the right conditions were created to enable this development. This belief gave Walras's general equilibrium theories a distinct moral dimension. They reflected a blueprint of an ideal society and as such could be used to develop and assess economic policies.

The introduction of mathematical theories of economic equilibrium by Jevons and Walras did not mean that the development of the neoclassical paradigm was now a run course. In fact, it took years before marginal utility theory and other aspects of neoclassical economics became an accepted part of the economic curriculum. Jevons did much to promote the cause of mathematical economics in England. Schabas (1990) even speaks of a Jevonian revolution to indicate his success. But he never established his own school of followers. The real breakthrough came with the highly influential textbook of Marshall. He was the first to offer an integrated analysis of the theories of individual and firm behaviour, consistently stated in terms of their supply and demand elements. It was his legacy which to a large extent determined the mold of neoclassical economics in England.

The proliferation of general equilibrium theory proved an even more difficult task. In Continental Europe the opposition from the German Historical School and its French equivalent prevented it from spreading very far, while in England the economics of Marshall became the ruling orthodoxy. Walras anyway had little chance of success in the English speaking world, because translations of his work were not available and he generally published his articles in obscure journals. Similar problems troubled Vilfredo Pareto, his successor at Lausanne, who with an occasional exception wrote in French and Italian. For years, Pareto remained Walras's most important follower. But even he believed towards the end of his career that general equilibrium analysis had reached a dead end, because he found it increasingly difficult to accept the incompatibilities between the highly abstract nature of the theory and the empirical evidence. As a result, he left the field of pure economics for what it was and turned to sociology.

Ingrao and Israel (1990) conclude that the period around 1910 was a moment of real crisis for general equilibrium analysis. After the demise of Walras and the conversion of Pareto, the intellectual heritage of general equilibrium analysis was in the hands of a very diverse group of economists in different corners of the world: Aupetit and E. Antonelli in France, E. Barone and G. Antonelli in Italy, Wicksell and Cassel in Sweden, Schlesinger in Austria and last but not least Irving Fisher and Henry Moore in America. Their work laid the germ of what was to become known as the Lausanne tradition, the study of the mathematical properties of general equilibrium theory.

However, the real breakthrough of general equilibrium analysis did not take place in Switzerland and came from an unsuspected corner. For years Walras in vain tried to arouse the interest of the mathematics profession in the development of mathematical economics. In the light of his efforts, it is ironic that in the 1930s a group of mathematicians led by Karl Menger, the son of the founder of Austrian school, rescued general equilibrium analysis from oblivion and gave it a decisive push forward. They founded general equilibrium analysis on proper mathematical grounds and turned it into a science that saw the mathematical problems of the existence, stability and uniqueness of general economic equilibrium as its leading questions. In the process, they pushed the theory in a direction that so many of Walras's opponents had detested, but that in the post Word War II era coincided much better with the preferences of the scientific community: general equilibrium analysis became a branch of pure mathematics with no more than a vague interest in the economic content of its propositions.

The how and why of this development will not detain us here and is the subject of Chapter 16. The next chapter is devoted to an economic tradition that did not favour the mathematical method in economics, the Austrian school.

NOTES

1. At times he found it necessary to remind the reader of his *History of Economic Analysis* that in spite of his admiration for Walras he was still objective. 'It is order for me to observe, neglecting my principle of effacing myself in this book, that the admiration I

keep for the ingenuity, nay, greatness of Walras' analysis, should not be understood to imply agreement in every respect' (Schumpeter 1954, 1019 fn.). See also Keizer (1997).

2. These changes were that the French economy moved from an agricultural stage to an industrial stage. This transition had put a strain on the economic relations within the existing social organization. Like many of his contemporaries, Walras tried to reform society by reformulating the economic relations. See Van Daal and Jolink (1993, 112).
3. As reality adjusts itself to the ideal model, Van Daal and Jolink (1993, 112 fn.) prefer to speak of a 'utopian reality'.
4. The general nature of the equilibrium meant that equilibrium was established in the four major sectors of the economic system: exchange, production, capital formation and money. 'Nor can we understand without mathematics why or how current equilibrium prices are arrived at not only in exchange, but also in production, capital formation and circulation, by raising the price of services, products and new capital goods when demand exceeds supply and lowering the price in the contrary case' (Walras 1954, 43).
5. French economics was still under the spell of Says's school which distrusted and disliked the use of mathematical formalization in economics. The key objection made to Walras was that mathematics is not applicable to political economy because it is a moral science. Practically, this meant that the rigorous determination and measurement of the amounts of pleasure and utility was impossible, as there was no psychological unit of measurement. See Ingrao and Israel (1990, 89 and 141–147).
6. Walras did not believe that Poincaré's comment applied to the foundations of his pure theory. In his reply he stated that correspondence with reality should be established at the level of applied theory. See his letter of 3 October 1901 in Jaffé (1965 vol. III, 167).
7. However, at some points in EPE Walras (1954, 146) clearly adopted a cardinal notion of utility. This was for instance the case when he argued that marginal utility is not just an individual concept but can be a measure of market prices as well, because the average marginal utility in the market will be proportional to the market price.
8. Mirowski and Cook (1990) who translated the article 'Economics and Mechanics' find numerous mistakes in his imitation of physics. They argue that he had insufficient knowledge of the energy physics he saw as a model for his economics and was unable to express the relevant physical theories in a correct mathematical manner. In their opinion, this seriously discredits his own economics as well, as they claim that all of the mathematics of Walras's general equilibrium was directly copied from energy physics. See also Mirowski (1989).
9. He stated that 'it is possible to witness the conditions of equilibrium of the steelyard and those of the sky . . . [but] . . . impossible to reveal all the conditions of exchange and those of the general equilibrium of the market' (Walras 1909[1990], 212).
10. The full title of EPE is: *Elements of Pure Economics, or the theory of social wealth.* Walras (1954, 65) defined social wealth as all things, material of immaterial, that are both scarce (that is limited in quantity) and useful (satisfy a certain desire).
11. Walras (1954, 79) summarized the differences as follows: 'The theory of property defines the mutual relations established between man and man with respect to the appropriation

of social wealth and determines the conditions of the equitable distribution of social wealth within a community . . . The theory of industry, on the other hand, defines those relations between man and things which at the increase and transformation of social wealth and determines the conditions of an abundant production'.

12. See Walras (1954, 64, his emphasis) about the characteristics of science, art and ethics: 'Their respective criteria are the *true*; the *useful*, meaning material wellbeing; and the *good*, meaning justice.'
13. Jolink (1991, 60) adds another subdivision to this classification, one according to method (pure and applied). Walras made a distinction between pure science and pure moral science. The latter covers the domain of human phenomena in table 8.1 and consists of applied natural science (arts) in case of the person-things relationship and applied moral science (ethics) in case of the person-person relationship.
14. *Etudes d'économie appliquée* (1898) and *Etudes d'économie sociale* (1896).
15. However, there is a discussion of methodological rules in early manuscripts of Walras. See Jolink (1991, 50–58). He concludes that 'Walras's contribution to the philosophy of science can, at most, be characterized as modest and is, in fact, primarily in the domain of economics' (ibid., 50).
16. Jolink (1991) therefore typifies Walras's complete economic system as evolutionary economics.
17. In any case, he did not claim any similarity between his (ideal) theoretical price-adjustement scheme to the actual pricing mechanism. Van Daal and Jolink (1993, 8).
18. Jaffé (1965 vol. I, 180, fn1) describes this this book as Walras's *vade mecum*.
19. In a footnote Walras added that is the task of applied economics 'to inquire whether free competition is always the best means [of bringing selling price into equality with cost of production]'.
20. The issue of the interpretation of the general equilibrium theory will be discussed further on in this Chapter.
21. The use of the term 'forces' seems adequate here, given the comparison made by Walras between this market equilibrium and the stable equilibrium of a suspended body due to the forces of gravity. See (ibid., 109–110).
22. The investigation of the dynamic characteristics of market equilibrium is often attributed to Alfred Marshall. Marshall himself claimed priority with regard to the theory of stable equilibrium in a letter to Walras. In this letter he maintained that he had read a short paper 'anticipating your doctrine of stable equilibrium' before the Cambridge Philosophical Society on October 20, 1873. But except for a few notes, there is no published record of this lecture and Marshall's first published elaboration of a theory of instability did not appear in print before 1879, whereas Walras's definitive version was published in 1874. See Jaffé in Walras (1954, 504, fn 5).
23. See Jevons to Walras, 12 May 1874 in Jaffé (1965 vol. I, 393–394) and Walras to Jevons on 23 May 1874 in ibid., 397–399.
24. D'Aulnis de Bourouill to Walras, 4 May 1874 in (ibid., 388).
25. L. von Bortkiewicz to Walras, 9 May 1888 in Jaffé (1965, vol. II, 248).

26. H. Amstein to Walras, 6 January 1877 in Jaffé (1965, vol. I, 516–517).
27. Walras (1954, 225) also suggested in equilibrium entrepreneurs make their living, not as entrepreneurs, but as land-owners, labourers or capitalists.
28. For unknown reasons, in the fourth edition of EPE Walras dropped the third conclusion that the whole amount of product is distributed among the productive services. See Schumpeter (1954, 1035).
29. Van Daal and Jolink (1993, 54) say that he considered it a kind of side issue not fitting within the framework of his models. If that is the case, then why did he call marginal productivity a 'cardinal theory in pure economics . . . for it shows the underlying motive of the demand for the services and the offer of products just as the theory of final utility shows the underlying motive of the demand for products and offer of services by landowners, workers and capitalists' (Walras 1954, 385)? This statement suggests that he placed marginal productivity and marginal utility on an equal footing. An alternative explanation may therefore be that he was not able to handle the analytical complications of marginal productivity theory in the context of his general equilibrium analysis.
30. But their related conclusions that the EPE is an unfinished research project is clearly wrong. Ingrao and Israel argue that 'none of the analytical theses the theory undertook to demonstrate were in fact clearly demonstrated in the *Eléments*' (ibid., 111). This conclusion is off the mark because Walras never intended to develop mathematical proofs of the existence, uniqueness and stability of general equilibrium in the first place. They interpret his work through the lense of modern economic theory and in the process give a false picture of his scientific intentions.
31. Jaffé (1980[1983], 348) claims that Walras had no liking for realism as such. 'In fact, he vehemently denounced it in all its manifestations: in art and in literature as well in philosophy, science and economics.'
32. Some of Walras's followers used to same argument to defend the abstract character of general equilibrium theory. Speaking about 'its hopeless discrepancy from any process of real life', Schumpeter (1954, 1015) invites the reader to consider 'if he ever saw elastic strings that do not increase in length when pulled, or frictionless movements, or any other of the constructs commonly used in theoretical physics; and whether, on the strength of this, he believes theoretical physics to be useless'.
33. Another argument that supports the conclusion of a continuous development is the fact that it took Walras many years to develop the appropriate mathematics in some cases. The examples that spring to mind are his use of differential calculus to derive the equimarginal principle in utility theory as a first order condition and marginal productivity theory. Both were introduced in the fourth edition.
34. The fact that it takes a system of perfect competition to produce this outcome motivates the claim of Koppl that Walras tried to synthesize liberalism and socialism. The welfare optimum produced in a state of general economic equilibrium is a relative one in the sense that Walras did not use a social utility function. He reasoned in terms of individual utility functions and anticipated Pareto's optimality condition in order to deduce consequences for the aggregate welfare level. See Jaffé (1977, 332 and 334).

35. Walras also realized that market forces produce only half of the ideal, namely commutative justice. In order to achieve distributive justice, deliberate institutional reform in the distribution of property was needed. Walras's lifelong campaign to promote the nationalization of land by the state falls into this category.

36. See Walras (1954, 147 and 179). Economic changes could also be determined by other types of research. 'For example, if we suppose a rise in price to coincide with the discovery of a remarkably new property in commodity B or with a catastrophe destroying part of the supply of this commodity, we could not possibly avoid associating one or the other of these events with the rise in price. Such inescapable inferences are not beyond the bounds of possibility. With their aid the primary causes and conditions of variations in prices are often determined.'

10. The Subjectivist Challenge of the Austrian School

INTRODUCTION

The Austrian school of economics is generally considered one of the three founding currents of the marginalistic revolution of the 1870s. However, with Streissler (1972) we may doubt whether the Austrian school was particularly 'marginalist' at all, despite the fact that it was Wieser who coined the term 'Grenznutzen', marginal utility. The last chapter showed that marginalism was a calculating technique borrowed from mathematics and applicable in various sciences. Austrian theory concentrated on the 'Nutzen', not on the 'Grenze'. Its real essence was the subjectivist approach to economics, the doctrine that states that the subjective perception of wants and the capacity of commodities to satisfy those wants is a determining factor of economic value (O'Driscoll and Rizzo 1996). Austrian economists believe that the introduction of subjectivism was a more radical part of the marginalistic revolution than the application of marginal calculation. As far as they are concerned, the proper name of the revolution that occurred in the 1870s should be the subjectivist revolution.

The subjectivist approach has had profound influences on the debates within the Austrian school about the meaning of economic equilibrium. First and foremost, it led the Austrians to reject the notion of equilibrium as a static proposition which states that all economic activity will cease when every individual feels himself fully content with his current and prospective options for production and consumption. In their vision, a state of this kind requires a degree of knowledge and foresight that is inconceivable to anyone who believes that people partake in the economic process on the basis of their subjective knowledge. Subjectivism raised the issue of coordination between individuals in a decentralized economy.

The Austrian answer to this coordination problem places the notion of disequilibrium at the heart of economic theory. The Austrians consider the market a crucial institution for the coordination of economic activities. The pressure of competition forces people to disclose information about their preferences and resources. Their offers and demands provide a hunting ground for entrepreneurs who respond to profit differentials and in the process close the gap between supply and demand. However, the essence of the Austrian tradition is the belief that they will never succeed in this endeavour. The market process may nudge production and exchange in the direction of full coordination but it will never actually reach this state. For the Austrians, the economy is an open-ended world of radical uncertainty. Knowledge is never a given factor and by just acting and seeking an opportunity for profit entrepreneurs probably upset the equilibrium which their mediating activities aim to establish.

The degree to which markets can be assumed to be equilibrating is one of the most contentious issues in modern Austrian theory. Four main positions can be discerned in this debate:

- Market equilibration is a real economic force and must be treated as an empirical trend. In the words of Rothbard (1970, 236) 'equilibrium is an ever-present force, since it is the goal toward the actual system is always moving . . . [the] concept, then, is of legitimate and realistic importance'.
- Market equilibration will be counteracted by disequilibrium forces. Hence the market process is a development without direction. The world displays so much volatility as to push any equilibrating tendency beyond the bounds of possibility. In the words of Lachmann (1976a, 331–332), 'in a kaleidic society, the equilibrating forces, operating slowly . . . are always overtaken by unexpected change, before they have done their work . . . What emerges is an image of the market as a particular kind of process, a continuous process without beginning or end'.
- Market equilibration is a fiction but a useful one. It is a benchmark for the study of dynamic forces. Mises (1949) described a state of static general equilibrium in terms of an 'evenly rotating economy'. This mechanistic metaphor represents an economy that is fundamentally unrealistic but that can be used as an imaginary construction to isolate and study forces that cause change in the actual world.
- Even as a metaphor, the word equilibrium is misleading because it has a mechanistic connotation. Boettke, Horwitz and Prychitko (1994) argue that a mechanistic metaphor insufficiently expresses the nature of the market economy as a process of incessant change. The use of this metaphor may lead one to commit the error of neoclassical mainstream economics, which is to conflate the metaphor and the field of study: in neoclassical economics economic theory and equilibrium have become synonymous. They therefore propose to use an organic metaphor instead and to see the market economy as an 'evolutionary ordering

> process'. This is 'a scientific alternative that works without reference to any equilibrium construct. An evolutionary process is open-ended, in that the process does not tend toward any end-state'.

This chapter claims that these four themes have a long history in the tradition of the Austrian school. In fact, they can be traced back to the work of the founding fathers of the school: Carl Menger (1841–1921), Eugen von Böhm-Bawerk (1851–1914) and Friedrich von Wieser (1851–1926). They launched the Austrian attack on the classical theory of surplus value on the basis of the subjective theory of value and marginal utility. But their contributions to the development of this theory did not endorse a common understanding of the meaning of economic equilibrium. The classical authors had stressed the capacity of market forces to bring about a supply and demand equilibrium, ultimately leading to a long-term equilibrium described as the 'stationary state'. This chapter intends to show that:

- Menger denied the validity of the equilibrium concept as an end-state but also refused to speak of a market process towards such a state. If there is a meaningful notion of equilibrium in his work, it is that of a secular trend that is best characterized as an evolutionary process taking place in historical time.
- Böhm-Bawerk stressed the indeterminacy of market exchange as a negotiating procedure. Nonetheless, he believed that in the real world the pull towards equilibrium was the dominant force behind the market process.
- Wieser had an ambiguous attitude towards the concept of economic equilibrium. On the one hand, he aimed to give realistic explanations of the market mechanism and its equilibrium tendency (in his view, perfect competition and static equilibrium were idealizations). On the other hand, he exaggerated the social costs of disequilibrium adjustments because he feared that such changes could lead to a collapse of the market system as a mechanism for the coordination of activities. This fear led him to advocate certain moral rules of conduct on the grounds that they would strengthen the stability of competitive equilibrium. For Wieser, equilibrium united the best of both worlds, economically and morally.

In addition, it will be shown that the issue of coordination is a unifying theme of the theories of equilibrium that occupied the first Austrians. In modern theory, Hayek is often credited as being the first to have defined equilibrium as a coordination process (O'Driscoll 1977a and Birner and Van Zijp 1994). This chapter claims that Hayek's contributions in this regard would have been unthinkable without the path-breaking work of his forerunners.[1] Menger was the real innovator, the one who introduced the crucial role of knowledge, plan making and foresight in the economic process. Wieser proved the able student who focussed attention more strongly on the relationship between knowledge and the production and distribution of commodities in the economic system. Finally, Böhm-Bawerk added the finishing touch by showing that one was addressing a dynamic problem. He understood that economic equilibrium is fundamentally an intertemporal concept involving the coordination of plans and expectations over time and so paved the way for Hayek's explicit recognition of economics as a problem of coordination in the 1920s and 1930s.

These claims will be explained in the following sections, but before we proceed to that task a few remarks are in order about the key characteristics of the Austrian school, the common ground from which Menger, Böhm-Bawerk and Wieser developed their theories of value, price and economic equilibrium. This chapter is therefore organized as follows. The first section introduces the Austrian vision of economics as a science of human action and its methodological aspects. I then discuss the key concepts of Menger's theory of value and marginal utility. The subsequent sections investigate the different conceptions of economic equilibrium in the work of Menger, Böhm-Bawerk and Wieser. I conclude with a critical discussion of these ideas in the context of the subsequent development of the Austrian School.

HUMAN ACTION AND THE METHODOLOGY OF THE AUSTRIAN SCHOOL

Why Equilibrium is Not an End State

There is a close relationship between the Austrian conception of economic equilibrium and the the key methodological aspect of this school. This is the notion that economics is a science of human action.

Mises (1949, 11) defined human action as 'conscious or purposeful behaviour'. He rejected the notion that economic individuals are 'automatons' who passively react to given means and given ends. Take the example of a rational agent who maximizes utility subject to constraints. The outcome of this maximization process is completely determinate given that one knows the objective function and the constraining conditions. The Austrians do not consider this type of choice-making meaningful, purposeful behaviour because it lacks a distinctive human element.[2] Anyone facing the same objective function and constraints would make the same decision, a rare condition for people of flesh and blood. The notion of human action gives a much richer portrait of human existence. It assumes that people select their own ends and choose means to attain those ends. For an individual to act is a personal affair and touches the heart of being human. In the words of Mises: 'Action is the essence of his nature and existence, his means of preserving his life and raising himself above the level of animals and plants' (ibid., 18). What makes action human is the fact that it is goal-oriented or purposeful behaviour. People are conscious beings and they use their brain to imagine a future in which life is better. Their actions are directed at making that dream become reality and although they know that disappointments are a fact of life, they will not stop trying. Man 'is not only *homo sapiens*, but no less *homo agens*' (ibid., 14) which is governed by the lifelong quest to improve his living conditions, whatever disappointments and setbacks he may find on his path.

One of the key tenets of the Austrian tradition is that human action implies a rejection of the notion of economic equilibrium as an end-state. When equilibrium means that every participant in a market realizes his plans, or in neoclassical terminology 'maximizes utility', no one has an incentive to change his or her behaviour. This is the end of economic activity and the negation of human action. 'A man perfectly content with the state of affairs would have no incentive to change things. He would have neither wishes nor desires; he would be perfectly happy. He would not act; he would simple live free from care' (Mises 1949, 13).

The concept of human action is nowadays associated with the name of Mises, but the root of this idea lies in the work of Carl Menger. Kirzner (1994a, viii–ix) speaks in this regard of Menger's 'original vision' which is that 'all economic phenomena and all human history are to be understood as the outcomes of human action, driven by dreams and expectations, the desires and hopes, of human beings living in an open-ended world of radical uncertainty'. Like Mises, Menger stressed that the economic activities of people have one overriding goal and that is to better their economic position. Menger (1871[1994], 96 and 128) called this goal 'economizing' which he defined as the whole of activities directed to the fullest possible satisfaction of people's needs. Furthermore, he believed that knowledge was a key element of the economic process. He argued that people need to have knowledge of their wants, of the commodities available to satisfy those wants and of the wants and resources of their competitors. Finally, they need to forecast their future wants and the ability of the current capital stock to supply the desired quantities of produce at the right time.[3] No wonder that Menger portrayed economizing individuals as always looking for knowledge.[4] But that did not mean that he considered them infallible. On the contrary, he stressed the subjective nature of economic knowledge and the capacity of humans to commit errors. Ingredients such as these give

Menger's interpretation of economic behaviour the undeniable flavour of human action.

From the outset Menger made it clear in his theory of price that he rejected the notion of equilibrium as a state, because it could not be reconciled with human action. He saw economics as a study of forces with a capacity of achieving something, of actually causing change. He therefore compared prices to the waves that appear on a water surface when the locks between two bodies of water at different heights are opened (Menger 1871[1994], 192). Such waves are symptoms of the operation of the forces we call gravity and friction. Similarly, prices are symptoms of the cause which ripples the water in the economic arena. In that sense, they resemble the waves on a water surface as a disequilibrium phenomenon, but the force that drives them to the surface is psychological rather than physical. It is the ultimate and general cause of all economic activity, 'the endeavour of men to satisfy their needs as completely as possible, to better their economic positions' (ibid.).

In Menger's view, the main task of economic science is to explain the causal chain of events running from the satisfaction of needs to the formation of prices. He rejected the notion of equilibrium as an end-state, because it implied the exact opposite of this task. Instead of showing prices as waves, the equilibrium metaphor depicts prices as a symbol of rest, for example as the surface of a tranquil lake. According to Menger, this was an image that had caused 'incalculable damage to our science' because it led economists to investigate a problem that in reality did not exist. Prices appear when people have an incentive to act, for example when they perceive opportunities for profit or believe that an exchange of commodities will better satisfy their wants. Menger's price theory aimed to investigate the formation of prices in terms of such causes. But when we assume that people are already fully content with their current situation, there is nothing to investigate. Such individuals have no incentive to offer something for sale and quote a specific price. According to Menger, the assumption of equilibrium involved the negation of the problem one aims to explain, namely human action and its economic consequences.

Causal–Genetic Explanation and the Role of Mathematics

From this perspective, the aim to investigate economic phenomena in terms of causes played an important role in the Austrian attitude towards equilibrium theory. This observation warrants a closer look. What is the Austrian interpretation of causes and what is its relationship with the equilibrium concept?

The focus on the role of causes becomes manifest from the preface of Menger's *Principles*. There he stated that he devoted 'special attention to the investigation of the causal connection between economic phenomena'. The lynchpin of this investigation was the relationship between human needs and the capacity of goods to satisfy those needs. This causal connection provides the clue to Mengers's subjective definition of an economic good and all the inferences from that, such as the theory of value, the concept of capital and the formation of prices.

For Menger, the concept of a cause referred to the tension between ends and means. Means were assumed to have a causal connection with a specific end, if they could further its goal. In addition, he believed that the operation of causes pointed to the passage of time. The actions to be explained in the means-ends framework took place in a sequence of steps, each involving a specific period of time. In this manner, he stressed the temporal nature of causes.

These two characteristics have led the Austrians to define Menger's mode of explanation as 'causal-genetic' (Cowan and Rizzo 1996). In 1932 Hans Mayer distinguished this approach from what he called the 'functional' mode of explanation of mathematical equilibrium theories (Mayer 1932, 148). In contrast to the subjectivist approach, mathematical general equilibrium theory cannot explain how a sequence of actions results in price formation, because it describes economic relationships in a system of simultaneous equations. This observation led Mayer to argue that this type of theory is unable to penetrate into the nature of economic decisions and henceforth cannot give a meaningful explanation of the problem of price determination.

Menger had used this same argument in a letter to Walras, which discussed their respective methods of inquiry.[5] In his eyes, mathematics could only be used to describe economic relationships already found by other methods of inquiry. Confined to this role, it could never penetrate into the real essence ('Das Wesen') of economic phenomena. The reason why Menger considered mathematics impotent in this regard is that it could not explain the motives that ultimately determine economic behaviour and therefore the exchange value of commodities. In a mathematical formulation, prices are ratios of quantities exchanged that do not provide insight into human needs and people's subjective estimation of the degree to which different commodities are able to satisfy those needs.

In spite of the vigour of the Methodenstreit, Menger's doubts about the use of mathematics were not shared by all Austrians alike. Böhm-Bawerk even stressed the advantage of the mathematical method in economics. According to him, one of these benefits was the precision with which one could apply the fundamental laws of price determination. For example, a mathematical expression allowed one to pinpoint an equilibrium of prices as the intersection between the continuous curves of supply and demand. He called this approach an 'immaculate procedure' and only retained a verbal explanation of his price theory for didactic reasons (Böhm-Bawerk 1921a, 289).

Likewise, Wieser underlined the usefulness of the mathematical method in economics. He said that in the case of the laws of value 'mathematics has a great task to fulfil' (Wieser 1893, xxxiii). But there were also several aspects of the problem of value that required a different approach. In this regard, he mentioned the need to clarify the definition of value, the study of the service of value in economic life and the connection of value with many other economic phenomena. These were questions for a 'philosophy of value which needs words, not numbers' (ibid.).

Wieser's doubts concerning the role of mathematics were better elucidated in his later book, *Social Economics*. There he stressed that mathematics had a limited domain of application in economics. It was only suited to study theory under the most abstract and idealizing assumptions (Wieser 1927[1957], 13). To him this was the theory of value and price in a static economy. But as one proceeded from the static to the dynamic domain and introduced notions of change (progress, development) the consequence would be that the mathematical approach had to be abandoned. In cases of increasing complexity, the explanatory power of mathematical theory would be lacking. Why this is the case is not completely clear. Wieser just observed that 'none of the great truths of economic theory … has been justified by mathematical means' (ibid.). Like Menger, he saw mathematics as a means to attach a numerical expression to already known magnitudes and relationships. This was an exercise that could have merit for its own sake. But the true nature of economic knowledge consisted of something else. One needed to know why the method of economic computation and the use of numerical money values was so widespread in real economic life. In the final analysis, Wieser aimed to understand the meaning of quantitative economic relations such as money prices and interest rather than describe them in a mathematical theory.

Empiricism and the Method of Decreasing Abstraction

By now it is clear that from its start the Austrian school rejected the notion of economic equilibrium as a point variable. But that does not mean that other conceptions of equilibrium played no role in the development of the school. The introduction to this chapter mentioned alternatives such as 'equilibration', 'market process' and 'evolution'. What can we say about the methodological role of these concepts?

All three founding fathers of the Austrian school stressed the fact that they were examining empirical reality. Menger (1883, 54) referred to his method as the 'realistic-empirical orientation of theoretical research'. The empirical part of his method consisted in the fact that theoretical concepts were derived from observed events and entities. Such phenomena were called 'empirical forms'. Menger criticized the German historical school for their attempt to derive universal laws from nothing but empirical forms. An attempt of this kind could only be successful if causes and effects followed a consistent and clearly observable pattern in time. But this condition did not correspond to the behaviour of forces in reality. As a result, he classified the scientific aim of the historical school as 'an unattainable goal of theoretical research' (ibid., 57).

The solution to the problem of complex forces was to abstract from certain aspects of reality in an attempt to isolate the main forces at play. In the opinion of Menger, abstraction was unavoidable in any kind of empirical research. In his *Principles of Economics* (1871) he claimed that he was following the scientific method that had proved so successful in the natural sciences (Menger 1871[1994], 47). This method aimed to explain causes and effects in universal statements by means of decreasing abstraction. The starting point of theoretical research was the construction of an idealized or simplified representation of observed events to study the working of isolated forces. This theory could in a subsequent step of the analysis be brought into closer conformity with reality by adding certain features and increasing the complexity of the case under scrutiny. This working method is clearly discernible in Menger's theory of prices which starts with the case of isolated exchange for a single monopolized good and proceeds to analyze cases with competing buyers of several units of this good.

Böhm-Bawerk and Wieser consistently copied this methodology. Böhm-Bawerk (1921a, 259–260) illustrated the complexity of economic forces and the need for abstraction by means of a metaphor. He said that one should study the theory of price formation by first addressing a simplified version of the problem at hand, just as one explained the erratic behaviour of the oceans' surf by studying the more tranquil behaviour of waves in ponds and rivers. For him, the appeal of the law of supply and demand was that it allowed us to construct this abstract image of economic exchange. As such, it had scientific value even when the behaviour of real markets seemed in violation of the law due to the operation of cartels, labour unions and other interfering causes.

Böhm-Bawerk proposed to proceed with the process of abstraction in the theory of prices in two parts (ibid., 264). The first part would address the basic law underlying the formation of prices. He called this law 'basic' because it formalized pricing behaviour in the case of a single economic motive, the desire to improve one's economic position through economic exchange. The second part would amend the basic law by considering other motives for economic exchange[6] and extend the analysis to different and more complex market conditions such as monopolies, cartels, boycotts, taxes, labour unions et cetera.

For two reasons, Böhm-Bawerk only dealt with the first part. In the first place, he found it important to establish a firm basis for theory before one proceeded to the laborious task of ferreting out the complexities of price formation on real markets (ibid., 265). Given the extent of this task, he considered it impossible to engage in a study of the second part as well.

Secondly, Böhm-Bawerk believed that the theoretical part was much more important than the extensions that would form the second part. The point was that he considered the economic motive behind his basic law the central force of most economic activities. He compared people's egoistic desire for economic gain to the force of gravity and averred that the presence of other economic motives would not significantly alter the outcome of the process of price formation as explained by this basic law. In his words (ibid., 266):

> wenn auch im tatsächlichen Leben das genannte Grundmotiv von hunderten von anderweitigen Motiven . . . durchkreuzt wird, so entfernt sich die tatsächliche Gestaltung des Preise doch gar nicht so sehr weit von derjenigen Richtung, der sie die ausschliessliche Wirkung des Eigennutzes allein zudrängen würde.

It will be shown that Böhm-Bawerk did not proceed on the path of decreasing abstraction beyond the point of the law of supply and demand in a simplified representation. For him, what started out as an ideal model to a large extent became a true representation of reality.

The same cannot be said of Wieser. Like his fellow Austrians, Wieser praised the empirical nature of the 'new' Austrian theory of value and price. According to him, 'the method of economic theory is empirical. It is supported by observation and has but one aim which is to describe actuality' (Wieser 1927[1957], 5). He understood that one cannot describe reality 'in every minute detail' which means that isolation and idealization are required. In line with this approach, Wieser framed his economic theories in terms of a model state, comprising of model markets and a model man. He stressed that in subsequent steps of the analysis, idealizing assumptions should be relaxed in order to better approach reality: 'Step by step by a system of decreasing abstraction, he [the economic theorist, BT] must render his assumptions more concrete and more multiform' (ibid., 6).

Of the first Austrians, Wieser best practiced what he preached. His *Social Economics* (1927) comprises four parts which form the different stages of decreasing abstraction.[7] The first part starts with the most idealized assumption and is called the 'simple economy'. This theory assumes that the economy consists of a single person. This person is an 'ideal economic subject' because he is 'in full possession of his powers' and liable neither to 'error, passion or weakness'. Wieser used this fiction to explain the doctrine of marginal utility, but also assumed that it represented an entire nation. This had the benefit that the operation of the national economy could be studied without the complexities of opposed interests involving what Wieser called the 'justice of relationships'.

The second part deals with the 'social economy' and explains the theory of exchange. This model consists of numerous subjects who meet in the course of exchange as they seek their own economic advantage. This process presupposes private property and takes place under the assumption that there is no interference on the part of the state. This stage of the analysis also formed the main focus of the classical school. But in the eyes of Wieser the classicists confined themselves to the main cases of well regulated, balanced competition while he went a step further. He aimed to erect a theory that could deal with monopoly and perfect competition alike as typical features of actual markets.[8,9]

Wieser therefore avoided the error of Böhm-Bawerk, the hasty conclusion that an idealization represents reality. His work also demonstrates the effects of another aspect of Austrian methodology, which is the use of introspection. This was a factor used by the Austrians as a scientific litmus test. It decided questions such as, how do we choose between rival theories? Or: why is a liberal economic order superior to central planning and other socialist alternatives?

The Austrians did not decide such questions on the basis of some empirical criterion like the predictive power of a theory. They claimed that the economic theorist had access to a unique source of cognition, the human mind. For this reason, Wieser designated economics as a 'psychological' science because it takes its point of departure 'from within, from the mind of the economic man' (Wieser 1927[1957], 3). For him, the problem of economic theory was 'to exhaust scientifically the content of everyday experience and to interpret it'. He saw it as a great advantage that every individual has an intimate knowledge of the information and deliberations that decide his or her economic actions. This was a common experience that the scientist could use to develop a theoretical explanation of these activities. In fact, it offered him 'a fountain-head so inexhaustible in its riches, so dependable in its purity' that one could impossibly ignore this source of knowledge (ibid., 4).

To use our mind as a source of inspiration is one thing, but the Austrians also used it as a tool of confirmation for their theories. In their view, the theory of a liberal economic order was superior because one could not doubt its validity, it was self-evident. For Menger, this type of argument was a manner to evade the problem of induction (see Milford 1990, 231 and Alter 1990, 105). He defined economics as an exact science. A science of this kind rested upon theories that only contained universal statements. He justified this approach by saying that some events are verified beyond doubt because 'our laws of thinking' and our experience leave no room for an exception. 'A critical mind' would find it simply inconceivable that the event in question was not true (Milford 1990, 234).[10]

The use of introspection and self-evident facts gives the Austrian theories of economic equilibrium a specific meaning. They are not only idealizations or empirical statements that are true by approximation. In some cases they are also items of belief. Why do the forces of competition move prices closer to equilibrium? That is a question one is almost not allowed to ask. Market equilibration is a result of the law of supply and demand, a law that in the words of Böhm-Bawerk (1921a, 290) is so self-evident ('von fragloser Wahrheit') that one need not question its validity (see also Dow 1996, 116).

SUBJECTIVE VALUE AND UTILITY

The first generation of the Austrian school intended to base the explanation of price formation on a new foundation, one that promised a unified theory of price. This theory saw utility rather than costs as the determining factor in price formation. For the Austrians the explanation of price formation was not a matter of demand theory versus supply theory. Rather, they rejected the claim of classical political economy that costs of production form an objective cause of prices. They stressed the perceived satisfaction of individuals as a subjective cause of value and argued that subjective value determined demand as well as supply.

Today the word 'value' is a suspicious term due its notorious ambiguity. Modern microeconomic theories take price theory as their starting point, given that prices can be objectivised as the ratio of quantities exchanged. Value in this conception is just another word for price and refers to the value in exchange.[11]

Menger, Böhm-Bawerk and Wieser lived in a different world. For them value was the all-important concept because of its meaning to economizing individuals. Value gave expression to their perception of the tension between means and ends and so guided their economic behaviour. Prices were seen as the end result of the process of exchange between such individuals and therefore considered of secondary importance.

The starting point of the Austrian theories of value was Menger's definition of an 'economic good' and the related notion of 'economizing'. He defined a good in terms of a number of characteristics. The first requirement was the existence of a causal connection between the properties of the good in question and the satisfaction of a human need. Secondly, the people expressing this need needed to have knowledge of the causal connection. The third condition was that they have the power to direct the good to the satisfaction of the need (Menger 1871[1994], 52).

The causal connection between commodities and needs is the defining characteristic of a 'good' but Menger also recognized that there are causal connections between goods. This fact led him to distinguish different orders of goods. Goods of the first order are those commodities and services that are able to directly satisfy a human need. Goods of a higher order lack this capacity. They are necessary to produce a good of the first order and therefore only indirectly satisfy a human need. The distance towards this moment of satisfaction determines their place in the rank order of goods. Goods of the second order produce goods of the first order; goods of the third order produce goods of the second order, etcetera.

A further division is that between goods that are scarce and those that are not. Scarcity is a characteristic of what Menger defined as economic goods (ibid., 96). Non-economic goods lack this characteristic. The distinction between economic and non-economic goods is important because scarcity induces people to economizing behaviour. This is the desire to 'obtain the greatest possible result with a given quantity of the good or a given result with the smallest possible quantity'. Only in this way does one direct the given quantities of consumers' and production goods to the satisfaction of needs in 'the most appropriate manner' (ibid., 95–96; see also 128).

It appears that, to Menger, value was more important than utility. In his scheme all commodities have utility, but not all goods have value. The missing link is the element of scarcity. According to Menger, any good that is capable of satisfying a specific need has utility, which basically applies to all commodities.[12] However, one cannot say that all goods are scarce. Non-economic goods lack this characteristic and therefore do not command value. From this perspective utility is a more common and hence less important aspect of commodities than value.

As a consequence, Menger never used the term marginal utility. He reasoned in terms of the value that a unit of a commodity represents to an individual. To him value was a purely subjective magnitude. He explained that 'value is nothing inherent in goods, no property of them, nor an independent thing existing by itself. It is a judgment economizing men make about the importance of the goods at their disposal for the maintenance of their lives and well-being' (ibid., 120–121).

Menger's marginal principle is then stated as follows: He argued that the value to a person of a given quantity of a good is equal to the 'satisfaction of least importance', assuming that this quantity is partitioned in equal shares (ibid., 132). This principle is supported by means of a diagram which shows that one needs to distinguish between the satisfaction of needs of *different* kinds and the more or less satisfaction of one and the *same* need. With regard to the same need, satiation causes a decline of the degree of satisfaction with the consumption of subsequent units of the good. Menger thus elaborated on Gossen's first law.[13] In his diagram he assumed that the degree of satisfaction declines in steps of one on a scale that begins with 10 and ends with 0.[14] As a thought experiment, Menger added a scale showing the degree of satisfaction per unit of different commodities. Thus the satisfaction of the first unit of commodity I is 10, while the first unit of commodity II gives 9 units of satisfaction, etcetera. The result is a diagram which is shown in Table 10.1.

Menger used this diagram to demonstrate that consumers' choice is guided by the equimarginal principle. He stated that people consume a specific good up to the point where the satisfaction of the last unit consumed matches that of other commodities and referred to this margin as an 'equilibrium' of different satisfactions (ibid., 127).[15]

Table 10.1 Degrees of satisfaction for different quantities and commodities

					Commodities					
	I	II	III	IV	V	VI	VII	VIII	IX	X
	10	9	8	7	6	5	4	3	2	1
	9	8	7	6	5	4	3	2	1	0
	8	7	6	5	4	3	2	1	0	
	7	6	5	4	3	2	1	0		
Quantity	6	5	4	3	2	1	0			
	5	4	3	2	1	0				
	4	3	2	1	0					
	3	2	1	0						
	2	1	0							
	1	0								
	0									

Böhm-Bawerk and Wieser closely followed Menger's system. They both adopted his definitions of economizing and economic goods and saw the relationship between scarcity and wants as the main ingredient of the theory of value (see Böhm-Bawerk 1921a, 167–169; Wieser 1893, 19–21 and Wieser 1927, 39–49). The difference between their theories and the work of Menger was one of semantics. Wieser had introduced the term 'Grenznutzen' into the Austrian literature and both men saw marginal utility as the 'Angelpunkt' of their theories of value.

Böhm-Bawerk (1921a, 181) copied Menger's diagram to explain that marginal utility determines value.[16] His *Habilitation* of 1881 had introduced expected utility as a new aspect of the Austrian theory of value (Streissler 1990b, 164), but on this plane his *Positive Theorie des Kapitales* offered little news. Here he went to great lengths to analyze the difference between use-value and marginal utility. He proposed to differentiate between objective value and subjective value, given that the economic meaning of a specific price could change according to circumstances. Further, subjective value should be subdivided into the categories of use-value and exchange-value. Böhm-Bawerk stressed that the actual use of a commodity and its exchange constitute two different economic activities with their own estimation of value. A divergence of these two values was therefore the rule rather than exception, but this fact did not pose a problem to economic theory. An economizing individual would treat the highest of these values as the 'true value' and hence as the measure of marginal utility (ibid., 205).

Further extensions included the value of complementary and production goods. Böhm-Bawerk explained that there is a similarity between these two cases, given that the marginal utility of both goods cannot be estimated directly (ibid., 223). A complementary good satisfies a specific need in conjunction with its complements. They have a joined marginal utility which makes it difficult to estimate the value of a complementary good in isolation. Likewise, a production good contributes to the satisfaction of a need in conjunction with other goods, only this relationship is sequential rather than simultaneously. Production goods produce goods of a lower order that are themselves production goods until at the end of the production chain a consumption good emerges that satisfies needs directly. The marginal product of a production good is therefore valued in terms of its contribution to the satisfaction of this need.

A final point that must be mentioned is Böhm-Bawerk's view on how people process their valuations in reality. He rejected the criticism that the calculation of marginal utility in concrete cases required 'Virtuosenkunst' because one had to assess needs and the available means of consumption for every purchase (ibid., 255). Critics had argued that this would prove a difficult task in the face of complexities such as complementary goods or a long production chain that obfuscates the causal connection between goods and the satisfaction of needs. According to Böhm-Bawerk, in reality the burden of calculating marginal utility was greatly reduced by the use of rules of thumb and other routines ('Gewohnheiten'). He stated that economizing individuals rely on past experiences to determine current choices and also follow on the examples set by others. Moreover, the division of tasks implied that the puzzle of marginal utility was broken up in many pieces of more manageable size. Entrepreneurs would specialize in the production of a specific production good rather than govern all the stages of the production process. As a result, their calculating task was limited to the maximization of revenues over costs. The optimal result for the entire production chain would be guaranteed by the fact that each stage of production was governed by a profit-seeking entrepreneur. Thus he assumed the coordination process to be solved automatically, 'as if led by an invisible hand', one is tempted to add.

As said, it was Wieser who introduced the term 'Grenznutzen' into Austrian theory. His other contributions include the development of a marginal productivity theory that was based on the notion of opportunity costs. Wieser also stressed the relationship between entrepreneurship and innovation, a theme later taken up by Schumpeter.

For this moment it suffices to note that Wieser placed the notions of utility and value in yet another perspective than Menger and Böhm-Bawerk. In the first place, he focused on the problem of 'natural value'. This is value as it would arise in a perfect rational society. For Wieser, this was the communist state because it lacked inequalities in the distribution of wealth and income. According to him, inequalities of this kind disturb the natural value that arises if goods are estimated simply according to their marginal utility.

Wieser used the notion of natural value as a benchmark for the economic analysis of different societal arrangements. It showed that the service of value in human societies is that it governs the allocation of resources and controls production. He saw this as a purely technical service that even in a communist state cannot be removed: it would leave the economy without the power of calculation and without control. The first task of his theory of natural value was to investigate this role. The second task was to study the effects of institutions that altered the course of natural value, such as the right of private property which introduces inequalities of wealth and income.

With regard to this second task, his theory of value became an instrument of welfare analysis. He believed that this analysis was 'neutral' towards the choice between alternative economic systems such as the liberal market order and a communist society.[17] However, a closer look reveals a bias that strongly favoured a liberal outlook on the economic organization of society.

This bias concerns the rationale of what Wieser called the 'upgrade' and 'downgrade' of value (ibid., 28). The upgrade and downgrade were the characteristics of a bell-shaped value curve. The value of a stock of goods would initially rise with the addition of subsequent units until it reached a maximum point after which it declined. Wieser presented a numerical example to explain the mechanism behind the rise and fall of (total) value that he saw as the root cause of the paradox of value. He defined the value of stock as the product of marginal utility and the number of units comprising this stock. This explains the upgrade of the value curve, as marginal utility is multiplied by an ever increasing number of units. However, given the law of decreasing marginal utility, total value is ultimately reduced to zero if marginal utility reaches this value. As a matter of logic, it follows that the value curve must have a maximum point. Wieser demonstrated that the downgrade emerges when the subtraction from total value (the units of stock are multiplied by a declining value of marginal utility with each addition and therefore 'lose' value) is greater than the utility of the last unit, which is, after all, the addition to the value of stock.

At this stage of the argument, Wieser made the surprising claim that, as a matter of fact, most commodities move on the ascending branch of their value curve: 'In most things we are so far from having a superfluity that almost every multiplication of goods shows a corresponding increase in the total value' (ibid., 31). This claim supports a liberal economic order because it implies that competition boosts economic welfare. In Wieser's scheme more exchange means higher total value as all goods are assumed to be on the upgrade of the value curve and a competitive economic order is more conducive to this goal than alternative arrangements. In the final analysis, Wieser's concept of natural value was not so neutral after all.

The introduction to this chapter underlined the distinguishing character of the Austrian school as one of the three founding currents of the marginal or marginalistic revolution. For the Austrians, the subjectivism of utility calculation by economizing individuals was the real innovation of this development, while Jevons and Walras focussed on the margin of utility as an opportunity to investigate prices as a mathematical theory. It is therefore not surprising that the equivalent of their equation of exchange is absent in the work of Menger and his followers. They focussed on the explanation of human action and aimed for a realistic explanation of price formation. This would be a theory that could deal with various motives for economic exchange and considered monopolistic market structures alongside perfect competition. The next sections aims to investigate how well they were able to meet this objective.

CARL MENGER: BARGAINING AND THE NATURE OF THE MARKET PROCESS

The conception of economic equilibrium that lies behind Menger's price theory still causes controversy. Some argue that he had no notion of economic equilibrium (for example Streissler 1972, Kirzner 1978 and Endres 1995), while others claim that he was addressing the problem of coordinative uncertainty in a decentralized economy. For instance, Moss (1978) attributes to him the notion of a market process that nudges prices in the direction of a supply and demand equilibrium as a response to the need for better coordinated prices. The question is, which is right? Can it be true that the founding father of the Austrian school ignored the dynamics of the market process, an aspect that nowadays is seen as a defining characteristic of this school?

The root of the controversy is the indeterminacy of prices as explained by Menger's price theory. This theory was based on the method of decreasing abstraction. It started by assuming a relatively simple case of barter exchange and gradually complicated the analysis by introducing more buyers and sellers into the analysis. The indeterminacy arises due to the fact that traders are assumed to buy and sell goods in discrete quantities. Their valuations are never exactly equal with the result that the rate of exchange hovers in a price range rather than settles at a specific level.

Menger's explanation of this price range proceeded in terms of what he called the 'price duel' (Menger 1871[1994], 195). This term symbolizes the rivalry between buyers and sellers that, according to him, was the driving force behind the exchange of commodities and the dynamics of price formation. However, a closer look reveals the limitations of his approach. The most striking aspect of Menger's price theory is the absence of a causal-dynamic explanation of prices, the sequential movements of prices in a temporal sense. The price duel explains the price range in terms of an external factor, namely the value judgements of the trading parties which are given and not endogenous to the exchange process. This robs Menger's theory of a truly dynamic factor and gives it the appearance of a static theory.

The key element of Menger's explanation of prices is the 'valuation of the buyer of the last unit', or 'marginal utility' as Wieser first called it. Menger explained the causal connection between value judgments and prices in several numerical examples. He first addressed the case of isolated exchange. This involved a price duel between A and B who aim to exchange grain for wine. A is assumed to possess 100 units of grain that to him has the same value as 40 units of wine. Menger argued that in order to conduct an exchange and buy a quantity of wine, A has to find someone to whom 40 units of wine has a smaller value than 100 units of grain. B is this person. He possesses 40 units of wine and is willing to trade this quantity for at least 80 units of grain. Menger concluded that as A and B start to negotiate about an exchange they must reach a price for 40 units of wine which lies between 80 and 100 units of grain (ibid., 195). Given that each of them will try to benefit from the exchange as best as he can, the exact exchange ratio will depend on their bargaining skills and their 'various individualities and upon their greater or smaller knowledge of business life'. These are contingent conditions which means that the ratio of exchange remains indeterminate (Endres 1995, 271).

However, the surprising fact is that Menger, while recognizing the limits of the price range, assumed away differences in bargaining skills and knowledge. He said that the negotiated price would converge upon the arithmetic average of the minimum and maximum price. As a result indeterminacy disappears through the back door (Menger 1871[1994], 196.):

> Under the assumption of economically equally capable individuals and equality of other circumstances, I venture to state, as a general rule, that the efforts of the two bargainers to obtain the maximum possible gain will be mutually paralyzing, and that the price will therefore be equally far from the two extremes between which it can be established.

In his numerical example this price would be 90 units of grain. Menger even maintained that the average price operates as a kind of 'natural middle position'. By this he meant that competition tends to even out differences between bargainers with the result that prices always move in the direction of this average level.

Competition Between Buyers

The analysis was subsequently extended to the level of market demand by considering the competition between buyers. Menger used the example of a horse market to demonstrate that marginal utility determines a unique market price in spite of the fact that each buyer has a different utility function for horses. Table 10.2 reproduces this example.

Table 10.2 Menger's horse market

	Horses							
Buyer	1	2	3	4	5	6	7	8
B1	80	70	60	50	40	30	20	10
B2	70	60	50	40	30	20	10	
B3	60	50	40	30	20	10		
B4	50	40	30	20	10			
B5	40	30	20	10				
B6	30	20	10					
B7	20	10						
B8	10							

This table shows that Menger assumed that all buyers experience decreasing marginal utility for subsequent horses. He used this example to demonstrate the steps by which marginal utility determines the market price. His explanation assumed a kind of auction: horses are subsequently sold to the highest bidder, which means that for each horse a price duel is fought. The first horse on the market will sell for a price that lies between 70 and 80 units of grain. The upper limit of this price range is determined by the fact that of all buyers buyer B1 is willing to pay the highest price for this horse. His maximum bid would be 80 units of grain. However, in order to procure the horse he has to outbid B2 who is willing to pay a maximum price of 70. As a result, B1 is in an exclusive position to bargain with the seller for any price between 70 and 80. The exact price depends on their relative bargaining positions and is therefore indeterminate, just as in the case of isolated exchange.

This bargaining process becomes more complicated as an increasing number of horses is offered for sale. For the second horse, the seller is able to bargain with two potential buyers: B1 and B2 who both value this horse at a maximum price of 70. The selling price will therefore be in the range of 60 and 70.[18] However, whatever the price, it must be a 'false' one in the sense that one of the bidders is excluded from the sale. This excess demand disappears when a third horse is offered for sale, but reappears for the fourth one when the sellers B1, B2 and B3 are all willing to pay a maximum price of 60.

Working through the subsequent price duels in this manner, a series of equilibrium price ranges can be constructed that suggests a declining demand schedule: the price of horses falls as the marginal utility of additional horses declines (Endres 1995, 277). However, the nature of this schedule is discrete due to the limited number of units (horses) sold and discontinuous. This latter characteristic reflects the indeterminacy of the price range.

Also, prices are not market clearing in a Walrasian sense. Depending on the number of units sold, a price emerges for which an excess demand exists. One may therefore conclude with Endres (1995, 275) that Menger's price theory 'does not predict a unique price ex ante. The essential unity of his theorizing on price formation is to be found in the focus on price distribution rather than in unique market clearing prices as point variables'.

Competition Between Sellers

So far the examples assumed the presence of a monopolistic seller. Menger did not relax this condition but approached the issue of sellers' competition in a more qualitative manner. He observed a historical trend from monopoly to competition in the development of human civilizations. According to him, monopoly preceded competition in this process, because anyone who sets up a new business temporarily enjoys a kind of monopoly. In the course of economic development the advantage of these first movers would disappear as high profits lured new competitors into the market. In this manner, he explained why monopoly was always 'the earlier and more primitive phenomenon' and competition the phenomenon coming later in time (Menger 1871[1994], 217).

It is essential to distinguish this analysis of sellers' competition from the notion of the market process, viewing equilibrium as a tendency. The classical interpretation of the market process is that competitive pressures in the form of entry and exit into the market erase abnormal profits and force market prices to comply with cost levels. This line of reasoning was anathema to Menger. He discussed sellers' competition as a secular trend that could be used to highlight the benefits of a competitive economic order. Endres (1995, 283) speaks of a 'a purely conjectural, developmental perspective . . . It is a long-term outlook that endogenizes a tendency of market conditions and institutions to change under a hypothetical regime of sellers' competition'.

The underlying aim of this analysis was to demonstrate the causal connection between the transition towards a more competitive economic system and the improvement of economic welfare. Menger argued that from a dynamic perspective competition prevents the abuse of market power that monopolists may enjoy. For two reasons this brings about an increase of consumer welfare. In the first place, the wants of consumers can be satisfied more fully due to a more differentiated composition of supply and, secondly, the prices of products can be expected to decline on a structural basis.

This conclusion shows that Menger approached the issue of competition from a different angle than the static theories of Jevons and Walras, discussed earlier. Their focus on the equation of exchange as the theoretical core of the theory of price was not shared by Menger, because such an approach defined away the problem one was trying to solve: the causal explanation of why people agree to conduct an exchange of goods and services. As a result, he rejected the static notion of economic equilibrium – the equality between quantities supplied and demanded – as a starting point for theoretical analysis.

But also as a dynamic conception there was no role for the conception of economic equilibrium in Menger's theory of prices. Menger addressed the relationship between competition and prices as a secular trend, but there is hardly any reference in his theory of price to the capacity of competitive markets to establish equilibrium between supply and demand. Surprisingly, Menger never stressed the capacity of the market process to safeguard the relative harmony of the exchange mechanism, a function that is usually associated with the tendency of prices to move towards a supply and demand equilibrium.

The Nature of the Market Process

This conclusion merits further investigation. In modern Austrian economics the notion of equilibrium as a tendency is considered in the perspective of the issue of coordination (O'Driscoll 1977a and Birner and van Zijp 1994). The starting point of Austrian theory is the observation that information is dispersed among the individuals partaking in a particular trade, because of the subjective nature of their perceptions of value. This raises the question of how suppliers and demanders are able to coordinate their activities. Hayek in his famous 1937 article was the first to realize that the price mechanism plays a crucial role in the solution of this problem. He saw prices as the monetary expression of people's subjective estimates of value. For him, the function of such statements was that they increase the stock of knowledge that market participants have of each others' plans. With competing bids, pricing differentials become visible which creates opportunities for arbitrage. In a competitive market suppliers and demanders will use this information to iron out such differences and move their bids into closer conformity. In this manner, the notion of equilibrium as a tendency and the issue of coordination are closely related.

It is clear that Menger contributed in several ways to the recognition of the Austrians that coordination is a central issue in economics. He strongly emphasized the relationship between knowledge and the pricing process and placed the price duel – the nucleus of the coordination issue – at the heart of his economic analysis. It is therefore not surprising that Menger is regarded as the true originator of what Moss (1978) calls the analysis of 'coordinative uncertainty'.

However, Moss also connects Menger's treatment of this problem with the conception of equilibrium as a tendency. He compares his notion of economic prices with what Marshall defined as 'true equilibrium prices', the price that is uniquely determined by the preferences of economic agents and is independent of their relative bargaining strengths. According to Moss, Menger believed that prices would tend towards an equilibrium level defined in this way, assuming that the number of buyers and sellers was very large. He therefore concludes that Menger's theory of price formation 'was similar in definition to Marshall's but generated by a market process more in the spirit of Edgeworth's notion of recontracting rather than the familiar auctioning or tatonnement process developed by Walras and his successors' (Moss 1978, 28).

The question is what the term market process means in this regard. Kirzner (1978) stresses that Menger's theory of price leaves no scope for a discussion of what the Austrians today consider the dynamic aspects of the market process. The puzzling fact is that Menger's explanation of prices is essentially static. The dynamic element of his theory is formed by the bargaining process, but this element is excluded from the analysis. Marginal utility only explains the outer limits of the arena for the price duel. This price range is wholly determined by an external factor, namely the value judgments of the trading partners, and therefore static. Menger assumed equal skills and information among the contestants with the result that the negotiated price would converge upon the arithmetic mean of the minimum and maximum price. Also he ignored the influence of error and learning that may cause individuals to revise plans and make a better choice in a next round of trading. As a result, bargaining has no effect on the minimum and maximum boundaries of the negotiated price which explains why there is no equilibrating tendency, for instance towards a market clearing price level or any other economic state that represents a situation in which the economic plans of the trading partners are better coordinated than before.

Therefore, the conclusion is that there appears to be a contradiction in Menger's *Principles*. In his theory of value he stressed the role of error and the continuous state of flux in which the economic system must always find itself. Yet in his theory of price he seemed to lapse into a fundamentally different world, one where the equilibrium price range is determined instantaneously and error plays no role. For that reason, Kirzner (1978, 38) concludes that interpretations, such as Moss (1978) who attributes to Menger a theory of price equilibration, are wrong. According to Kirzner, Menger's price theory does not belong to the domain of what the Austrians nowadays call market process theory. This theory uses the pull towards equilibrium as a benchmark for the analysis of the causes behind the dynamics of the market process. The main elements of this process – entrepreneurial activity and the notion of exchange as a time-consuming bargaining process – are absent in Menger's price theory. He can therefore not be considered a forerunner of this branch of the Austrian school. But Menger had solid reasons to develop a different mode of explanation and by doing so generated another fundamental insight, namely that the process of institutional change is of crucial importance to the functioning of the modern economy.

Evolution and Institutions

To understand why Menger never described the market process in terms of a tendency towards equilibrium, one needs to revoke the metaphor of the water locks in the opening sentences of Menger's chapter on prices. Here he explained that he found the image of economic forces in, or tending towards, equilibrium uninteresting and one may add unrealistic, because it leads to a dismissal of the core economic questions. But if that is the case, then why did he state his explanation of bilateral exchange in terms of a static condition?

The solution of this apparent contradiction is that it forms an abstract, and therefore ideal, representation of actual market conditions. First and foremost Menger abstracted from the element of time. His explanation of bilateral exchange is like a snapshot that freezes the flux of the actual market process. The benefit of this frozen image is that it illuminates the causal connection between marginal utility and economic prices. The static condition of an equilibrium price range explains why people with diverging subjective perceptions of value have an incentive to trade commodities and on what terms they will be able to agree on the terms of the exchange. In that sense the minimum and maximum values of the price duel can be compared to the different height of the water levels on the exact moment when the locks are opened. It is this act that unleashes the forces that ripple the water surface, just as exchange constitutes a wave of economic activity that upsets economic equilibrium.

Conclusion

The notion of a bargaining solution in terms of a frozen image of the market has some drawbacks. In the first place, it lacks the dimension of time. The negotiated price that ends the price duel signals equilibrium in the sense that both parties to the exchange rest content with this result. But this condition is only valid during the time frame of the snapshot. To paraphrase Adam Smith, the state of inertia lasts as long as the urge to 'truck, barter and trade', is not felt. One may assume that Menger believed that for economizing men in real life situations this would have been an exception, just as one always feels the impulse to breath in order to stay alive.[19] Secondly, from an aggregate point of view it seems impossible to define equilibrium as a point of rest. Menger's analysis of multilateral exchange showed that the negotiated price may cause excess demand to persist. Therefore, it does not necessarily reflect a supply and demand equilibrium and leaves some of the market participants discontented.

In these circumstances, the words of Streissler (1972, 438) come to mind that 'Menger . . . could not even conceive of equilibrium as anything precisely describable'. A general economic equilibrium in the market economy requires a group of people experiencing a state of rest at the same time. Without structural forces to bring about such a situation the chances of such a simultaneous equilibrium are extremely small, just as the surface of a lake is never really tranquil.

It appears that Menger did not believe that learning and entrepreneurship would endow the market process with this sense of order, because he did not explain the market process in these terms. However, he did locate an equilibration tendency elsewhere. His discussion of the institutional changes of markets in the course of economic progress shows that he envisioned a kind of social learning process. This process involved the standardization of goods, the creation of institutions for gathering information and the emergence of a class of middlemen. Such changes were the driving forces behind the transition of monopolistic markets into more competitive exchange processes. According to Menger, this boosted the growth of economic welfare in general but it would also bring about a more equitable distribution of wealth among the classes of society. This effect would occur because in a competitive environment there is less scope for suppliers to exploit consumers and reduce the consumer surplus in favour of their profits. The transition towards the competitive market economy forces prices to better comply to the law of one price. In that sense Menger did foresee an equilibrating tendency of the market economy. However, as Streissler (1972, 439fn) puts it, this would be an extremely slow process, possibly lasting a century. Compare this speed of adjustment to Walras who claimed that the adjustment (tatonnement) of the market towards equilibrium would be a matter of minutes.

EUGEN VON BÖHM-BAWERK: PRICE DYNAMICS AND INTERTEMPORAL EQUILIBRIUM

The main achievement of Böhm-Bawerk in the field of price theory was the extension of Menger's analysis of multilateral exchange in terms of a price duel. Menger discussed the effects of competition on the demand side but always assumed a situation of monopolistic supply. Böhm-Bawerk was able to relax this condition and explain price formation when there is competition on both the demand and the supply side of the market.

This result is praised by some for its theoretical superiority when compared to Menger. For example, Endres (1996) says that he much better perceived the significance of bargaining and strategic considerations to the process of price formation. As a result, his price theory must be counted as an early example of game theory. Moreover, according to Endres, Böhm-Bawerk explored the issue of price formation in a truly intertemporal framework. This led him to stress the tendency of prices towards supply and demand equilibrium as an outcome of the bargaining process. Endres even attributes to him a conception of intertemporal equilibrium that strongly resembles Hayek's ideas of the 1930s. According to this definition, equilibrium involves the coordination of plans for current and future activities. This section aims to critically discuss this interpretation of Böhm-Bawerk's price theory and its conception of economic equilibrium.

The Price Dynamics of Two-sided Competition

Böhm-Bawerk's price theory was probably just intended as a restatement of Menger's ideas and contributed little to this subject. He adopted the same assumptions about the indivisibility of the commodities traded and the role of information and bargaining skills. Like Menger he worked through the cases of isolated exchange and multilateral exchange to demonstrate the role of marginal utility in the price setting process and the scope for bargaining within the equilibrium price range. He even used the same example, namely that of the horse market.

Table 10.3 The horse market of Böhm-Bawerk

		Valuation of one horse			
	A1	300	100	B1	
Strong buyers	A2	280	110	B2	Weak sellers
	A3	260	150	B3	
	A4	240	170	B4	
	A5	220	200	B5	
	A6	210	215	B6	
	A7	200	250	B7	
Weak buyers	A8	180	260	B8	Strong sellers
	A9	170			
	A10	150			

However, Böhm-Bawerk was able to give a more consistent analysis of price setting in the horse market, because he was able to include competition on both sides of the market. His example involved a market with ten buyers and eight sellers which is summarized in Table 10.3. This table shows the different valuations that buyers and sellers have concerning the sale of a horse. Böhm-Bawerk assumed that the price mechanism in this case operates as what Endres (1996, 95) calls a two-sided auction, even though his market lacks a central figure that collects bids and quotes prices. Negotiations take place spontaneously in a process that Böhm-Bawerk (1921a, 274fn) described as 'sondieren'. Buyers first deliberately offer a low price to invite a counteroffer that gives them information about the eagerness of suppliers to sell. In the example of Table 10.3 this was a price of 130 which meant that all ten buyers would be willing to purchase a horse. However, at this price only two sellers would offer their horse, leaving an excess demand of eight buyers. According to Böhm-Bawerk, competition among the buyers would raise their asking price, thus excluding some of the buyers and attracting more sellers. Multiple rounds of bidding so push the price towards an equilibrium level, which in this case must be lie between 210 and 215 when five buyers and five sellers are willing to conclude a deal.

This example highlights that marginal utility from a buyers's perspective is not enough to determine the market price. Ultimately, the price is set by what Böhm-Bawerk called the 'Grenzpare', the marginal buyer and seller (ibid., 279). In his example, this pair is formed by buyer A5 who is willing to offer a maximum price of 220 for a horse and seller B5 who wants a minimum price of 200. Their negotiations establish that the price is pushed above 210 so that A6 is eliminated but remains below 215 in order to prevent that B6 will find it worthwhile to enter the duel and offer his horse for sale.

Knowledge and Bargaining

In these terms it is evident that information and learning play an important role in the price setting process. Böhm-Bawerk referred to this role in the following sense. In the first place, he stressed that custom and familiarity facilitate the negotiating process and greatly shorten the time necessary to establish a price (ibid., 274 fn). Buyers who are familiar with a particular trade follow a different strategy than newcomers. Their first offers will be less conservative because they are better able to estimate the final outcome of the bargaining process and therefore more quickly move their price offers in the direction of the equilibrium price range. Secondly, from Table 10.3 it is clear that knowledge of the preferences of one's competitors likewise helps to speed up to negotiating process. For Böhm-Bawerk knowledge of this kind had two dimensions, namely space and time, as trade could take place in different localities but also in different time frames (ibid., 276 fn2). He argued that the transparency of the negotiations determined the degree to which prices would converge with the equilibrium price range. The more people were able to (literally) oversee the bargaining process of their competitors, the smaller would be the chance that price differentials would persist and that real market prices would therefore diverge from the 'ideal price' of his abstract representation of exchange.

To what extent can this type of reasoning be called an early example of game theory? The focus on the role of bargaining and the dispersion of information may suggest that strategy is a key aspect of the price setting process. Endres (1996, 96) compares the zone of actual trading in Böhm-Bawerk's horse market to the core of a cooperative game because it takes repeated negotiations to establish the market price. Also, he argues that his analysis includes a form of strategy. This concerns the case where the five remaining sellers in the horse market form a coalition to force the market clearing price as close as possible to the maximum price of 215. Endres admits that Böhm-Bawerk failed to explore this strategic dimension systematically, but nonetheless concludes that 'he came to the brink of perceiving the significance of bargaining and strategic behaviour in price formation' so that his work 'must be counted as one early game-theoretic prototype'.

In my opinion even this cautious wording overstates the importance of game theory to Böhm-Bawerk's analysis of price formation. Like Menger, he left the process of bargaining unexplained and simply assumed that the negotiated price would be the arithmetic average of the minimum and maximum price (Böhm-Bawerk 1921a, 270). For both Menger and Böhm-Bawerk, the notion of a price duel was a metaphor to express their conviction that rivalry was the essence of the competitive process. The true meaning of price theory was not the analysis of strategic considerations in the price setting process, but the study of the subjective nature of all economic decisions. This notion is omnipresent in Böhm-Bawerk's price theory. After all, the key idea of this theory is that the market price is determined by the subjective estimations of value of the marginal pair (ibid., 279). He called the theory of subjective value the 'unentbehrliche Grundlage der Preistheorie' (ibid., 299). Reviewing the lessons of his price theory, he said that 'Von alle Ergebnissen, die wir in diesem Abschnitt gewonnen, ist weitaus das schwerwiegenste daß wir sämtliche bei der egoistischen Preisbildung wirksamen Einflüsse aufgelöst haben in subjektive Wertschätzungen und ihre vernunftgemäße Würdigung' (ibid., 285). The role of bargaining and strategy was in that regard nothing but a side issue.

The focus on game theory leads Endres to misinterpret Böhm-Bawerk in another sense as well. He says that Böhm-Bawerk deliberately ignored cases of perfect competition because he considered them unrealistic. 'To be sure, a Walrasian price-auction market where the number of competitors is sufficiently large, where traders are faced with parametric prices and where equilibrium price is determinate, all implied reasoning from a level of abstraction well beyond Böhm-Bawerk's purview' (Endres 1996, 96).

Nothing could be further from the truth. The degree of abstraction applied in his theory was a matter of convenience, not a matter of principle. Böhm-Bawerk demonstrated what would happen if one relaxes a number of conditions and assumes, for example, that the commodities traded are infinitely divisible or that the number of market participants is 800 or 1000 rather that eight or ten. Such changes would cause a reduction of the range in which the marginal pair must establish the market price. As a consequence, 'die Zone, in welche der beiderseitige Wettbewerb die Preisbildung drängt und innerhalb welcher der Markt sein momentanes Gleichgewicht finden konnte, verschmälert sich zu einem Punkt' (Böhm-Bawerk 1921a, 287). In this point, equilibrium is determinate as even the marginal pair of buyers and sellers lacks the market power to significantly affect the market price. In other words, Böhm-Bawerk recognized a continuum of market structures between the extreme cases of monopoly and perfect competition and discussed the implications of parametric prices in a determinate equilibrium point.

In line with this extension of his theory, he argued that one could just as well use a mathematical theory to explain the formation of prices or represent market equilibrium as the intersection of two continuous curves of supply and demand (ibid., 289). He even admitted that mathematics formed a sharper theoretical instrument (Edgeworth had corrected him on a number of occasions), but he preferred a verbal explanation for didactic reasons. His main point was that supply and demand were household names in economics and for that reason terms with a very vague meaning. Applied in a mechanical fashion, the law of supply and demand added no new insights to the corpus of economic knowledge. It simply stated that in equilibrium the quantities supplied and demanded would be equal which, according to Böhm-Bawerk, was a mere truism. Attempts to explain the underlying causes of this equilibrium missed the mark because they lacked the Austrian notion of subjective value. 'So schwebte und schwankte die alte Lehre von Angebot und Nachfrage gleichsam zwischen des Scylla einer inhaltsarmen, unbefriedigenden Vagheit und der Charybdis einer ebenfalls unbefriedigenden Inkorrektheit' (ibid., 291). The Austrian theory of subjective value and its verbal mode of reasoning was intended to avoid these pitfalls.

Intertemporal Equilibrium

In spite of his criticism, Böhm-Bawerk's horse market is a classic example of the law of supply and demand and its conception of equilibrium as a tendency: the forces of competition push the market price towards an equilibrium that is determined by the equality of supply and demand. However, as Endres rightfully stresses, this notion misleadingly suggests that his price dynamics was restricted to the explanation of short term economic changes because he assumed a given stock of horses. In fact, this was one of Marshall's main criticisms of Böhm-Bawerk. He accused him of giving one-sided consideration to the causes of temporary changes and short-term value fluctuations.[20]

Böhm-Bawerk went to great lengths to prove that Marshall's reading was wrong and that the essence of the Austrian analysis of price formation was the exact opposite of what he had claimed. In his own words, the Austrians aimed to explain the relative permanent establishment of a certain price 'bis in seine letzte Wurzel' (Böhm-Bawerk 1921b, 193). This required an intertemporal conception of economic equilibrium for which he used the metaphor of a walking man (ibid., 168):

> Gleichgewicht einer lebendige Wirtschaft ist nicht mit dem Gleichgewicht eines ruhig stehenden Menschen in Parallele zu stellen, sondern es ist zu vergleichen dem Gleichgewicht eines gehenden Menschen, der mit jedem Schritt eine bisherige Gleichgewichtslage verlässt und verliert, um sie mit dem nächsten Schritt wiederzugewinnen und abermals wiederzuverlieren.

The controversy with Marshall on this issue brought to the fore for the first time an essential difference between Austrian economics and its fellow neoclassical schools of thought. The Austrians see the issue of coordination in a decentralized economy as one of the core economic questions and approach this issue from an intertemporal perspective. This means that equilibrium involves more than a match between the supply and demand for current products. In its proper context, equilibrium is a condition of the coordination of plans that economizing individuals make, both current and forward looking. For a full coordination of plans, future prices must be in line with the expectations of future costs. The tendency of current prices towards cost is therefore part of the dynamic process of adjustment.

Hayek (1928) was the first to fully account for the intertemporal structure of the price mechanism in this sense. He referred to Böhm-Bawerk as someone whose work was replete with hints to the importance of the intertemporal price system, but according to Hayek he had little to offer in the way of positive conclusions for this problem. In particular, Hayek said that he lacked a definition of equilibrium that would allow us to assess the significance of the temporal pattern of prices for the undisturbed functioning of the economy.

For Hayek, equilibrium essentially involved a state of rest, which implied that no one would have an incentive to change his current behaviour and plans. This required, firstly, that each individual currently believed that he would be able to realize his expectations and, secondly, that those plans were mutually compatible (Hayek 1928, 75–76). Stated in these terms, his intertemporal conception of equilibrium included the notion that relative prices vary over time as the conditions of supply and demand are expected to change. He was adamant to demonstrate that 'even in a stationary economy, in which the same processes are repeated in the same order, the same goods will not necessarily realize the same prices at every point in time' (ibid., 72).

The elaboration of this point formed the main challenge of Hayek's business and monetary theory of the 1930s and was also the reason why his opponents failed to grasp the significance of this work (McCormick 1992). How can one assume that economic processes are changing and stationary at the same time? A claim of this kind is bound to cause confusion. Moreover, Hayek used the terminology and theoretical concepts of the Austrian school which in the 1930s were still largely unknown in the English speaking world and were therefore easily misunderstood. Famous in this regard is Keynes's scathing review of Hayek's *Prices and Production* (1931) and his exclamation that 'God knows what the Austrians mean by "period of production". Nothing in my opinion' (Keynes to Robertson, 20 February 1935, in Keynes 1973, 517).

Böhm-Bawerk (1921b, 179) was well aware that his controversy with Marshall stemmed from similar problems and he therefore wanted to state his argument as clearly as possible. He emphasized that he addressed the causal relationship between value and costs from a much broader perspective than that of short term adjustments towards equilibrium. He did not assume that supply is a given quantity, but argued that supply at a specific time is the result of some dynamic equilibrating process going on behind the scene (Endres 1996, 101). In this regard, Hayek's words of praise for Böhm-Bawerk appear slightly ungenerous, for like himself Böhm-Bawerk was aiming to explain the process of coordination in a framework of intertemporal equilibrium.

The key to this framework was the distinction between consumers' and producers' goods. As was explained above, producers' goods refer to the goods of higher order that form the means of production of goods of lower order and ultimately consumer goods. Citing Menger, Böhm-Bawerk argued that the value of producers' goods is not determined by the value ascribed to consumers' goods in the present, but by their anticipated value in future periods when today's producers' goods will have ripened into ready products (Böhm-Bawerk 1921b, 189n; Endres 1996, 100). The causal connection between the different stages of the production process was therefore the channel by which prices in different time periods were able to mutually influence each other.

In his *Prices and Production* (1931) Hayek tried to visualize this process by showing how a change in the natural rate of interest would affect the capital structure through an elongation or contraction of the period of production (Hayek 1931a, 39–40). This explanation consisted of a series of triangles that showed the different stages of production. The value of the original means of production was expressed by the horizontal projection of the hypothenuse, while the vertical dimension, measured in arbitrary periods from the top to the bottom, expressed the progress of time. The bottom of the triangle showed the value of the current output of consumers' goods, so that the area of the triangle represented the total amount of intermediate product bound up in production. It also showed the successive stages through which the several units of the original means of production pass before they become ripe for consumption. This meant that the lengthening of the period of production, in Austrian terms a more roundabout production process, could be visualized by including more production stages which results in a vertically elongated triangle.

Böhm-Bawerk never explained the dynamics of equilibrium adjustment in such detail but proceeded in a more qualitative fashion. He described the capital structure as a gigantic 'Pumpwerk' because it needed to adjust the allocation of producers' goods in the different stages of production to the needs for consumers' goods. Hence: 'Jeders Bedürfniszweig hat sein besonderes Saugrohr in das Reservoir des originären Produktivkräfte eingesenkt und sucht sich daraus, konkurrierend mit allen anderen Zweigen, seine Deckung saugend an sich zu ziehen' (Böhm-Bawerk 1921a, 313).

This image shows that Böhm-Bawerk treated the subjective valuation of the end product as the force controlling the allotment of scarce resources over the different stages of production (Böhm-Bawerk 1921a, 309; 1921b, 180, 184 and 186). For each stage considered in isolation, supply and demand would determine the price of the producers' good in question, which meant that the law of cost would apply: value would tend towards equality with the cost level. But for Böhm-Bawerk this did not imply that cost was the determining factor of value and prices. On the contrary, he saw the law of cost as nothing but a special case of the law of marginal utility (Böhm-Bawerk 1921a, 315). After all, what is the marginal utility of a producers' good? A good of this kind does not satisfy a want directly. Its value is derived from the fact that it forms a link in the chain of production activities that ultimately produces a consumers' good. This pointed to the problem of imputation. The estimated value of the end product is the factor that guides the demand and hence the value of the producers' goods in every single step of the production chain (ibid., 217 and 221).[21]

Costs are of secondary importance to this process. Böhm-Bawerk wrote that from a layman's point of view costs are always determining value, but if one considers their source a different picture emerges (ibid., 223). In the intermediate stages of the production structure, producers' goods produce other producers' goods. This means that the costs of goods of the n-th order should equal the value of the goods of the order n+1 that were used as input into the production process at this stage. In that regard costs and utility are nothing but two sides of the same coin, as value is imputed from the end product to all foregoing stages of production.[22]

Taken to its extreme conclusion, one could therefore argue that the value of the producers' goods in the different stages of a specific production line should be identical because they all facilitate the production of the same consumers' good. Böhm-Bawerk (1921a, 315) saw this as an ideal situation that would only materialize under very strict conditions, such as perfect foresight of the wants of consumers, the availability of resources and the development of technology. Under these conditions

> [würden] auch die originären Produktivkräfte mit idealer mathematischer Genauigkeit in die lohnensten Verwendungen investiert und das Kostengesetz würde in idealer Reinheit gelten. Es würden die komplementären Gütergruppen aus denen schließlich ein Genußgut hervorgeht auf allen Etappen des Werkfortschrittes genau denselben Wert und Preis behaupten, also das Genußgut genau seiner Kosten, die wieder ihren Kosten usf. gleich gelten, bis zu den letzten originären Produktivkräften herauf, aus denen schließlich alle Güter entspringen.

This view has two implications. First, the issue of imputation demonstrates the links between factor and consumer markets and so points to general equilibrium analysis as a natural corollary. This link will have influenced Hayek who in the early steps of his career wrote a thesis on the subject of imputation, later reworked into Hayek (1926).[23] Second, there is a strong suggestion of a price equilibrium stretching over time, in other words of Hayek's (1928) conception of an intertemporal equilibrium of prices.[24] Böhm-Bawerk realized that the conditions for an equilibrium of this kind would be extremely hard to fulfil (ibid., 316). In particular, he isolated two causes that are likely to disturb the ideal symmetry between prices and costs. The first one concerned all kinds of frictions between supply and demand such as the indivisibility of commodities and calculation or planning errors. The second source of disturbances involved the influence of time. Depending on the nature of the product, it could take 'weeks, months and even years' before raw materials and other means of production were being processed into end products. Böhm-Bawerk said that the assumption of perfect foresight essentially means that one abstracts from the influence of time in this sense. He believed that in reality the duration or period of production played a crucial role in the price setting process in a manner that should be differentiated from other kinds of frictions. According to him, time structurally affects prices because people value present consumption more than future consumption. This fact explained the phenomenon of interest and formed the heart of his capital theory.

The details of this theory will not detain us here. This section concludes with the observation that for Böhm-Bawerk frictions between supply and demand and the duration of production explained why the economy is not continuously in a state of intertemporal equilibrium. In all stages of the production process supply could be in disequilibrium with demand. However, disturbances of this kind did not imply a chaotic process of adjustment. The law of cost meant that all producers' goods at least showed a tendency towards a supply-and-demand equilibrium (ibid., 219). Moreover, the stages of production formed a chain of causal connections, or in Austrian terms a means-end framework, directed to a common goal, namely the satisfaction of human wants by means of the end product.

This connectedness can be likened to a roadmap to keep the walking man on his planned course. Hayek later better succeeded in explaining the nature and details of this roadmap by considering the process of coordination in more detail. But without doubt Böhm-Bawerk was the first Austrian to argue that equilibrium involves more than the mechanistic adjustment of demand to a given supply. For him a stable price or a constant supply was like a snapshot of a dynamic process of adjustment that never ends and involves the ramifications of a capital structure with many intermediate stages. The bottom line of this process was that prices always tend towards costs, even when we are addressing the exchange rate between present and future commodities. He would have certainly agreed with Hayek (1931a, 34) who argued that

> if we want to explain economic phenomena at all, we have no means available but to build on the foundations given by the concept of a tendency towards an equilibrium. For it is this concept alone which permits us to explain fundamental phenomena like the determination of prices or income, an understanding of which is essential to any explanation of fluctuation of production.

FRIEDRICH VON WIESER: COMPETITION AND LEADERSHIP

Equilibrium as a Benchmark

Wieser is another one who would have liked the words of Hayek but for a different reason. He was not so much interested in the explanation of intertemporal equilibrium, but used the notion of economic equilibrium as a benchmark to study the effects of institutions on the formation of value and price in particular and economic progress in general.

The notion of equilibrium allowed Wieser to get a better grip on what he considered to be the key element of the economy, production (Streissler 1990). Naturally, production was the engine of growth, but it was also the channel by which markets and therefore the economic activities of individuals are interrelated (Wieser 1927, 50). He described the problem posed by production to economic theory by comparing the natural, simple economy to the social economy which for him represented modern economic production. Characteristic of the simple economy was the absence of exchange; Wieser assumed that in the natural economy each household is a self-contained economic system. This assumption gave the economy a natural unity because households are producer and consumer at the same time. They would have a natural drive to produce because everyone seeks to maximize satisfactions, but this drive would also have a natural limit. As the theory of value explains, this would be the marginal utility of the resulting products which would keep the productive efforts of the household in a kind of natural balance.

Wieser found this unifying principle lacking in the social economy where exchange is possible and production involves 'thousands and millions of individual establishments' (ibid., 49). Here households have lost their economic autarky, because production and consumption are dependent on what others do. Wieser asked if one could still assume that households are able to maximize satisfactions under this condition. Moreover, how does one safeguard a harmonious operation of the economy as a whole and can this harmony lead to a maximum of total utility?

Wieser believed that the theory of what he called 'economic statics' gave a false answer to this question. This theory used the conception of economic equilibrium to argue that the social economy operates as a harmonious system controlled by some inner law. This was the tendency towards equilibrium, which meant that disturbing influences would automatically call forward compensating movements to reestablish equilibrium. Wieser stressed that this conception of economic equilibrium was useful to economic theory. It involved a simplification that was of great aid to the understanding of certain fundamental economic relationships (ibid., 52–53). However, he also warned that this act of simplification could easily lead one astray. Equilibrium theory suggested a method of research that was unsuited to the subject matter of economics. In particular, Wieser feared that economics would be treated as a physical science of economic goods, which ignored the fact that it was the 'active impulse' of economizing man which put life into the economy. Furthermore, he argued that the theory of economic equilibrium required simplifying assumptions which contradicted the facts of experience. In the first place, it could not explain why a condition of superabundance or scarcity tends to persist because it assumes that an excess supply or demand will quickly disappear. Secondly, Wieser did not believe that for a specific commodity marginal utilities would everywhere tend to the same level, as the theory of equilibrium predicts. The heterogeneous nature of wants prevented that one could compare them on a homogenous scale of utility, which suggested that a perfect equilibrium was simply unattainable.

Given these unrealistic features of the equilibrium model, why use the assumption of equilibrium at all? For Wieser, the aim of equilibrium theory was not to give an accurate description of present economic conditions but to perform a thought experiment. He used the simple economy and its sense of unity as an imaginary construction to investigate the inner force of a complex economy with production and exchange. This thought experiment aptly shows how Wieser studied the theme of coordination by imagining an economy in which this problem was solved by definition. Moss (1997) refers to this experiment as the 'benevolent dictator model' (see also Lavoie 1985, 80–82). Wieser's simple economy assumed ideal conditions for production by abstracting from disturbing influences, such as error and social inequalities. But the real leap of imagination was the assumption that production was guided by what he called 'a single intelligence' (Wieser 1927, 19 and 49). The simple economy 'answers its purpose in an impeccable manner because a systematic and penetrating mind guides it. This director foresees ends, weighs them without error or passion and maintains a discipline which ensures that all directions are executed with the utmost precision and skill and without loss of energy' (ibid., 19–20). In short, the benevolent dictator took care that the incentives of each person were perfectly aligned to the purpose of the system as a whole, which was to attain the greatest possible total utility.

Wieser used the fiction of the benevolent dictator to discuss the *modus operandi* of the social economy with all its imperfections and complex relationships. This economy lacked the guiding hand of the dictator but was governed by an alternative organizational principle, the law of value and price. The service of value and price in this regard could be studied by comparing the social economy to the ideal operation of the simple economy. In modern parlance, the simple economy and its equilibrium of marginal utilities was a benchmark for the analysis of economic systems with less perfect qualities.

This type of questioning gave Wieser's analysis of value and price a certain normative meaning. If the acts of the dictator are benevolent to society, can the same be said of value and price? It was one of Wieser's main contentions that in many cases value and price could not live up to this ideal. He argued that

> even in the most favourably circumstances – say when there is no disturbing element, no suspicion of force, dishonesty, or error and when the transaction is one we are accustomed to call free and just, – exchange value is calculated to render its service in economic life in an imperfect manner and with consequences which society feels to be serious evils (Wieser 1893, 56).

Compared to Menger and Böhm-Bawerk, as well as present day Austrians, Wieser was surprisingly critical about capitalism as a blueprint for the economic organization of society.

Natural Value and Economic Calculation

The main obstacle for natural value was the institution of private property and the related phenomenon of an unequal distribution of wealth and income. Menger had already argued that utility was not the only formative power of value and price. For him, effective demand was a matter of preferences and the availability of sufficient purchasing power. This meant that one had to assess the effect of incomes and the distribution of wealth on the formation of value and price before one was able to give a balanced judgement about their service to society.

Wieser (1893) introduced the notion of natural value to remove the distorting effect of incomes and wealth from the analysis of value. This notion is an example of the method of imaginary constructions that he more explicitly introduced in his later book *Social Economics* (1927), first published in 1914. Natural value is the product of a perfectly rational society that lacks the institution of private property. Wieser (1893, 60–61) therefore referred to this society as a communist state. He stressed that he was not describing an existing economic system but a state he called a 'dream' because 'it will be ordered in the best possible way'. There will be no misuse of power on the part of its officials, or selfish isolation on the part of its citizens; no error or any kind of friction will ever occur.

Wieser remarked that taken to its extreme a rational society would be one in which exchange and hence prices would be superfluous (ibid., 39). Possessing perfect knowledge, each household would already satisfy its needs in the best way possible, so why produce or trade commodities?

Wieser relaxed this condition to the extent that he wanted to be able to analyze the economic role of value, even in a society that possessed the characteristics of this dream-like state. He argued that even in a communist state, where money prices played no role, value would be indispensable. How else would one be able to distribute scarce resources among competing ends? Wieser referred to the example of land rent. In order to control the agricultural production efficiently, the communist state needed to calculate the return from different portions of land and judge if the returns would merit the outlays necessary to maintain the land. Here value provided the same 'economic-technical' service to the control of production as in a society with private property.

This is the leading thread of Wieser's discussion of natural value. He believed that the technical or coordinating service of value was something that could never be given up because that would leave the economy 'without power of calculation and without control' (ibid., 63).

The role of natural value in this process was that it simplified economic calculations at the level of the individual decision-makers. Wieser argued that for consumers natural value was uniquely determined by marginal utility which rendered their choice-making process 'infinitely more easy' (ibid., 43). On the supply side, natural value gave the measure for production and for the expenditure of costs. 'Goods should be produced according to the rank of their value, and other goods should be sacrificed for them as costs only on so far as the comparison between the value of amount produced and the value of costs allows' (ibid., 57).

The introduction of money as a unit of account further increased the efficiency of calculation and could be assumed to lower transaction costs. In the words of Wieser (1893, 36):

> Where money is the medium of exchange everything is measured equally, for purpose of trade, according to its money value; all utility in its illimitable variety is reckoned by the value of coin, the separate items of which are all equal to each other, and the amounts of which appear in the calculations as multiples of one and the same unit. It is the possibility of calculating utility in terms of value which puts us in a position to draw out exact economic plans and foresee their necessary limitation. Thus value becomes a controlling power in economic life.

However, as a store of value money introduced complexities that violate the assumptions of Wieser's simple economy. The ability to hoard money or other commodities requires property rights and such rights are a feature of the social economy. In this economy value is no longer a natural phenomenon but a monetary phenomenon. According to Wieser, this changes the service of value. A price is the monetary expression of value which means that people have to estimate the marginal utility of money in addition to the marginal utility of the good in question (ibid., 43). As a result, differences in wealth and income will have an impact on prices, given that the poor will value a unit of coin more than the rich. This changes the perspective of value in the following way: Natural value depends on just one causal factor, marginal utility, but exchange or monetary value measures a combination of utility and purchasing power (ibid., 57).

Wieser believed that the causal effect of purchasing power on the process of price formation changed the nature of economic calculation in a way that could have serious consequences for the economic well-being of society. He argued that it disturbed the natural pattern of production and consumption and so frustrated the economic-technical service of value. In particular, it led to a 'perverted employment of goods' because 'production is ordered not only according to simple want, but also according to wealth. Instead of things which would have the greatest utility, those things are produced for which the most will be paid' (ibid., 58). It is clear that Wieser did not identify commutative justice with distributive justice. He stressed the social ills of an unequal income distribution and condemned such effects in a sharp tone. According to him (ibid.):

> The greater are the differences in wealth, the more striking will be the anomalies of production. It will furnish luxuries for the wanton and the glutton, while it is deaf to the wants of the miserable and the poor. It is therefore the distribution of wealth which decides how production is set to work and induces consumption of the most uneconomic kind: a consumption which wastes upon unnecessary and culpable enjoyment what have served to heal the wounds of poverty.

These words underline that Wieser was not an uncritical adherent of the capitalist order of society. He used the notion of natural value to assess the function and therewith the danger of the institutions that form the corpus of different economic systems. The fact that the concept of natural value referred to the process of value formation in a communist state did not mean that Wieser was prejudiced towards communism. On the contrary, he believed that natural value was a neutral phenomenon that played a part in any kind of economic system. As such, the examination of natural value proved nothing for and nothing against socialism (ibid., 63).

Prices and Costs

Wieser's analysis of price formation closely followed the lines set out by Menger and Böhm-Bawerk. He explained that prices are determined by the negotiations between a marginal buyer and a marginal seller. His law of price was therefore that 'price must at all times settle between the equivalents of the marginal buyer and that of the buyer who stands next under him; viz. that one among the excluded competitors who has the greatest purchasing power' (ibid., 43).

Depending on market conditions, this process could be explained in terms of 'indices' of supply and demand (Wieser 1927, 173). These showed the numerical relationship between prices and the quantities offered and demanded. Wieser recognized the usefulness of such schedules but added that a theory of price based on them is incomplete (ibid., 182–183). First, he assumed that goods are traded in discrete quantities and that the intersection of supply and demand schedules merely indicates the margins within which the price will rest. Therefore, the exact point of equilibrium remains unexplained. Second, he argued that the indices describe an empirical pattern of prices and quantities. As such, they do not penetrate into the underlying causes of price formation, namely value and its motivating factors. The real objective of price theory was to 'understand the whys and wherefores of the decisions of parties as to price' (ibid., 173).

There are two remarkable aspects about Wieser's price theory. In the first place, it offers a general explanation of price formation in the sense that its scope was not limited to commodity markets but included factor markets. Wieser complained that even in his day the theory of price was confined within too narrow limits. In part, this was due to the distinction that the classical school had made between the theory of commodity prices and the theories of income, dealing with the phenomena of interest, wages and land rent. Wieser found this distinction untenable, given that income is just another word for the price of the service of capital, labour and land respectively. He provided the foundation for this general theory by clarifying the concept of costs. In his words it was 'probably the greatest triumph of the theory of marginal utility that it fully explains the obscure conception of costs, with which every other theory had to reckon and with which no theory could come to any reckoning' (Wieser 1893, 185). Wieser argued that the utility of a unit of a producer good was more than just the use-value of the product in question. For a proper account of its marginal utility, one also had to consider the utilities it could have satisfied had it been employed in alternative directions. In other words, cost is a 'sacrifice [that] consists in the exclusion or limitation of possibilities by which other products might have been turned out, had the material not been devoted to one particular product'. (Wieser 1927, 99). Nowadays this concept is known as an opportunity cost.

The second outstanding aspect of Wieser's price theory is that it examines price formation under perfect as well as imperfect competition. As a result, it covers a much broader spectrum of market structures than the theories of Menger and Böhm-Bawerk. They had been principally interested in the element of bargaining in the price setting process. For Wieser, the main objective of price theory was to explain price formation in terms of the institutional differences between markets. What is the effect of monopoly on price formation? What causes monopoly and is a monopoly from the demand side different from a monopoly on the supply side? What is the effect of intermediary forms that occur in great variety between competition and monopoly? Wieser enlivened his answers to these questions with examples of the competitive case in question. It is this casual empiricism which gives his price theory a specific sense of realism that is missing in the theories of the other Austrians. Also, the examples support his contention that perfect competition is not always the best safeguard of economic welfare. Wieser argued that under specific conditions (for example increasing returns to scale) a monopolistic market structure may produce better results and that in some cases government intervention is needed.

Institutional Analysis

This conclusion made it necessary to carefully weigh the benefits and disadvantages of the institutions that support a free market society.

The greatest benefit in this calculus was the effect on the efficiency of the general economy. Wieser (1927, 204–205) believed that competition was a motivating factor that pushes agents to produce the best results. For producers this meant that they offered the largest quantity of goods at the lowest cost. Moreover, their supply would accommodate demand in the best of possible ways and so produce a welfare maximum. The competitive market also had the capacity to maintain this position of equilibrium, as there are 'movements of equalization constantly at work' (ibid., 207).

The beauty of this system was that the benevolent dictator performed his role without conscious and deliberate economic management. Here we find the kernel of the notion of a spontaneous order. The competitive economy produces order and welfare for all, although no one intends this result.[25] In the words of Wieser (ibid.):

> The spirit of a social economy is complied with, although there is not a unitary social management. The personal interest is expressed thru the mechanism of excess-supply and unsatisfied demand. The quest of gain by producers and the pressure of competition are in themselves sufficient to result in a social effect.

But this harmonious order is threatened from many corners. A first source of disturbances is the fact that income effects upset the valuations made on the basis of marginal utility. As a result, the price-cost law works in a sub-optimal fashion and 'does not operate to reach the highest, universal satisfaction of needs' (ibid., 206).

A second risk of a competitive market society is the possibility of disorganized markets. This possibility arises in the case of violent and unforeseen changes in supply and demand. Such changes may have many causes. Well-known examples are self-enforcing panics among buyers or sellers which result in large price swings. As Wieser (ibid., 196) put it: 'Once a few of the alarmists have set the example of selling at mad prices, the entire market may follow in their train, with never a man left to stand off the stampede.' He stressed that under such conditions the economic organization of the market breaks down. The competitive pressure of supply and demand is no longer controlling price movements and value cannot play its coordinating role. One might say, a market society in disarray produces a worse result than a communist state where value can still be assumed to provide guidance for production decisions.

The worrying fact is that the collapse of markets may be a natural result of the competitive process. Wieser expressed his doubts about the competitive practices of modern industries. The economic gains of new methods, new products or new territories were becoming so great that 'friendly rivalry' turned into a 'deadly contest' (ibid., 209). Wieser feared that the spur of competition would tempt industries to over-competition with excessive production as a result. Especially the 'rich' were bent to 'economic extravagance' of this kind without taking note of the serious consequences of their actions. Or: 'How many unjustified expenditures a nervously eager or apprehensive competition imposes on the economy of a people!' (ibid.).

Thirdly, a related point concerns the duration of the disequilibrium adjustments that are necessary to restore equilibrium between supply and demand. Wieser believed that actual economic conditions violated the assumptions of the model of perfect competition on many accounts. He observed numerous intermediate (monopolistic) market forms that he considered more important than the perfect ones (ibid., 217). Furthermore he stressed that, depending on the circumstances, the transition towards market equilibrium could be a slow and costly affair. In this regard, he pointed to the influence of the growing number of 'mammoth enterprises' on the labour market. Lay-offs by such firms would have serious impact on the rate of unemployment. The 'displaced multitudes' would not quickly find new jobs and during this period would be handed over to abject misery (ibid., 210). In other words, measured in terms of human happiness the transition from one equilibrium state to another would have serious costs that forced one to regard the model of perfect competition with caution.

Equilibrium Requires a Just Price

In sum, Wieser's analysis of value and price reflected his doubts concerning the viability of a free market society. He attacked what he called the 'dogma' of the classical school that perfect competition is the optimal economic model for a market society (ibid., 210). Wieser was conscious of the restrictions of economic theory and tried to avoid the pitfall of what Schumpeter later called the 'Ricardian Vice', the hasty application of theoretical deductions to the problems of the real world.[26] Wieser faithfully followed the method of decreasing abstraction and treated the model of perfect competition as an idealization. He recognized that real markets hardly ever meet the conditions of this theoretical ideal, which called for a nuanced and realistic view on the economic role of the competitive model. As a result, he believed that there could be grounds for government intervention and even argued that, depending on the economic characteristics of a market (for example increasing returns to scale), monopolistic forms of competition would be better for economic welfare than perfect competition. Indeed, compared to the work of his fellow-Austrians Menger and Böhm-Bawerk, Wieser offered the most detailed and variegated analysis of price formation in the market economy.

But there is another aspect of Wieser's analysis of value and price which sets him apart from Menger and Böhm-Bawerk. He blended his economic analysis with a form of social analysis that seemed to favour a position of competitive equilibrium for normative reasons. His economic analysis had shown that the pressure of competition was not always sufficient to ensure that the private interests of profit-seeking individuals run parallel to the general interest of society. But if that was the case, then what force would guarantee the orderly operation of the free market society?

Wieser criticized the classical school for their blind faith in the beneficial operation of the invisible hand. 'Their healthy optimistic thinking left them in no doubt of the parallelism of individuals and social economic interest' (ibid., 153). According to Wieser, this attitude emerged from a neglect of an aspect of social intercourse that in his view had dramatically changed economic conditions since the times of the classical authors. This was the fact of social power. Writers like Smith and Ricardo recognized that individual freedom was restrained by law and morality, but they never attempted to investigate the economic consequences of social inequalities due to differences in talent and income. For Wieser, this had become a question that economics could no longer afford to ignore, given that 'capitalist development reduced great strata of the population to the direst straits'. As a result, 'an economic theory that should suffice for our times is inconceivable without a social theory that is consistent with the fact of power' (ibid., 154).

Wieser then turned to social theory in order to explain the unity of a free market society. He stressed that there are two types of social force that work as the cement of a social group. The first concerned what he called the natural controls of individual behaviour. These are the rules of conduct that people consciously or unconsciously adopt and that promote social organization. For example, he argued that in the course of history people learned to attune their egoistic motives to a level that is agreeable to society at large (ibid., 185). According to him, they came to understand that 'social egoism' is more profitable than unrestrained 'personal egoism'.

However, he doubted that in most cases the self-control of people would be sufficient to safeguard social harmony, as there was always 'the seductive temptation of personal egoism'. The second social force, compulsion, did not have this drawback. This force could work in a direct manner, such as the power exerted by political or military leaders. But for economic questions, the indirect mechanisms of compulsion were considered by Wieser of more importance. Here leadership took the form of a role model. He believed that people followed the example of leaders, because they represented social success. In addition, the decisions of the common man could be shaped by the power of education and the widespread practice of others who had been placed in like circumstances. As a result, certain rules of conduct could be imposed on the masses. One might say that Wieser replaced the invisible hand of the competitive market by the visible hand of a leader whose job it was to unite a group of individuals in a common purpose of action (see also Streissler 1990b, 177).[27]

Wieser was not very outspoken about the consequences of these lessons of social theory for his economic policy agenda. Did they impose a limitation on economic liberalism? One is inclined to answer this question with 'yes' but the reality is that for Wieser they broadened the agenda of economic liberalism.[28] *Laisser faire* did not mean 'doing nothing' but creating the right conditions for individuals to exert their free choice. This included the instalment of a proper legal framework to protect private property, rules of morality to moderate the personal egoism of profit-seeking individuals and a social policy to redress the negative economic effects of social inequalities.

This aim put the applied economics of Wieser in a specific normative perspective. He did not trust the self-adjusting capacity of competitive markets in the real world. His analysis of economic exchange treated many examples of markets that lacked stability and in some cases balanced on the verge of total collapse. Wieser believed that it was the task of economic policy to suppress such disruptive forces and support the self-adjusting capacity of competitive markets.

This required a program of moral education and guidance as well as a social program aimed at a reduction of the inequalities between social groups. The aim of the moral program was to promote an attitude of social behaviour and counter the seduction of personal egoism.[29] In part, this learning process took place automatically as the economy went through the different stages of economic development. But in those parts of the economy where markets still lacked stability, economic leaders had a task in trying to mould the morality of their followers. The task of the social program was no less daunting and involved the differences in economic power between social groups. For Wieser, this was a subject of particular importance, as he observed that capitalism tended to promote social stratification. It remains unclear how ruling powers could affect the class structure of society, but it is evident that he envisioned a society based on efficiency and equality. In his words:

> Where the general conditions are considered socially satisfactory and morally and legally correct, the general price [the equilibrium price according to Wieser's law of price, BT] is found also to be the just or equitable price. No one does injury to the other in demanding the just and common price; one and all, they can subsist

> under it. The general interest is well taken care of if, man by man, they adhere to it. The individual, cooperating in the establishment in the market of this price by looking out for his individual interest, protects at the same time the social interest; he fulfills a personal and a social duty . . . In this way the struggle of price-competition will be purged of its objectionable elements and will cease to be a struggle at all at the height of social progress, but it will become a cooperative endeavour of supply and demand to socially appraise stocks and needs (Wieser 1927, 184).

In the final analysis, for Wieser economic equilibrium embodied the ideal of both commutative and distributive justice, making the equilibrium price a just one as well.

CONCLUSION

Equilibrium Metaphors

This chapter bears testimony to the custom in economics to describe the meaning of economic equilibrium in terms of natural or mechanistic metaphors. Menger used the image of a water lock to argue that the goal of price theory is to examine forces that cause disequilibrium rather than equilibrium. Böhm-Bawerk added a walking man to our vocabulary to explain that the economy is an ongoing process between forces that move it closer to a state of equilibrium and forces that threaten to upset it. The fact that walking takes time even gives us a chance to define equilibrium as an intertemporal concept. The swing of the economy around a position of equilibrium can be compared to a map that traces the route taken by this walking man, his footsteps marking the connection between past and present. Suppose that competition keeps the economy near a position of equilibrium and our map will probably show a relatively straight line. But where the stability of competitive markets is uncertain, as Wieser made out so clearly, the map will show an erratic path, apparently without a sense of direction.

Wieser himself never used the metaphor of a map to describe the equilibrium pattern of economic activity, but this image is useful to describe the following three conclusions of this chapter. Firstly, a map is a tool to explain to someone how to travel from A to B. In economic terms one may translate this function as a statement about how to attain a position of equilibrium. As liberals in the true sense of the word, Menger and Böhm-Bawerk would not interfere with the economic course of the market economy, nor with the path taken by a walking man. The liberal approach would be to let him walk and afterwards check if the pattern that emerges confirms our suspicion (generated by introspection) that walking is most efficient in a relatively straight line. But Wieser was a maverick among the older Austrians and would have used the map in a different way. He knew from previous experiences that disequilibrium and disorder are important aspects of the actual functioning of markets. He would therefore not assume a priori that a walking man takes a straight path. He would give him a map in order to prevent diversions and show him the right direction to economic well-being.

Second, a map is a metaphor of an economic model because, like a model, it abstracts from many details of reality in order to better comprehend a certain part of the world: both map and model are what we call ideal representations. Building theories on the basis of such ideal concepts is usually a first step in the scientific process. An important question is therefore how accurate we believe that our map of the economic world should be. This chapter shows that the first Austrians answered this question differently. Böhm-Bawerk was quickly convinced that his model of two-sided competition satisfied the goals of his price theory. He believed that the ideal of a tendency towards competitive equilibrium and reality were not far apart. However, Wieser did not trust the road map of his fellow-Austrians to this extent. He always emphasized that his theories represented idealizations of reality and stressed that the road towards equilibrium was littered with many obstacles.

Finally, in evolutionary theory 'path' is a metaphor for the time-dependency of events. It captures the notion that what happens at a specific moment in time crucially depends on what went on before. As a consequence, such processes are irreversible, because one cannot turn the clock backwards. This characteristic is also known as path-dependency.

This chapter shows that this notion is relevant to our understanding of Menger's position on equilibrium theory. Menger never described the free market society as an equilibration mechanism, but focussed on the importance of institutional change. In particular, he discussed the transition of monopolistic markets into more competitive exchange processes in the course of economic development. In our terms this transition embodies an attenuated equilibrium process, because it tends to strengthen the economy's capacity to establish equilibrium. But as an evolutionary process, it proceeds very slow and treats time as a causal factor. It is unidirectional through time and therefore path-dependent.

For Menger, then, the notion of a map towards equilibrium would have had typical features. It indicates a road that one is unable to travel more than once. Also, the value of this map as guide for future action would be limited, as it would be difficult to predict exactly where and when the current road would end. All one could do was to investigate the generative causes behind the process of evolution and to that purpose Menger considered the notion of equilibrium, seen as either a static concept or a tendency, of limited use.

The Novelty of the Austrian Paradigm[30]

The differences between Menger, Böhm-Bawerk and Wieser are typical for the start of a new paradigm. Characteristic of an emerging paradigm in science is that it abounds in new ideas but also struggles to find its place among existing schools of thought. In particular it needs time to develop a scientific core that unites its followers and sets it apart from competing paradigms.

The Austrian school followed a similar pattern of development. Its initial source of inspiration was Mengers's subjectivist revolution in economics which generated a flood of new ideas. Alongside the theory of subjective value, the Austrians were among the first to study the role of bargaining, knowledge and entrepreneurship in price formation. They viewed economic decisions in terms of human action which led them to reject equilibrium as a static notion. In addition, subjectivism raised the question of the coordination of the economic activities of individuals with different goals and means and the role of the market mechanism in this process. Their examination of these issues took them beyond the boundaries of static theory into the unmapped terrain of truly dynamic processes where time plays a crucial role and where the future is shrouded in clouds of uncertainty. If that was not enough, they defined a structure of production (the different orders of commodities) which made it possible to examine the interdependencies of the markets for consumer and investment goods and generated an alternative explanation of capital, interest and the business cycle.

However, in spite of these developments it took the Austrians at least fifty years to recognize the distinctiveness of their paradigm. In the 1870s the Austrian and neoclassical paradigms were both part of the revolt against classical economics, a revolution that consisted of two parts. The first part involved the theory of value and price. Jevons (1879, xvi) referred to the classical theories of price as 'chaotic' because they offered different explanations for factor and commodity prices, as well as national and international values. His revolution consisted in the aim to develop a unified and comprehensive body of theory and this goal was shared by Menger and Walras. The second part of the neoclassical revolution concerned the methodology of economic research. The Austrians and the neoclassicals both advocated a purely theoretical economics based on deductive reasoning. In their endeavour to provide this they had a common cause and a common opponent, the German and English Historical schools, then also in the ascendant. As a result, both the Austrians and the neoclassicals believed for many decades that they belonged to the same broad marginalist stream of thought.

The correspondence between Walras and the first Austrians (Menger, Wieser and Böhm-Bawerk) is a clear example of this common spirit. In part the letters deal with the methodological differences between their theories. Especially Walras wanted to know the Austrian position on the use of mathematics in economics, something that Menger was fundamentally objected to. But this disagreement did not cause a breach between the originators of the marginalist-subjectivist revolution. Menger still saw Walras as an ally in his battle to defend the cause of an 'exact' or 'analytical' method against his German opponents (letter of February 1884 in Jaffé 1965, vol. II, 5). Although their methods differed, Walras and the Austrians were aware of the novel character of their work and felt they were pursuing a common goal.[31] Their main aim was to develop a unified theory of prices and to give economics a sounder theoretical footing.

The common cause for theoretical economics made the marginalists 'comrade-in-arms' (Kirzner 1990, 246). It is this sense of alliance which is ignored in Jaffé's erroneous contention that the differences between them were more important than anything they had in common (Jaffé 1976, 511). In fact, the sense that they were fighting for a common cause lasted well beyond the point when the Historical school ceased to exist. It led to such a degree of convergence between the marginalists that in 1932 Mises remarked that although 'we usually speak of the Austrian and the Anglo-American schools and the school of Lausanne . . . [the fact is] that these three schools of thought differ only in their mode of expressing the same fundamental idea and that they are divided more by their terminology and by peculiarities of presentation than by the substance of their teachings' (Mises in Kirzner 1990, 245).

By then most Austrians believed that their ideas had been absorbed into the neoclassical mainstream to such an extent that they felt no reason to maintain a doctrinally distinctive Austrian label (Kirzner 1994a, xvii).

The Austrian school did not really start to realize and emphasize its distinctiveness as a research programme different from mainstream neoclassicism until the great debates of the 1930s. It was in this period that important developments were made in mathematical general equilibrium analysis. Before this time the Austrians probably never perceived mathematical economics as a genuine threat to their science. The programme of Jevons and Walras to mathematize economics never attracted many followers and economics remained a verbal science for several decades to come.

However, in the 1930s more able mathematicians entered the scene such as Hicks and Samuelson in the Anglo-Saxon and Wald and von Neumann in the German-speaking countries. They rescued Walras's equilibrium analysis from oblivion and gave it a powerful new impetus. This development made the Austrians realize that the rift between their ideas and the neoclassical programme was bigger than they had anticipated. Mayer (1932, 148) distinguished between the causal-genetic mode of explanation of Austrian theory and the functional mode of explanation of the mathematical equilibrium theories. He argued that by pursing economics as a branch of mathematics the neoclassical economists were adopting a methodology alien to the Austrian approach. This remark was a sign of the growing discomfort of the Austrian economists with the direction microeconomics was taking in the 1930s. It showed that, in contrast to Mises's earlier statement, not all of the ideas fundamental to the Austrian tradition had been or could be accommodated in the neoclassical paradigm.

The best example of this transformation is the work of Hayek. In the late 1920s Hayek still saw the equilibrium theory of the Lausanne school as the starting point for all economic explanation (Hayek 1933a, 42n, 86, 95–96). He argued that economic theory builds on 'the fundamental thesis of static theory' which states that prices always keep supply and demand in equilibrium (ibid., 76).[32] However, by 1933 he started to realize that a theory dealing with the complexities of an economy developing in time could not start from these static premises. To explain how the price mechanism coordinates the activities of millions of individuals and thereby moves the market in the direction of equilibrium the concept of equilibrium itself had to be changed. Equilibrium theory could not start by, ab initio, assuming the full coordination of plans. Instead, it should explain how the economy reaches this state. According to this reformulation, equilibrium refers to that situation in which all market participants expect to be able to realize their planned activities. But this question could not be addressed in the static framework of the equilibrium theory of the Lausanne school. Consequently, Hayek's reformulation of equilibrium as a problem of coordination had the effect of widening the gap between Lausanne and Vienna (and Londen, Hayek's residence as of 1931).

In addition, the Hayek-Keynes debate in the 1930s acted as the catalyst to bring out the idiosyncratic nature of Austrian macroeconomic theory. Upon his appointment in 1931 at the London School of Economics, Hayek wrote a highly critical review of Keynes's *Treatise on Money*. This was the start of a particularly acerbic exchange of reviews and letters between them (Tieben 1997). The exchange established Hayek's name as a leading theorist but it also had the unwanted effect of his isolation. Hayek's scientific efforts were focused on the theoretical problems of inflation, while the reality of everyday showed that it was deflation which caused the problems of mass unemployment. The disregard for this reality alienated even his closest allies.

In 1971 even Robbins regretted having opposed Keynes on the issue of public spending, calling it 'the greatest mistake of my professional life' (Robbins 1971, 153). In the end, Hayek failed to stem the Keynesian tide and by the end of the 1930s the Austrian school had almost disappeared as a separate school of thought.

More than anything else it was the socialist calculation debate which led Hayek and Mises to realize and articulate the distinctiveness of their ideas (Kirzner 1988). The debate can be divided into different phases all of which were important for the gradual crystallization of the Austrian paradigm (Keizer 1994). The first phase was a controversy between Mises and a number of Central European Marxists over the need for economic calculation and rational prices to achieve a welfare-maximizing allocation of scarce resources. This phase of the debate was conclusively won by Mises who thereby established the importance of scarcity pricing for economic rationality. The next challenge came from more theoretically sophisticated socialist economists who responded by employing concepts from the other two marginalist approaches, the Walrasian and the Marshallian. Some advanced E. Barone's 1908 proof that a Walrasian general equilibrium model, yielding a set of optimal prices, could also be established for a society in which the means of production were owned by the state. Mises refuted this criticism by attacking the methodological foundation of general equilibrium analysis. This concerned its static premises and its abstraction from change and fundamental uncertainty. According to Mises, general equilibrium only applied to a stationary (Mises's evenly rotating) economy which is an imaginary and unrealistic construct.

In 1935 Hayek augmented Mises's case with his knowledge-argument saying that socialist planners can never possess the knowledge required to allocate resources as efficiently as the market system. All human knowledge is subjective and therefore dispersed over millions of individuals. It is often of a tacit nature and can therefore only be manifested in free market prices, which by definition are lacking in a socialist economy. However, this argument created the impression that the Austrians considered the problem facing the socialist planners as merely impossible-in-practice, on account of the complexity of the calculating task to solve a real-life general equilibrium model. The socialist answer to this 'practicality' charge was to circumvent it by means of a decentralized trial-and-error procedure using markets for consumer goods and labour. This market socialist model (introduced by O. Lange in 1936) was based on Marshallian partial equilibrium theory. Hayek and Mises in turn responded to this solution by attacking the methodological and theoretical underpinnings of all neoclassical equilibrium theories, whether Walrasian or Marshallian.

In brief, the socialist calculation debate made Hayek and Mises aware of the essence of Austrian thought and of the extent to which it differed from the approach taken by neoclassical microeconomics. It now appeared that the confluence of all marginalist currents that Mises had believed in earlier was wrong; in fact it had not occurred at all. As a result of this insight, Hayek and Mises came to distinguish sharply between their efforts to establish a science aiming at understanding the systematic forces leading the market economy towards the coordination of individual plans and the neoclassical paradigm focusing on the mathematical analysis of equilibrium states. It is the difference between a science of purposeful human action in an institutionally specified environment characterized by fundamental uncertainty and a mathematically formulated pure logic of choice of a Robbinsian maximizer.

NOTES

1. For example, Hayek (1937, 41) defined equilibrium in the following way: 'a society in a state of equilibrium [means that] compatibility exists between the different plans which the individuals composing it have made for action in time. And equilibrium will continue, once it exists, so long as the external data correspond to the common expectation of all the members of society.'
2. For that reason, Gunning (1997) prefers to speak of *distinctly* human action.
3. This was an aspect of knowledge that Menger (1871[1994], 91) considered of special importance. In his words, 'knowledge of requirements for goods in future time periods is the first prerequisite for the planning of all human activity directed to the satisfaction of needs. Whatever may be the external conditions, under which this activity of men develops, its success will depend principally upon correct foresight of the quantities of goods they will find necessary in future periods'.
4. For example, see Menger (1871[1994], 90–91).
5. Letter of February 1884 in Jaffé (1965, vol. II, 3). This is probably Menger's only remark concerning the value of mathematics as a tool of research in economics. See the comment of Hayek who believed that 'Menger has nowhere commented on the value of mathematics as a tool of economic analysis'. Introduction to Menger (1871[1994], 15).
6. He mentioned custom, niggardliness, culture, empathy, pride, discrimination by nationality and race.
7. The German original was first published in 1914 as *Theorie der gesellschaftlichen Wirtschaft*.
8. In the classical conception monopoly was nothing but an exception to the general case of perfect competition. Wieser explained the need for a broader scope of analysis by the fact that the economic organization of actual markets had changed. He believed that 'at the present day monopoly and other inequalities of power make themselves felt more sharply

than during the classical period' (ibid., 10). As a result, one needed to include the degree of market power as an integral part of one's price theory.

9. The final two stages introduce respectively the state as an active player in the economic field and the international economy. They are not treated here, but bring with them their own idealizing assumptions.
10. In similar vein Wieser (1893, 5) acclaimed 'how else shall we better prove our scientific statements than by appealing to the recollection which every one must have of his own economic actions and behaviour? For this reason, every expression which may be taken as confirming this recollection, is welcome as an aid to our investigation'.
11. For example, Jevons (1879[1957], 79–81) discussed the different meanings of the 'dangerous name' value and decided not to use this word in his *Theory of Political Economy*. He substituted it for the 'wholly unequivocal expression' ratio of exchange.
12. See Menger (1871[1994], 119): 'Utility is the capacity of a thing to serve for the satisfaction of human needs, and hence (provided the utility is recognized) it is a general prerequisite of goods-character.'
13. Although there is no direct proof that Menger had read Gossen's *Entwicklung der Gesetze des menslichen Verkehrs* (1854), it is noteworthy that they analyzed utility in terms of the same dimensions, intensity and duration. On the likelihood that Menger knew the work of Gossen, see Georgescu-Roegen (1983).
14. The steps represent the 'separate acts of satisfaction that can be realized by means of individual goods'. As such, the schedule is the result of successive equal additions to the quantity of the good consumed (ibid., 126, 127 and 139).
15. In order to perform this comparison, the schedules of Table 10.1 must represent cardinal indices. In other words, the economizing individual must be able to compare his satisfactions for different goods in terms of a homogenous unit of satisfaction. See (ibid., 128, fn 8).
16. In his words, 'Der Wert eines Gutes bestimmt sich nach der Größe seines Grenznutzens' (ibid., 185).
17. Wieser (1893, 61) argued that natural value 'can prove nothing for and nothing against socialism'.
18. Endres (1995, 276) refers to the ex post ratio of exchange as an 'equilibrium price' because it indicates a state of rest for the trading partners involved. But Kirzner (1978, 39) says that it is odd to call such ex post ratios equilibrium prices. He proposes that they are better called 'correct' prices. Prices are correct in the normative sense that sensible market participants would (each in his own interest) immediately agree to pay these prices, had they been aware of all the relevant circumstances. The opposite case is that ignorance and information asymmetries force agents to accept 'wrong' prices.
19. Mises (1949, 13) speaks of a certain 'uneasiness' that compels man to act.
20. See Endres (1996, 97). For example, in the eigth edition of his *Principles* Marshall said that 'there seems to be no good foundation for the suggestion made by Böhm-Bawerk that value must be determined generally by demand, without direct reference to cost, because the effective supply of labour is a fixed quantity' (Marshall 1920, 528fn).

21. To be precise, Böhm-Bawerk argued that if a producers' good has alternative uses, then its value is determined by the marginal product ('Grenzprodukt'). He defined this product as the marginal utility of the resulting consumers' good with the lowest value. The rationale behind this definition is that for a given quantity of the producers' good in question, the consumers' good with the lowest estimated value per unit will be the final one to be taken into production. See Böhm-Bawerk (1921a, 221–222).
22. Strictly, imputation points to the problem of what Menger called complementary goods. This refers to those goods which cannot by themselves satisfy certain needs, but which are able to do so only in combination with other goods. The question then is: how to isolate the utility of each individual good and hence determine its value? See Hayek (1926).
23. It is uncertain how important the issue of imputation was to Hayek's development of the equilibrium concept. He does not refer to this his work on imputation in Hayek (1928), the first exposition of his ideas on equilibrium. Also, he later degraded the importance of his work on imputation and expressed the hope that no copies of his thesis had survived. See Hayek in Kresge and Wenar (1994, 65).
24. There is an important difference between the intertemporal equilibrium of Hayek and Böhm-Bawerk. Hayek tried to show that an intertemporal equilibrium does not mean that equilibrium prices remain constant. They vary between the different stages of the production process according to anticipated changes in consumer demand. However, Böhm-Bawerk did assume that equilibrium prices would remain constant during the entire period of production.
25. The spontaneous order is the product of human action, but not of human design. See Hayek (1967, 96–105).
26. He spoke in similar terms about the 'optimistic thinking' of the classical school about the harmony of interests. According to him, this dogma was an example of the belief that the ideal situation is in fact reality: 'The methodological instrument of idealization was carried by them to the point at which it became idealized observation' (ibid., 153).
27. In the course of his life Wieser became more and more obsessed by the meaning and function of leadership in society. His latest book dealt with *Das Gesetz der Macht* (1926) and argued that political power was justified by success alone. On Wieser's latent facism that is associated with this book, see Streissler (1990b, 165–166).
28. Although it has to be stressed that there are interventionist strands in Wieser's work. In this regard his economic views differed from Menger and Böhm-Bawerk who were outright classical liberals. See Streissler (1990b, 165).
29. Wieser called private interest attuned to a level agreeable to the social interest, social egoism.
30. The remainder of this conclusion builds on Tieben and Keizer (1997).
31. Walras to Böhm-Bawerk, 1 August 1888 in Jaffé (1965, vol. II, 256); Böhm-Bawerk to Walras, 7 August 1888 (ibid., 260); Wieser to Walras, 18 June 1890 (ibid., 413).
32. This book concerns the English translation of Hayek's doctoral dissertation from 1929: *Geldtheorie und Konjunkturtheorie*.

11. Monetary Equilibrium

INTRODUCTION

This chapter addresses the historical development of theories about monetary equilibrium. The definition of monetary equilibrium is one of the most controversial issues in economics. For most people, money and economics are synonymous, given that in real life virtually every economic transaction is conducted in terms of money. Whether it be in commodity, fiduciary, digital or plastic form, money represents purchasing power now and in the future and is thus an asset that people demand for transaction, precautionary or hoarding purposes.

However, today economic science is still not able to fully integrate money and general equilibrium analysis, generally considered to be the theoretically most advanced part of our science. The reasons for this failure are not difficult to explain. The main problem is to explain why people demand money in equilibrium. Do we hold money as a precaution against unforeseen circumstances? In general equilibrium with a full set of forward markets nothing is unforeseen and money is a mere accounting unit. By the same token it would be foolish to hoard money for investment purposes, given that it bears no interest while other assets do. Hahn (1981) concluded that money transactions can only be explained as a transactions technology for which money is an input. But that runs into circular reasoning because we cannot explain why a particular asset performs this function: money is used to conduct transactions because it is money. It is possible to explain the transactions demand for money in terms of the mutual trust of transactors or a kind of network externality in which it is advantageous to use money if others already use it, but these explanations all point to factors that fall outside the scope of the general equilibrium framework or violate one of its assumptions (that is the assumptions of perfect foresight or negligible search and information costs).

The difficulty of integrating money into the equilibrium framework gives us an interesting perspective on the history of economic thought in this field. Ironically, the question of monetary equilibrium played such an important role in the development of our science exactly because it allowed us to study the impact of money and monetary changes on real equilibrium and real magnitudes. In other words, the main question addressed by theories of monetary equilibrium was whether money was neutral or not. However, the term neutral money is somewhat confusing as it has been used for different concepts (Visser 2002, 527):

- Money is a veil in the sense that the economy behaves as if it where a barter economy;
- It points to the absence of disturbances from the monetary sphere;
- It means neutrality in the comparative static sense (that is the quantity theory of money);
- Or it implies superneutrality, that is the phenomenon that the real economy is indifferent to the rate of inflation.

These conceptions of neutrality and hence of monetary equilibrium played a role in different stages in the history of economic thought. Probably the oldest conception of neutrality is the absence of disturbances from the monetary sphere, which is closely linked to the development of the quantity theory. This chapter therefore starts by discussing the development of the quantity theory. My discussion of this subject follows Laidler (1991) who distinguishes three periods of development.

The first period runs from the end of the sixteenth century to 1776. This period produced a wealth of ideas about the monetary economy, but it did not lead to a coherent account of the quantity theory of money. For example, many writers endorsed the money-stimulates-trade doctrine, a view which was contested by thinkers like Hume who followed the quantity theorem to its logical conclusion.

Hume stressed the neutrality of money to the extent that in the classical period (1776–1870) money hardly played a role in economic analysis. At least, that is the textbook interpretation of the quantity theory in what Laidler isolates as its second period of development. Schumpeter (1954, 282) referred to the classical period as 'the victory of Real Analysis that was so complete as to put Monetary Analysis practically out of court for well over a century'. This appraisal strikes me as rather odd, given the important monetary debates of this period (Bullionist controversy; Banking School versus Currency School). But fact is that real economic analysis stood central in classical economic thinking with monetary analysis in a secondary role. An example is the peculiar monetary economics of Adam Smith who at certain points followed a line of thinking that opposed one of the basic lessons of the quantity theory, namely that money is the cause of higher or lower prices.

The third period is dated 1870–1914 which Laidler calls the 'golden age of the quantity theory'. This is the period in which the quantity theory reached the peak of its development and enjoyed a more central position in monetary economics than it has enjoyed at any other time.

The thread of these three periods of development is the unclear dividing line between the statics and dynamics of the theories dealing with the conditions of monetary equilibrium. Neutrality and superneutrality of money are modern terms that refer to the comparative static and 'steady state' analysis of monetary changes. It is quite common to attribute such comparative static interpretations to the early progenitors of the quantity theory. Thus Keynes (1936, 343) claimed that 'Hume began the practice amongst economists of stressing the importance of the equilibrium position as compared with the ever-shifting transition towards it'. Similarly, Vickers (1959, 52) praised Locke's exposition of the quantity theory for its 'static, equational' nature.

I believe that it is necessary to avoid these modernistic interpretations of the early quantity theory. It is well-known that in the course of history the quantity theory inspired a host of 'dynamic' explanations of the causal connection between money and real magnitudes such as the growth of trade and production. Vickers averred that such theories were the product of the autonomous development of monetary theory. In his eyes, '[i]t is one of the achievements of the period that the theorems of monetary analysis which were seen to be potentially the most fruitful were transformed from the static form in which Locke had set them, into an essentially dynamic analysis' (Vickers 1959, 27). From statics to dynamics in preclassical monetary analysis? As if the mercantilists and their successors had been locked up in some ivory tower, labouring to turn a research program called the quantity theory into a progressive science in the sense of Lakatos.

I shall argue that for a long time the dividing line between the statics and dynamics of the quantity theory was not very clearly drawn. Many seemingly 'dynamic' investigations of monetary changes that started from the quantity theory were in fact ad hoc or ill-defined attempts to comprehend specific monetary problems. This is related to the fact that until the 'golden age' of the quantity theory the basic principles of this theory were not yet well-understood.[1] To begin with most writers treated the quantity theory as a long run proposition about the causal connection between money and prices. Alongside this long-run theory about neutral money ran the notion that money in the short run was almost certainly non-neutral (Blaug 1995, 30). This explains why many of the early monetary theorists seemed to embrace the quantity theory, while simultaneously advocating statements that ran counter to it, such as the money-stimulates-trade doctrine.

The impact of the quantity theory as developed by Locke, Hume and others and the related notion of the specie-flow mechanism for international transactions is well-known: money only affects nominal magnitudes, but leaves the real economy undisturbed (temporary influences excluded). This conclusion gave rise to the familiar image of money as a veil that could be safely removed to expose the working of the real economic mechanism. The 'money as a veil' image is the reason why Schumpeter ascribed to classical economics the victory of real analysis. As a counterargument, in this chapter I will stress the theoretical developments that contributed to a meaningful monetary analysis in the dynamic sense, in other words theories aimed at linking the monetary and real economy. Cantillon is an important stepping stone in this regard. He argued that the ultimate price effect of a monetary change crucially depends on the channel (transmission mechanism) by which money enters the economy. Such notions were carried further by men like Thornton who introduced the distinction between a natural and monetary rate of interest as a source of monetary disturbances and J.S. Mill who placed the analysis of monetary equilibrium in the context of Say's law and thus provided an analytical framework for the dynamic analysis of disequilibrium adjustments on the basis of the quantity theory.

In a later stage of development the meaning of neutral money was deepened by explicitly using it as an equilibrium benchmark. For example, Hayek defined neutral money as an ideal unit of exchange which allowed the monetary economy to function like a system of barter. One could for that reason use the familiar instruments of equilibrium analysis to investigate the behaviour of this monetary economy. Hayek developed his monetary analysis on the basis of Wicksell's definition of monetary equilibrium in terms of the distinction between the natural and monetary interest rates. Here neutral money signified monetary equilibrium, a situation characterized by stable prices which was brought about by the equality of saving and investment. Wicksell demonstrated that a deviation of monetary equilibrium would cause all kind of dynamic effects, mainly in nominal terms (cumulative process) but with potential effects on the real sector of the economy.

In this chapter I shall argue that Wicksell is exemplary for the fact that even during the heyday of the quantity theory – its so-called golden age – the dynamic analysis of monetary changes was never far away. However, such dynamic extensions were difficult to reconcile with the static framework of the quantity theory. Thus, Fisher isolated 'transition periods' in his account of the business cycle during which the quantity theory would not strictly hold. Similarly, Wicksell ascribed the business cycle to real causes independent of price movements, such as the speed of technological advance. It became one of the main challenges of economic theory in the post-1914 period to integrate such real and monetary effects and to offer a more comprehensive account of the business cycle.

I continue with a discussion of the difficulties that were raised by this effort and which put economics at a crossroad. The new dynamics, which often started from Wicksell's definition of monetary equilibrium, raised complicated problems involving the leads and lags of the dynamic movement under scrutiny. Such problems highlighted the analytical benefits of the equilibrium method which could be used to cut through this Gordian knot. This is one of the reasons why Keynes adopted a static equilibrium theory (the income-expenditure model) as the basis of his *General Theory* when his true intent had been to bring about a kind of monetary revolution. The consequences of this choice were far-reaching, because the end result of Keynes's revolution was a new standard in macroeconomics which was anything but founded on a dynamic method. This was the IS-LM version of Keynesian economics. In this chapter I shall discuss the how and why of this outcome.

The related story why the monetary dynamics of Keynes's competitors, most notably the Stockholm school and the Austrian school, failed to conquer the economics profession is treated in the next chapter.

This chapter concludes with a brief look at the challenges to modern monetary theory. The problem of integrating money into the general equilibrium framework is well-known but there are all kinds of developments to overcome that obstacle such the overlapping generations model and the application of game theoretic concepts. Can we report successes in the field of monetary equilibrium theory or is money still treated as a veil in the (neoclassical) mainstream of contemporary economics?

THE QUANTITY THEORY IN ITS EARLY STAGES

In the course of history the quantity theory of money underwent many changes. It started as a rudimentary theorem about the relationship between the quantity of money and the general price level and culminated into the familiar equation of exchange MV = PT. This equation states that the quantity of money M multiplied by the number of times it changes hands in a given period of time (velocity, V) is identically equal to the total volume of trade (T) multiplied by the average price of these goods (P). The quantity theory studies the interrelations of the constituent elements of this equation. That M causes P is the popular but inaccurate image of the quantity theory. Blaug (1995, 29) summarizes the meaning of the quantity theory in terms of three interrelated propositions (see also Schumpeter 1954, 703):

- Money M causes changes in the price level P and not the other way round, which implies that the initiating change in the supply of money must be assumed to be exogenous;

- The velocity of circulation V is an institutional datum that varies slowly or not at all. This suggests a stable demand for money balances which is unrelated to changes in the money supply;
- The volume of transactions T or the volume of output Y (depending on which version of the quantity theory one follows) is determined independently of the quantity of money or the level of prices but rather by real variables such as endowments, preferences and technology.

The starting point of the quantity theory must be located in the 16th century. In this century commentators such as Bodin and Davanzati began to comprehend that the influx of gold and silver from the New World was a more important reason for the gradual rise of the general price level than the debasement of coinage (Monroe 1923, Vickers 1959 and Guggenheim 1989). Subsequently, the quantity theorem, linking the size of the money stock to the rate of inflation, quickly diffused throughout Europe and became something of a commonplace. This theorem stated that an increase in the stock of money would raise the general price level, or as the well-known catch phrase reads, 'plentie of money maketh generally things deare' which is commonly attributed to E. Malynes (Bowley 1963, 125).

Step by step intuitive ideas about the influence of money on prices developed into a more formal theory. John Locke was one of the first to offer a more or less systematic theory about the quantity of money (Vickers 1959, Vaughn 1980 and Eltis 1995). The basis of his theory was the role of money as a medium of exchange. Previous statements of the quantity theorem used a rudimentary form of supply and demand analysis to explain that the inflow of precious metals would reduce the value of the money unit. Locke recognized that this explanation of the relationship between money and prices ignored the essential feature of role of money as a medium of exchange. Money was not a stock that like other commodities was offered for sale at a specific market at a specific time. Money was the 'counterbalance' of all exchanges and therefore commanded a price that was determined on all markets taken together (Locke 1691, 45). Most commodities were purchased for consumption purposes and were seldom sold more than once. In contrast, money was demanded not for its intrinsic value but because people would universally accept it as a means of payment. It would therefore enter the process of exchange again and again, a flow that in Locke's view formed the counterpart of the trade of goods.

Locke incorporated this notion of money demand as a flow, a stream of payments over time, in his theoretical explanation of the relationship between the quantity of money and its value. The ingenuity of his argument was that he was able to formulate his quantity theory as part of a general theory of value (Negishi 1989). This theory defined the demand for money in terms of its 'vent', a concept that indicates the rate of turnover or velocity of circulation of money.[2] Locke believed that the vent of money rarely varies so that the value of money was affected by changes in the quantity of money alone (Locke 1691, 62).[3] He even demonstrated that, assuming a constant output of all other commodities, a given change in the quantity of money will bring forth a proportional change in the price level (Locke 1691, 62, 73–74, 77–78 and Vaughn 1980, 39).

The main contribution of Locke to the development of the quantity theory was that he defined its constituent elements and studied some of the relationships involved. Vickers (1959, 52) describes his formulation of the quantity theory as 'static' because Locke failed to address the transmission mechanism between money and prices, which led to a fragmented approach of the quantity theory. For example, he recognized that a reduction of the quantity of money could affect both the volume of trade and the general price level. But he never explained the causal mechanism behind the scene, nor did he conceive the possibility of a combination of effects.

Likewise, Locke's analysis of the velocity of circulation as part of the quantity theory was innovating for its time but far from complete (Vickers 1959, 69). He observed that the economy would be better off if the quickness of circulation could be increased, because less money would then be needed to drive the trade (Locke 1691, 39–40).[4] Further he implied that a fixed amount of money could support a greater volume of transactions when velocity increased. But he never reached the conclusion that an increase in the velocity of money could also raise the price level with a fixed amount of output.

However, we may question whether it is justified to call this fragmented account of the quantity theory a 'static' theory. Indeed, Locke did not provide an explanation of the transmission mechanism, which would have allowed us to trace the change of the dependent variable – the price level – over time, given the changes in the independent variables. But it is undeniable that his perspective for developing the quantity theory was the secular change in the money stock. This change caused a tenfold increase in the world stock of silver in a period of 200 years (since the discovery of the West-Indies). The result was that the price of money decreased by nine-tenths, ceteris paribus the velocity of circulation and the 'vent' of other commodities.[5] It appears, then, that Locke was addressing a process of long-term change, rather than comparing one equilibrium price level to another.

Locke's analysis was carried further by men like Hume and Cantillon. Hume is renowned for his description of the quantity theory in a static framework (Vickers 1959, 221; Laidler 1991, 11 and Rothbard 1995, 426). He introduced the notion of a neutrally distributed change in the supply of money (in modern terms 'helicopter money') to explain why a change in the money stock causes a proportional change in the price level. To this purpose he assumed that each inhabitant of Great Britain would overnight, and 'by miracle', find five pounds slipped into his pockets. A monetary impulse of this kind would have no real effects whatsoever but 'would only serve to increase the prices of everything' (Hume 1752, 51, see also 62–63).

Compare this overnight monetary shock to the secular change in the world silver stock addressed by Locke, a development that lasted centuries. Seen from this perspective, Hume's approach was certainly more of a static nature than Locke's, analyzing the comparative statics of a 'neutral' monetary impulse. But it must be stressed that Hume's method of analysis was untypical in 18th century economics (Blaug 1995, 30). In other words, his mental experiment involving an exogenous increase in the money supply is not indicative of a generally accepted static approach to monetary issues in the preclassical period. The opposite is probably closer to the truth.

The author who, after Locke, described the phenomenon of the velocity of circulation with the greatest depth of insight is Cantillon (Guggenheim 1989, 43). Like Petty and Locke before him, he used the notion of a circular flow to calculate the quantity of money needed to finance a given amount of output and trade in a state. But his analysis of the flow of money and incomes reached much deeper than his forerunners (see Chapter 5). Unlike Locke, he knew that a quicker velocity of circulation would have the same effect on prices as an increase in the quantity of money. He demonstrated the interaction between money and the velocity of circulation by showing that a higher frequency of payments implied that a smaller quantity of money would suffice to make the same amount of annual payments. As a result, he argued that 'an acceleration or greater rapidity in circulation of money in exchange is equivalent to an increase of actual money up to a point'.

Money Stimulates Trade

In spite of the broad acceptance of the quantity theorem in the late 17th and early 18th centuries, money was for most of the writers in this period anything but a neutral phenomenon. Money was seen as a policy instrument that could be used to promote the growth of output and employment, the money-stimulates-trade doctrine. The proponents of this doctrine were mercantilists like John Law, Jacob Vanderlint and George Berkeley (Vickers 1959). They believed that an addition to the money stock would provide a stimulus for industry by allowing investors to borrow more cheaply, while it also provided the purchasing power for new consumers' demand. From the perspective of the quantity theory this appears a self-defeating strategy because the changes involved will be purely nominal. But the mercantilists believed that a gradual increase of the money supply would not disrupt the level of wages and prices, or the price level was simply held constant as part of a ceteris paribus clause. Even Hume, who was certainly not a mercantilist, argued that money could have real effects during a transition phase (Rothbard 1995, 427). He argued that prices and wages respond with a lag to a change in the money stock so that an inflow of gold provided stimulus to trade and employment. But he hastened to add that 'it is only in this interval or intermediate position, between the acquisition of money and rise of prices, that the increasing quantity of gold and silver is favourable to industry' (Hume 1752, 38 see also 48).

Richard Cantillon went a step further than Hume. For him the non-neutrality of money was a fundamental characteristic of a monetary economy. Cantillon put the microeconomic process of price adjustments at the core of monetary analysis (Vickers 1959, 187; Rothbard 1995, 355). He argued that money enters the economy in a step-by-step process and does not simply increase prices in a homogenous aggregate.[6] A silver or gold discovery means that the new money first boosts the purses of the owner of the mine, the smelters and all the other workers; in the case of a balance-of-trade surplus it is the 'industrial inhabitants' who are the channel by which the extra money enters the economic system. The propagation of the monetary impulse subsequently depends on a kind of cash-balance mechanism. The first receivers of the extra money experience higher cash-balances because prices in general have not yet risen. They are likely to spend the extra cash and so raise the cash-balances of an expanding range of people. As subsequent receivers of the extra money also raise their consumer demand, price increases will spread like oil throughout the economy.

However, the question is whether the diffusion of the monetary impulse will be general enough in order to raise all prices in an equal manner. For several reasons, Cantillon believed that such a proportionate increase of the general price level was unlikely to occur. First, he argued that the process of adjustment would affect the proportion between supply and demand in individual markets and therefore change relative prices. This effect became later known as the Cantillon effect. Its rationale is that in some markets people are unable to raise their prices or wages, while the ferocity of competition will also differ between commodities. Cantillon observed that bread, for example, will not rise as fast as meat, given that the consumers' competition for the latter product is much stronger. Such differences explain that a change of the money stock involves more than a nominal change of prices; it also alters economic decisions. This effect is amplified because, second, the extra money supply affects the velocity of circulation. Some people change their payment habits (use cash money instead of credit, or vice versa). Furthermore, Cantillon recognized that specific groups are likely to save the extra gains rather than to spend them for consumption purposes.

Hence, it matters for the ultimate price effect of a monetary impulse whether the new coins wind up in the hands of entrepreneurs (industry) or in the coffins of those who hoard cash for precautionary purposes and keep it out of circulation.[7]

Both effects combined led Cantillon (1755, part II, Chapter 7) to conclude that

> an increase of money circulating in a state always causes there an increase of consumption and a higher standard of expense. But the dearness caused by this money does not affect equally all the kinds of products and merchandise, proportionally to the quantity of money, unless what is added continues in the same circulation as the money before, that is to say unless those who offer in the market one ounce of silver be the same and only ones who now offer two ounces when the amount of money in circulation is doubled in quantity, and that is hardly ever the case. I conceive that when a large surplus of money is brought into a state the new money gives a new turn to consumption and even a new speed to circulation. But it is not possible to say exactly to what extent.

It can be concluded that Cantillon had a clear notion of the microeconomic process that determines the dynamic adjustment of prices. However, the end result of these price changes is still a trend towards market equilibration. Cantillon is often credited as being the first have defined an economic order in terms of market equilibration. He stressed that markets are driven by an entrepreneurial spirit that explains why a competitive market economy has a strong tendency towards an equilibrium between intrinsic values and market prices in all sectors of the system (Spengler 1954, 424).

Sir James Steuart copied Cantillon's process approach to monetary theory, but he reached the opposite conclusion, namely that the monetary economy lacked equilibrating forces at all. For our purposes, Steuart is an intriguing figure. He explicitly defined the conditions of economic equilibrium (Milgate 1987), but unlike many of his contemporaries he did not believe that the pressure of market competition would be sufficient to maintain this 'perfect balance' between supply and demand and keep the system 'in equilibrio' (Steuart 1767[1973], 159). Like Cantillon, he argued that the effect of a monetary shock depends on the channel by which the money enters the expenditure stream. Steuart believed that the first receivers of the extra cash would change their propensity to consume. As a result, the new money would never reach the market and leaves prices unaltered. In addition, where price changes would occur commodities' intrinsic values would be changed as well. This suggested that the 'overturning' of the equilibrium between market prices and intrinsic values would not be automatically corrected. For Steuart, state intervention and active economic management were necessary to maintain the balance between supply and demand for goods and money and keep the economy on a road to prosperity (Vickers 1959, 268). The gap with the liberal outlook of Smith's *Wealth of Nations*, published just nine years later, could hardly have been greater.

The Specie-flow Mechanism

In the preclassical period it was soon recognized that metallic money is a liquid asset that in the form of bullion can be exported and imported. Cantillon was one of the first to analyze the consequences of the international scope of the money trade for the value of money. The crux of the specie-flow mechanism is the interaction between international price differences and the balance of trade. Cantillon observed that an increase of the money stock would not just raise the national price level, it would also worsen the terms of trade for a nation and thus cause a balance of trade deficit. This implies that part of the increase in the money stock will be exported until the balance of trade has again reached an equilibrium level. Seen from this perspective, the specie-flow mechanism allows one to extrapolate the quantity theory to the case of many countries.

However, Cantillon himself never reached the conclusion that the specie-flow mechanism would push national price levels to an international equilibrium level that eradicates any trade imbalances between countries. He observed all kind of endogenous changes and frictions that in reality made international monetary equilibrium an improbable affair.[8]

Hume voiced similar objections but he did take the specie-flow mechanism to its logical conclusion. He used one of his examples of neutrally distributed new money to demonstrate the nature of international monetary equilibrium (Hume 1752, 62–63). In his opinion it did not matter whether the money stock in Britain was in one night diminished or multiplied by a factor five. The resulting change in the international competitive position implied that the money lost or gained would quickly return or disappear again through a shortage respectively a surplus of the balance of trade. Accordingly, Hume believed that in an open economy it would be impossible for the national authorities to regulate the national money stock unless they would take very drastic measures to stop imports, to stockpile money at the national bank or to issue paper-money. But he did not consider such measures recommendable because they constitute impediments to free trade and therefore cause great harm to the economic wealth of nations (ibid., 75–76).[9]

The Nature of Economic Equilibrium

Summing up, the quantity theory in the preclassical period was not based on a unified approach to equilibrium theory. There was no consensus about a static version of the now familiar equation of exchange. At best the writers of the preclassical period had a very rough notion of this equation at the back of their minds. We have seen in this section that most notably Locke and Hume fostered ideas that with some credibility can be interpreted as static applications of the quantity theory. But it is something different altogether to suggest, as Vickers does, that a scientific development took place which led economists of this era to give up a (non-existing) static quantity theory in favour of a more dynamic version of it. Certainly the writers of this period would have accepted the quantity theory as a long run proposition about the neutrality of money. But as a short run proposition almost everyone, including Hume, believed that money was non-neutral, which explains the popularity of the money-stimulates-trade doctrine. Cantillon presented us with probably the finest analysis of why money is able to generate such effects on real variables. In terms of the quantity theory, this implied that the volume of output Y is not determined independently of the quantity of money or the general price level. In the next section I shall argue that the classical economists treated money as non-neutral in a similar (short-term) sense, implying that the victory of real analysis in the period 1776–1870 was not so complete as is commonly believed.

THE CLASSICAL THEORY OF THE PRICE LEVEL

Schumpeter (1954) considered the classical period 1776–1870 something of a watershed in the history of monetary theory. According to him, the classical period marked a 'victory of Real Analysis that was so complete as to put Monetary Analysis practically out of court for well over a century' (Schumpeter 1954, 282). Smith's *Wealth of Nations* exemplifies the trend towards real analysis in classical economics. For him money was not part of the national capital and could therefore not affect the process of capital accumulation and economic growth. Smith's theory of money and banking touches several important issues, but the quantity theory of money plays no role whatsoever in his analysis. Indeed, his monetary ideas reflect a position that is better described as anti-quantity theory.

However, that does not mean that real analysis fully dominated the scene in the classical period. The quantity theory played a role in several of the economic debates of the period, most notably the Bullionist controversy of the 1810s and the debate between the Banking and Currency Schools in the

1840s. Thornton, Ricardo, Mill and others further developed the thinking of Hume and Cantillon on the quantity theory. Their work concerned a wide range of monetary issues such as the transmission mechanism between money and prices, the role of paper money and credit, the explanation of interest and the nature of business cycle fluctuations.

Real Bills and the Law of Reflux

For certain Adam Smith's monetary theory was antithetical to the quantity theory in one crucial respect. He saw the quantity of money as a purely passive variable which adjusted itself to the price level rather than the other way round (Smith 1937, 188, 323–324). He believed that the price mechanism would always and everywhere prevent the 'wheels of circulation' to hamper due to a lack of money. Greater wealth implied higher prices for gold and silver and thus an increase in the money supply by means of either the production of gold and silver from the mines or importation. As 'metals naturally fly from the worse to the better market' there is always a tendency towards an equilibrium distribution of gold and silver between the trading nations of the world (ibid., 189).

This conclusion applies to a metallic currency system. In addition, Smith was one of the first classical economists to extend monetary theory to accommodate paper money, but this extension did not fundamentally alter his view about the causality between money and prices. He expounded what later became known as the real bills doctrine and the law of reflux. Both are mechanisms to prevent an overexpansion of bank credit. The reflux principle relies on price differentials to explain that paper money replaces metallic money so that the total quantity of money remains unchanged. Paper money issued domestically tends to raise domestic prices. This causes an outflow of specie until the total quantity of money returns to its previous equilibrium level. Alternatively, excess (convertible) paper will be offered to the banks in exchange for gold, which will then be exported. In either case, in a mixed currency system the quantity of money regulates itself and the issuing of paper money will not cause inflation.[10] It was this thesis which stood at the centre of the Bullionist debate of the 1810s.

The cause of this debate had been the suspension by the British government of the convertibility of bank notes in 1797. Bullionists such as Henry Thornton and David Ricardo plead for restoration of convertibility in order to control the supply of paper money and prevent inflation. Their adversaries appealed to some form of the real bills doctrine that had previously been used by James Law, James Steuart and Adam Smith. Smith pointed to the problem that banks not always acted rationally and as a consequence frequently overstocked the market with paper money (Smith

1937, 286–288). To prevent this from happening, he advocated that banks would accept 'real bills of exchange' as collateral for bank notes and other forms of credit (money). As long as the repayment of these bills is credible, banks experience an automatic check against the over-issue of paper money. They merely advance a sum of money in expectation that goods now being produced will soon enter the market and generate the revenue needed to repay the bill of exchange. In this manner, the demand for notes from the business community is limited by the needs of their trade. Hence, even without convertibility, the supply of money will necessarily expand in pace with the volume of goods produced.[11]

Henry Thornton in his *Paper Credit in Great Britain* (1802) produced the most forceful rebuttal of this line of thinking.[12] He pointed out that the demand for loans is insatiable and that real bills do not stop that demand. In the first place, real bills 'may be multiplied to an extremely great extent' (Thornton 1802[1939], 253). Bank loans are a form of near money and thus increase the total quantity of money and lead to higher money incomes and demand. As a result, they also justify additional borrowing and inflate the stock of paper money still further. As Thornton (ibid., 241–242) put it:

> An enlarged issue of paper, produces an increased facility of borrowing . . . It communicates an additional power of purchasing, not only to the original borrower at the bank, but successively, also, to all the other individuals into whose hands the new bank notes pass in the course of their circulation.

Secondly, the real bills doctrine led Thornton to pose the logical question, what governs business's demand for bank credit and money? His answer was the rate of interest in comparison to the 'mercantile gain' to be obtained by the employment of the borrowed capital (ibid., 254). Thornton was the first to make the distinction between a natural and a market rate of interest, the germ of the later cumulative process of Knut Wicksell. In Thornton's analysis, the main problem was that the laws against usury often restricted the rate of interest that could be asked by the banks. As a consequence, a divergence between the natural and market rates of interests emerged which implied that merchants obtained their loans too cheap. And '[t]hat which they obtain too cheap, they demand in too great quantity' (ibid., 255). It was therefore 'erroneous' to believe that it would be safe to permit bank paper to limit itself (ibid., 254).

The real bills doctrine runs as a thread through the classical period. Ricardo copied Thornton's critique of the doctrine but allowed for 'reflux' to occur in the case of a convertible currency (Hollander 1987, 290). The issue gained new impetus in the Banking-Currency schools debates of the 1840s. The Bank Charter Act of 1844 gave the Bank of England the monopoly on note issue which raised the question whether or not it was necessary to regulate the currency. The Banking school endorsed the reflux principle in a very simple form: excess note issue might induce inflation, but that would lead to a race to redeem notes in gold, thereby removing the excess money supply. From that perspective there was no need to regulate the currency as long as convertibility was maintained. The details of the debate will not detain us here. For present purposes, it suffices to note that John Stuart Mill shared the views of the Banking School. However, like Ricardo, he also followed Thornton's analysis of the transmission mechanism between money and prices via the interest rate and recognized that in a speculative state of the business cycle credit creation would indeed proceed unchecked, even if banks obey the rule of 'real bills only'.

The Transmission Mechanism between Money and Prices

The issue of the transmission mechanism between money and prices can best be discussed in the context of Say's law of markets. This law formalized the insight of amongst others Locke, Boisguilbert, Cantillon and the Physiocrats that the economy consists of a circular flow of incomes and expenditures with the supply of money acting as the counterpart of the supply of commodities. A crude form of the law states that the excess supply of money should equal the excess demand for commodities so that the money and commodity markets simultaneously reside in equilibrium. The question is how this equilibrium comes about and whether it is possible to conceive of disequilibrium at all.

Adam Smith introduced a version of the law of markets in the form of the saving-is-spending theorem (Smith 1937, 321). Strictly, this theorem implies that the money value of aggregate supply is identically equal to the money value of aggregate demand, a condition known as Say's identity. Under this condition there cannot be an excess supply or demand of money, which makes it impossible to investigate the relationship between money and prices. By definition money and commodity markets reside in equilibrium for any price level. In the world of Say's identity the general price level has no meaning.[13] The economy operates as a barter system in disguise, given that money is only an accounting unit. Without a more elaborate role for money, this version of the law of markets is inconsistent with the quantity theory which, after all, implies a determinate level of prices for every given money supply.

Say's law in the form of the equality between aggregate supply and demand avoids this problem. In this case the aggregate price level is determinate and may fluctuate in order to restore an excess supply or demand for money. The question is how money acts upon prices so that it is able to perform this equilibrating role.

Cantillon and Hume had pointed the way to the direct mechanism relating the quantity of money to the price level. They showed that an increase of money raises prices equiproportionally only if the extra money is neutrally distributed ('helicopter money' in modern terms). The assumption implicit in their analyses is that the extra cash raises people's cash or real balances above their equilibrium level. The excess supply of money mirrors an excess demand for commodities which raises prices until cash balances return to their equilibrium level. The direct mechanism in this comparative static form was anticipated by Ricardo and Mill (Hollander 1987, 269 and 272).

In addition, Thornton's criticism of the real bills doctrine provided the key to the indirect mechanism linking money and prices. According to this mechanism, monetary equilibrium requires that the market rate of interest equals the natural rate of interest. Thornton pointed out that an expansion of bank loans tends to reduce the price of such loans, the market rate of interest. Assuming that the natural rate of interest remains constant, this reduction will boost the volume of loans and the demand for investment goods. The result will be inflation which continues until the rate of interest returns to its natural level. This may occur automatically, given that the demand for loans overtakes the supply so that the bank rate will begin to rise again. If the rate of 'mercantile' profit has remained invariant, the end result will be that the transition phase has merely increased prices. As Thornton (1802[1939], 255–256) pointed out, in the new equilibrium the bank rate has returned to its previous level, so that we only have a larger quantity of money and higher prices without any lasting real effects. In his own words, 'the power of purchasing will be the same; the terms of lending and borrowing must be presumed to be the same; the amount of circulating medium alone will have altered, and it will have simply caused the same goods to pass for a larger quantity of paper'.

Ricardo in the *High Price of Bullion* (1815) adopted this argument but did not improve upon Thornton's analysis (Ricardo 1951–1955, vol. III, 91 and Grubel 1961). It was left to John Stuart Mill to better clarify the transition between two equilibrium states when an expansion of loans or an inflow of gold tends to push the market rate below the natural rate of interest (Hollander 1985, 531–541). His exposition of the loanable funds theory is justly praised by Patinkin (1956, 259 fn10), even though his account of the interaction between the commodity and the loan markets did not involve more than a spelling out of what in 1865 was already well understood.

Real Effects and the Credit Cycle

The standard view of classical monetary theory is that it led to a dichotomization of the pricing process, the so-called classical dichotomy (Grandmont 1983, 10). According to this view, the classical economists had different theories for the determination of prices in the commodity and money markets respectively.[14] However, Patinkin (1956, 454) claims that he was unable to find an example in the classical literature which succeeded in spelling out in detail the dichotomy between money and prices. There are many suggestions which point in the right direction and state that a change in the quantity of money causes a proportionate change in prices. But they generally do not explicitly add the obvious implication that relative prices remain unaffected.

One of the main obstacles to a more precise statement of the quantity theory was the unclear dividing line between value theory and monetary theory. The classical economists treated (metallic) money like any other commodity implying that its value was determined by cost of production.[15] As a result, they argued that absolute prices are determined by comparative costs of gold and of goods in general. But this conclusion ran into conflict with the quantity theory, which linked the long term price level to the quantity of money.

To add to the confusion, the classical economists generally did not accept the quantity theory as a short-term proposition (Blaug 1995). Short-run non-neutrality was explained by a variety of phenomena such as sticky prices, sticky nominal wages and fixed nominal incomes of wage earners and rentiers (Reisman 1971, 86–87 and Blaug 1995, 32). Obstacles of this kind implied that a neutral injection of cash into the economic system was simply impossible. Hume and Cantillon had already shown that real effects could occur depending on where the new cash would be disbursed. Their argumentation was taken over by Thornton, Malthus, Cairnes and J.S. Mill.[16] The latter argued that:

> It is of course possible that the influx of money might take place through the medium of some new class of consumers, or in such a manner as to alter the proportions of different classes of consumers to one another, so that a greater share of the national income than before would thenceforth be expended in some articles and a smaller in others; exactly as if a change had taken place in the tastes and wants of the community' (Mill 1909, Book III, Chapter 8).

Such disturbances would, however, be temporary, lasting until production had accommodated itself to the changes in relative demand.[17]

The issue of the lags involved in the monetary adjustment process pointed the way to another effect with real implications. This was the doctrine of forced savings. Thornton (1802[1939], 239) observed that the supply of new bank loans would 'for a time' lift up the cost of goods but not the price of labour. As a result, workers are 'forced to consume fewer articles', a 'saving' that led to 'an augmentation of stock' but also caused 'hardship and injustice'. Ricardo, Cairnes and Mill copied this line of reasoning. The latter two offered the clearest exposition of the fact that a continuous flow of new bank credit is able to bid away resources from consumers through forced savings. Hence, they maintained that capital accumulation at an increased rate would accompany monetary expansion (Hollander 1985, 539–544 and Laidler 1991, 18).

With the concept of forced savings and the distinction between the market and natural rate of interest Thornton developed the two core elements of what Hayek later combined into a monetary explanation of business cycle fluctuations. The first steps towards such a theory can be found in the writings of various classical authors. But it would be too farfetched to attribute them to a monetary theory of the business cycle. As Laidler put it, the classicals possessed all the ingredients but failed to put two and two together. They focused on the dynamics of price fluctuations rather than on cyclical swings in national output. The typical cycle would start as a result of speculation arising out of overconfidence about the economic opportunities for gain. According to Mill, the root of the problem lay in the 'universal propensity of mankind to overestimate the chances in their own favour', so that 'every event which stimulates hopes, will give rise to extensive miscalculation; and every miscalculation upon a sufficiently extensive scale, will terminate in the ruin of multitudes' (quoted in Hollander 1985, 550).

The expansion of credit was therefore not treated as the cause of an upswing of the cycle, as Wicksell and the Austrians would later argue. In contrast, in classical monetary theory variations in the money supply were passive reactions and symptoms of inflation rather than its cause (Hollander 1985, 547).[18] The argument here is that merchants' optimism fuels both the demand and the supply for credit. The increase in the demand for credit is intended to finance new investment projects and banks are inclined to accommodate that demand, given that they foresee a further rising of the price level. As such, the availability of credit and the banks' response to the optimism of the business community is a crucial factor for the propagation of the credit cycle.

In spite of the focus on price dynamics, the implications of the classical credit cycle for real output and employment are highly interesting and point forward to monetarist and new classical theories of the 1960s and 1970s. Mill's insistence that the stimulating effect of a monetary expansion crucially depends on expectations by each producer that his own output will sell at a higher relative price when it reaches the market, recalls Phelps' island model (1969). Lucas and Barro used this model to apply the rational expectations hypothesis to the general equilibrium analysis of the business cycle. Further, Mill showed that the optimism about future gains will only temporarily boost real magnitudes. Phelps and Friedman would later argue that in this framework a more permanent increase of output is impossible because people (partially) adjust their expectations about the rate of inflation, so that in due time rising prices are no longer a stimulating force.

In addition, Mill stands out among the classical economists as the one who incorporated Say's law into the analysis of the credit cycle (Forget 1990 and Skaggs 1994). It is one of the accomplishments of Mill that he gave a clear definition of Say's law as an equality between aggregate supply and demand. He used this definition to reject the explanation of the glut theorists (he mentioned Malthus, Simonde de Sismondi and Chalmers) of a commercial crisis in terms of a general excess of production. According to Mill, this explanation committed a 'great error' for it ignored that an excess of aggregate supply has as its mirror an excess demand for money (Mill 1848[1909], 560). He therefore recognized that money could be more than a medium of exchange. In his view, speculation and precaution formed additional motives for people to acquire cash balances in order to hold them. Such behaviour would mean that a temporary, but nevertheless general oversupply of commodities would accompany a financial crisis. Mill's analysis of the credit cycle in terms of Say's equality is another indication that classical monetary theory did anything but dichotomize the pricing process.

THE NEOCLASSICAL THEORY OF THE PRICE LEVEL

The quantity theory of money was brought to full fruition in what Laidler called its 'golden age', the period 1870–1914. In this period exponents of the theory, such as Marshall, Fisher and Wicksell, succeeded in developing the quantity theory into a logical consistent body of theory. In doing so, they solved the problems that had bothered their classical predecessors such as the distinction between the quantity theory and the cost of production explanation of the value of money. However, in many other respects they were faithful heirs of the classical tradition. Laidler (1991, 82) describes the continuity of the neoclassical theory of the price level with the classical analysis that preceded it as the 'most striking characteristic' of the quantity theory in this period. Most importantly, the neoclassical quantity theorists retained the idea that in the long run money is nothing but a veil and that the object of monetary economics is the explanation of price level behaviour.

This approach suggests that the quantity theory of money was the domain of comparative static analysis and in general terms that impression is correct. The main exponents of the quantity theory (Marshall, Fisher and Wicksell) all explicitly stated that they were dealing with the analysis of the equilibrium price level and that dynamics involved the transition from one equilibrium level to another. But that was not the whole story. The neoclassicals also used the quantity theory as a starting point for business cycle analysis and in some cases this endeavour led them to revise their interpretation of the equilibrium concept. This section briefly discusses their problems with the comparative static framework of the quantity theory and their attempts to develop a monetary explanation of the business cycle.

The Transmission Mechanism

The peak achievement of neoclassical monetary theory was the development of the quantity theory as a logically consistent body of theory. Most importantly, it removed the uneasy blend of the quantity theory as a short run explanation of the general price level and the cost of production theory as its long run explanation. The neoclassical cash balance approach clarified the sequence of events between a monetary impulse and the subsequent change of the price level. As a by-product, it showed that cost of production is merely one of the several factors that (indirectly) act upon the price level through its influence on changes in the quantity of money.

The cash or real balance effect is the essential regulating mechanism of what in the modern literature is known as the short run Walrasian monetary equilibrium (Grandmont 1983). This mechanism explains people's demand for commodities in terms of the purchasing power of their money balances. Ceteris paribus, a change in the total quantity of money means that people perceive a change in their nominal money balances. They will try to preserve the real value of their cash balance and therefore supply (in case of an increase of the money stock) or demand (in the reverse case) extra cash. Given that an excess supply or demand is reflected in an excess demand respectively supply of commodities, the general price level will adjust until cash balances have regained their real equilibrium value.

This is the transmission mechanism that appears in the work of Marshall, Fisher and Wicksell. With the cash balance effect the transactions demand for money can be graphically described as a rectangular hyperbola, as both Marshall and Wicksell (1935, 142) demonstrated.[19] The analysis of Fisher differed from that of the Cambridge school and Wicksell in that he put transactions velocity at the heart of his monetary analysis. He remained much more in the classical tradition and approached the demand for money as a flow concept. Like his classical predecessors, he looked at the factors which determine the frequency of payments as a measure of people's desire for cash. In line with this approach he classified people's habits towards 'thrift and hoarding' as belonging to the determinants of the velocity of circulation, rather than as something that directly affects the demand for money.

However, Marshall considered velocity an inconvenient concept and substituted it for the concept of 'the amount of commodities over which people keep command in a ready form' (Laidler 1991, 59). This is the demand for a stock of real balances, the 'k' in the well-known Cambridge equation, linking the demand for money to its quantity. But this difference should not obscure the similarity between his views and those of Fisher on the nature of the quantity theory. Both used the cash-balance mechanism to explain why changes in the money supply cause a proportional change in the price level, an adjustment which pushes the monetary economy from one static equilibrium to the next.

Marshall spoke about an influx of gold as 'a sort of ripple on the surface of the water', meaning that this would simply cause prices to rise proportionally, while the supply of gold 'exercises no permanent influence over the rate of discount' (Laidler 1991, 66). Fisher adopted an intricate mechanical metaphor to demonstrate the equilibrium tendency of the monetary price mechanism. This metaphor consisted of a hydraulic diagram showing two reservoirs of gold, one for its monetary and the other for its non-monetary uses. Market forces, represented by a pipeline between the reservoirs, tended to equalize the levels of the gold, in spite of leaks (industrial consumption of gold) and new supplies in the form of gold production. In Fisher's view, such irregularities explained that '[t]he exact point of equilibrium may seldom or never be realized, just as in the case of a pendulum swinging back and forth through a position of equilibrium, there is always a tendency to seek it' (Fisher 1911, 108).

The diagram also convincingly showed that the equilibrium price level did not depend on something like a natural value for commodity money, like the classicals had argued. Cost of production did have an effect on prices, but it was an indirect one, operating through the quantity of money, as the supply pipeline of the diagram clearly indicated.

Monetary Aspects of the Business Cycle

Faced with this line of reasoning, one is tempted to draw the conclusion that neoclassical monetary analysis treated money as a veil and restricted its study of monetary affairs to comparative static analysis. However, it should not be inferred that price level behaviour was the only problem taken up by neoclassical monetary economists. There was also a strong monetary element in their analysis of the business cycle which was developed as an extension of the quantity theory.

Again the investigation of this issue was greatly influenced by the classical analysis of the credit cycle. Recall that the typical classical credit cycle, as developed by John Stuart Mill, stressed the role of speculative behaviour as the cause of rising prices that marked the upswing of the cycle. Neoclassical monetary analysis brought this type of analysis a step further by showing that speculative behaviour could be investigated in terms of the distinction between nominal and real interest rates.

The effect that generates the dynamics of this credit or price cycle is nowadays known as the Fisher-effect. The classical theory of the interest rate had been a theory of the real interest rate. As Thornton, Mill and others showed, the interest rate is determined by the supply and demand for loanable funds. But this rate is ultimately determined by the same real forces that govern the rate of profit on capital, for in equilibrium the two rates are equal. The effect of rising prices on the interest rate will therefore only be a nominal one.

Fisher empirically investigated the influence of price level movements on the interest rate and observed that in practice this conclusion is not entirely true. Indeed, inflation will be compensated for by an offsetting adjustment of nominal interest rates, but this adjustment comes with a long time lag. It is this difference between the nominal and the real interest rate that in Fisher's theory causes the characteristic swings of the business cycle.

Fisher's analysis of the different stages is as follows. The typical cycle starts when prices rise due to an increase in the quantity of gold, but the cause may also lay elsewhere. The rate of interest will start to rise in response to inflation, but not sufficiently. This creates overly optimistic profit expectations and encourages entrepreneurs to expand their loans. The result is an expansion of deposit currency, which causes prices to rise still further. Thus, the 'rise of prices generates rise of prices, and continues to do so as long as the interest rate lags behind its normal figure' (Fisher 1911, 60). The turnaround occurs because banks are unable to indefinitely expand loans relative to reserves. Banks respond with a lag but when they finally act they do so too strongly. The interest rate overtakes the inflation rate, pushing the nominal interest rate above the real interest rate which marks the onset of the downswing of the cycle. The crisis is the mirror image of the upswing. Prices fall in response to the contraction of credit, but the nominal interest rate again reacts with a lag. The crisis will come to a natural end when the interest rate does catch up with inflation but overshoots and the whole process starts again.

For a proper understanding of this cycle, it is crucial to point out that Fisher followed the classical example and treated the cycle as a price phenomenon only. To be sure, he recognized that the quantities of goods produced could expand a little during the upswing and contracted as a result of the crisis, but such real movements were incidental to what constituted the essence of the cycle, 'the culmination, fall and recovery of prices' (Fisher 1911, 70). But in spite of this focus, the price dynamics of this cycle did not fit the mould of the quantity theory. Fisher made it quite clear that what occurred during the movement of the cycle was not the path taken by the price level from one stationary equilibrium value to another (Laidler 1991, 78). He referred to them as transition periods that violated the quantity theory. Prices did not just respond to changes in the quantity of money but other kinds of feedback also occurred. As mentioned, the volume of transactions changed during the cycle and could therefore not be assumed constant, and more importantly, the velocity of circulation could not be assumed independent of the inflation process. Fisher was careful to note that the quantity theory did not strictly hold during the transition periods that marked his account of the credit cycle. In other worlds, in the real world price movements did not always comply with the mechanistic image of a hydraulic system that continually tends towards a position of equilibrium.

In general terms, Marshall's account of the cycle was similar to that of Fisher. He also used the notion of speculative behaviour and the extension of loans to explain a cumulating of price rises. However, he never deeply investigated the price dynamics of this cycle and, more importantly, did not treat it as an extension of the quantity theory. In particular, he did not regard changes in the quantity of money as an important cause of cyclical dynamics. Price changes had an amplifying effect on the cycle but compared to Fisher, Marshall and after him Pigou, placed more emphasis on changes in real output and the possibility of unemployment. Pigou stressed variations in agricultural output and the comparative attractiveness of investment as impulses driving the cycle. Like Marshall, he used money wage stickiness as one the factors responsible for the propagation of the cycle, showing that this element already had a long tradition in Cambridge before Keynes entered the scene. For the moment, it suffices to note that also in the case of the Cambridge school, the comparative static framework of the quantity theory was considered inadequate to handle the complexities of business cycle behaviour.

The Cumulative Process

Knut Wicksell is the next pawn in the development of the quantity theory. He introduced the distinction between the market rate of interest and the natural rate of interest and explained inflation as a cumulative process of price changes instigated by a difference between these two rates. In addition he is also presented as one who grounded the monetary analysis of the business cycle on a much firmer basis, using the capital theory of Böhm-Bawerk and introducing the notion of forced saving in monetary theory. According to later Austrian writers, the notion of equilibrium underlying this type of analysis differs in a crucial sense from neoclassical quantity theory. As Mises and Hayek would argue, the focus on the analysis of equilibrium positions implies that there is no role for coordination, learning behaviour and other aspects related to the passing of time. The answer of the Austrian and Swedish schools to this challenge was process or period analysis and Wicksell is considered to be the father of this type of inquiry. As Ebeling (1997, 43) put it:

> Wicksell opened the analytical horizon for inquiring as to what the market conditions are for intertemporal plan coordination, what may cause discoordination of intertemporal plans and, if such plans do not match, what the sequential effects and consequences may be of the adjustment process that leads (perhaps) back to a condition of coordinated plans.

What is often overlooked in this discussion is the remarkable continuity of thought between Wicksell on the one hand and Marshall and Fisher on the other hand. As Laidler (1991, 67) points out, Wicksell was familiar with Marshall's work and adopted some of his ideas to develop his account of the cumulative process. In particular, this concerned the cash-balance mechanism as an explanation of the price dynamics following an inflow of gold in an international money commodity case. Moreover, we have also seen that a cumulation of price rises was the essence of Marshall's and Fisher's analysis of the credit cycle.

Where Wicksell did break new ground was the explicit definition of monetary equilibrium. He argued that monetary equilibrium requires three conditions. The first condition is that prices are stable. Secondly, the market rate of interest should equal the natural rate of interest which indicates that, thirdly, ex ante investments equal ex ante savings.[20]

Wicksell explained the nature of the equilibrium mechanism underlying this concept by comparing it to the operation of a barter economy. He argued that in the latter case prices always have a tendency to return to their former equilibrium level when the equality between supply and demand is disturbed, like a 'freely suspended pendulum or a ball at the bottom of a bowl' (Wicksell 1935, 197). But when money is used as a medium of exchange, the nature of this equilibrium mechanism slightly alters. Concerning the general price level, equilibrium exists at what Laidler (1991) calls a meta-level. After a disturbance, prices do not return to their former level but establish equilibrium at a different position. In the words of Wicksell, this is an 'indifferent equilibrium of the same kind as that of a ball or cylinder on a plane'. Characteristic of the movement of a ball on a plane is that it has a tendency to roll on because it lacks the automatic operation of an opposing force (abstaining from friction). It comes to rest again somewhere else on the plane when the forces that set it in motion cease to operate.

Translated to the economic arena, the force that upsets equilibrium is that unleashed by a difference between the market rate of interest and the natural rate of interest. Wicksell recognized the limits of the cash balance mechanism as a regulating principle in an economy that uses credit alongside commodity money. The availability of credit implied that the interest rate exerts an influence on the price level. To highlight this indirect mechanism, Wicksell constructed the fiction of a pure credit economy.[21]

For Wicksell, the natural interest rate represented the neutral or normal rate of interest that he defined in a variety of ways, amongst others as 'the rate of interest at which the demand for loan capital and the supply of savings exactly agree, and which more or less corresponds to the expected yield on the newly created capital' (Wicksell 1935, 193).[22] The inflation process is set in motion when, assuming equilibrium, banks lower the loan rate below its natural level. As was well-known from the classical literature, this increases the demand for loans and causes an expansion of the volume of credits. But this is not the effect that directly causes prices to rise. Here the role of capital is crucial. Wicksell stressed that entrepreneurs use the extra credit to finance the purchase of capital goods. In other words, the reduction of the interest rate causes a shift of resources in favour of the production of consumption goods for a more future period. In terms of the Austrian capital theory, demand shifts from consumption goods to goods of higher order resulting in a longer period of production. Current prices are affected because a competition ensues for the scarce resources of production such as labour, raw materials and intermediate products. The result is that wages are driven up which in turn increases the demand for consumption goods. So, while the production of consumption goods is likely to be reduced (resources are shifted to production of investment goods), the demand for such goods will probably increase. From both the supply and the demand side, a pressure emerges that tends to raise the prices of consumption goods.

For Wicksell, the rise of the general price level was not a one-time affair. He emphasized that prices would increase period after period as long as the interest rate would remain below the natural rate of interest. This is the cumulative process.[23] But, given that the demand for loans in nominal terms rises accordingly, would the banks not experience a pressure to again raise the loan rate, realign it with the natural rate and stop the process of inflation?

Wicksell acknowledged this tendency that in theory could provide an automatic brake to inflation (ibid., 101). However, he also argued that the credit system is relatively insensitive to changes in the general price level. He seemed to have endorsed a kind of real bills doctrine and stated that banks will continue issuing loans as long as they trust the capacity of borrowers to repay their debt. Consequently, the demand for credit simply generates its own supply.[24]

The cumulative process has a remarkable similarity to the operation of the Fisher-effect. Both are the products of the sluggish adjustment of the loan rate by the banks. Recall that Fisher described how banks underestimate the rate of inflation and raise the interest rate too slowly. In similar terms Wicksell stated that the market rate always lags behind changes in the natural rate of interest. To put this remark in context, it is important to note that for Wicksell a change in the natural rate of interest was a more likely source of inflation than a change in the market rate of interest. An increase in the natural rate would generate the same pressure for higher prices as a lowering of the market rate of interest. The banks should now raise the loan rate to take away the pressure for inflation but they only reluctantly do so. According to Wicksell, the problem is that banks set their interest rates routinely. They are risk-averse and a change of the interest rate may have unforeseen consequences. Moreover, in a competitive banking system banks experience a kind of prisoner dilemma. The one to first raise its rates runs the risks of losing customers to its competitors. As a result, the market rate of interest will only adjust itself 'langsam und zögernd' to changes in the natural rate of interest (ibid., 110).

This issue of a lagged adjustment of interest rates is almost never discussed in modern interpretations of Wicksell's monetary theory. In contrast, he is seen as the originator of a period analysis that stresses the role of time and the forward-looking character of economic decisions. Ebeling (1997) is an example of those who stress the pioneering role of Wicksell in this regard. He argues that Wicksell used an abstract model consisting of two periods to analyze the causal sequence of events that generates the cumulative process. According to him, the essence of this model is that it produces real as well as nominal changes due to the effect of forced savings. A reduction of the market rate of interest stimulates entrepreneurs to begin two-year investment projects in excess of the planned savings of consumers. This causes an excess demand for consumers' goods and a rise of prices at the end of period one because productive resources have been moved to the production of intermediate products. Consumers are forced to save via higher consumer goods prices, an effect which allows the entrepreneurs to complete their two-year investment projects.

This dynamic interpretation of Wicksell may be criticized from different angles. In the first place, the notion of intertemporal equilibrium of this two-period model is meaningful, but it is also a weak conception. It suggests a two-period planning horizon for entrepreneurs, but entrepreneurs are also extremely myopic. They simply assume prices to remain constant, even when inflation repeats itself period after period. Also, Wicksell did not distinguish between ex ante and ex post decisions. That distinction was first made by Erik Lindahl and one may argue that the disequilibrium approach of the Swedish school owed more to the latter's investigation of the adjustment process of economic dynamics than to Wicksell's cumulative process.[25]

Second, there are important differences between Wicksell's account of the cycle and Austrian monetary business cycle theory. Austrians such as Mises and Hayek saw the cycle as a monetary phenomenon because they believed that changes of the monetary rate of interest were the main cause of cyclical fluctuations. Wicksell, on the other hand, ascribed the trade cycle to 'real causes independent of movements in commodity price, so that the latter become of only secondary importance' (Wicksell 1935, 209). These real causes were for instance the speed of 'technical and commercial advance' that manifested itself in the natural rate of interest. In short, it was the natural and not the monetary rate of interest that caused the cycle.[26]

Concerning the propagation of the cycle, Hayek put much effort in showing that the misalignment of investment and saving decisions affects the economy's capital structure and causes the real economic adjustments that we commonly associate with the different phases of the business cycle.[27] In Wicksell's work, real adjustments of the capital structure play a very minor role. In fact, the effect of forced savings in the two-period model of Wicksell's *Geldzins und Güterpreise* is the only place in which this argument appears. I therefore conclude that he anticipated some of the core elements of the Austrian cycle theory such as the distinction between the natural and market rate of interest and the concept of forced savings, but not its most distinctive feature which is the explanation of business cycle *dynamics* in terms of the elongation or contraction of the period of production (see also Siven 1997, 211–213).

In contrast, Wicksell stood closer to the classical tradition that treated the cycle as a purely nominal affair. He merely offered an intuitive explanation of the trade cycle, a phenomenon that according to him is related to price movements in 'good' and 'bad' times (Wicksell 1935, 209). This explanation highlights the importance that he attached to the lagged response of the market rate of interest. Like Fisher, he treated the general price level as a the connecting variable between two interest rates, in his case labelled the natural and market rate of interest. In his opinion, price changes were of crucial importance to the establishment of monetary equilibrium, for there was 'no other connection between the two than *variations in commodity prices* caused by the difference between them' (ibid., 206, italics in the original).[28] Wicksell used the metaphor of a spring ('Spiralfeder') to explain how the equilibrium dynamics of a monetary economy would change depending on the system's institutional set up. In a barter economy the spring would be 'kurz und stark' given that a difference between the monetary and natural rate of interest could not persist (Wicksell 1898, 125). But as credit money enters the scene and an increasing share of transactions proceeds through the channels of banks and other financial institutions, the spring between the two interest rates becomes longer and longer indicating increasing slackness of the price adjustments called forth by a disruption of monetary equilibrium.[29] Wicksell's version of the quantity theory was first and foremost an instrument to examine the impact of money and monetary institutions on the economy's capacity to maintain monetary equilibrium. In retrospect, Wicksell appears a more consistent successor to the classical monetarist tradition than his fellow travellers Marshall and Fisher who at some point felt that their thinking ran counter to the comparative static methodology that underpinned the quantity theory.

KEYNES, MONEY AND EQUILIBRIUM

In the interwar period economics found itself at a crossroads. By 1914 the quantity theory of money had blossomed into a fairly consistent and widely accepted body of doctrine.[30] The natural complement of this theory of the general price level was the neoclassical theory of consumer and producer behaviour, which had been highly successful in explaining the mechanics of economic exchange at the micro level. All in all, it seemed that neoclassical economics had brought economic science a significant step further, as it could now satisfactory deal with such issues as public finance, growth, distribution and international trade. However, there was one issue which still lacked adequate treatment and that was the short-term instability of the economy, the question of industrial fluctuations or business cycles. We have seen in the previous section that the neoclassicals tried to address this issue through the lense of the quantity theory, which implied that it was mainly seen as a nominal affair. Attempts by, for instance, Jevons to develop a real theory of the trade cycle ran into difficulties precisely because they ignored the monetary factor. In other words, what was called for was a new approach, one that integrated the real and monetary aspects of the business cycle.

The interwar period marked the transition to a business cycle theory along this line. Characteristic of this development was its diverse nature, for it comprised several schools of thought that adopted different and sometimes conflicting approaches to economic theory. In Austria Mises and Hayek developed a monetary theory of the business cycle that focussed on the dynamic changes of the economy's capital structure. In Sweden Lundberg, Lindahl, Ohlin and Myrdal introduced the ex ante – ex post distinction as a framework to analyze the misalignment of saving and investing. Finally, following the lead of Marshall, Cambridge economists like Lavington, Pigou, Hawtrey, Robertson and Keynes used specific market failures like fixed money wages and other lags to explain why disequilibrium between saving and investment was not automatically corrected, giving rise to the swings of the business cycle.[31]

However, the eclecticism of these approaches cannot conceal the fact that a number of common themes was at stake. In the first place, the aim of all schools was to develop a dynamic analysis of the business cycle. Here dynamics meant that explicit recognition was given to the leads and lags that exist between the development of economic variables like prices, incomes and output over time. The approach is therefore also known as sequence or period analysis. Secondly, money was seen as a crucial causal element for the explanation of the sequence of changes that comprise the business cycle. Money was therefore certainly not a veil that could be ignored because it did not belong to the set of variables that determine real equilibrium. This aspect distinguishes the monetary analysis of the 1920s and 1930s from the real analyses of the classical and neoclassical periods.[32] Thirdly, due to the influence of Wicksell, the saving-investment relationship was seen as the main theoretical framework for analyzing the causes of cyclical swings. That put the definition of monetary equilibrium at the heart of what may be called the 'monetary revolution' in the interwar period.

However, the surprising fact is that this revolution failed to materialize. The legacy of what Shackle (1967) called *The Years of High Theory* was a theoretical doctrine that is nowadays known as Keynesian orthodoxy. The key to this Keynesian victory was the IS-LM model, a general equilibrium model which treats money as inessential and is unable to address genuine dynamics due to its static nature. What explains this sudden shift of tactics? Why did economics not continue on what seemed such a promising road, namely the monetary explanation of the disequilibrium changes during the different phases of the business cycle? With IS-LM we are back in a world where equilibrium perpetually reigns and money is a form of transactions technology that leaves real equilibrium undisturbed. In other words, we re-enter the world of the classical dichotomy where neoclassical real equilibrium is assumed to explain relative prices, while the quantity theory dictates the conditions of monetary equilibrium which is only valid for the general price level.

I shall try to explain this victory of monetary equilibrium over monetary disequilibrium in two steps. Sticking to the theme of this chapter, the present section aims to explain the Keynesian victory by looking at the strengths of the static equilibrium model. Like many of his Cambridge colleagues, Keynes in the 1920s and 1930s tried to incorporate the lessons of Wicksell in a dynamic explanation of the business cycle. His *Treatise of Money* (1930) is considered an example of the sequence analysis that also occupied his Swedish and Austrian contemporaries. In his *General Theory of Employment, Interest and Money* (1936) he still professed to treat money in an essential way and to explain why unemployment is a feature of a monetary economy. However, the end result was not what one would have expected, for the GT reinvokes the static equilibrium method. Kohn (1986) even calls the abandonment of sequence analysis in favour of the method of equilibrium the true nature of Keynes's revolution. In this section, I shall discuss the rationale of this surprising turnaround, which led to an unhappy marriage between money and equilibrium.

The natural complement of this issue is the question why the focus of the Swedish and Austrian schools on the dynamics of monetary disequilibrium failed to establish a new standard for macroeconomic theory. Their efforts to develop the dynamic approach as a viable alternative to static equilibrium theory are discussed in the next chapter.

Money and the Need for Economic Dynamics

What typifies monetary analysis if we look at the use of the equilibrium concept? In Chapter 2 I have argued that real equilibrium can be defined as a repetitive flow, a situation in which behaviour is unchanging over time. In such as situation it is as if production is instantaneous and current production is immediately consumed. To facilitate this cycle, the circulation of money is precisely suited to real activity and does not constrain it in any way. Given that we are dealing with an unchanging and endless cycle of events, it is only natural to assume that expectations are fulfilled and that there are no windfall profits or losses.[33]

This definition of the repetitive flow allows us to analyze the conditions of (stationary) equilibrium by assuming that economic exchange takes place in real terms, that is without the intervention of money as a medium of exchange. Here money is indeed a veil and nothing is lost by drawing this veil aside. What remains is a system of virtual barter where equilibrium emerges as the result of the frictionless and instantaneous exchange of goods for goods. The nature of this equilibrium is static or stationary because it consists of a cycle of events that is unchanging over time. This characteristic makes it unsuited to address truly dynamic questions which involve the disruption of the repetitive flow and the movement of economic variables outside of equilibrium.

In monetary analysis the situation is entirely different. If we give money a meaningful role, then exchange is no longer frictionless, which means that the medium of exchange must exert some influence on the process of exchange and hence on relative prices. In that situation we can no longer study the conditions of equilibrium by assuming that the economy operates as a virtual barter system that always resides in real equilibrium. Furthermore, with a store of value expenditures can be postponed, which means that production and consumption or incomes and expenditures need no longer instantaneously match. This means that the introduction of money also necessitates explicit consideration of the leads and lags in the economic process. Accordingly, the subject matter of monetary analysis is *changing* flows of money incomes and expenditures that may or may not converge on the repetitive flow that characterizes real equilibrium.

The 1920s and 1930s saw the development of monetary analysis along this line. In general terms, the aim of this monetary analysis was to study the stability of the economic system with the real equilibrium of classical and neoclassical economics as the central point of reference. This equilibrium signified an ideal that would never obtain in reality. The actual economy would deviate from this ideal position because real or monetary shocks could shift either the actual economy or the position of equilibrium itself. While the veil of money could be safely ignored in characterizing the nature of the ideal equilibrium position, monetary factors were of the essence in understanding the movement of the economy toward or around equilibrium.

This aim of monetary analysis gave monetary policy a clear task, namely to prevent the disruption of monetary equilibrium and to help the actual economy to track real equilibrium as closely as possible. This was called a policy of neutral money because it assumed that in equilibrium a monetary economy operated just like the exchange mechanism of a barter economy.[34] The schools of thought that contributed to the neutral money debate widely disagreed about the degree of state intervention needed to maintain neutral money, but these differences shall not detain us here. For the moment what matters is that the development of monetary analysis in the interwar years put the definition of monetary equilibrium and the dynamic analysis of changes outside equilibrium at the heart of the economic debate.

Keynes's *Treatise on Money* (1930) is an outstanding example of this type of monetary analysis. In the first place, the theoretical structure of the *Treatise on Money* (henceforth: TM) has a typical Wickellian flavour. Keynes defined monetary equilibrium on the basis of Wicksell's distinction between the natural and monetary rate of interest.[35] This means that his theory also makes a sharp distinction between the nominal changes that accompany monetary disequilibrium and the real effects of that disruption that constitute the motions of the business cycle. In the second place, the TM is an example of sequence analysis, because it addresses the dynamics of the business cycle in a step-by-step approach that attributes a central role to expectations and the passage of time.

The main ingredient of the equilibrating mechanism of the TM is the saving-investment relationship. Following Wicksell, Keynes (1930, 120–124) defined the conditions for monetary equilibrium in two so-called fundamental equations. These equations differentiate between short-term and long-term prices to distinguish the permanent causes of price changes from temporary ones.[36] The economy resides in monetary equilibrium if the two price levels coincide. The long-period equilibrium norm is given by what Keynes called the money-rate efficiency earnings of the factors of production, while the actual purchasing power oscillates below or above this equilibrium level as the cost of current investment is running ahead of, or falling behind, savings. In this manner, Keynes explained why the equality of saving and investment is of crucial importance to the maintenance of monetary equilibrium.

Keynes incorporated the element of time in this static framework by giving profits a dynamic role. They are what he called 'the main spring of action' and explain how entrepreneurs respond to price changes and effect transitions between equilibrium states (ibid., 141). Profits are able to play this dynamic role due to Keynes's peculiar definition of profits in the TM. In equilibrium, entrepreneurs are assumed to earn a normal reward, but this reward may not be called a profit. Keynes defined profits as windfall gains that only arise in a state of disequilibrium. They are realized gains that arise when the current-sale proceeds exceed the cost of production and are thereby equal to the difference between saving and investment.[37] In other words, profits signal the positive or negative disappointment of entrepreneurs about the level of their income which consists of the normal reward plus an unexpected component. It is this latter factor which upsets monetary equilibrium and becomes the cause of the real adjustments that accompany it.

However, the two fundamental equations assume a given level of output and hence determine nominal income. They are static equations which means that the dynamic adjustments referred to above cannot be addressed as part of this theoretical framework. Keynes investigated output changes in a second, separate stage of the analysis. We shall later see that Keynes's dissatisfaction with this construction was an important reason why he reformulated his monetary theory in the *General Theory* (henceforth GT). In the TM he started his dynamic analysis by assuming a constant level of aggregate output. In the first stage of analysis the fundamental equations were used to investigate the types of inflation that occurred as result of monetary disequilibrium during the different phases of the business cycle.[38] The second stage of the analysis informally discusses the impact of these changes on the investment decisions of the business community. For Keynes these behavioural adjustments were the motive force of the changes in the levels of output and employment during the cycle.[39]

The exact sequence of events during the cycle need not be discussed at this time, but a number of issues warrants further attention. The first one is the role of expectations. We have seen that in Keynes's theory (unanticipated) profits are the mainspring of action, so that changes in output and employment levels take place in the stages that Keynes characterized as profit inflations and deflations. Keynes described such real effects as a kind of chain reaction, which implied that expectations would endogenously change during the cycle. Thus an important part of the propagation mechanism was the fact that financial opinion could turn bearish or bullish as a result of a decrease or increase in investment and output. Keynes even discussed the case where pessimism would spread throughout the economy generating a bust as a self-fulfilling prophesy (ibid., 217–230).

However, it has to be remarked that Keynes's analysis of such sequences of price and output adjustments in the TM were not logical deductions based on a solid set of first principles. He merely discussed what he considered as typical examples of the trade cycle (ibid., 262). He argued that many other schemes are conceivable, given that circumstances are likely to change from case to case and depending on the origin of a the cycle. In other words, for Keynes the sequence analysis of the business cycle was a heuristic device, which could help the economist to discuss the several phases in an informal way. In his view, business cycle analysis was a kind of art that depended on the plausibility of the analysis and not on its truth content to be determined by logical or empirical assessment of the case at hand. This aspect of his approach explains the lack of theoretical rigour that marks the TM which, following the publication of the TM, provoked severe criticism from different corners of the economics profession.[40]

Keynes's approach of economics as an art may explain why the main innovation of the TM went largely unnoticed. In the TM Keynes developed a rudimentary portfolio-balance approach to monetary theory explaining why the interest rate could fail to coordinate saving and investment appropriately.[41] He began his analysis of the interest mechanism by differentiating between the decision to save current income instead of consuming it and the decision to loan savings to investors (Keynes 1930, 127 and 154–158). This second step reflects Keynes's insight that in a capitalist economy the public has the choice between a variety of financial assets, such as bonds, securities and assets, to determine the form in which savings must command future consumption. In deciding what to do with savings, a person thus considers the yields on assets that compete with money and balances the advantages of keeping money assets and buying investments.[42] Keynes did not fully work out this idea in the TM but the message was clear. The interest rate does not automatically equate the supply and demand for loanable funds, as the decision to invest savings partly depends on asset prices and speculative sentiments.[43] As a result, monetary disequilibrium in terms of an unbalance between saving and investment could well persist for a while with negative consequences for output and employment.[44] Viewed in these terms, it is clear that in spite of Keynes's later disappointment, the TM was an important stepping stone towards the development of the GT.

This conclusion provides us with a vital clue to interpret the nature of the equilibrium concept used by Keynes in the TM. The fundamental equations show that the TM was well rooted in the tradition of the quantity theory of money. This characteristic leads commentators to interpret Keynes's monetary equilibrium in the classical fashion. As Barens (1989, 112) puts it, 'in the *Treatise*, the actual behaviour of the economy is analysed, quite traditionally, in terms of the short period deviations from a full-employment long-period position'.

In my opinion, there is a very important footnote to that conclusion if we consider how Keynes applied the notion of monetary equilibrium in the TM. The conventional view of equilibrium described by Barens suggests that the long period equilibrium provides a stable point (or a point of gravitation) around which short-term developments will fluctuate. However, Keynes described the relationship between long-term and short-term equilibrium prices exactly the other way around. He believed that during the trade cycle the natural rate of interest was always the initiating factor due to its inherent instability.[45] Laidler (1999, 144) shows that this assumption places Keynes firmly in the Cambridge tradition. Like his colleagues, Keynes assumed that fluctuations in the rate of investment in fixed capital were the main component of changes in the demand for output.[46] In his view, this implied that the level of output was liable to violent fluctuations due to changes in what he called the influence of mob psychology (Keynes 1930, vol. II, 324).

The typical trade cycle would thus see a change in the natural rate of interest which upsets monetary equilibrium. The market rate of interest would try to catch up with this adjustment, but it did so with a lag because of the workings of the monetary system. In the words of Keynes (1930, vol. II, 182):

> I think that the market rate of interest . . . is very 'sticky' in relation to the natural rate of interest . . . [W]hen savings are abundant or deficient in relation to the demand for them for investment at the pre-existing levels of interest, the rate does not adjust itself to the new situation quick enough to maintain equilibrium between saving and investment.

The result was that the market rate of interest would overshoot the equilibrium level giving rise to the typical swings of the business cycle.[47]

This view of the nature of monetary equilibrium gives monetary policy a clear task. In the early 1930s Keynes was an advocate of a counter-cyclical policy by the central banks (Laidler 1999, 146–154). He believed that properly timed bank-rate variations would be sufficient to stabilize the economy under normal circumstances. If the market was not quick enough to close the gap between saving and investment, then the monetary authorities should push the market rate of interest in the right direction and ensure that it would follow the changes in the natural rate as closely as possible. By the same token, Keynes argued that open-market operations were a weapon powerful enough to deal with deep depression, unless international complications inhibited their deployment. All in all, it is clear that he saw money as a crucial element of the disequilibrium dynamics of the economic system, which made the central bank the guardian of monetary equilibrium. We shall later see that the Austrians, one of the other schools discussing the dynamics of monetary disequilibrium, reached exactly opposite conclusions concerning the desirability of active monetary management.

Keynes's Turn Towards Static Equilibrium Theory

Keynes's transition from the TM to the GT is difficult to assess and gives rise to conflicting interpretations. On the one hand, in the years following the publication of the TM he often expressed his dissatisfaction with this book and presented the GT as a revolutionary contribution to economics.[48] On the other hand, in the introduction to the GT Keynes presented his new book as a 'natural evolution' of his thought (Keynes 1936, xxii). Like in the TM he stated that his subject of analysis was the monetary economy, but that his emphasis had shifted from the 'traditional' analysis of price changes that marked the TM to the investigation of changes in the levels of employment and output. In addition, there are numerous references to the TM in the GT which reflect on the level of agreement between the two books. Keynes even claimed that the theory of effective demand, the main theoretical innovation of the GT, was a tool that fitted the theoretical corpus of the TM (ibid., 78). The only thing that was lacking in the TM, one reads in these cases, was clarity due to a confusing and incomplete exposition of arguments.

Viewed in these terms, one should almost forget that the GT adopts a method that radically breaks with the approach that Keynes had followed before. In the GT he abandoned the sequence analysis of the TM in favour of the equilibrium method. The key to this change was a new set of definitions for income, saving and investment that made saving and investment identically the same. In the TM Keynes had stressed disequilibrium between saving and investment as the main cause of monetary disequilibrium and the price dynamics that followed it. In the GT, adjustments of this kind were simply impossible because saving and investment were assumed to be equal by definition. Keynes never reflected on the consequences of this change of method for the analysis of a monetary economy. He even suggested that the analysis of the aggregate levels of employment and output in terms of the theory of effective demand could also be done using the definitions of the TM (ibid., 78). He thereby completely ignored the tension that may exist between the assumption of equilibrium and the analysis of a monetary economy. The results of this neglect were far-reaching. The GT set the stage for a 'revolution' in macroeconomics that favoured the use of the static equilibrium method and swept the dynamic analysis of rival schools in monetary thought aside.

There are two main reasons why Keynes abandoned the dynamic analysis of the TM in favour of the equilibrium method: first, Keynes's dissatisfaction with the TM and, second, the fact that he wanted to criticize 'classical economics' from within by showing that it was internally inconsistent.

In the first place, Keynes's dissatisfaction with the TM focussed on the separate analysis of the nominal and real effects of monetary disequilibrium. The fundamental equations only stated the conditions of equilibrium in nominal terms and assumed a given level of output. This was the reason why the TM could not thoroughly deal with the effects of changes in the level of output (ibid., xxii). Keynes could have remedied this lacuna by rewriting the conditions of equilibrium and introducing explicit linkages between price and output changes. This would have required a truly intertemporal definition of equilibrium, which recognized the leads and lags of economic changes. It appears that Keynes toyed with this idea, but that he believed that a definition of this kind was unworkable and would lead to complex theories that did not suit his goals.

The fundamental objection that Keynes developed in the 1930s to the further development of macroeconomics on the basis of sequence analysis is clearly explained in correspondence with Bertil Ohlin, one of the leading members of the Swedish School. He explained to Ohlin that he had written 'many chapters along what were evidently the Swedish lines' but that he had 'scrapped the lot' and felt that his new treatment was much safer from the logical point of view. He stated that his reason for giving up was that he failed to establish a definite unit of time that one needs to make the leads and lags in sequence analysis explicit. He found that the solution to that problem only led to very artificial constructions that prevented him from stating his theory in precise terms.[49] As Kohn (1986, 1204) puts it, it was Keynes the mathematician who abandoned sequence analysis because he recognized that it would lead to intractable problems.

However, secondly, Keynes also had another side. Keynes the economist was not just an academic writer, but perhaps first and foremost someone who was actively engaged in the political debate. This had made him acutely aware of the powers of persuasion. According to Keynes, in economics debates were not concluded on the basis of watertight logical conclusions, but by convincing one's opponent of the plausibility of a certain view. In this process the choice of the right economic model was of the upmost importance, for economics was 'a science of thinking in terms of models joined to the art of choosing models which are relevant to the contemporary world'.[50] It is clear that the TM failed in this regard, because the economic situation had changed drastically since the it was conceived. But probably equally important was what Skidelsky (1992, 439) describes as its 'artistic failure'. The TM pursued monetary theory along the traditional lines of the quantity theory. As a result, the economics audience did not appreciate the heretical nature of the TM because its theory was not presented as an explicit challenge to the orthodox way of doing economics (ibid., 442). In the GT he tried avoid this pitfall by openly attacking the methodology of what he called classical economics. In his view, classical economics failed to explain the behaviour of modern economies because it abstracted from money, which ruled out all the problems created by its existence. Monetary forces were not temporary disturbances to placid waters; they entered fundamentally into the determination of equilibrium states. There was no better way to bring this message across than by presenting an equilibrium explanation of the monetary economy, which had the combined benefit of being relatively simple and focussing directly on the main issue at stake.[51] The introduction of an intertemporal definition of equilibrium, like the Swedes and the Austrians had done, would just have diverted the attention by raising difficult questions about the choice of the unit period and so on. In other words, in Keynes's view the disequilibrium approach to monetary theory lacked persuasive power.

Keynes launched his attack on classical economics by showing that it lacked a proper theory of supply and demand for output as a whole. This failure was due to Say's law which states that aggregate supply and demand will always be equal, assuming that markets have sufficient time to adjust to the underlying real causes of equilibrium. In Keynes's view, this restricted the scope of classical theory because it was only valid for the special case of full employment (Keynes 1936, 26). Keynes argued that a more general account of equilibrium theory could be given, which included the possibility of unused resources and hence of unemployment. This general theory assumed that while competitive pressures would be able to equilibrate supply and demand in a single market, a coordinating device of this kind was lacking with regard to the behaviour of supply and demand for the economy as a whole.

The attack on Say's law took place along several lines. Keynes first showed that the classical treatment of the aggregate supply function was wrong because it pegged real equilibrium at the position of full employment, which by definition ruled out the possibility of deficient effective demand. Secondly, he rejected the loanable funds explanation of the interest rate, which secured the establishment of equilibrium on the goods market through the equality of savings and investment.

The GT opens with a frontal attack on what Keynes called the postulates of classical economics, such as the assumption that the real wage equals both the marginal productivity of labour and the marginal disutility of labour. This had the unfortunate effect of suggesting that Keynes was merely explaining disequilibrium in the labour market in terms of market failures at the microeconomic level. But the true nature of his rejection of the classical theory of employment concerns the fallacy of composition. Keynes believed that for the economy as a whole the marginal disutility of labour would not equal the real wage, because changes in factor rewards have a feedback on the level of aggregate spending. The key to this feedback mechanism lies in Keynes's definition of effective demand. This is the aggregate income which the entrepreneurs expect to receive from the amount of current employment which they decide to give (ibid., 25 and 55). This means that for the economy as a whole the level of employment is determined by effective demand. But through the state of technology the level of employment is also related to the real wage and this connection establishes the causal link between effective demand and the real wage rate. In Keynes's view of the macro economy, the real wage is an endogenous variable, partly determined by effective demand, and not an exogenous one pegging the labour market at the position of full employment.[52]

The practical implication of this conclusion is that if the propensity to consume and the rate of new investment result in a deficient effective demand, the actual level of employment will fall short of the supply of labour potentially available at the existing real wage; the economy gets stuck in an unemployment equilibrium (ibid., 30, 289). This occurs at a wage rate that exceeds the marginal disutility of labour, which is why in this case Keynes defined unemployment as 'involuntary' (Keynes 1936, 15, 30, 128, 289). The possibility of unemployment in this micro-macro framework so stresses the importance of the equilibrating mechanism behind the constituent elements of effective demand, consumption and investment expenditures. Why does aggregate demand cause production to fall below the full employment level?

This question concerns the conditions for equilibrium on the goods market. In the GT consumption demand is determined by current income and the propensity to consume, which Keynes described as a psychological law. This means that investment demand needs to equal the amount of savings in order to clear the goods market. In classical theory, it is assumed that the interest rate automatically establishes equilibrium between savings and investment, given the level of aggregate income. Keynes disabled this equilibrating mechanism by assuming that saving and investment depend on different causes and not solely on the interest rate. In his scheme, the amount of savings is determined by the fraction of current income that individuals decide not to consume (one minus the propensity to consume), but investment demand depends on *prospective* income and therefore introduces the element of expectations and uncertainty.

The precise details of Keynes's theory of investment[53] shall not detain us here, because the essence of the principle of effective demand is the macroeconomic insight that aggregate saving and investment are necessarily equal.[54] This means that in the Keynesian system the equilibrium level of income may land anywhere, which therefore also applies to the quantity of employment demanded. Income and employment are indeterminate because they depend on a factor that we cannot explain in economic terms, the expectations that underlie current investment (Garretsen 1991, 23–35). In this system, there is no equilibrium tendency towards a full employment level of aggregate output. A boost to investment increases effective demand and employment and pulls the economy out of a slump like Baron Munchhausen who escaped from a swamp by pulling himself up by his hair. Conversely, a decrease in investment demand has the capacity to push the economy into a depression without calling forth counteracting forces to remedy the lack of effective demand. Any level of aggregate income and output must therefore be termed an equilibrium position and employment 'is what it is', as Keynes (1937, 122) put it, due to the uncertain and volatile nature of the expectations that govern investment.

This brief exploration of the theory of effective demand leads to the conclusion that the definition of monetary equilibrium in the GT is radically different from that of the TM (Kohn 1986). The most notable difference is that in the GT equilibrium does not operate as a point of attraction, which was the meaning of the natural rate of interest (the long term equilibrium price level) in the TM. The practical implication of this change was that Keynes could not address the stability of the economic system as the main question of his monetary analysis. Keynes's turn towards static equilibrium theory in the GT robbed him of the tools that are needed to explain the development of the monetary economy over time. There were no leads or lags between the variables of the system nor a tendency towards a point of attraction that could be strengthened or corrected by means of monetary management. In other words, this new view had implications too for the potential role of economic policy. Instead of being able to improve stability in order to reduce inappropriate fluctuations about real equilibrium, policy was now presumed to be able to determine the position of equilibrium itself.

The Impact of IS-LM

As is well-known, the impact of Keynes's static formulation of monetary equilibrium was enormous. Able mathematicians like Hicks were quick to assimilate the theory of effective demand, in conjunction with the theory of liquidity preference, into the general equilibrium framework. The result was the IS-LM model, which depicts Keynes's unemployment equilibrium as a special case of a more general theory, which also allow us to derive the contested classical results. Later, the debate focussed on the necessity of a fixed money wage for the existence of a Keynesian equilibrium over time. Keynes himself had initially assumed fixed money wages as a 'simplification' (Keynes 1936, 27), but he also stated that he would dispense with this assumption at a later stage of the analysis. However, the IS-LM model showed that a fixed money wage was a *sine qua non* of his analysis (Kohn 1986, 1216). It then appeared that the unemployment problem of Keynes's monetary economy was not a fundamental one. On the contrary, all that was needed to derive the Keynesian results was a market failure that prevented the labour market from clearing. This type of analysis could also be conducted in terms of a real equilibrium model like IS-LM with the added feature of a fixed money wage. All in all, the IS-LM model fully capitalized on the equilibrium method that Keynes adopted in the GT. As Hicks put it in his famous article on *Mr. Keynes and the Classics*, 'The *General Theory of Employment* is a useful book; but it is neither the beginning nor the end of Dynamic Economics' (Hicks 1937[1982], 115).

In a subsequent stage of development multiplier-accelerator models would add a dynamic quality to Keynesian analysis. These models introduced leads and lags between variables over time by using difference equations to formulate multiplier-accelerator interaction. This allowed precise mathematical analysis of the business cycle in a manner that resembled the period analysis of the Swedes and Austrians in the 1930s. However, multiplier-accelerator models did rely on the notion that output is determined by a level of aggregate demand equal to the sum of consumption and investment. It was this feature that gave them a typical Keynesian twist and in time this type of analysis came to be taught as a natural dynamic extension of IS-LM analysis.

However, multiplier-accelerator models had trouble dealing with money. The analysis of the cycle in terms of multiplier-accelerator interaction could be conducted entirely in real terms. Thus the role of money often came in as an afterthought.[55] In order to accomplish that link the LM-curve had to be accounted for and that could be done by assuming that it was horizontal. As Laidler (1999, 336) stresses, in that way one cut out any feedback from the monetary system that might disturb the smooth operation of whatever linear-difference-equation dynamics were to be analyzed. Thus even with explicit dynamics it appeared that the role of money was not so fundamental as Keynes had claimed it to be.

Kohn (1986) attributes this failure of the Keynesian revolution to a basic error in Keynes's thinking. In his view, Keynes had tried to do what was undoable, namely to reconcile money and equilibrium. In order to explain the role of money, one needs to introduce uncertainty or specific market failures, assumptions that are incompatible with the conditions of equilibrium, which requires perfect knowledge, plan coordination or market clearing on all markets et cetera. This internal inconsistency of the GT was quickly resolved by those who further developed Keynesian economics. They dropped the monetary factor and retained the assumption of equilibrium as the foundation of their work. Thus, the attacks by Keynes and his followers on neoclassical monetary analysis had the paradoxical effect of making monetary analysis hopelessly unfashionable.

Of course, we cannot hold Keynes directly accountable for the development of Keynes economics after 1936. He only briefly commented upon Hicks (1937) with the outlines of the IS-LM model and never used the multiplier or the accelerator to construct a dynamic mathematical version of his theory. In that sense, it is odd to speak of Keynes's 'failure', as Kohn does with regard to his choice to study the workings of a monetary economy in terms of an equilibrium method. The inconsistency of money and equilibrium is typical of the general equilibrium method that is the starting point of the IS-LM model. But Keynes never adopted general equilibrium analysis with its assumptions about market clearing and perfect knowledge. For Keynes, equilibrium signified a state of rest, a position in which there are no endogenous forces to change the current values of economic variables (Asimakopoulos 1992). This is a definition of equilibrium that can be reconciled with phenomena such as trading at false prices that in the setting of a general equilibrium model are classified as disequilibrium events. This is why Patinkin (1992) prefers to speak of disequilibrium analysis when he discusses Keynes's method of analysis in the GT.

Patinkin's judgement shows that a debate about the method of the GT runs the risk of becoming a quarrel about words. The meaning of what is called equilibrium or disequilibrium depends on the substance of one's analysis. In the case of Keynes, the linkage with Marshall is of the utmost importance (Patinkin 1976). Marshall had shown that the assumption of equilibrium could be used to deal with the element of time in economics. By choosing a proper time period, one could study the price mechanism of a specific market for given supply and demand curves. This partial equilibrium approach required that the period under investigation was short enough to assume that the general conditions of this market (tastes, technology et cetera) would remain unchanged (Marshall 1920, 366). In short:

> The element of time is a chief cause of those difficulties in economic investigations which make it necessary for man with his limited powers to go step by step; breaking up a complex question, studying one bit at a time, and at last combining his partial solutions into a more or less complete solution of the whole riddle. In breaking it up, he segregates those disturbing causes, whose wanderings happen to be inconvenient, for the time in a pond called *Ceteris Paribus*.

Keynes adopted the same method in the GT to deal with an issue which he felt was grossly neglected in classical economics, namely the influence of uncertainty on economic decisions.[56] He highlighted this problem in his answer to the early reviewers of the GT (Keynes 1937[1973]). He argued that 'Ricardian analysis' either ignored the influence of expectations or reduced knowledge to some kind of certainty equivalent. In his opinion, this abstraction was in conflict with reality, which in itself may be excusable but not in this case because uncertainty about future events is closely related to the use of money and thus to the operation of a monetary economy. Assuming perfect knowledge, classical economics could not explain the use of money as a store of wealth, for money was the only asset that did not yield some interest or profit. Thus, Keynes exclaimed, 'Why should anyone outside a lunatic asylum wish to use money as a store of wealth?' (ibid., 115–116).

For Keynes money could act as a store of wealth because it allows us to deal with uncertain knowledge. He described the possession of money as a 'barometer of the degree of our distrust of our own calculations and conventions concerning the future' (ibid.). According to him, the demand for money is related to the fact that it is the most liquid of all assets, which means that it gives us the freedom to quickly respond to changing circumstances.[57] In other words, the possession of money does have a yield, but this yield is determined by yet unforeseen future events. Each investor will try to balance this expected marginal yield to the marginal cost of holding money, which is the interest rate. This is the basis of Keynes's liquidity preference theory of interest, because 'the premium which we require to make us part with money is the measure of the degree of our disquietude' (Keynes 1937[1973], 116).

The fact that the interest rate depends on uncertain expectations makes the volume of investment a highly volatile determinant of output and employment. Keynes dealt with this problem in Marshallian fashion by applying partial equilibrium analysis. The theory of effective demand is defined for a very short period because this time frame was sufficient to show the consequence of the fact that investment demand depends on current income as a convention.[58] In this manner, Keynes could explain why output and employment are so liable to fluctuation (ibid., 121). For this exercise, long term expectations could be assumed constant, but Keynes relaxed this condition when he discussed the effect of expectations on the investment function in Chapter 12 of the GT and addressed the motions of the trade cycle (in Chapter 22). All in all, Keynes argued that it depended on the problem at hand which variables are taken as given and which are not (Keynes 1936, 247).

The meaning of this brief digression into the partial equilibrium method of the GT is to support the claim that Keynes considered uncertain knowledge essential in order to explain the role of money. It is therefore absurd to argue that Keynes committed an error because he developed an equilibrium theory of a monetary economy. It is true that in general equilibrium analysis the use of money is difficult to reconcile with the conditions of equilibrium, but in partial equilibrium analysis this is not the case. Keynes applied partial equilibrium analysis to reduce the complexities of time and uncertain knowledge in economics to manageable proportions. The equilibrium assumption allowed him to rule out any source of change as a first approximation. The dynamic effects of uncertainty and investment could then be analyzed by relaxing this assumption in a step-by-step analysis that consisted in formulating a ceteris paribus clause that was appropriate for the problem at hand.

This approach allows us to explain where the Keynesian revolution went wrong. In the aftermath of the GT, the crucial choice was not that between money and equilibrium, as Kohn contends, but between general equilibrium analysis and partial equilibrium analysis. A general equilibrium formulation of the theory of effective demand like IS-LM had the benefit of logical consistency. It had a theoretical structure that could be reduced to first principles, which allows one to check the validity of one's conclusions as logical deductions. A partial equilibrium model lacks this transparency because it crucially depends on what is assumed constant in the ceteris paribus clause. This introduces a subjective element into the analysis. Without decisive empirical evidence, it is inevitable that one disagrees about which variables to assume constant and which not. This is exactly what Keynes meant when he wrote to Harrod (Letter to Harrod of 4 July 1938 in Keynes 1973, 296–297):

> Economics is a science of thinking in terms of models joined to the art of choosing models which are relevant to the contemporary world. It is compelled to be this because, unlike the typical natural science, the material to which it is applied is, in too many respects, not homogenous through time. The object of a model is to segregate the semi-permanent or relatively constant factors from those which are transitory or fluctuating so as to develop a logical way of thinking about the latter, and of understanding the time sequences to which they give rise in particular cases.

The partial equilibrium method proved the Achilles heel of Keynes's theory of effective demand. As Hodgson (1985) argues, the GT suffered from an uneasy juxtaposition of the determinism of Keynes's post-Marshallian model of the economy with the indeterminacy of expectations. Theoretically, this tension could elicit two kinds of responses from the economics community. The first was to reject the undetermined part as being too difficult or simply irrelevant and to erect a holistic determinism as that of the IS-LM model. The second response was to regard the indeterminacy of expectations as the essential and all-encompassing explanatory variable of economic activity, as the Austrians have done. Garretsen (1991, 43) argues that without a further analysis of how economic agents deal with the indeterminacy of expectations caused by uncertainty, Keynes's economics was prone to a 'takeover' by either one of these extreme positions.

However, history has shown that Hayek and the Austrian school were unable to counter the Keynesian avalanche (McCormick 1992). Modern macroeconomics has been thoroughly reshaped by the rational expectations hypothesis, which is just another version of holistic determinism. The Keynesians of our time have only recently begun to realize that they need to reintroduce the element of uncertainty into economic analysis, or 'fundamental indeterminacy' as Garretsen calls it, if they want to build a new future for monetary analysis along the lines of Keynes.

THE CHALLENGE FOR MONETARY THEORY

Keynes's general theory focussed on the money economy seen as a whole. However, that did not prevent him from thoroughly discussing the functions and properties of money from a microeconomic perspective in chapter 17 of the GT. The loophole of his approach consisted in connecting these two analytical levels: how does individual behaviour relate to the changes in macroeconomic variables and, *vice versa*, can macroeconomic behaviour be explained in terms of individual choice making? These questions formed the substance of the microfoundations debate in macroeconomics that started in the 1960s (Weintraub 1979 and Van Ees and Garretsen 1990).

An important driver behind the microfoundations puzzle was the development of neoclassical general equilibrium analysis, which in the post war period became the standard approach in microeconomic theory. General equilibrium analysis forms the core of modern theories of consumer and producer behaviour, but is also a theory of the economy as a whole, discussing the feasibility of supply and demand equilibrium on all market simultaneously. Thus, assuming that money acts as the medium of exchange and that one of these markets is the money market, it is unavoidable that general equilibrium analysis raises the question of the integration of value theory and the theory of money.

This section discusses the challenge that is posed by this problem to contemporary monetary theory. I shall start this query by first briefly looking into the history of this problem. How did the pioneers of general equilibrium analysis integrate money into their analysis? Secondly, I shall discuss the problems and some of the answers that haunt the integration of monetary theory and the theory of value in modern economic analysis. Finally, I ask whether modern equilibrium analysis still condemns money to being a kind of veil. This question bring us back to the starting point of this chapter: Does money have real effects and what is the nature of monetary equilibrium?

Money in the Development of General Equilibrium Analysis

The tension between the role of money in the theory of the general price level and the theory of value respectively was already apparent in Walras's own statement of general equilibrium theory. The name of Walras is generally associated with general equilibrium analysis. It is not well-known that he was also a very able monetary theorist who presented a precise statement of the quantity theory of money, including among other things a mathematical specification of the cash balance mechanism long before Fisher developed his famous equation of exchange. It is in that sense not surprising that Walras devoted much effort to include money in the general equilibrium framework. He dealt with several functions of money in this context and came on the verge of achieving an integrated approach of value and monetary theory.[59] However, Van Daal and Jolink (1993, 105) argue that the treatment of his different monetary models was so confusing that Walras nor his followers recognized the fundamental implication of his work: the real and monetary sectors are strongly interrelated and should be modelled in a comprehensive theory. In contrast, Walras believed that the results of his monetary models converged upon the conclusions of his real analysis, leading him to conclude that the monetary factor could as well be dropped. Accordingly, he stated that the quantity theory of money should be used to explain the value of money and retained this monetary dichotomy throughout his career (Van Daal and Jolink 1993, 93).

The later pioneers of neoclassical general equilibrium analysis did not fare much better. From the start, Cassel (1927) recognized the need to include the monetary factor in the treatment of the theory of value, but he failed to explain what role money should play in a general equilibrium model of exchange. He merely postulated the existence of money and felt that he was entitled to do so because a comprehensive theory of all economic events was in his eyes simply impossible (Cassel 1927, 43). In the real economy all events are interrelated, which according to Cassel meant that one had to partition the analysis in 'different chapters'. He argued that the explanation of the general price level deserved a chapter of its own and strictly separated his analysis of the quantity of money from the general equilibrium explanation of (nominal) price formation.

Hicks (1939) was keenly aware of the fact that the appointment of a *numeraire* or standard of value in general equilibrium analysis does not mean that one has introduced genuine money into the system. This 'shadow money', as he called it, is merely a commodity with no other quality than that it forms an object of desire, like all other commodities. Nevertheless, Hicks believed that the inclusion of shadow money was validated by the results of his general equilibrium analysis. It allowed him to quickly produce results that 'have a good prospect of being true for a monetary economy, even if they are not the whole truth' (Hicks 1939, 59). In the dynamic part of his *Value and Capital* (1939) Hicks extensively discussed the motives for holding money, which he summarized in a function that linked the demand for money to the interest rate and the volume of investment in the near future. He then addressed the question of the stability of general equilibrium in terms of the elasticity of expectations.[60] This could only succeed when he assumed that the expected prices of a specific commodity are only affected by the current price of that same commodity, not by other current prices (ibid., 257).[61] This assumption is at odds with the general equilibrium nature of his analysis.

Patinkin (1956) put the integration of monetary and value theory once more on the agenda and gained wide recognition for his solution of this problem, which linked real cash balances and consumption in the IS-LM model. However, he was well aware of the fundamental problem of explaining the role of money in a general equilibrium model. He observed that, by assumption, no transactions are completed until the auctioneer determines the equilibrium set of prices. Hence, no rational individual will have a desire to hold money balances. Patinkin circumvented this problem by using what he considered highly unrealistic assumptions, such as using an exogenous random process to explain the timing of payments of individuals.

He justified this strategy by evoking the methodological defence of Friedman (1953): a theory cannot be tested by the realism of its assumptions. The proper way to judge the merit of a theory is to assess the accuracy of its predictions. Accordingly, he claimed that his theory 'explained' the role of money in a real economy, for it implies that:

> individuals have a positive demand for money balances, that the extent of this demand is dependent upon the price level and rate of interest . . . All of these implications are in accordance with our observations of the real world. Conversely, the extent to which the neglect of dynamic or uncertain expectations makes our model unrealistic can be determined only by the extent to which there are real phenomena which cannot be explained by our model (Patinkin 1956, 87).

It is interesting that Patinkin refers to the positive demand for money balances as one of the facts that is accurately predicted by his model, because it is this aspect that would prove the Achilles heel of his monetary general equilibrium. In his famous critique of Patinkin's theory, Hahn (1965) showed that Patinkin's model always has a general equilibrium in which fiat money is worthless. This means that it is not enough to demonstrate the existence of general equilibrium, because this knowledge does not establish the existence of a monetary equilibrium, that is an equilibrium in which the real value of money is positive. The conclusion must be that Patinkin failed to develop a general equilibrium model in which money plays an essential role.

Walrasian and Non-Walrasian Equilibrium Models with Money

Hellwig (1993) argues that monetary theory has still not recovered from the blow of Hahn's dismissal of monetary equilibrium. He believes that economics lacks a suitable theoretical framework for studying the functioning of the monetary economy. In his opinion, the main cause of this lacuna is 'our habit of thinking in terms of frictionless, organized, that is Walrasian markets'. The problem is that Walrasian general equilibrium models accommodate money without explaining what the role of money in the economy is. In other words, the existence of money is still postulated like Cassel and other early pioneers of general equilibrium analysis did.

The best example of this practice is the Clower or cash-in-advance constraint.[62] This constraint means that goods cannot be exchanged for goods, but only for money. Thus each individual wants to enter a new trading period with sufficient money balances to finance the purchase of consumer goods. This will certainly generate a demand for money and, under certainty, the demand for money will be just equal to planned and actual purchases.

The question is, of course, why one should impose the cash-in-advance constraint. In the context of a general equilibrium model, the requirement that people pay with money is simply counterintuitive and generates paradoxical results (Hellwig 1993, 221). In the Walrasian system all exchanges are effected simultaneously, so there is no need for a constraint that ensures that people actually pay for what they buy. In general equilibrium the requisite *quid pro quo* is automatically ensured. In this case the use of money as a medium of exchange just appears cumbersome; it is an extra constraint imposed upon the freedom to exchange that impedes rather than facilitates trade. This is at odds with the general notion that the use of money as a medium of exchange enables the economy to exploit trading opportunities that would not be available under barter.

There are ways to circumvent this problem, but they lead to problems of their own. A popular workhorse of modern monetary theory is the overlapping generations (OLG) model, which focusses on the role of money as a store of value. The OLG model offers a sensible explanation of why money can have a positive value in equilibrium, but runs into problems when people may choose between money and other assets to carry wealth across generations. A very simple OLG model with money and storable goods shows that we face a fundamental choice (Blanchard and Fischer 1989, 160–161). If the rate of return on money is less than the return to storage, nobody wants to hold money and thus money is not valued. This generates the result that, if there is a barter equilibrium which is a Pareto optimum, there cannot be a monetary equilibrium with a constant money stock. *Vice versa*, in case a monetary equilibrium exists, it must be a Pareto optimum and there cannot be a barter equilibrium that is also a Pareto optimum. In the OLG world, the barter and monetary economy are mutually exclusive.

Faced with such difficulties, Blanchard and Fischer (1989, 155) state that 'building a model that formally explains why money is used in transactions when it is dominated as a store of value has proved a difficult task'. That is an understatement. OLG models generally invoke the Clower constraint to circumvent this problem. Hellwig (1993) considers the explanation of the role for money a fundamental question for monetary theory. Why does 'worthless' fiat money have a positive value in exchange against goods and services when there are other assets whose own rates of return in each period exceed the own rate of return on money? According to Hellwig, the answer to that question is still forthcoming with disastrous results, because 'it undermines practically all our textbook models of closed-economy and open-economy macroeconomics' (ibid., 219).

The rescue must come from the abandonment of the Walrasian auctioneer. We must replace the assumption of a centralized market system by a decentralized system of multiple bilateral exchanges. This can be done by modelling the matching process of agents in a random way. Agents are matched in pairs and when they meet they must decide to trade bilaterally or not. In pairwise meetings there is a certain chance of a double coincidence of wants, but it is more likely that agents decide to exchange good A for good B if they estimate that the possession of B will give them a better chance of eventually meeting a trading partner that is willing to exchange the good that they desire. In other words, the assumption of decentralized exchanges allows us to model the process of indirect exchange and to investigate the properties that make money the most desired medium of exchange.[63]

The result is an equilibrium that is non-Walrasian because there is no central figure that collects the data on ex ante supply and demand and establishes the price vector that simultaneously clears all markets. Agents face a price distribution rather than a single (equilibrium) price and their choices reflect the history of their exchanges. In any one meeting, the price at which agents trade depends on their inventories of goods and money balances. These inventories, in turn, depend on the time that passed since their last trade. In other words, in the non-Walrasian approach the demand for money and therefore the resulting monetary equilibrium is to a considerable extent path-dependent.

However, the models of decentralized trading also face the question why agents engage in indirect exchange through money rather than general indirect barter. This question cannot be answered without using a restriction that resembles the cash-in-advance constraint. It can be shown that if agents are free to exchange *all* goods and money, a monetary equilibrium fails to exist in the random-meetings model. That is to say, in all equilibria the value of fiat money in all bilateral exchanges is zero. As Hellwig (1993, 236 and 238) argues, the fundamental problem of Walrasian general equilibrium analysis simply reappears in the models that assume decentralized trading. The use of fiat money as a medium of exchange in competition with other assets and goods depends on special assumptions about storage or marketing costs of all assets and goods other than fiat money. Thus Kiyotaki and Wright (1989) show that if the inventories of goods have higher storage costs than fiat money, one can have monetary equilibrium without exogenously imposing the constraint that all indirect exchange use fiat money.[64] Another way is to assume frictions related to the poor marketability of goods or the indivisibility of the money unit (Trejos and Wright 1995).

Alternatively, an inventory approach *à la* Baumol and Tobin can be used to model the timing for money withdrawals at the bank (Romer 1986). This is a powerful tool to endogenize the decision making process that underlies the choice between money and competing assets. The advantage of this model is that it reduces the restriction of the Clower constraint, because the demand for money depends on the chosen frequency of money/bond transactions and not just on the requirement to pay in cash for certain purchases. Suppose, for example, that it was possible for people to convert interest-bearing assets into money just five minutes before the actual purchase. This would greatly reduce the average holding period of money to the extent that the impact of the cash-in-advance constraint on the aggregate demand for money becomes fairly insignificant.

In combination with decentralized trading, this seems like a promising development to tackle the role of money in equilibrium theorizing. However, this is also a direction that involves difficult mathematical formalizations due to the explanation of transaction dates as endogenous variables. Clower (1998) proposes a numerical approach using computer simulation techniques to circumvent this problem. He refers to a computer experiment which he performed in collaboration with Peter Howitt. This experiment involved 2000 undifferentiated transactors, which starting from an initial situation of transactor autarky and evolves through time (iterations) into an organized system with a limited number of market makers (<10), trading with all other transactors using a single commodity as an exchange intermediary. Clower says that the benefit of the numerical approach is that it forces one to develop explicit algorithms about the logistics of exchange. Whether one adopts the theoretical or numerical approach, one thing is clear, the role of money continues to challenge the wits of the monetary theorist.

Is Money a Veil?

Putting aside the microfoundation of money demand and just assuming that money exists, this final section briefly asks what the effect is that money generates in the equilibrium theories of contemporary economics. Does monetary equilibrium theory still lead to the conclusion that money is best seen as a veil?

We have seen in this chapter that the role of expectations is of crucial importance to underpin the function of money in equilibrium. Keynes grappled with this issue because he relegated the formation of expectations to a ceteris paribus clause and focussed his analysis on the conditions of static equilibrium. The introduction of the rational expectations hypothesis allowed macroeconomics for the first time to deal with expectations and equilibrium in a comprehensive theory, which explains price expectations as an endogenous variable (Sheffrin 1983).

The Lucas model has been one of the most influential theories in what became known as new classical economics. Lucas (1975) explained why equilibrium models with decentralized markets and imperfect information can account for the effects of nominal as well as real shocks on output. The basis of his model was Phelps's representation of the market system as an island economy (Phelps 1969). The fact that markets are isolated on islands explains why individuals have to deal with imperfect information. In particular, suppliers in each market are unable to distinguish between aggregate demand shocks (a change in nominal money) and sector-specific shocks that affect relative prices, that is, there is a problem of signal extraction. This leads to both types of shocks, thus including nominal shocks, to have an effect on output. Lucas formalized this notion in what is now called the Lucas supply function, which shows output as an increasing function of the price surprise, the unanticipated increase in the aggregate price level.

The implication of this equilibrium model is that money can have a real effect on output and employment when price changes are unanticipated. However, this effect is not very long lasting. The hypothesis of rational expectations entails that individuals update their 'model' of the economy in the quickest of time (one unit of time in the original Lucas model), leading to stochastically correct predictions of price changes. This implies that the public can never be systematically 'fooled' about the inflation rate. The quick response to unanticipated price changes in nominal money results in a short term Phillips curve that is vertical at the natural unemployment rate. Money may not be entirely sterile, but it is at least very close to it.[65]

The problem of the Lucas model is that the assumption about imperfect information does not seem very sensible. The notion of information 'islands' conflicts with technological development such as the internet, which facilitates the spreading of information and reduces the cost of such knowledge. It is therefore not likely that the public suffers from a lack of knowledge about prices and money. In this day and age, the reverse may be closer to the truth. The availability of a large number of information sources at virtually no cost causes the public to suffer from an overload of information. The problem is to interpret the wealth of information that is just a mouse click away and to isolate the right source to satisfy one's need for information.

In the light of such developments it is remarkable that the proponents of the equilibrium approach did not try to develop alternative explanations for the Lucas setup of the coordination problem in a decentralized economy.[66] An alternative is to study the consumption-saving decision in an intertemporal context, which requires an OLG model. A general equilibrium model of this type, assuming money and interest-bearing bonds to coexist, can be used to characterize money demand and to study the effects of money growth on the real allocation in general equilibrium. It can be shown that in this model money affects real allocation, but that these effects are quite small in a steady state. Blanchard and Fischer (1989, 181) therefore conclude that the OLG model with money shows that 'under realistic assumptions' one may ignore the presence of money and conduct the analysis, of for instance business cycles, in real terms.

It has to be remarked that one of these assumptions is the Clower constraint which ensures that people use money and nothing else to buy goods. This limits the scope of the analysis because it rules out the study of coordination failures related to the use of money as a medium of exchange. There is no transactions technology in the OLG model that allows us to address a question of this kind. As Garretsen (1991, 130) concludes, the OLG model with money is far too restrictive to obtain results that show us how money causes real effects like unemployment. The obvious way forward is therefore to focus more clearly on the issue of coordination, exploring the idea that imperfections can lead to strong effects on aggregate demand and output.

This branch of macroeconomics is called New Keynesian because it introduces specific Keynesian themes like fixed nominal prices and wages.[67] However, it also fits the general equilibrium approach because it is based on the assumptions of rational behaviour and studies the conditions of equilibrium for a multi-sector economy as a representation of the economy as a whole.[68] This approach implies that the fixity of prices and wages is not an assumption but an equilibrium outcome of the model. In this New Keynesian branch of the theory imperfect competition or asymmetric information is used to explain why disequilibrium (in the sense of a persistent gap between supply and demand on some market) can be an optimal solution and therefore another sort of equilibrium. The meaning of equilibrium here is simply that at the microeconomic level everyone is content with his or her choices, leaving the economy without an endogenous force to change. There is no automatic correction of what, on the level of the economy as a whole, appears to be a sub-optimal outcome, namely unemployment. With this result we are back in the Keynesian world. The government is needed as an outside force to accomplish what the market system itself cannot achieve, to equilibrate aggregate supply and demand for the economy as a whole.

To explain why profit maximizing producers and workers decide to leave prices unchanged one also needs to assume that the adjustment of prices is costly (Blanchard and Fischer 1989, chapter 8). The costs of changing prices may be related to the costs of collecting information at discrete intervals of time. It may then be optimal for price setters to change their prices at fixed intervals of time, to use time-dependent price rules. If, instead, the costs of changing prices are physical or 'menu costs', it may be optimal to change prices as a function of the state, to use state-dependent rules. In both cases, price setters may choose not to adjust their prices, or to change them infrequently, if the costs of doing so are relatively low. It can be shown that it may take just small private costs of changing prices to generate substantial nominal price rigidity and long-lasting effects of changes in aggregate demand on output.

However, a necessary ingredient is that price-setters do not want to change relative prices very much in the first place. In the case of the labour market, this means that the opportunity cost of not adjusting wages is not very large. This is a counterintuitive result. Why would wage-setters accept large variations in employment as the price of little change in the real wage? The answer is that the labour market does not function like a market with atomistic agents. The institutional setting of the labour market generally involves wage setting between representative organisations and results in collective bargaining agreements. Hence, we need to take account of a different price setting process, wage determination through bargaining between firms and labour unions.

The presence of collective bodies like unions creates perverse incentives, explaining the a-typical behaviour of wages in corporatist labour markets. Consider the reward scheme for the members of the labour unions as the insiders to the wage-setting process. They reap a return to their union membership in addition to their wages. The membership return consists in sharing part of the monopoly rent with the firm. This creates an incentive for the union members to accept wage rate cuts in order to shield their part of this rent. In other words, union members may care more about employment stability than wage stability. After all, losing their job would change their status from insider to the wage bargaining process to becoming an outsider. Collective wage bargaining so provides an explanation for the phenomenon of less employment fluctuation and more real wage flexibility in corporatist labour market than in competitive labour markets. This result is corroborated in modern empirical labour market studies.

The efficiency wages hypothesis offers a more sensible explanation of sticky wages. The starting point of this theory is the observation that workers differ in their abilities and that the productivity of a worker can vary considerable depending on the amount of effort that he devotes to his work (Shapiro and Stiglitz 1984). But neither ability nor effort is easy for the firm to assess or monitor. This leads to the result that it may be optimal for the firm to raise wages in order to increase the opportunity cost of shirking. Efficiency wages thus predict a positive relationship between the real wage rate and the productivity of workers. This means that there are costs to changing wages. These costs may cause firms to 'resist' adjusting wages when the unemployment rate changes. In other words, the wage rate may be sticky, generating involuntary unemployment and aggregate demand effects, which stand central in Keynesian macroeconomic analysis (Akerlof and Yellen 1985a).

The New Keynesian analysis of the labour market seems a long way from our main question: what are the real effects of monetary equilibrium? The reason why I discussed this branch of theory is that it shows how modern macroeconomics deals with the issue of coordination failures in a monetary economy. Money matters in these models because there exist nominal inertia that may explain why aggregate demand changes have an effect on output and employment. We have seen that New Keynesian economics offers a variety of explanations of such nominal inertia, which make money more than a veil. But that is not the whole story. There is also the issue why people use money in the first place. New Keynesians deal with this question in the same way as their neoclassical opponents: they simply postulate the existence of money. One may argue whether an explicit micro foundation for money use would improve the analysis. Garretsen (1991, 207) comments that criticism of this kind misses the mark because 'the coordinating device *par excellence* in a general equilibrium framework, our friend the Walrasian auctioneer, is also in need of choice theoretic foundations'. It appears that economists of all directions still face a difficult task of explaining the relationship between money and the real economy. One way of going forward is to drop the equilibrium assumption and to study the role of money in disequilibrium. It is to this branch of theory that we now turn.

NOTES

1. Blaug (1995, 34) even maintains that not a single pre war writer in the neoclassical tradition ever succeeded in developing a rigorous statement of the proportionality theorem. In his view, they failed to recognize that long-run neutrality depends on the precise way that new money is injected into the economy (the new money must increase the nominal money holdings of all individuals in the same proportion).
2. In Locke's words, 'the vent is nothing else, but the passing of commodities from one owner to another in exchange; and is then called quicker when a greater quantity of any species of commodity is taken off from the owners of it, in an equal space of time' (Locke 1691, 67)
3. Locke's price theory explained prices in terms of the ratio between a commodity's vent and its supply. This is a clear example of the ratio theory of value that was one of the first expressions of the supply and demand mechanism in economics (Bowley 1973).
4. Locke's analysis of monetary demand is a clear example of the dominance of the transactions motive in pre-classical (and for that matter, classical) monetary analysis. He tried to estimate how much money was needed to drive the wheels of trade, a calculation which crucially depended on the 'quickness of its circulation' (Locke 1691, 33). Locke was not able to give an absolute estimate of the quantity of money to support a given amount of transactions. Instead he related the quantity of money to the income velocities

of the different income groups. Thus, if labourers are paid once a week, one-fiftieth of their yearly income is a good approximation of how much money labourers need to complete their transactions. See further, Vickers (1959, 48–49) and Vaughn (1980, 42).

5. In particular Locke was referring to the vent of wheat which, as a basic necessity, he believed 'being the constant and most general food, not altering by fashion, nor growing by change'. This implied that it maintained a constant ratio between vent (rate of turnover) and supply making it the best standard to judge the change in the price of (silver) money. See Locke (1691, 74).
6. He criticized what he called the 'fundamental maxim' of Locke's quantity theory that a change in the total supply of money causes a uniform proportionate change in all prices. His main objection was that Locke had only looked at the effects of monetary changes but left the transmission mechanism unexplained. In his words, Locke had 'clearly seen that the abundance of money makes everything dear, but he has not considered how it does so'.
7. According to Cantillon, all classes of society had an inclination to save money as 'many miserly and timid people bury and hoard cash for considerable periods' (Cantillon 1755, Part II, Chapter 7).
8. Although Cantillon believed in the self-governing nature of a free market economy, in the field of international monetary relations he can at best be described as a 'semi-equilibrium' theorist. He did not think of the world economy as tending firmly to equilibrium. See Vickers (1959, 189) and Rothbard (1995, 359).
9. At the same time, Hume did not dismiss all levies on imports as harmful because they could protect employment and industry in specific sectors. See Hume (1752, 76).
10. Smith used a numerical example to demonstrate that one pound of paper money exactly displaces an equivalent value of currency, so that the total quantity of money remains unchanged. Smith (1937, 277–278).
11. One could say that before 1797 the policy conditions were simply not conducive to the development of the quantity theory. As Blaug (1995) argues, the suspension of convertibility in 1797 for the first time established that money was an exogenous variable, as the conditions of the quantity theory demand. But the mainstream of the classical and neoclassical tradition focused on commodity money to which the quantity theory does not apply. Hence, the quantity theory is described as 'the illegitimate sideline of the classical tradition, the classical theory of unclassical fiat money' (Niehans quoted in Blaug 1995, 35).
12. For an in-depth analysis of Thornton's approach to monetary analysis and monetary policy, see Reisman (1971). Skaggs (1995) traces the influence of Thornton's work on the monetary theorists of the classical period, most notably those belonging to the Banking School.
13. The logic of the argument is this. An excess demand or supply only arises if people have an incentive to hold money in the form of a cash balance. However, under Say's identity people are assumed to immediately disburse any money in exchange for other commodities. No one will hold on to money and any positive amount of money will

therefore cause a lasting state of excess supply of money which drives prices up to infinity. Hence Say's identity and money involve a logical contradiction.

14. The classical dichotomy approaches the determination of equilibrium prices in two steps. First, the markets for goods (the 'real sector') determine equilibrium relative prices, that is the price ratios and quantities of goods exchanged in equilibrium. Second, the consideration of the money market then determines the level of equilibrium money prices, which will be proportional to the money stock. See Grandmont (1983, 10) and Patinkin (1956, 106).
15. In the words of Mill (1909, 519), the value of money is determined 'temporarily by demand and supply, permanently and on average by cost of production'.
16. Blaug (1995, 32) adds that 'Ricardo and especially James Mill only grudgingly admitted non-neutrality in the short run but admit it they did'.
17. Even Ricardo conceded that 'the operation of an increased currency is not instantaneous, but require some interval of time to produce their full effect' See Hollander (1987, 268).
18. This is the issue of reverse causation, which shows that classical monetary theory violated one of the core assumptions of the quantity theory, namely that money is an exogenous variable. See Blaug (1995, 35–36).
19. It has to be noted that in 1886 Walras was the first to give an explicit algebraic treatment of the cash-balance approach to the quantity theory. See Patinkin (1956), 386–412 ('Suppl. Note C') and Van Daal and Jolink (1993).
20. For a critical discussion, see Myrdal (1939). Myrdal claimed that the stability of the price level and the equality of the market and natural or normal interest rate were unnecessary for the maintenance of monetary equilibrium. See further, Chapter 12. In a review of Wicksell (1898) in 1899 D. Davidson already pointed at the implicit assumption of Wicksell's definition of monetary equilibrium, namely that the economy is stationary. When one allows for factor productivity growth, neutral money (that is monetary equilibrium) no longer requires that the price level remains stable. See Visser (1971, 396).
21. Wicksell believed that a fully developed credit system would be able to replace the use of money in its physical form as a medium of exchange. See Wicksell (1898, 101).
22. In his earlier book *Geldzins und Güterpreise* (1898) he defined it as the rate of interest that is determined by supply and demand if no use were made of money and if all lending were in the form of real capital goods. See Laidler (1991, 130ff) for a discussion of the difficulties surrounding Wicksell's different definitions of the natural rate of interest.
23. In the words of Wicksell (1898, 87): 'Verhart die Zinsrate längere Zeit auf jenem niedrigen Stand, so muss ihre Einwirkung auf die Preise eine *akkumulatorische* sein, d.h. in gleichen Zeiträumen sich in gerade derselben Art wiederholen' (emphasis in the original).
24. 'Das "Angebot an Geld" wird also durch die Nachfrage selbst geschaffen.' Wicksell (1898, 102).
25. See for example Siven (1997, 215) who argues that Wicksell's cumulative process is not based on disequilibrium analysis. In his view, the cumulative process (as described by

Wicksell in *Interest and Prices*) consists of a sequence of partial equilibria because all agents expect their price expectations to be correct.

26. This conclusion concerns the operation of the indirect mechanism linking money and prices. The direct mechanism is of course a second channel that may cause a cumulative process and the related phenomenon of the trade cycle. In this regard Wicksell pointed to the constant flow of gold to the non-gold-producing countries as a cause of the progressive increase in prices there. See Wicksell (1935, 162–163 and 205).

27. An important difference between Hayek and Wicksell is that according the former the cause of the business cycle would be exclusively monetary (that is through a change in the monetary rate of interest), while the real adjustments that followed it constituted the essence of the business cycle. See Hayek (1931a).

28. 'There exists . . . no other connection between the two than the *variations in commodity prices* caused by the difference between them. And this link is elastic, just like the spiral springs often fitted between the body of a coach and the axles' (Wicksell 1935, 206).

29. 'Die Gleichheit der beiden Zinsraten stellt sich schliesslich nichts destoweniger, aber nur und infolge einer vorangehenden Aenderung der Preise her. Letzere sind sozusagen eine Spiralfeder welche die Kraftübertragung zwischen der natürlichen under der Geldzinsrate vermittelt . . . Bei reiner Barwirtschaft ist die Feder kurz und stark, sie wird länger und nachgiebiger, in dem Masse als sich Kredit- und Bankwesen entwickelt' (Wicksell 1898, 125).

30. It is odd that Laidler completely ignores the hostile reception of the quantity theory in Germany, even in what he calls its Golden Age. Karl Helfferich (1872–1924) was one of the German economists of this period who was at pains 'to set himself off from contemporary quantity-theorists' (Williamson 1971, 45). Helfferich considered the quantity theory a too simple explanation of the price level. In his view, the price level was determined by a manifold of causes, many of which were not included in the quantity theory. Unfortunately, such views also affected the policy of the German *Reichsbank* during the hyperinflation of the 1920s. See Hardach (1980, 22–23): 'The Reichsbank had followed the nineteenth-century Banking School holding that supplying the business world with additional money against genuine commercial bills could not have an inflationary effect.'

31. In this chapter, I ignore the American contributions to the development of the analysis of money and the cycle. Laidler (1999) extensively discusses the development of American macroeconomics in the interwar period.

32. Real analysis can be distinguished from monetary analysis by defining it as the branch of the theory which assumes that all essential features of the economy may be understood in real terms, that is by reducing them to real determinants like tastes and technology. The use of money in actual transactions can be ignored, if the monetary mechanism functions properly. We may then analyze the economic process as if it takes place in a barter economy. See Schumpeter (1954, 276–282).

33. This definition does not preclude the possibility that we are dealing with a growing rather than a stationary economy, as long as the rate of growth is correctly foreseen by all agents. See Hayek's definition of equilibrium as an intertemporal concept (Hayek 1928).
34. The main question of the debate about neutral money was what such a policy would entail. It could mean stabilizing the price level, stabilizing the quantity of money or something quite different. However, Koopmans (1933) showed that Fisher's equation of exchange could not be used to develop an operational criterion to determine monetary equilibrium. The problem was that monetary equilibrium could be reconciled with changes in either the price level P, the volume of trade T or the flow of monetary payments MV. See also Myrdal (1939). This conclusion meant that it was futile to use monetary equilibrium as an operational concept, as even Hayek conceded.
35. Leijonhufvud (1981) speaks of the Wicksell Connection when he addresses the development of interwar macroeconomics, because in this period most schools of thought used Wicksell's definition of monetary equilibrium as the starting point of their theories. In his view, this implies that the interest-rate mechanism was the main bone of contention between the competing currents of thought in economics focusing on the ability of market forces to appropriately coordinating saving and investment.
36. Keynes (1930, 139) explicitly stated that his distinction between these two price levels corresponds to Wicksell's distinction between the market and the natural rate of interest.
37. In this connection it has to be remarked that Keynes also defined saving and investment as *ex post* and not as prospective quantities (ibid., 111).
38. Keynes called these stages commodity, profit and income inflation respectively. For a discussion of these stages, see Tieben (1997, 104–105).
39. Hicks (1967a) points out that there are in fact three stages of analysis. The third stage is formed by the adjustment of rigid prices (for example wages).
40. See Patinkin (1982, 11–32) and Patinkin (1993). For a review of the reviews, see Dimand (1989).
41. Indeed, this theory is an embryonic account of the liquidity preference theory of interest rate determination that stands central in the GT. See Laidler (1999, 139–141).
42. Keynes (1930, 31) defined different kinds of deposits, called the cash, business, income and savings deposits, in order to elucidate the financial decision making process. See also Chapter 15 of the TM.
43. Leijonhufvud (1981, 161) therefore describes this theory as a stock-flow problem, given that interest rate determination is not just a matter of the financing of new investment, but also of trading in the outstanding stock of 'old' securities.
44. Keynes even spoke of 'involuntary unemployment' and discussed the conditions of what in the GT he would call an unemployment equilibrium. See Chapters 19 and 20 of the TM and the comments of Robinson (1933).
45. Keynes (1930, 139) defined the natural rate of interest as the discount rate used by entrepreneurs to capitalize the prospective income that they anticipated from current investment. It is therefore not some physical characteristic of the economy's production

process, but a factor that reflects changing expectations about the future business climate. This makes it an inherently unstable factor. See also Laidler (1999, 136).

46. In the GT Keynes (1936, 78) stressed that the dependence of the volume of employment on what entrepreneurs expect to be the level of effective demand, is an issue that links the GT with the theoretical framework of the TM. According to Keynes, in that latter book 'an expected increase of investment relatively to saving . . . being a criterion of an increase in effective demand'.

47. With regard to this conclusion, it is odd that Barens (1989) stresses the instability of the short-term equilibrium price as the key characteristic of the TM. Barens reaches this conclusion by placing the famous banana parable at the heart of the monetary theory of the TM. This parable discusses the disastrous effects of a thrift campaign on an imaginary plantation where bananas are the only good produced and consumed. Barens thereby ignores the crucial role played by the interest rate mechanism in preventing that a disequilibrium between saving and investment is timely corrected. The banana parable is simply not characteristic for the trade cycle analysis of the TM. Barens makes matters worse by arguing that Keynes introduced the liquidity trap in the GT as an afterthought in order to rescue his conclusion that the economy can get stuck at an unemployment equilibrium, even when money wages are flexible. This conclusions ignores that Keynes stressed that liquidity preference was an important ingredient of the explanation why the interest rate fails to coordinate saving and investment, a line of thinking that Keynes first developed in the TM.

48. See Keynes's letter of 1 January 1935 to G.B. Shaw, in Keynes (1973, 492).

49. Letter to Ohlin of 27 January 1937 in Keynes (1973, 184–185). He referred to 1931 and 1932 as the time when he abandoned sequence analysis.

50. Letter to R. Harrod of 4 July 1938 in Keynes (1973, 296). See also the letter to Harrod of 16 July 1938.

51. See how Hicks judged the merit of the GT in his review of this book. He referred to the great complexity of the factors determining output in general 'even under static assumptions' and stated that 'a great part of Mr Keynes's work may be regarded as an endeavour to cut trough this tangle, by grouping complex factors together into bundles. This process is one of drastic simplification, but it is necessary if the theory is to become an instrument of practical thought' (Hicks 1936[1982], 87).

52. Another way to state this conclusion is by saying that the dependence of the level of employment on effective demand means that there exists a macro foundation or macro constraint for the behaviour at the micro level.

53. Keynes explained investment demand in terms of the equality between the interest rate as a price for liquidity preference and the marginal rate of efficiency, which in turn depends on the expected yield on new capital investments and the supply price of capital. See Laidler (1999) and Garretsen (1991).

54. The identity of saving and investment appears in conflict with the statement above that saving and investment depend on a different set of causal factors. However, this contradiction is only apparent given that different motives for saving and investment at

the micro level need not preclude that, when we turn to the economy as a whole, they must be seen as identically equal. For an individual savings and investment may not be equal, but in the macro economy saving and investment always imply a two-sided transaction, which leads to the conclusion that in the aggregate they must be seen as equal by definition. See Keynes (1936, 63–64 and 81–82).

55. As Hicks put it in his *Theory of the Trade Cycle* (1950): 'This emphasis on the real (non-monetary) character of the cyclical process has of course been entirely deliberate; it has been one of the main objects of this work to show that the main features of the cycle can be adequately explained in real terms. But now that our real analysis is substantially complete, it is natural to turn around and inquire whether the part played by money has not been underrated. Even if the factors we have been considering are the main causes of the cycle, may it not be that there are some subsidiary monetary causes, which should not be left entirely on one side?' (Hicks 1950, 136).

56. Keynes addressed uncertainty as a logical concept and not as a statistical concept that could be analyzed in terms of a frequency distribution. See Keynes (1936, 148, 152, 162–163) and further Lawson (1985) and Klant (1985). There is a clear resemblance between Keynes's work in this field and Knight's distinction between risk and uncertainty (Knight 1921).

57. On the analysis of the liquidity premium, see Chapter 17 of the GT and Garretsen (1991, 156–168).

58. See Hicks (1936[1982], 86 and 89). According to Keynes, short-term expectations are likely to gradually adjust because the future of tomorrow is not so far away, but long-term expectations have a much more violent character. That is why he initially assumed them constant. Short-term expectations are subsequently assumed to always match current receipts, because people treat current outcomes as a reliable guide to future action as a convention. According to Keynes, this is one of the techniques they use to beat 'the dark forces of ignorance and time'. See Keynes (1936, 152–158) and Keynes (1937[1973], 114).

59. Van Daal and Jolink (1993) reconstruct Walras's monetary models and demonstrate how he used money as either circulating capital, fiat money and commodity money.

60. Technically, the dividing line between stability and instability is the case where elasticities of expectations are equal to or greater than unity. See Hicks (1939, 255).

61. Hicks (1939, 257) felt that this restriction was justified when one assumed that a proportionate rise in all current prices raises all expected prices in the same proportion.

62. It is noteworthy that Clower (1998) himself considers the failure of economics to account for an explicit mechanism for the logistics of exchange, one of the greatest lacunas in economic theorizing.

63. Kiyotaki and Wright (1989) has become a standard model for this type of analysis. See also Trejos and Wright (1995) for the case of divisible rather than indivisible goods. Wright (2005) discusses the recent developments in this field.

64. There remains the problem that we need to assume that everyone believes that others will accept fiat money. If no one believes in fiat money, then it cannot get off the ground. This

is a problem of rational expectations that likewise plagues the OLG model. See Blanchard and Fischer (1989, 159) and Kyotaki and Wright (1989, 943).

65. Assuming rational expectations, a constant money growth rule will not be able to 'fool' economic agents because it systematically raises the money stock each period. This lead to money being 'superneutral', which means that a constant money growth rule is not able to change real equilibrium. See Blanchard and Fischer (1989, 162).

66. The Lucas model lost its appeal in the early eighties when empirical studies showed that, in contrast to the central prediction of the model, output appeared to be affected by the currently perceived money stock. See the evidence cited in Blanchard and Fischer (1989, 360).

67. See Mankiw and Romer (1991) and Romer (1996). For a review of New Keynesian economics, see Gordon (1990) and Hargreaves Heap (1992).

68. This is not true of all New Keynesians. Gordon (1990) complains that a large part of this school just adopts the partial equilibrium method and ignores the very obvious relationship with the fix-price general equilibrium models of Leijonhufvud (1968), Barro and Grossman (1971) and Malinvaud (1977). In contrast, the New Keynesian literature that descends from Cooper and John (1988) does explicitly recognize the kinship with such non-market-clearing models of general equilibrium.

12. Dynamic Analysis in Monetary Theory

INTRODUCTION

This chapter discusses the dynamic methods of two schools in economics that both enjoyed their greatest popularity in the interwar period, the Stockholm school and the Austrian school. These schools were at the forefront of monetary theory in the 1920s and 1930s and aimed to develop an explicit dynamic theory of economic changes with money in a leading role. The interesting fact is that the Swedes and the Austrians have common theoretical roots, for both schools took the work of Wicksell as their starting point (Ebeling 1997; Laidler 1999). The importance of Wicksell in this regard is that he had shown that the interest rate is a key variable for the allocation of scarce resources over time. This placed the relationship between saving and investment at the nexus of the dynamic theories of the Swedes and the Austrians.

However, this common starting point cannot conceal the important differences that exist between the macroeconomics of these schools. As Laidler (1999, 52) puts it: 'It might seem, at first sight, utterly astonishing that two bodies of economic analysis, developed at the same time and in response to the same theoretical puzzles bequeathed by a single person, could move apart so rapidly.' The aim of this chapter is to shed some light on the different approaches of the Swedes and the Austrians towards the dynamic analysis of the monetary economy. This comparison shall be used to answer the question that I raised in the last chapter: why did the dynamic approach, focussing on the analysis of disequilibrium rather than equilibrium, fail to establish a new standard for macroeconomic theory?

The organization of this chapter is as follows. The next section addresses the dynamic method of the Stockholm school. I shall discuss the main features of this dynamic method by clearing up a few inconsistencies and misunderstandings in the recent literature on this subject. In the process I shall investigate what the different members of this school contributed to the development of this method and what their dynamics implied for the role of monetary theory and policy. The two following sections separately discuss the monetary theories of Mises and Hayek as the main representatives of the Austrian school. These sections investigate what Mises and Hayek took from Wicksell and what they left out. In particular they address the question why they believed that the neutrality of money had to be rejected as a fundamental principle. That seems like contradiction, for in the early stage of his career Hayek was also one of the pioneers to adopt neutral money and the conditions of monetary equilibrium as the starting point of monetary analysis. I shall try to resolve this contradiction by showing what the monetary dynamics of Mises and Hayek was assumed to achieve. One of my main arguments is that Mises and Hayek developed a method of analysis that was unique of the Austrian school, but that is often misunderstood. This method used the equilibrium assumption as a thought experiment. I shall also argue that it was Hayek himself who, in the later stages of his career, abandoned this method in favour of a different concept of equilibrium. The final section reviews the lessons of this chapter.

THE DYNAMIC METHOD OF THE STOCKHOLM SCHOOL

The term Stockholm school suggests a degree of coherency in the methods of the Swedish economists that is not in all cases warranted. Especially in the field of dynamic economics the method of the Swedes is described by Laidler (1999) as 'eclectic' from both a theoretical and a policy perspective. Kohn (1986) even states that each author devised a sequence analysis of his very own by adopting his own set of definitions for common terms such as saving and investment. The problem was that economics in this period was conducted mainly in verbal terms, while the Swedes and others addressed complicated dynamical problems that asked for mathematical tools that were not yet available. Theoretical problems were then often 'solved' by a clever adjustment of one's definitions (Andvig 1991). The result was that debates about the proper approach to dynamic theory generally ended in a quarrel about terminology.[1]

However, Hansson (1982) has shown that this lack of coherency does not stand in the way of a useful reconstruction of what with hindsight can be seen as the common vision behind the dynamic method of the Stockholm school. The following sections discuss this method and its rationale. In addition, I shall highlight the individual contributions of the members of the Stockholm school to the development of this method and critically discuss some of their more significant differences.

Sequence Analysis and Disequilibrium Analysis

What is the dynamic method of the Stockholm school? It is clear that it originated in an attempt to provide an alternative for the static method that the Swedes found lacking, but beyond that there is a surprising lack of clarity about the nature of the dynamic method that came in its place. Laidler (1999) devotes a whole chapter to the Macrodynamics of the Stockholm School, but does not define what this method is. Ebeling (1997) in one breath introduces the terms 'period analysis', 'plan analysis' and 'process analysis' to describe the dynamic method of both the Austrian and the Stockholm school, but it is left to the reader to figure out for himself what these methods involve. Whether they are just different names for the same thing or represent different solutions to the same problem remains unknown. Finally, Hansson (1982) reconstructs the dynamic method by discussing the work of all the Swedish economists in this field in painstaking detail. However, his reconstruction regularly leaves the reader lost in the woods, as his general statement of what the dynamic method entails is unclear and at certain points inconsistent.

The problem is that Hansson uses the terms dynamic and disequilibrium method interchangeably. This method starts by analyzing a single period out of equilibrium and is said to signify that 'the ex ante plans are not consistent but the ex post values are equal' (Hansson 1982, 27). This is the starting point for two versions of the disequilibrium method: the equilibrium sequence analysis and the disequilibrium sequence analysis. Hansson says that the former is basically the same as intertemporal equilibrium. But how can a disequilibrium method that rests on the assumption that ex ante plans and ex post outcomes are unequal support the notion of a perfect foresight intertemporal equilibrium? Hansson presents an unintelligible mix of the terms equilibrium and disequilibrium that makes it hard for the reader to grasp his reconstruction of the dynamic method.

The solution to this muddle is to carefully separate the disequilibrium feature from the dynamic method. The reason for this is simple. Imagine a stationary state, which describes the motion of an economy that regularly reproduces itself over time. This is a form of dynamics because the economic variables of this system are dated. However, it also has an equilibrium feature because the values of the variables involved are unchanged when the system progresses through time. Lindahl (1939, 32) called a repetitive flow of this kind a stationary state and considered it part of a more general dynamic theory. One may therefore call it a form of equilibrium dynamics.

But this was not the type of dynamics that the Stockholm school was primarily interested in. The method of the Swedes has in common with the equilibrium dynamics of the stationary state that it addresses the changes of economic variables over time in distinct time frames. It analyzes economic change as a sequence of adjustments, hence the name sequence analysis.

Sequence analysis is very common in economics and can be applied to any system that can be formulated in terms of difference equations. The distinctive treat of the Stockholm school is the definition of disequilibrium which, indeed, reflects the incompatibility of ex ante plans at the beginning of a period as a contrast to the equality of ex post outcomes at the end of the period. This is the familiar description that Myrdal (1939) gave of the ex ante – ex post method, one of the corner stones of the Swedish method. The point is that Myrdal explicitly constrained his analysis to the study of points in time (Myrdal 1939, 43). He believed that the investigation of instantaneous moments was a necessary preliminary of the study of changes during periods. The problem of period analysis in this sense was that it required all kind of auxiliary assumptions in order to reduce the complexity of temporal changes.[2] One could therefore better focus on the points between such periods and conduct the analysis in terms of the tendencies to change. The introduction of the ex ante – ex post distinction was meant to facilitate this kind of analysis. I therefore conclude that Myrdal developed a disequilibrium method, but that he lacked a mechanism to connect the effects of disequilibrium forces to the dynamic changes during periods. In other words, in his framework we have disequilibrium theory but no dynamics in the proper sense.

For a clear exposition of the dynamic method of the Stockholm school, we need a definition of disequilibrium dynamics in a more meaningful way. This can be done by combining sequence analysis and the ex ante – ex post definition of disequilibrium. The trick is to realize that a fully developed sequence analysis consists of two parts, an analysis of the single period and an explanation of the causal link between periods, 'continuation theory' in the terminology of Hicks (1956[1982], 223). This latter part explains how the outcomes of the current period determine the initial conditions for the next. The ex ante – ex post analysis is an example of continuation theory, which allows us to define disequilibrium for an instantaneous moment. The question that remains is what disequilibrium means for changes during a single period.

Table 12.1 sketches the different options. The first possibility concerns the definition of intertemporal equilibrium that was first developed by Hayek (1928) and was quickly taken over by Lindahl (1929[1939]). This equilibrium concerns the case of full compatibility between plans and outcomes in the single period and continuation theory ensures that each subsequent period also resides in equilibrium. That means that there are no disappointed expectations at the end of the period and that there are also no endogenous or exogenous changes to generate a change of the plans for the next period. The result is a chain of equilibria which shows that at the beginning of period one we have what is called perfect foresight.

Table 12.1 Classification of equilibrium and disequilibrium dynamics[3]

Type	Single period theory	Continuation theory	Who?
Intertemporal equilibrium	equilibrium	equilibrium	Lindahl, Hayek
Temporary equilibrium	equilibrium	disequilibrium	Lindahl, Hicks
Disequilibrium dynamics	disequilibrium	equilibrium/disequilibrium	Lindahl, Lundberg

In temporary equilibrium continuation theory explains the working of causes that upset rather than maintain equilibrium. We may use Hicks's definition of equilibrium to illustrate this conception. Hicks used a week as the relevant period to define temporary equilibrium (Hicks 1939, 130ff). He assumed that on Monday trading would start for the coming week. If on Monday prices would not be able to equate supply and demand in all markets, prices would adjust to change plans for supplies and demands to establish equilibrium. Hicks assumed that this adjustment would be instantaneous so that he could ignore the process of equilibration. He conceived of the economic system as being always in equilibrium. We shall later seen that Lindahl developed a similar notion of temporary equilibrium.

The dynamic part is here played by continuation theory. Hicks argued that price expectations for the present week may be consistent with equilibrium, but the plans may be not be. This causes disequilibrium on the second Monday. This may also occur if people have consistent plans, but incorrectly foresee their own wants for the second Monday or make wrong estimates of the results of the technical processes of production. Inconsistencies of this kind mean that the equilibrium of the first week is not carried over to the second week. The second Monday will again see a process of instantaneous equilibration to remove the imbalances bequeathed by the first week. The result is a chain of temporary equilibria to form what Hicks called 'Equilibrium over Time' (ibid., 132).

The disequilibrium method of the Swedes rejects the assumption of instantaneous equilibrium on Monday. According to Myrdal, ex ante quantities (planning) at the beginning of the period are in disequilibrium for each period, but the quantities ex post (outcomes) at the end of the period are by necessity in equilibrium in terms of a bookkeeping balance (Myrdal 1939, 46-47). The purpose of dynamic analysis is to study how a tendency to disparity develops into an ex post balance. It is the task of the single period theory to explain how this process takes place as a dynamic change involving the duration of time. Continuation theory then links disappointed expectations or unforeseen exogenous events to a revision of plans for the subsequent period.

The problem of the dynamic method of the Stockholm school is that the nature of the connecting links is not entirely clear. In the hands of Myrdal, the tendencies to change at the points between the periods are clearly of a disequilibrium nature. However, Hansson (1982, 27) suggests that they have an equilibrium feature in the sense that 'there are constant rules of conduct which determine how the ex post results from one period influence the ex ante plans for the subsequent period. These rules represent the equilibrium notion within disequilibrium sequence analysis'. Hansson's suggestion points to the problem that at the individual level people must have a theory about how to update their expectations when they are faced with outcomes that do not meet their prior expectations. This theory will not change from day to day, because in this case it would be useless to have expectations at all; one could as well adjust one's actions in a random way (Heiner 1983). Hansson is therefore right to assume a stable basis for the revision of expectations. The point is that people's theories of expectations also need to be regularly updated.[4] As Hansson puts it, the rules cannot be assumed to stay constant for more than a few periods. This raises the question how to characterize this process. Is it an equilibrium or a disequilibrium notion? We shall later see that the difficulty of explaining how one period is causally connected to the next in terms of the revision of expectations formed the major stumbling block for the development of the dynamic method of the Stockholm school.

From Dynamics to Statics

The aim of the dynamic method of the Stockholm school was to increase the realism of economic theory by giving time an explicit role in the analysis. Thus Myrdal (1939, 32) declared that the main purpose of his book *Monetary Equilibrium* was 'to *include anticipations in the monetary system*. A criticism of Keynes and Hayek would have to begin by pointing out the fact that in their theoretical systems there is no place for the uncertainty factor and for anticipations' (emphasis in the original).[5]

For the Swedes, static theory epitomized a timeless approach to economics, which meant that expectations, planning and other dynamic causes simply fell outside the scope of the analysis. Lindahl and his colleagues believed that a truly dynamic theory could not start by first assuming static equilibrium. In contrast, the proper approach was exactly the other way round: static theory needed a foundation in dynamic economics. Failure to do so could lead to serious economic errors.[6]

However, the confusing aspect is that the Swedes did not reject the equilibrium method altogether. They presented the dynamic method as a continuum of methods, which in some cases also had a role for the equilibrium method. This complicates the interpretation of the dynamic method and is an aspect that is often misunderstood. Thus Zappia (2001, 59) claims that Lindahl's ultimate aim was to abandon the equilibrium approach. He refers to Hansson (1982) as a source confirming that Lindahl gave up the temporary equilibrium approach as a result of the critiques of Lundberg and Myrdal on this method. In contrast I shall claim that Lindahl did not give up the temporary equilibrium but that he considered it a useful, and in specific circumstances even realistic, application of the dynamic method. In other words, for Lindahl the dynamic method had a disequilibrium branch, but certainly also an equilibrium branch.

This ambiguous attitude towards equilibrium theory is also present in the work of Lundberg. Lundberg is one of the members of the Stockholm school best known for his criticism of the equilibrium method. This was in fact the subject of his licentiate thesis (Lundberg 1930). It is in that sense somewhat surprising that Lundberg did not altogether reject the equilibrium method. He stated that '[t]he value of equilibrium theory cannot be denied simply by pointing to its lack of realism' and called the notion of general equilibrium 'indispensable to economic thought' (Lundberg 1930[1996], 369 and 383). His ideas on the relationship between statics and dynamics warrant a closer look.

The essence of Lundberg's criticism on the equilibrium method was that it generally involved an extremely sloppy use of the ceteris paribus clause.[7] He complained that economists used this clause to hide the dynamic influences on the equilibrium position. In his opinion this was an illegitimate procedure. He argued that one could not isolate economic equilibrium from the dynamics outside equilibrium. *Vice versa*, the assumption of equilibrium could play a useful role in dynamic analysis, provided that one made careful use of the ceteris paribus clause.

The main part of Lundberg (1930) consists in an elaborate attempt to demonstrate the implicit dynamics in the basic partial equilibrium model of the market mechanism. Every student of economics learns to investigate the equilibrium properties of a specific market by shifting one or both of the supply and demand curves and comparing the new equilibrium with the previous one. A comparative static exercise of this kind proceeds under the assumption that everything else remains constant as part of the ceteris paribus clause. But Lundberg stressed that everything does *not* remain constant in comparative statics (Lundberg 1930[1996], 363 and Lundberg 1937, 10–11).

By shifting one of the curves, one has changed the preconditions of equilibrium that existed before the change took place. In other words, one has altered the ceteris paribus clause and is no longer justified to assume that, for instance, the shape of the curves will remain unaltered during the transition. Static theory simply has nothing to say about the transition phases between different equilibria. Lundberg used a simple cobweb model to demonstrate that the dynamics between two equilibrium points may have devastating effects on the nature of the equilibrium. Such equilibria may be explosive or implosive, oscillating or non-oscillating et cetera, but static theory cannot address such issues. According to Lundberg (1937, 11), if we ignore the time element in the adjustment process, the theoretical equilibrium becomes 'wholly illusory'. There is no equilibrium without dynamics and we have no option but to base the study of economic equilibrium on a thorough analysis of the dynamics behind the scene.

Lundberg (1937) studied a range of dynamic models as an alternative to static theory. In this book he rejected the concept of monetary equilibrium on the same grounds as the partial equilibrium model. He argued that the sequence of changes that constitute economic development will continuously upset the given conditions to which adjustments are supposed to take place. In other words, there is no such thing as neutral money or any related neutrality concept. In his view, the dynamic approach to the monetary economy relates the decisions to save and invest to the sequences of changes during the different phases of the expansion. He formalized this dynamics in numerical economic models that anticipated the multiplier-accelerator mechanism of Keynesian economics (Laidler 1999, 66).

The crux of Lundberg's macroeconomic analysis is the same as his earlier article: in real life reaction speeds matter and need to be assessed before one models the economy as being in equilibrium or disequilibrium. This view about the nature of economic changes explains why he still believed that equilibrium theory could be useful.[8] He remarked that in reality 'the concepts of statics and dynamics cannot be separated' (Lundberg 1930[1996], 382). The dynamic method may be more realistic, but has the drawback of being often vague and complicated. The problem is that there exists no standard unit for a sequence analysis of economic changes. There are almost innumerable possibilities regarding assumptions about the quantitative size and duration of changes (Lundberg 1937, 46-50). Lundberg claimed that a dynamic theory can only be developed if we constrain these possibilities to the course of events actually observed and this is where the concept of equilibrium may play a role. He advocated an empirical approach to the business cycle as one of the means to investigate the reaction speeds of economic changes. Such knowledge allows us to better specify the ceteris paribus clause and may lead to the conclusion that certain independent variables of the case under scrutiny change comparatively slowly. This conclusion may warrant the assumption of equilibrium to greatly simplify the study of dynamic changes. Or, in the words of Lundberg (1930[1996], 382): 'Here the concept of equilibrium has proven to be highly useful although not in its general form, but rather in restricting its applications to a smaller number of variable factors.'

Lindahl developed his dynamic method in a similar way. His earlier work in this field followed the conventional approach. He aimed to gradually approach a realistic economic theory beginning with a simplified static analysis and introducing successively more complicated assumptions. Thus he introduced 'dynamic problems within the static framework' (Lindahl 1939, 10). In the late 1930s he developed a dynamic approach to economics which he called 'the general theory of development'. Static theory was a special case of this approach which meant that statics had to be approached as a problem within the dynamic framework rather than the other way round.

The first ideas of Lindahl on the nature of dynamic theory originated in the late 1920s. Like Hayek in this period, he aimed to incorporate the notion of time into the static framework by redefining the concept of equilibrium itself (Zappia 2001). This led to the development of intertemporal equilibrium as a perfect foresight equilibrium and the concept of temporary equilibrium. Lindahl found the latter concept more useful and realistic than intertemporal equilibrium, because he believed that the assumption of perfect foresight would again reduce economics to static theory. The problem with this assumption is that it precludes real action in the sense of disappointed expectations, the revision of plans and a change of choices. Everything that is foreseen complies with the actual outcomes, which means that no one feels the urge to change his plans once the time counter starts running. All action takes place at $t = 0$ and the rest is of no interest from a dynamic perspective.

Lindahl developed the concept of temporary equilibrium as a more realistic alternative. He proposed to study dynamic processes by describing them as a series of temporary equilibria. The benefit of this approach was that one could isolate the factors causing change at the transition period between periods. Thus: 'In order to analyse such a dynamic process, we imagine it to be subdivided into periods of time so short that the factors directly affecting prices, and therefore also the prices themselves, can be regarded as unchanged in each period. All such changes are therefore assumed to take place at the transition points between the periods. The development of prices can then be expressed as a series of successive price situations' (Lindahl 1939, 158). Moreover, these price situations would be equilibrium states in the sense that there would be equality of supply and demand during the period.

Zappia (2001) claims that Lindahl dismissed this approach in his 1939 essay *The dynamic approach to economic theory*. Under the influence of Lundberg and Myrdal, Lindahl (1939, 55) pointed out that even during a short period it is unlikely that individuals with imperfect foresight may find their plans wholly feasible. The fact that the plans are not synchronized with respect to the moment of their revision merely worsens this problem. According to Zappia, this was the main reason why Lindahl abandoned the temporary equilibrium approach.

My reading of the 1939 essay leads to a different conclusion. It is true that Lindahl was critical of the temporary equilibrium approach, but his dynamic framework left sufficient room for an equilibrium dynamics of this kind. He even stated that an equilibrium explanation of dynamic change had the advantage of being 'simple and clear' (Lindahl 1939, 69). His position can therefore be compared to the views of Lundberg. Both stated that under specific conditions the assumption of equilibrium could fulfil a useful role in the analysis of a dynamic process.

Lindahl's general dynamic theory comprises both static and 'special' dynamic theory. For Lindahl static theory involved the analysis of a repetitive process. Statics therefore also describes the motion of a system over time, but the variables studied do not change their values with the lapse of time. In these terms, the benefit of the static approach is immediately clear. One may drop the time coefficient from the analysis which greatly simplifies the analysis. In dynamics this is not possible because the system under scrutiny is changing or evolutionary (Lindahl 1939, 33).

The relevance of this categorization is that it allowed Lindahl to argue that we cannot understand the nature of a static simplification if we do not begin with what he called a 'broad formulation of the problem' (ibid.).

> As in mechanics, the concept of equilibrium can be defined only on the basis of a theory of forces, so the significance of a reiterating process which, as stated above, is the central concept of static theory in economics, can be explained only on the basis of a more general theory of economic development.

Lindahl argued that it is customary in economics to start with static theory and then to directly proceed to dynamic theory. According to him, the neglect of the detour through an all-encompassing general dynamic theory only made life more difficult and could easily lead to mistaken ideas about the nature of dynamic change. He pointed to the seemingly very natural construction of a theory of variations as a complement to a theory of equilibrium. This could easily lead to the idea that dynamic changes must be seen as fluctuations around a centre of gravitation, a notion that is not generally true.

Lindahl proposed to begin with general dynamic structures and to critically assess whether static assumptions can have relevance for the treatment of the particular dynamic problems in the real world. He considered several reasons for justifying static assumptions such as their pedagogic value, the benchmark function of a hypothetical case and the use of statics as an approximation to real phenomena. The latter argument is of special interest if we consider what Lindahl had to say about equilibrium dynamics. He considered approximations useful because 'even in the real world, all factors do not alter continually. There is always a good deal of invariability. In some field, fairly stationary conditions may prevail for a comparatively long time'. Most interestingly, he added that '[s]tatic structures are also very helpful for the explanation and exposition of economic motives, expressed in the planning activity of business men and consumers' (Lindahl 1939, 34).

In the remainder of his essay Lindahl tried to give a systematic exposition of a general dynamic theory of economics. Part of this theory was what he called the theory of economic planning, which aimed to explain how individuals change their plans for the future under different assumptions.[9] This was an innovative part of his dynamics and certainly one of the first attempts in economics to explain how the microeconomic process of plan revision may underpin our conception of economic dynamics.

Lindahl explicated his analysis of plan revision by looking at the concrete example of the pricing process (ibid., 60ff). He argued that pricing is a discontinuous process because it involves two different kinds of action. First, there are offers by seller or buyers quoting a certain price whereby goods and services are placed in the market and, second, those actions whereby these offers are accepted by the other party. Lindahl stressed that these actions take place at definite moments of time. He assumed that the offers, but also the responses to them by for example competing sellers or buyers, would take place at the points of time between periods. The acceptance of the prices offered would then take place during a time period giving the parties concerned sufficient time to carry out all actions necessary to complete the transaction, to produce the good or to deliver it, to consume it et cetera.[10] Lindahl believed that firms would generally not change their business plans very sudden. 'A seller will generally sum up the result of all transactions during a certain period before he decides to alter the price of what he is selling.' Accordingly, he felt that it was realistic to assume that all decisions about price changes and the business and consumption plans to be adopted, take place at the transition points between the periods during which all transactions are actually carried out (ibid., 62). In this manner, the pricing process could be described as a series of disequilibria, because there was no reason to believe that the expectations that guided the decisions at point A in time would be validated by the outcomes of the transaction process during the period between points A and B or any subsequent period (see also Hicks 1956[1982], 223-224).

Surely, this description of pricing as a process in disequilibrium spelled the end of equilibrium concepts like temporary equilibrium? Not according to Lindahl. He explained that at a certain point in time a disequilibrium process of the kind described above may lapse into a temporary equilibrium state. This occurs when after several periods of trading a situation is established which the sellers see no reason to alter under the prevailing conditions. According to Lindahl, the result is temporary equilibrium in two different senses. The first one is a kind of partial equilibrium when the market price is adjusted to the supply and demand as they appear currently in the market. In subsequent periods, costs and incomes affected by the market price may also be adjusted to the new situation as the process continues from one temporary equilibrium to the next. Lindahl stressed that under certain conditions temporary partial equilibrium may develop into a temporary general equilibrium 'of the Walrasian type' (Lindahl 1939, 66).

This continuum of dynamic methods is overlooked by authors like Zappia who stress the importance of the ex ante–ex post method, but underestimate the importance of the equilibrium branch of the dynamic method. Lindahl approvingly referred to the fundamental equations of Keynes's *Treatise on Money* and Hick's *Value and Capital* as important examples of the partial and general temporary equilibrium method respectively. He recognized that temporary equilibria of this kind rested upon some highly unrealistic assumptions such as the 'abrupt transition' from one equilibrium to another. Accordingly, '[i]n real dynamic development such equilibria are probably found only sporadically' (ibid.). That limited the range of applications but did not imply that the equilibrium method was useless in a dynamic setting. Lindahl valued it most as an approximation to real conditions and as a pedagogic instrument. In his own words (ibid., 68):

> The advantage of this method is that the entire static apparatus may be employed in the analysis of a dynamic sequence. It thus bridges the gap between statics and dynamics. The cumbersome ex ante and ex post terminology becomes superfluous, for the individuals are assumed to have knowledge at the beginning of the period of all transactions and of the relevant prices valid for the period.

According to him, the equilibrium method would yield the best results if one aimed to describe 'the main lines' of a dynamic development. In that case one needed clarity, which was the main strength of the equilibrium method and would in this case counterbalance the apparent disadvantages of the equilibrium method (ibid., 69).

So, temporary equilibrium could form a bridge between statics and dynamics, but how about the pure disequilibrium method itself? Lindahl developed a classification scheme that could be used to investigate disequilibrium sequences in terms of the initial conditions, the revision of expectations during the sequence and the changes in the external conditions. The most challenging part was to explain the dynamics generated by the revision of expectations. Zappia (2001) concludes that Lindahl was unable to develop a convincing theory of the price mechanism based on this consideration. Lindahl said that he had only dealt with the theory of planning, as he called it, in the most general and abstract manner. To get specific results one needed more specific theories that differentiated, for instance, between different classes of individuals and their different valuation attitudes. However, that lacuna does not make his disequilibrium dynamics a failure. On the contrary, one of the important lessons of his general theory of development is that we cannot take equilibrium prices for granted. Even within a very short period of time we must be able to explain why equilibrium emerges or why it continues to reign for a single period. Lindahl demonstrated that it is the process of price adjustments that causes the revision of expectations as an endogenous result. The implication of his analysis is therefore a familiar one: whether in equilibrium or disequilibrium, a dynamic theory necessarily entails the discussion of the organization of exchanges (see also the closing section of Chapter 11).

Monetary Theory

At this stage of our argument the reader may wonder what money has to do with the dynamic method of the Stockholm school. The Swedes developed their dynamics on the basis of the naive notion that time and expectations are necessary elements of a realistic economic theory. What was the role of money in this process?

The answer to that question lies in Wicksell's definition of monetary equilibrium in terms of the equality of the natural rate of interest and the monetary rate of interest. We have seen in the previous chapter that monetary equilibrium in this sense suggested a natural anchor point for monetary policy. Faced with the prospect of cumulative price changes outside monetary equilibrium, the goal of monetary policy became to establish and maintain equilibrium between the natural and monetary interest rates. All that was left was to find an operational way to discover when the interest rate did in fact reside at its natural level.

The members of the Stockholm school, most notably Lindahl and Myrdal, revealed the error of this approach by showing that it rested on quicksand. They demonstrated that the natural rate of interest cannot be defined independently of the loan rate and hence of the price level. This conclusion destroys two of the three conditions for monetary equilibrium, namely the requirement that the natural rate matches the market or loan rate of interest and the condition that in monetary equilibrium prices remain stable.[11] It is therefore not difficult to understand why the Swedes considered the saving-investment relationship of vital importance to the maintenance of monetary equilibrium.

The key to the reformulation of monetary equilibrium by Lindahl and Myrdal was the conception of capital that formed the basis of Wicksell's definition of the real or natural rate of interest as the marginal physical productivity of capital. Lindahl (1939, 248) pointed out that a definition of this kind was only possible under very strict conditions, namely when inputs and outputs could be measured in terms of the same physical unit such as a quantity of corn. In the real world with heterogenous capital we lack the means the define the interest rate in terms of a physical unit and therefore cannot restrict the analysis of the natural rate to technological considerations. Both Lindahl and Myrdal realized that in realistic conditions the yield on real capital needs to be assessed in terms of exchange values. Thus Myrdal (1939, 51) proposed to replace the concept of physical productivity by that of an 'exchange value productivity' and Lindahl (1939, 248) redefined the real rate in terms of 'the relation between future product values (with appropriate reductions for risk) and the values invested during the period'.

The definition of the real rate of interest in terms of expected capital values has far-reaching implications for Wicksell's definition of monetary equilibrium. The most serious one is the impossibility to differentiate between a natural and a monetary rate of interest, which was the prime mover behind Wicksell's monetary dynamics. Lindahl explained this problem as follows. He argued that the real rate of interest on capital has a tendency to adjust itself to the loan rate because the loan rate determines the demand for services to be invested in the production of real capital (ibid.). As a result, the price of these services may be expected to rise or fall to the point where the invested capital values are supposed to bear the same interest as the loan rate (see also Myrdal 1939, 63). Moreover, this also means that the interest rate is not independent of the price level, as Wicksell's conditions for monetary equilibrium assert. When the real interest rate on capital is linked to the loan rate, it is also affected by the pricing process that brings about the equality of saving and investment (and by extension equilibrates the goods market). Lindahl and Myrdal therefore concluded that it is impossible to analyze the problem of the intertemporal allocation of resources in a monetary economy by comparing it to the problem of capital formation in an idealized barter economy without money or credit, as both Wicksell and the Austrians had tried to do.

But there is more. The Swedish focus on the role of expectations in the process of capital formation revealed another problem. This problem is closely related to the influence of expected inflation on nominal interest rates, the Fisher effect. Lindahl used this effect to demonstrate that the equilibrium rate of interest could be reconciled with any price level as long as the inflationary component of the nominal interest rate is correctly forecasted (ibid., 252). This implies in the words of Myrdal (1939, 133) that 'the development of the price level would seem to have nothing to do with monetary equilibrium'. The result is that another of Wicksell's conditions needs to be dropped, namely the requirement of a stable price level, if one assumes perfect foresight. Under imperfect foresight the situation is slightly more complicated, given that one needs to account for the process by which individuals change their expectations. As is currently known, this may either foster price stability (if one falls back on rules of thumb and other conventions) or lead to cumulative price changes in case of self-fulfilling prophecies.

Both possibilities play a role in the Swedish analysis of the influence of expectations on the process of price formation under imperfect knowledge. Lindahl, for example, is ambiguous about the course of events. On the one hand, he stressed that unforeseen events may cause sudden and severe adjustments of the interest rate and other prices. In his view uncertainty causes people to lose all sense of direction leading to 'such an avalanche of price level movements that no equilibrium could be established between the factors determining prices, even for very short periods' (Lindahl 1939, 251). On the other hand, he pointed at the 'frictional conditions' of the real world that immobilize the price level to a certain extent. The interest rate may then vary within certain limits without immediately disturbing the equilibrium of the price level (ibid.). Lindahl found it impossible to offer a more precise explanation of the price dynamics under uncertainty. He stressed that any attempt to do so means that one needs to descend to the analysis of 'individual functions' describing how people deal with expectations (ibid., 349). This is a problem that Lindahl did not work out for the theory of capital. He merely stated that in this case the problem of equilibrium 'of course' becomes more complicated than when one deals with the theory of capital in the temporary equilibrium framework (ibid., 350). In his view, this framework had the advantage of allowing us to assume perfect knowledge for at least the single period, while the analysis of uncertainty and its consequences could be concentrated at the points between such periods. In short, it appears that also in this field Lindahl valued the temporary equilibrium approach as a bridge between statics and dynamics.

Myrdal put the incompatibility of ex ante plans at the heart of his monetary analysis, so it is evident that he stressed the importance of imperfect knowledge to a much greater extent than Lindahl. He developed the ex ante–ex post distinction with the explicit aim to introduce 'anticipations' into the monetary system (Myrdal 1939, 32). The next step was to determine the conditions of a non-cumulative price situation, that is a position of equilibrium in which money serves as an intermediary for both present and intertemporal exchanges. We have seen that Myrdal considered two of Wicksell's three equilibrium conditions irrelevant to this aim, namely the equality of the natural and the money rate of interest and the requirement of a stable price level. That meant that the equality of ex ante saving and investment was the determining factor of a non-cumulative price situation. Or, in his own formulation of this equilibrium condition (Myrdal 1939, 96, italics in the original):

> The money rate is normal if it brings about an *equality between gross real investment on the one side and saving plus total anticipated value-change of the real capital, that is expected decreases in value minus increases in value of the existing real capital, on the other side.*

The question then arises what happens when this condition is violated and a dynamic process of cumulative price change sets in. Will this process reestablish the equality between saving and investment? In other words, is monetary equilibrium a stable condition? In Myrdal's reading it is not. Like Wicksell, he stressed the nature of monetary equilibrium as a 'labile' equilibrium (Myrdal 1939, 36). Ebeling (1997, 52-53) demonstrates that there are three conditions which may upset monetary equilibrium in Myrdal's formulation and cause a cumulative process:

- The profit expectations of entrepreneurs may change for a given money rate of interest. This means that more (or less) funds will be borrowed at this rate and incomes will rise (fall). This will result in higher (lower) prices for consumer goods which supports the initial change in expectations and feeds a next round of price changes.
- Given entrepreneurial expectations, the money rate may change causing a similar chain reaction of price and income changes fuelled by self-fulfilling prophecies.
- Savings may increase but the interest rate does not adjust quickly enough to reflect the new underlying conditions. This causes a paradox of thrift. Consumer demand will fall lowering prices and expected profit margins. Incomes decline and consumer demand falls even further, thus reinforcing the initial change.

All these cases illustrate that the disappointment and subsequent adjustment of expectations form a crucial part of the chain of events that sets the cumulative process in motion.

Myrdal's monetary dynamics is exemplary for the emphasis of the Stockholm school on the potential instability of monetary equilibrium (Laidler 1999, 66). This characteristic explains why the Swedes advocated a monetary policy that favoured active monetary management and thereby strongly opposed the monetary teachings of the Austrian school, a doctrine that started from the same theoretical framework, namely Wicksell's. The tendency of price changes to cumulate as a consequence of monetary disequilibrium logically leads to the conclusion that price stability should be one of the goals of monetary policy. The rationale for this objective was also found in the role of price expectations. We have seen that monetary equilibrium can be reconciled with any absolute level of prices as long as price changes are fully foreseen. The practical implication of the impact of price expectations on the saving-investment behaviour of agents was that monetary policies would have a maximum effect if the policy effects were already foreseen. As Myrdal (1939, 193) put it, 'publicly declared monetary policy can hardly serve its purpose if it is not stated in simple terms and in terms which are of direct importance to the anticipations of entrepreneurs'. This supported the cause of a price stabilization policy as a policy goal that was relatively easy to comprehend.

In addition, the realistic outlook of the members of the Stockholm school brought them to consider the presence of sticky prices as an important aspect of the pricing process in real markets. They believed that sticky prices – money wages in particular – were subject to changes emanating from non-monetary sources, such as the balance of market power between buyers and sellers and a host of other institutional circumstances (conventions, consumption habits et cetera). Obviously, monetary policy could not control this part of the economic system, which meant that one could better aim to adapt the flexible part of the price system to these (fixed) prices (Myrdal 1939, 142). Moreover, 'maintaining a monetary equilibrium becomes a question not only of monetary policy but of economic policy as a whole, social policy and the institutions which rule the labour market, cartel legislation and all related factors' (ibid., 184).

Conclusion

To conclude, it appears that money played an important but not a decisive role in the dynamic method of the Stockholm school. Their realistic and pragmatic approach to economics allowed them to investigate the question of monetary equilibrium and its dynamic aspects from a much broader perspective than is customary in modern theory. The aim was not just to deduce the right formula for the maintenance of equilibrium in a monetary economy, but also to study the pragmatic usefulness of such a concept. We have seen that in some circumstances one had to concede that it was better to adjust monetary policy to the frictions of the real world than the other way round. That does not mean that the Swedish approach to monetary theory was ad hoc or lacked theoretical substance. The role of price-expectations in the monetary process is just one example of the theoretical advance achieved by the Stockholm school.

Nowadays, economic theory stares itself blind at the question of how to reconcile money and equilibrium. In the realistic approach of the Swedes this issue raised no problems at all. We have seen that most notably Lindahl and Myrdal dispensed with the idealized general equilibrium theory as the foundation of monetary theory. They postulated the existence of imperfect knowledge and used the ex ante–ex post framework to examine the dynamic consequences of money use in an environment that is characterized by uncertain prospects. This approach relieved them of the need to construct a decent microfoundation for the role of money in equilibrium. Money was simply there and quite naturally so, given that people had to cope with the problems caused by an uncertain future. However, without equilibrium as an anchor the equality between saving and investment was not a self-evident fact. The main question of Swedish monetary theory was therefore how saving and investment would change in case of a disturbance of monetary equilibrium and how the equilibrium conditions could be restored. According to the Swedes, the maintenance of monetary equilibrium was a fragile affair that required the active management from the government and the monetary authorities.

Another main lesson of the Stockholm school concerns the difficulty of developing dynamic analysis without using some kind of equilibrium assumption. We have seen that for pragmatic reasons Lundberg and Lindahl applied the equilibrium assumption at different stages of their dynamic theories, even though they clearly understood the shortcomings of the equilibrium method. They wrestled with the problem that one cannot base a dynamic explanation of economic change on the assumption that everything changes all the time. In order to achieve theoretical progress at least some of the independent and given variables need to be stable or constant for a while. That is why Lundberg adopted a 'mechanical' theory of expectations formation, just as Lindahl looked for 'constant rules of conduct' in the process of plan revision and tried to build a bridge between statics and dynamics.

In the remainder of this chapter we shall see that the Austrians likewise found it impossible to dispense with the assumption of equilibrium as a means to organize their investigation of monetary dynamics, even when the logic of their own arguments suggested that something like equilibrium could impossibly exist in the real world.

AUSTRIAN ECONOMICS: EQUILIBRIUM AS A THOUGHT EXPERIMENT

The Austrians Mises and Hayek clearly belonged to the Wicksellian family and one may even surmise that their monetary theories were more Wicksellian than those of the Stockholm school.[12] We have seen that the members of that school were highly critical of Wicksell's definition of the natural rate of interest as the anchor point of monetary theory. I shall argue that, in contrast, the Austrians considered the use of an ideal equilibrium construct such as the natural rate of interest of vital importance to the development of their theories. However, that does not mean that they were 'slavish' imitators of Wicksell. They went beyond Wicksell in arguing that money is fundamentally non-neutral due to the influence of distribution effects (Cantillon effect) and other irregularities like imperfect knowledge, which allowed them to explain the business cycle as a monetary phenomenon. The interesting fact is that their journey into the unknown field of monetary dynamics started by assuming a highly abstract equilibrium which Mises called the Evenly Rotating Economy and Hayek defined as a neutral money economy. In the following I shall try to explain how they aimed to reconcile these two seemingly incompatible theoretical constructions – perfect foresight equilibrium and monetary dynamics – by using equilibrium theory as a thought experiment.

Human action and the Evenly Rotating Economy

Mises's conception of economic equilibrium as an Evenly Rotating Economy is closely related to the notion of human action and the subjectivist theory of value that follows from it. Mises saw economics as a branch of a more encompassing general theory of human action that he called 'praxeology'. As I explained earlier, human action is purposeful or goal-oriented behaviour with the main goal being that all humans strive to better their conditions. Praxeology is the study of the theoretical consequences of the action theorem. As a true student of Menger, Mises took the task of theory seriously and sharply distinguished between theory and history. For him all data were historical data. Thus the domain of history is 'the collection and systematic arrangement of all the data of experience concerning human action. It deals with the concrete content of human action' (Mises 1949, 30). Praxeology, on the hand, approaches human action from the theoretical angle. The relationship between the two constituting branches of the science of human action, is like a faint echo of the Methodenstreit. Mises believed that history as such could tell us very little.[13] One needs some kind of theoretical structure to select and interpret historical data. Praxeology provides this structure and is therefore needed to give history context and meaning. Theory itself, on the other hand, is decidedly ahistorical. Its field of study is 'human action as such, irrespective of all environmental, accidental and individual circumstances of the concrete acts . . . It aims at knowledge valid for all instances in which the conditions exactly correspond to those implied in its assumptions and inferences'.

For Mises the distinguishing characteristic of praxeology was its emphasis on logical deduction. Like mathematics, it forms an axiomatic structure that can only be penetrated by means of logic. However, in contrast to mathematics the conclusions of praxeology also are a priori true, given that they ultimately rest on the axiom theorem. Mises saw the notion that human beings act in order to improve their condition as a self-evident fact in the sense that it can be checked by means of introspection. The only reasonable scientific test in praxeology is thus a test of its logical consistency. It cannot reach false conclusions unless some logical error is made, which effectively shields it from refutation by empirical test.

Moreover, Mises believed that all human life can be seen as a manifestation of this fundamental axiom. Praxeology would therefore provide a unified social science with a firm theoretical foundation. Concerning the economic domain of this unified science, he defined catallactics as the science of all market phenomena (ibid., 233) and economics as the study of 'the determination of money prices of goods and services exchanged on the market' (ibid., 234).

The definition of economics as a branch of praxeology raises several issues that require further elaboration. The first is the emphasis on the determination of money prices. Mises argued that monetary calculation is an indispensable catalyst of human action. In his view, without money as a medium of exchange it would be almost impossible to conceive of human action. Human action involves a process of comparing alternatives and making a choice between the means one may employ to further some end one considers beneficial to our well-being. Vaughn (1994, 79) points out that choosing in this sense does not mean that acting individuals already have fully articulated preferences. Such preferences are formed during the process of market exchange when people literally face the choices open to them and are able to negotiate the terms of the exchange. According to Mises, this process requires a mediator and that role is performed by money. The importance of money is that it provides a system of accounting that helps people to form preferences over an array of goods. Entrepreneurs use this same tool to compare inputs and outputs and judge the profitability of various ventures. Accordingly, for Mises all aspects of economic calculation – capital and income, profit and loss, spending and saving, cost and yield – are inseparably linked to the operation of a market in which goods and services are exchanged against a universally used medium of exchange, that is money (Mises 1949, 212). Money literally is 'the only vehicle of economic calculation' (ibid., 204) which suggests that the analysis of price formation and human action outside the context of a market economy with monetary exchange is simply a meaningless endeavour.[14]

This line of reasoning affected Mises's work in several ways. To start with it constituted his key contribution to the socialist calculation debate. He believed that the manager of a socialist system would be powerless because there is nothing to calculate in a system without markets. 'There is no way which could lead one from the money computation of a market economy to any kind of computation in a nonmarket system' (Mises 1949, 206). 'The paradox of planning is that it cannot plan because of the absence of economic calculation. What is called a planned economy is no economy at all. It is just a system of groping in the dark' (ibid., 696 and also Mises 1920 and 1936). In addition, the focus on the meaning of monetary calculation led Mises to dismiss the notion of neutral money as a 'serious blunder' (ibid., 203). He argued that money could not be lifted as the well-known veil, given that it performed an essential role as a calculating instrument. As a result, it would be impossible to analyze the monetary economy assuming that it operates as a system of barter where prices are the exchange ratios between commodities in real terms. Without money there would be no exchange, production or investment, in short, there would be no prices.

In line with the demands of praxeology there is a logical relationship between equilibrium as a state of rest and the notion of human action. Human action is driven by what Mises described as 'uneasiness' because people perceive opportunities to better their position. In the world of monetary calculation these opportunities are weighed as the possibilities of profit and loss that motivate consumers, entrepreneurs, speculators and other folk to partake in the economic process. Mises (1949, 244) stated that all human action aims at making itself superfluous. It tends to remove the uneasiness that set acting man in motion and therefore pushes him towards a state of rest. In that sense, human action logically includes the notion that all behavior is equilibrating. As van Zijp (1992, 25) put it: 'On the level of the individual actor all successful action is equilibrating because it eliminates profit opportunities. It is in this sense that praxeologists regard the position that action is equilibrating as a priori true.'

However, we cannot a priori assume that all activities of acting man will be successful. It is therefore uncertain if people are actually able to attain a state of rest; there is only a tendency towards such a state. Van Zijp (1992) points out that this raises the question of coordination on an economy-wide scale. What can we logically deduce from the principle of human action about the behaviour of the market system as a whole?

The way in which Mises dealt with this question is often misunderstood. Cowen and Fink (1985) are an example of the common misconception that Mises simply ignored the issue of coordination and assumed that the market economy always tends towards a state of general equilibrium. In Mises's (1949, 247) terms, this equilibrium is called the 'evenly rotating economy' (ERE). The characteristic of this equilibrium is the complete absence of causal changes that require the lapse of time. There is change in the sense that production takes place, goods are exchanged and prices are formed; there is even population dynamic because people are born, get old and die. But all these changes are regular movements that are repeated again and again without altering the course of the system as a whole. The ERE is therefore 'in perpetual flux, but it remains always at the same spot' (ibid., 248).

Mises himself raised the suspicion that he ignored the issue of coordination by stating that there is 'in every action [a tendency] towards the establishment of an evenly rotating economy' (ibid., 250). He added to the confusion by offering two other conceptions of equilibrium in addition to the ERE. Firstly, he defined equilibrium as a 'plain state of rest' which is a temporary state in which all currently desired transactions have been made and, for the moment, no one wants to trade. According to Mises, this is a kind of equilibrium that can often be observed in real economic life, for example when trade ceases on a market due to a lack of new supply or new demand. It signifies a situation in which all market participants for a moment rest content with their current situation and accordingly feel no impulse to act. In reality such a state will never last for long, given that new consumers enter the market or a new shipment of goods is bound to arrive. To examine how such changes affect prices, one needs a conception of equilibrium that is valid for a longer period of time. Mises's second conception of equilibrium falls into this category and represents a 'final state of rest'.[15] This is the state toward which the market economy tends, if there is no change in the data.

The point that is often misunderstood is that the final state of rest and the ERE are of a radically different nature than the plain state of rest. The plain state of rest only looks at what is going on right now. In that sense it strives to give an adequate description of what happens in actual markets (ibid., 246). But the other two equilibrium concepts adopt a longer time perspective (the final state of rest) or dispense with the elements of time and economic change altogether (ERE). For that reason they do not offer a realistic description of what happens in the actual economy.[16] On the contrary, Mises used them as 'imaginary constructions', mental tools to be used in a thought experiment about the operation of the market system (ibid., 246).

This kind of thought experiment had a long tradition in classical economics and was revived by the older Austrians.[17] Mises (1949, 237) described an imaginary construction as 'a conceptual image of a sequence of events logically evolved from the elements of action employed in its formation'. The function of this construction is that we may better understand the operation of the prime movers of the economic process by first assuming that they are not present and then introducing an isolated factor to provoke change. Mises called this the *argumentum a contrario* (ibid., 251). Thus the ERE excludes all phenomena related to the lapse of time so that we can study what a world without change would look like. This knowledge helps to understand the nature of entrepreneurship as a source of economic change, as well as other events that are indissolubly related to the passage of time, such as uncertainty and the use of money. That is why the Austrians also refer to equilibrium as a 'foil' that can be used to shed light upon the real world by method of contrast (for example Hayek 1941, 23).

The crucial point to grasp is that the ERE and other imaginary constructions are wholly unrelated to the real world. To put it in Mises's words (ibid., 237):

> In designing such an imaginary construction the economist is not concerned with the question of whether or not it depicts the conditions of reality which he wants to analyse. Nor does he bother about the question of whether or not such a system as his imaginary construction posits could be conceived as really existent and in operation.

For that reason, the criticism often levelled against Mises and other Austrians that you can not describe a real economic process of tendency in terms of an ideal concept like the ERE, simply misses ground. Mises no more intended to use the ERE in this manner than Debreu aimed to describe a real economy in terms of his GE-theory.

Nonetheless, this is a point that returns again and again in the commentaries on the Austrian doctrine. Cowen and Fink (1985) criticize Mises and Rothbard for their attempt to establish a real world tendency towards equilibrium on the basis of the ERE. In their view, the ERE merely assumes away the problem to be explained, which is the manner in which acting individuals strive to better coordinate their plans. Thus they exclaim 'How can an imaginary construction illuminate an institution [the system of markets and prices] that performs absolutely no function within that construct?' (Cowen and Fink 1985, 868). In a related way, Trautwein (1996) attacks Hayek for his attempt to explain the disequilibrium adjustments in a monetary economy in terms of his concept of intertemporal equilibrium. He argues that 'there is no link between disequilibrium and equilibrium. Intertemporal equilibrium and the business cycle imply logically disparate assumptions about the role of money and banking'. What these authors overlook is the fact that the ERE and other imaginary constructions are intended to be a logically distinct category and only help to understand reality by providing a contrast.[18] But that is a different type of exercise than the analysis of the ERE or intertemporal equilibrium itself, as Hayek would later point out.[19]

Entrepreneurship, Competition and Market Order

All this does not mean that Mises satisfactorily solved the problem of order that he found so important for the market process. Without question Mises assumed that a market system proceeds in an orderly and harmonious way. He often remarked that market prices are relatively stable and adjust cautiously to changed circumstances. In this way money prices are best able to play their role as the calculating device that helps acting man to determine his preferred choices. Like Adam Smith, Mises (1949, 669) argued that the division of labour and exchange is responsible for increasing wealth. He argued that the higher productivity of the division of labour removes the conflict of interests that naturally exists among humans. In the capitalist system of unhampered market exchange and private control of the means of production, everyone shares in the winning and thus everyone has an interest in preserving this type of social arrangement. For Mises, this was social cooperation in its most pure form. In his vision, an alternative arrangement in which people were assumed to shed the shackles of their egoism and to labour for the common good (that is as the socialist writers assumed would be the case under socialism) was a fantastic fable. Socialism simply could not work, so the choice was that between 'capitalism and chaos' (ibid., 676).[20]

Characteristic of Mises's liberalism is that it is blind to anything that may upset the harmonious operation of the market economy under a capitalist rule.[21] As Vaughn (1994, 90) concludes, for him disorder was a relatively minor problem. Mises never investigated the possibility that disorder could be internal to the market. The manner in which he treated the issue of monopoly is a case in point. Mises conceded that with regard to monopoly prices there is not harmony, but a conflict of interest because the producer has no incentive to accommodate the wishes of consumers. However, he believed that monopoly was not a natural feature of a capitalist market economy (Mises 1949, 677). Monopoly prices were always the outgrowth of some kind of government intervention. 'They are not the products of capitalism, but precisely of the endeavours to counteract the forces determining the height of the market prices'. That is why he preferred to speak of 'monopoly statism'.

This is a telling example of Mises's belief that market disorder could only be an exogenous phenomenon brought about by government intervention. The surprising fact is that in spite of his focus on the nature of the market process, he never studied how competitive forces bring the state of equilibrium closer, that is how entrepreneurial activity helps to better coordinate plans in a decentralized economic structure.

At this point of the analysis the limitation of Mises's logic of choice framework becomes apparent. Mises saw the notion of time as a crucial aspect of praxeology, for 'the notion of change implies the notion of a temporal sequence . . . Action aims at change and is therefore in the temporal order' (ibid., 99). But Mises merely paid lip-service to the importance of time and never seriously investigated the consequences of the passing of time for the action theorem.[22] The process of exchange that is fundamental to the elimination of profit opportunities simultaneously generates new knowledge and so pushes the goal of the ERE further out of sight. Such sources of endogenous change put the onus on learning behaviour and the revision of expectations. But Mises ignored these aspects of economic behaviour in a market context (Van Zijp 1992, 26 and Vaughn 1994, 91). He adopted what is called a static version of subjectivism (see O'Driscoll and Rizzo 1996). The key to this approach is that preferences are subjective and at the same time exogenous. In such a construction there simply is no room for the dynamics of learning and information gathering. Mises only implicitly incorporated expectations and knowledge.

Two examples may serve to support this conclusion. The first concerns the role of expectations in the process of price-formation. According to Mises (1949, 334), for acting man knowledge in the form of 'experience about past prices' was crucial to see his way in the unknown and uncertain future. However, he simultaneously stressed that the importance of knowledge should not be overstated. He said that '[i]f the memory of all prices of the past were to fade away, the pricing process would become more troublesome, but not impossible' (ibid.). To be sure, more mistakes would be made and price fluctuations would be somewhat larger, but all in all the smooth working of the market process would be soon restored. In that regard, the role of knowledge in the form of accumulated experience does not seem so meaningful after all.

It appears that for Mises the explanation of the tendency towards the ERE did not crucially depend on the ability of economic actors to learn from and adjust to the changes that are brought about by the market process. He used a different force to explain the equilibration of market prices, competition. In his own words, '[t]he essential fact is that it is the competition of profit-seeking entrepreneurs that does not tolerate the preservation of false prices of the factors of production' (ibid., 335). As Hayek (1978) would later point out, competition may also involve a process of learning and information gathering, but that was not the kind of equilibrating mechanism that Mises had in mind. For him the crucial aspect of competition was selection. It 'weeds out' the entrepreneurs that fail on two accounts: they are either less efficient than their competitors or fail to anticipate correctly the future demands of consumers.[23]

This brings us to our second example: entrepreneurship is a matter of talent and not something that can be learned or depends on learning behaviour. Mises stressed that entrepreneurs are not 'soulless automatons' that blindly apply some kind of algorithm to instantaneously accommodate changes in demand. Entrepreneurship is the work of humans and therefore by its very nature fallible. In his view 'entrepreneurs often err' (ibid., 582). The point is: do entrepreneurs learn from their mistakes and are they able to thereby improve their track record? Mises's answer to that question is clearly negative. He saw entrepreneurship as a 'specific anticipative understanding of the conditions of the uncertain future [that] defies any rules and systematization'. As a result '[i]t can neither be learned nor taught' (ibid.).

The entrepreneurial capacity of the economy as a whole is therefore a constant and given factor, for the number of successful entrepreneurs simply depends on the distribution of talent among the acting individuals of society. This means that the tendency towards the ERE is likewise driven by an exogenous force. I conclude that a society with more talent for entrepreneurship will have a greater capacity to push the economy towards the ERE. Competition will not alter this tendency but merely affects the speed of adjustment. Stronger competition enhances the quality of entrepreneurship through the selection mechanism. Consequently, market processes are able to faster establish equilibrium when the economy in general shows a higher degree of competitiveness.

This warrants the conclusion that Mises's process analysis only partly succeeded. His definition of human action as a temporal process of choice-making put entrepreneurship, expectations and knowledge formation on the agenda of Austrian economics. However, Mises himself never followed this lead and adopted the typical custom of the classical authors to rely on the force of competition to explain why a market economy always tends towards a state of equilibrium, even when it never actually reaches this position. It was Lachmann who would later show that this view on the nature of the market process involves a contradiction with the action theorem when seen in truly dynamic terms.

Business Cycle Dynamics

The publication of Ludwig von Mises's *Theorie des Geldes und der Umlaufsmittel* (1912) put monetary theory on a radical new course. Mises presented a subjectivist explanation of the value of money which led him to reject the quantity theory as a framework for monetary analysis. His objection to the quantity theory was that it mechanistically linked changes in the quantity of money to changes in the general price level. This was a 'holistic' approach that ran counter to the subjective theory of value that forms the heart of the Austrian economic doctrine (Mises 1949, 396 and 402). The quantity theory looks at the total supply of money and not at the actions of individual men and firms. For the Austrians, aggregate magnitudes such as the quantity of money are like fata morganas – illusory objects that have no real existence, let alone that one can speak of a causal relationship between such magnitudes.[24] The theory of money has to be build up from the basis. Mises understood that from a microeconomic perspective the supply and demand for money depend on the willingness of individuals to exchange money for goods and vice versa. The theory of money was therefore nothing but a special case of the theory of value. Just as for any commodity, for an individual the value of money depends on the subjective perception of the utility of the final exchange.[25] It was the contribution of Mises that he was able to extend the price theories of Menger and Böhm-Bawerk to the case of indirect exchange and the value of money.

The subjectivist approach to monetary theory was of great importance to Mises's interpretation of monetary equilibrium. He rejected the static notion of monetary equilibrium that underlies the quantity theory. According to Mises, money was never neutral in the sense that an increase (decrease) of the money stock proportionally raises (lowers) the general price level, so that real equilibrium in terms of relative prices remains unchanged. For him it was inconceivable that an injection of cash would leave relative prices unaltered. He followed Cantillon in his reasoning that the manner in which the extra cash enters the system and finds its way to people's purses causes income and wealth effects (ibid., 121). He stressed that even in the extremely unlikely case of a neutrally distributed increase of the money stock (Hume's magical overnight doubling of people's purses), relative prices would be affected, given that the demand for commodities would not change in the same neutral manner (ibid., 122).[26]

The meaning of the Cantillon effect can be elucidated by showing that is incompatible with the image of monetary equilibrium as a ball resting at the bottom of a bowl. Mises never liked mechanistic metaphors in the first place, but he certainly would have rejected this one.[27] He saw money as a dynamic agent of irreversible changes. The economy would, after a monetary impulse, never return to its previous equilibrium position. Mises made it quite clear that income and wealth effects would push it on a trajectory to a different equilibrium. His image of monetary equilibrium was more like Wicksell's ball on a plane, but with a crucial difference. Recall that according to Wicksell's metaphor, a ball disturbed from its equilibrium position would keep running until the force that moved in the first place would cease to operate (the cumulative process stops). Mises would probably see a ball running on very edged and roughed plane. Once in motion, it would eventually stop somewhere but exactly where would be impossible to foretell. By the same token, the ball could never return to the position it had been before.

In Mises's mind, the road towards equilibrium has a certain dynamic of its own and the static framework of the quantity theory is not the right kind of instrument to explore where it leads (Mises 1924, 133, see also 126).

> Die mechanische, auf fehlerhafter Übertragung eines statischen Gesetzes auf die Dynamiek beruhende Auffassung versagt aber in diesem Falle gerade so wie in jenem; sie kann uns nicht genügen, da sie uns das nicht erklärt, was wir erklärt wissen wollen.

To put the Austrian contribution to monetary theory into context it is important to dehomogenize Mises and Hayek. The latter was more a 'Wicksellian' than Mises. Hayek consistently used the distinction between the market rate and natural rate of interest in his monetary analyses and saw forced savings as an important part of the transmission mechanism between monetary and real effects. In contrast, Mises just once referred to the notion of a natural rate of interest in his magnum opus *Human Action* and adopted a distinction of his own (the loan market rate of interest and the gross market rate of interest).[28] Moreover, the doctrine of forced savings was one of Mises's main objections against Wicksell's cumulative process.

Forced saving is essentially a comparative static argument and, for that reason alone, suspect. It played a role in Wicksell's two-period model (see Chapter 11) which showed that the cumulative process could proceed unchecked as long as the market rate of interest remained below the natural rate. The essence of this model was that it showed the interaction of monetary and real effects that are caused by a disruption of monetary equilibrium. The fact that the market rate is lower than the natural rate of interest provides an incentive to invest in production processes with a longer time horizon. This development reflects an intertemporal coordination failure, for the time preferences of consumers have not shifted accordingly. Forced saving neutralizes the potentially disturbing effect of this mismatch. Inflation forces consumers to save in real terms and it is this effect that allows producers to finance their overoptimistic investment plans. The end result is that producers are not corrected and continue their mistake in the next two-period cycle, causing subsequent rounds of inflation as long as the market rate remains below the natural rate of interest.

Mises's rebuttal of the cumulative process focused on the feedback mechanism (or rather the lack thereof) between inflation and the interest rate. He asked why a divergence between the two interest rates was not automatically dissolved and monetary equilibrium restored (ibid., 369).[29] He followed Wicksell's analysis of the interaction between the interest rate and the capital structure. A lowering of the interest rate below the natural rate provides a false signal to investors to elongate the production period (ibid., 371). However, in contrast to Wicksell Mises did not believe that this elongation would be sustainable. He presented what in the end amounts to a crisis theory of the monetary business cycle. He argued that the loan fund and the stock of intermediate products would in time prove insufficient to fully complete the new investment projects. Sooner or later some of these projects would have to be abandoned due to a lack of resources. According to Mises, this provokes a reaction of the price mechanism that is concomitant to a higher market rate of interest: the price of consumers' goods rise while the price of producers' goods fall.[30]

This effect may be counterbalanced if the banks decide to increase the money stock again and supply the financial means that allows producers to continue their projects a little longer. This will temporarily put off the increase of the interest rate. However, Mises stressed that sooner or later producers will again run short of resources and return to their banks for yet another infusion of credit. The banks may set the interest rate at whatever rate they like, but there is a downward limit to how low it can sink. According to Mises, this limit is formed by people's belief that money is still an objective standard of exchange value. The moment that an ever increasing rate of inflation causes people to distrust the value of money as the common unit of exchange a panic breaks out with all the familiar symptoms of a currency crisis: galloping inflation and a likewise panic-driven increase of the interest rate (ibid., 373). The end result is that the banks are forced one way or another to restore the equality between the market rate and the natural rate of interest.

So there is a mechanism that automatically restores monetary equilibrium, but this equilibrating tendency cannot be used as the basis of a comparative static exercise. Mises argued that the new equilibrium is simply incomparable to the old one. The fall of the interest rate has distributive effects that changes relative prices. More importantly, it takes a crisis to restore monetary equilibrium. Equilibration is a euphemism for a very costly process of adjustment in both human and economic terms. According to Mises, a large part of the capital stock will go to waste because it cannot be employed in an alternative fashion. This constitutes an important loss of wealth that will impoverish society at large.[31] However, the destruction of capital as part of the process of reconstruction is unavoidable. It is therefore in society's interest to undergo this process as soon as possible and not to prolong the artificially created investment boom.[32] A prolongation of the investment boom would simply mean that the correction cuts deeper and causes a greater amount of economic destruction.

Conclusion

From this brief exposition of Mises's ideas it is clear that he had a lot in common with the Swedes. With the Stockholm school he believed that money played a vital role in the economics process and that the explanation of this process required a dynamic theory. For Mises it was simply inconceivable to have a market economy without the use of money as a medium of exchange. Without money there would be no calculation and hence no price formation or exchange.

Furthermore, like the Swedes, Mises aimed to give a dynamic explanation of economic changes, because in static conditions there would be no human action, no choice making, no error and disappointed expectations; in short no economic problems that require explanation. In line with this view he rejected the static interpretation of the quantity theory and related concepts like forced saving. According to Mises, monetary changes induce adjustments of individual choices in a historical sense, which means that the choices made are unidirectional in time and cannot be undone. As a result, the economy does not smoothly move from one equilibrium position to the next but undergoes a process of change that is determined by uncertainty and path-dependent effects.

At this point the agreement with the dynamic method of the Stockholm school radically breaks off. We have seen that the Swedes like Myrdal believed that monetary equilibrium was unstable and their aim was to explain the dynamics of the disequilibrium adjustments. Their dynamics consisted in investigating the causal chain of events in distinct sequences or periods regardless of the direction of those changes (away or towards monetary equilibrium). This reflects their conviction that active management of the money supply was needed to ensure that the conditions of monetary equilibrium would be met.

This call for monetary intervention is in stark contrast with Mises's business cycle theory, which concludes that intervention of any kind will merely deepen the economic crisis that results when monetary equilibrium is disturbed and prolongs the period needed to restore equilibrium. In that regard, Mises's monetary dynamics is rather one-sided. It stresses the healing powers of free competition and the equilibrium tendency of the market system. We have seen in this section that Mises simply ignored the possibility that market exchange generates disequilibrium forces as an endogenous outcome of the trading process. Austrian dynamic analysis focusses on disequilibrium adjustments but has a blind spot for any change that does not comply to the image of the market economy as a harmonious process leading towards equilibrium.

In the next section we shall see that Hayek's work in this field showed the same bias in spite of his efforts to redefine the concept of economic equilibrium and to provide Austrian dynamic analysis with a better theoretical underpinning.

THE PROBLEM OF ECONOMIC ORDER

Hayek and Equilibrium Theory

In the late 1920s and the 1930s Hayek further developed Mises's theory of a monetary business cycle. In this field of research Hayek owed much to the theoretical foundation laid by Mises. Like the latter he put the time structure of production – the Austrians called this the period of production – central to the analysis and assumed that money was the unique cause of the cyclical fluctuations in real output. Hayek surpassed Mises's achievement in that he was able to give a much more systematic exposition of this theory. His aim was challenging as he attempted to integrate monetary and price theory. As he put it in *Prices and Production* (Hayek 1931a, 127):

> The task of monetary theory is a much wider one than is commonly assumed . . . its task is nothing less than to cover a second time the whole field which is treated by pure theory under the assumption of barter, and to investigate what changes in the conclusions of pure theory are made necessary by the introduction of indirect exchange.

In the process, Hayek critically examined the underlying assumptions of his business cycle theory and posed important questions about the nature of several key concepts. Recurring themes in his work are questions like 'what is capital?', 'what does saving mean?' and, for our purposes of specific importance, 'what is the nature of equilibrium?'.

Hayek's studies on monetary equilibrium and business cycle theory have been the subject of many commentaries and interpretative studies. However, there are two issues in particular that need to be addressed in the context of this chapter.

The first issue is Hayek's aim to develop a meaningful notion of monetary equilibrium. Hayek tried to solve the dilemma of equilibrium in a monetary economy by developing the concept of neutral money. This concept refers to the conditions under which it would be conceivable that in a monetary economy prices would behave as they are supposed to behave in an ideal barter economy. The problem with this concept is that Hayek left a fundamental question unanswered, namely: What are the foundations of this monetary economy, that is, what are the functions that money performs? (Klausinger 1990, 63). Colonna (1990, 63) argues that Hayek made very little progress in this area: 'In his theory the role of money is the traditional and very limited one of "disturbing" the normal course of events in the short run and of being "neutral" in the long run.' According to her, it was the neutrality concept which prevented Hayek from breaking new ground and putting monetary theory on a radically different course.

Moreover, he used monetary equilibrium as a benchmark for his business cycle analysis which means that his efforts in this field are likewise susceptible to criticism. Trautwein (1996, 143) puts the finger at the sore spot. He argues that Hayek's equilibrium benchmark:

> . . . has serious defects at various stages in the sequence of the [business] cycle. First, there is no link between equilibrium and disequilibrium. Intertemporal equilibrium and the business cycle imply logically disparate assumptions about the roles of money and banking. Therefore, both states cannot be connected by transitions from neutrality to non-neutrality of money.

The second issue concerns the strategy of Hayek's equilibrium analysis in general. Caldwell (1988) is an example of those who argue that Hayek's seminal 1937 article *Economics and knowledge* constituted a radical change in Hayek's thinking about economic equilibrium, a change that ultimately caused him to abandon the field of pure economics in favour of social and political theory. According to Caldwell, until 1937 Hayek adopted the static framework of neoclassical general equilibrium as the basis of his work; Desai (1994) even calls him a 'staunch defender' of the Walrasian general equilibrium approach. However, the focus on the role of knowledge in the economic process gradually made him aware that the static approach led economics into a dead alley. In order to examine dynamic questions such as that of the business cycle, the concept of equilibrium itself had to be reformed. Hayek met this challenge by defining equilibrium as plan coordination, assuming that market participants only have local and thus imperfect knowledge. Caldwell, Desai and others argue that this was a substantial departure from Walrasian general equilibrium.

The implications of this alleged break in Hayeks's thinking on equilibrium are highly significant. The discovery of a new and scientifically improved conception of equilibrium makes it hard to explain why in 1941 Hayek returned to the Walrasian general equilibrium as the basis of his *Pure Theory of Capital*. Was he being inconsistent or is there another reason why he continued his pre-1937 research programme? Another question is what became of the new Hayek programme which intended to examine the dynamics of plan coordination? Desai (1994) expresses great disappointment in the results of this new approach. He argues that by 1945 Hayek had abandoned his quest for a solution of the problem of equilibrium. He substituted a vision which entailed that by operating as a telecommunications mechanism the price system could be assumed to automatically solve the coordination puzzle. For Desai, at this stage the problem of knowledge had again become a non-problem. This U-turn may explain what Caldwell (1988) calls Hayek's transformation; his turning away from technical economics to other fields of study.

I shall argue that there is a missing link in this discussion which allows us to view the development of Hayek's conception of economic equilibrium in a different light. This link is Mises's approach to equilibrium analysis as a thought experiment in the Austrian tradition. Following Moss (1997), this chapter argues that Hayek treated equilibrium theory in the same manner. This interpretation sheds new light on a number of old issues, such as the concept of neutral money and the meaning of the equilibrium benchmark in his business cycle theory. Additionally, it shows that the real break in Hayek's approach towards equilibrium theory did not occur in 1937 when he redefined equilibrium, but much later in the 1960s when he stopped pursuing equilibrium theory as a thought experiment. The next sections intend to investigate the cause and consequences of this change of tactics.

The Role of Imaginary Constructions

It is often thought that Hayek rejected Mises's approach to equilibrium theory because the latter used the notion of a stationary equilibrium as a benchmark for analysis, whereas Hayek, from the very start of his career, defined equilibrium as an intertemporal concept (van Zijp 1992). It is true that Hayek rejected the notion of a stationary equilibrium over time which assumes that prices remain constant as the economy reproduces itself. Hayek believed that a stationary state in this sense was simply impossible. The crux of his argument was the insight that in order for self-reproduction to take place the prices of the same goods at different points in time have to be different (Hayek 1928, 73). Put differently, even when commodities are identical in terms of physical characteristics, if they are traded at different points in time then in economic terms they are best seen as different commodities. The reason for this is that the economic conditions under which production and exchange take place will change over time. Hayek (1928) recognized that such changes are no problem for a definition of equilibrium as long as it includes the assumption of perfect foresight. Thus even when the economy regularly reproduces itself it is necessary to view the equilibrium concept in terms of the intertemporal price system.

However, Hayek's rejection of the stationary equilibrium concept that had occupied a central place in Mises's monetary analysis obscures the common base from which both members of the Austrian school developed their ideas on equilibrium analysis. This was the method of imaginary constructions, one of the core features of the work of their teacher Friedrich von Wieser (see Chapter 10).

Recall that Mises used his ERE as a mental construction that is wholly unrelated to the real world but is nonetheless of great value to better understand the causal forces at play in everyday processes. It can perform this paradoxical task by showing what will happen in the economic world if we abstract from certain aspects of economic life such as money, uncertainty or entrepreneurship. Mises used the ERE in this manner to investigate the features of economics as a science of human action.

On his part Hayek was from the start fully committed to equilibrium analysis calling it an 'indispensable tool' for economic analysis (Hayek 1928, 75). That he saw equilibrium theory as a thought experiment is best described in the opening chapters of his *Pure Theory of Capital* (1941) where he explained his conceptual method in painstaking detail. One finds in these chapters a synopsis of all issues that inspired his earlier writings on equilibrium theory, such as the discussion of why capital theory is a problem of general equilibrium theory, the goal and limits of equilibrium theory in economics, the relationship between money and equilibrium, the difference between stationary and dynamic equilibrium and the definition of equilibrium as plan coordination.

This definition is clearly based on what Desai (1994) sees as the key elements of Hayek's redefinition of equilibrium in the 1937 article. There is first of all the compatibility of the plans based on the subjective data of different individuals. This condition states that 'correspondence between plans prevails' because people 'correctly foresee what changes will occur in the actions of others' (Hayek 1941, 18–19). In brackets he added that there is no reason to believe that an equilibrium of this kind will actually come about, which shows that the congruence of the subjective expectations with objective outcomes is the second aspect of the definition of equilibrium as plan coordination (Desai 1994, 37-38). In the words of Hayek (1941, 23–24): 'The state of equilibrium as here understood is a state of complete compatibility of ex ante plans, where in consequence (unless changes occur in the external data about which economic theory cannot say anything in any case) the ex post situation is identical with the ex ante.'

Another innovation of the 1937 article was the discovery that the knowledge on which individuals base their expectations is necessarily imperfect. People only have what Hayek called 'local knowledge' concerning the prices and quantities of economic goods under their control. Their economic activities are nothing more than a single step in a long chain of successive operations; they perform part of a larger process of the rest of which they know little. This raises the question whether all these bits of information are sufficient to ensure that the larger process can be completed at all. Hayek solved this problem by assuming that the fragments of knowledge are connected. For equilibrium to exist at the macroeconomic level, there must be some overlap between different individuals' bits of knowledge to span the entire set (Desai 1994, 41–42).

This insight led Hayek (1937) to define the division of knowledge as one of the central problems of economics. The challenge for economic theory was to discover the dynamics behind the coordination of decentralized activities. What role do prices play in revealing the knowledge individuals have? People have incomplete knowledge so false trading (in a Walrasian sense) must occur. Does false trading eventually get eliminated as people learn from experience? If so, what are the conditions on the process of revising expectations to guarantee convergence?

In 1941 Hayek simply ignored these questions, assuming that it will be possible to coordinate all these different plans into one single plan, although this plan will not exist in any one mind (Hayek 1941, 26). He even evoked the fiction of the benevolent dictator, the person who is assumed to direct the actions of the different individuals in accordance with this single plan. Small wonder that commentators like Desai (1994) and Rosner (1994) believe that by 1941 Hayek had returned to his Walrasian general equilibrium programme of the pre-1937 period.

However, I claim that the issue at stake is merely a shift in emphasis, not of principles. In the quoted passages from the 1941 book Hayek was preparing ground for his pure theory of capital, an exercise which he considered possible only in the context of general equilibrium theory. Before proceeding with this task, Hayek felt the need to justify this type of equilibrium analysis as part of his general approach to economics. This vindication consisted in explaining that the benevolent dictator model which guarantees plan coordination is nothing but an imaginary construction. For Hayek (1941, 22–23) equilibrium analysis begins 'by constructing as an intellectual tool, a fictitious state under which these plans are in complete correspondence without, however, asking whether this state will ever, or can ever, come about'.[33]

Hayek's description of equilibrium analysis as an imaginary construction is in complete agreement with Mises's use of the ERE. First, like Mises Hayek stressed that equilibrium theory is not realistic in the sense that it aims to explain or describe events as they take place in real life situations. He made it quite clear that equilibrium refers to an ideal state that will never be fully realized. In fact, he stated that 'in order to derive full advantage of this technique [equilibrium theory, BT] we must abandon every pretence that it possesses reality' (ibid., 28).

This bold claim raises the question whether a thought experiment of this kind has any purpose apart from studying the logical aspects of some abstract economic system. It is at this point that we encounter a second agreement with Mises's treatment of equilibrium analysis. Hayek described the imaginary state as a 'kind of foil' (ibid., 23). In line with Mises's *argumentum a contrario*, he stated that equilibrium provides a contrast that allows us to predict what will happen if the conditions for equilibrium are not met. An example explains how this method of contrast is supposed to operate. Equilibrium requires the mutual compatibility of all individual plans. Hayek argued that by studying the conditions for equilibrium in this sense we gain a better understanding of the mutual interdependence of individual decisions. According to him, this knowledge helps us to explain people's reactions when the economy is not in equilibrium, which forces people to readjust their decisions. This is the meaning of Hayek's rather puzzling conclusion that '[t]he statement of the conditions under which all individual plans will be compatible is therefore implicitly a statement of what will happen if they are not compatible' (ibid., 23). In other words, Hayek clearly saw a bridge between equilibrium and disequilibrium.

At this point the ways of Mises and Hayek part. Mises treated the thought experiment as an exclusively mental process that required no empirical proof in order to validate its conclusions. For him, equilibrium analysis was a logical operation that proceeded from the self-evident axioms of human action and therefore reached conclusions that were a priori true as long as one did not violate the rules of logical reasoning. However, Hayek did not rely on the power of logical reasoning to the same extent. In fact, he distinguished between two types of analysis. He saw equilibrium analysis as an exercise in economic logic, an example of what Hayek (1937) called the Pure Logic of Choice. Complementary to this field was a causal analysis of the economic changes that bring the economy closer towards equilibrium. Dynamic analysis of this kind could profit from the insights gained from logical analysis, but the ultimate test of theorizing about causation was an empirical one. Hayek was not very clear about the nature of this test. In one place he asserted that one needed to demonstrate a theory's usefulness by applying it to a particular problem (Hayek 1941, 27). In another case, he stressed that what was at stake was the verification of an empirical proposition (Hayek 1937, 26).

I argue that Hayek's distinction between equilibrium analysis as a form of pure logic and the empirical investigation of the causal process that pushes the economy towards equilibrium is a vital clue to the interpretation of his work. It is hardly ever mentioned that one of the reasons why Hayek published his article *Economics and knowledge* was to emphasize the importance of this distinction, because he believed that the 'economists of the older generation' mixed up the two kind of propositions, the logical and the empirical (Hayek 1937, 53-54). The main purpose of the article was therefore not to reject Walrasian general equilibrium theory or another form of pure equilibrium analysis, as some are prone to maintain (for example Desai 1994 and Rosner 1994). Hayek merely set out an agenda for research and economic analysis in terms of static and highly unrealistic equilibrium theories was a valid part of that agenda. In un-Austrian fashion he even promoted the cause of mathematical formalism in economics. As Hayek (1937, 35) put it:

> My criticism of the recent tendencies to make economic theory more and more formal is not that they have gone too far, but that they have not yet been carried far enough to complete the isolation of this branch of logic and to restore to its rightful place the investigation of causal processes, using formal economic theory as a tool in the same way as mathematics.

To a large extent Hayek (1937) was devoted to the question how one should investigate the tendency of a market economy towards equilibrium as an empirical proposition, that is as a form of causal analysis. It is in the context of this question that he launched his ideas about the division of knowledge and people's learning behaviour as elements of the process of disequilibrium coordination. The sharp distinction between logical and causal analysis in economics returns in Hayek (1941), which underlines the consistency of his research agenda in this period. The major difference with the 1937 article is that Hayek now focussed on the further development of real equilibrium analysis, the logical part of the agenda. He undertook this study because he considered it 'logically prior' to the study of the monetary mechanism (ibid., 36). For him, monetary analysis belonged to the domain of causal analysis, because there is no role for money in an equilibrium theory which assumes that individuals have perfect foresight and compatible plans. However, to better understand the effects of monetary prices on the process of coordination, it was necessary to first examine the working of the price mechanism in real terms and its interaction with the structure of production. It was this objective that Hayek's *Pure Theory of Capital* aimed to realize.

Hayek originally intended to extent this analysis by adding the monetary factor and using the pure theory of capital as a framework for causal analysis in the monetary domain. However, his intention to publish a work on the applied theory of capital never materialized (Hayek in Kresge and Wenar 1994, 79). He pointed to the outbreak of the war as the reason why he had ceased his research in this direction, but the more likely explanation is that he failed to make sufficient progress. He admitted that laying a proper theoretical foundation for the dynamic inquiry of capitalist production had cost him much effort and that he had come to a point where he doubted whether further effort on his part would be repaid by the results (Hayek 1941, viii). I shall further on consider the reasons for Hayek's pessimism in this regard and his subsequent abandonment of technical economics.

Neutral Money as an Equilibrium Benchmark

From the start, the notion of neutral money was one of the key concepts of Hayek's redefinition of monetary equilibrium. For him neutral money was nothing but a theoretical concept on a par with Walras's *numeraire* and Menger's assumption of an 'inner objective' exchange value of money. The aim of neutral money was to examine the impact of the assumption that people use an indirect medium of exchange on the formation of prices. Barter exchange is characterized by what Hayek called 'the basic identity of supply and demand' (Hayek 1933b, 160). By this he meant nothing else than that Say's law applies to the total quantity of supply and demand in a barter economy (Hayek 1941, 32). The introduction of money disrupts the identity between supply and demand and turns it into an equality: excess supply or demand for goods must now be matched by an equally large excess demand or supply for money.

The point is that Say's equality did not explain why the introduction of money affects relative prices and the capacity of the price mechanism to maintain equilibrium between supply and demand. The quantity theory of money assumes that money leaves relative prices unchanged as the general price level proportionally increases (decreases) with an increase (decrease) of the money stock, assuming other things constant. By introducing the concept of neutral money, Hayek aimed to investigate whether it was valid to assume that money was neutral in this sense. To this purpose he defined neutral money as the study of 'the conditions under which it would be conceivable that in a monetary economy prices would behave as they are supposed to behave in equilibrium analysis' (Hayek 1941, 30-31, n1).

It is very tempting to compare neutral money in this sense with Walras's *numeraire* in general equilibrium theory. Conceptually, there is indeed a similarity because both concepts define a fictitious unit of money to effectuate indirect exchange in an equilibrium model. However, there is also an important difference that is closely related to Hayek's strategy to approach equilibrium theory as a thought experiment. This difference is that Hayek used the concept of neutral money as a contrast to better understand the economy's dynamics when the conditions for neutral money are violated. He therefore applied neutral money to a specific dynamic setting, while Walras's analysis of monetary problems never ventured into areas where knowledge is imperfect, that is where false trading is allowed and expectations may be disappointed.

Hayek's definition of neutral money received much criticism on the grounds that it failed to explain the role of money in a state of equilibrium (Klausinger 1990). Criticism of this kind misses the mark because Hayek was well aware of the fundamental tension that exists between the use of money as a medium of exchange and the definition of equilibrium in terms of perfect foresight.[34] His *Pure Theory of Capital* (1941) is a study of general equilibrium in real terms because he acknowledged that people have no incentive to demand and hold money when there is no uncertainty about future plans and conditions. Under such conditions 'there is indeed little room for money in the picture at all, except as "mere counters"' (ibid., 29).

This raises the question why Hayek used the definition of monetary equilibrium as the starting point of his business cycle analysis. Better than anyone else, he knew that a definition of this kind is internally inconsistent, so why build business cycle analysis on quicksand?

The answer to this riddle lies in the meaning of equilibrium analysis as a thought experiment. It is easily forgotten that for an Austrian economist the assumption of neutral money was a bold conjecture. One of the pillars of Austrian thought is the notion that money is essentially non-neutral in both the short-run and the long-run. Mises was one of the first Austrians to explain the dynamics behind the non-neutrality of money in terms of distribution and income effects. Hayek contributed to his analysis by defining money as a 'loose joint' between the decisions to produce and sell things on the one hand and decisions to buy them on the other hand (Yeager 1997, 31). In his view money was an inherently unstable factor because a monetary change would always bring about changes in the real structure of production (Hayek 1941, 33–34). To make matters worse, such changes would be self-reversing without ever leading the economy back to the original equilibrium in real terms. In short, for him as for Mises, money was the ultimate and only cause of cyclical fluctuations.

From that point of view, it is highly paradoxical to start business cycle analysis by assuming that money is neutral. The rationale for this approach was the vision outlined above: the study of a deliberately unrealistic assumption like neutral money allows us to better comprehend the mechanism that causes money to be a non-neutral factor. This objective of Hayek's monetary business cycle analysis materialized in what became known as the 'traverse', Hayek's intertemporal monetary equilibrium that functions as a growth-path reference for the analysis of the cycle.

We need to discuss Hayek's cycle analysis in some detail because the role of the traverse and the neutrality assumption is frequently misunderstood. The view of Trautwein (1996) in this regard has already been cited. He argues that Hayek adopted an illegitimate procedure because he analyzed a process of disequilibrium adjustment in terms of an equilibrium model. This is impossible, given that the equilibrium state and the disequilibrium process are founded on different assumptions. Rosner (1994) even goes a step further and typifies Hayek's business cycle analysis as un-Austrian because it involves comparative static analysis. It thereby ignores crucial aspects of the market process approach such as information-processing via markets.

The error involved in these commentaries is that they misunderstand the meaning of Hayek's equilibrium approach to business cycle analysis as a thought experiment. In this role the traverse or equilibrium adjustment towards a new monetary equilibrium acts as a benchmark for the analysis of the disequilibrium coordination process that constitutes the dynamics of the business cycle. But the benchmark function of equilibrium does not mean that equilibrium and disequilibrium are founded on a different framework. In fact, both are based on Hayek's (1928) definition of equilibrium as an intertemporal concept in terms of perfect foresight.

Recall that Hayek (1928) defined equilibrium as an intertemporal concept because he believed that price changes are necessary to keep supply and demand in equilibrium when the economy reproduces itself over time. Price adjustments of this kind are the proper response of the market mechanism to changes in external conditions such as preferences and technology. It was the contribution of Hayek that he recognized that future changes of this kind pose no threat to economic equilibrium as long as they are foreseen by all relevant parties. In his hands perfect foresight became the defining characteristic of economic equilibrium.

In his business cycle analysis, Hayek made the time factor explicit by introducing the period of production and heterogeneous capital. In Hayek's structure of production, goods are time specific and therefore heterogeneous in the sense that they require a different period of production in order to be transformed from basic materials into consumer goods. Thus consumer goods have a short period of production because they are almost ready for consumption. Capital goods on the other hand require a long period of production because they support production processes that will turn out consumer goods at some future date. The average period of production of all production processes, therefore, is an indication of society's willingness to invest current resources in the production of future consumption.

The period of production thus provides a key to analyze equilibrium dynamics over time. Hayek assumed that in equilibrium the price margins (over costs) between the stages of production equal the rate of interest. This is equivalent to Wicksell's second equilibrium condition which states that the monetary rate of interest equals the natural rate of interest. A change in one of the real determinants of equilibrium, like a shift in consumer preferences, sets in motion a chain of price changes between the stages of production and thus breaks this equilibrium condition. Hayek's traverse concerns a change in the time preferences of consumers, such that they are willing to give up current resources in exchange for future consumption. This raises the supply of savings in the loan market which, ceteris paribus, causes a fall in the rate of interest. The money rate of interest thus follows the shift in the natural rate of interest and restores monetary equilibrium, while the production structure smoothly adjusts itself to the intertemporal shift of resources and demand.

The key in this equilibrium adjustment process is that the price signals in all stages of production set in motion a change of production plans in the right direction. The shift in the savings rate of consumers implicitly involves a change in demand from consumer goods towards capital goods (goods of higher order). As a result, price margins of the production of capital goods will relatively increase. Entrepreneurs now shift resources from the production of consumer goods towards the production of capital goods causing the price differential to disappear. The price margins of the different stages of production will swiftly tend towards a new uniform level, albeit a lower one than the former. In the process, the structure of production adjusts itself because producers elongate their production processes, that is the average period of production will rise. This raises the productivity per unit of capital but also means that in general consumers will have to wait longer before they are able to enjoy the fruits of their savings. The adjustment of real production processes thus swiftly follows the change in the time preference of consumers that started the equilibrium adjustment in the first place.

The essence of the Austrian monetary theory of the business cycle is the claim that a monetary expansion does not result in a smooth and coordinated adjustment of this kind, but causes a chain reaction of malinvestments and upsets the intertemporal equilibrium in real terms. The typical case treated by Hayek is that of a credit injection by the banks.[35] An increase of the money stock in this manner causes a fall of the monetary rate of interest which disrupts monetary equilibrium because the natural rate has not changed. However, Hayek treated the natural rate of interest as a notional concept that cannot be observed. Entrepreneurs perceive the monetary rate of interest as a signal for changes in the economy's real determinants. Hence they believe that the fall in the interest rate indicates that consumer preferences have changed in a manner which improves the relative profitability of longer, more capital-intensive, production processes. As a result, they engage in an investment boom generating an excess-demand for the original means of production such as labour and other non-specific capital goods.

We are now in the middle of a cumulative process of price changes that had already been explained by Wicksell and Mises. A fall in the interest rate causes entrepreneurs to bid away resources from the consumer goods industries and so causes inflation of consumer goods but also raises the incomes of workers. At this stage in the process an effect occurs that is crucial for the sustainability of the credit-induced investments that mark the boom phase of the business cycle. This is the Ricardo effect that in Hayek's scheme works as a counteracting force on the expansion of output and ultimately causes economic crisis, the inescapable turning point of the cycle.[36] The Ricardo effect occurs due to a double pressure on the price of consumer prices. On the one hand, the supply of consumer goods decreases as a result of the shift of resources towards the production of intermediate and other capital goods. On the other hand, the demand for consumer goods has also increased due to higher nominal incomes for workers. The result is that consumer prices are rising faster than nominal wages causing real wages to fall. Hayek described this process by saying that in the upswing of the cycle wages are always 'lagging' behind consumer prices (Hayek 1931a, 90 and 146).[37] The Ricardo effect states that falling real wages motivate producers to substitute labour-intensive for capital-intensive production processes. In Hayek's theory the upswing thus automatically calls forth a counteracting force to the investment boom which set the cycle in motion. The question to be answered is what force will dominate: the credit-induced investment in longer production processes or the inflation-induced pull towards shorter production processes?

Hayek's answer to that question was that the banks who ignited the investment boom in the first place also keep it running. Entrepreneurs, determined to complete their endangered long-term capital projects, return to the banks for more credit and the whole process repeats itself. An infusion of new credit-money lowers the interest rate and supports the expectations of entrepreneurs that the economy's fundamentals are changing. They invest in longer production processes, pulling resources away from the consumer goods industry and causing a next round of inflation. But, as product process always rise ahead of wages, the Ricardo effect again emerges and acts as a break on the expansion of investment. In each market period, it so provides a signal to investors that opposes the expectations fed by the fall of the interest rate. Hayek stressed that there is no right or wrong in this struggle for scarce investment resources. Rather, both product prices and the interest rate are incorrect in the sense of being inconsistent with the underlying objective conditions of supply and demand for consumer goods. As long as capital creation is financed through expanding bank credit, the signals that communicate the objective conditions to entrepreneurs are distorted, leading to incorrect investment decisions. In Hayek's view, there was no gentle escape from this process of competing errors. The lesson had to be learnt the hard way by means of an economic crisis.

The business cycle reaches its turning point when the banks finally deny the claims of producers for new loans. Hayek offered several explanations for the stop of the credit expansion. First, he argued that the money rate of interest is a function of the default risk, which, in turn, increases with the debt-equity ratio. Second, in the course of a credit boom the need for cash will increase along with money incomes and prices. The ensuing cash drain will force banks to restrict the credit supply. Finally, he adopted Mises's argument that even if there is no reserve restriction in terms of outside money, a credit expansion must stop before an accelerating rate of inflation invalidates money as the unit of account.

In Hayek's reading, any of these causes will stop the expansion of credit and raise the interest rate. This is the signal which awakens entrepreneurs and makes them realize that they have been building their production plans on false expectations. They have invested their loans in longer, more roundabout production processes, but the projected demand for the products of these processes is not forthcoming. The change to more productive methods of production turns out to be futile. The result is a massive restructuring of investments between the stages of production. Many of the longer processes under construction will remain incomplete. Entrepreneurs try to salvage some of the non-specific capital goods by investing them in shorter processes, but capital goods that lack this flexibility will be abandoned and constitute a significant economic loss. Needless to say, the hands employed by these capital goods will likewise become redundant.

Hayek regarded the crisis as a cure for the price mechanism that has to be waited out. The turmoil of the crisis breeds uncertainty that probably causes entrepreneurs to overreact and to over-shorten the period of production. But he did not say much about where interest and prices end up in the crisis or how the bottom of the downswing is determined. The only certainty is that the business cycle will not return the economy to its initial equilibrium (Hayek 1941, 35n2). Like Mises, Hayek stressed the redistribution of incomes in the process of forced saving (Cantillon effect) and the real capital losses in the wake of the crisis. Frictions of this kind cause long-term deviations which force the economy onto a new path of equilibrium growth. Whether it will actually reach this new traverse remains highly uncertain, given that Hayek believed that any money using economy is inherently unstable. Without the proper controls on the money supply, the most likely scenario for the monetary economy is a random walk from one equilibrium growth path to another, meanwhile going through the motions of the business cycle. Seen in this way, there is no escape from the conclusion that for Hayek money was non-neutral in both the short and the long run.

At this stage, it is necessary to return to the starting point of this analysis. I claimed that Hayek approached business cycle theory as a thought experiment with the concept of monetary equilibrium (neutral money) as its anchor point. What lessons can be learned from comparing this equilibrium benchmark with the discoordination dynamics of the business cycle? In my opinion, there emerge four main lessons.[38]

First, the behaviour of banks is a crucial factor for the explanation of the start of the business cycle. Banks initially reduce the interest rate and so cause the coordination failure that starts the malinvestment in capital goods. For Hayek, banking behaviour in this regard was not an accidental or empirical factor. Rather, he aimed to give an endogenous explanation of the cyclical fluctuations and linked the banks' behaviour to the elasticity of the credit supply.

Second, comparison of the business cycle with the traverse highlights forced saving as a propagation mechanism of the upswing. In the traverse, consumers voluntarily expand savings and so allow the construction of more roundabout production processes to take place. But characteristic of the business cycle is that during the upswing new investment in more capital-intensive production processes lacks the support of new savings. This gap is closed by forced saving, which emerges as a result of the lag between rising consumer prices and nominal wages.

Third, propagation of the cycle is accompanied by a counteracting force. This is the Ricardo effect that ultimately arrests investment and turns the boom into an economic crisis.

Fourth, the Ricardo effect will not become fully operative as long as the banks accommodate the claims of investing firms for new loans at an increasing rate. Once the banks are forced to raise the interest rate, entrepreneurs realize that they have been building their plans on false expectations and start to redress their investment portfolio. This marks the actual start of the crisis.

This summary underlines the specific dynamics of Hayek's business cycle analysis. It shows that a coordination failure between savers and investors is the root problem of the cycle. Typical for the Austrian tradition, Hayek focussed the analysis on the microeconomic foundation of major macroeconomic disruptions. Monetary disequilibrium causes real adjustments in production because it provides an incentive to entrepreneurs to jointly miscalculate their profit opportunities. The drama that unfolds is explained in a sequence of steps marking the start and propagation of the boom as well as the onset and actual start of the crisis that follows. In contrast to the smooth adjustment of the traverse, these steps take place in disequilibrium. Hayek stressed that he aimed to explain 'what happens in the interval before a new equilibrium is attained.' (Hayek 1931a, 85). The business cycle involved 'a prolonged period during with the relations corresponding to the real equilibrium are greatly distorted by monetary changes' (Hayek 1978, 178). In short, Hayek's approach to the study of business cycle is an outstanding example of what in the 1930s became known as period or process analysis, dealing with the dynamics of disequilibrium adjustment.

This conclusion is highly relevant, for in the 1930s and 1940s and even today, Hayek's business cycle theory was not seen in these terms. From the start, a debate ensued about the validity of the Ricardo effect which had the unfortunate side effect that it turned all attention to the comparative static qualities of this proposition and by extension of Hayek's theory. Commentators such as Wilson (1940) and Kaldor (1942) argued that his explanation of the upper turning point of the cycle involved a logical inconsistency because the Ricardo effect could not explain a reduction of total investment demand. According to them, Hayek overlooked the scale effect of a reduction in investment, which neutralizes the substitution of labour for capital brought about by the Ricardo effect.[39] However, this argument is entirely based on comparative static reasoning. It studies the push and pull of respectively real wages and the marginal costs of borrowing on capital formation by comparing two equilibrium situations. But for Hayek the Ricardo effect operated in a setting of false trading: neither wages nor product prices were correct in the sense of being consistent with the underlying objective conditions of supply and demand. The gap between Hayek and his adversaries could almost not have been greater (Moss and Vaughn 1986).

Unfortunately, the debate about the Ricardo effect and several of the other controversies surrounding Hayek's business cycle (*vis-à-vis* amongst others Keynes and Sraffa) failed to clarify this difference in method. Language and scientific tradition proved important stumbling blocks in the communication between Hayek and his British colleagues. Most English speaking economists were not familiar with the theoretical features and terminology of the Austrian capital theory that formed the heart of Hayek's business cycle theory. Hicks (1967b, 204–205) later described this communication failure as follows. He said that Hayek's *Prices and Production* 'was in English, but it was not English economics. It needed further translation before it could be properly assessed . . . what emerged, when we tried to put the Hayek theory in our own words, was not Hayek. There was some inner mystery to which we failed to penetrate'.

It may well have been that part of the problem was that Hayek himself did not fully realize the extent to which his disequilibrium analysis differed from mainstream economics. As Moss and Vaughn (1986) put it, he struggled to free himself from the precepts of comparative static analysis and the debates about the Ricardo effect may have helped him in this regard. For one, it showed him that the comparative static approach could not handle such thorny issues like the formation of expectations and the processing of information via markets. However, I shall argue that in the next step of his career, the complexity of these questions would prove a stumbling block for himself as well.

The Problem of Economic Order

Why did Hayek abandon his quest for neutral money and the definition of monetary equilibrium? I have argued that in the 1920s and 1930s there was a remarkable continuity in his definition of economic equilibrium, which focused on the compatibility of individual plans. Hence, I find it unlikely that he suddenly (in 1937) changed his approach to equilibrium analysis and as a result devoted his energies to a different field of study. In my opinion, Hayek's farewell to economics was a far more gradual affair and was inspired by a different motivation. It was not the shift from a static, Walrasian conception of equilibrium to a dynamic conception of equilibrium that set him on a different course. Rather, for a long time he retained the idea that fictions like the static general equilibrium theory served a useful role in economic analysis. But somewhere after the 1940s he decided that his efforts to pursue economics as a thought experiment would not generate the results he had hoped for. As a consequence, Hayek abandoned his quest to develop economics on the basis of equilibrium theory seen as a thought experiment.

Moss (1997) attributes Hayek's abandonment of the thought experiment to his growing awareness that a decentralized market system is fundamentally different from the theoretical representation of competitive economic equilibrium. In the 1940s Hayek started to realize that the dispersion of knowledge created a degree of complexity to economic problems that could not be handled by conventional economic theory. This awareness was not a sudden insight but developed over the course of many years. Hayek's progress in this regard can be shown if we consider the development of his ideas along a number of dimensions (see Table 12.2).

Table 12.2 Hayek's ideas concerning equilibrium theory, 1928–1992

Role of....	Time period		
	1928–1945	1945–1967	1967–1992
Theory	Deduction; focus on logical reasoning; generates testable predictions	A priori search for patterns; generates testable predictions	Focus on unintended consequences of individual action (invisible hand explanation): how does the interplay between individuals produce social order?
Empirics	Study of causal relations in terms of temporal sequence (process analysis)	Pattern prediction; may lead to falsification of theory; supports options for policy	Study of the role of rules, conventions and knowledge in the establishment of social order; empirical testing cannot decide relevant cases
Policy	Active monetary management disrupts process of market coordination	Create general conditions for maximization of output	Very limited scope for public policy; focus on market forces that may act as an automatic countervailing power to government action
Equilibrium	Ideal concept and instrument of logical reasoning, used to study the operation of causal forces in the real economy	Ideal concept and instrument of logical reasoning; precedes empirical analysis to search for orderly patterns	Focus on the concept of social order as the unintended outcome of individual action.

When Moss (1997) speaks about Hayek's use of the equilibrium concept as a thought experiment, he is referring to what he calls the benevolent dictator model. This is the fiction of a centrally directed communist state that Hayek used as the central assumption in his *Pure Theory of Capital* (1941). Moss argues that sometime prior to 1944 Hayek realized that the thought experiment involving the benevolent dictator model was fundamentally flawed as a device for organizing thought experiments about the market system, which led him to abandon this type of model. The flaw is that the market system is not analogous at all to a household economy under the direction of a single patriarch whose preference ordering can represent the entire group (Moss 1997, 158).

However, it is my contention that in the post-1944 period Hayek abandoned the benevolent dictator model but retained the equilibrium concept as a thought experiment, albeit in a different form. In its new role, equilibrium theory became a method for finding patterns of order in the market process. To appreciate this function, it is necessary to explain pattern prediction as a goal for economic theory that Hayek introduced in his *Theory of Complex Phenomena* (Hayek 1967a). Key to this theory is the recognition that economics, as all social sciences, has a degree of complexity that far exceeds that of the natural sciences.[40] The main factor causing this complexity in economic issues is the presence of feedback mechanisms, such as the dynamics of expectation formation. People respond to changed economic conditions by revising their expectations, which leads others who took these expectations as given to adjust their expectations as well, and so forth and so forth. Hayek recognized that chain reactions of this kind make it virtually impossible to speak of given data when dealing with the manifestation of a complex phenomenon.[41] As a result, the study of such events requires a method that is able to accommodate uncertainty and causal indeterminacy because one lacks the knowledge to connect complex events in a straightforward manner.

Hayek's answer to this challenge was the introduction of pattern prediction and it was in the context of this approach that he formulated a new task for equilibrium theory. Hayek defined a pattern as the recurrence of a certain class of events in time. For him, the main issue at stake was the degree of detail with which one could describe and henceforth analyze such patterns. Complex events would only allow the analyst to describe very general patterns. Patterns of this kind lack information about the particular manifestation of the pattern in specific circumstances. For example, in economics one is able to make general statements about the movements of market prices, but the prediction of specific prices at a specific date is generally beyond our grasp. Likewise, Hayek (1967a, 24) stressed the importance of making a distinction between the prediction of the appearance of a pattern of a certain class and the appearance of a particular instance of this class. In complex sciences like economics the scope of analysis is confined to the first category, while in more simple sciences like physics one has the ability to generate valid scientific statements about the second class of events.

Hayek's point was that this limitation did not invalidate the scientific status of the study of complex events. He argued that the prediction that in certain general conditions a pattern of a certain kind will appear is also a significant and falsifiable prediction.[42] Accordingly, he advocated falsification as the main criterion for empirical economics (Hayek 1967a, 24). Was Hayek, a prominent member of the Austrian school, turning economics into an empirical science? Far from it. In his conception of science, theory still had the leading role because, due to the complexity of forces, it would be impossible to generate testable hypotheses by means of induction.[43] In his own words: 'in the case of more complex phenomena [compared to the discovery of regularities in two-variable relations, BT] it is more obvious that we must have our theory first before we can ascertain whether the things do in fact behave according to this theory' (ibid., 42). One therefore starts looking for patterns by first making them up (ibid., 24).

It seems that, at this stage in the development of his thinking, Hayek was far from giving up equilibrium theory. On the contrary, throughout his entire career Hayek believed that order was one of the most pervasive characteristics of the market economy. Up to the 1960s this belief inspired him to put the theoretical notion of equilibrium at the core of economic theory. In his vision it was this assumption which allowed us to literally imagine how the market mechanism could, in theory, produce an orderly outcome. He even cited Walras's general equilibrium theory as a prime example of the general patterns that form the core of economics (ibid., 35). Thus the role of equilibrium theory underwent a subtle change in Hayek's postwar work. He no longer used the concept of equilibrium as a deliberately unrealistic assumption in order to provide a contrast for the analysis of causal forces.[44] In his theory of complex phenomena he introduced a different 'leap of the imagination', namely equilibrium theory as an instrument to a priori impose order on the field of study.[45]

A more drastic change in Hayek's attitude towards equilibrium theory came when he got interested in the theory of evolution as an explanation of the development of institutions. It was at this point that he proposed to abandon the concept of equilibrium altogether and to replace it by the notion of order.

This change was inspired by the realization that economic equilibrium as conventionally defined (for example plan coordination) cannot represent the essence of the spontaneous order produced by the market. In 1967 Hayek argued that the quintessence of the market order is that it arises as the unintended consequence of people's self-interested economic actions (Hayek 1967b, 1967c and 1978). This order is dynamic because it implies a continuous process of adjustment, but it is also undetermined. No one knows what the market process will produce in terms of end results because it is the product of countless individual economic arrangements. Hayek (1978) stressed that the notion of economic equilibrium fails on both accounts. First, equilibrium is static because it presupposes that all relevant facts have already all been discovered and that competition has therefore ceased. Second, the economy as described by equilibrium theory has a final goal and is in that sense deterministic. In the words of Hayek (1978, 182), it forms 'a single organized community serving a given hierarchy of ends'. But such a hierarchy of ends is not relevant to the complex structure of the market order where people's wants and desires are subjective and therefore incomparable. Hayek finally reached the conclusion that 'equilibrium' and 'order' are fundamentally different concepts. As a result, he stated that equilibrium cannot represent the spontaneous order of the market, not even as an ideal type (ibid., 184).

This spelled the end of equilibrium theory as a thought experiment. In the words of Hayek (1978, 185), 'we do injustice to the achievement of the market if we judge it, as it were, from above, by comparing it with an ideal standard [that is economic equilibrium, BT] which we have no known way of achieving'. Compare this statement to Hayek's earlier approach when he had praised the 'purely fictitious character' of the equilibrium concept and argued that 'to make full use of the equilibrium concept we must abandon the pretence that it refers to something real' (Hayek 1941, 21).

Indeed, as Moss (1997) maintains, Hayek gave the thought experiment that had such a long tradition in Austrian economics its final death blow. But this break with the past was not a sudden affair and did not occur as a result of his alleged redefinition (in 1937 and 1945) of economic equilibrium as plan coordination. For a long time after 1945 he retained the idea that equilibrium was a useful assumption because it imposed order on the field of study. Hayek clearly rejected the notion of equilibrium, for the first time, in the 1960s when he started to realize that the spontaneous order of the market process cannot be compared to economic equilibrium as a state of plan coordination. It was this insight which led him to formulate an alternative research strategy for economics which introduced evolution as the main driving force towards the establishment of economic order.

The main theme of Hayek's theory of spontaneous order is that society and its institutions are neither natural formations nor the outcome of human design (Hayek 1967b, 1967c and 1978; see also Petsoulas 2001). Instead, they originate in the unintended and unforeseen spontaneous coordination of a multiplicity of action by self-interested individuals. This theory emerged as a (rather belated) response to the theory of knowledge that Hayek developed in the 1930s. According to this theory, individual knowledge is fragmented, temporary and partly tacit, so that it is impossible for a central planner to access all information required to match supply and demand on all markets. The complexity of the price system is simply too great for the human mind to comprehend. Thus any form of coherent behaviour at the micro level, and order at the macro level, cannot be the result of deliberate design and choice. It can only emerge from the interaction of all members of society as an unintended and unplanned outcome. For Hayek, the spontaneous order was something to which everyone contributes, from which everyone benefits, which everyone normally takes for granted, but which individuals rarely understand (Witt 1994).

Hayek saw the investigation of social and economic order as the unintended outcome of human action as a new challenge for the social sciences (Hayek 1967a). He proposed to answer this challenge by developing the theory of cultural evolution as an explanatory tool. In fact, for Hayek spontaneous order and evolution were 'twin ideas' (Hayek 1967c, 77). First, Hayek used the principle of selection to explain how people adopting certain rules of conduct would produce social order as an unintended outcome of their actions. But, secondly, in his view, the process of evolution was itself a manifestation of the spontaneous order because no one could foresee or design the products of evolution.

It has to be said that the close association of the terms spontaneous order and evolution makes it difficult to give a precise statement of Hayek's theory of social evolution, because he failed to clearly define either of these terms (Witt 1994; Hodgson 1993). The scope of his theory of social evolution is wide. It focusses on the emergence of rules of conduct, morals and traditions that govern human interaction and induce an order in culture, society and economy likewise. Extending the ideas of the Scottish moral philosophers, he saw these rules of conduct, morals and traditions as the product of the development process taking place over thousands of years, during which these patterns of behaviour have been learnt without much reflection on their meaning.

The drivers behind this process are genetic and cultural evolution that take place in both the individual and the group levels (Hayek 1967b). The former case involves what Hayek called the transmission of rules of conduct from individual to individual. By contrast, the natural selection of rules of conduct is something that takes place between competing groups and operates on the basis of the greater or lesser efficiency of the resulting order of the group. A group adopting superior rules will enjoy a better social and economic life and thus create potential for growth due to more successful procreation and integration of outsiders. By the same logic, groups not adopting appropriate rules, whether inventing or imitating them, will decline in number. Through this selection process, the rules of conduct, norms and morals that eventually prevail are suited for the survival of more and more members of the group.

The challenges posed by the theory of evolution to the theory of equilibrium in economics will be studied in more detail in the next chapter. For the present time, it suffices to say that for Hayek the theory of evolution and spontaneous order drastically changed his outlook on the problem of monetary equilibrium. He abandoned all attempts to explain monetary processes in terms of some abstract and highly unrealistic monetary equilibrium embodying, for example, neutral money. In the world of evolution there is change and adaption to changed circumstances without equilibrium as a point of gravitation towards which all developments must tend. The spontaneous order moves without a predetermined goal or a road map drawn by some central planner or designer. The notion of order therefore describes a different kind of organizing force that Hayek himself explained as follows. Interviewed about the relevance of GE-analysis, he said that:

> Of the direct significance of equilibrium analysis to the explanation of the events we observe, I never had any doubt. I thought it was a very useful concept to explain a type of order towards which the process of economics tends without ever reaching it. I'm now trying to formulate some concept of economics as a stream instead of an equilibrating force, as we ought, quite literally, to think in terms of the factors that determine the movement of the flow of water in a very irregular bed. That would give us a much better conception of what it does (Hayek in Kresge and Wenar 1994, 147).

Of course, the question is where this flow is taking us if it is not to some kind of social optimum or maximum. Hayek (1967b, 1978) explained that qualifications of this kind have no meaning to evolutionary processes. However, he also added that the absence of a tendency towards a predetermined equilibrium does not imply that the spontaneous order moves without a goal because 'it may yet be highly conducive to the achievement of many different individual purposes not known as a whole to any single person, or a relatively small group of persons' (Hayek 1978, 183). In other words, the social value of the establishment of economic order can only be assessed by individuals themselves but is meaningless as an aggregate measure of the collective well-being.

In this context, policy making must also assume a different role. The irrelevance of a social optimum implies that policy makers lack a point of reference to plan and control the execution of social and economic policies. According to Hayek, evolutionary processes are so complex that there is no one who possesses sufficient knowledge to direct the economic and monetary processes that arise spontaneously as a consequence of people's individual choices (Hayek 1967b, 1978).

Over the years this insight deepened Hayek's repugnance of any form of government intervention in the economy. He saw it as a main task of economic and legal science to develop the proper checks against the irrepressible urge of government officials to abuse their legislative and executive powers. In the 1970s this task briefly revived Hayek's interest in monetary theory (Hayek 1976, 1979). Previously, he had always argued that the severe economic damage of monetary disequilibrium meant that a constant money supply was the best policy that any government or central bank could pursue, because it best constrained the discretionary power of public policy.[46] However, evolutionary theory focussed his attention on the institutional setting that gave public bodies the power to issue money in the first place. He realized that it was public control of the money supply that was the root cause of monetary disequilibrium. In his view, with 'public' money there was always the risk of unwanted intervention by public officials and no institutional check could prevent that.[47] The logical conclusion was therefore to take away from government the monopoly of issuing money and to hand it over to private industry. Hayek (1976) argued that a monetary system based on a competitive money supply would be far more effective in keeping the purchasing power of money stable. In such a system every issuer of money has a financial incentive to safeguard the value of the monetary unit that he brings on the market. Failure to do so would mean that he would at once lose his extremely profitable business to a competitor who offers better money. Hayek concluded that the free market monetary system is better suited to the needs of capitalism and promoted the denationalization of money as a remedy against the great fluctuations in credit and economic activity that in the history of economic development were the cause of prolonged periods of depression.[48]

Hayek's brief return to monetary analysis in the 1970s is interesting because it shows how he applied to economics the notion of the spontaneous order as a flow rather than as a tendency towards equilibrium. First, by addressing the issue of who controls the money supply he aimed to develop an institutional framework that would guarantee an unhampered flow of monetary expenditures and receipts. This is the familiar story of government intervention that blocks the automatic adjustment of supply and demand that can also be explained in comparative static analysis. The novelty of a flow as a metaphor for economic order is the unpredictability of where the monetary river runs in the long run. In geological terms a river is not a static entity but a flow that adjusts itself to changes in its natural environment. The river will simply leave its current bed if forced by blocks and other irregularities below the water surface. It thus creates a new river bed. Hayek believed that the institutional setting of the money market should be able to adjust itself in a similar manner. In this case it is evolution driven by the force of competition which allows us to predict the changes in monetary institutions as a general pattern. In the words of Hayek (1979, 5):

> The interesting fact is that what I have called the monopoly of government of issuing money has not only deprived us of good money but has also deprived us of the only process by which we can find out what would be good money. We do not even quite know what exact qualities we want because in the two thousand years in which we have used coins and other money, we have never been allowed to experiment with it, we have never been given the chance of finding out what the best kind of money would be.

The criticism that can be raised against Hayek's explanation of spontaneous order as an organizing force in economics is that evolution in his view is an unidirectional process: it is always aimed at the establishment of order, but the possibility of disorder is completely overlooked (Hodgson 1993, 178). Why is order and not chaos the unintended outcome of the interaction between self-interested actors in the economic arena? We know from dynamic systems theory that even stable systems may encounter a point called bifurcation. Working latently during the periods of peaceful development, built-in mechanisms can prepare for eventual catastrophic change. At the point of bifurcation, the system loses its relative macrostability and enters a phase in which it is highly sensitive to minute changes. Small variations can affect the entire course and trajectory of development.

Austrian predecessors like Wieser pointed at the risk of a systems' breakdown in a free market society (see Chapter 10), but like Mises Hayek never discussed this possibility. The entire emphasis is on the emergence and stabilization of the economic order, as the unintended consequence of individual actors. Hayek accepted that to some extent the focus on economic order formed an unproven premise, for the economic success of the competitive market system could never be empirically tested (Hayek 1978, 180). This was one of the areas where the scientific method of economics was simply inadequate due to the complexity of the problem. As a result, '[a]ll we can hope to find out is that, on the whole, societies which rely for this purpose [the discovery of facts, BT] on competition have achieved their aims more successfully than others' (ibid.). Not surprisingly for the author of *The Road to Serfdom* (1944) and *The Fatal Conceit* (1988), Hayek stated that '[t]his is a conclusion which the history of civilisation seems eminently to have confirmed'.

However, in my opinion this conclusion just shows that Hayek ignored the many examples recorded in history where the free market system did produce chaos or some form of a systems' breakdown.[49] It seems that his liberal political agenda (favouring laissez faire policies) strongly coloured his outlook on the nature of the market process. As Hodgson (1993, 178) puts it, he invested the idea of the spontaneous order with a hallowed and inviolable mystery: suggesting that in general it should not be tampered with. Yet if the possibility of spontaneous disorder was accepted, then perhaps some grounds for interventionist policies could be readily sustained.

CONCLUSION

In the introduction to this chapter I posed the question why the disequilibrium approach failed to conquer the economics profession in the interwar period. The obvious answer to that question is that there was no single dynamic or disequilibrium method that could form the basis of a new approach to macroeconomic theory. We have seen in this chapter that the dynamic methods of the Swedes and the Austrians started from a common theoretical framework, but developed into widely different theories with policy conclusions that were in complete conflict with each other. Armed with the dynamic method one could either advocate active monetary management in order to maintain monetary equilibrium or strongly reject it. Add to that the fact that even within the schools themselves there was no agreement about the proper approach to dynamic problems and it is not hard to see why the dynamic method did not stand out as an appealing alternative to conventional neoclassical theories that favoured the equilibrium approach.

If we would summarize this conclusion in terms of Lakatos's methodology of scientific research programs, we could say that both the Swedes and the Austrians failed to establish a progressive research program that could rival that of Keynesian economics in the post war period. In this regard it is interesting to compare the dynamic method of the Stockholm school to the approach taken by Keynes himself in the GT. Both the Swedes and Keynes stressed the subjective and highly volatile nature of expectation as a prime cause of economic dynamics. Keynes choose to deal with this powerful source of change by first ignoring it altogether and focusing on the very short period for which one could assume that equilibrium existed. This approach allowed his followers to fully exploit the analytical benefits of the equilibrium assumption, which greatly facilitated the establishment of a generally accepted hard core of the Keynesian research program. In contrast the members of the Stockholm school like Lindahl and Lundberg approached the dynamic problem exactly the other way round. We have seen in this chapter that they took the dynamic method as the general theory and treated equilibrium theory as a special case which involved the analysis of a steady state. The problem of this approach was the absence of an unequivocal method to measure changes over time. There was no criterion to define the length of a period, the basic measure of the sequence analysis of the Stockholm school. As a result, one could describe a sequence of periods in many different ways, which explains the lack of coherency in Swedish dynamic analysis. This research program may be called the opposite of a hard core. It consists of an open-ended set of applied models and is for that reason best described as 'eclectic' (Laidler 1999). Moreover, the lack of theoretical consistency was a deliberate choice. The Swedes believed that fitting a dynamic model to the case at hand was the best way to keep track of the changing nature of economic reality. Their theoretical aspirations were simply far less ambitious than those of Harrod, Hicks and other exponents of the Keynesian model (see the foreword to the 1955 edition of Lundberg 1937). Unfortunately, this eclecticism ran counter to the spirit of the time, which increasingly favoured mathematical modelling (Blaug 2003). It is in that regard not surprising that the Stockholm school failed to attract sufficient new followers to become a serious rival to the developing Keynesian paradigm.

The demise of the Austrian school is a more complicated affair. In the 1930s the fate of Austrian economics was at least partly determined by the rise of Hitler and the Nazis. Their ascent to power forced Jewish members of the Austrian school like Ludwig von Mises to flee their home country (Vaughn 1994). It goes without saying that it is not easy to develop the hard core of a scientific program when its members are in exile.[50]

However, this chapter has shown that there are also other reasons why Austrian economics failed to counter what has been called the Keynesian avalanche (McCormick 1992). Compared to the Stockholm school, Austrian economics was a more unified paradigm with a considerable history in economics. The Austrians stressed the importance of deductive reasoning and by the 1930s had developed a set of theories like Menger's theory of subjective value and the capital theory of Böhm-Bawerk that were generally accepted among the members of the school. As a result, Austrian economics was in a much better position to make advances in the field of economic dynamics and to become a progressive research program. The reasons why it failed to do so can be summarized as follows:

- Keynesian economics turned the attention of the economics profession towards macroeconomics. As an essentially microeconomic research program, Austrian economics was seen as a 19th century, and therefore outdated approach to economics.
- This impression was confirmed by the fact that the Austrians raised methodological objections against empirical testing in economics, while econometric modelling became one of the new spearheads of research in the aftermath of the Keynesian revolution.
- Austrian business cycle theory focuses on inflation as the main cause of economic crisis, while the Great Depression of the 1930s was

characterized by deflation. This incongruence made it hard to sell Austrian policy prescriptions as the right cure to the economic crisis. Hayek later stated that his business cycle theory was designed to explain a type of cycle that was common of the 19th century, which adds to the suggestion that he tried to fight Keynes using the wrong theory at the wrong time.

- Hayek failed to solve important theoretical problems concerning the role of capital in dynamic theory. He stressed that Austrian capital theory ended with the publication of his *Pure Theory of Capital* in 1941, as later generations did not follow the leads that he had suggested in this book (Hayek in Kresge and Wenar 1994, 96).[51] This is not a sign of theory development and even suggests that in the field of capital theory the hard core of Austrian economics was retrogressive instead of progressive.

However, in other respects Austrian economics was making important advances that were not fully appreciated until much later, largely due to the waning reputation of the Austrian school. I am here referring to the Austrian contribution to the socialist calculation debate and Hayek's work on the role of knowledge in economics. It seems that the Austrian school was both outdated and ahead of its time, a split that was certainly not conducive to becoming a successful paradigm in economics.

Faced with this muddle of dynamic theories, the static alternative of a Keynesian model that could be expressed in five equations (IS-LM) must have appeared like a haven of clarity. In addition, the static model promised rapid advance into the field of dynamic analysis, as the multiplier-accelerator models demonstrated. In that respect it is not difficult to see why the Keynesian revolution advanced at such a rapid pace.[52]

Yet I conclude that Keynes took an extreme position in a trade-off that the Swedes and the Austrians could not avoid.[53] This trade-off is the difficulty of developing a dynamic explanation of economic changes without the use of some kind of equilibrium assumption. Equilibrium is a great facilitator of economic theory because it allows us to freeze economic conditions for a while and to study dynamic questions in a more simplified form. Keynes adopted this strategy to the extent that his formal theoretical framework could not handle dynamics at all. The Swedes, on the other hand, designed their dynamics with the explicit aim to fully account for the changes in economic variables over time. We have seen that they only partly succeeded in this aim, because they were unable to solve the problem of the complexity of dynamic changes. Myrdal tried to evade this problem by ignoring the explicit dynamics during a period and focusing on the tendency of certain forces to bring about change. But Lindahl and Lundberg used the assumption of (temporary) equilibrium to simplify dynamic analysis and so reintroduced partial and even general equilibrium theory through the back door.

In Austrian analysis the role of equilibrium theory is more prominent but often misunderstood. I have argued that the Austrians used the concept of equilibrium as an imaginary construction, as a mental tool to be used in a thought experiment. This imaginary concept was deliberately unrealistic in order to provide a contrast to those aspects of reality that the Austrians considered of specific importance to the dynamic operation of the actual market process – like money, uncertainty and entrepreneurship. The use of equilibrium theory as a thought experiment explains a number of confusing elements in Austrian economics, such as Hayek's definition of neutral money as the starting point of his monetary analysis, while the essence of his monetary theory was to show that money was essentially non-neutral. Similarly, Mises adopted the Evenly Rotating Economy as the benchmark of his investigation of the economic consequences of human action, while the ERE represented an equilibrium in which human action was not present.

In the history of economic thought the method of imaginary constructions has caused heated controversies about the meaning and relevance of Austrian economics. To a certain extent these controversies were misguided because they rested on a misunderstanding of the Austrian method of imaginary constructions and the meaning it had for the interpretation of equilibrium theory. However, I have shown in this chapter that the Austrians themselves applied the lessons of their thought experiments with a strong normative bias. Unlike their teacher Wieser, Mises and Hayek were blind to any kind of dynamics that could upset the harmonious nature of production and exchange in a free market society. In their view, dynamic adjustment always tended to bring the economy closer towards equilibrium, while the possibility of disorder as an endogenous outcome of the market process was simply never conceived.

I have argued that Hayek long retained the conception of equilibrium as an imaginary construction, even after 1937 when he explicitly introduced the dissipation of knowledge as a factor influencing the coordination process. Hayek believed that as a benchmark of dynamic analysis the fiction of equilibrium (in the sense of plan coordination) served a useful role because it imposed order on the field of study. In that regard his use of equilibrium theory can be compared to the approach of the Stockholm school. But the nature of the dynamic process that emerged as a result of this analysis, was radically different. We have seen that the Swedes focused on the disequilibrium process, whether it would move towards or away from an equilibrium position. The principal interest of Mises and Hayek was always a process leading towards economic order, and in due time Hayek came to realize that equilibrium theory proper was not the right instrument to study this process. This moment occurred somewhere in the 1960s and was inspired by the insight that the market process as a spontaneous order cannot be compared to economic equilibrium as a state of plan coordination. This conclusion marks the end of the Austrian thought experiment and led Hayek to formulate an alternative research strategy for economics, which introduced evolution as the main driving force towards the establishment of economic order. For the Austrians, dynamic analysis had become a problem, not of equilibrium, but of economic order.

The question that remains to be answered is what lessons we can draw from the dynamic economics studied in this chapter for the direction of contemporary research. Is there a future for the dynamic analysis of economic change along the lines set out by the Stockholm school and the Austrians? Are there new developments in economics that promise to base dynamic economics on a stronger foundation and what does this mean for the role of the equilibrium concept? We have seen that in spite of their dynamic outlook both the Swedes and the Austrians built their theories on specific definitions of the equilibrium concept. This raises the question whether it is possible to conceive of economics without equilibrium at all. These questions will be addressed in the next chapter.

NOTES

1. This was a problem that also plagued the Cambridge approach to business cycle theory. See Andvig (1991). The Keynes-Hayek controversy in the 1930s is one of the finest examples of such a misguided controversy that mainly revolved around the meaning of words, but failed to address substantive differences in scientific method. See Tieben (1997).
2. Myrdal believed that the return to this type of analysis was minimal, for 'the element of greater realism which the period analysis gains by introducing the time-sequences as an object for study must be paid for by certain very unrealistic approximations. In fact, such a study must assume most of the world unchanged and the rest changing in a very regularized way'. According to Myrdal, the assumptions adopted could be varied in an endless number of combinations, leading him to assert that the value of period analysis will only be casuistic. See Myrdal (1939, 43–44).
3. It has to be stressed that the definition of equilibrium in this table is ambiguous. Intertemporal equilibrium implies a perfect foresight equilibrium with all markets in supply and demand equilibrium. In the other cases a degree of imperfect foresight must be allowed for. However, we may speak of equilibrium in these cases because imperfect foresight does not prevent markets from (temporarily) clearing, which means that agents (yet) feel no impulse to change their plans. In other words, in this table equilibrium indicates the absence of an endogenous tendency to change.

4. Rational expectations theory is an example of a theory which assumes that the revision of expectations takes place in the shortest of time. According to this theory, people are always able to correctly forecast any systematic change in the value of exogenous variables like the money stock. They are only 'fooled' by truly random changes in such variables. However, Heiner (1983) points out that highly flexible expectations of this kind may be have a hidden price in terms of transaction costs. Interpersonal exchange may benefit from stable and therefore predictable behaviour. This means that in such cases rules of thumb that are relatively rigid may be more efficient than rational expectations.
5. See also the opening sentence of Lundberg (1937): 'The ultimate purpose of all economic theory is to analyze changes in economic life with respect to time.' Or the opening sentence of Lindahl (1939): 'The final aim of economic science it either to explain the economic phenomena of the past or to forecast the economic events that will, under given conditions, probably occur in the future.'
6. From a theoretical point of view, the Swedish criticism is correct. Without a dynamic explanation of economic changes, we cannot rule out the possibility of multiple equilibria. This greatly reduces the scope of comparative static analysis because the economy does not tend to uniquely determined equilibria. However, from a methodological point of view, the Swedish approach cannot be said to overrule alternative strategies. Theoretical reasoning always requires a degree of abstraction, but there is no scientific criterion for determining the exact degree of abstraction for equilibrium analysis or any other kind of theory (Occam's razor excepted). Hence one cannot rule out that Keynes's approach, who preferred to reason from statics to dynamics (see Chapter 11), generates better results.
7. Lundberg (1930[1996], 361) defined statics as the study of a system of forces at rest. As such it 'states the conditions for their equilibrium when no motion occurs'.
8. Hansson (1982, 226) even argues that equilibrium constructions play a 'fundamental role' in Lundberg's development of sequence analysis. He points to the fact that Lundberg causally connected the different sequences of a dynamic change by assuming given response functions. Thus his continuation theory rested upon a mechanical adjustment of behaviour in response to disappointed expectations. In other words, he assumed that people do not change their theory of expectations but respond mechanically just as, for example, the adaptive expectations hypothesis assumes. Hansson says that Lundberg later rejected this assumption in favour of the expectational dynamics of Lindahl that does not link sequences in a mechanical way, but allows for genuine surprise, unexpected errors et cetera. See further below.
9. The other two parts of the general dynamic theory concerned the technological, institutional and psychological conditions for planning and the theory of economic development that traces the dynamic process on the basis of certain assumptions regarding planning and external conditions.
10. Lindahl assumed that a day was a realistic time period for such activities to take place.
11. In a review of Wicksell's *Geldzins und Güterpreise* in 1899 D. Davidson already pointed at the implicit assumption of Wicksell's definition of monetary equilibrium, namely that

the economy is stationary. He argued that when one allows for factor productivity growth, neutral money (that is monetary equilibrium) no longer requires that the price level remains stable. See Visser (1971, 396).

12. Quite correctly, therefore, Laidler (1999) discusses Mises and Hayek under the heading 'The Wicksellians'.

13. The problem is the complexity of all social phenomena which form the subject of the science of human action. This complexity implies that controlled experiments like in the natural sciences are impossible. Hence '[t]he information conveyed by historical experience cannot be used as building material for the construction of theories and the prediction of future events. Every historical experience is open to various interpretations, and is in fact interpreted in different ways . . . It is impossible to reform the sciences of human action according to the pattern of the physics and the other natural sciences. There is no means of establishing an a posteriori theory of human conduct and social events' (Mises 1949, 31).

14. It has to be stressed that Mises's theory of monetary calculation is only referring to the use of money as an accounting unit. He explicitly stated that this theory 'does not belong to the theory of indirect exchange. It is a part of the general theory of praxeology' (Mises 1949, 394, n1). The role of money as medium of exchange is explained in different terms. Mises described money as the 'most marketable good' and its price is determined by supply and demand, as is the case with the prices of all vendible goods and services. However, to avoid running into circular reasoning (money has a price because it has value in exchange), he then adopted a regression theorem which stated that money commands a price because it must at one time had exchange value on account of the services it rendered directly to consumption or production (ibid., 398, 407 408). In other words, there is no need for a distinct quantity theory of money. The subjective theory of value can be applied to money as well.

15. Here Marshall's distinction between short-term and long-term equilibrium naturally springs to mind.

16. The final state of rest is unrealistic because we cannot expect that it will ever be reached, given that it moves with every change in the data. Mises (1949, 47) said that the final state of rest 'pays full regard to change in the temporal succession of events', whereas the ERE is characterized by the elimination of any kind of change in the data. For that reason the ERE is also an unrealistic concept. Nonetheless, the distinction between the two equilibrium concepts remains rather vague. In spite of Mises's words, the ERE also describes a temporal succession of events, albeit it around a fixed centre. See the quotation above.

17. An example is Wieser's construction of the benevolent dictator. See Moss (1997). Böhm-Bawerk drew the following parallel with the mode of operation in the natural sciences: 'Wie der Experimentator die Bedingungen künstlich vereinfacht, unter denen er die Wirkungsweise gewisser Kräfte oder Stoffe erproben will, und dadurch kreuzende 'Störungsursachen' . . . seinem Experiment fernhält, so auch der deduktive aber keineswegs aprioritischer Theoriker; auch er isoliert die Wirkungsweise typischer sozialer

oder ökonomischer Kräfte in seinem Denken, um sich zunächst in ihren Reinheit 'störungsfrei' zu verfolgen, und um aus den gewonnenen Teilerkentnissen erst auf einer Folgestufe des Erkennens die Erkenntnis der vollen, bunten empirischen Wirklichkeit zusammenzusetzen.' Quoted in Klant (1972, 114).

18. See Gunning (1989) for a defence of Mises along this line.
19. See Hayek (1941).
20. Assuming that human nature would not miraculously change, in a socialist society selfishness would merely incite inertia and laxity. In addition, there was the point that socialism is unrealizable because it cannot develop a method for economic calculation.
21. In the next section I shall argue that same conclusion applies to Hayek.
22. It is in that sense telling that the chapter dealing with the subject of Time is, with six pages, one of the shortest of *Human Action*.
23. 'The market is a process of selection in continual operation.' Mises (1949, 580).
24. Aggregate magnitudes such as the quantity of money have no scientific meaning in a science of human action. After all: '[d]er Geldbedarf der Volkswirtschaft is nichts anderes als die Summe des Geldbedarfes der Einzelwirtschaften' (Mises 1924, 112).
25. 'Der Prozess, der durch den Angebot und Nachfrage sich solange anzupassen suchen, bis der Gleichewichtszustand hergestellt ist und beide sich sowohl quantitativ als auch qualitativ decken, ist das Um and Auf der Vorgänge auf dem Markte. Angebot und Nachfrage sind aber nur die vom Markte aus sichtbaren Schlussglieder von Verknüpfungen, die tief in die menslichen Seele hineinreichen. Von der subjektiven Wertschätzungen hängt es ab, ob sie mit stärkerer oder schwächerer Intensität auftreten, mithin auch, in welcher Höhe die Austauschrelation gefunden wird, in der beide zur Deckung gebracht werden. Das gilt nicht nur von der Bildung des zwischen den anderen Gütern untereinander im direkten Tausche bestehender Austauschverhältnisses, sondern in der gleichen Weise auch von der Gestaltung des Austauschverhältnisses zwischen dem Gelde einerseits und den einzelnen Tauschgütern anderseits' (Mises 1924, 112).
26. The crucial point is that a money injection sets in motion a process of change that leads to all kinds of additional endogenous changes. Mises (1924, 126) stressed that the only case where the quantity theory holds is that of a comparison between two identical economies in a static state. Assuming that the only difference between them is that the stock of money in economy A would be double that of economy B, the purchasing power of a unit of money in A would be half of that of B's money. Note that in this case there is no process of change due to a monetary injection so the Cantillon effect has no chance to blur the comparison between the two equilibrium states.
27. Mises (1924, 89) rejected mechanistic analogies because by definition they lacked the subjectivist perspective. In his view, a mechanism of whatever making is not a man of flesh and blood with preferences and an urge to act.
28. The distinction between the market rate and the natural rate of interest does appear in his earlier monetary work. See Mises (1924).
29. Wicksell had at an earlier stage argued that banks do experience an incentive to raise the interest rate due to inflation. This occurs because banks fear that their reserves will be

depleted, eventually even causing a bank run when people try to convert their credit money for gold or another kind of commodity money. Mises (1924, 365) criticized this explanation because it implied a violation of Wicksell's own presuppositions. Analyzing the dynamics of the cumulative process, he had assumed that there is only fiduciary money. So why fear conversion?

30. 'Die Preise der Konsumgüter steigen, die der Produktivgüter sinken, das heißt der Darlehenfußes steigt wieder, er nähert sich wieder dem Satze des natürlichen Kapitalzinses' (Mises 1924, 372).

31. Mises would later further develop this argument in a theory of the business cycle that consists of the alternation of booms and busts. See Mises (1949).

32. The fear of inflation is an evident motive underlying the monetary analysis of Mises. As part of this fight against inflation, he also attacked the popular fallacy that a shortage of credit is the cause of underemployment and a low level of economic activity. According to this fallacy, banks are the key to economic recovery. They should provide easier access to supply, that is lower the rate of interest. Needless to say, Mises's analysis showed why this call for credit was best left unanswered.

33. Lest one forget, the overall aim of Hayek's theoretical efforts was not to develop a general equilibrium theory of price formation, but to explain the dynamics of cyclical fluctuations in terms of monetary theory, just as Wicksell and Mises had done. The notion of equilibrium was just the starting point of this exercise.

34. Klausinger (2008, 9) warns that we should not identify Hayek's notion of correct expectations with the notion of perfect foresight in modern theory. According to Klausinger, for Hayek, foresight did not extend into the indefinite future. This would open up the possibility, in my opinion, that Hayek saw his concept of intertemporal equilibrium as a kind of temporary equilibrium.

35. It should be emphasized that for Hayek the business cycle always started due to a monetary disturbance, while the dynamics of the cycle constituted a real phenomenon. This differentiates him from Wicksell who always linked the start of the business cycle to changes in the natural rate of interest and hence to causes in the sphere of the real economy.

36. Birner (1999) discusses the place of the Ricardo effect in Hayek's overall research programme. His conclusion is that the Ricardo effect formed a link between his monetary business cycle analysis, starting from a general equilibrium concept, and his capital theory. In the end, Hayek's formulation of the Ricardo effect gained much more attention than is warranted by its actual role. According to Birner, this undue attention occurred due to Hayek's inability to fully execute his initial research programme. Likewise, Klausinger degrades the importance of the Ricardo effect in Hayek's work.

37. However, Hayek later denied that lags of this kind are responsible for the dynamics of the business cycle because all prices are the result of false trading, which is the real cause of the upswing. See Hayek (1978, 173–174).

38. Reviewing these lessons, it is necessary to understand how Hayek interpreted his business cycle analysis. In the 1930s he was criticized for assuming that inflation was a dominant

feature of economic crisis, while reality showed that deflation was the real problem of the economic depression in this period. Hayek (1978, 174) responded by saying that his theory never claimed to do more than account for the upper turning point of the typical nineteenth-century business cycle. This underlines the hypothetical nature of his business cycle analysis.

39. Hayek had assumed an upward-sloping supply curve of credit to explain the capital scarcity that causes banks to raise the interest rate towards the end of the boom phase. A fall in total investment thus levels off the rising marginal borrowing cost for firms and the effect of the fall in real wages on capital intensity dies away. See Blaug (1985, 544) and van Zijp (1992, 60–61).
40. Complexity is here defined as 'the minimum number of elements of which an instance of the patterns must consist in order to exhibit all the characteristic attributes of the class of patterns in question' (Hayek 1967a, 25).
41. It is apparent that Hayek's theory of complex phenomena involved a generalization of the argument that stood central in Hayek (1937) and Hayek (1945), namely that it is absurd in economics to assume that people have perfect and therefore given knowledge when the main purpose of science is to explain how they acquire this knowledge.
42. Hayek (1967a, 32) underlined that the characteristic of a theory explaining a general pattern is that is describes a range of possibilities. In doing so, it excludes other conceivable courses of events and thus in principle can be falsified. In other words, the empirical content of a theory of complex phenomena consists in what 'it relegates to the realm of the impossible'.
43. Hayek (1978, 180) stated that in those cases in which it is interesting the validity of theories of competition can never be tested empirically. All we can hope to find out is that, on the whole, societies which rely for this purpose on competition have achieved their aims more successfully than others. According to Hayek, this is a conclusion which the history of civilization seems eminently to have confirmed.
44. One of the factors explaining this change is that Hayek realized that for complex events the notion of causality is of very limited use. See Hayek (1967a, 41–42).
45. A good example of this approach is Hayek (1945) which praises the 'marvel' of the price system as a mechanism for communicating information. According to Hayek, it is this aspect of the price system which explains why free market exchange produces such an efficient allocation of scarce resources. Desai (1994) complains that in this article Hayek merely assumed that a competitive economy establishes equilibrium and failed to demonstrate how an equilibrium solution is produced by the interactions of people each of whom possesses only partial knowledge. It was the latter aspect which Hayek (1937) had isolated as the main problem of economic theory. According to Desai, in the 1945 article Hayek abandoned the tough quest for a solution of the problem of equilibrium and substituted equilibrium as a vision of how the market economy should function.
46. By the same token, Hayek advocated a return to the Gold Standard.
47. Hayek had always been pessimistic about the prospect of ensuring that monetary policy would not cause cyclical fluctuations. See Hayek (1931, 125).

48. In the Austrian literature the issue of a competitive money supply or 'free banking' was subsequently taken up by White (1984) and Selgin and White (1994).
49. For examples, see Kindleberger (1978).
50. Mises arrived in the United States in 1940, but never acquired a tenured academic position. Until the Austrian revival of the 1970s he worked relatively isolated from the rest of the profession. See Vaughn (1994).
51. The aim of the *Pure theory of capital* was to integrate capital and money into a dynamic explanation of the business cycle. Hayek later explained that he worked seven years on the capital theoretic foundations at which point he became, in his own words, 'dead tired of the subject' (Kresge and Wenar 1994, 91). That explains why the monetary part of the theory was left unwritten.
52. According to Blaug (1991a), the definite breakthrough of the Keynesian revolution in America and Britain took just 12 years, which for a scientific revolution is an amazing rapid success. He argues that the quick ascendancy of Keynesian economics can be explained in terms of Lakatos's methodology of scientific research programs. That means that the Keynesian program must be classified as progressive because it predicted novel facts such as the prediction that the value of the instantaneous multiplier is greater than unity. The relative simple theoretical structure of the static equilibrium model of the GT enlarged the appeal of these novel predictions and thus contributed to the rise of Keynesian economics.
53. As Shackle (1972, 441) put it, Keynes 'moved towards concessions of method in exchange for tremendous heresies of content'. The concession that Shackle mentions was the use of equilibrium theory as an instrument to generate determinate solutions, while equilibrium was the antithesis of Keynes's vision of business life. According to Shackle, the real subject of the GT is the 'Economics of Disorder' (ibid., 427).

13. The Impact of Uncertainty

INTRODUCTION

In modern economics, the equilibrium concept elicits many critical comments. It is said to be unrealistic or to be unworkable. It supports theories like Walrasian general equilibrium analysis which revel in mathematical modeling, but are unable to generate empirical claims about the behaviour of actual economic systems. This has led to a situation in which even the founding fathers of GE theory concede that 'the cost of that mathematization sometimes outweighs its benefit' (Debreu 1991, 5). There is danger that in the training of economic researchers 'the part of economics will become secondary' (ibid.). In addition, theories adopting the equilibrium framework like GE theory wrestle with difficult analytical problems, such as explaining the role of money or finding a suitable notion of stability to prevent that equilibrium is nothing more than an end-state. Problems of this kind motivate economists to look beyond the equilibrium framework. What are the disequilibrium foundations of equilibrium theory? Would economics without the equilibrium concept generate better results? In sum, what are the alternatives to the dominance of the equilibrium concept in economics?

Strictly, one would not expect an investigation of the prospects for disequilibrium analysis in a book discussing the role of economic equilibrium. However, I consider the question of disequilibrium theorizing closely related to the track record of equilibrium theorizing. The former often arises as a result of the criticism of the latter and, what is more important, in spite of its criticism disequilibrium analysis always adopts its own version of the equilibrium concept. It seems as if equilibrium is truly indispensable in economics, even in those branches which fundamentally reject its role. The proof of this proposition is one of the main goals of this and the subsequent chapters.

Hence, this book continues with an investigation of the prospects for economics without equilibrium. This term indicates that the focus is on theories which do not a priori assume the existence of equilibrium. These theories take the task of explaining the process of improving coordination among decentralized economic decision makers very seriously. As I have said in Chapter 2, disequilibrium theory is all about trying to achieve coordination in the decentralized economy. The result is often a theory trying to explain what I have called generative causation in an open economic system. In other words, time plays a crucial role in disequilibrium theory and indicates that the issues of dynamics and disequilibrium are generally closely intertwined.

We shall see that economics knows many different approaches to disequilibrium theory seen in this way. This investigation of disequilibrium economics is organized along doctrinal lines. It will be shown that there are many common themes in the disequilibrium analyses of the different schools of thought in economics. This means that there is considerable scope for inter-doctrinal or joint analysis in this field. To isolate these common themes and approaches it is necessary to first explain what distinguishes the different economic traditions when they address the economy as being in disequilibrium. I shall subsequently discuss Post Keynesian Economics (this chapter), Austrian Economics (Chapter 14), Evolutionary Economics (Chapter 15) and the disequilibrium foundations of equilibrium analysis, which can be seen as sub-discipline of neoclassical economics (Chapter 16). In Chapter 17 I draw conclusions and answer the question whether we should prefer economics with or without equilibrium.

WHAT IS POST KEYNESIAN ECONOMICS?

Post Keynesian Economics is one of those schools in modern economics which represent themselves as disequilibrium approaches (Eichner and Kregel 1975; King 2003). This branch of theory claims to expand the message of Keynes's *General Theory*, especially as it concerns the economic effects of what Keynes called the 'dark forces of time and ignorance' (Keynes 1936, 155). According to the Post Keynesians, time must be seen as real (that is calendar) time and not as a logical concept, the role it plays in most formal economic models of neoclassical making.[1] To the Keynesians this distinction implies a fundamental criticism of equilibrium economics. The reason for this is that calendar time is associated with genuine uncertainty, path dependency and historical contingencies. These are factors that make it impossible to assume that one can travel forward and backward in time, as is customary in neoclassical models. This may seem like a harmless assumption, but the ability to travel through time greatly facilitates the ability to establish and maintain equilibrium. Take the example of errors in decision making. In logical time one simply turns back the clock to improve the decision making process until the outcome converges with the optimal choice. That is why the assumption of perfect foresight is a *conditio sine que non* for most equilibrium models. In contrast, Post Keynesians like to stress the bounded rationality of human decision making and the unique nature of historical events. For them, an economy expanding over time in the context of history is most likely a system in disequilibrium.

The problem with Post Keynesian Economics is that its main message is not always presented with the greatest clarity, to put it mildly. The Keynesians are internally divided on the true intent of their message, which means that it can hardly be used as a shared conviction to combat competing paradigms. Today Post Keynesian economics is anything but a homogenous school of thought. As Harcourt (1985, 125) somewhat sarcastically noted: 'The people who come under this umbrella [Post Keynesianism, BT] are a heterogeneous lot, sometimes only combined by their dislike of orthodox or neoclassical economics – all brands, or at least their conception of it/them.' It goes without saying that this dissension greatly imparts the thrust of the Keynesian assault on neoclassical equilibrium thinking. I shall argue in this section that the root of the problem is that Post Keynesians struggle to free themselves of the equilibrium concept. In fact, it is hard to find another branch of economics which quarrels so much about the proper definition of equilibrium and its meaning to economic theory. In light of their aim to engage in disequilibrium theorizing, this struggle is slightly ironic.

The intriguing question is if it is possible to define Post Keynesian Economics as a school of thought. After all, the label 'school' suggests that the people working in this field adopt a common research agenda or share a belief in a set of principles. So what is it that binds the members of this paradigm beyond their repugnance of neoclassical doctrines?[2]

To answer this question I shall distinguish between Post Keynesians who more or less claim to extend the lessons of Keynes and those who, paradoxically, do not. I shall denote this latter group as the non-Keynesian Post Keynesians. The former category knows two main constituent groups, which I shall refer to as the short-period and the long-period Post Keynesians.

What characterizes both short-period and long-period Post Keynesians is their shared belief that the main message of what Keynes had to say in the *General Theory* is not adequately represented by the neoclassical synthesis of Keynes's theories in terms of the IS-LM model. This message is that unemployment is a persistent and inherent feature of the capitalist economy caused by a lack of effective demand (Dow 1996, 101). At this point, there is a fundamental split among Post Keynesians caused by disagreement about the nature of this problem, that is, the ultimate causes of the lack of effective demand. On the one hand there is a group which stresses the short run nature of this problem, while others believe that Keynes's revolutionary contribution must be seen as a theory of the long period levels of output and employment.

Hence the prefixes used to distinguish these Post Keynesians from each other.

The non-Keynesian Post Keynesians share the conviction of the latter group that the ultimate goal of economic theory must be to explain long period levels of economic activity, but their allegiance to Keynes is much weaker. Like Keynes, they believe that economics is in need of a major overhaul. However, whereas Keynes selected classical economics as his main target, these Post Keynesians advocate a return to the classical doctrines of Ricardo and his followers. Following Sraffa (1960), they argue that the surplus approach of the classicals provides the foundation of a radical conversion of the theory of value, growth and distribution (Eatwell and Milgate 1983). Above all their neo-Sraffian or neo-Ricardian alternative is anti-equilibrium in the sense that it dispenses with the familiar supply and demand framework of neoclassical making. In its place, they put a theory that relates value to the physical aspects of the means of production. This theory focuses on the distribution of surplus production between workers and capitalists as one of the crucial relationships determining the rate of profit and the growth of production over time.

Why call these Sraffians/Ricardians 'Keynesians' on a par with the short-period and long-period Post Keynesians? A very pragmatic reason to do so would be that Sraffa launched his critique of neoclassical theory from Keynes's home base, the university of Cambridge, UK. Moreover, in 1960 his long period perspective nicely corresponded to the contemporary attempts of more typical Keynesians like Robinson and Kaldor to develop a distinctive Cambridge approach to income distribution, growth and capital theory.

Seen in this manner, there are at least three characteristics that may serve as the common base of this Post Keynesian school, including its Sraffian current.[3] The first element is the aim to infuse economic theory with a considerable dose of realism. This is partly where the Post Keynesian critique of neoclassical equilibrium comes from. Post Keynesians believe that the formalistic equilibrium models of this paradigm, such as the Arrow-Debreu elaboration of the basic Walrasian model, are unrealistic because they ignore several empirical facts of life that Post Keynesians find important. These facts concern the role of money in exchange, the uncertainty of future events, the bounded rationality of economic actors, the degree of competition on real markets and the role of firms in this process.

Secondly, part and parcel of this institutional set up is the notion that the income distribution affects the way in which the market system works. This is probably the only point that Post Keynesians of every kind wholeheartedly embrace, which explains why they give it a pivotal role in economic theory and policy. They argue that institutional factors determine a historical division of income between the different classes of society such as workers and capitalists. This recalls the world of classical economics with its twofold class structure and the assumption that capitalists carry out and finance all investment, while workers consume all their income. This type of argument is a marked difference to the neoclassical way of thinking that solely relates the distribution of income to the marginal productivity of variable factor inputs. The practical implication of the institutional approach is that income distribution may play a role in the process of price formation on both a microeconomic (allocation) and macroeconomic scale (inflation) as well as in the process of economic development.

This conclusion automatically points to the third defining characteristic: the economy is modeled as extending over time in a meaningful way. The qualification 'meaningful' refers to the fact that time must be seen as calendar time as opposed to logical time, the concept that is the basis of most neoclassical models. For Post Keynesians, a step forward in time is a significant activity and, moreover, one that cannot be reversed (Clark 1987 and Rogers 1989). Time thus plays a role in the explanation of uncertainty and the use of money as a medium of exchange. To other Post Keynesians time refers to the dynamics of the business cycle and the growth process. For example, they address the question how the distribution of income and differences in the propensity to save out of different incomes affect aggregate saving ratios and, by implication, economic growth. A process of this kind is unidirectional through time as the historical conditions shaping the structure of society and the distribution of income cannot be reversed.

With these three shared elements of Post Keynesian Economics in mind, we may continue by elaborating on the characteristics of the different strands within this school and their meaning to the development of disequilibrium economics.

THE IMPACT OF UNCERTAINTY

The group which I typified as the short run Post Keynesians concentrates on what it believes is the forgotten aspect of Keynes's revolution and that is the role of money. These Post Keynesians argue that the role of money in Keynesian theory is closely related to the impact of uncertainty, because in the GT Keynes explicitly drew attention to the distinction between a monetary and a barter economy. According to him, it was only in the latter type of system that market forces could be assumed to automatically establish equilibrium between aggregate supply and demand. But in a monetary economy a macroeconomic equilibrium would not arise because the interest rate would fail to play its coordinating role on the market for financial assets, that is the supply and demand for saving and investment. In other words, in the monetary economy Say's law would not apply, which opened the door to the Keynesian explanation of unemployment in terms of a lack of effective demand.

The short period Post Keynesians like Davidson, Minsky and Shackle continue this line of analysis. They focus on what they consider is the key element of Keynes's thinking; his explanation of the essential properties of money in chapter 17 of the GT and the role of uncertainty as he explained it in Keynes (1937). This research takes different directions such as the study of why money matters (impact of nominal contracts) and why money must be seen as endogenous rather than exogenous (Cottrell 1994). These elaborations will not detain us here. To our purpose what matters is the relationship between money and equilibrium in this branch of Keynesianism.

The key notion here is uncertainty and its relation to the process of expectation formation (Hoogduin 1991). Keynes defined uncertainty in a fundamental sense, that is, as a concept that cannot be described as the mathematical property of a frequency distribution (for example Keynes 1936, 152, 162–163). He believed that individuals are able to cope with this kind of uncertainty by relying to a considerable degree on conventions. For example, conventional judgments are rules of thumb that we use to update expectations. Keynes (1937[1973], 114) mentioned several of such rules that play a role in the process of expectations formation. He argued that:

- Expectations are backward looking rather than forward looking, because people take the past as a reliable guide to future action;
- People assume that current market prices and quantities express a correct summing up of future prospects;
- Expectations tend to converge upon an average opinion, because people believe that others are better informed. They therefore tend to copy their behaviour and beliefs.

With the notion of fundamental uncertainty the future remains an impermeable mist. Post Keynesians use this concept to reject any kind of perfect foresight or perfect knowledge equilibrium. In their view, uncertainty stands in the way of probability calculations that technically allow us to determine the certainty equivalent of future events (Shackle 1972, 15–24). As a result, economic decisions are to a large extent undetermined and rely on non-rational considerations like guesswork, routine behaviour and emotions.[4] This destroys the possibility of a perfectly foreseen and hence predetermined equilibrium position as error and conflict must be part and parcel of the economic process.

What are the consequences of Keynesian uncertainty in this sense for the character of equilibrium? The effect is, to be frank, ambiguous. On the one hand, rules of thumb may promote the stability of economic changes. These are to a certain extent fixed rules, perhaps periodically updated to reflect changing conditions, which may lead to highly predictable behaviour (Heiner 1983). On the other hand, uncertainty is a source of genuine surprise and thus of sudden revisions when agents are confronted with events that cause them to abandon their rules of thumb. This is exactly the kind of behaviour that Keynes envisioned when he discussed the determinants of investment. He believed that investment demand could undergo violent fluctuations because it depends on the 'animal spirits' of entrepreneurs (Keynes 1936, 161 and 249; 1937[1973], 121). It goes without saying that the economy may be liable to quick changes that are anything but equilibrating, when it is propelled by such uncertain forces.

How do the short-run Post-Keynesians cope with this prospect? Some argue that the Keynesian critique of equilibrium economics leads to untenable conclusions. For example, Coddington (1983) describes the monetary branch of Keynesianism as 'fundamentalist' because he believes that their rejection of equilibrium theorizing has nihilistic implications for the entire corpus of economic theory. In his opinion, this applies in particular to the work of G.L.S. Shackle who presented the essence of Keynes's thought as the liberation from equilibrium theory, as an escape from the restriction that it imposes on our thinking.

My reading of Shackle leads to a different conclusion and I therefore present the contribution of the short run Post-Keynesians in a different light. I believe that their most important lesson is a call for modesty. It is true that Shackle saw economics as a science of 'disorder' (Shackle 1972, 429) and that he believed that timeless concepts like static equilibrium are simply unable to address the questions that are relevant to such a science. However, he also realized that equilibrium is an indispensable tool to the study of dynamic processes, because it allows us to isolate specific forces by means of a ceteris paribus clause. Shackle called this construction a 'kaleidic equilibrium', because it unites two seemingly incompatible magnitudes, namely timeless equilibrium and dynamic change in a world ruled by uncertainty.

The kaleidic method is Shackle's way of achieving a union of reason and realism. He argued that Keynes in the GT correctly perceived that the nature of equilibrium in economics is not that of an optimum. Equilibrium simply means that the economy undergoes a period of stagnation caused by the absence of endogenous sources of movement. In the vision of Shackle such periods never last for long. He believed that these equilibria are vulnerable in the extreme to any expectation changing news (Shackle 1972, 433). Hence:

> The method implicit in the General Theory is to regard to economy as subject to sudden landslides of re-adjustment to a new, precarious and ephemeral, pseudo equilibrium, in which variables based on expectation, speculative hope and conjecture are delicately stacked in a card house of momentary immobility, waiting for 'the news' to upset everything again and start a new dis-equilibrium phase.

But how does one analyze the dynamics of this disequilibrium that Shackle also described as a kind of turmoil? Surprisingly, he argued that the development of theories about disequilibrium is possible if one adopts the assumption of equilibrium, the state of rest that in reality is such a rare event. Shackle was the first to admit that this role for equilibrium theory is paradoxical, but his kaleidic method ascribes to equilibrium a position that is akin to that of Mises's Evenly Rotating Economy in Austrian Economics (see Chapter 12). Both methods define equilibrium as a state of rest so that it can be used as a contrast to analyze the events that occur in disequilibrium. As Shackle put it, equilibrium allows us to study the abstract adjustments which expectations and beliefs prevailing at some moment would lead to, given 'a breathing space or moratorium to work out their logical interactive consequences' (ibid., 435). This state of rest can then be compared to the 'cascade of real events' which occurs when a change in expectations upsets equilibrium.

Shackle strongly stressed the limitations of his kaleidic method. The analysis of the disequilibrium adjustments is not aimed at forecasting future developments, but merely at enhancing our understanding of the dynamic process. The method offers insight of a very 'tentative, modest and short range kind, not seeking to show what must happen, but what is the range of diversity of the immediate developments that various situations are capable of'. The reason for this modesty is that it is impossible to assess all the dynamic influences that we assume constant in the ceteris paribus clause. Shackle used the image of a sailing boat in tempestuous and tide swept waters to support this point. Knowing the design of the boat, the training of the crew et cetera, we can predict how the boat responds to this or that shift of the surrounding forces. But the complexity and interaction of the forces of the environment is such that we cannot hope to know what those shifts will be.

I believe that the modest approach to the analysis of the monetary economy of what I have called the short-period Post Keynesians may generate valuable insight to economic theory. One of the main topics of their research concerns the impact of nominal rigidities. The Post Keynesians regard rigidities of this kind as a fact of life. As such it forms an aspect of the monetary economy that can be used to support the Post Keynesian disequilibrium analysis of dynamic change. In their view money contracts can be seen as a natural complement to the possession of cash. Liquidity means flexibility, while a money contract provides stability in terms of value that is needed to arrange transactions that apply to future periods. As Davidson (1991, 59) puts it, a forward money contract permits the contracting parties to possess a measure of control over future performance and cash flows in an otherwise unpredictable future. This line of reasoning suggests several topics for research:

- *The role of contracts in individual decision making*: A contract can be a rational response in the face of uncertainty, but it can also be guided by custom, law and other factors. This can be combined with behavioural economics that is used by Post Keynesians in their short period analysis. This analysis studies the actual behaviour of consumers and producers with emphasis on the institutional environment and employs a kind of social psychology reminiscent of the GT (Dow 1996, 104-105).
- *Effect of contracts in specific markets*: Here a fruitful crossover with New Keynesian analysis seems possible. Contracts like collective labour agreements can improve the functioning of specific markets such as the labour market (prevention of labour unrest, counter veiling power against monopsony of employers), but they have the drawback of blocking the price mechanism. Take the example of complete wage rigidity. This creates the possibility of stable labour market equilibria, but only at the cost of the dismissal of the allocative role of wages (Teulings and Hartog 1998). So, what are the implications of such contracts for economic welfare?
- *The optimal degree of nominal rigidity*: The example of the labour market shows that full price flexibility is not always a Pareto optimal outcome. Assume that the wage setting process is a bargaining game that can be analyzed as a Nash equilibrium. Just as in the prisoners' dilemma the optimal solution involves a coordinated strategy, which involves a degree of nominal wage rigidity. But now every individual agent has an incentive to cheat. This occurs when each agent gets the highest individual payoff if he sticks to full flexibility, given that the other agents maintain some degree of nominal inertia. As a result, the labour market may tend towards the non-cooperative solution with full price flexibility, despite the fact that a Pareto superior outcome exists. Such issues call for a cross-fertilization of Keynesian analysis and insights from other theoretical corners, such as game theory.

Questions of this kind show that Post Keynesian theory may offer a positive contribution to modern economics. By way of comparison, in GE theory there is no need for contracts and nominal rigidities. Contracts are either superfluous because the future is perfectly foreseeable or, if based on imperfect knowledge, an impediment to reaching equilibrium and therefore inefficient by definition. Post Keynesian theory shows that outside general equilibrium it may be rational for the individual to calculate in nominal terms and that full price flexibility is no universal recipe for economic wealth and welfare.

THE ACCUMULATION OF CAPITAL

The next branch of the Post Keynesian family tree intends to extend Keynes's theory of effective demand to the long period. As early as 1933 Joan Robinson suggested that Keynes's analysis of the problem of unemployment in a monetary economy should be seen as a problem of long term economic development (Robinson 1933, 25). The problem was that the static framework of Keynes's GT ruled out any kind of analysis in this direction. He focused on the role of income changes in closing the gap between saving and investment and establishing macroeconomic equilibrium. But the effect of net positive saving on the stock of capital and thereby on the economy's future earnings capacity was beyond the purview of his analysis. There are even good reasons to believe that he fundamentally opposed the use of long period equilibrium constructions (Asimakopulos 1991). We only need to refer to his famous quotation that 'in the long run we are all dead' to underline his distrust of such concepts (Keynes 1923, 80). Yet it was exactly in this direction that Keynes's colleagues in Cambridge tried to extend his lessons in the post-GT era.

The static nature of Keynes's *General Theory* was the result of his definition of the short period. This period was so short that changes in the stock of capital resulting from investment could be ignored. The growth models in the tradition of Harrod and Domar removed this obstacle and allowed the Keynesians to extend the lessons of Keynes to the investigation of long period changes and the process of capital accumulation.

The Oxford economist Roy F. Harrod was the pioneer of this approach (Harrod 1936 and 1939). Harrod developed his notion of a dynamic Keynesian theory in the context of his trade cycle theories, which he explicitly presented as an extension of Keynes's static theory of unemployment and output (Asimakopulos 1991, 139). The crux of his approach to dynamic theory was that saving entails growth and that the resulting growth in income must be allowed for in working out equilibrium conditions. This strongly suggests that for him dynamic theory was just another department of equilibrium theory. For Harrod, the crucial difference between statics and dynamics was the temporal aspect, the fact that the former type of analysis just looks at the levels of output and investment, while a dynamic theory examines the rates of growth of such variables. His dynamic theory therefore studied the conditions of a 'moving equilibrium', a steady state of advance that could be described as an equilibrium rate of growth. I shall briefly examine the properties of this dynamic equilibrium theory and study how it may support the development of a Keynesian theory of dynamic disequilibrium.

Harrod's theories led to the development of what we now know as the Harrod-Domar model of economic growth. The basis of this model consists of three equilibrium conditions. Equilibrium on the product market is specified by the two familiar conditions: full capacity use of capital stock ($K=vY$) and a flow condition expressing the equality of planned investment and saving (in the absence of lags). Equilibrium of the labour market is given by the single condition of full employment of the labour force. On the supply side, the labour force is given as growing at the constant proportional rate *n*. Further, the simplifying assumption is made that there is a single homogenous capital good used both for consumption and as a perfectly malleable stock of capital (there is no technical progress).

Harrod used the multiplier and accelerator mechanism to generate steady state growth.[5] Any additional investment is 'multiplied' into output (income) by the multiple 1/s, as given by the flow condition ($I=sY$). The multiplier having generated rising output, the accelerator then takes over ($I=vY$) and generates further investment, to be converted by the multiplier in its turn into further rises in output, and so on. As long as output is raised at some point, the multiplier and accelerator combine to produce steady state growth at the equilibrium or, as Harrod (1939, 17) called it, the 'warranted' rate $g_w=s/v$.

Harrod stressed that the warranted rate of growth entails the possibility of unemployment, a crucial Keynesian feature. But the full employment condition of the Harrod-Domar model implies an equilibrium at the natural rate of growth $g_n=s/v=g_w$. Mathematically, this is the only solution that is consistent with the three equilibrium conditions of this model, specified above.[6] This is also the only unique solution to the model. The warranted rated of growth, stressed by Harrod as the core of his trade cycle theories, is not a unique solution, which presented him with some major problems of interpretation.

To unravel these problems it is necessary to first explain the nature of the steady state solution to the Harrod-Domar model as an equilibrium concept. In mathematical terms, this is clear enough (all variables grow at the same constant rate), but what does this moving equilibrium mean in economic terms?

Following Keynes, Harrod himself focused on the impact of entrepreneurial decisions. The Keynesian feature of the Harrod-Domar growth model is the fact that investment is an autonomous factor (albeit partly induced) and that saving adjusts itself (through income changes) to ensure that the investment plans of business can be carried out (Allen 1967, 215 and 305ff). For Harrod, the steady state therefore represented a kind of entrepreneurial equilibrium. The warranted rate is the rate of growth of output in a specific period that will give entrepreneurs the feeling that they have made the right investments for the current period. Consequently, 'it will put them into a state of mind which will cause them to give such orders as will maintain the same rate of growth' (Harrod 1939, 16).

Expectations play a role in Harrord's definition of the steady state, but a very limited one. The quotation above shows that the plans of business are not forward looking. Rather, their expectations recall one of the rules of thumb explained by Keynes (1937): we take the past as a reliable guide to future action. The entrepreneurial equilibrium that underlies Harrod's steady state is therefore based on a specific form of rule-guided behaviour.

But we have seen that Keynes used this kind of rule-guided behaviour to explain the erratic nature of investment, while in Harrod's theory it supported the notion of steady-state growth. This caused a tension that Harrod was unable to resolve. With Keynes he believed that economic theory needs to take account of uncertainty and this was a demand that especially applied to economic dynamics (Harrod 1948, 65). He tried to include this factor by stating that the warranted rate of growth reflects some 'average' experience. Just as in real life some producers would find to their surprise that their investment is more than justified by the increase in demand for their produce. Others are not so lucky and find the outcome of this period's trading disappointing. The warranted rate of growth is the collective result of these successes and failures and in this manner seems to include a notion of uncertainty.

But what kind of average would be the result of these individual experiences? Investment decisions are made by a very large number of entrepreneurs producing different types of goods in a world characterized by uncertainty. It would be fluke if these individual decisions added up to the investment corresponding to that required by the warranted growth path. It would be even more remarkable if they continued to do so. Harrod (1948, 86) realized this all too well. But in spite of this recognition, he implicitly assumed the existence of a 'state of mind' that will keep the economy growing at this warranted rate. In short, Harrod's dynamic equilibrium was at odds with one of the key Keynesian principles.

Other Keynesians, like Joan Robinson, were more explicit about the forward looking character of expectations (Asimakopulos 1991). They based their conception of a long period equilibrium on the assumption that current conditions are expected to continue indefinitely and that expectations are immediately adjusted in the case of a change (for example Robinson 1956, 67). But that did not improve matters, for it only stressed that the uncertainty of business prospects in real life could not be handled by equilibrium theory, in static or in dynamic form. Robinson was well aware of this limitation. She stressed that '[a] world in which expectations are liable to be falsified cannot be described by the simple equations of the equilibrium path. The out-of-equilibrium position is off the page, not in the same era of logical time as the movement along the path' (Robinson 1962a, 25).

In that light it is not surprising that Robinson used the term *Golden Age* to describe a situation in which growth is occurring at a steady rate with full employment of labour. This term indicates that it represents 'a mythical state of affairs not likely to obtain in any actual economy' (Robinson 1956, 99). This raises the question why anyone should be interested in the development of such abstract models, if the final goal is to understand the operation of actual economies. The long-period Keynesians never clearly answered this question, but the key is probably that they believed that steady-state growth is the essential basis of more realistic and less mythical models (for example Allen 1967, 175).

Theoretically, the Harrod-Domar growth model has proved a fertile tool of research. Popular extensions include the possibility of technical progress, income distribution, two-sector models and heterogeneous capital (vintage models). Robinson (1956 and 1962a) demonstrated the flexibility of the Keynesian growth model by studying a variety of growth situations, which she gave colourful names like the limping, bastard or restrained *Golden Age*, the *Leaden Age* and the *Platinum Age* (galloping or creeping).[7] But what was the use of this variety of models? Did they support the rise of a competitive Keynesian paradigm based on the notion of disequilibrium rather than equilibrium?

To answer that question we need to be precise about our terminology. The Harrod-Domar growth model belongs to the domain of dynamic equilibrium analysis, because it assumes the existence of a steady state. This kind of analysis can be developed into disequilibrium theory when the following conditions are met (Allen 1967, 185). First, we need to determine the disturbance, which explains how the variables Y and K get out of line. Second, we must add a specific and appropriate error-adjustment mechanism designed to bring Y and K back into line. Finally, one may solve the model to give the disequilibrium paths of Y and K and compare the solution with the steady state growth of the equilibrium model.

The Keynesian-style dynamic disequilibrium models more or less comply to this format. The first step received the most attention, due to the instability of the basic Harrod-Domar model, described by Solow (1956) as a 'knife's edge'.[8] A divergence between the actual rate of growth and the warranted rate causes a growing rather than a shrinking gap between these growth rates (Harrod 1939, 22). This explains why Harrod believed that an equality of the natural and warranted rates of growth would be a case of sheer coincidence. He never tried to resolve the instability issue in a theoretical manner, that is by introducing an error-adjustment mechanism. He used the tension between the actual and the warranted growth rate as a framework to explain the movements of the trade cycle in a verbal rather than mathematical analysis. For him, the exact nature of the instability of dynamic equilibrium was an empirical question. He doubted that the disequilibrium forces would be powerful enough to quickly move the growth rate away from the steady state in case of a disturbance, as the image of a 'knife's edge' suggests. He preferred to speak of a 'shallow dome' and concluded that it needs empirical study rather than theory to evaluate the slope of the reaction curve in case the actual growth rate deviates from the steady state growth path (Harrod 1970).

In the late 1950s the knife-edge (or instability) principle of the Harrod-Domar model would literally drive a wedge between the economic schools dealing with questions of the trade cycle and growth theory. This division was caused by the fact that there are two ways of overcoming the knife-edge. Solow (1956) pointed the way to the neoclassical solution by introducing a variable capital-output ratio with continuous substitution along a smooth production function. Unaware of Solow's progress in this regard, Kaldor (1956) demonstrated the Keynesian alternative. He introduced the income distribution into the growth framework via the principle of variable relative income shares and a flexible average savings ratio, an extension never considered by Harrod himself.

Putting doctrinal warfare aside, it is evident that the disequilibrium dynamics based on the Harrod-Domar model can be deepened by formulating an error-correcting mechanism of some kind. A popular candidate for this extension is the formulation of a lag that relates actual investment to the desired level. This type of analysis supported the development of Post Keynesian models investigating the disequilibrium dynamics of growth off the steady-state growth path. It allowed the Post Keynesians to study the swings of the trade cycle, the interaction between the cycle and the trend of economic growth as well as the interaction between the real and monetary sectors of the economy.[9]

At this point a split occurred in the Post Keynesian tradition dealing with the analysis of long term economic developments. The logical way forward from the Harrod-Domar model in a disequilibrium setting was advanced (mathematical) theorizing on the leads and lags of disequilibrium adjustment and the subsequent empirical testing of the resulting models. This approach has tempted some to conclude rather prematurely that the Keynesian system is 'complete', as epitomized by Allen (1967, 409): 'What remains is to turn the models in econometric form and to try them out with the aid of modern simulation on a computer – and to pass on, in theory and in econometrics, from positive economics to problems of planning and optimisation'.

But the development of increasingly complicated mathematical models explaining the disequilibrium adjustment path towards or away from a long period equilibrium was not followed by all Keynesians. In particular, pioneers in the field of growth theory like Kaldor and Robinson lost their belief in the validity of this formalistic approach to Keynesian dynamics, if they ever possessed it in the first place. Kaldor and Robinson began their careers as equilibrium economists. They both ended up as severe critics of both the concept itself and of its relevance to any actual capitalist economy. King (2003, 77) argues that this position was 'powerfully reinforced' by their experience as growth theorists.

What was their criticism and what did it mean for the development of Post Keynesian disequilibrium analysis? The main reason why Robinson and Kaldor distrusted the use of equilibrium concepts in either static or dynamic analysis was the likelihood of path-dependent effects. For Kaldor technical progress and increasing returns to scale were factors explaining why the economy's production frontier would be changing while the system was moving towards it. According to him, this was an endogenous response of the system that economists were unable to explain in their equilibrium theories of whatever variety (Kaldor 1972). Robinson expressed her objections in a similar manner. From the start her distrust caused her to abstain from using mechanistic metaphors like equilibrium. For example, she described the steady-state growth path not as an equilibrium but as a 'state of tranquillity' or a 'smooth development' (Robinson 1956, 26 and 59). The problem with the equilibrium concept was that it assumes changes to take place in logical time which rules out path-dependent effects. As a result, the course of economic development was very difficult to describe in mechanical terms. In her own words (Robinson 1956, 58):

> When a market reacts to a change in circumstances, we cannot liken it to the reaction of the balance to a one-for-all change in the weights. However the balance wobbles about, it will come to rest in exactly the same position; but in most economic reactions the path the market follows, while it is adapting itself to a change, has a long-persisting effect upon the position that it reaches.

This insight results in an approach to disequilibrium analysis that does not rely on mathematical and deterministic models, but handles growth in a manner that is open-ended (King 2003, 190).[10] The different growth models of Robinson (1956 and 1962a) are an example of this approach. They discuss the interplay between the factors that drive economic growth, like the propensity to accumulate, the propensity to save, the rate of growth of the labour force, technical progress and institutional features. The result is a variety of possible growth situations to examine the broad factors that will influence the rate of investment in actual economies.

Which model is the 'true' model of economic growth? Robinson and Kaldor would answer that there is no true model. In the real world with an uncertain future and complex interactions the determination of investment cannot be reduced to a simple formula. Every disequilibrium adjustment needs to be examined as something of interest in its own right. The equilibrium growth path can no longer be used as a standard of comparison to draw general lessons about the growth process (Robinson 1974). All that can be done is to sketch out some of the important elements that affect the rate of accumulation over time. The values for these elements depend on historical and institutional circumstances, as well as psychological factors affecting the decisions of the business community. It is the complexity of such factors which explains why Robinson (1956, 244) concluded that 'over the long run, the rate of accumulation is likely to be whatever it is likely to be'.

THE CAPITAL CONTROVERSIES

What is Capital?

As could be expected, there is no agreement in the Keynesian school about the implication of this kind of critique for the nature of equilibrium theory. Referring to Robinson, Kregel (1973, 39) says that the notion of equilibrium employed in Keynesian theory concerns the study of structural relations needed to keep the system moving. Kregel here refers to the use of equilibrium as a long period concept that played a role in the capital controversies that raged between members of the two Cambridges (UK and Massachusetts, USA) in the 1950s and 1960s (although, according to some, it never ended).

In this section, I shall address the meaning of this debate and its implications for equilibrium theory. As the name suggests, the capital controversies revolved around the vexing question; what is capital? I shall not discuss the different conceptions of capital in economic theory, but one is of particular importance to the capital debate. This is Böhm-Bawerk's conception of capital as the time factor in production. It was the insight of Böhm-Bawerk that besides land and labour there does not exist a separate, third category of production factors called capital. In his conception, capital can be any service or commodity provided that it furthers production and is bound up in the production process for at least one period of time. This latter condition is crucial, because it means that capital services or commodities cannot be used for consumption in the current period. A capitalist production process implies waiting. One postpones direct consumption to free resources to build a more refined, and therefore more productive, production process.

The production factor capital is therefore closely related to land and labour, the primary sources of production. In the words of Wicksell (1935, 150): 'We may thus regard capital as a single coherent mass of saved-up labour and saved-up land, which is accumulated in the course of years.' In contrast, his Austrian colleagues liked to stress the heterogenous nature of capital. They defined capital as goods of the *n*th order, where the number *n* marks the distance to the final stage of production (see further Chapter 10). The nature of a capital good is therefore related to its position in the time structure of the production cycle of a specific consumers' good.

The question is why anyone would go through the trouble of building factories rather than consuming the means of production required for its production. The answer is that the aid of capital goods raises per capita output, because it allows one to exploit economies of scope and scale. Additionally, it may raise production through a physical improvement of the production process (stronger, quicker, longer lasting et cetera). The reduction of current consumption thus finances the production of a larger stock of consumption goods at some future date. So there is a reward for the postponement of consumption and that is the surplus of output when compared to the input in terms of production goods (and deducting the costs of the other production factors land and labour). This surplus expressed as a percentage of total output may be called the profit or interest rate and is in a very literal sense the reward for waiting.[11]

The key proposition of the Austrian theory of capital is that an increase in the capital intensity of production (or 'roundabout production' in Austrian terminology) always raises per capita output, albeit at a decreasing rate.[12] Neoclassical capital theory allows us to state this conclusion in more precise (mathematical) terms and to relate the interest rate to the demand for capital. Assuming a simple one-commodity aggregate production function $Q = f(K,L)$ it follows that a greater quantity of capital leads to a lower marginal product of additional capital and thus to a lower rate of interest. In other words, capital can be handled as any normal good with a downward sloping demand curve, so that the standard neoclassical analysis of substitution can be applied. The main lesson of this analysis is that factor inputs are determined by relative factor prices yielding the following analytical results:

- Explanation of the interest rate: the rate of interest equals the real return on capital which is determined by the technical properties of the diminishing marginal productivity of capital.
- Explanation of the income distribution: relative factor scarcities and supplies determine relative factor prices and the shares of labour and capital in total output.
- Explanation of the equilibrium growth rate: Factor substitution among a smooth production function can be used to eliminate the Harrod instability problem, as shown by Solow (1956).

Reswitching and Capital Reversal

These are all useful lessons, but the question that emerged when economists started using aggregate production function of the type mentioned above was: in what units should one measure the quantity of capital K?

This was an old question that had originally been posed by Wicksell (1935). Commenting on the capital theory of Böhm-Bawerk, he remarked that with labour and land the law of marginal productivity applies to both the economy as a whole and to every private undertaking. But in the case of capital one could only assess productivity from the point of view of the individual entrepreneur.

Wicksell (1935, 149) explained that the cause of this divergence lay in the units of measurement of the production factors. Land and labour can be measured in terms of their own technical units (working days, acres per annum), but capital must be reckoned as a sum of exchange value. In other words, each particular capital good is measured by a unit extraneous to itself. This value can be the cost of production or the present value of the future output stream the capital goods may produce. In either case, a time element is involved (looking forward or backward) which leads to circular reasoning. Capital is assumed to explain the interest rate, but in order to determine the quantity of capital we need to take the interest rate as given (it is the rate at which costs or future earnings are discounted).

The nature of this problem can be elucidated by referring to what are now called the Wicksell effects (Harcourt 1972, 39). These effects involve changes in the value of the capital stock associated with different interest rates, arising from either inventory revaluations of the same physical stock due to new capital goods prices (price Wicksell effects) or differences in the physical stock of capital goods due to changes in techniques (real Wicksell effects).

These effects came to play an important role in the capital controversies. For example, Robinson (1954, 81–82) used them to argue that the rate of interest must be known independently of the production function and cannot, therefore, be determined by it. This critique provoked several responses from the neoclassical camp that were all aimed at defending the production function as the proper tool to investigate the price of capital in terms of its marginal productivity (Solow 1956, Swan 1956 and Samuelson 1962). The least one can say of the ensuing debate is that it led to a better understanding of the Wicksell effects, which were now named reswitching and capital reversal.

The nature of these problems can be demonstrated using Samuelson's (1966) famous 'Summing Up' of the capital controversy in which he reflects on the Austrian conception of capital as a time factor. For example, take two techniques for making wine using only labour and time as inputs. Technique A requires 7 units of labour at (t - 1) to produce one barrel of wine. This barrel subsequently needs another year to ferment and to obtain the required taste and alcohol percentage. Technique B employs 2 units of labour in the first year (t - 2) followed by 6 units of labour in the third year (t = 0) elongating to the total production period with one year.

The problem of reswitching emerges when we compare the cost equations of these techniques to determine the most profitable one. The equiprofitable options are given by the equation:

$$7(1 + r) = 2(1 + r)^2 + 6$$

This equation has two roots ($r = 0.5$ and $r = 1.0$), which suggests that we have two rather than one switching point in the choice of technique. At very high interest rates ($r > 1.0$) the compounded interest on the two units of labour invested for two years makes technique B more expensive, so A is chosen. At zero interest only labour cost counts making A also cheaper. But at interest rates between 0.5 and 1.0 the relative late employment of six units of labour starts to count, resulting in B being the cheapest technology to produce wine.

Mapping the choice of technique against the interest rate then shows what reswitching and capital reversal is all about. The 'reswitch' occurs because the same technique is preferred at different interest rates. This violates the proposition that the interest rate is determined by the marginal productivity of capital, which assumes a given technology. The term 'capital reversal' refers to the change in the capital-labour ratio that is associated with the switch in techniques. Technique B produces with more labour and thus a lower capital-labour ratio for any value of the interest rate. But this means a decrease in the capital-labour ratio when the interest rate falls below the switch point $r = 1.0$, where technique B is substituted for A. We are now operating a production process that is less capital-intensive, where theory predicts that it should be more capital-intensive due to the fall in the interest rate which makes capital relatively cheaper. Therefore, the practical implication of capital reversal is that the demand curve for capital is not always downward sloping, which violates the neoclassical explanation of relative income shares in terms of the marginal productivity of the production factors vis-à-vis their relative scarcities.

It is not surprising that this kind of criticism provoked a salvage operation from the neoclassical side. The work of Robert Solow embodies the effort of Cambridge, Massachusetts to defend the use of aggregate production functions as an empirical proposition. His argument was not that the aggregate production function accurately describes economic reality in the sense that one can measure the aggregate stock of capital. Rather, he claimed that his empirical research followed the dictum of Friedman's 'as if' methodology. The neoclassical growth model using the aggregate production function predicted empirical outcomes that are the same 'as if' they were the result of the actual growth process. Whether or not the steady state growth path of the model is the end of an actual economic process is irrelevant. All that matters is the predictive accuracy of the model.

The 'predictions' of the neoclassical growth model include the well-known fact that the historical trends in relative income shares portray a remarkable constancy. But Solow also realized that the prediction of a constant income per person (no one gets richer) is hardly a valid picture of industrial capitalism. One needs technical progress to allow for long run growth in real wages and the standard of living. His efforts to empirically estimate the aggregate production function generated the famous Solow residue: more than 90 percent of the rise in gross output per hour of work in the U.S. economy between 1909 and 1949 could be attributed to 'technical change in the broadest sense' (measured as total factor productivity) and only the remaining part (< 10 percent) could be attributed to conventional increases in capital intensity (Solow 1957).

Solow (1988) seemed reasonably satisfied with the advance made in growth accounting in the thirty years since his first steps in this field. However, he also acknowledged the limitations of this empirical approach in macroeconomics. He said that he was 'very sceptical' about the use of the aggregate production function in empirical work, but pressed on nonetheless (Solow 1988, 309, see also Solow 1957, 312). He also admitted that the empirical results could never express more than a 'qualitative truth' given the problematic foundation of the theoretical concepts in growth theory and the fact that the econometric analysis of historical time-series could never constitute a critical experiment (Solow 1988, 311 and 314). What remained was what he called methodological opportunism: 'One cannot do macroeconomics without aggregative relationships; and at least for the moment there is no substitute for macroeconomics' (ibid., 313).

Solow later described the Cambridge controversies as a 'playing out of ideological games'. The playground for these games was the field of analytical economics, rather than the domain of applied growth theory. In his opinion, the controversies were closely related to the attempts of several MIT-economists to find a theoretical answer to the challenge posed by heterogeneous capital. Solow (1963) himself tried to avoid the problem of capital in terms of the concept of the 'social rate of return'. Inspired by Fisher (1930), this was capital theory without any mention of either capital or its marginal product. The social rate of return gives the ratio of the present value of the additional stream of future income generated by investment and the total costs of that investment. This concept served as the basis for empirical estimates of rates of return in actual economies. However, this attempt to apply the marginalistic calculus in growth theory without the concept of capital has met with severe criticism. For example, Pasinetti (1969) criticized the concept of capital as a rate of return (in both Fisher and Solow) arguing that it was based on an 'unobstrusive postulate' that ruled out capital-reversing from the start (see further Harcourt (1972, 159–167)).

Swan (1956) entered the capital controversy by stressing the substitutability of capital through the metaphor of 'putty capital'. He argued that even heterogeneous capital goods may work to equalize the rates of return as long as they are sufficiently malleable. To that purpose he compared capital to a meccano set, the pieces of which can be timelessly and costlessly reshaped into appropriate quantities of capital in response to the pull of relative factor prices. With metaphors of this kind we are back in the world of Solow where capital is one all-purpose commodity and where the problems posed by reswitching and capital reversal are avoided rather than solved.

The best known neoclassical attempt to salvage the production function is the Surrogate Production Function of Samuelson (1962). This construction was intended to show that even in cases with heterogeneous capital goods some rationalization can be provided for the validity of simple neoclassical 'parables' which assume that there is a single homogeneous factor called capital, the marginal product of which equals the rate of return. The model that was designed to achieve this assumed a two-sector economy in which both a consumer good and a capital good are produced by means of nonproducible labour and a single produced capital good. Samuelson assumed that there is a large number of techniques to produce the consumer good, all using a different kind of capital good, and the problem is to choose among them. This choice is facilitated by assuming that all techniques employ an equal proportion of labour to capital. Samuelson demonstrated that in stationary equilibrium, for given wage rate, there is always one technique for each sector which is the most profitable, or for a given interest rate there is always one technique that pays the highest wage rate. This result allows the derivation of an aggregate factor-price frontier with a slope that can be used as an index of capital per man in the economy.

However, writers from the opposite camp like Garegnani (1970) were quick to discover the loopholes in this approach. They showed that the fixed proportions assumption turned the Surrogate Production Function into the despised aggregate production function. As there are equal factor proportions in all industries, the income distribution between wages and profits does not affect relative prices. By this token the real economy with heterogeneous capital collapses into the imaginary economy with homogenous output. Or as Blaug (1985, 525) has put it, Samuelson adopted a many-products-one-technique simplification which rules out switching and assures that the capital-labour ratio is always uniquely associated with a particular rate of interest.

Samuelson (1966) openly admitted defeat in his 'Summing Up'. He concluded that the basic neoclassical 'parables' in capital theory like the inverse monotonic relation between the interest rate and the capital-labour or capital-output ratio are not universally valid. Thus the general consensus in the economic literature is that on a theoretical level 'Cambridge, UK' won the battle over aggregate production functions. They fell out of favour in the 1970s, but that was certainly not the end of the affair.

The Retreat to General Equilibrium Analysis

Samuelson's defeat shifted the capital controversy into the next round, which took place on the field of general equilibrium analysis. With some exaggeration one might say that the demise of the one-sector models in the tradition of Solow and Swan with homogenous capital and output caused a neoclassical retreat to general equilibrium models. The advantage of the general equilibrium framework is that it allows one to explain the prices of any set of heterogeneous commodities, including those of capital goods, while retaining the main elements of the neoclassical theory of price determination. Thus factor returns are equal to the disaggregated marginal products, while (assuming well-behaved production functions and profit maximizing producers) the factor demand functions can be derived as the inverse forms of the marginal product equations. If factor and product markets are perfectly competitive, the firms will employ workers and capital until wage rates and the rate of return on capital are equal to their respective marginal value or marginal revenue products.

The protagonists of this approach like Hahn (1975) and Bliss (1975) were quick to seize the opportunity. They acknowledged the problems of the traditional theory of capital caused by reswitching and capital reversal, but only with reference to the neoclassical model conceived in aggregate terms.

They argued that the problems do not apply to neoclassical general equilibrium theory, which handles price formation and production in disaggregated terms. In the domain of microeconomics the production function is a valid (albeit not entirely unproblematic) concept and this conclusion helped the neoclassical to fend off the Post-Keynesian/Sraffian attack on the foundation of their price theory.

The unsuspected pay-off of the shift of the capital controversy into the domain of neoclassical general equilibrium analysis was that it placed the controversy in a different light. From the start the capital controversy seemed to revolve around the problem of capital valuation with the issue of constructing an aggregate measure of capital as a by-product. However, this latter question now emerged as the main problem involving the pricing of all factors of production, while the specific problem of valuing the capital stock moved out of sight. In general equilibrium analysis product prices, factor prices, marginal products and the interest rate are all determined simultaneously. This invalidates the accusation of circular reasoning that the Cambridge Keynesians were accustomed to use against neoclassical capital theory. Or as Blaug (1985, 466 and 472) puts it: the Cambridge school is right, but for the wrong reasons. The insistence of the Cambridge critics on the difficulties of measuring the stock of capital without assuming the existence of a predetermined rate of interest may be called a 'red herring'. The true problem is that of achieving consistent aggregation of micro-production functions.

I shall briefly digress on this matter to explain the nature of this problem. Recall how Wicksell originally posed the problem of capital valuation as a problem related to the absence of a specific physical unit that could serve as the basis for measuring the quantity of capital. For him 'acres of land' and 'hours of labour' were physical units that allowed one to calculate the quantity of land and labour on either the microeconomic or macroeconomic scale. But he felt that in the case of machines and other capital goods a physical unit of comparable significance was simply unavailable. It was this lacuna which obliged one to assess the quantity of capital in terms of exchange value rather that in terms of some physical magnitude and which subsequently caused the problem of circular reasoning when one tried to establish this value.

But why is it more difficult to aggregate a quantity of capital than it is to aggregate a quantity of labour? We should question the conclusion of Wicksell on this point. Even Adam Smith, who called labour the 'only universal, as well as the only accurate measure of value', recognized that labour is not a heterogeneous quantity and that (real) wages reflect differences in hardship and skill. Such differences require that we weigh the quantity of labour in terms of efficiency or productivity. In a one sector model this is an easy exercise, as input (and therefore wages) and output are the same commodity. But in multi-sector models labourers consume a basket of goods, while output is also heterogeneous. It is clear that in this situation one needs to solve an index number problem that is commensurable with the problem of aggregating capital. In other words, as Blaug (1985, 468) has put it, all factors of production can somehow be measured in their own technical units, but such measurements have no obvious economic meaning. Wicksell too quickly isolated the problem of measuring capital as a problem specific of this production factor. The difficulty of applying the law of marginal productivity to the economy as a whole applies to all factors of production.

Related to this issue is the technical problem of the construction of a macromodel with a proper microfoundation. It has been known since the 1940s that the aggregation of utility and production function requires stringent conditions. Generally these functions have to be assumed separable in all terms. Introducing product diversity and imperfect competition complicates matters still further, as can be shown by the New Keynesian literature building on Dixit and Stiglitz (1977).

General equilibrium theory 'rescued' the general approach of neoclassical price theory based on marginalistic calculation, but at the cost of dropping all causal claims involving, for instance, the connection between the interest rate and the demand for capital. After all, in general equilibrium analysis all prices and quantities are simultaneously determined, which invalidates any attempt to develop partial hypotheses of causal effects under a ceteris paribus assumption.

Moreover, the general equilibrium approach deepened the rift between the contending parties. For example Hahn (1982) adopted the trick of Keynes (1936) to qualify the analyses of other schools as special cases of one's own analysis. Thus he reduced the importance of Sraffa (1960), which Post Keynesians saw as the foundation of their alternative approach to economics, by saying that 'there is not a single formal proposition in Sraffa's book which is not also true in a General Equilibrium model constructed on his assumptions' (Hahn 1982, 353). This special case referred to the original heterogeneous goods in the given initial set being in exactly in those proportions to generate a uniform rate of profits. To Sraffa the assumption of a uniform rate of profit was a key assumption. The non-uniformity of interest rates was therefore presented by Hahn as a sign of the generality of the general equilibrium model.

The Post Keynesians did not appreciate Hahn's dialectical skill. Pasinetti (2000, 37) called his paper 'incredibly polemical and dogmatic' and 'explicitly intended to heap discredit on those economists whom he calls "Neo-Ricardians"'. Was this a tempest in a teapot or was there a fundamental disagreement between the neoclassical general equilibrium theorist and the Sraffians?

The Classical Revival and its Meaning to the Capital Controversy

It is time to elucidate the importance of Sraffa to the present discussion. Like Robinson and Kaldor, Sraffa (1960) explained the problems of reswitching and capital reversal to the theory of capital. His 'Prelude to a Critique of Economic Theory' started a revival of the classical tradition in economics. This revival consisted in the formulation of a new theory of price that rejected a number of the cherished neoclassical concepts. For example, in Sraffa there is no marginalistic calculus to determine optimizing behaviour and the interplay of supply and demand is irrelevant, because in the long term framework of Sraffa only supply conditions matter. Likewise the concept of factor substitution is irrelevant, because Sraffa's prices are, to a large degree, independent of changes in the distribution of income.

The essence of Sraffa's work was that he tried to reinstate the classical theory of value of Smith and Ricardo. I have just cited Smith in this regard, who considered labour the only universal and accurate measure of value. Ricardo later reworked the labour theory of value to establish an invariable measure of value, a standard of measurement that was invariant to changes in the distribution of income. With this standard, one would be able to distinguish changes in relative prices from changes in the price level itself, that is in the price of the money unit. But the problem of constructing a standard of this kind in the labour theory of value is well-known. The price of a product in the long run is equal to its wage cost plus a profit margin on the capital advanced. Let us now compare the prices of two commodities with different periods of production. In this case the relative price of these commodities will no longer match their relative labour requirements, because the cost of capital for thc one product will accumulate over a longer period and so affects the relative price. We may therefore conclude that the labour theory of value cannot account for relative prices when capital as well as labour is involved in the productive process.

Ricardo tried to solve this problem by means of an invariable standard of value with a few very special properties. He stipulated that the invariable standard (Ricardo used both corn and gold) was a commodity produced by a constant quantity of capital and labour. In addition he assumed that the average period of production for the whole economy would equal the average period of production in agriculture (12 months), the sector which also delivers the invariable yardstick, corn. This was a convenient assumption, as it implied that on average the costs of capital would not affect relative prices, thereby ruling out the problem mentioned above. To secure the same result for the problem of commodity pricing, he confined himself to comparing goods produced by the same ratio of capital to labour. But this procedure resolves problems by defining them away.

This problem reemerged 140 years after Ricardo's *Principles* in Sraffa's *Production of Commodities by Means of Commodities* (1960). Sraffa approached the problem of pricing head on by formulating the cost equations of *k* products in a system that is assumed to revolve in a self-replacing state. Production requires both labour and capital goods, but in the class of goods a vital distinction is made between basic commodities and non-basic commodities. The difference between these commodities is that the basic commodities are directly or indirectly inputs into the production of every commodity in the system. Their costs therefore determine the prices of all other commodities, while for non-basic commodities this is not the case. This class of goods only enters into final consumption and represents the surplus of value over costs, that is the rate of profit.

The next step of the argument is the construction of a standard commodity, which is to serve as the yardstick of value of the system. This standard commodity is made up of all basic commodities. They enter its production in a standard ratio, which is the same proportion as they enter into their own production. The details of this construction will not detain us further. What matters is that the non-basics do no enter the production of the standard commodity. Henceforth relative prices depend only on the technical conditions of producing the standard commodity and are not affected by the prices of non-basic commodities. Moreover it can be shown that an exogenous change in wages or the profit rate (whichever is given) has no effect on relative prices measured in terms of the standard commodity. The reason for this lies in the standard ratio which implies that the measuring rod (that is the standard commodity) and the other output prices are affected to the same extent. As a corollary, the pricing process in Sraffa's system is immune to changes in the distribution of income, solving Ricardo's old quest for an invariable measure of value.

Looking backwards, the question is what the Post Keynesians ever saw in the ideas of Sraffa. In the capital debates they were combating the highly formal growth theories of the neoclassicals in favour of a more realistic view on the nature of economic development. But with Sraffa they sought to ally with someone who modeled the economy just as formalistic as Walrasian general equilibrium analysis and seemed equally far removed from economic reality.

There are two interrelated answers to this apparent contradiction. The first answer is connected to the implications of Sraffa's theory of value for the theory of distribution. The second answer is related to the promise of an alternative paradigm to the neoclassical programme, based on a different conception of equilibrium.

One of the reasons for the Post Keynesians to embrace Sraffa's rehabilitation of the classical value theory is that it provided an additional argument to reject the neoclassical explanation of income distribution in terms of marginal productivities. Sraffa provided an explanation of price determination for both factors and final products in which the concept of marginal productivity plays no role. Moreover, his theory suggests that the income distribution cannot be determined within the theory of value, as either the wage rate or the profit rate must be taken as given in order to derive a determinate solution. This opened the way to a number of possibilities that were highly valued in Post Keynesian circles. Sraffa himself suggested that the rate of profit is fixed by conditions in the money market. Another possibility is to link the profit rate to the Kaleckian degree of monopoly or to the outcome of the class struggle between capitalists and workers.[13] The supporters of Sraffa claim that the analysis of the income distribution along Sraffian lines has made considerable progress (Pasinetti 2000).

The second pillar of support for the Sraffian approach is the criticism of the static equilibrium approach of the neoclassical paradigm. The retreat of the neoclassical economists after Samuelson's defeat in the reswitching debate to the general equilibrium defence of capital goods pricing fuelled the criticism in Post Keynesian corners of this specific type of equilibrium analysis (Cohen and Harcourt 2003, 207). A familiar point is the lack of stability results in general equilibrium analysis, undermining the logical coherence of this theory and introducing some highly unrealistic features into the theory (Pasinetti 2000, 36-39). Further, from the Keynesian perspective intertemporal general equilibrium is a timeless concept, because it cannot accommodate what the Keynesians have termed fundamental uncertainty. The knowledge attributed to individual agents in a general equilibrium setting is such that one may calculate the optimal set of choices for any point in time. In other words, this equilibrium is predetermined and thereby unaffected by the actual progress of production and exchange over time.

Sraffa's return to the surplus approach of the classical school offered an alternative. He opposed the classical standpoint to the marginal method saying that this approach requires attention to be focused on change, for without change there can be neither marginal product or marginal cost (Sraffa 1960, v). But in a system in which production continues unchanged day after day, the margin of activities is irrelevant and that opens the door to an entirely different set of questions. Sraffa placed the 'self-replacing state' central to his analysis. This assumption implied that the output of each commodity was at least equal to the inputs of it that are used to produce itself and all other commodities. The production of commodities by means of commodities thus became the vehicle to address the theory of value and distribution without reference to marginal productivity or to the equilibrium of supply and demand.

But the question is: what kind of equilibrium do we get when we replace the timeless equilibrium of the neoclassicals by the Sraffian one? The classical economists generally addressed issues of long term economic development governed by competitive forces, such as the stationary state. Sraffa's construction may be seen in similar terms, given that he assumes a uniform rate of profit in all sectors. In Sraffa, this is clearly a simplifying assumption, but the Post Keynesians also interpreted it in the classical sense as the end point of a long term economic development of an actual economic system (Harcourt 1972, 181). This allowed them to confront the unrealistic and timeless concept of equilibrium in neoclassical economics with the Keynesian alternative, addressing 'the analysis of a system undergoing change through historical time' (Kregel 1973, 33).

In the 1970s Joan Robinson even started to present this issue as the essence of the capital controversies. To the surprise of many she claimed that 'the argument was not really anything to do with the problem of valuing capital' (Robinson in Kregel 1973, xii, see also Robinson 1974, 213). The real problem was the assumption of a timeless equilibrium implied by such metaphors as 'malleable capital' and other constructions required to secure the establishment of a full employment equilibrium in the neoclassical theories of growth and distribution.[14] She aimed to trace the errors and 'sophistries' of the neoclassical doctrines to their neglect of historic time in their static equilibrium theory and at the same time 'to find a more hopeful alternative in the classical tradition, revived by Sraffa, which flows from Ricardo through Marx, diluted by Marshall and enriched by the analysis of effective demand of Keynes and Kalecki'.

But Robinson grew increasingly dissatisfied with the notion of equilibrium and in due time her criticisms turned against the Sraffians themselves (King 2003, 209). The weak spot of Sraffa's theory is the familiar one of focussing on equilibrium states to the neglect of the dynamic changes that are needed to establish that state (Cohen 1993, 235). Sraffa (1960, vi) literally ruled out the possibility of changes in output in order to shield his theory against the accusation that it rests on a tacit assumption of constant returns in all industries. Nonetheless, modern Sraffians like Pasinetti and Garegnani developed this theory as the corner stone of a long period theory of production (Kurz and Salvadori 1995). The key to this method is the examination of persistent forces in establishing centers of gravitation in the economic system. As Caravale (1997, 19–20) puts it:

> The definition of equilibrium requires the identification of the forces which play a central role; that is, of those forces which – to adopt the expression used by the classical economists – have the characteristic of being 'dominant' or 'systematic' and which are, therefore, held to be different from those other forces which have a transitory, and not systematic, character.

The question that occupied the Sraffians in the aftermath of the capital controversy was the nature of these systematic forces. In their opinion, supply and demand were typical examples of the transitory forces mentioned by Caravale, which led to the conclusion that the classical conception of equilibrium was fundamentally different from the neoclassical notion which succeeded it. According to Garegnani (1976), 'equilibrium' is an incorrect term to describe the long period method of the classicals, because they discussed the tendency towards a uniform rate of profit under competitive conditions without referring to supply and demand as opposite forces. In a similar sense, Walsh and Gram (1980) draw a sharp distinction in the theory of general equilibrium between the classical theme of the accumulation and allocation of surplus output and the neoclassical theme of the allocation of given resources among alternative uses.

The issue at stake is the interplay between market and natural prices that stands central in the classical theory of price determination. Market prices are assumed to always tend towards a natural level determined by the cost of production and Adam Smith introduced the term 'gravitation' to describe this equilibrium tendency. The modern reader is accustomed to interpret the classical natural prices as the normal prices of Marshall, who explained such prices in terms of the long run schedules of supply and demand (Marshall 1920, 363–380). But Sraffa (1960) showed that we do not need the Marshallian scissors to explain relative prices. In the Sraffian self-replacing state relative prices are fully determined by the technological conditions of supply without any role for subjective factors like demand. Moreover, one of the conclusions of Sraffa's theory is that we cannot explain both the wage rate and the profit rate in terms of the same set of supply prices. In other words, supply and demand are not the omnipotent forces that Marshall and the neoclassical school assume them to be.[15]

This observation led the Sraffians to reject the neoclassical approach to simultaneously determine prices and quantities in terms of supply and demand. In their view, the distinction between structural forces underlying the long period position and transitory – supply and demand – forces suggested a stratified approach. This approach consisted in separating the determination of, on the one hand, outputs and, on the other hand, prices and profits. As a result, 'the adjustment of individual outputs involved in the gravitation towards natural prices could be conceived of as an *adaptation towards quantities already fixed, that is determined in another part of the theory*' (Garegnani 1976, 76: italics in the original text).

The structural forces ruling this 'other part' of classical theory are closely connected to the generation, extraction and distribution of surplus output. This is what Walsh and Gram (1980) isolate as the distinguishing characteristic of the classical as opposed to the neoclassical paradigm. The production of surplus output is contingent on the development of society and thus on specific social conditions. In brief, in the classical model it is assumed that technology has developed to the stage where it is possible to produce a social surplus. Thus the purpose of classical economics is to exhibit the special historical form assumed by the surplus under capitalism, to show how the production and distribution of surplus output depends on social class and technical relationships in capitalist production and to analyze how this distribution affects the division of the surplus between capital accumulation and luxury consumption, thereby affecting the development of the economy. In neoclassical economics this question does not occur at all. Surplus value is only defined in a model in which among the outputs there are commodities used as inputs into further production. If instead all resources are treated analytically, as if they were primary non-produced factor of production (in the manner of Walras), the question of defining a surplus of net output simply cannot arise.

This conclusion points to different conceptions of equilibrium in the neoclassical paradigm and the classical paradigm, as the Sraffians define it. The classical notion of equilibrium is that of a circular flow as commodities are used to produce commodities in successive cycles of production. In the timeless world of neoclassical equilibrium analysis, equilibrium is established through a one-way street leading from given factors to final outputs.

The Sraffian interpretation of the classical long period method is necessary to explain the debate between Joan Robinson and the Sraffians on the validity of equilibrium analysis (even when the Sraffians are unwilling to call it that). We have addressed Robinson's criticism in this regard earlier in this chapter. In her opinion, equilibrium is a fleeting concept because it is highly uncertain that the conditions which determine it today will be present tomorrow. Moreover, one cannot sequentially compare different equilibrium states, like 'flipping stills through a projector', in order to assemble an image of a process moving through historical time (Robinson 1974, 212). The reason for this is that such historical processes are governed by path-dependent effects, which means that those equilibria must be treated as interdependent.

Garegnani (1983, 75) reconstructed Robinson's argument by saying that she focuses on the analysis of historical processes in terms of a sequence of short-period positions. According to him, this is not the type of 'traditional' long period method used by himself, because the comparative statics dismissed by Robinson relies on the use of supply and demand as controlling forces.[16] Demand factors are controlled by subjective causes like beliefs and expectations, which explains their erratic nature. This was one of the reasons of Keynes in the GT to dismiss the notion of a long term equilibrium and to focus on short period equilibria in which expectations could be assumed constant (Garegnani 1976, 141ff and Asimakopulos 1991, 120–137).[17]

Garegnani rejected this argument as a valid criticism of the long period method employed by Sraffa and his followers. We have already explained that the Sraffians conducted their long period analysis independently of supply and demand considerations. According to Garegnani, this invalidated Robinson's criticism. The gravitation towards a uniform rate of profit does not depend on price expectations.[18] Therefore, this tendency cannot be upset by the potentially labile animal spirits which guide investors' behaviour in Keynes's GT. Subjective factors of this kind belong to the domain of the transitory forces, which will not have a lasting impact on the resulting long period position. Garegani (1983, 76) even suggested that we should interpret the tendency towards a long period position not only as an analytical proposition, required to isolate specific systematic forces, but also as an empirical one. Thus he argued that 'long period theory analyses what will happen *over an average* of such "short periods"' (Garegnani 1983, 76, italics in the original text). The natural or normal rate of profits is therefore the rate which is being realized 'on an average (as between firms and over time) . . . because these firms will receive, on average, the normal price for their product and pay, on an average, besides normal wages and rents, normal (supply) prices for the means of production to be replaced' (ibid., 77).

In my opinion, Garegnani's reply to Joan Robinson is incorrect on at least two accounts. The first error concerns the role of the supply and demand mechanism in the Sraffian explanation of the long term 'position'. Sraffa gets rid of demand in the explanation of prices by the assumption that in the steady state all commodities are produced under conditions of constant costs, in which case the scale of output of a commodity makes no difference to input proportions. As stated above, Sraffa himself wanted to avoid any discussion about the returns to scale by ruling out the possibility of a change in output. But this question cannot be avoided if one applies Sraffa's theory in a comparative static analysis of dynamic change. As soon as we consider alternative stationary states, which differ in the scale of output, the structure of the standard commodity itself will change unless constant returns to scale conditions obtain. The long period method therefore requires one to explicate the assumptions concerning the returns to scale or to assume a given pattern of demand (Kurz and Salvadori 1995, 33–34). The existence of increasing returns to scale poses major problems to the Sraffian framework, because it rules out profit maximization and the equality of the rate of profit between industries.[19] Moreover, the moment we have increasing returns to scale the pattern of demand is vital to the explanation of relative prices. This invalidates the attempt of Garegnani and others to present Sraffa's theory of value and distribution as independent of traditional supply-and-demand considerations and in that respect as an anti-neoclassical approach.

The second objection to Garegnani's position on Robinson concerns the nature of the long period forces that are supposed to overrule the transitory effect of supply and demand. Robinson not only stressed the impact of uncertain expectations, but also of path-dependent effects in the movement towards equilibrium. In my opinion, path-dependency also affects the structural forces which occupy a central role in the Sraffian long period method. The point to emphasize is that such forces are anything but given when we consider the tendency towards a long period equilibrium. Take the state of technological knowledge that plays such an important part in the neoclassical and Keynesian explanation of the growth process and in Sraffa's theory also in the process of price formation. Evolutionary economics shows that there is a complex interaction between the choice of technology and the tendency of the economic system towards a long period position. Technology choices are characterized by lock-in effects that may occur during the process of development. Such effects arise as a result of what Nelson (1995) calls 'dynamic increasing returns' in combination with network externalities. Alternatively, chance events which occur during the process may push the system to one of multiple equilibria (Arrow 2000). Accordingly, the end result of a process of development is significantly influenced by what happened earlier.

The implication of path dependency in this sense is that the long period position of the Sraffians is unlikely to be a unique equilibrium. Depending on the course of economic development over time, there exist multiple equilibria which may operate as the center of attraction in the long period. This means that we have no way of knowing what direction the economy will take unless we have some knowledge of the dynamic mechanism forcing the system to take route A or B. Let alone that it is possible to draw conclusions about the nature of dynamic changes by comparing two different long period positions, as the Sraffians do. One might as well argue that it is possible to explain the dynamics of ebb and flow by comparing two random kernels of sand on the beach.

CONCLUSION

So, who is right? Robinson and the other short period Post Keynesians like Hyman Minsky who fundamentally oppose the use of long period equilibrium constructs (King 2003, 209–211) or Garegnani and the Sraffians who accuse Robinson of theoretical nihilism? The answer is that both parties are partly right and grossly overstate the errors of the opposite camp.

To start with Robinson, Cohen (1993) argues that in spite of her scathing criticism of equilibrium theory, she did not denunciate all kinds of equilibrium theorizing. According to him, she did accept a role for equilibrium theory in a very general sense: to provide the abstraction or simplification that is the essence of theorizing (Robinson 1962b). Equilibrium theory could therefore be part of what Cohen calls a three-stage theoretical process that allows one to examine the out-of-equilibrium process in an open model operating in historical time. The stages of this process are (Cohen 1993, 232):

- Building a closed, deterministic equilibrium model;
- Embedding it in a historical context to create an open, historical model, and
- Confronting the open historical model with empirical data.

In other words, the equilibrium model must be loosened up and combined with specific factual information to create an open historical model that will be useful for the analysis of actual outcomes. This factual information will consist of what Robinson (1962b, 124ff) called the 'rules of the game', behavioural responses, institutional description and historical parameters.

Surprisingly, the Sraffians claim that the long period model must be seen in similar terms. For example, Pasinetti insists that we understand the principles of an institution-free system before we take into account the role of institutions and particular historical episodes (Harcourt and Kerr 2003, 351).[20] This approach at least suggests a two-stage theoretical process consisting of 'building a closed, deterministic equilibrium model' and 'embedding this model in a historical context'. Seen in this way, it appears that there is substantial common ground between Robinson and several of her (former) Cambridge colleagues like Pasinetti and Garegnani. Why, then, were they unable to agree on the proper way to address typical Keynesian questions like the analysis of unemployment and income distribution and the way to incorporate institutions and economic development into economic theory?

It is evident that Joan Robinson felt that the Sraffians were exclusively concerned with the development of a closed, deterministic equilibrium model. In her terms, their work firmly remained within stage one of the theoretical process and never reached stage two, the loosening up of the Sraffian model to include institutional factors. Let alone that the Sraffians confronted their models with empirical data.

The reason for their unwillingness or inability to go beyond the deterministic equilibrium model inspired by Sraffa (1960) can be found in the capital controversies. This debate provided the initial impetus for the Sraffian 'revolution' but also marked it as a theoretical development, given that the capital controversies largely revolved around the treatment of capital as a theoretical issue. In the process of spelling out the consequences of his prelude to a critique of economic theory, Sraffa's followers were primarily engaged in building a Lakatosian hard core of a scientific research program that could compete with the neoclassical doctrine.

A hard core of this kind consists of theoretical propositions that are shielded from empirical testing and thus automatically lead to a focus on the first stage of Robinson's theoretical process. Moreover, the nature of this hard core is such that a loosening up of the assumptions which support it is not an attractive prospect. In Lakatos's terms, the confrontation of the positive and negative heuristic of the hard core easily leads to conflict.[21] An example of this problem is the positive heuristic 'assume a uniform rate of profit in all sectors, operating as a centre of attraction for long period changes'. This rule is combined with the negative heuristic 'do not use supply and demand schedules to explain prices and quantities'. But we have seen what happens when we try to examine the dynamics behind the assumed tendency towards a uniform profit rate. The inclusion of a time factor implies that output may vary, which raises the question of the returns to scale. In Sraffa's theory the returns to scale need to be assumed constant in all sectors in order to prevent that demand factors emerge as price determining causes. It is therefore impossible to relax this assumption of the Sraffian model in response to actually observed economies of scale. One must either abandon the attempt to loosen up the Sraffian model on this point or drop one of the constituent parts of the Sraffian hard core, namely the negative heuristic that precludes analysis in terms of the supply and demand mechanism.

The Sraffians, on the other hand, criticized Robinson for not fully joining their camp. As King (2003, 99) puts it, there was in her case always some 'residual attachment' to neoclassical analysis.[22] This attachment included, for example, the use of the supply and demand mechanism as a tool of analysis and her reluctance to reject the main basis of the neoclassical theory of distribution, the notion of a technical substitutability between capital and labour (Garegnani 1976, 144 n39).

Such arguments may explain the animosities between theorists with a common scientific goal. An 'error' that applies to both parties to this debate is that neither practiced what she/he preached. The Sraffians never succeeded in incorporating institutional factors into their theoretical structure or to confront their analyses with empirical data. The root of this problem may have been a theoretical one. As Blaug (1985, 141) described it: 'Sraffa's model is so restrictive as to rule out any meaningful discussion of its empirical implications for the real world.'

However, the failure to close the gap between theory and the real world also partly applies to Robinson. Her analyses of the golden and not so golden growth paths are testimony of her attempt to create an open historical model of economic growth (Asimakopulos 1991, 179–185). But this catalogue of possible growth situations is based on postulated conditions, not all of which can be considered plausible. What misses is the confrontation with 'hard' empirical evidence. A test of this kind could have helped to assess the validity of the Robinsonian growth paths in actual economic conditions. This would have provided vital information about the need to adjust the theoretical models in a next round of theory development.

One aspect that could have benefitted from such an approach is Robinson's treatment of instability. Her examination of possible growth situations assumed conditions of tranquillity with no disturbances or other incompatibilities to disrupt growth (Robinson 1962a). Surely, this was an aspect of her analysis that cried out for a confrontation with real growth conditions. But Robinson rested content by saying that her analysis of long run growth would still be cogent 'in a broad way' even under the conditions which give rise to inherent instability without testing whether this was actually the case. In sum, Robinson succeeded in developing the second stage of her theoretical process – the open historical model – but failed to make the subsequent step and confront this model with empirical data. This third stage of the theoretical process remained a promise that was never fulfilled.

This conclusion brings me to a final assessment of the capital controversies. The outcome of this debate is well-known. The quarrels between the two Cambridges were never resolved and deepened the impression that their members were working in two rival paradigms. In other words, the end result was an ideological rather than a scientific debate (Cohen and Harcourt 2003, 210).

In retrospect, this split should have been avoided. On a theoretical level the differences between the neoclassical and Post-Keynesian camps were not that great as both sides have made us believe. As Blaug (1975b, 68–69) pointed out, the main difference between the growth theories belonging to these 'paradigms' can be reduced to the question of whether investment adjusts to an autonomous saving rate or vice versa. In his opinion, the road forward is a practical one, applying the right model in the right economic conditions. This means that in conditions of less than full employment a

Keynesian treatment of growth would have been logical, while the analysis of growth with full employment calls for the application of neoclassical models. As a third layer, attention may be given to the impact of income distribution along Sraffian lines.

Even on a methodological level there could have been a meeting of minds. Neoclassical economists are sometimes just as critical of their equilibrium tools as their Post Keynesian adversaries. Frank Hahn moved the capital controversy into the domain of general equilibrium analysis, but at the same time he expressed great concerns about the progress made in this branch of theory (Hahn 1981 and 1984). He argued that there are all kinds of economic features which are yet not integrated into general equilibrium analysis such as asymmetric information, money, the formation of expectations, the possibility of missing markets, market power, involuntary unemployment et cetera. Questions of this kind threaten the logical consistency of general equilibrium theory and also limit its explanatory power for process in the real world. According to Hahn, general equilibrium theory gives a fairly good account of how production and exchange are organized in the decentralized economy, but we are just beginning to understand how this system behaves outside equilibrium.

Robert Solow has similar worries about recent developments in the endogenous growth theory of Kydland and Prescott (1982), Paul Romer (1986) and others. In the highly abstract world that lies behind this theory, consumers and firms are assumed to continuously solve a Ramsey-optimal growth problem through time, disturbed only by stationary stochastic shocks to taste and technology. The result is a model of the capitalist world which is always on an equilibrium growth path. What we used to call business cycles are now to be interpreted as 'optimal blips in optimal paths' in response to random fluctuations in productivity and the desire for leisure. Solow (1988, 310–311) is not at all convinced by this of kind of progress in his field of research. 'The markets for goods and labour look to me like imperfect pieces of social machinery with important institutional peculiarities.' In his opinion, the image of markets as 'transparent and frictionless mechanisms' does not enhance our understanding of how the economic process works in the real world. We need theory and thus employ abstractions to organize our thinking, but the other side of the medal is that 'we have no choice but to take seriously our own direct observations of the way economic institutions work'. In addition growth theory needs to come to grips with that other intriguing question in dynamic economics: How to account for the behaviour of the system in disequilibrium and the possibility of path-dependent effects? Failure to do so may lead to a line of inquiry that Solow typifies as 'foolishness' (ibid., 311).

This kind of criticism raises the question why the members of competing paradigms like Post Keynesians and neoclassicals are often incapable of working together on a common agenda. Solow (1988) provides a vital clue: economists cannot perform critical experiments. We lack the laboratory that in other sciences helps to settle academic disputes. As a result, a host of other arguments enter the ring which muddle rather than clarify the issue at stake. Political preferences and other ideological concerns are well-known examples, but also the social psychology of research groups to prefer one particular method over another.

The capital controversies are a prime example of the problems caused by the inability to settle arguments by way of a critical test. Even worse, the controversies show that economics is a predominantly theoretical science. Its members have a remarkable dislike for doing muddy empirical work. Take the Post Keynesians. They define their own *raison d'être* in terms of the need to build a more realistic economic theory. But their contribution to the capital controversies is best described as 'theory without measurement' (Blaug 1975b). The so-called realistic assumptions of Post Keynesian theory like fixed coefficients of productions or increasing returns to scale produced a string of theories that were never submitted to an empirical test of any kind.[23] Meanwhile they provided the ammunition to combat rival neoclassical theories.[24] Reswitchting and capital reversal played an important role in the theoretical victory of the Keynesian Cambridgians over their neoclassical namesakes, but no Keynesian tried to establish whether these phenomena are also empirically relevant. To the surprise of many, they simply considered the empirical issue beside the point (Cohen and Harcourt 2003, 209). The Keynesians habitually stated that this was a theoretical debate in which all models assume a given technology.[25]

Are the neoclassicals, then, the heroes of this story? That would be too simple. There is a large literature trying to measure growth and its determinants using the Solow-Swan fiction of the one sector model with infinitely malleable capital. It should be clear by now that the theoretical basis for this kind of approach is rather shallow, given the difficulties surrounding aggregate production functions.[26] The complement of this empirical approach is the general equilibrium defense of the neoclassical theory of value and distribution which is so abstract as to rule out any kind of practical application. In the words of Blaug (1975b, 80): 'It is almost as if one-half of mainstream economics consisted of 'measurement without theory' and the other half of "theory without measurement"'. This, in my opinion, does not stand out as a 'best practice' either.

Some say that we should prefer the neoclassical paradigm over its Keynesian rival, because its equilibrium theories have demonstrated great flexibility in handling new questions. This may be true of the partial equilibrium theories that have been the bread and butter of economics since the days of Marshall. But with regard to general equilibrium theory I doubt whether it has effectively incorporated the new (and partly non-Walrasian) issues mentioned by Hahn (see further Chapter 16). Besides theoretical flexibility, there is a more important feature at stake, which, however, lies in the hearts of people rather than in the hearts of theories. This is what Robinson (1962b, 147) described as the 'first essential' for economists when arguing among themselves: 'try very seriously to avoid talking at cross purposes'. Unfortunately, it is typical of our profession that she continued these wise words by saying that we should 'combat, not foster, the ideology which pretends that values which can be measured in terms of money are the only ones that ought to count'.

As the expression runs: Is the glass half empty or half full? Economists like to stress the empty part and continue to quarrel among themselves, while the more constructive attitude would be to explore the potential for joint research, exploiting the benefits of cross-fertilization.

NOTES

1. See Dow (1996) for a discussion of this distinction.
2. It is perhaps telling that King (2003, 5) evades this question in the following manner. Referring to an Israelian joke concerning the definition of a Jew, he argues that all those who call themselves Post Keynesian qualify as a member of this school.
3. The classic definition of the Post Keynesian paradigm is Eichner and Kregel (1975). See also King (2003).
4. 'Generally speaking, in making a decision we have before us a large number of alternatives, none of which is demonstrably more 'rational' than the others, in the sense that we can arrange in order of merit the sum aggregate of the benefits obtainable from the complete consequences of each. To avoid being in the position of Buridan's ass, we fall back, therefore, on motives of another kind, which are not "rational" in the sense of being concerned with the evaluation of consequences, but are decided by habit, instinct, preference, desire, will, etc.' Keynes (1979, 294).
5. Domar (1946) used a different economic construction. He based his growth model on the assumed constancy of the capacity output-capital ratio ($1/v=Y/K$) from the production function. This construction produces a mathematically equivalent solution of Harrod's result, namely a unique equilibrium or 'warranted' rate of growth with full employment: $g=s/v=n$. See Allen (1967).
6. It was Kaldor (1957) who stressed that the assumption of full employment was a matter of theoretical necessity. He also postulated that the system tends towards an equilibrium rate of growth at which the natural and warranted rates are equal.

7. With this taxonomy Robinson (1962a, 51–59) in effect provided a summary of the various logical possibilities in the relationship between the actual, warranted and natural growth rates (although she never used this terminology). In the various *Golden Ages* (GA) there is (a) steady growth, but full employment is normally unattainable because of deficient animal spirits (limping GA), (b) a maximum growth rate that is too low (restrained GA) or (c) an inflation barrier (bastard GA). In the various *Platinum Ages* steady growth itself is precluded by unsuitable initial conditions: the capital stock is either above or below that desired by entrepreneurs, so that the actual growth rate is either increasing or decreasing rather than steady over time.
8. Harrod's 'fundamental equation' of the warranted growth rate explains this instability. He defined v as the desired incremental capital-output ratio (C in his equation). If the actual growth rate G outruns the warranted growth rate, the actual increase in the capital stock per unit of output C must be lower than the increase in capital that is desired by entrepreneurs. Consequently, they will respond by increasing investment orders, raising G still further.
9. There is of course the related issue of the microfoundations underlying such disequilibrium dynamics. The microfoundations project starting in the 1960s tried to reconcile macrotheory with the choice-theoretic foundations of neoclassical economics. I shall discuss the implications of this approach in Chapter 16.
10. See Cohen (1993) for an explanation of this open-ended model in terms a three-stage theoretical process.
11. Without going in detail, there are several competing explanations of the profit rate. Firstly, profit may be seen as a return to uncertainty bearing (Knight 1921); secondly, it may be expressed as the reward for innovation in the sense of Schumpeter (1942), and lastly it can be explained as a return to arbitrage, as Kirzner (1973) stressed. See further Blaug (1985, 462–465).
12. Böhm-Bawerk (1921a, 13–14) called this claim the 'most important and fundamental principle of capital theory'. But he stressed that the justification of this principle rests on nothing else than casual empiricism: 'Es muß ausdrücklich ausgesprochen werden, daß seine Stütze die praktische Lebenserfahrung und nur diese ist. Die nationalökonomische Theorie beweist nicht und kann nicht a priori beweisen, daß es so sein müsse, aber die einmütige Erfahrung aller Produktionstechnik lehrt: es ist nun einmal so. Und das genügt, um so mehr, als die bezüglichen Erfahrungstatsachen allbekannt und jedermann geläufig sind.'
13. The importance of this point is illustrated by Kregel (1973, 48) who isolates the conflict between the interests of different classes as a defining characteristic of the Post Keynesian paradigm. He rejects the notion of distribution as a process of free bargaining between equal partners. He says that workers are not in the same position as capitalists, for if workers cannot find employment 'they must cease eating'. Thus, according to him, the social relations are much as Marx saw them, in the terms of the class struggle between labour and capital. See also Nell (1967, 17).

14. In the opinion of Robinson, 'the purpose of malleable capital is to overcome the difference between the future and the past'. See Robinson in Kregel (1973, xii).
15. As Garegnani (1976, 76) puts it, '[t]he forces which Marshall and post-Ricardian theory introduced to determine the normal rates of wages and profits were fundamentally different from those envisaged by Ricardo for his natural rates.' Garegnani (1983, 77) also points to Marx as a prime exponent of the classical long period method, which operates independently of the supply and demand mechanism.
16. 'The persistence of the traditional notion of a demand-and-supply equilibrium provides, we submit, the main explanation of Robinson's position regarding the impossibility of studying changes by means of comparisons.' See Garegnani (1976, 144–145).
17. Robinson went even further and at times suggested that uncertainty is sufficient reason to dismiss any kind of equilibrium theory. In her own words: 'As soon as the uncertainty of the expectations that guide economic behaviour is admitted, equilibrium drops out of the argument and history takes its place.' See Robinson (1974, 202).
18. 'In traditional theory, not only the long period position, but also the gravitation towards it were generally explained without introducing price expectations.' See Garegnani (1976, 140).
19. Of course, it is evident that the possibility of increasing returns to scale poses problems to neoclassical general equilibrium theory as well. See for example Kaldor (1972). The main problem is that Arrow-Debreu existence proofs of competitive equilibrium in terms of fixed point theorems like Brouwer's crucially rely on convexity assumptions. However, more recent insights have led to the developments of techniques to handle non-convex technologies in the context of general equilibrium theory. See Brown (1991).
20. See also Pasinetti (2000, 22): 'Sraffa's most important contribution was to open up the issue of the determination of the rate of profits – and, with it, the whole problem of income distribution – to an investigation that did not stop short at purely economic considerations but would go beyond them, up to including the entire institutional organisation of an economic system, as a subject of analysis.'
21. In common language, the positive and negative heuristic of the hard core describe the do's and don'ts of theoretical development in the belt of a scientific research program. See Chapter 3.
22. In private correspondence with Robinson, Kaldor said it even more forcefully: 'But the main point on which we differ is your thorough-going neoclassicism which, despite all your protests, permeates your thinking on this whole business.' Quoted in King (2003, 100).
23. There is a sense of irony in this, since the empirical irrelevance of general equilibrium theory was a favorite Post Keynesian argument to dispel the neoclassical competition. See Kaldor (1972).
24. Blaug (1975b) says the Post Keynesians themselves fell victim to the malady of formalism, treating abstract phenomena as though they were real, which they were constantly ascribing to their neoclassical opponents. See also Blaug (2003) for a discussion of this malady in general.

25. See for example how Kurz and Salvadori (1995, 450) reject all attempts to disprove reswitching in terms of wage-profit curves constructed from input-output tables for different years. They call this approach 'fundamentally mistaken', because reswitching refers to technical knowledge at a given moment of time. Interestingly, Han and Schefold (2006) recently published the first Keynesian attempt to empirically prove the existence of reswitching by means of the same method. They estimated the *w–r* envelopes for 32 input-output tables for nine OECD countries for 1979–1986. Reswitching appeared in one case, and in 3.65 percent of tested cases there was a 'perverse' substitution of labour, that is capital-labour substitution that contradicts the neoclassical parable. Whatever one may find of the method, this at least suggests that reswitching is a rare phenomenon.
26. An additional difficulty is the problem isolated by Franklin Fisher. He showed that as long as factor income shares remain constant, an aggregate Cobb-Douglas production function will fit the data well, 'even though the underlying technical relationships are not consistent with the existence of any aggregate production function' (Fisher 1971, 325).

14. Creative Entrepreneurship: Chaos or Coordination?

INTRODUCTION

In the history of economic thought the Austrian school is the tradition that has most persistently pursued the analysis of processes in disequilibrium. We have seen in Chapter 10 that the founding fathers of the school – Menger, Böhm-Bawerk and Wieser – developed a subjective theory of value which treated price as a range of possible outcomes rather than as a determinate point of equilibrium. Chapter 12 argued that the second generation of Austrian economists used this theory to explain the business cycle as a disequilibrium phenomenon that is typical of monetary economies. Hayek introduced a new, dynamic definition of equilibrium into business cycle analysis and put the role of knowledge on the agenda of economic science. His contributions in these areas are said to have inspired a host of modern developments like the economics of information (Zappia 1997) and the new classical analysis of the business cycle (van Zijp 1992). Ample reason to investigate what contemporary Austrians may contribute to the modern analysis of economic processes in disequilibrium.

This objective is hindered by the fact that the Austrian treatment of disequilibrium processes is far from uniform. Chapter 10 concluded that Böhm-Bawerk was the only one of the Austrian grandfathers to stress the capacity of real markets to continuously tend towards a position of supply-and-demand equilibrium. Menger and Wieser did not unconditionally share this conviction and discussed several aspects of the market processes that would disturb rather than establish economic equilibrium. Similar disagreements mark the later development of the Austrian school. Mises (1949) used the fiction of an Evenly Rotating Economy as a benchmark of analysis. But Hayek (1928) rejected a stationary equilibrium concept of this kind, arguing that, viewed in dynamic terms, equilibrium prices must reflect the expected changes of preferences and resources over time.

In this chapter, I shall argue that the modern Austrians have still not digested all the problems of this inheritance. The main Austrian problem is the position of disequilibrium vis-à-vis equilibrium. Is the nature of the market process to show a tendency towards equilibrium, seen in Hayekian terms as a state of plan coordination? Or is Shackle's kaleidic society a more accurate description of the market process? According to this view, markets are pushed hence and forth by both equilibrating and disequilibrating forces, resulting in a process without any sense of direction.

I shall address these questions in three steps. First, I discuss the role of entrepreneurship as a driving force behind the market process. According to Kirzner and his followers, it is this force which ensures that free markets always tend towards a position of enhanced coordination. This view is criticized by Lachmann, Rizzo, O'Driscoll and others who claim that uncertainty is endogenous to the market process. Their arguments contra to the equilibrium view are my second topic for this chapter. Finally, I shall inquire what economics has learned from the confrontation of these two disequilibrium views within the Austrian school.

CREATIVE ENTREPRENEURSHIP AS THE KEY TOWARDS COORDINATION

One of the leading voices of the Austrian revival in the final quarter of the last century was that of Israel Kirzner. His classic *Competition and Entrepreneurship* (1973) firmly focused the attention of the economics profession on the distinctive trait of Austrian economics as a doctrine that stressed the importance of competition as a process and the role of entrepreneurship therein. For Kirzner, the market was a dynamic process that proceeds in disequilibrium. This view placed him in opposition to neoclassical microeconomics, which defines competition as perfect competition and assumes markets to reside in perennial equilibrium. Kirzner (1997a, 64) called this approach 'blatantly false' because it leads economists to ignore exactly those aspects of the market process which form its governing force in real economies. However, for an accurate understanding of Kirzner's position it is crucial to note that he does not reject the neoclassical paradigm completely. He shares with the neoclassicals the belief that in real life competitive markets are always moving in the direction of equilibrium. The focus of his market process theory is not on equilibrium as an end state, but on equilibrium seen as a tendency, a change in the direction of improved coordination among market participants. Kirzner has devoted his work since 1973 to explaining the uniqueness of this approach – it represents a disequilibrium theory of the market, whereas neoclassical theory focuses on the analysis of equilibrium states – and the persistence of entrepreneurship and competition as forces that will not fail in bringing the free market economy closer to equilibrium.

The latter part of this mission has increasingly brought Kirzner into conflict with other Austrians. This conflict has reached a state in which Mario Rizzo, one of Kirzner's closest associates, has isolated him as virtually the last Austrian to believe in the market process as a predominantly equilibrative tendency (Rizzo 1996, xviii). These opponents argue that entrepreneurship is more than a means to exploit and reduce price differentials. Entrepreneurship is also a source of innovation, a function that Schumpeter (1942) has described as 'creative destruction'. The impact of creative entrepreneurship in this sense is disruptive rather than coordinative. In other words, entrepreneurship calls forth a mix of forces which fosters both equilibrium and disequilibrium. Kirzner's opponents complain that he systematically overlooks the latter part of the entrepreneurial role and thus gives an one-sided image of the market process. They argue that by doing so he even risks losing the distinctive character of the Austrian market process approach. For, why not follow the assumption of equilibration-always to its logical conclusion and ignore the process in favour of its end state? This is the strategy chosen by neoclassical economics and Kirzner now risks being drawn into the same camp. As Rizzo (1996, xix) argues, '[t]o the extent that the equilibration-always view eschews endogenous disruption of coordination, it must degenerate into the complete-stasis position of extreme neoclassical economics'.

It is odd to find that the author of *Competition and Entrepreneurship* is on the brink of being labeled a hard core neoclassical by his own brethren. The Austrian revival as a disequilibrium tradition seems to have imploded. Surely, this is an issue that calls for further exploration. Why is it that Kirzner so stubbornly maintains that the essence of entrepreneurial discovery in competitive markets is a systematic tendency towards equilibrium? I shall answer this question by isolating the key components of Kirzner's market process, entrepreneurship and competition.

Alertness as a Quality of Entrepreneurship

The background of Kirzner (1973) is that in standard neoclassical equilibrium theory there is, by definition, no role for the entrepreneur. Assuming conditions of perfect competition, both sellers and buyers are price takers. Every market participant instantly knows the equilibrium price and adjusts his or her activities accordingly. The result is that there is no scope for profit in this market en henceforth there is nothing to do for the entrepreneur.

It goes without saying that for Kirzner this was not an acceptable description of the market process as we observe it around us. He argued that the neoclassical explanation of a competitive equilibrium price demands too much from all concerned. Take the Marshallian explanation of the equilibrating process in a market for any normal good with a downward sloping demand curve and an upward sloping supply curve. Now assume that a technology shock suddenly shifts the supply curve to the right. What happens? Neoclassical theory assumes that the market already knows that the demand price of the quantity now available exceeds the supply price. As a result, suppliers will start to produce a higher quantity in order to exploit the difference and thereby move the market from the old to the new equilibrium. Everyone instantly knows the new equilibrium price, so the adjustment will be as quick as (physically) possible.

Kirzner objected that this process of equilibration misinterprets the nature of the market process as a mechanistic response to changes in exogenous conditions, like a change in technology. According to him, the market process operates in an entirely different fashion. The urge to change comes from within rather than outside the market. Kirzner (1976, 117) stressed that disequilibrium occurs precisely because market participants do not know what the market clearing price is. By implication, it is also not clear how the fact that the quantity on the market is less than the equilibrium quantity assures the decisions of market participants to be so modified as to increase it. Clearly, there is something missing in our theoretical framework that actively seeks for profit opportunities and urges producers to modify their plans in the required direction. This is the role of what Kirzner (1973, 35) called 'alert' entrepreneurs.

Alertness is a quality of entrepreneurs which presses them to constantly seek for unexploited opportunities for profit. By doing so, they take advantage of the differentials between supply and demand prices, a gap which through their actions tends to become reduced. This simple story of the entrepreneur as an arbitrage trader is the basis of Kirzner's contention that entrepreneurial activity will bring markets closer to equilibrium. In this version, it seems nothing more than a theory which complements the neoclassical theory of market equilibrium by providing an explanation of what occurs during the transition from one equilibrium point to another. However, to reduce Kirzner's theory of entrepreneurship to a case of 'neoclassical Austrianism', as some maintain (for example Boettke, Horwitz and Prychitko 1994, 65), would fail to do credit to his true intentions. In my reading, the Austrian content of his theories is far more important than any sympathetic allegiance to neoclassical economics he might portray.

The key to the Austrian element in Kirzner's theory of entrepreneurship is the open-ended character of entrepreneurship as Kirzner sees it. In neoclassical economics, equilibrium is for every individual partaking in exchange or production the outcome of a constrained optimization problem. They all operate with a given objective function (regarding utility, costs or profit) and a given set of resource constraints (income or inputs). They are what Kirzner (1973) called 'Robbinsian maximizers' (see also Kirzner 1979, 166). Robbins (1932) defined economics as the study of economizing behaviour. This concerns the question of the most efficient allocation of scarce resources among multiple competing ends. According to Kirzner, it is this framework which gives the neoclassical choice-theoretic framework its closed, deterministic character. Mises (1949), on the other hand, emphasized the much broader notion of purposeful human action, embracing the deliberate efforts of men to improve their position. This framework also involves economizing in the sense that it focuses on the connection between means and ends, but the crucial difference is that in Mises's conception of human action the means-ends framework is not given. Men actively seek new ends to improve their well-being. Along the way they may encounter new means to help them along but which they did not know existed beforehand. Uncertainty and surprise, in other words, play a large role when purposefully acting people apply means to ends and it is this aspect which gives Kirzner's theory of entrepreneurship its distinctive Austrian flavour.

Competition as Rivalry

For Kirzner, entrepreneurship is not a specific economic function, but a quality that every supplier and demander possesses.[1] Every agent on the market is alert to opportunities which may help him to better satisfy his goals. Generally, this means that they are looking to reap a profit which someone else has overlooked. According to Kirzner, the hunt for unexploited profits is the main driver of the market process. Market exchange means competition in the classical sense of a rivalrous struggle. Sport is probably the best metaphor to explain the degree to which competition in this sense differs from the model of perfect competition in neoclassical economics. Perfect competition is literally a zero-sum game. The most efficient allocation of given resources in a competitive market leads to a state in which the scope for profits is reduced to zero. This is a world that no entrepreneur wishes to enter. In Kirzner's world of rivalrous competition affairs run very differently. His market is like the play ground for an unending sports contest. The players in this contest have a drive to beat their opponent and they do not labour for nothing. He or she who crosses the finish line first gets a prize, in terms of social esteem (the admiration of others) and generally in terms of money. Certainly, this is not a zero-sum game.[2]

To understand this aspect of Kirzner's market process we need to combine the elements of alertness and discovery. According to Kirzner, every market agent is alert to profit, but when he finds it, it will come as a total surprise to him. Running through his work is the notion that the entrepreneurial process is governed by uncertainty in the Knightean sense or 'ignorance', as he prefers to call it (Kirzner 1992, 23–26; Kirzner 1997a, 70–72). He stressed that there are always unexploited profit opportunities to be found in the market, but no one knows what they are. Everyone is utterly ignorant of their existence. We cannot even estimate the chance of finding one in terms of a probability distribution.[3] In Kirzner's world, profit is a discovery in the true sense of that word. 'It may have been right under your nose, but you didn't see it', as Kirzner often formulated the sense of genuine ignorance. Consequently, the market process does have something of a gathering of individuals all blindfolded looking for success. 'Without knowing what to look for, without deploying any deliberate search technique, the entrepreneur is at all times scanning the horizon, as it where, ready to make discoveries' (Kirzner 1997a, 72).[4]

This may sound like a highly constrained and artificial conception of entrepreneurship. In a sense it is, because in the Austrian tradition Kirzner approached the study of entrepreneurship as a mental experiment (Kirzner 1999, 10–12). This means that he treated entrepreneurship in first instance as a pure analytical concept, an imaginary construction as Mises (or Hayek) would call it. In practice this means stripping the notion of entrepreneurship to its bare essence. For Kirzner (1999, 11), this is 'to recognize the *arbitrage* element in *all* entrepreneurial activity' which he summarized in the conception of alert entrepreneurship. In his opinion, other qualities like boldness, imagination and leadership involve complications to be added in a later stage of theoretical development and do not necessarily 'bite' the notion of the alert entrepreneur as essentially an arbitrage trader (ibid.).

Kirzner readily admitted that the strategy to marry alert entrepreneurship as a pure concept with the strict notion of Knightean uncertainty involved a risk. This risk is that entrepreneurship cannot be seen as a force systematically nudging markets towards equilibrium, because the success of the entrepreneur constitutes a case of sheer luck. After all: Why waste time hunting for profit, when the rate of success cannot even be estimated? At this point it is fruitful to reinvoke the sports metaphor. For Kirzner successful entrepreneurship is not a case of sheer luck, because some entrepreneurs are more alert than others (Kirzner 1979, 179–180).[5] They are the ones that look harder for profits and try harder in being successful. Like on the race track, success involves a combination of effort (for instance, training to become to best) and natural ability (having the physique and mentality of a world class athlete). Concerning the degree of alertness, Kirzner always tended to downplay the first element, the ability to learn for and train entrepreneurship. He referred to alertness as a natural ability which rests on the attitude of receptiveness to available (but hitherto overlooked) opportunities (Kirzner 1973, 35 and 65). It is this attitude which urges human beings to actively look for profit opportunities and thereby increases the (non-quantifiable) chance that they will find it. Compare it to the drive of athletes to beat their opponent, even when there is no money price at stake. Only, in the world of Kirzner the most able athlete (in a physical and mental sense) is the one most likely to win the race, no matter the amount of training he has endured.[6]

However, the focus on alertness as a natural ability does not mean that 'learning' is ruled out as a coordinating device. In Kirzner's scheme, learning does not take place on an individual level, as we have just seen, but on the level of the market as a whole. This process can be explained as follows.

According to Kirzner, profit opportunities arise as a result of previous entrepreneurial error (Kirzner 1992, 21–23 and Kirzner 1997a, 71). It appears that alertness is not a universal recipe for success. Some entrepreneurs have been insufficiently alert, which resulted in choices that afterwards turn out to be errors. Errors of this kind cause malinvestment of capital goods, unsatisfied demand and thereby missed opportunities for profit. Luckily, if other entrepreneurs are alert enough, they will perceive such opportunities and employ actions to seize them. This is the essence of Kirzner's claim that in competitive markets entrepreneurial errors tend to become corrected, driving supply and demand in the direction of improved coordination. In brief, it is alertness which assures that the market as a whole 'learns' from entrepreneurial mistakes and displays a continuous tendency towards equilibrium.

The reader may object that learning is an individual activity which has no meaning in the context of a collective body like a market. I shall explain this facet of Kirzner's coordinative process in terms of Hayek's knowledge problem: How to coordinate dispersed and partly tacit knowledge in a decentralized market system? (Van Zijp 1992, 66). Kirzner answered this question by focusing on the discovery of previously unknown knowledge by alert entrepreneurs. The fact that an alert entrepreneur raises a profit from discovering a hitherto unknown profit opportunity starts a process which Hayek (1945) described with the famous metaphor of the price mechanism as a telecommunications system. It spreads the news that a realignment of productive resources in the direction chosen by this successful entrepreneur is, in economic terms, a superior choice. The entrepreneurial process so set into motion is a process tending toward better mutual awareness among market participants, because it reveals information which no one was aware of its having been lacking. In other words, the market 'learns' from the correction of past mistakes as it moves toward equilibrium.[7]

An example may help to understand what Kirzner is driving at. Kirzner (1999) discussed the invention of the automobile as an example of an entrepreneurial discovery which unmasked the errors of investing in the horse-drawn carriage industry. He presented this industry as being in grave disequilibrium before the automobile actually appeared, although to the superficial observer at the time the industry seemed normally prosperous and secure. The point is that with hindsight we know that the technology was available to replace the expensive and time consuming horse-drawn transportation by lower cost and rapid motorized transportation. In other words, there was a profit opportunity, but before alert entrepreneurs like Henri Ford appeared on the scene no one seized it. As a result, investments were being made in the wrong type of industry, while consumers were wasting their money on a too expensive form of transportation. 'Production was, in this sense being conducted inefficiently; capital and labour were being misallocated – invested and specialized in direction and skills that were (in the light of the true conditions which hindsight reveals to have existed) utterly mistaken' (Kirzner 1999, 14). It goes without saying that this is a qualification of a market in serious conditions of disequilibrium.[8]

The successful introduction of the automobile with a combustion engine constituted the big bang which changed all this. Kirzner stressed that this innovation disrupted the plans of many investors and workers in the industries it displaced. But in doing so, it constituted not an act of destruction, as Schumpeter would call it, but a development which revealed the wastefulness and the misallocated character of the investor and labour decisions that mistakenly committed resources to the horse-drawn carriage industry (ibid., 15).

> The essential entrepreneurial contribution of the automobile pioneers was unmistakably to make clear what that disequilibrium situation really was. Those entrepreneurs alertly saw better ways of using resources; their putting into effect the productive possibilities they saw was coordinative in the sense that it brought the pattern of resource allocation into a higher degree of coordination both with the true pattern of technological possibilities and the pattern of consumer preferences, than had the leaders of the horse-drawn carriage industry.

In other words, the discovery of new information and knowledge is a key facet of the mechanism which explains why alert entrepreneurship incessantly pushes the economy towards equilibrium.

THE STRUGGLE BETWEEN EQUILIBRIUM AND DISEQUILIBRIUM

The focus of Kirzner on the market process as a tendency towards equilibrium has its strongest opponent in the person of Ludwig Lachmann (Vaughn 1992). Like Kirzner, Lachmann focused on the indeterminateness of human action, but unlike the latter he extended this lesson to the market process as a whole. As a result, he believed that even a competitive market would not systematically move in the direction of improved coordination, one of Kirzner's main conclusions. The outcome of his thinking is a view on the nature of economic processes which some have described as 'nihilistic' (for example O'Driscoll 1977b, Littlechild 1979 and Kirzner 1994b), but which nowadays seems to attract a growing number of Austrians (High 1990 and O'Driscoll and Rizzo 1996). This view is that the market moves as a 'continuous process without beginning or end, propelled by the interaction between the forces of equilibrium and the forces of change' (Lachmann 1976a, 61). The present section intends to investigate the nature and consequences of the delicate balance between equilibrium and disequilibrium in Lachmann's view of the market process.

In a sense the German economist Ludwig Lachmann was predisposed to become the leading Austrian proponent of a radical disequilibrium approach. In the 1930s he studied at LSE under the guidance of Hayek, which resulted in a number of papers on typical Austrian subjects like the role of capital in the business cycle. For example, he tried to make Hayek's business cycle theory more dynamic by combining it with Schumpeter's analysis of technological change (Lachmann 1940). This line of research brought him to reflect on the importance of expectations formation as a source of cyclical fluctuations (Lachmann 1943). He argued that the Austrian conclusions in business cycle theory crucially depend on the assumption that investment demand is elastic with regard to interest rate expectations. This caused a problem, since his analysis concluded that investment demand is fairly inelastic with regard to interest rate expectations. According to Lachmann, the root of the problem lay with the fact that the Wicksellian framework, which the Austrians used as a starting point, links investment demand to the natural rate of interest. However, since this rate is unobservable, agents are assumed to use the market rate of interest as a proxy (see Chapter 12). Hayek (1931a) had argued that a change in this rate fools agents in making the wrong type of investment decisions when the natural rate does not change accordingly, in other words when monetary equilibrium does not prevail. This incongruity marks the onset of a new round of business cycle fluctuations.

Hayek never asked why rational economic actors would continue to use a compass that has proven unreliable. But Lachmann argued that agents would learn not to trust each change in the market rate of interest. In other words, they would become reluctant to revise their expectations about the natural rate on the basis of the market rate only. As a result, investment demand will not respond to short-term fluctuations in the market rate of interest. This finding demolished a crucial building block in Hayek's explanation of the business cycle. According to Lachmann, to salvage it, the Austrians needed to explain why elastic expectations would prevail.

This line of inquiry brought Lachmann to take up the question how (price) expectations are formed (Lachmann 1945). He argued that agents form expectations on the basis of past price experiences. That is, they learn inductively. This causes a degree of slack in the speed of adjustment of expectations, as recent experiences will only partly adjust current expectations. In this manner, Lachmann rejected Lange's mathematical interpretation of the elasticity of expectations. This elasticity suggests that each and every price change leads to a proportional change in price expectations, given a certain degree of elasticity. But Lachmann's inductive theory of expectations formation suggests otherwise. He argued that expectations do not mechanistically follow price changes. In his view, agents do not form what may be called point-expectations about a price, but they formulate a range in which they expect the future price to fall. If it falls outside this range, expectations are disappointed and agents may then react by adjusting the range.

Van Zijp (1995, 421) argues that this inductive theory means that Lachmann could not logically conclude that the economy would tend towards a situation of coordination. In his theoretical framework, the existence of this tendency can only be established on empirical grounds. This may explain the admiration of Lachmann (1947) for the sequence analysis of the Swedish school. Lachmann (1977, 143) praised this method, developed by Lundberg (1937) and Lindahl (1939), as one of the first attempts in economics to develop a dynamic theory of economic change with a central role for expectations and the process of plan coordination (see Chapter 12). Key to this method is the investigation of a sequence of discoordination situations in terms of people's decision situations. For Lachmann (1947, 118), this was also an empirical question, as it enables us to 'follow up, sector by sector, the chain of changes set in motion by the impact of the original change'. It is evident that sequences of this kind need not lead to a situation of coordination. It is here, in other words, that we find the root of Lachmann's contention that the market process cannot be seen as always tending towards equilibrium.[9]

This conclusion stresses that from the start of his career Lachmann isolated expectations and thereby the role of time as a crucial factor in the economic process. I argue that this focus marks a crucial distinction between him and Kirzner who, as we have seen, downplayed the role of expectations as an aspect of entrepreneurship. Lachmann's focus on the importance of expectations was in subsequent years sharpened by his two main fields of interest, capital theory and subjectivism. I shall briefly sketch the implications of his view of economics as the study of processes in real (as opposed to logical) time along these two lines.

In true Austrian spirit Lachmann treated capital as a heterogeneous stock of capital goods (Lachmann 1956). He was fascinated by the fact that the stock of capital goods is continuously being reshuffled and reused. Entrepreneurs make production plans, but these plans are often impossible to complete because of mistaken expectations about the plans of others. This line of thinking pointed to an aspect that Lachmann stressed again and again: In the market economy people have widely differing expectations and it is not very likely that the market process will bring these expectations into closer alignment.[10] On the contrary, Lachmann (1976a, 59) pointed in this regard to the difference between knowledge and expectations. The assumed equilibrium tendency of Kirzner and others rests on the assumption that competitive pressures help to coordinate existing knowledge scattered over many parts of the economic system and to disseminate the market knowledge thus gained. Lachmann asked if the market can play the same role in closing the gap between diverging expectations. According to him, this is by no means obvious. The success of bits of knowledge can be judged in terms of the profits attributed to them. But by definition expectations concern future events the relevance of which cannot be judged in terms of an ex post criterion like profitability. As Lachmann argued, how successful an expectation is we can only know when it is too late for others to embrace it. It is therefore very unlikely that the market process can bring about (or even promote) the coordination of people's plans and expectations.

Lachmann's opinion in this regard was heavily influenced by the subjectivism of G.L.S. Shackle. According to Lachmann, Shackle was the man who put the importance of expectations on the agenda of economic research. Of course, Keynes had incorporated expectations in his GT, but he had done so in what Lachmann (1977, 142) called a 'haphazard fashion.' In particular, he failed to grasp the nature of the problem posed by the existence of inconsistent expectations. Hayek dealt with expectations in 1933 in his Copenhagen lecture (Hayek 1939) and his 1937 article 'Economics and Knowledge', but like Keynes he presented an one-sided analysis. He treated expectations as being of analytical interest only to the extent to which they converge, but he ignored the causes and consequences of their divergence (Lachmann 1976a, 58).

For the Austrians, the importance of Shackle's work was that he extended the scope of subjectivism from tastes to expectations. By doing so, he supported Lachmann's belief about the divergent nature of people's expectations. According to Lachmann, it is simply unimaginable that individuals will agree on the meaning of future events. Such interpretations are shaped by subjective experiences, beliefs and feelings which are unlikely to match for any group of people. As Lachmann (1976a, 59) worded it, '[d]ivergent expectations are nothing but the individual images, rather blurred, in which new knowledge is reflected, before its actual arrival in a thousand different mirrors of various shapes'. It is here that we find the root of Shackle's famous metaphor, the kaleidic society, which Lachmann wished to apply to the domain of Austrian economics.

There is some need to review Shackle's interpretation of economic reality, an approach that Lachmann (1976a) described as a form of 'extended subjectivism'. According to Lachmann, Mises (1949) had firmly rooted the subjectivist approach of Austrian economics in his theory of human action. But the great omission in his work was the role of expectations. 'Mises hardly ever mentions expectations, though entrepreneurs and speculators often enough turn up in his pages' (Lachmann 1976a, 58). Lachmann felt that Shackle's work could be used to remedy this lacuna.

However, in the Austrian literature the result of this 'fusion' is often misunderstood. O'Driscoll and Rizzo (1996) have interpreted 'extended subjectivism' as meaning a different kind of subjectivism. They have defined a distinction between what they call 'static' and 'dynamic' subjectivism. According to the first form, the mind must be seen as a passive filter through which the data of the decision making process are perceived. This results in an explanation of this process which is perfectly determinate. The consumer theory of the older Austrians (Menger, Wieser) is said to constitute an example of this type of subjectivism. In contrast, the dynamic form views the mind as an 'active, creative entity' in which decision making bears no determinate relationship to what went before (O'Driscoll and Rizzo 1996, 22).

In my opinion, this distinction between two types of subjectivism suggests a schism in the Austrian school that in reality does not exist. The obvious attraction of labels like static and dynamic is that you can attach names to them. This is exactly what has occurred. Mises was the first to be labeled a static subjectivist of the old kind (O'Driscoll and Rizzo 1996, 23). Others have followed suit. Van Zijp interprets Mises's subjectivism as a deterministic variant which leaves no scope for the vagaries of the mind, and even places Hayek (partly) in the same camp (van Zijp 1992, 40 and 69). According to van Zijp, the Austrian revival of the 1970s must be seen as a revival of dynamic subjectivism, aimed at making plausible why a tendency towards coordination exists (ibid., 102). But this was exactly the view which the arch subjectivist Ludwig Lachmann tried to fight. I conclude that the distinction between static and dynamic subjectivism is misleading and hinders us to grasp the true meaning of the latter's 'extended subjectivism'.

The root of the problem is that static subjectivism is defined in terms of a given means-ends framework. In other words, it is the working field of the

Robbinsian maximizer who has no choice but to adopt the option which maximizes his objectives, given his resource constraints. This what Latsis (1976, 16) called single exit decision making situations. In contrast, with dynamic subjectivism the assumption of given means and ends is dropped, which opens up the decision making process for so-called multiple exit situations that are not deterministic.

If we adopt this distinction, we have no choice but to conclude that either all or none of the Austrians are static subjectivists. Did Mises confine his analysis to the examination of single exit situation, as exemplified by the Robbinsian maximer? I would say that his concept of human action is the exact opposite of this figure. Kirzner (1973, 33) described Mises's approach as follows:

> The decision, in the framework of the human action approach, is not arrived at merely by mechanical computation of the solution to the maximization problem implicit in the configuration of the given means and ends. It reflects not merely the manipulation of given means to correspond faithfully with the hierarchy of given ends, but also *the very perception of the ends-means framework* within which allocation and economizing are to take place . . . Mises's *homo agens* is endowed not only with the propensity to pursue goals efficiently, once ends and means are clearly identified, but also with the drive and alertness needed to identify which ends to strive for and which means are available.

On the other hand, Lachmann repeatedly stressed the need to adopt a notion of individual equilibrium, which strongly suggests a static subjectivist view on the nature of economic decision making. With regard to the individual in household and business, he argued that 'there is no doubt that here equilibrium has a clear meaning and real significance. Men really aim at bringing their various actions into consistency. Here a tendency towards equilibrium is not only a necessary concept of praxeology, but also a fact of experience' (Lachmann 1977, 189). Elsewhere he said that equilibrium in this sense was simply tantamount to 'rational action', a notion he considered so important that it is to be retained 'at all costs' (Lachmann 1976b, 131).[11]

This comparison illustrates that with some effort we may argue that Mises is a dynamic subjectivist and Lachmann a static subjectivist, showing that the distinction between these labels is meaningless. Mises and Lachmann are both subjectivists who adopt the theory of human action as the starting point of the Austrian theory of decision making. Lachmann surpassed Mises by arguing that the subjectivist interpretation of expectations may have implications for the nature of the market process. He was thereby stepping from the level of individual decision making, firmly rooted in praxeology, to the level social interaction and group behaviour. It was at this point that the neoclassical treatment of rational action went astray, because it fell victim to what Lachmann (1977, 189) called the 'vice of formalism'. This implied that various phenomena which have no substance in common are pressed into the same conceptual form and then treated as identical. 'Because equilibrating forces operate successfully in the individual sphere of action, we must take it for granted, so the formalists tell us, that they will also do so outside it. From Walras to Samuelson we find the same manner of reasoning, the same arbitrary assumptions, the same unwarranted assumptions' (ibid.). The main omission here is that the neoclassicals assume that the process of coordinating different individual plans is solved automatically by the invisible hand, an auctioneer or another *deus ex machina*.

For Lachmann, it is at this stage that Austrian economics raises crucial questions. As Hayek (1937) argued, people do not have the same knowledge and hence do not share the same expectations of future developments. Consequently, some plans are bound to be disappointed when the market process unfolds, leading to plan revision and a next round of trading and producing. Lachmann (1977, 190) isolated two elements of this coordination failure that he saw as the core of the market process; unexpected change in exogenous variables and the inconsistency of human plans. The former element is related to the fundamental uncertainty of economic processes. In real life people are bound to be surprised by developments, which are impossible to predict in detail. This means that the market process is constantly disrupted by exogenous forces, causing agents to reformulate their plans. But, secondly, Lachmann considered the endogenous forces of change an even more potent source of market disruption. The fact that expectations are people's subjective images of future events implies that they are not very likely to agree on the same plan concerning future action. In addition, people respond to the assumed changes in each other's expected behaviour.[12] According to Lachmann, this flexibility of expectations formation, constitutes an important reason why the incompatibility of plans is such a powerful disequilibrating tendency of the market process (Lachmann 1976a, 60 and Lachmann 1977, 190).

This conclusion must be seen in its proper context. Lachmann supported the notion that the market process harbours important equilibrating tendencies of the kind explained by Kirzner's theory of entrepreneurship. However, he stressed the volatility of expectations as part of an 'extended subjectivism' to underline that in real life the market process is a mix of equilibrating and disequilibrating forces. In his opinion, neither the occurrence of unexpected change, nor the incompatibility of individual plans can be seen as a sufficient condition for a disequilibrating tendency of the market process. Lachmann (1977, 190) argued that without the first, that is in a stationary world, it is likely that plans gradually become consistent as agents come to learn more and more about their environment including one another's plans. On the other hand, without the inconsistency of plans prompted by divergent expectations, it is at least possible that all individuals would respond to exogenous change in such a way that general equilibrium in the sense of full plan coordination can really be established. In other words, in addition to entrepreneurship, Lachmann presented learning as a strong force behind the equilibrium tendency of the market.

However, in the end he did not consider it very likely that the market would actually move towards equilibrium when individuals have to deal with both unforeseen changes in the data and the incompatibility of plans (Lachmann 1976a and Lachmann 1977). The reason for his conviction in this regard concerned the speed of the equilibrium enhancing adjustments. It is easy to see that when disequilibrium swiftly calls forth equilibrating forces of the kind here described, the chance is considerable that equilibrium is actually reached or at least closely approached before the next unexpected change occurs. But Lachmann did not believe that equilibrium would overtake disequilibrium so easily. For him, the main stumbling block would be the assumed quick spreading of coordination enhancing information throughout the market. He doubted whether this can be at all regarded as a rapid process. The problem is that not all participants have the same ability to asses the informative significance of the events they observe. Further, there is an information distraction problem. Nobody can be certain whether an event he has observed constitutes a structural change or a random fluctuation. One has to wait for confirmation and this takes time. Moreover, in a changing world information which is relevant today may have become obsolete tomorrow. Accordingly, Lachmann (1977, 192) concluded that the information diffusion process is bound to be a rather slow process, which is hampered by the divergence of expectations and overtaken by unexpected events. Therefore, the end result of his deliberations is the image of the market as a 'continuous process without beginning or end, propelled by the interaction between the forces of equilibrium and the forces of change' (Lachmann 1976a, 61, see also Lachmann 1986, 35).

DISEQUILIBRIUM THEORY AND THE FUTURE OF AUSTRIAN ECONOMICS

The strife between Kirzner and Lachmann has left the Austrian school in disarray (Vaughn 1994). Some proclaim victory for Lachmann and other proponents of a radical disequilibrium approach (Rizzo 1996). Others still consider Lachmann a side figure and feel that Austrian economics is firmly grounded on Kirznerian principles (Baird 1987 and Garrison 1995). Who is right in this issue and what is the best way forward for Austrian economics?

The answer to that question requires us to consider that there are at least three different strands in Austrian economics trying to cope with the challenge of disequilibrating forces. Kirzner heads the first development which aims to defend and deepen the analysis of the market process in terms of Kirzner's theory of entrepreneurship. Secondly, there is a group of Austrians trying to find a midway position by adjusting the concept of equilibrium in order to account for the presence of disequilibrating forces. O'Driscoll and Rizzo (1996) are the prime exponents of this approach. The third group believes that the Austrians need to follow Lachmann's radical subjectivism to its logical conclusion. In their opinion, this means that Austrian economics must reject any kind of equilibrium metaphor and related mechanistic concepts. For them, the proper way forward is what they call 'order analysis', an institutional approach to economic questions based on the insight that there is a close link between history and economic theory (Boettke, Horwitz and Prychitko 1994).

The Market Process as an Equilibrating Tendency

The suggested relationship between history and economics is exactly the reason why many Austrians have condemned Lachmann's work as nihilistic. In the view of Rothbard (1985, 284) the Lachmannian economist becomes 'a mere institutionalist and historian, recording the past choices and trends'. He argued that this historicist approach would imply 'the scrapping of economic theory all together' and that Mises would have called such a doctrine 'anti-economics'.

Kirzner (1994b) formulated his concerns in similar words. The ferocity with which such condemnations are made is explained by the fact that Rothbard and Kirzner perceive radical subjectivism as an attack on the very foundation of Austrian economics. In their opinion this school emerged as a scientific discipline in the late 19th century in the famous *Methodenstreit* between Carl Menger and the German historical school of Gustav Schmoller. The historical school rejected the validity of universal laws and thereby the scope of theory as a tool to logically connect lawlike statements with basic premises. Menger and the Austrians defended the cause of theoretical research, which in their case was aimed at understanding the powerful and systematic character of market forces. For Kirzner (1992, 20), 'the victory of the theoretical approach over the historicist approach was a victory for the recognition of the coordinative properties of the market'. According to him, the 'bizarre irony' of the radical subjectivist approach is that its acceptance among Austrians would completely undo this revolution after more than a century (Kirzner 1994b, 40).

The ongoing discussion about the impact of disequilibrium forces has forced Kirzner to clarify his position on the assumed dominance of equilibrating tendencies in the market process. Firstly, he reconsidered his interpretation of Schumpeter's entrepreneur, which in 1973 he had portrayed as essentially disruptive. In Kirzner (1999) he still believed that Schumpeter's and his own view of entrepreneurship were partly contrasting, but he now also stressed that they should be seen as pointing to different aspects of the market process. In that sense they are complementary rather than conflicting views. For example, by varying the level of abstraction, one can include the typical features of Schumpeter's entrepreneurship like boldness and leadership in Kirzner's theory of entrepreneurship, which starts by assuming as an ideal concept that the entrepreneur is an arbitrage trader driven by alertness. According to Kirzner, in this more extended and realistic image, Schumpeter's entrepreneur can be seen as part of the sequence of affairs moving the economy closer to market equilibrium rather than removing it further from this state. In other words, Kirzner effectively warded off the threat of Schumpeter's disequilibrating entrepreneur by pulling him into his camp and presenting him as a special case of his more general theory of entrepreneurship.[13]

Secondly, Kirzner was forced to counter the criticism that his theory of alert entrepreneurship neglected those aspects of the market process related to the role of time, such as learning and uncertainty.[14] He responded by explaining, firstly, that entrepreneurial discovery of profit opportunities is closely related to the presence of genuine uncertainty and, secondly, that profit opportunities arise as a result of previous errors because they enforce a misallocation of resources. Kirzner (1997, 81) even conceded that error making may be a self-enforcing process. New entrepreneurs entering a market may in fact be more mistaken than their predecessors, so that 'instead of correcting the earlier misallocation of resources, the entering entrepreneurs may be making matters even worse. And such errors may generate still more errors' (Kirzner 1997, 81).

Therefore, Kirzner acknowledged the influence of Lachmannian disequilibrating forces as part of the market process. In his words, '[i]t is easy to imagine circumstances where the power of the coordinative market process is completely swamped by the volatility of change and by the high incidence of entrepreneurial error' (Kirzner 1992, 35). But he never conceded that such processes would block the trend towards market equilibrium as a dominant tendency. As a general rule, the market 'obviously works' (ibid.). Why this stubbornness? The most obvious reason is the fear for the nihilism associated with Lachmann's radical subjectivism and the fact that it seems to conflict with the opposition of the Austrians against historicism as a scientific doctrine in the *Methodenstreit*. This inheritance may certainly have played a role. Rothbard (1985, 284) even suggested that Kirzner originally developed his theory of entrepreneurial alertness in reaction to Lachmann's introduction of radical subjectivism into the Austrian arena.

But there also are two substantial arguments that warrant consideration. Firstly, time and again Kirzner stressed that while errors occur and must be seen as part and parcel of the market process, there is no tendency for entrepreneurial errors to be made (Kirzner 1997a, 82). According to Kirzner, it defies logic that the market process should display a tendency in the direction of diminishing rather than increasing mutual awareness among its participants. Garrison (1995, 76) stresses that this is a fundamental point of logic for Austrian economics. Without this notion of market equilibration there is no notion of order to underpin the Austrian analysis of market processes in terms of Mises's praxeology, which in Mises's eyes is a purely deductive science.

This focus on the logic of choice and its consequences for the dynamic of the market process cannot conceal the fact that a second, empirical argument plays a role. This argument is that Kirzner and many other Austrians believe that under a system of free competition actual markets will always tend towards equilibrium. According to Kirzner (1992, 35), '[t]hat the market works is perhaps the most significant lesson of modern history.' There is a large measure of belief involved in this conclusion, as this branch of Austrian economics eschews empirical and historical research. Thus Kirzner defended the superiority of the free market order as a matter of 'casual' and 'historical experience' (ibid., 36, 43 and 51).

In my opinion, the question arises whether, in modern economics, this tactic is convincing enough, even for the present day adherents to the Austrian school. There is some merit in presenting the focus on market equilibration as an analytical assumption, needed to support the Austrian analysis of the market process. But in practical terms, what are the scientific pay-offs of this approach? Like many Austrians, Kirzner had no penchant for applied research. At best he discussed the applied results of his theory of entrepreneurship in terms of 'new perspectives' on subjects like the economics of advertising and the economics of anti-trust (Kirzner 1997b, 54–75). The point is that there is nothing new in these perspectives. Kirzner has discussed the practical relevance of his work in terms of these same subjects for the past thirty years.

The market process approach in Austrian economics needs to break new ground. I argue that they will only succeed in doing so, if the Austrians manage to cast off the shadow of a methodological debate that took place almost 120 years ago. They need to recognize that Kirzner's alert entrepreneur and his vision of the market process as an equilibrating tendency are ideal concepts. In order to increase the policy relevance of such Austrian tools, the level of abstraction needs to be reduced by filling in some of the blanks and testing the relevance of assumptions like market equilibration. This need not boil down to doing hard core econometric research. Why not systematically investigate the role of entrepreneurship in actual markets? This may shed light on the motives for entrepreneurship and whether they can be seen as alertness. Also it may generate knowledge of the institutions supporting the operation of market processes, like the methods of trading in different countries and at different times. I claim that a research strategy along these lines will prove more viable for Austrian economics than a continuation of the doctrinal warfare about the question whether markets are equilibrating or not.

The Fusion of Disequilibrium and Equilibrium Theory

A second strand in modern Austrian economics aims to counter the disequilibrium critique on the market process approach by a refinement of its core analytical concept, the notion of equilibrium (seen in dynamic terms as a process). This attempt was made in what some consider as a pathbreaking contribution to the Austrian tradition, namely *The Economics of Time and Ignorance* by O'Driscoll and Rizzo (first published in 1985). The key to this book is the desire to give real time (as opposed to logical time) a central role in economic analysis, which results in the aforementioned distinction between static subjectivism and dynamic subjectivism. The preferred approach is of course the dynamic variant, which runs parallel to the radical subjectivism of Lachmann. However, without saying so, O'Driscoll and Rizzo believe that they can salvage the market process approach from the nihilistic consequences of the latter's approach (Baird 1987, 201). Following Hayek, they aim to marry time and equilibrium, because they believe that 'some concept of equilibrium is an indispensable ingredient in all economic explanations.' (O'Driscoll and Rizzo 1996, 85, see also 71 and 118).

In order to achieve this goal O'Driscoll and Rizzo introduce the concept of pattern coordination as a substitute for equilibrium. Pattern coordination refers to the typical aspects of economic processes taking place in real time. The idea of this concept is that actions can be coordinated with respect to such typical aspects, because they are not affected by the mere passage of time (ibid., 76ff). In contrast, unique features concern the time-dependent features in the flow of events. It is here that events are the products of endogenous change and genuine uncertainty. By definition, such events are impossible to predict, which means that they are outside the reach of the coordinative forces of the market process. But the typical features are not.

The concept of pattern coordination thus retains the benefits of the traditional neoclassical notion of equilibrium by showing that there exist relatively stable types of patterns, which are, in the short run, only affected by exogenous shocks to the system (ibid., 87). In other words, something more than the mere passage of time is needed to induce pattern reorganization, which keeps the threat of Lachmann's nihilism at bay. However, at the same time the unique aspects of events are time-dependent and hence change from within the system. This factor allowed O'Driscoll and Rizzo to account for the endogenous market process, without losing sight of the forces that provide the market process with a sense of stability.

Whatever one may find of this new equilibrium concept, it is refreshing to observe that O'Driscoll and Rizzo devoted more than half of their book to what they called 'applications'. This term is a bit confusing, because the majority of the applications concern the explication of the market process approach in specific theoretical fields, like capital theory and monetary theory. Nonetheless, the analysis of several applied policy problems like anti-trust, pollution regulation, rent control and the deregulation of the airline and telecommunications industries is thoroughly Austrian in character and illuminates one major point: None of the cases discussed crucially depend on pattern coordination as a novel equilibrium concept. The distinction between unique and typical features of events in the flow of time is nowhere decisive for the policies advocated by O'Driscoll and Rizzo. What they see as endogenous market change generally refers to the feedback mechanisms between market participants and policy makers that also stand central in public choice theory.[15] Another main theme is the familiar critique of Hayek and Mises in the socialist calculation debate, namely the informational and calculational dilemma's that limit the scope of successful policy interventions in fields like anti-trust policy. No Austrian would dispute the relevance of this approach. Baird (1987, 204) adds that many of their points have long been recognized even in neoclassical analysis. In sum, the economics of time and ignorance is not the watershed that its authors claim it to be.

In light of this conclusion, one may ask what pattern coordination as a new equilibrium concept adds to our understanding of the market process. Nothing in my opinion. The notion of pattern coordination heavily leans on Hayek's idea of 'pattern explanation' (Hayek 1967a). As an aside, O'Driscoll and Rizzo (1996, 27) remark that pattern explanation is consistent with dynamic subjectivism, but when they introduce pattern coordination they do not refer to Hayek. To the contrary, Hayek's focus on plan coordination is used as an example of 'exact coordination' which they see as a form of static equilibrium and thereby the opposite of a dynamic equilibrium concept like pattern coordination (ibid., 80-82).

The main point is: does pattern coordination really embody a marriage of equilibrium and real time? I argue that the definition of coordination in terms of the typical aspects of events in the flow of time implies that it fails to do so. Consider how typicality is defined. It refers to those aspects that are repeatable in the sense that they are not affected by the mere passage of time (ibid., 76). A pattern of this kind may be the result of stable physical laws or the stabilizing effects of rules of thumb. Whatever the source, the fact is that where coordination of activities is achieved the time factor is ruled out. One might say that it is nothing but the exact coordination of Hayek's (static) equilibrium. Uncertainty and real time only enter the picture in the conditional statement that a pattern equilibrium prevails if plans are coordinated with respect with their typical features, *even if their unique aspects fail to mesh* (ibid., 85). In this construction endogenous change becomes a fringe event. It is the sort of statistical noise neoclassical economists generally assume away in order to focus on the state of exact coordination.

Of course, ignoring the role of time is the last thing O'Driscoll and Rizzo want to achieve. But if they want to marry equilibrium and time, they need to give endogenous change a more prominent role in their theoretical corpus. For example, this can be achieved by explaining the causal connection between unique and typical features. After all, viewed at a specific point of time each event is unique. One may speak of typical features when a sequence of such unique events in the flow of time seems to embody certain shared elements. In other words, with regard to change as a process in time, there exists a relationship between typicality and uniqueness.

This connection has proven the Achilles heel of pattern coordination as an equilibrium concept. Kirzner (1994b) accused O'Driscoll and Rizzo of inconsistency on exactly this point. His complaint was that O'Driscoll and Rizzo treat what they call 'creative entrepreneurship' as a force which on net balance strives to make the coordination of plans possible (O'Driscoll and Rizzo 1996, 79–80). That is, the typicality of the market process as an equilibrating tendency arises as a result of entrepreneurship guided by the lure of profit. However, at the same time they acknowledge that entrepreneurial activity creates 'some uncertainty of its own'. Now, if that is true, Kirzner asked, then it remains a mystery why any aspect of reality can be relied upon to be other than 'unique'.

O'Driscoll and Rizzo did provide a clue to the solution of this mystery but they failed to state it clear enough. This opened a 'window of opportunity' for Kirzner to discredit them as nihilists. The latter prefers to defend the Austrian market process approach as the 'middle ground' between the two polar views of, on the one hand, neoclassical static equilibrium theory which assumes rapid equilibrating market forces and, on the other hand, the kaleidic world of Lachmann and Shackle which displays such volatility as to push any equilibrating tendencies beyond the bounds of possibility (for example Kirzner 1992, 6–8). Kirzner (1994b) accused O'Driscoll and Rizzo of seeing this middle ground as a 'razor's edge'. They criticized the neoclassical approach for its neglect of the distinction between uniqueness and typicality, in order to 'rush headlong into the abyss represented by the opposite polar view' (ibid., 39).

O'Driscoll and Rizzo could have countered this attack if they had presented their research program in a different and more consistent manner. The clue to the connection between typical and unique features of events in time lies in their claim that the difference between these aspects of reality is one of degree. They argued that what makes typical features a stable pattern in time is that they change so gradually relative to the changes in the unique elements (O'Driscoll and Rizzo 1996, 79). The practical consequence of this dependence is that stable patterns carry within them the seeds of change. It is the accumulation of knowledge gained from the observation of unique aspects of reality which will eventually upset the stable patterns that form the basis of pattern coordination. O'Driscoll and Rizzo, therefore, too hastily concluded that typical features are not affected by the 'mere passage of time' (ibid., 76). They should have stated that stability arises because typical features are relatively unaffected by the passage of time.

In my opinion this nuance is relevant because it can be used to show where the Austrian middle ground lies. I agree with Kirzner that the analytical framework of O'Driscoll and Rizzo does not allow us to draw the logical conclusion that the entrepreneurial market process is equilibrating or disequilibrating. The broadness of the Austrian middle ground depends on the speed of, on the one hand, the coordinative process driven by entrepreneurship and, on the other hand, the disruption caused by endogenous entrepreneurial uncertainty. The balance of these forces is an empirical issue, which can be tested by measuring the span of time during which a specific market process develops itself within a relative stable framework.

O'Driscoll and Rizzo could have addressed this question as an application of their framework. But their Austrian methodological principles dictated an approach which does not follow this route. I consider this is a missed opportunity. In itself the concept of pattern coordination does not lead to novel insights into the market process. The discussions following the publication of *The Economics of Time and Ignorance* demonstrated that it may even have been counterproductive in this regard. But stated as an empirical proposition, pattern coordination and its underlying distinction between typical and unique features of processes in time, could have fostered an attitude among Austrian economists to investigate what the fusion between disequilibrium and equilibrium amounts to in actual markets. In my opinion, this would have been a shift in the right direction.

Evolution as a Non-Equilibrium Alternative

It is now time to see how Lachmann proposed to study the interaction between equilibrating and disequilibrating forces. His solution lay in developing a much richer understanding of markets than is customary in Austrian economics. He considered the notion of uniform market theory unhelpful, because 'different markets characterized by the encounter of different classes of agents with different interests and functions, will give rise to market processes of various kinds' (Lachmann 1986, 124). In other words, to disentangle the complex interaction between equilibrating and disequilibrating forces we need to decrease the level of abstraction to a level sufficiently low to permit us to designate price setters and their ranges of action in various markets.

Lachmann developed several ideal concepts to accomplish this task. He distinguished between different types of entrepreneurs like arbitrageurs, speculators and innovators. They are active in different kinds of markets like asset markets, production markets, fix-price or flex-price markets. Lachmann (1986) used the distinction between such ideal types to explain the different ability of markets to react to change. This approach is instructive, but leaves one main question unanswered: It says nothing about the problem of order in society (Vaughn 1992, 270). Is there reason to believe that a free market society inhabits a fundamental coherence and order? The ad hoc framework of Lachmann's ideal types does not provide the tools to address this question.

Inspired by Hayek and Lachmann, a growing stream in the Austrian literature is trying to fill this gap by using the concept of evolution as an alternative principle of organization (Birner and Van Zijp 1994). This approach suggests that there is a generalized perspective that brings into focus creativity and open-endedness in the evolution of non-equilibrium systems (Buchanan and Vanberg 1991). The *leitmotiv* of this perspective is that the future is not given, but is created in an unfolding evolutionary process. A characteristic feature of such systems is the presence of nonlinearities that can amplify small causes into large effects. Such processes exhibit a mixture of necessity and chance that produces a unique and irreversible 'historic' path along which the system evolves.

This brief characterization of evolutionary processes shows that it contains all the elements that should interest Austrian economists. It provides a fundamental critique of static equilibrium by describing the market as a process driven by unpredictable changes. That is why Boettke, Horwitz and Prychitko (1994) propose to abandon all mechanistic concepts like equilibrium and replace them by evolution as the key organizing principle. According to them, evolutionary theory demonstrates that unpredictable change and open-ended processes need not result in nihilistic consequences for economics as a science. There are systematic forces driving the process of evolution and these forces can be scrutinized in a systematic analysis of the market economy.

There are at least three questions about markets seen as evolutionary processes. First, there is the issue of the emergence of evolutionary processes as the unintended consequences of individual action. Small actions can have large effects and these effects need to be studied in a market context. Second, at the macroscopic level, the unintended outcome of individual actions is a stable order that most economists know through the metaphor of Adam Smith's invisible hand. But seen through the lens of evolutionary theory it is necessary to typify this order. Which factors further the emergence of a stable process at the macroscopic level? What threatens this sense of relative stability? Third, in evolutionary terms the market process traces an irreversible path through historical time. This historical record forms a knowledge base that can be used to study the drivers of the evolutionary process. It leads to theory being informed by history, while vice versa theory can be used to interpret history. According to Boettke, Horwitz and Prychitko (1994, 68), it is in this sense that the Austrian study of the market process can become an empirical theory.

The proponents of the evolutionary approach in Austrian economics realize the delicacy of this task. In Austrian circles the accusation of historicism is always just a small step away. But this threat can be countered by showing that evolutionary theory allows the Austrians to approach a key question of the market process approach from a different angle. This question is the issue of the coordinative properties of the market system. Since Menger, the Austrians know that institutions like money and property rights are coordination devices on a par with the price mechanism. However, in contrast to the latter, the relationship between plan coordination and the functioning of non-price institutions is hardly ever addressed in modern Austrian economics. Evolutionary theory provides a tool to fill this lacuna and thus opens new vistas for an alternative research strategy. This will be an Austrian paradigm without the concept of equilibrium.[16]

I shall discuss the contours of this research agenda in the next chapter. The reason for the separate treatment of the evolutionary agenda of Austrian economics is that evolution is not an exclusive Austrian concern. Other paradigms like institutional economics likewise develop their arguments in terms of evolutionary processes. The parallel between these developments is widely recognized among the members of the different paradigms. The next chapter investigates the common basis of these theories and studies their criticism of equilibrium economics.

NOTES

1. In this regard, Kirzner approvingly quotes Mises (1949, 253): 'In any real and living economy every actor is always an entrepreneur.'
2. Kirzner (1976, 124) literally refers to alertness as 'the incentive to try to get something for nothing'.
3. In that case entrepreneurship would be a process of search rather than a process of discovery. According to Kirzner (1997, 72) search involves the production of information one knew one had lacked. We may calculate the marginal benefits and marginal costs of this process in order to determine the equilibrium quantity of search. In that sense, it belongs to the closed framework of neoclassical decision making which Kirzner wishes to avoid. For him, the entrepreneurial process involves the discovery of a hitherto unknown profit opportunity. This involves a series of steps that cannot be rationalized in a frequency distribution, mapping profits and the quantity of search.
4. Drawn to its logical conclusion, this vision would lead to the conclusion that every profit is a pure windfall gain, accompanied by what Shackle (1972) called an 'absolute maximum potential surprise'. This is a position that Kirzner wished to avoid by introducing expectations as a kind of intuition. 'Now it *may*, of course, happen that while our market participant had no inkling that the price would rise, he nonetheless realized that it *might* rise. And his actions in buying may have reflected his judgment that the price would not fall. So his act of purchase *may* perhaps be seen as entrepreneurial in character, with any gain qualifying as entrepreneurial profit' (Kirzner 1979, 178, italics in original text). This is why Kirnzer often speaks about entrepreneurs 'seeing' or 'glimpsing' an opportunity for profit.
5. 'Market profits of the kind under discussion will not be attributable to sheer luck, since they resulted from the exercise of deliberate profit-seeking individual action' (Kirzner 1979, 179–180). Although he also admitted that the fate of entrepreneurial undertaking is determined to a certain degree by 'fortuitous change'.
6. Kirzner never explained why he ignored the possibility of learning to become an alert entrepreneur. I suspect that the reason is that Mises (1949, 586) explicitly ruled out this route to successful entrepreneurship. In his view, entrepreneurship 'can neither be learned nor taught' See further Chapter 12.
7. In the words of Kirzner (1997, 72): 'Enhanced mutual awareness, via the entrepreneurial discovery process, is the source of the market's equilibrative properties.'
8. This should not be seen as an argument denying the toils and troubles needed to develop technological innovations. The example is intended to give the correct interpretation of disequilibrium, seeing it as a development towards equilibrium, rather than as a movement away from it, as Schumpeter's notion of creative destruction suggests.

9. In the view of Van Zijp (1995, 421) the adoption of the Swedish sequence analysis led Lachmann to reject the importance of the Hayek problem, which in his opinion implicitly assumes a tendency towards coordination.
10. See Lachmann (1956, 46); Lachmann (1976a, 59); Lachmann (1976b, 129); Lachmann (1977, 190); Lachmann (1986, 17, 56).
11. This refers to Mises's conception of human action. 'Action controlled by one mind is, as Mises showed, necessarily consistent' (Lachmann 1976b, 131).
12. Well-known parables illustrating this principle are Keynes's beauty contest (Chapter 12 in the GT) and the Sherlock Holmes-Moriarity chase of Morgenstern (1935). See O'Driscoll and Rizzo (1996).
13. Kirzner (1999, 15) admitted that there is certain semantic ambiguity in this new portrait of Schumpeter's entrepreneurship as being coordinative and equilibrative. He warned that his interpretation must not be taken to mean that each and every Schumpeterian technological innovation is equilibrating. He stressed that in a Walrasian state of affairs which fully incorporates all currently available technological knowledge, Schumpeter was right in seeing the role of the entrepreneur as being disruptive and disequilibrating. But of course, no self-respecting Austrian would ever accept the conditions of Walrasian general equilibrium analysis, which reduces the value of this case to virtually zero. Thus, following Kirzner's logic, the Austrians face a choice, seeing Schumpeter's entrepreneur as either a Kirznerian entrepreneur or as an entrepreneur not belonging to the corpus of Austrian theory.
14. See Vaughn (1994, 145–150) and O'Driscoll and Rizzo (1996, 100) for the critique that Kirzner ignored the role of time and uncertainty. High (1990, 40) stresses that when uncertainty is present, entrepreneurship not only involves alertness, it also involves judgment. This refers to the mental process of weighing the factors that will influence the outcome of an event.
15. As O'Driscoll and Rizzo (1996, 117) put it, bureaucratic controls generate a process of response, where each stage generates changes in the environment that cause further responses. Each control breeds evasion of the control. Each evasion produces further changes in the market environment and additional adaptations. There is literally no end to this process so long as there are calculating entrepreneurs, economic and political, who can profit from existing opportunities. It is this argument which leads O'Driscoll and Rizzo to conclude that there is 'simply no static equilibrium to which anything will settle down' (ibid.).
16. In a very literal sense evolution and equilibrium as an end state are mutually exclusive concepts. If institutions like money and prices foster the development towards a general market equilibrium, then human society tends towards a state of affairs without these very institutions. From that point of view, it seems internally inconsistent to discuss market equilibration in terms of evolutionary theory. See Boettke, Horwitz and Prychitko (1994, 64).

15. Evolutionary Economics

INTRODUCTION

Like the Post Keynesian and Austrian schools, the broad movement known as evolutionary economics is highly critical of neoclassical economics. Nelson and Winter (1982), one of the classic works in this field, introduce their subject by noting the growing chorus of dissenters in contemporary theory. Hodgson (1993) motivates his efforts to ground economics on evolutionary principles by pointing to the crisis and chaos in economics. Invariably, general equilibrium theory is the main bone of contention. Hodgson says that GE theory has now reached a serious impasse. Langlois (1986) grounds the rise of rise of new institutional economics on a similar discontent with neoclassical equilibrium theories. Nelson and Winter list the following shortcomings of neoclassical equilibrium theory: it is unable to accommodate uncertainty or bounded rationality; it can cannot account for the presence of large corporations or institutional complexity, and it fails to give a credible explanation of actual adjustment processes. Evidently, in the face of such shortcomings a new kind of theory is needed, one that is able to handle all these things. This alternative is evolutionary economics.[1]

The theoretical developments summarized under this heading are versatile and differ in their degree of criticism on neoclassical (general) equilibrium theory.[2] Nonetheless, there are a number of common themes which allow us to investigate them as a more or less unified approach. The first of these themes is realism (Vromen 1995). Evolutionary theorists believe that the formal way of theorizing, which is the trademark of general equilibrium analysis, has widened the gap between economic theory and its subject matter to indefensible proportions. Therefore, the aim is to restore economic theory on its proper foundations and to increase the realism of economic explanations. The second characteristic of the evolutionary movement naturally follows from this aim. In evolutionary theory, economic behaviour is often described as bounded rational or non-rational, because there is an overwhelming amount of empirical evidence that *homo economicus* is nothing but a fiction (Kahneman 2003). The third characteristic is closely related to this point. To explain the driving forces of economic behaviour a sense of context is needed, which is offered by institutions like social networks, rules and the legal and political framework (Hodgson 1988, 1998 and 1999).

Finally, but not lastly because it explains the common denominator, evolutionary economics aims to give an explicit account of the dynamic path of development underlying economic changes. This dynamics sees economic change as evolution, because it shares several aspects with the biological processes which are commonly associated with this term. Both may involve changes requiring a substantial amount of time,[3] but even more important is the categorization of the main causal forces in three distinct classes: selection, mutation and inheritance (Nelson and Winter 1982, 9–11; Hodgson 1993, Chapter 3). Evidently, a theory grafted on these principles will not result in a static equilibrium view on the nature of economic changes. The essence of evolutionary thinking in economics is the espousal of disequilibrium theory as the preferred tool for economic analysis (Nelson and Winter 2002, 40). This chapter is devoted to the question of what this theory has to offer to economists looking for an alternative to the equilibrium-dominated approach of modern economics.

Like in the previous chapters, the answer to this question will not be unequivocal, given the variety of the theories bearing the label evolutionary. An important watershed in evolutionary economics is the distinction between evolutionary game theory, which can be seen as complementing mainstream neoclassical economics, and the market and institutional approaches which reject the current orthodoxy and consider evolutionary theorizing as a full blown alternative to the neoclassical equilibrium paradigm. I shall start by drawing out the implications of evolutionary game theory. What is the use of modelling evolution as a game? The subsequent section introduces the work of Nelson and Winter and their 'fight' against what they consider the neoclassical orthodoxy. I then focus on the evolutionary aspects of market process theory. Does evolution promote economic order and can it thus be used as an alternative organizing principle? Finally, I turn to the prospects of institutional analysis as an evolutionary theory. Do we need to see institutions through evolutionary lenses and what does that mean for the nature of economic theory?

GAMES AS EVOLUTIONARY PROCESSES

Evolutionary game theory is the branch of evolutionary economics that stands closest to neoclassical economics, in evolutionary circles the paradigm case of the non-evolutionary approach to economic questions. Like the latter, game theory is profoundly mathematical. It relies on equilibrium concepts like Nash equilibrium and can be used to support the microfoundation of both

Walrasian and non-Walrasian equilibrium analysis (Janssen 1990). However, game theory also shares one of the shortcomings of neoclassical economics, especially as represented by general equilibrium theory. This is the lack of stability results. It is quite able to investigate the analytical properties of different equilibrium constellations, but cannot answer the question which equilibrium will be selected as the final outcome of all the negotiating and bargaining that goes on in the economic arena. In that respect it lacks the ability to explain the dynamic steps required to bring the economy from disequilibrium to equilibrium.[4]

For many, this result will not be surprising, given that standard non cooperative game theory proceeds by endowing its players with an impressive (some call it heroic) degree of rationality and knowledge. Firstly, it is assumed that every economic agent is a rational decision maker who will try to maximize the pay-offs from the bargaining options he encounters. Secondly, he is helped in achieving this goal by the assumption of common knowledge. All players know that their counterparts are also rational maximizers. They also know that their adversaries know that they know they are rational maximizers. The result is that each player's predicted strategy must be that player's best response to the predicted strategy of other players. That is, under this assumption play will result in a Nash equilibrium, which indicates that no single player wants to deviate from his or her predicted strategy.[5]

However, the problem is that a Nash equilibrium need not be a unique equilibrium. The question therefore is how to select the 'right' Nash equilibrium. Over the years non-cooperative game theory has been unable to solve this question. The attempt to differentiate between the Nash equilibria of specific games led to the development of still stronger notions of equilibrium like subgame-perfect Nash equilibrium, Bayesian Nash equilibrium et cetera. The aim of this so-called refinement literature is to find rationality-based criteria to exclude implausible Nash-equilibria. But this hunt for the right equilibrium concept just led to frustration with the limitations of the rationality-based models and its unrealistic assumptions concerning the calculatory power and common knowledge of individual agents (Samuelson 2002). What use is a theory that staples one equilibrium concept on another without prospect of ever finding the definitive solution concept?[6] Moreover, the rise of game theory facilitated the development of experimental economics, which showed that actual decision making lacks the rationality that game theory attributes to its players (Kahneman 2003).

Evolutionary game theory provided a way out of the impasse. Key to this approach is the elimination of implausible equilibria through the process of evolution. It has to be stressed that the origin of evolutionary game theory is not economic; it first appeared in biology.[7] But economists were quick to seize the opportunity and started using the main solution concepts like the evolutionary stable strategy (ESS) and the replicator dynamics (RD) (van Damme 1994). The advantage of evolutionary game theory is that it allows a much richer picture of economic incentives. This theory often describes economic behaviour as naïve rather than rational as in standard non cooperative game theory. But in order to explore this field, the step had to be made from biology to economics. What do selection, mutation and inheritance mean in economics? Does evolution really help us to solve the problem of equilibrium selection?

To address this issue, we need to introduce the basic concepts of evolutionary game theory. The basis of this theory is the concept of an evolutionary stable strategy. This solution concept assumes a large population of agents who are repeatedly, randomly matched in pairs to play a game. Now suppose that everyone in the population plays a common strategy, except for a tiny toehold of mutants who play an alternative strategy. If the common strategy earns a higher expected pay-off than the mutant strategy, then we can expect selection to eliminate the latter. If this outcome holds for any possible mutant strategy, then the common strategy can be said to be evolutionary stable. That is, an ESS can repel any sufficiently small mutant advance (Vega-Redondo 1996, 14).

It is evident from this result that selection is the force which propels the population towards the ESS. The obvious economic connotation here is that of selection through the price mechanism. Pay-offs in this game can be seen as 'fitness' in the sense that the competitive process favours those who earn higher pay-offs. Others are selected out and will eventually be driven from the market. However, an important difference with the regular interpretation of the competitive game is the absence of a notion of rational choice. In the economic context rationality is interpreted as behavioural adaptation (Vanberg 1994, Chapter 2), but in the evolutionary game there is no conscious choice (at least in first instance, see further below). Individuals are programmed to play certain strategies (van Damme 1994, 848). The ability to adapt is introduced into the system by means of a link between generations: players leave offspring of exactly the same strategic type (asexual reproduction).[8] This allows more successful strategies to reproduce faster than others, so that eventually only the most successful strategies survive. In addition, mutation is the force that generates new and previously non-existent behaviour. One may think here of the Schumpeterian entrepreneur who upsets market equilibrium by introducing an entirely new product into the system. Such mutation is able to enrich prior patterns of behaviour so that adaption to the environment is possible at all. The ESS thus also represents fitness in the sense of being best adjusted to changed external circumstances.[9]

I shall discuss further on the interesting option of letting the degree of rationality be the endogenous outcome of the evolutionary process itself (Does evolution wipe out irrational behaviour?). But first the analytical consequences of the ESS need to be mentioned. In static analysis, ESS is a refinement of Nash equilibrium. It can be shown that in the bilateral game assumed above if some strategy is an ESS, then it must be a Nash equilibrium (Vega-Redondo 1996, 20). The introduction of explicit dynamics, the so-called replicator dynamics, further deepens this analysis. RD describes the process by which successful strategies drive out less successful ones, which adds the element of stability to the ESS.[10] It can then be shown that a Nash equilibrium is a stationary point of the dynamical system. Conversely, each ESS induces an asymptotically stable stationary state, which is a Nash equilibrium (Vega-Redondo 1996, 55).

The problem is that stability results from this literature are insufficient to draw general conclusions about the trajectory of evolutionary developments (Samuelson 2002). There are many cases where ESS does not exist and where it does arise the results mentioned above are only valid for local stability.[11] So there is only a conditional answer to the question: Do people actually play Nash equilibrium? We need to assume that the Nash equilibrium in question is stable. According to Samuelson (2002, 58), this result puts game theory on much the same footing as the rest of economics. We know that markets do not always reside in equilibrium, that agents are not always rational and that firms are not always profit maximizing. But we hope that disequilibrium behaviour is sufficiently transient, so that we may proceed 'as if' the economy is actually approaching or close to equilibrium. Likewise, evolutionary game theory provides little reason to believe that equilibrium behaviour should characterize all games in all circumstances. But it gives hope that the behaviour that comes into our field of study is likely to be equilibrium behaviour.

The introduction of stochastic noise into the system may help to improve the selection mechanism. Noise in these models is an upsetting or perturbing force, as it introduces a deterministic flow of mutations into the system of individuals adopting every possible strategy. This perturbation entails a test of the robustness for each of the several limit sets which will typically result from the exclusive operation of the (mutation free) selection dynamics. Allowing for mutation, one may discriminate among these sets, based on the fact that not all of them are equally robust under mutation. Only those which are most resistant to mutation may qualify as long run outcomes. This, then, opens the door to selecting RD that is most likely to emerge as the outcome of the evolutionary process under fairly general conditions. The analytical power of this result is profound. Vega-Redondo (1996) demonstrates that the noise-perturbation model can be used to explain the evolution of Walrasian behaviour. In a simple evolutionary model of Cournot oligopoly, a Walrasian equilibrium can be shown to exist which is unique. This result is obtained without placing a restriction on the number of firms (that is the population is infinite), which underlines the power of evolutionary game theory as a support for regular equilibrium analysis in economics.

However, the model of Vega-Redondo assumes that all players are imitators. Firms are postulated to adjust their output by simply copying that of a firm which is earning the highest profit. There are voices which find this kind of naïve behaviour implausible (Mailath 1998, 1356). Is it not possible to find a better balance between the extremes of assuming that players are either inhumanly rational or incredibly stupid? The evolutionary answer to that question is, of course, to model the degree of rationality as an endogenous outcome of the evolutionary process. Let the players themselves decide the level of rationality they find appropriate to the game theoretic situation at hand. The interesting question then is: Will evolution wipe out irrational behaviour?

This issue requires us to explicitly incorporate the process of expectations formation into stochastic evolutionary models. Unfortunately, the results of this class of models are mixed. If the choice set facing players allows a high degree of sophistication, then the outcome is a state which Vega-Redondo (1996, 185) calls 'equilibrium volatility'. This term indicates the impossibility of anchoring the system at a particular equilibrium. To reach a determinate outcome, the choice set facing individual players needs to be restricted. This means placing an upper boundary on the degree of sophistication, so that the highest level of smartness is static optimization. Alternatively, sophistication can be postulated costly. This will lead to a situation where, even though higher sophistication levels might be possible, the lowest one must in the end prevail. It can be shown that both these cases – constraining the degree of smartness or assuming costly sophistication – restore efficiency as the long run criterion of equilibrium selection (ibid., 194). But consider the cost of this result. With costly sophistication we reach efficient equilibrium assuming that evolution promotes instead of eradicates irrational behaviour. This anomaly indicates that the search for a proper long term interpretation of the process of evolution in stochastic evolutionary game theory is not yet completed.[12]

This brings me to a final assessment of evolutionary game theory as a tool of disequilibrium analysis.

The first conclusion is that evolutionary game theory allows us to explicitly model the dynamic adjustments needed to bring about equilibrium. This perspective is an improvement of the dynamics underlying non-cooperative game theory in the sense that is based on minimal rationality requirements. However, it shares with non cooperative game theory the focus on solving the puzzle of selecting the right equilibrium. In the words of Mailath (1998, 1371), 'it shows that there are primitive foundations for equilibrium analysis.' We have seen the progress of evolutionary game theory in this regard, for example when we apply a model with stochastic noise to explain the emergence of a Walrasian equilibrium in evolutionary terms. However, the limits of this approach must not be underestimated. Evolutionary game theory does not provide the ultimate clue to the identification of the unique 'right' equilibrium. There are many cases in which ESS does not exist. Likewise, in dynamic stochastic analysis evolutionary games need to converge on an equilibrium state.

Secondly, the question is whether this shortcoming is really a disadvantage. After all, even when dynamic adjustments do not converge on equilibrium, we can still analyze the disequilibrium process for its own sake, for example in order to typify to process of long term change as open-ended or to address questions of path-dependence. But the question is whether the protagonists of evolutionary game theory really want to take this road. My impression is not. The stress lies first and foremost on refining the Nash equilibrium, that is on underpinning the equilibrium approach. This means that evolutionary game theory risks the fate of the refinements literature: too many equilibrium concepts and little basis for choosing among them (Mailath 1998, 1372 and Samuelson 2002, 62–63).

Thirdly, a justification for the perusal of so many equilibrium concepts might be that they have a role in generating useful applications. Unfortunately, evolutionary game theory is generally far too abstract in order to be applicable to cases close to economic reality. Mailath (1998) considers it still too stylized for this role. Moreover, so-called applications often concern theoretical cases rather than empirical questions and where theoretical applications are considered, they are often directed to demonstrating that equilibrium may come about along an evolutionary route. By and large, evolutionary game theory firmly stays within the realm of theoretical equilibrium economics.

Fourthly, one may doubt whether a truly open-ended process is possible in the current state of evolutionary game theory. An important limitation to modeling a process of this kind is the assumption that the strategy set of the game remains fixed. This makes it impossible to analyze mutations that in economic terms can be seen as innovations (Vega-Redondo 1996, 195). It is evident that Schumpeterian innovation involves a strategy that was not previously in the choice set of the players. Innovation of this kind is highly relevant to the process of technological change and hence to the explanation of economic dynamics in the long term. But at present evolutionary game theory is not able to handle dynamic processes belonging to this category.[13]

THE FIGHT AGAINST 'ORTHODOX' NEOCLASSICAL EQUILIBRIUM THEORY

Evolution as a Support for Neoclassical Economics

In the previous section we have seen that a central focus in evolutionary game theory is to determine the right equilibrium. This theoretical effort of evolutionary game theory is challenged by evolutionary theorists who want to discard with equilibrium theory altogether. In their view, evolutionary economics must be seen as a radical alternative that displaces rather than complements neoclassical equilibrium analysis, a branch of theory which in evolutionary circles is often referred to as 'the orthodoxy'. In this section I aim to investigate what this alternative entails and what benefit it will bring to economics. The leading question therein will be whether economics without the equilibrium concept as its main building block will degenerate into an a-theoretical (and some will argue anti-theoretical) discipline, a science that lacks the ability to deduce valid conclusions from theoretical models. Evolutionary theorists try to keep such fears at bay by presenting evolutionary forces as the foundation of a new paradigm with highly promising theoretical and empirical features. So, can evolution function as an organizing principle for economics just as the equilibrium concept has been for so many years?

The natural starting point for answering this question is a discussion of the way neoclassical economics introduced evolution as a support rather than a challenge of its equilibrium approach. The root of the introduction of evolutionary arguments in neoclassical circles was the criticism of anti-marginalists like Hall and Hitch in England and Lester in the USA (Vromen 1995, 14–17). The anti-marginalists argued on the basis of empirical research (conducted with questionnaires sent to individual firms) that entrepreneurs do not actually follow the marginalist principles of profit maximization and/or cost minimization in running their firms. Hall and Hitch (1939) found that almost all businesses prefer a 'full cost' pricing rule over a pricing rule in terms of marginal revenue and marginal cost. Likewise, Lester's (1946) results casted doubt on the relevance of marginal costs (especially concerning the costs of labour) as a factor affecting the actual pricing decisions of entrepreneurs. The result of such findings was a call for a new theory of the firm, as the neoclassical theory of firm behaviour in terms of profit maximization appeared in conflict with the actual behaviour of business men.

In the 1950s, this conclusion provoked a response from the defenders of the neoclassical theory of the firm like Alchian (1950) and Friedman (1953) (Machlup and Stigler preceded them). They introduced natural selection as an evolutionary argument explaining why it was unnecessary to assume that all business men are always and everywhere maximizing their profits without rejecting profit maximization and its associated marginalistic principles as the core concepts of neoclassical economics. Alchian defended what Vromen (1995) called the 'ultimate claim'. He argued that the neoclassical theory of the firm is not about firms as such but industries. Individual firms may follow a variety of routines such as full cost pricing, but the selection taking place through the process of price competition will ensure that at the level of the industry only firms with positive profits will survive. Hence, in view of this end result, one can maintain the assumption of profit maximization as a convenient generalization, even if with regard to individual firms it does not correspond to fact at any point in time.[14]

However, the approach of Alchian leaves open the option that one could in principle test the behavioural assumption of profit maximization. Friedman (1953) went one step further and dismissed a test of this kind as methodically unnecessary. Vromen (1995, 33) has termed this argument the 'intermediate' claim to indicate that it dispenses with the need to ground assumptions about firm behaviour on any kind of realistic notion. Friedman's instrumentalism dictates that consistency with profit maximization is the only requirement to validate the intermediate process of one's market theory. According to him, business behaviour may be anything at all, 'habitual reaction, random chance, or whatnot' (Friedman 1953, 22). One may approach firms as if they are profit maximizers, as long as the neoclassical theory of the firm generates better predictions than rival theories. In Friedman's eyes, the need to beat rival firms in the process of price competition formed an evolutionary explanation that the neoclassical theory of the firm meets this criterion. Friedman here introduced the famous analogue of the expert billiard player that is assumed to play as if he has mathematically calculated the best shot possible, but in reality plays on the basis of his routine and other tacit skills. He argued that it is unknown which tactic players choose in reality. But on the basis of the selection criterion, we do know that the surviving tactics must be consistent with the idealized image of the expert billiard player, otherwise players would not be able to win any games.

A Radical Alternative

It is this type of argumentation that is attacked by the evolutionary theorists that present themselves as a radical alternative to neoclassical economics and its focus on the analysis of equilibrium states. The criticisms levied by this group against the evolutionary theories of Alchian and Friedman is that it forms an implicit dynamic theory that is just used to sanction the exclusive focus on the analysis of equilibrium states, but does not form a field of research in itself. In this regard, evolutionary theorists often refer to the words of Tjalling Koopmans (1957) who said that if market selection is the basis for the belief in profit maximization, then we should postulate that basis itself and not profit maximization which it is said to imply in certain circumstances. The proponents of evolutionary economics as a radical new paradigm try to do just that. They aim to explicate the process of evolution, which forms the foremost instrument to demonstrate the nature of economics as an essentially dynamic science in opposition to the static image of our science in the neoclassical orthodoxy.

The Evolutionary Theory of Economic Change (1982) of Nelson and Winter has been one of the key publications in the attempt to develop evolutionary economics as a new paradigm. The reader of this book cannot fail to miss its main message. Economics is a science dominated by the equilibrium theories of neoclassical making. This approach is consistently labelled as the 'orthodoxy' reflecting the belief of Nelson and Winter that it has brought economics on the brink of a scientific crisis. According to them, the approach of neoclassical economics is patently false, given that it relies on assumptions that are in stark contrast to the conditions of the real economy. The assumption that agents are rational in the sense that they optimize is considered one of the main examples of this abstract and unrealistic methodology. Nelson and Winter argue that it is this kind of formalism in defiance of reality which explains the bad track record of neoclassical economics. In particular, even after so many years of theorizing, the orthodoxy is still unable to give a plausible account of the most pervasive aspect of economic events, namely the fact that changes in the economic realm take place in historical time. Neoclassical economics is a theory of equilibrium states, not of economic change.

Nelson and Winter propose two radical changes as part of their evolutionary revolution. In the first place, they reject the exclusive focus of orthodox theory on the study of the conditions that are necessary or sufficient to bring about a state of equilibrium. In evolutionary theory, the emphasis lies on the explication of the process of dynamic adjustment underlying economic changes, which may or may not bring the system to a state of equilibrium. These mechanisms are organized according to the classification of evolutionary theory. That is, they explain economic change in terms of selection, inheritance and mutation. Secondly, as an outflow of the denial to model change as a sequence of static equilibria, Nelson and Winter reject the assumption that economic agents operate as rational consumers and producers that manage to select the optimal choice in any imaginable situation. Instead, they place routines at the heart of their behavioural theory. The characteristic of routines is that they describe those elements of firm behaviour that are regular and predictable, which makes them relatively fixed patterns of behaviour. For Nelson and Winter this is an aspect of routines which increases the realism of rule-guided behaviour as an explanatory principle. Actual firms do not change their decision rules for the key characteristics of the business process overnight, such as the technical routines for producing things, the procedures for hiring and firing, ordering new inventory or allocating funds to research and development. The assumption of rule-guided choices in the form of routines may account for this aspect of firm behaviour in actual economic conditions.

More importantly, Nelson and Winter see routines as the basis of an evolutionary explanation of economic change. They give them the role that genes play in biological evolutionary theory. Like genes, they are a persistent feature of the behaviour of the organism that one wishes to explain, in this case the firm. The evolutionary theory of Nelson and Winter subsequently models the dynamic of economic change in terms of the selection, inheritance and mutation of routines. The selection argument is geared in terms of the profit and loss mechanism that we know from orthodox neoclassical theory. Firms with profitable routines have a better chance for survival than rival firms and thus the relative importance of these firms in the population (industry) tends to increase over time. This trait can be inherited by subsidiary, acquired or merger firms, which extends the life time of routines. But this does not mean that routines are transferred in an unchanged form. To the contrary. The essence of the economic outlook of Nelson and Winter is that the economy is a source of unlimited variety which translates itself in the mutation of routines. Firms experiment with new routines (innovation) or copy the ones of successful competitors. In either case, they alter the routine pool and so allow it to adjust to changed circumstances.

The Janus-faced Evolutionary Theory of Nelson and Winter

What can we say about this kind of evolutionary dynamics? Is it really the sort of alternative that disequilibrium theorists are looking for? There is one aspect of the evolutionary approach of Nelson and Winter that from the outset distinguishes it from the Post Keynesian and Austrian theories discussed earlier. This is the aim to use mathematics as the main tool of analysis which neatly complies with the preferred mode of reasoning in modern economics. In short, Nelson and Winter aim to increase the realism of economic explanations, but they not eschew mathematical analysis like (some) Post Keynesians and (generally all) Austrians. They even argue that '[j]ust as some orthodox ideas seem to find their most natural mathematical expression in the calculus, the foregoing verbal account of economic evolution seems to translate naturally into a description of a Markov process

– though one in a rather complicated state space' (Nelson and Winter 1982, 19).

The mathematical focus of Nelson and Winter is closely related to the fact that their general message is not unambiguous. Vromen (1995) has correctly drawn attention to this aspect of their evolutionary project. He warns against exaggeration. The claim of Nelson and Winter that their evolutionary theory defeats the orthodox competition on all accounts is grossly overstated. In particular, he argues that their basic mathematical model, addressing the mechanics of static selection equilibrium in evolutionary terms, underwrites rather than undermines orthodox market theories, inducing selection arguments like that of Friedman's intermediate claim (Vromen 1995, 69). The real bite of their evolutionary theory is in the informally stated list of 'complications and snags' to their model, which discusses the problems that they consider relevant to their position, but were unable to include in their formal model.

I agree with Vromen that Nelson and Winter fail to consistently develop their argument. In general, their rhetoric carries them away to a position that they are unable to substantiate in theoretical or empirical terms. In some cases, they do not even want to accept the criticism suggested by their own rhetoric. The result is a muddle, which makes it hard to assess the scientific value of Nelson and Winter's evolutionary theory. Let me explain.

The main problem of the approach chosen by Nelson and Winter is that it aims to criticize orthodox theory, but at the same time wants to convince the practitioners of orthodox theory of the relevance of a superior alternative, namely evolutionary theory. In terms of Lakatos's methodology of scientific research programs, Nelson and Winter argue that their evolutionary theory of economic change has 'excess content' over the theoretical and empirical results of orthodox theory.[15] The rational, that is career-oriented, economist is therefore well advised to switch from the degenerating orthodox program to the promising ('progressive') research program of evolutionary economics.

In less scientific terms, one might say that there is a part of Nelson and Winter (1982) which tries to 'please' its audience in order to gain access to the scientific community. If you want to convince the mainstream into changing its current working methods, you are well advised not to antagonize them too much (the focus on mathematical modelling is a sign of this). A full-blown criticism of orthodox theory would very likely have this effect. However, the troubling fact is that many passages in Nelson and Winter (1982) do suggest a critique of this kind. It is this Janus-face of their book which causes the confusion about the exact purpose and meaning of the new evolutionary paradigm.

A few examples may help to explain this point. I have already mentioned that Nelson and Winter describe the current state of knowledge in economics as a 'general malaise' (ibid., 5). An important reason for this malaise is the fact that orthodox theory fails to generate successful (quantitative) predictions about the future course of economic events. Nelson and Winter call the predictive record of orthodox theory in this regard 'inadequate' (ibid., 184). Consequently, they consider the entire theoretical apparatus of the orthodoxy 'excess baggage' that will seriously encumber theoretical progress in the long run.[16]

But then look at how they proceed to prove the superiority of evolutionary theory. The starting point of their formal analysis concerns the selection mechanism generating static market equilibrium. Nelson and Winter (1985, 153) conclude from this analysis that their selection equilibrium does not correspond to orthodox market equilibrium. But Vromen (1995, 69) shows that the opposite is true. Their model assumes that firms choose their routines in a stochastic search process. Competitive selection then explains that market equilibrium comes about with equilibrium prices and production at full capacity for all firms, even when firms try all kinds of non-orthodox pricing rules such as full cost pricing during the process of reaching this equilibrium. Nelson and Winter present this aspect of the adjustment process, which in their view entails a rejection of the algorithms of optimal calculation, as a success of their evolutionary approach. But Vromen argues that what they have done is just show that Friedman had been right all along: We do not need to be mathematical geniuses to play like an expert billiard player. In economics terms, the business strategy of actual firms is irrelevant to the question whether the neoclassical theory of the firm is successful or not. That is, Nelson and Winter underwrite rather than reject Friedman's intermediate claim, which is a support of the orthodox neoclassical theory. Whither excess baggage?

In the discussion following the presentation of their model in Chapter 6 Nelson and Winter concede that they consider the static equilibrium approach a 'fruitful' starting point of their evolutionary exploration, 'in spite of the artificiality' (ibid., 157).[17] Apparently, realism is a pragmatic argument, a demand that one need not maintain equally strict in all stages of theoretical development. To make matters worse, they even validate orthodox theory on epistemological grounds. Throughout their book, the ignorance of the neoclassical creed towards a truly dynamic theory of economic change (that is one that does not treat the generative mechanism as a black box), is presented as the all important reason why orthodox theory fails as scientific tool. But when the reader reaches Chapter 7 on the 'Firm and Industry Response to Changed Market Conditions' he is told that 'standard' orthodox results of neoclassical comparative statics are correct, because 'they describe the typical patterns of firm and industry response in the dynamic, evolving economy of reality' (ibid., 175). The true intent of evolutionary theory as a radical alternative to orthodox neoclassical equilibrium analysis gets more mystifying by the chapter.

Evolution as a Scientific Research Program

At this point the reader may start to wonder whether the evolutionary challenge of Nelson and Winter to orthodox economics theory is a hoax. I do not think so. They should have restrained their rhetoric so that it becomes evident that evolutionary theory has a lot in common with the theory it aims to replace. In this regard, there is merit in the Lakatosian reconstruction of the evolutionary theory of Nelson and Winter as a research program, which claims to be progressive and thus fit to replace a degenerating orthodox program. A claim of this kind entails that evolutionary theory covers the entire *explanandum* of orthodox theory and more, that is it has excess content.[18] In other words, the value of evolutionary theory as a scientific undertaking can be assessed by investigating this 'extra' that the theory is said to offer over its neoclassical rival.

I am not so pessimistic about the potential that the evolutionary theory of Nelson and Winter has in terms of excess content. But I also feel that they have insufficiently exploited this potential. This potential is clearly sketched in their summing up of the results of their formal analysis of static selection equilibrium. The question arises whether it matters that non-optimal rules survive in selection equilibrium. Their answer is a clear yes because the existence of such rules may cause path-dependent effects which seriously jeopardize the stability of equilibrium as an end state. Nelson and Winter argue that in this case it is likely that a disruption of an orthodox-type equilibrium will be followed by an adjustment process which takes the economy to a state that does not have this characteristic (ibid., 154). It may even occur that if the system is not initially in equilibrium, 'the selection forces operating in disequilibrium states may prevent it from ever reaching equilibrium' (ibid., 159). In other words, the evolutionary system may demonstrate unstable if not chaotic qualities.

It is this kind of disequilibrium theorizing that one would like to see developed in a far more extensive degree than achieved by Nelson and Winter. One might say that their replication of orthodox equilibrium economics succeeded a bit too well. By developing a formal theory that is able to combat neoclassical economics on its own domain, they pressed evolutionary theory into a corner where it proved unable to generate non-orthodox results. The main problem is that they modeled routines as fixed rules, while in reality they should be treated as the outcome of a dynamic learning process. This simplification allowed them to model industry behaviour in a relatively simple way, but according to Vromen

(1995, 128), they paid a double price for it. 'Not only can their model not be said to give a "realistic" account of industry behaviour, it also cannot but reproduce standard "orthodox" results'. Vromen argues that the more elaborate models in the later chapters of Nelson and Winter (1982) do not alter this conclusion, because they fail to relax the particular assumptions of the simple static selection model (ibid., 70).

The basic problem is that there are two distinct evolutionary mechanisms at the heart of the evolutionary theory of Nelson and Winter, operating at different levels. These are natural selection (operating at firm level) and satisficing, which concerns individual learning. These processes occur simultaneously, but the formal theory of Nelson and Winter only addresses natural selection. The problem of changing decision rules as a result of adaptive learning is 'swept under the carpet' by assuming routines to be fixed for the duration of the search and selection process (Vromen 1995, 125). Vromen suspects that the explanation for this act of ignorance concerns the difficulty of mathematically modeling the complex interaction of the process of co-evolution.

I agree with Vromen that the scope of the more extended models in Nelson and Winter (1982) is limited due to their decision to exclusively focus on competitive selection as the main evolutionary mechanism. They rank the nature of search processes among the most important for those trying to understand economic growth (Nelson and Winter 1982, 229). Their evolutionary theory of growth is therefore framed in terms of a 'pure' selection process (ibid., 234–245). This opposes the current trend in growth theory to focus on human capital and schooling as an important determinant of the GDP-growth rate (Barro and Sala-i-Martin 1995). But the results of this exercise are certainly worth mentioning. The growth theory of Nelson and Winter is used in a simulation model that is able to mimic the familiar macroeconomic time series data that are generally used to support standard neoclassical growth accounting analysis of the type developed by Solow (1957). The merit of the reconstruction by Nelson and Winter is that it does not portray the economy as being in equilibrium. That is, it does not assume that economic growth proceeds along a warranted rate of growth or another kind of equilibrium growth path. Nelson and Winter reject the illustre aggregate production function and instead formulate a stochastic search process for heterogeneous capital goods. The result is a considerable diversity in the realized rates of return rather than a pull towards an economy-wide equilibrium rate of profit (ibid., 227).

The other formal contribution of Nelson and Winter concerns the dynamics of Schumpeterian competition. The main result of this model is that it shows that free competition is not the automatic and harmonious regulator of the market economy that economic liberals take it to be. The disturbing element in the notion of Schumpeterian competition is the introduction of innovation. Successful innovation may reward firms with supranormal profits, so that a process emerges that tends to produce winners and losers. Nelson and Winter argue that this process is self-enforcing. Winners tend to prosper and grow due to their technological leadership, while decline breeds technological obsolescence and further decline. As these processes operate over time, there is a tendency for concentration to develop even in an industry initially composed of many equal-sized firms. This may eventually lead to self-destruction of the market system. Nelson and Winter claim empirical support for this finding. They estimate the resulting size distribution of firms by calibrating a numerical model, which in their opinion shows that their model should be taken serious as 'an illustration of realistic opportunities' (ibid., 325).

This brings me to a final assessment of the evolutionary theory along the lines promoted by Nelson and Winter. The results reported above show that Vromen's criticism is valid, but also underestimates the progress made by Nelson and Winter. As Hodgson (1999, 166) argues, formal modeling plays a significant but not a central role in their evolutionary approach. They try to strike a balance between empirical research and formal theorizing by demanding that the two go hand in hand. Thus mathematical modeling should guide and frame empirical study, while vice versa empirical findings should be able to influence formal theory. The evolutionary theories of economic growth and the dynamics of Schumpeterian competition demonstrate the progress that can be made by this kind of cross-fertilization.

It is this multi-faceted approach directed towards the analysis of disequilibrium situations that explains the appeal of the evolutionary approach to economists in heterodox circles. Austrians, Post Keynesians and Institutionalists, they have all expressed their acclaim for Nelson and Winter (1982).[19] The result has been a steadily growing attention for this book. In the period of the 15 years following its publication both the annual number of citations and the annual citation share have shown a clear upward trend.[20] As Nelson and Winter (2002, 42) themselves observe, 'the citations to our 1982 book suggest that the evolutionary approach has had broad appeal to a wide range of scholars from a variety of different disciplines working on business organization and strategy'.

Nelson and Winter thus succeeded in building a bridge across the different paradigms of economics, but they missed one of their main targets. Hodgson (1999, 167) argues that the impact of the book on mainstream economic theory has been detectible but no more than marginal. It is much more frequently cited in management and business publications, rather than in the core theoretical journals of mainstream economics. Nelson and Winter (2002) seem to have accepted this fate. Reviewing the lessons of the twenty years since the publication of their book does not bring them to formulate a new agenda for research. To the contrary, they continue to combat old enemies such as Alchian and Friedman, but ignore the new developments in neoclassical economics, which in some cases have important implications for their work. The theoretical and empirical literature in industrial organization is a case in point. This quickly expanding field is covered in a footnote (see Nelson and Winter 2002, 28n3). The implications of human capital theory for economic growth are not mentioned at all. The same applies to the development of search theory in microeconomics, which finds applications in labour economics and beyond. How is it possible that two economists whose main task in academic life has been to open up the eyes of their colleagues to the conservative elements of their discipline, now themselves turn a blind eye to new developments that directly concern their field of study? What remains in their 2002 review article is a rather placid summing up of what their followers have achieved in the business and strategy literature. Looking to the future, I conclude that evolutionary economics is in dire need of a new impetus if it wants to have a more lasting impact on economic theory.

DOES EVOLUTION PROMOTE ECONOMIC ORDER?

This conclusion warrants a closer look at parallel developments in economics that likewise present the evolutionary mechanism as a radical alternative to neoclassical equilibrium analysis. These approaches have diverse roots, but can nonetheless be grouped under a common heading. This binding element is the question: Does evolution promote economic order? For the Austrians, this question refers to the invisible hand explanation of the market order. In this role it focuses on the function and historical emergence of institutions that support market order, such as property rights and money (Koppl 1992). Post Keynesians and Institutionalists pose similar questions, but address the issue of evolution from a different angle. They consider the emergence of institutions in the evolutionary process as a sign of the macro stability of certain social structures such as rules and norms. For them, the force of evolution endows the economy with a sense of stability, which can be used to promote a specific kind of social analysis (in term of collectives or other aggregates) and to underpin the need for active government involvement in the economy. I shall briefly discuss the merits and disadvantages of these different approaches.

I have already discussed Hayek's approach towards evolutionary theory in Chapter 12. For Hayek, the study of evolution marked his final rejection of equilibrium analysis as a main tool of analysis. He replaced equilibrium as a mental construct by the notion of the spontaneous order that was closely embedded in the institutional structure of the market system. This order arises as the unintended consequence of acting human beings. According to Hayek, the new objective of the social sciences (which included economics) was to study the causal drivers behind this process, for which evolution was the main explanatory tool. That is why he saw evolution and the concept of the spontaneous order as twin ideas.

I shall presently ignore the details of Hayek's theory of evolution as a process of group selection.[21] For my current purposes what matters is that this paradigm shift caused Hayek to approach economic questions from a different angle. Equilibrium presents the economy in an ideal state that will never become reality because the tendency towards it is obstructed by all kinds of disturbing effects. With the notion of the spontaneous order one might say that these disturbing elements are built in from the start. It constitutes a process in historical time that cannot be organized by a benevolent dictator or another central planner, because the evolving process of order generates effects that are impossible to predict by anyone. This ordering process will, in general, be beneficial to the society at large, but it has no predetermined goal that can be used to assess its success or efficiency. This is mainly caused by the fact that the market order consists of so many exchange and production relationships that it has a complexity which far outruns the cognitive capacity of the human brain or the calculation power of the computers it devices.[22]

Hayek's theory of complex phenomena introduces instruments that are designed to shortcut the complexity of such questions. The notion of pattern prediction is one these tools, the concept of spontaneous order as the unintended outcome of human action is another. However, as I stressed in Chapter 12, this approach leads to a biased view on the nature of the market process and the principle of evolution that underlies it. Evolution is always seen as promoting rather than disrupting the establishment of order. It is evident that this view on the nature of adjustment processes dovetails with Hayek's *laissez faire* policies, but it ignores an important feature of evolutionary processes in real life situations. As a non-equilibrium and open-ended system, evolution may inhabit nonlinearities causing violent changes that are anything but orderly. An occurrence of this kind can be compared to the self-destruction of the market system alluded to by Nelson and Winter above. This was an aspect of evolutionary theory that Hayek overlooked when he substituted the concept of spontaneous order for that of equilibrium as the central organizing concept of economics.

The work of Ludwig Lachmann seems more promising in this regard. Lachmann did not take the tendency towards market order as his starting point. For him, 'in every conceivable situation there are "destabilizing" as well as "stabilizing" forces at work' (Lachmann 1971, 69). In Chapter 14 I concluded that Lachmann depicted the market process as a seemingly steerless process on a par with Shackle's kaleidic society. It is now time to delve further into this issue and to investigate how Lachmann grounded his disequilibrium analysis of the market process on a more general theory of institutions that has strong links with evolutionary theory.

Viewing Lachmann through the lenses of evolutionary theory, I am treading on dangerous soil. Lachmann himself strongly opposed the use of analogies of any kind and especially warned against using 'some dubious biological analogy' when assessing the modus operandi of institutions (Lachmann 1971, 9). My choice to violate this ban is motivated by the fact that Lachmann's theory of institutions needs clarification. Vaughn (1994, 157) even concludes that he said many interesting things about institutions, but failed to develop a general theory of institutions. I shall argue that with the concepts of evolutionary theory we may better explain what Lachmann was trying to achieve.

The starting point for this exercise is the concept of institutional order. This concept refers to the origin and coherence of the institutional structure underlying the market economy. Lachmann (1971) used Menger's 'organic' interpretation of institutions to explain the origin and function of this institutional set up.[23] This function was to aid to process of coordination in a decentralized economic system. He described institutions as 'recurrent patterns of conduct' that 'coordinate activities to a common signpost' (ibid., 49 and 75). This commonality was related to the predictability of institutionalized behaviour. Institutions formed 'a point of orientation' that could help acting individuals to reduce the impact of uncertainty. In this role, he considered the existence of institutions fundamental to civilized society because they allow us to solve Hayek's knowledge problem. 'They [institutions, BT] enable each of us to rely on the actions of thousands of anonymous others about whose individual purposes and plans we can know nothing' (ibid., 50).

The reference in this citation to the purposes and plans of individuals is crucial. Lachmann (1971, 57) consistently promoted his theory of institutions as part of the more general theory of praxeology, which stands central in modern Austrian economics.[24] Menger had used this theory to explain how institutions could emerge and adapt to changed circumstances. In this view, institutions arise as the unintended result of the pursuit of individual plans by a large number of actors, not as a product of social design (ibid., 57).[25] According to Lachmann, the process by which new institutions emerge could be compared to the process of innovation. Both are driven by alert individuals who realize that there exist unexploited opportunities for gain. They will seize such opportunities and, if they are successful, their example will be followed by others. By this process, '[s]uccessful plans thus gradually crystallize into institutions' adding new 'orientation points, which may take the place of older institutions that became obsolete' (ibid., 68).

Until this stage Lachmann's theory of institutions follows the outlines of Hayek's theory of cultural evolution. They share the focus on the explanation of institutions as the unintended result of human action. Further, this spontaneous order is the product of an evolutionary process. Lachmann did not use this term, but it is clear that selection, inheritance and mutation play an important part in his theory.

Firstly, the role of selection is evident in his claim that 'successful plans' crystallize into institutions. The success alluded to is the success of the market place. Lachmann literally presented his theory of institutions as the sociological counterpart of the theory of competition in economics (ibid., 68). It is therefore clear that selection through competitive pressures is an important driver behind the process that creates and adjusts institutions.

Secondly, once an institution is in place, it has a certain permanence and is henceforth inherited by subsequent generations. Here imitation is the main causal factor. People copy successful patterns of behaviour and so extend the life time of an institution. The result is what Lachmann called the problem of the intergenerational succession of plans (ibid., 47). According to him, in historical time institutions may cast a shadow, which is often centuries long.[26]

Thirdly, mutations are a crucial component of Lachmann's theory of institutions. Institutions need to be flexible enough to adjust with changed circumstances. No society can function with continual flux in its institutional structure, but a society that never permits its institutional structure to change will suffer increasing inefficiencies (ibid., 89). The forces that allow institutions to adapt to changed circumstances are the same that explain their emergence. They are set in motion by the 'entrepreneurial skill' of the innovator who perceives an unexploited profit opportunity. The changes resulting from this innovation are subsequently promulgated by his successful imitators (ibid., 64 and 78).

Having explained the origin and function of institutions, Lachmann then addressed the difficult question of the institutional order. If institutions are to serve as the instruments of coordination, do they not themselves have to be coordinated? For Lachmann, this concerned the question of what binds different institutions into a comprehensive structure, but also what may cause this structure to fall apart. In other words, the question of the institutional order pointed to the conditions of integration as well as disintegration (ibid., 51).

It is here that Lachmann probed much deeper than Hayek in his theory of cultural evolution. The two questions raised above indicate that, unlike the latter, Lachmann did not approach the problem of the institutional order from the one-sided viewpoint of the tendency towards an economic order. For him the exact nature of the institutional order was an open question to be studied in terms of the friction between the need for coherence and permanence in the institutional structure on the one hand and the need for flexibility on the other hand.

Vaughn (1994, 156–157) finds this an interesting setup, but she complains that it does not allow him to solve his problem of order. According to her, Lachmann failed to develop a clearly articulated theory of institutions 'that generates confidence in the relative beneficence and coherence of the market order'. I agree with Vaughn that Lachmann did not present us with a tightly argued theoretical explanation of institutions which underpins the stability of the market order. But I do not think that a theory of this kind was his principal aim, so it is unfair to criticize him for failing to accomplish this goal.[27] What he considered a general theory of institutions consists of several reflections based on the aforementioned tension between permanence and flexibility. It is this aspect of the institutional structure which led him to conceive of the social world as a series of nested institutions. In a society of this type we may distinguish between external and internal institutions. The former constitutes, as it were, the outer framework of society such as the legal order. It is here that the need for permanence is most immanent. The latter refers to the institutions which gradually evolve as a result of market process and other forms of spontaneous action.

The theoretical core of this framework is the theory of praxeology which, as we know, can also not be used to support the stability of the economic order.[28] But Lachmann brought the analysis of this problem one step further by allowing us to assess the organizing force of society in terms of the different steps of the evolutionary process: What causes new institutions to arise? Why do they continue to exist and what makes them adjust to a changed world? These are valid questions which led Lachmann to assess the characteristics of the institutional order and to formulate several specific proposals how the institutional order can be strengthened in actual cases.

The limit of this theoretical exercise is formed by the fact that in reality institutions have a specific social and historical background. In terms of the evolutionary metaphor, this background is not surprising. Evolutionary forces exhibit path-dependency, which means that the process of building and reforming institutions takes place in historical time. Therefore, the precise functioning of the institutional structure can only be investigated if this historical track record is taken into account.

Lachmann (1971) showed a few powerful examples of what this type of analysis can teach us. One of his cases concerns the explanation of how the adoption of the system of collective bargaining in most countries in the Western world resulted in what he called 'deformation of social space', which is a nice term for what others would call economic crisis (ibid., 83–88). The deformation in question is the process of mounting wage and price inflation which in the 1960s and 1970s seemed unstoppable. Lachmann isolated collective wage bargaining as the main cause behind this process, but that is not the whole story. He stressed that when collective wage bargaining became accepted in many countries around the 1920s as the preferred institution for settling wage demands in the labour market, it seemed a valid answer to the economic conditions of this time. In particular, collective bargaining was embedded in an economic order sufficiently strong and stable to vouchsafe their beneficial character. However, the economic changes following the crisis of the 1930s and later developments led to the removal of several conditions which supported the checks and balances of the system. Under these conditions collective bargaining no longer formed the right answer to the right problem and started to form a threat to the coherence of the institutional order.

It is clear that this type of investigation does not promote our confidence in the relative beneficence of the market order, but the subject choice of this case study indicates that Lachmann had no intention of doing so.[29] For him, stabilizing and destabilizing forces were both valid parts of the institutional structure and thus had to be accounted for. His theory of institutions shows how this can be done. For all its shortcomings, it allows us to study the question of economic order and disorder in a unified theoretical framework, which treats evolution as an open process in historical time.

EVOLUTION AND INSTITUTIONS

The question whether evolution promotes economic order underlines the close relationship between evolutionary theory and institutional economics. This connection is studied in different corners of the economic discipline (Witt 1989, Hodgson 1993 and Loasby 1999). I shall highlight a few aspects of the importance of evolutionary theory for the role of institutions in economic theory. These are:

- The focus on routines as the basis of human decision making and the criticism of neoclassical rational choice theory that follows from it;
- The notion that institutions provide a sense of stability of the economic system but do not form an optimal solution to coordination failures. Uncertainty generates a process of institutional adjustment that contains both stabilizing and destabilizing elements;
- The call for a more multifarious approach to economic theory, which takes institutions seriously and is willing to combine the insights of

formal economic theory with other types of economic research such as historical analysis.

The Limits of Human Cognition

Like other parts of evolutionary economics covered in this chapter, institutional analysis rejects rational choice theory and focuses on routines and habits as the foundation of economic decision making. However, the distinctive contribution of this approach is that it treats the theory of decision making as an integral part of institutional analysis. We have seen that in evolutionary game theory non-rational rule-guided decision making is at best weakly underpinned. Likewise, Nelson and Winter (1982) merely assume that firms place routines at the heart of their business process, because casual empiricism suggests that they do. Proponents of the institutional approach in economics like Hodgson (1988) and Loasby (1999) take a more integral approach and argue that the economic decision making process is made up of rules that like other institutions are the product of an evolutionary process. As Hodgson (1998, 188) puts it, the human mind did not fall from the sky. It is a part of the human body that co-evolved with society and thus we need to explain the behavioural assumptions of economics in evolutionary terms. Likewise, Loasby (1999) explores the (physical) limits of human cognition in terms of network theories which present the brain as a classification structure shaped by the forces of evolution.[30]

To the average economist, this link between routines and the physiological characteristics of the human brain on the one hand and the economic decision making process on the other hand must seem outlandish, but it leads us to the very heart of the meaning and importance of institutions in economic theory. There is widespread agreement in this part of the literature that institutions must be seen as routinized forms of behaviour. Hodgson (1988, 125) adopts Veblen's definition of institutions as the 'settled habits of thought common to the generality of men'. They are the 'commonly held patterns of behaviour and habits of thought, of a routinized and durable nature, that are associated with people interacting in groups or larger collectives' (Hodgson 1993, 253).[31] The theory of institutions therefore comprises a theory of how people make decisions when they engage in economic decision making.[32]

This is a question that generally falls outside the scope of economic theory. Friedman's (1953) defence of the 'as if' approach to rationality has already been cited in this chapter. Today economists still habitually adopt rationality as one of their basic assumptions without ever questioning the relevance of this postulate. 'There are no $100 notes lying on the side walk' is one of the more popular phrases used by economists to support the plausibility of the rationality postulate.

Evolutionary theory shows that this complacency is unwarranted. Loasby (1999, 32) argues that there is a scarce resource involved in the process of decision making, namely cognition. This resource should be priced like other scarce resources, but rational choice theory simply ignores this question. It accords to agents the mental capacity to optimize any decision rule regardless of its complexity and the number of variables involved. But there is a real cost here that should be included in the calculation. This the energy cost of the supposedly rational procedures. According to Loasby, this cost is not trivial. Brain tissue is energetically among the most expensive tissues in the body and the brain accounts for about one-fifth of human energy requirements. In sum, there is nothing more economical than including this cost in the problem set of economics. Evolutionary theory should help to open up rather than close the black box of economic decision making.

When confronted with this issue, the proponents of rational choice theory retort that institutions will not resolve this problem. In their view, rule-governed behaviour imposes constraints on the free will and constraints of this kind demand a shadow price that needs to be accounted for in the optimization procedure (Hodgson 1998, 179). Implicitly, they argue that adding constraints via rules and other institutions leads to suboptimal outcomes, because as a matter of logic it reduces the maximum result attainable under the decision rule. According to this position, increasing the set of choices available to individual producers and consumers – that is more flexibility in the individual decision making process – is always welfare-improving.

Two remarks are in place. First, there is the ontological question of what free will means. What is the nature of freedom in rational choice theory? This theory assumes that self-interested individuals mechanistically choose the optimal outcome of the decision situation. Latsis (1976) called this a 'single-exit' decision situation to indicate that there is really only one option available, the optimal outcome. The rational choice is fully determined by the decision rule (that is, maximize utility) and the constraints such as prices and income, which are treated as givens. As a result, the notion of freedom in this context is a limited one. The individual is not even allowed to choose his own decision rule, which would open the door to decision situations that Latsis ascribed the label 'multiple exit'.

Second, in rational choice theory the freedom of will has the status of an absolute principle. But we need to probe deeper and ask what really determines economic decisions. It may then appear that people actually choose to constrain their set of options by wilfully adopting a rule of thumb. Hodgson (1988, 126) argues that the adoption of rules and habits can be an efficient response to deal with the complexity of everyday life. People economize on the need to gather information and to calculate the optimal choices by following a fixed rule. This is a choice that can be seen as rational and amenable to an optimization procedure. But Hodgson stresses that there is a part of human behaviour which is essentially unconscious and therefore requires another kind of explanation. Polanyi's 'tacit knowledge' is an example of this class of behaviour. To explain the emergence and function of such rules in economic decision making, we need to go beyond rational choice theory and allow for both conscious and unconscious aspects of human deliberation (Loasby 1999, 12 and Hodgson 1988, 144).[33]

From the institutional perspective, this conclusion is crucial because it touches upon the main problem of economics: How to explain the coordination of activities in a decentralized economic system? Institutions are a key factor in this process and if one ignores them, one misses a key aspect of how markets actually operate. A basic example of the coordinative role of institutions concerns imitation. People economize on cognition as a scarce resource by consciously or unconsciously copying the behaviour of others. The unintended by-product of this attempt to cope with the consequence of uncertainty is that it provides a basis for successful interaction with other people. We find ourselves using similar assumptions, similar taxonomies and similar methods of arguments. Such shared conventions make it easier to predict the behaviour of others and thus facilitate coordination. As Loasby (1999, 46) argues:[34]

> The institutions which we have already found indispensable for our own private purposes now suggest interdependent solutions to the problems of interdependence; our reliance on conventions and procedures, many of them adapted from other people, as a consequence of our cognitive limitations helps to resolve the coordination problem which result from those limitations.

However, Vanberg (1994, 64–65) argues that one should distinguish between cooperative rules like the one cited by Loasby and prisoner-dilemma-type rules, which are typically not self-enforcing. In the latter case there is no natural harmony between the private and social interests of the members of society due to the pay-off structure of the game in question. One may, therefore, not conclude that all rules and social institutions promote coordination.

Stabilizing and Destabilizing Forces

We have seen in this chapter that evolutionary game theory addresses the issue of coordination in terms of the evolutionary stable strategy, ESS. Here, the focus is foremostly on proving the stability and uniqueness of the ESS as an equilibrium result. In contrast, the institutional branch of evolutionary theory investigates coordination in terms that remind us of Lachmann: Economic change is not controlled by a strong tendency towards equililbrium. Evolution proceeds as a tug of war between stabilizing and destabilizing forces.

The essence of equilibrium in the institutional variant of evolutionary economics is that of a stable process through time. This notion is used loosely and does not rest on precise definitions like ESS and replicator dynamics in game theory or stochastic search equilibrium in Nelson and Winter (1982). Loasby (1991) isolates equilibrium as a characteristic of one of the three stages of the evolutionary processes. These stages are the generation of variety (mutation), the reduction of variety (selection) and the persistence both of the variants selected and their environment. He argues that the factors which are responsible for the persistence, which is necessary for evolution, might be analysed in terms of equilibrium. Similarly, Hodgson (1998, 171) argues that institutionalism substitutes the concept of socio-economic order, arising upon variety at the micro-level, for equilibrium as a mechanistic metaphor.

Loasby believes that equilibrium analysis in this sense may provide useful insights, but in evolutionary theory its role is necessarily a limited one. The problem is that there are many evolutionary processes which depend on very different timescales of persistence (Loasby 1999, 25). The result is that equilibrium must be defined over different time frames and is therefore context-dependent. Equilibrium in institutional theory is 'history-laden' which means that it cannot perform the central theoretical role it has in neoclassical economics (Hodgson 1998, 174).

Another inference is that we are dealing with processes over time that lack stability and are liable to quick changes. It is necessary to stress this point, because it marks an important difference with biological evolution. Darwin's process of natural selection works slowly over a long period of time, because for species to become established a stable environment is generally necessary so that their distinctive characteristics can show their superiority in the contest. Compare this slow process of gradual adjustment to the fickleness of the economy. The environment faced by the consumer, the firm or the national economy changes rapidly and sometimes suddenly as prices fluctuate, stock markets boom and bust, governments change, wars erupt and natural disasters strike. A smooth Darwinian process of gradual natural selection of the fittest is thus ruled out (Hodgson 1988, 141).

This conclusion refers to the question whether economic changes must be seen as mutations of a gradualist type or of a saltationist type, involving leaps and jumps (Vromen 1995, 215). It is clear that economic evolution does not proceed in classic Darwinian terms, where slow changes occur in generation after generation, and the typical or 'equilibrium' form of an organization changes gradually over time (Rosenberg 1994). Instead, it can proceed by succession of periods of stability and crises, of apparent equilibrium and cumulative instability (Loasby 1999 and Hodgson 1988). Two questions now emerge. First, how does one explain the establishment of relative permanence that make up the equilibrium phase? And, second, does evolutionary theory provide the tools to investigate the complex interaction between stabilizing and destabilizing forces?

We have seen in the previous section that the Austrians address the first question in terms of the spontaneous order that is said to arise as the unintended consequence of profit seeking entrepreneurship in a free competitive system. Institutionalists like Hodgson find this explanation lacking, because it constrains analysis to a given means-ends framework.[35] The theory of human action addresses purposive behaviour which takes the preferences and purposes of the individual as given. But Hodgson (1988, 138) argues that such preferences should be seen as endogenous, which opens the door to dynamic processes that disrupt rather than promote economic order. The appeal of the Austrians to an evolutionary conception of economic order is therefore 'laudable', but it lacks a crucial part of the evolutionary process. In evolutionary terms, the spontaneous order stresses the reduction of variety through competitive selection rather than the generation of variety that may push the market process off the path towards equilibrium.

The answer to a more complete image of economic evolution must come from the study of habits, rules and other social institutions.[36] They form semi-permanent structures that may give the economic process a much needed sense of stability (Hodgson 1998, 171). But how to explain the emergence of such routinized patterns of behaviour? To achieve this task, we need to answer the difficult question when individuals require fixed rules as a response to uncertainty and complexity and when flexibility and adjustment of fixed rules is wanted as a reflection of changed circumstances (Lachmann 1971, see the previous section). This trade-off between permanence and flexibility is studied in a variety of ways. We have seen that Nelson and Winter (1982) apply Markov chain analysis to explain the formation of routines as the outcome of a trial and error process. Witt (1997) uses first order cubic difference equations to model the interplay between what he calls self-regulating and self-augmenting features of the economic process.[37] Evolutionary game theory has also increasingly been used to study how stable, self-sustaining social patterns of behaviour can emerge spontaneously (Binmore and Samuelson 1994, Peyton Young 1998). Evolutionary psychology provides another example of a theory aimed to explain why the human brain is willing to adopt fixed rules of conduct.

On closer inspection, it appears that evolutionary theory does not provide us with a definite answer to the question why routines and habits emerge. The proponents of the evolutionary approach do not even agree on what social level this equilibrium should pertain. For Hodgson (1993) the stability of social relations is above all an issue of macro theory. Without much underpinning, he argues that macrostability of economic relations arises as the result of the evolutionary higgling and haggling that goes on at the micro- and mesoeconomic level. For him, this result justifies the autonomy of macroeconomics as a scientific discipline and allows economics to study where government intervention may improve economic welfare by controlling the course of macroeconomic variables (see also Hodgson 1998, 171–173).

In contrast, the Post Keynesian Brian Loasby strongly leans towards the Austrian research agenda of Lachmann and the transaction cost economics of Coase. Like the Austrians, he investigates the impact of institutions on economic order bottom-up. His starting point is Menger's conception of economic planning under uncertainty. His leading thought is that 'uncertainty does not mean an end to planning; indeed it makes planning more important, because now, instead of being a prelude to action, it becomes a part of the process of managing a business, or one's life' (Loasby 1999, 117). Institutional analysis, then, is meant to study how institutions help the individual to cope with the consequences of uncertainty. This leads Loasby to investigate transaction costs, the scope of the firm and the rationale of market exchange. Potentially, an agenda of this kind may become very broad, given the variety of such institutional arrangements in actual economic conditions. But Loasby tries to maintain a degree of theoretical coherence by adopting Menger's typology of goods and markets as an analytical benchmark. As we have seen earlier, this typology centers on the time structure of consumption and production, which brings the element of uncertainty into focus (Loasby 1999, 115).[38]

The evolutionary perspective broadens the scope of analysis and traces the development of institutions through time in terms of their intended and unintended consequences. Perhaps surprisingly, this approach does not lead Loasby to support a kind of hydraulic Keynesianism like Hodgson. The role of the equilibrium concept remains the modest one that I have noted above. Permanence is necessary for evolutionary development to continue, but this element of equilibrium is bound to be disturbed by the forces of selection and mutation. The role of the familiar notion of market equilibrium is a case in point (Loasby 1999, 127). It is clear that, on the one hand, the particular institutions which shape a market are the result of supply and demand, given that they are ultimately responsible for the existence of this particular market. On the other hand, it also clear that the pattern of supply and demand in a market is a consequence of the institutions of that market. Put differently, it matters whether a central auctioneer is trying to match supply and demand on one of today's (electronic) stock markets, or whether people negotiate the terms of exchange bilaterally on a typical street market. Viewed on an evolutionary time scale, we must accept that equilibrium seen as a balance of forces is of a transient nature and henceforth of limited analytical value.

TOWARDS A MORE MULTIFARIOUS ECONOMICS

Shall the concept of evolution supersede the concept of equilibrium in the future of economics? I do not think that this race is yet run. Rosenberg (1994) clinically dissects the differences between evolutionary theory in biology and economics. He concludes that there is little chance that the evolutionary conceptions that proved so successful in biology will also work in economics. Ironically, the main problem, according to Rosenberg, is that we lack the most important feature that justifies evolutionary thinking in biology: independent evidence that there is a stable equilibrium to be explained like the distribution of gene frequencies. In biology, equilibrium is a proposition that can be submitted to empirical tests. But in economics, Rosenberg (1994, 399) observes, there is nothing comparable to the observed stability of gene frequencies that needs to be explained. We may appeal to phenomena like price stability, but the occurrence of this event is conditioned by a strict ceteris paribus clause, which makes it hard to test. Moreover, economic theory does not even have a theoretical proof of price stability in the case of interdependent markets. Rosenberg concludes that it is senseless to apply the toolkit of Darwinian evolution to economic questions, which focuses attention on Lamarckian evolution. However, the surrender of the Darwinian approach to economic evolution in favour of a Lamarckian one is dangerous, given that in the latter approach 'anything can evolve into anything by any means' (ibid., 405). Hardly a recommendation, one is inclined to think.

Most evolutionary economists are not so naive to believe that the transplantation of biological conceptions to economics can be done without problems. There is widespread understanding that Darwinian evolution functions differently than economic processes. Theorists like Loasby, Witt, Lachmann and Hodgson warn their audience against bold evolutionary generalizations based on dubious biological laws.[39] The focus should be on those elements of biological evolution that may aid our understanding of economic processes. The scope of this overlapping area is still an open issue. People like Hodgson (1993) believe the shared field of study to be so considerable that economists should consider building a new paradigm on the basis of evolutionary concepts. He argues that biology is about to overwhelm the prestige that physics has enjoyed for three centuries and is earmarked to become the leading science of the twenty-first century. He states that the world may be impoverished by 'rapacious economic activity' if economics does not partake in this success and continues to disregard what he calls the 'biotic foundations' of economic life (Hodsgon 1993, 267).

This is a challenging claim, but I doubt whether Hodgson himself lives up to his own promise. Take the difficult question of the balance between stability and flexibility that comes to the fore in institutional analysis. Can evolutionary biology help us solve this question? Hodgson (1993) does not provide the definite answer. He merely treats his readers on several difficult sounding new conceptions that are said to capture the nature of biotic life in economics. In one place he refers to the idea of autopoiesis that comes from the modern theory of complex systems. Like living animals and plants, autopoietic systems maintain an autonomy and continuity of pattern despite the endless turnover of their constituents. 'Clearly, economic systems may well exhibit autopoietic self-replication and growth' (ibid., 262). But in another place he adopts the term chreodic development to capture the butterfly effect in dynamic, non-lineair systems (ibid., 205). The result of this effect is that very different evolutionary outcomes may emerge from small variancies in initial conditions, an outcome which seems in conflict with autopoiesis. But in a more general sense chreodic development seems to include a similar notion of stability, which Hodgson describes as 'homeorhetic' (from the Greek *rheo*, to flow). This term indicates the stabilizing tendency of evolutionary changes taking place over time. Combined, an image results of economic evolutionary processes, where small perturbations can take place but the system often is pulled back on to a 'chreodic channel'. In yet a third place we find Hodgson supporting the socioeconomic equivalent of 'punctuated equilibria' in biology, which has a similar function (ibid., 264).

Are these evolutionary conceptions internally consistent and what is their practical use in economics? Hodgson does not tell. His quest for the biotic roots of economic life ends with a plea for the revival of old-fashioned Keynesianism involving the analysis of economic aggregates. This is a field where we can apply the chreod, because in the economic context state intervention is said to be able to change the contours of chreodic development (ibid., 207). However, autopoiesis is also operative in the shape of the macroeconomic system that can be regarded as a self-organizing system due to its own intrinsic set of institutional structures (ibid., 265). Without any evidence Hodgson then claims that the national economic systems of most developed industrial countries satisfy this latter criterion and can thus be called an autopoiesis. The justification for this statement is the 'one important unifying component' of national economic systems, namely culture. Through a common culture, agents form compatible perceptions and complex modes of communication and interaction. This establishes self-reinforcing norms of perception and behaviour which allow the economy to exhibit some structural stability for long periods of time.

From the perspective of today, the identification of national borders with a common culture raises many questions. In my opinion, if there is any lesson to be drawn from the globalization of economic trade in recent years, it is that cultural identity is at stake in virtually all countries of the world (Huntington 1996 and Wetenschappelijke Raad voor het Regeringsbeleid 2007). Of course, Hodgson recognized that institutions like national culture are liable to change. He remarked that even gradual change can put such strain on a system that there can be outbreaks of conflict or crises, leading to changes in actions and attitudes (Hodgson 1993, 263). I would argue that it is this kind of institutional realignment that we are currently experiencing in the Western world and far beyond.

The question is how to investigate such processes that may have profound economic and social impact. Evolutionary theory offers many valuable hints. However, if the application of evolutionary theory leads to a stapling of vague concepts like those introduced by Hodgson, I fear that this approach has limited value added. It confuses rather than clarifies the analysis. In the end, Hodgson does not offer a ready made theory that is able to replace the neoclassical mainstream. His principal contribution is the description of a methodology that could help us build an alternative economics based on the biological metaphor. The starting point of this alternative is the insight that a grand unifying theory on a par with general equilibrium analysis is not forthcoming. In the domain of disequilibrium analysis, economics needs to join forces with other disciplines such as sociology, psychology and history (Hodgson 1993, 266).[40] What we need is specific and historically located approaches to analysis (Hodgson 1998, 168). Hodgson sees this as an important lesson of evolutionary biology. This science has a limited number of laws and general principles by which origin and development can be explained. But investigation of the evolution of a specific organism requires detailed data concerning the organism and its environment, and also specific explanations relevant to the species under consideration. Compare this to physics – the hallowed example of economics in the past 100 years – and its hunt for a 'theory of everything'.[41]

The general lesson of evolutionary economics is therefore that our science requires a multifarious approach to the analysis of economic change. As Hodgson (1998) states, the institutional approach to evolutionary theory must follow the example of biology and move from general ideas concerning human agency, institutions and the evolutionary nature of economic processes to specific ideas and theories, related to specific economic institutions or types of economy. Accordingly, there are multiple levels and types of theory linked by the common interpretation of core concepts like habits and institutions. This leaves scope for the application and combination of many different theories that in economics are often seen as belonging to competing paradigms, such as Keynesian macroeconomics, old and new institutionalism, Austrian market process theory, Coase's transaction cost economics and in some cases even old-fashioned neoclassical price theory (Hodgson 1988, 140). However, specific theories allow us to raise specific questions such as: what is the explanatory power of this particular theory? It is in this sense, by moving from the abstract to the concrete, that evolutionary economics still has to prove its value as a tool for the analysis of disequilibrium phenomena.[42]

NOTES

1. Nelson and Winter deny that they are setting up a straw man version of neoclassical economics. They say 'that it is a caricature to associate orthodoxy with the analysis of static equilibria, but it is no caricature to remark that continued reliance on equilibrium analysis, even in its more flexible forms, still leaves the discipline largely blind to phenomena associated with historical change' (Nelson and Winter 1982, 8).
2. For a description of the different meanings of evolutionary economics, see Hodgson (1999, Chapter 6).
3. As Hodgson (1993, 32) puts it, the evolutionary approach in economics 'enhances a concern with irreversible and ongoing processes in time, with long-run development rather than short-run marginal adjustments'. See also Nelson and Winter (1982, 10).
4. The history of game theory forms an important part of the history of equilibrium theory and should for that reason deserve a more elaborate discussion than is possible in the context of this chapter. The reader is referred to Schmidt (1990), Myerson (1999) and Giocoli (2003) for an analysis of the historical development of Nash equilibrium and other aspects of game theory.
5. For a formal definition, see Gibbons (1992, 8).
6. One answer is that such equilibrium concepts help to understand the strategic structure of different games. See Mailath (1998, 1349, n5). The question remains what the scientific value of this knowledge is, given that it rests on assumptions that are evidently in conflict with reality.
7. The classic reference is Maynard Smith (1982).
8. This type of evolution is defined as Lamarckian, because it assumes that the behavioural traits themselves are the object of inheritance. This reproductive mechanism is generally opposed to Darwinian evolution, which operates on the level of genes. However, Vromen (1995, 94) calls this opposition false. He argues that the acquired traits produce a change in the genotype and these altered genes are inherited by the organism's offspring. Biologists generally reject Lamarckianism, because no mechanism has been accepted as

an explanation of how an acquired character would be encoded in the genes and thus passed on to future progeny. See Hodgson (1993, 40).

9. This result must not be seen as an optimal outcome of the adjustment process. 'Best adjusted' is here defined as relative to the strategies that are available in the strategy set. For evolutionary economists, optimality is a concept that is directly related to the equilibrium tools of 'orthodox' neoclassical economics, which need revision or, in some cases, are rejected altogether.
10. Formally, the replicator dynamic states that the share of the agents playing a given strategy grows at a rate equal to the difference between the average pay-off of that strategy and the average pay-off of the population as a whole. See Vega-Redondo (1996, 48).
11. For example, ESS does not exist in most asymmetric games. A game is asymmetric when a player's strategy depends on his role in a specific matching. In symmetric games players can switch positions (row versus column player) without affecting the outcome. The problem with asymmetric games is that ESS in such a game is a strict equilibrium (this is an equilibrium that cannot be improved upon). But most games do not have strict equilibria and so ESS's do not exist for most asymmetric games. See Mailath (1998, 1361–1363).
12. An additional complexity is that it may take a very long time for a stochastic evolutionary model to establish equilibrium. See Samuelson (2002, 60).
13. This conclusion is related to the criticism of Vromen (1995, 190) that in evolutionary game theory rules are analyzed in an institutional vacuum. Another example of this vacuum concerns the assumption of global random matching. This mode of interaction is postulated, but a truly dynamic theory should be able to analyze how patterns of interaction endogenously evolve. See also Vega-Redondo (1996, 195).
14. Alchian struggled with the fact that due to uncertainty in actual markets it is impossible to establish a firm relationship between the attempt to maximize profits and realizing positive profits. He therefore proposed to focus directly on the actual result and to use the assumption of optimization calculus as a plausible approximation. See Alchian (1950, 213).
15. Nelson and Winter do not use the vocabulary of Lakatos's methodology of scientific research programs, but their approach naturally suggests interpretation in terms of the MRSP. For an example, see Langlois (1994, 35).
16. Reference is made to modern general equilibrium theory and related theorizing of the past two decades. See Nelson and Winter (1982, 5).
17. In another place, they claim that they have no choice but to build a static equilibrium model, given that their aim is to scrutinize the evolutionary defense of orthodox 'from within'. Since this theory is restricted to the domain of static equilibrium analysis, they argue that their model must likewise be a static equilibrium model, for '[o]rthodoxy offers no other target' (ibid., 144).
18. This interpretation is validated by the claim of Nelson and Winter (1982, 184) that the quantitative track record of orthodox theory is a poor one. They argue that the

'econometric equations consistent with an evolutionary approach' have the potential to improve on this result. In addition, they claim that their evolutionary theory constitutes a broader 'master theory', because formal orthodox theory fails to explicate the problems involved in the dynamic process of economic change. This means that orthodox theory tends to neglect a number of important issues such as the dynamics of search and selection. The explicit recognition of these dynamic issues in evolutionary theory 'brings a whole new range of phenomena into theoretical view'. See Nelson and Winter (1982, 175).

19. See for example Langlois (1994), Loasby (1999) and Hodgson (1999). Hodgson praises the leading role Nelson and Winter have played in putting evolutionary economics on the agenda, but he also says that their book has had a limited positive reception among heterodox economists. This was due to the fact that it occupies 'the uncomfortable no-man's land between neoclassical theorists who do not care about empirical realism, on the one hand, and institutionalists and allies who reject neoclassical assumptions, on the other' (Hodgson 1999, 167).
20. For the graph marking this ascent, see Hodgson (1999, 168).
21. The interested reader is referred to Vanberg (1986), Chapter 12 of Hodgson (1993) and the special issue of *Cultural Dynamics* dealing with this subject, see Lavoie (1990).
22. Hayek (1967a, 34) also believed that the conception of a mind fully explaining itself involves a logical contradiction. The root of this contradiction lies in the theory of complexity. Hayek (1952, 185) argued that the capacity of any explaining agents must be limited to objects with a structure possessing a degree of complexity lower than their own. The explanation of neurological processes generating human thought does not satisfy this condition.
23. Note that by following Menger in this regard, Lachmann inadvertedly incorporated a biological metaphor into his theory of institutions.
24. 'The theory we are attempting to establish [the general theory of institutions, BT] aims at the reduction of certain social phenomena to human mental acts as manifested in plans' (Lachmann 1971, 74).
25. However, Lachmann did recognize that in reality many institutions are the deliberate design of humans and he incorporated this fact into his theory. He therefore saw the institutional structure as being a mix of institutions of deliberate and undeliberate design.
26. He stressed that the world in which we are planning today with its houses, streets, parks, means of communications et cetera is largely the result of the cumulative result of the plans made by our ancestors. As part of this inheritage, '[s]uccessful institutions often bear the unmistakable imprint of the spirit of their creators even after centuries of change' (Lachmann 1971, 47 and 71).
27. Lachmann developed his theory of institutions as part of his reflections on the *Legacy of Max Weber* (1971). As a student of Gustav Schmoller, Weber was strongly attracted to the methods of the German Historical School, but unlike Schmoller he did not reject theoretical analysis as a matter of principle. Rather, his method can be seen as occupying a midway position between theoretical and historical research. Weber's intention to end

the *Methodenstreit* by trying to mediate between Schmoller and Menger bears testimony to this aim.

28. See Chapter 12.
29. The evident extension of Lachmann's analysis is to ask why an institution like collective bargaining did not timely adjust to the changed economic environment. After all, the 'deformation of the social space' caused by this institution crucially depends on the speed by which this adjustment process takes place.
30. Vromen (2004) classifies this approach as 'revionist', because it leads the practitioners of this discipline to call for a 'friendly' amendment of standard (neoclassical) economic theory. But in the case of Loasby and Hodgson this label is inappropriate. They are clear examples of what Vromen defines as the 'revolutionaries'. However, there is a clear link with evolutionary psychology that tries to identify psychological mechanisms which allowed individuals to overcome past evolutionary problems.
31. In similar vein, see Lachmann (1971), Nelson and Winter (1982), Vromen (1995) and Loasby (1999).
32. It has to be stressed that the notion of an institution has a wide scope. It encompasses not simply organizations such as firms and banks, but also integrated and systematic social entities, such as money, language and law. Hodgson (1998, 179) discusses the common characteristics of institutions in this broad definition.
33. There is also the ontological issue that Hodgson (1988, 128) believes that habits are real. He concludes this on the basis of what we know about the working of the human brain. He also cites different empirical studies which indicate that habit-governed behaviour has real economic existence. An example is that consumer spending is subject to inertia, because it depends on preceding consumption. Hence consumers are not forward-looking and hence rational planners, but to a certain extent rely on fixed rules while planning their consumption expenditures.
34. For a similar view, see Hodgson (1988, 132–133). One consequence of the coordination-enhancing role of institutions is that in a highly complex world, and despite uncertainty and information overload, regular and predictable behaviour is possible. See Heiner (1983).
35. We have seen in Chapter 14 that Austrians like Kirzner, O'Driscoll and Rizzo strongly deny this.
36. I here use rules and habits interchangeably. However, in a more precise definition a distinction can be made. For example, Hodgson (1998, 185) argues that rule-following may be conscious and deliberative, while habits lack this quality. According to him, habitual action is characteristically unexamined. He also says that rules do not necessarily have a self-actuating or autonomic quality but, by repeated application, a rule can become a habit. This latter possibility motivates my use of the terms as close substitutes.
37. Witt (1997, 506) defines self-augmenting features as the self-destabilizing forces of the economic system. The driving force behind this disequilibrium force is the search of agents for new knowledge and innovative products and services.

38. A typical Keynesian element in Loasby's work is that he also emphasizes the role of money as an institution which role it is to reduce transaction costs. See Loasby (1999, 115–117).

39. For example, Witt (1997) sees the interplay between self-regulating and self-augmenting forces as an essential similarity between biological and economic processes. But he also warns that the laws governing these processes are of a very different nature. In biophysical systems self-organizing structures are governed by a complicated chain of chemical reactions. In the economic domain, by contrast, it is intelligent human action and imagination that drive the development, and these follow their own laws. See Witt (1997, 497).

40. There is a certain irony in this, since, as Vromen (1995, 216) remarks, evolutionary theory was once seen as attractive to economists, because it held out the hope of getting around troublesome psychological and historical issues which emerged in institutional analysis. It is now evident that this hope was a chimera. Vromen concludes that '[p]sychological and historical issues will have to be tackled even by those who are willing to accept an economic evolutionary theory in which all forces and factors but one are accepted' (ibid.).

41. It should be noted that the proponents of general equilibrium analysis in economics like Debreu (1991) concede that GE analysis will not furnish a grand unifying theory, a hope that once turned the attention of economists towards this modeling technique.

42. By this I mean that I would like to see greater stress in evolutionary economics on the need to use the evolutionary approach in applied economic studies. See for example the collection of applied studies in Saviotti (2003).

16. Disequilibrium Foundations of Equilibrium Analysis

INTRODUCTION

The previous chapters discussed a variety of approaches towards the analysis of disequilibrium phenomena. It has been shown that the common motive of these approaches is the dissatisfaction with the current state of knowledge in mainstream equilibrium analysis. This type of analysis is said to lack a relevant economic meaning. It is generally considered excessively mathematical, said to rely on unrealistic assumptions and to derive results that are never confronted with the conditions of economic reality. In short, economic equilibrium is a condition that pertains to a certain class of mathematical models, but it seems entirely disconnected with the mechanisms that rule actual economies.

The aspect that plays a crucial role in this analysis of the current state of knowledge in equilibrium economics is the problem of disequilibrium adjustments. This problem refers to the ability of a competitive economy to improve coordination between decentralized decision units through price and quantity adjustments. The lay public considers the explanation of this coordinative process one of the key achievements of economic science. It is not for nothing that the invisible hand has become one of the best known metaphors in economics. But what is the actual state of affairs in the field of disequilibrium theory? For sure, in partial analysis there is a rich variety of explanations for adjustment processes in many different cases. But in general analysis this is not the case. On the contrary. The theory of global stability in general equilibrium analysis is said to have reached a complete impasse. Ingrao and Israel (1990, 359) conclude in their review of this literature that research in this direction must be considered as having come to a 'dead end'.

This conclusion raises serious questions about the validity of general equilibrium analysis. What use is the existence proof of general economic equilibrium if we have no clue whether the establishment of a state of this kind has a chance of survival, that is, whether it is stable and does not risk tumbling down like an egg standing on its head? In addition, for the policy conclusion that one wishes to ground in equilibrium analysis, it is useful to know which equilibrium adjustments will converge upon, if equilibrium is not unique. This chapter explores the answer to these questions by looking at the disequilibrium foundation of equilibrium analysis. The scope of this section is therefore different from that of the previous ones. The economic schools previously discussed generally considered their disequilibrium approach a radical alternative to the equilibrium analysis of the neoclassical school. I now explore the potential that the neoclassical doctrine itself offers for the development of disequilibrium theories as a support of equilibrium analysis.

STABILITY AND DISEQUILIBRIUM TRADING

The first issue to be addressed in this context is the question of the disequilibrium explanation of the coordination process underpinning the establishment of a competitive general economic equilibrium. As the classic question of Koopmans (1957) and Arrow (1959) runs, if everyone is assumed to be a price taker, then who changes prices? It appears that without the fiction of the Walrasian auctioneer, there is a serious theoretical lacuna in general equilibrium analysis. This theory explains equilibrium prices in an existence proof of equilibrium via a system of simultaneous equations. But about the dynamic behaviour of this price system outside equilibrium very little is known. I shall briefly sketch the developments in this field.

Why is the question of dynamic price adjustment so important to general equilibrium theory? We have seen that Walras believed that real markets would solve the problem of finding the equilibrium price vector in a matter of minutes (see Chapter 9). In light of this belief, it is not remarkable that the issue of stability did not play a large role in the equilibrium analysis of Walras and his followers.[1] This attitude lasted until well in the 1940s when Samuelson in his influential text *Foundations of Economic Analysis* (1947) questioned the very existence of something like an unstable equilibrium. He considered the question of out-of-equilibrium behaviour of secondary importance and called upon his readers to consider the number of times that they had seen 'an egg standing upon its end' (Samuelson 1947, 5). However, he also realized that dynamic analysis is a necessary supplement of equilibrium analysis. The determination of equilibrium is the first step towards a comparative static analysis of economic changes. But in order to compare two equilibria, one needs a to assume a degree of stability. How can one otherwise assume that the disruption of equilibrium A leads to the establishment of a new equilibrium position B? Or that B is that is end point of the changes set in motion by the disruption of A, instead of a yet unknown position C? To answer such questions we need an explanation of dynamic changes. As Samuelson (1947, 262–263) put it:

> The problem of stability of equilibrium cannot be discussed except with reference to dynamical considerations, however implicit and rudimentary. We find ourselves confronted with this paradox: in order for the comparative-statics analysis to yield fruitful results, we must first develop a theory of dynamics.

Fisher (1983) put the need for a disequilibrium foundation of equilibrium analysis a bit stronger. He raised the simple question, why focus on the analysis of equilibrium positions in the first place? The classical answer to that question is that such positions seem to have a permanent and therefore structural character, because they operate as centers of attraction. Disequilibrium is considered transient and of a temporal nature. Why waste energy on the study of things that have no lasting effect?

But Fisher (1983, 3) argued that this defense of the equilibrium approach involves a logical error. He argued that showing that disequilibrium points will not be maintained is far from sufficient to justify analyzing only equilibria. In his opinion, equilibrium analysis logically requires two assumptions about the dynamics of what happens out of equilibrium. The first one is the point mentioned above. The system must be stable. That is, it must converge to some equilibrium. Second, such convergence must take place relatively quickly. We cannot use comparative statics, unless we know that the move from A to B is sufficiently rapid, so that the system, reacting to a given parameter shift, gets close to B before parameters shift once more.

The point to stress at this stage is that in GE analysis disequilibrium theory has a specific goal. This is the need to substantiate the assumption of stable rather than unstable equilibrium positions. Samuelson not only raised this point, but also gave stability theory an important new boost. This was done by formalizing Walras's idea of tatonnement as a set of price adjustment equations:[2]

$$dP_i = F^i[Z_i(\mathbf{P})] \text{ unless } P_i = 0 \text{ and } Z_i(\mathbf{P}) < 0$$

In which case: $dP_i = 0$.

This is the well-known aggregate excess demand function, expressing that the price of the *i*th commodity adjusts in the same direction as excess demand for that commodity, the exact adjustment being a continuous function of excess demand. The exception to this occurs where such a rule would require that a good which is already free and in excess supply be given a negative price, in which case the price is simply left at zero.

The early literature addressing the local and general stability of the tatonnement process used this function under the assumption of gross substitutability.[3] This investigation did not get very far, because it introduced conditions which lacked economic meaning. For example, a necessary and sufficient condition for local stability is that the principal minors of the Jacobian of the excess demand functions alternate in sign. But what is the economic meaning of this condition?[4] The problem of the proof of global stability is that it requires severe restrictions on the aggregate excess demand function, such as the weak axiom of revealed preference. This axiom makes excellent sense in terms of individual behaviour, but there is no good reason to impose it on aggregate demand functions. The Sonnenschein-Debreu-Mantel results of the 1970s destroyed the initial conjecture of Arrow, Block and Hurwicz (1959) that the tatonnement process was always globally stable.[5] The disappointment caused by these negative results explains the long period of standstill in research in this field (Ingrao and Israel 1990, 343).

A parallel development followed a different approach and casted off the straightjacket of tatonnement. This inspired the non-tatonnement process of price adjustment, which allowed for trading at false prices. The best-known result of this approach is the Hahn-Negishi theorem of global stability of non-tatonnement. This provides a process of price adjustment converging at equilibria without specifying the form of the demand functions, but at the price of the very strong assumption that the markets are orderly at all times.[6] Even Hahn himself has more than once conceded that this assumption casts doubt on the realism and relevance of this approach (for example Hahn 1961). Another problem is that the Hahn-process of non-tatonnement combines the idea of trade taking place at disequilibrium prices with an auctioneer who changes prices. The two processes alternate. Hahn assumed that as long as individuals can gain from trading, they will engage in disequilibrium trading. But as soon as trade stops, prices change as a function of aggregate excess demand, until new trading opportunities arise. Of course, the retention of the illustre auctioneer does not add to the realism of this disequilibrium theory and fails to answer to the core question: Who changes prices in the competitive economy?

A number of authors have subsequently tried to extend this type of analysis. For brevity's sake, I shall restrict the present discussion to the follow-up of Fisher (1983). Fisher developed a proof of global stability based on the aforementioned Hahn-process. His core innovations were the following two elements. First, he rejected Hahn's assumption of a central price setting body like the auctioneer. In his model prices are negotiated bilaterally. Each good is assumed to represent a seller who calls a price for his good. The other side of the market is made up of buyers who are searching for the right match to satisfy their demands. Second, Fisher considered it essential that individual agents are consciously aware of the fact that they face disequilibrium trading opportunities. He thus substituted a vector of individual excess demand function for the aggregate excess demand function mentioned above.

Fisher (1983, 32) argued that the Hahn-process is a very convenient way to formalize a disequilibrium price setting process based on these assumptions. For one, in the Hahn process target utilities fall out of equilibrium. These are the utilities which agents would achieve if they could complete their transactions. Such declining target utilities are a sign that in disequilibrium plans are not all compatible. In the Hahn process, this leads to the adjustment that such people have to lower their expectations until equilibrium is reached and everyone can in fact attain the utility he anticipates.[7]

However, this does not mean that the Hahn process is conceptually without its problems. The main problem remains the familiar question, who sets prices? In Fisher's model, individual sellers operate like little auctioneers. This means that they adjust their prices in exactly the same way as the Walrasian auctioneer does on the basis of the aggregate demand function, given above. They call a price believing that it represents a kind of market clearing price. When they perceive excess demand or supply, they move their price up or down, depending on the sign of the perceived excess demand. In other words, they behave as if they are setting equilibrium prices. But, then, what is the difference between the equilibrium and the disequilibrium perspective? Now we do assume that every agent is a price setter rather than a price taker, and no one takes this opportunity to do something different. The disequilibrium approach taken by the Hahn process just mimics the outcome of the Walrasian model. From a disequilibrium perspective, we would like agents to take advantage from the fact that they face a declining demand curve, but in the Hahn process they seem to ignore this fact.

This raises difficult problems for the theory of stability in general equilibrium analysis. Fisher has demonstrated that global stability can be proved, provided we assume that all sellers foolhardedly maintain their equilibrium beliefs and fail to explore and exploit their ability to control prices and quantities demanded. Suppose, however, that we allow sellers to realize what is happening and to know the declining demand curves they face. Can we nevertheless get to competitive equilibrium allowing sellers to use that information in a profit-maximizing way? Fisher considers this a wholly open question in general equilibrium analysis. Attempts to develop disequilibrium theories along these lines have been typified by him as 'fairy tales' (Fisher 1983, 50 and 156).[8]

The current state of affairs in the theory of stability using the non-tatonnement process is that it cannot be shown to result in a Walrasian competitive equilibrium. In the model of Fisher (1983), the end point of the disequilibrium process is left open. Fisher stated that he was unable to include an element of learning in his model to eradicate the monopolistically competitive elements, which can characterize disequilibrium. As a result, his model is silent on the question whether or not the equilibrium asymptotically attained is Walrasian.

However, it is interesting to note that as a follow-up of the Fisher model, Schinkel (2001) did manage to develop a disequilibrium theory with learning elements. But his Bayesian extension of the Fisher model neither generates a Walrasian competitive equilibrium as the outcome of the disequilibrium adjustment process. Nor does Schinkel want to find such equilibria. The outcomes of his model are non-Walrasian by construction, because he believes that only equilibria should be considered that are the outcome of interesting dynamics (Schinkel 2001, 213). Hence, he rejects the hunt for conditions to rule out unwanted equilibria. In his vision, the onus should be on the characteristics of the dynamical disequilibrium process and equilibria should be appreciated for the fact that they are the limits of this process.

There is another important proviso to Fisher's disequilibrium foundation of equilibrium analysis. In his model, individual agents are aware of disequilibrium opportunities and act upon this recognition. This is a fundamental aspect of Fisher's disequilibrium theory. But what if agents perceive similar impulses when the system finally reaches equilibrium? Fisher (1983, 87) considered the following scenario. 'Equilibrium is about to be attained. Church bells are ready to ring announcing the great moment. Just as celebrations begin to break out, however, a non-negligible number of agents sit up and say: "Wait a minute. The price of gold-plated chocolate bars will go up tomorrow"'. It is clear that such insights lead to actions which delay convergence to equilibrium. And if it keeps being repeated, convergence may never occur.[9]

For Fisher, this outcome was unacceptable. He introduced the assumption of 'no favourable surprise' to rule out the occurrence of sudden optimistic revisions in agents' expectations. Of course, he did not pretend that this is a realistic assumption. But he considered it a necessary first step, if we want to prove that the economy at least has a tendency to return to equilibrium when it is hit by an exogenous shock.[10] In the model with Bayesian updating of Schinkel (2001), this assumption is reformulated as the condition of 'no statistical surprise', which states that no individual agent shall be confronted with a sale- or purchase-possibility which was not initially included in the support of his beliefs. In other words, no exogenous or endogenous events should occur that were initially given zero probability.[11]

No favourable or statistical surprise is a strong restriction, but if one adopts it, it is not necessary to restrict price adjustment processes in other ways to secure stability.[12] One such candidate would have been Hahn's assumption of orderly markets. In the context of individual price adjustment processes of the kind developed by Fisher and Schinkel, the assumption of orderly markets would require one to assume costless search or perfect information (Fisher 1983, 191). Of course, the condition of no favourable surprise also raises questions that may prove awkward, such as the need to explain the kind of expectations formation process that underlies it.[13] Fisher conceded that his model fails to address this issue. His explanation of the individual price adjustment process observes that prices will reflect perceived demand and supply curves, but it says nothing about how such perceptions are formed. According to himself, this is far from a minor matter. 'The way in which prices are formed and the role they play in the allocation of resources is the central topic of economic analysis. It is no small thing that we are uncertain as to how this takes place' (ibid., 215).

In brief, we now know who changes prices, but we have little knowledge about how he or she does it. From this perspective, disequilibrium analysis based on the non-tatonnement process is hardly an improvement over the current state of affairs in general equilibrium analysis.[14]

COMPUTATIONAL ALGORITHMS

This conclusion underlines a common critique of general equilibrium analysis and its disequilibrium foundations, namely that its highly complex mathematical structure obfuscates its economic meaning (for example Ingrao and Israel 1990). Supporting this argument, Smale (1976) argued that equilibrium theorists have used the wrong kind of mathematics to formalize their ideas. For example, the existence theory in general equilibrium analysis is deeply rooted in the mathematics of fixed point theory. But proofs of fixed point theorems traditionally use difficult ideas of algebraic topology. According to Smale (1976, 290), this has obscured the economic phenomena underlying the existence of equilibria. He therefore proposed to bypass the fixed point approach and to investigate the system of supply and demand equations directly by using a simpler kind of mathematics.[15]

Herbert Scarf is the grandfather of the computational modeling methodology in general equilibrium analysis. Key of this method is the development of computational algorithms for the approximate numerical determination of equilibrium based on the use of the techniques of combinatorial topology. Scarf (1973) used this method to calculate the fixed points of general equilibrium models (see also Scarf 1984). Smale adjusted the Scarf algorithm to free it from the fixed point theorem. His 'global Newton' method, involving ordinary differential equations, allowed him to obtain a proof of the existence of economic equilibrium without using fixed point theorems or algebraic topology (see Smale 1987).

Schinkel (2001, 88) questioned the relevance of the computational approach, stating that it proved unable to provide insights into the behaviour of markets out-of-equilibrium. Two remarks are in place here. First, in my opinion the dismissal of computable or empirical general equilibrium models is too quick. Especially in the Netherlands, computable general equilibrium (CGE) models are considered 'state of the art' in economic modeling and have an important impact on economic policy decisions. Should we consider this approach a dead alley and its policy advice therefore ill-conceived? Second, van der Hoog (2005) used computational algorithms to generate results that cannot be ignored in the context of this survey. He shows that, contrary to Schinkel's conclusion, CGE modeling may teach economic theory some interesting lessons.

I shall start by explaining the latter point. van der Hoog advocates the use of computational algorithms in fields of study where the application of mathematics only leads to highly complex models. He argues that in such cases the adoption of a computational algorithm can be a useful way to circumvent cumbersome and complex mathematical calculation and to derive results that have a more economical meaning. For him, 'more economical' means that the numerical model in question satisfies the following six conditions:

- The model is formulated as a non-tatonnement process;
- Trade takes place at false prices and hence transactions are irreversible;
- There is no central coordinating device between agents on different markets; the trading process is decentralized;
- Trading takes time and the adjustment process takes time to converge (often there is sequential trading);
- The expectations formation process of agents is explicated;
- The process includes money, so that issues related to income, liquidity and financial constraints, as well as debts accumulating over time, are able to play a role.

These are the well-known points of criticism often raised against general equilibrium analysis and it is therefore useful to inquire what role they can play in computable models of disequilibrium processes. The general advantage of using computable models is that in analytical models assumptions like those mentioned above often lead to intractable problems. The numerical model allows us to investigate problems in far greater detail, that is with higher dimensions (Shoven and Whalley 1984, 1008). Of course, the drawback is that the numerical solution cannot be considered a formal proof of an analytical problem like the existence and stability of general economic equilibrium. But van der Hoog argues that the numerical inferences from the computational model can be useful for understanding the analytical problem and the underlying economic theory.[16]

What are the lesson that we may draw from this numerical approach to disequilibrium analysis? These are first and foremost that the institutional set up of the trading system has an important impact on the stability of the equilibrium the system converges upon. By and large, this set up consists of two elements, behavioral assumptions and parts of the market mechanism like price adjustment mechanisms (flexible or not) and exchange methods (via a medium of exchange or not). For example, van der Hoog demonstrates that in a credit exchange model 'money' may act as a soft correction mechanism on the fluctuations of the balance of account. The possibility to accumulate debt in the form of credit allows the model to converge upon equilibrium. But in a cash exchange model without bank credit, the cash-in-advance constraint acts as a hard correction mechanism on fluctuations.[17] This causes the system to overshoot rather than dampen in response to a disequilibrium shock. However, with regard to assumptions about the degree of foresight attributed to agents, the dynamic adjustment pattern does not show a similar sensitivity. This leads van der Hoog (2005, 244) to conclude that in general 'the market mechanism and the market institutions play a much greater role for the stability of the exchange process than the question of whether agents are in fact using optimal trading strategies by taking into account all of the relevant and observable market signals'.

This study is a good example of the type of analysis that allows us to investigate the role of different institutions for the functioning of the market exchange system.[18] The question that logically follows is whether such effects actually occur in the operation of the real economy 'out there'. This is the second line of research inspired by computional general equilibrium models. This field covers a vast literature that cannot be reviewed in this brief section, but a few remarks are in order. To start with, the key to computable general equilibrium models is the use of an algorithm to calculate the fixed point of an equilibrium model. As a result of this (computer) exercise, we find the equilibrium solution and thereby know it exists. But this proof of existence does have a drawback. The algorithms developed by Scarf and Eaves are such that the system is unable to cycle (Schinkel 2001, 84). This construction overrides the problem of stability, but then runs into another. Who guarantees that the solution found is unique? The proper answer is nobody, which creates serious problems if one employs these algorithms in applied models (Ingrao and Israel 1990, 333 and 348).

There is a clear link between computable general equilibrium models and the socialist calculation debate that I discussed earlier in Chapter 10. Scarf (1987) explicitly referred to the vision of the neoclassical socialists like Barone and Lange to develop the general equilibrium model as a calculation device for the central planner. This is a vision that appealed to Scarf, but he was certainly realistic enough to realize that its practical execution was impossible. Decades of development in this field have allowed us to calculate equilibrium prices in a Walrasian model in which the number of variables is in the order of 100 (ibid., 90).[19] But the coordination problem of the actual economy is infinitely more complex and requires us to handle models with millions of prices and activity levels. Hence, Scarf's important lesson (ibid., 90):

> The computer, while expanding our capabilities immeasurably, has taught us a severe lesson about the role of mathematical reasoning in economic practice and forced us to shift our point of view dramatically from that held by our predecessors. We realize that our preoccupations are not with universal laws which describe economic phenomena with full and complete generality, but rather with intellectual formulations which are an imperfect representation of a complex and elusive reality. The application of general equilibrium theory to economic planning, and more generally, to the evaluation of the consequences of changes in economic policy, must be based on highly aggregated models whose conclusions are at best tentative guides to action.

Others, like Shoven and Whalley (1984, 1048), issue similar warnings about the limitations of computable equilibrium models as input into the policy decision making process.

As a side-issue, we may raise the question what policy makers can learn from such models. The question of successful application does not, of course, solve the theoretical issue of proving the stability of general equilibrium. But it does give us a notion of the plausibility of this type of approach. The computational algorithms generate feasible GE-models that can be used as a tool to evaluate concrete policy proposals. This shows that GE-theory is more than just black board science and does find applications in the real world with all its uncertainties and dynamic effects.

The Netherlands Bureau for Economic Policy Analysis (CPB) is one of the leading institutes in the world working with computable general equilibrium models.[20] Models like MIMIC (focus on labour market) and Worldscan (focus on international economy) show the value added of this type of models for the policy making process (Don and Verbruggen 2006). It allowed the CPB to investigate the different scenarios and policy packages for a range of subjects like ageing, reform of the welfare state and climate change.[21] The researchers of the CPB are generally well aware of the limitations of the CGE-approach.[22] Outcomes are presented as long term effects, since the short term dynamics underlying these changes remain a black box. This underlines that the computable GE-approach does not solve the theoretical issue of proving the stability of general equilibrium. The assumed stability of the convergence process is regularly checked by means of a sensitivity analysis, which is of course just a second best option. But the advantages of the CGE-method are often said to balance its shortcomings. CGE-models like MIMIC allowed applied research to focus on structural parameters and to derive macroeconomic outcomes from explicit microeconomic behaviour. The weakness of this approach for policy purposes is its empirical foundation. Given the weight put on the structural parameters, the question arises how to generate numerical values for these sometimes thousands of parameters. This presses researchers in this field to obtain estimates with a firm empirical base. But, so long as a complete econometric estimation of general equilibrium models is excluded, it is unavoidable that some parameters have a weaker empirical base. This should caution our use of CGE-models when assessing the effects of specific policy proposals.

In sum, this computable approach in empirical economics does not allow us to open up the black box that hides the balancing mechanism of general equilibrium. This exercise requires a different approach, more piece-meal and partial instead of general analysis and qualitative instead of quantitative analysis. It shall also probably need a combination of insights from different corners of economics like evolutionary theory, institutional analysis and market process theories. This is generally not the kind of expertise of the typical researcher working at institutes like the CPB. The research tradition in such institutes rewards and therefore attracts knowledge of mathematics and econometrics.[23] For a greater focus on disequilibrium analysis in applied research, it is necessary to counter this trend. This can only be achieved when applied research institutes like the CPB give this kind of research a higher priority and when economic faculties around the globe are able to train a sufficient number of scientists with expertise in disequilibrium analysis to carry it out.[24]

INFORMATION AND SEARCH THEORY

Fisher (1983) suggested that one should not use an equilibrium theory of economic decision making as the starting point of an analysis of disequilibrium events. Yet this was exactly the research strategy of the economics of information in the past thirty years (Stiglitz 2002). The reason why Fisher did not want to start with assuming equilibrium was that he believed it would constrain the scope of one's disequilibrium analysis. How to perform disequilibrium analysis in a world ruled by equilibrium forces? Proceeding in this way, it would be very hard to gain significant insights into the nature of disequilibrium adjustments. The present section shall investigate whether Fisher was right. We have seen in this book that several schools of thought in economics consider information and related topics like search and uncertainty powerful sources of disequilibrium changes. What happens if we introduce a force of this kind into the equilibrium paradigm? Will it prove useful or a chimera? I shall argue that the former is the case, but with an important disclaimer. The economics of information allowed the reigning neoclassical doctrine in economics to handle important cases of market disequilibrium, but it failed to generate the accompanying dynamic processes. In this sense, the information revolution in economics is still partly an unfulfilled promise.

It is well-known that information is a crucial variable when we consider the conditions for general competitive equilibrium. The highly stringent conditions underlying the general equilibrium model, such as perfect foresight or common knowledge, are a favorite target of rival paradigms. The problem with information is that it affects beliefs and behaviour. As Stiglitz (2002) put it, the fact that information is imperfect means that the choices of individual agents disclose information. Other market participants know this and respond accordingly. This changes the way markets function and explains why information imperfections have such profound effects.

This difficult relationship between information and economic equilibrium has been known for some time, but the surprising fact is that until the 1970s the majority of the economics profession remained silent on this issue.[25] They rested content with assuming that economies in which information was not too imperfect would look very much like economies in which information was perfect. Stiglitz (2002, 466) noted that in the classic formulation of the Arrow-Debreu model of general competitive equilibrium perfect information was not even listed as one of the conditions of the model. 'The perfect information assumption was so ingrained it did not have to be explicitly stated.'

The information revolution in economics, which started around the beginning of the 1970s, changed all this. It turned out that even with an arbitrarily small amount of imperfect information a competitive market equilibrium often did not exist. The classic references here are Akerlof (1970) and Spence (1973 and 1974). In the models of Spence, prices act as signals, feeding selection mechanisms which ruled out a unique market equilibrium solution. His results even indicate the possibility of a continuum of equilibria.[26] Self-selection mechanisms of the kind developed by Rothschild and Stiglitz (1976) further complicate this process. In their model of the insurance market two types of equilibria are possible: pooling equilibria in which the market is not able to distinguish among the different types of risk and a separating equilibrium in which these types can be isolated. Rothschild and Stiglitz showed that a pooling equilibrium could always be broken by the offer of a superior contract which was able to separate risks. But the same applied to the separating equilibrium. Any putative separating equilibrium could be broken by a profitable pooling contract, a contract which would be bought by both low risk and high risk types. In the follow-up of these developments in the economics of information, it began to dawn that the standard model of competitive equilibrium was simply not robust.

In the 1970s, these results rekindled the interest in microeconomics, but it did not lead to a rejection of the equilibrium paradigm. One might say that the response was above all a change in the modeling strategy of economists working in this field. The principal victim of this change was general equilibrium analysis, which during this time had run into a few problems of its own (see the previous section). It appeared that the troublesome features of information could best be studied in simple models of specific markets. This led to a flurry of activity aimed at understanding the different effects of information in markets like insurance, used cars, labour, education et cetera. Stiglitz (2002) has described the benefit of this research strategy as follows. He observed that the use of highly simplified models of particular markets allowed researchers to carefully scrutinize assumptions and conclusions of these cases. This led to the identification of general principles, which could be checked by applying them to other cases. Trial and error so generated an understanding of the general features of information in different cases, but also of the features which seemed to be more relevant in one market or another. After all, the nature of competition in the labour market is different from that in the insurance market and the capital market, though these markets have much in common.

The basic models of this new age of information economics shared with each other that they were equilibrium models. As Stiglitz (2002, 469) worded it, 'perhaps the hardest problem in building the new paradigm was modeling equilibrium'. Why go through this trouble and retain equilibrium at all cost, even when one is attempting to understand the role of something which so evidently belongs to the domain of disequilibrium analysis? Stiglitz did not provide a clear answer to this question. But it seems that the formalistic approach of microeconomics played a large role. Given the mathematical structure of the basic microeconomic theories, addressing the behaviour of firms, consumers and markets, it might have been even more difficult to build a disequilibrium model explaining what information does to the behaviour of these entities.

However, we need to be careful here. What Stiglitz called equilibrium models did not take market clearing as an assumption. In fact, in many cases the principal aim of introducing information into this framework was to explain why certain markets like the labour market failed to clear. The theory of efficiency wages is a clear example of this approach (Shapiro and Stiglitz 1984). The equilibrium feature which Stiglitz referred to was the theory of rational economic decision making. In his view, both sides of the market had to be modeled as rational in order to logically deduce the consequences of informational asymmetries for the beliefs and behaviour of suppliers and demanders (Stiglitz 2002, 469). In this sense, information economics followed a modeling strategy that was similar to the disequilibrium or fixed-price literature of the same period (see for example Malinvaud 1977). The difference was that informational asymmetries could be used to explain why prices were fixed or why there existed certain constraints (for example in the credit market) which prevented markets from clearing, in specific sectors but also on a macroeconomic scale (Akerlof 2002).[27]

What can we say of the results of this equilibrium approach in the economics of information? I believe that the results have been impressive and important to the development of economics. First, it helped to understand the incentives which agents have to disclose or hide information. Does the seller of a used car tell the truth about the quality of his car? How do we prevent buyers of an insurance lying about their risk profile? How can workers be seduced in disclosing their true productivity? In all these cases, the working of the market mechanism crucially depends on the incentives to use or hide information. A second key issue concerns the question of what you can do with such information. How does one appropriate the returns to creating information? Modeling information as imperfect allowed us to answer these questions. The results had serious implications for policy, because they could be applied to design mechanisms to overcome informational asymmetries and affect behaviour. The price setting behaviour of insurers is a clear example of this. In the labour market, efficiency wage theory demonstrated how one could make use of incentives to hide or disclose information. The basic idea of this theory is that it might pay a firm to offer a higher wage in order to attract more able workers. Shapiro and Stiglitz (1984) showed that even with identical workers efficiency wages may act as an incentive for workers. Only now it is the existence of unemployment which explains why workers pay a price for shirking.[28]

The third lesson is related to the working of the market mechanism. The economics of information greatly reduced the value of supply and demand theory as a universal law. Supply and demand are of course still important for understanding markets, but with imperfect information we can no longer rely on the forces of competition to push these magnitudes towards equilibrium.

In addition, it can be used to explain an often cited empirical fact, namely that in actual markets the law of one price does not hold. There is a standard wisdom in economics which says that not everyone has to be informed to ensure that the market acts perfectly competitive. But the economics of information shows that this statement is simply not generally true. Salop and Stiglitz (1982) constructed a model which demonstrated that even in situations with small search costs markets might be characterized by a price distribution. In a similar sense, efficiency wage theory can be used to explain the existence of wage distribution as an equilibrium feature of the market. All this means that our view of the competitive equilibrium model of the market mechanism has to be adjusted in a significant way. It also suggests that there might be a stronger reason for the active involvement of the government with the functioning of markets than economists have long believed.

From a scientific point of view these lessons of the economics of information have proved valuable. They provided the key to the solution of many anomalies which had bothered the neoclassical paradigm for many years. I have already mentioned the examples of a plausible explanation of involuntary unemployment and the inability to verify the law of one price in empirical studies. Another well-know failure of neoclassical theory is the efficient market hypothesis which holds that stock prices convey all the relevant information from the informed to the uninformed. Grossman and Stiglitz (1976) showed that, when information is costly to collect, stock prices necessarily aggregate information imperfectly. In their view there is a fundamental conflict between the efficiency with which markets spread information and the incentives to acquire information. One might say that to induce people to gather information there must be an equilibrium amount of disequilibrium. The final point I want to mention concerns the theory of monopoly which lacked a firm foundation in a general theory of price discrimination.[29] The economics of information was able to provide this foundation and to explain why firms would have an incentive to extract the full consumer surplus from each individual consumer (Stiglitz 2002, 474).

These examples all refer to theoretical developments. In addition, there have been some contributions to the empirical literature. In this regard, one of the most promising fields has been the application of equilibrium search models in the empirical analysis of labour markets. In equilibrium search models, supply, demand and wage determination in the labour market are jointly modeled.[30] The supply side is represented by a partial job search model with sequential search. Workers looking for a job are confronted with a sequence of job offers from employers, representing a given distribution of wage offers for a given job offer arrival rate. In equilibrium, the flow of workers out of jobs with a given wage is equal to the inflow into such jobs. Similarly, the flows into and out of unemployment match each other. The key feature of such equilibrium search models is that the equilibrium wage rate is affected by the presence of informational frictions or search frictions. Put simply, it takes time to find the right job or the right candidate to fill a vacancy. This fact explains why the equilibrium wage rate will be dispersed even in a market with homogenous workers.[31]

The literature on partial job search models has made considerable progress in explaining supply-side behaviour, unemployment durations and job durations of workers looking for a new job (van der Berg 1999). The structural estimation of these models enabled the investigation of the underlying parameters of the search process. This knowledge is needed to formally test the theory and to estimate the effects of policy changes. In general, these studies focus on the effects of changes in the level of unemployment benefits, the impact of taxes or the effect of a mandatory minimum wage.

To assess the value of equilibrium-search models, it pays to briefly discuss their two key ingredients. These are the matching function, which determines how workers and firms get together, and the bargaining solution, which determines wages once they do. The matching function models the flow of contacts between firms and workers. A common assumption for this function is that the probability distribution explaining the frequency of a match is exogenous, that is the process of meeting a suitable worker or firm is random. This implies that the actual mechanics of the process by which agents make contact is left unexplained. Nonetheless, researchers value this approach to matching for its flexibility and consider the exact specification an empirical issue. However, there is a class of models which tries to open this black box a bit by including 'directed matching'. This means that workers do not encounter firms completely at random, but try to locate those posting attractive terms of trade.

For the bargaining solution a similar dilemma exists. The standard approach is to assume that employers offer a job for a given wage and the job seekers accept or reject this offer. But wage posting is a strong assumption, since it means that agents commit to the posted terms of trade. If the market is really decentralized, there is no reason why they should not try to bargain for a different wage after they meet. Game theory provides the tools to explain these bargaining solutions.[32] This approach runs into a number of identification problems, which may explain why most of the empirical work is done with the wage posting model (van der Berg 1999, 300).

Bargaining or not, a crucial feature of the equilibrium search model is that the wage offer distribution is endogenous. It is explained within the model. The partial search model with a fixed and exogenous distribution of wage offers leads to a degenerate equilibrium outcome, which makes it uninteresting from an empirical point of view.[33] With an endogenous distribution of wage offers, the wage offers are the result of optimal wage setting by firms that take account of the behaviour by job seekers and other firms. For example, in this case firms know that a job seeker's reservation wage is an increasing function of unemployment benefits and they anticipate on the effect of changes in such policy variables. Wage offers are therefore affected by all structural parameters, including policy parameters as well as the frictional parameters that indicate how frequently individual labour market transitions occur. The benefit of this approach is evident: it answers the Lucas critique. Equilibrium search models with endogenous wage offer distribution properly take into account changes in employer behaviour in response to policy changes. This, of course, enhances the ability of this type of model to study the effects of labour market policies.

The empirical success of this approach can be measured in many different ways. One way is the explanation of wage dispersion. There are three sources which are empirically relevant for this exercise: (a) workers heterogeneity (observed and unobserved), (b) firm productivity heterogeneity (observed and unobserved) and (c) market frictions. Eckstein and van der Berg (2007, 552) claim that the equilibrium framework of this type of search models has successfully measured the quantitative importance of each source.[34]

So, returning to our initial question, was Fisher too pessimistic about the prospects of exploring disequilibrium events like information and search in terms of equilibrium models? Not quite. He did underrate the importance of equilibrium search theory, as I have argued, but there is a downside to this class of models that I have not yet discussed. This is the lack of dynamics explaining the change of the equilibrium system over time. As Stiglitz (2002, 486) says, information economics has alerted us to the fact that history matters; there are important hysteresis effects.[35] I have argued throughout this book that equilibrium models have trouble describing such effects. In models with imperfect information, we need to develop a mechanism to select the right equilibrium outcome otherwise the model is undetermined. Structural empirical analysis of the equilibrium search model may help us to devise this mechanism and to solve dynamic selection effects.[36] But the current class of models in this field is still limited in the sense that the dynamics explaining search are not 'rich' enough. That it, the black box hiding the mechanics of matching and bargaining, is not opened wide enough. We have seen that the probability distribution explaining the frequency of a match is often considered exogenous, which rules out all kinds of dynamic responses. Likewise, the assumption of wage posting also rules out feedback effects, which are important to the bargaining solution of a match. Finally, when bargaining is included in the model, the tools of standard non-cooperative game theory are used to determine the equilibrium solution. But we have seen earlier in Chapter 15 that this branch of game theory, at best, provides a partial answer to dynamic effects, such as the stability of the equilibrium solution. As a result, there are many important dynamic inferences that remain outside the purview of equilibrium search models.

How can we judge whether history matters? Stiglitz (2002) postulated that dynamics may be better described by evolutionary processes and models, than by equilibrium processes. This brings us back to the topic of Chapter 15 and indicates a field were the new developments of information economics may lie. A possible inference would be to use evolutionary game theory in describing the bargaining solution to equilibrium search models. But this approach requires us to drop the assumption of rational decision making, which plays a central role in the current literature on this subject. Another possibility is to drop the formal approach and study the evolutionary aspects of institutions related to the production and dissemination of information. In Chapter 15 I have discussed an example of this type of study in the labour market.

Whether the economics profession shall follow this lead is questionable, because there is an important reason why researchers dealing with information and search cling to a formal equilibrium model as their prime tool of analysis. This is that equilibrium allows us to study the welfare implications of policy proposals based on these models. As Eckstein and van der Berg (2007, 533) put it, '[t]he main advantage of the analysis of equilibrium models is that it enables us to measure the implications of the inefficiency due to the market structure with imperfect imperfection'. The framework for executing this exercise is the neoclassical one of the Pareto welfare theorems. Rogerson, Shimer and Wright (2005) demonstrate that the first welfare theorem holds for an equilibrium search model with a combination of wage posting and directed search under quite general assumptions, showing how efficiency can be obtained for economies with frictions. I conclude that it is the desire to give a formal explanation of such welfare implications which explains why economists do not fully follow the example of Fisher (1983) to reject optimal choice theory as the proper foundation for the study of disequilibrium phenomena like stability, unemployment and wage or price dispersion.[37]

In the next section I shall return to the link between information and evolution and the question of what this connection means to the conception of equilibrium.

POST WALRASIAN MACROECONOMICS

Information and search have implications beyond the field of microeconomic theory. This final section explores these implications. That informational imperfections have macroeconomic consequences, such as unemployment, was already established in the previous section. I now turn to the question of how macroeconomic theory responded to such lessons and what it means for the future agenda of macroeconomic research.

I shall argue that one result of the inclusion of information in the macroeconomic framework is the recognition that equilibrium may not be stable and certainly not unique. This message has led to a new, Post Walrasian branch on the family tree of macroeconomics. Colander (2006) defines the characteristic of this branch as follows. He compares it to the recent synthesis between New Keynesian, New Classical and Real Business Cycle analysis called the dynamic stochastic general equilibrium approach (DSGE). According to Colander, DSGE endows individuals with high-level information processing capabilities and a rich information set. The background of this assumption is that individuals in a general equilibrium framework need to possess perfect foresight and information for equilibrium to exist. Post Walrasians consider this assumption far too stringent and seek to relax it. Hence, they assume that agents possess low-level information processing capabilities and a poor information set.[38]

Seen in this way, information imperfections generate a fundamental divide in current macroeconomic practice. For completeness, it should be noted that we need to broaden this perspective by including imperfections in the market structure. These issues are closely related. As Stiglitz (2004) argues, informational advantages may give firms an instrument to exploit their market power. In other words, imperfections of information give rise to imperfections of competition. I shall argue that these two imperfections may have comparable effects on macroeconomic theory and can therefore be fruitfully discussed under the same heading, even though the developments they feed into do not take an exact parallel course.

Imperfect Information

The most far-reaching consequence of imperfect information and/or imperfect competition is that it causes researchers to consider a much broader class of equilibrium outcomes. That is, in this case we cannot a priori assume that the macroeconomic outcome will be a unique and stable equilibrium. Colander (2006) explains this aspect of the Post Walrasian research agenda in the following terms. He says that Post Walrasians return to a set of questions that an earlier generation of economists was unable to answer due to a lack of analytical and statistical tools. Recent developments have provided us with such tools and the much improved computing power of PCs allows us to execute the highly complex calculations that are needed to employ them.

So, what are these old questions that give rise to the new and complex calculations? They are the familiar objections which since the rise of the general equilibrium paradigm in the 1940s have been part and parcel of economic discourse (Kirman 2006 and Colander 2006):

- Economic agents are not clones of a species called *Homo Economics*. Agent heterogeneity is a relevant aspect of economic reality and should therefore be the starting point of economic analysis;
- If agents are not identical, we cannot use the fiction of the representative agent. This means that we have to model the economy as a system in which there is a direct interaction among individuals;
- Agents do not act rationally or optimally. Behavioral assumptions should be grounded in empirical knowledge about how people actually choose among competing ends;
- Due to the existence of imperfect information, we are unable to assume that agents know the true model of the economy. This means that we have to dispense with the assumption of rational expectations. However, since learning has powerful implications for macroeconomic outcomes, we need to include a theory about how people learn from past experiences;[39]
- Macroeconomics has important implications for applied policies. Hence, a model based on these Post Walrasian considerations should have testable conclusions.
- The Post Walrasian system should have meaningful dynamics, showing how it functions over time but without assuming that it necessarily converges to any particular state. The question then emerges whether this means that 'anything goes' or that we need to develop a new equilibrium concept corresponding to an economy in continual movement.

Post Walrasian Macroeconomics tries to achieve all this, which is really a daunting task. The benchmark against which to judge its success or failure is the Walrasian synthesis mentioned above. The essence of this dynamic stochastic general equilibrium is that it portrays the macroeconomy as a gigantic dynamic optimal control problem. This means that it assumes that individuals are rational consumers and producers who are all dynamically optimizing their intertemporal objectives subject to budget and resource constraints. This element of DSGE is what links it to the New Classical and the Real Business Cycle literature, adding the element of stochastic risk. The New Keynesian element in DSGE concerns the institutional setting. It has often been remarked that Arrow-Debreu general equilibrium theory operates in an institutional vacuum. DSGE changes this by including institutional and nominal rigidities.

This set up gives us a good perspective to compare the visions behind DSGE and Post Walrasian Macroeconomics. DSGE explains macroeconomic fluctuations in terms of exogenous supply shocks, which are not perfectly dampened because of nominal and institutional rigidities. The underlying assumption is therefore that the economy is inherently stable, but that rigidities prevent the stabilizing forces to do their job. The Post Walrasian perspective is fundamentally different. It relies on complex interactions among agents and expectations formation processes that are very likely not based on the true model of the economy. As a result, the competitive macroeconomy is described as a system with strong tendencies towards chaotic behaviour. The factors controlling this behaviour are institutions like rules of thumb or nominal contracts.[40] The Post Walrasians, therefore, aim to study how institutions are able to play this stabilizing role, which is the exact opposite of the question central to the DGSE view.

Post Walrasian macroeconomics rejects the assumption of rational expectations, but it needs another kind of anchor to make its models tractable. This is the assumption of agent-modeler consistency. Post Walrasian analysis builds on the assumption that the agents populating the theoretical economy have as much knowledge as the researcher modeling this particular economy. Agents inside the model are assumed to each formulating their own 'model of the model' (Mehrling 2006, 78). These are models that are subsequently adapted in the light of experience. Behaviour will thus always be model-consistent even though agents never learn the 'true' structure of their world. Colander (2006) calls this assumption 'metamodel consistent expectations'. It can help to determine a solution if one can specify precisely how selections can be made among alternative models. But it can also be a powerful source of volatility, since expectations are likely to generate large changes as expectations shift from one model to another.

It is evident that this kind of complexity presents a serious problem for formal modeling. Post Walrasians therefore often short-circuit the search for an analytical solution by simulating the outcome. This is called agent-based computational economics (ACE). It is a modeling strategy which endows heterogenous virtual agents with local optimizing strategic rules and allows them to compete in a virtual economy. In this virtual system different learning rules and strategies can be tested. This information can be used to the study the dynamics of the model with no external equilibrium condition imposed. It can even be used to pretest the effectiveness of various policies in the virtual economy. This kind of modeling is still in its infancy, but it offers hope of an alternative to finding analytic solutions of complex systems (Colander 2006, 12).

Macroeconometrics is another way to relax the strain on the need to provide an analytical solution to complex systems. Post Walrasians use data-driven empirical methods with less reliance on theory than their Walrasian counterpart. The difference is that Walrasians generally start with the presumption that the DSGE model is the correct model and look to the data for confirmation of that model. Post Walrasians try to extract as much information as possible from available data sources using cointegrated vector autoregressions. They use econometric analysis to choose among assumptions and alternative theories, not to test a particular theory. This requires a looser theoretical, but more highly disciplined statistical approach than characterizes the Walrasian approach (ibid., 13). This explains why Post Walrasians tend to be more open to case studies and institutional research.

The question is what this means for the concept of equilibrium in Post Walrasian Macroeconomics. Mehrling (2006) stresses the open-endedness of disequilibrium dynamics in the Post Walrasian model, which suggests Knightian uncertainty. He says that 'Post Walrasians [emphasize] that the future is not a knowable fact, not even in principle, and not even in probabilistic terms' (Mehrling 2006, 76). This recalls the position of the fundamentalist Keynesians like Shackle and Minsky (see Chapter 13).[41] We have seen with the Post Keynesians that equilibrium is likely to play a limited rule in a world ruled by the dark forces of time and ignorance. One finds this same attitude among the Post Walrasians. Kirman (2006) is frank about this. He says that '[p]erhaps the most important idea here is that we should not regard learning as a way of justifying the static or steady state equilibrium that we are interested in, but we should accept the economy to have interesting dynamics that do not converge to an equilibrium in the standard sense' (ibid., xviii–xix). This does leave scope for another kind of equilibrium, which Kirman indeed finds in specific applications. He mentions a model with constantly changing prices, which nonetheless seems to exhibit a certain structure in that the time averages will converge and that a unique limit price distribution will exist. This may be the case. I merely observe that an equilibrium of this kind is a probabilistic equilibrium explicitly ruled out by Mehrling. It seems that the Post Walrasian have not made up their mind among themselves whether they will fully embrace fundamental uncertainty and the possibility that anything can happen, or allow probabilistic measures of future events and use them to generate alternative conceptions of equilibrium.

Imperfect Competition

The implications of imperfect competition in macroeconomic models are just as interesting, but also have a few characteristics which we need to distinguish from Post Walrasian macroeconomics. To start with, this approach, building on the Dixit and Stiglitz (1977) model of monopolistic competition, is in a far more developed stage than the imperfect information approach discussed above. Unavoidably, this means it values different features of its modeling strategy. Researchers exploring this field do not worry about heterogeneity of agents. The Dixit and Stiglitz model assumes identical firms and consumers and the monopolistic competition literature in macrotheory builds on this foundation. Proponents recognize this feature as 'somewhat unrealistic' but that did not prevent the Dixit-Stiglitz approach from becoming the workhorse model in many areas like international trade theory, macroeconomics, growth theory and economic geography (Brakman and Heijdra 2004, 12). In addition, strategic interaction between agents is ruled out, given that they compete for a large number of product varieties (Stiglitz 2004, 137). This feature is actually considered an advantage, because simplifies the structure of the model and thus improves its tractability (Brakman and Heijdra 2004, 27).

This would be a good reason not to include this approach in this section, given that it fundamentally conflicts with the basic tenets of the Post Walrasian approach set out above. However, just like Post Walrasians try to distinguish themselves from the DSGE approach, there are voices calling for a change of tactics in the field of monopolistic competition models of the macroeconomy. Dixit himself is critical of the absence of strategic interaction in the basic Dixit-Stiglitz model. He wants to go beyond its simplifying assumptions and explore new perspectives from game theory and numerical simulation models (Dixit 2004). But his concerns are not shared by the other name-giver of the theory, Stiglitz. The latter still cherishes the simplicity achieved by ruling out strategic interaction. Likewise, he recognizes that agent heterogeneity is a crucial feature of actual economics, but he values the simplifications for one reason: They keep the analysis simple and allow for clear welfare analysis (Stiglitz 2004).

The dissident macroeconomist must look elsewhere and may find inspiration in Solow (1998). Solow prefers the Hotelling model of monopolistic competition which Stiglitz eschews as a foundation for macroeconomic theory. This model describes competition in terms of firms on a circle. In the Dixit-Stiglitz approach, a new firm produces a new product, competing symmetrically with all existing firms. In the circle model, a firm has two nearest neighbours and primarily competes with them. This image gives competition a different dynamics. The competition between the new entrant and the market focuses on the struggle of the new firm to establish a niche between two existing firms. This may give rise to predatory tactics and expectations about the beliefs and actions of rivals.

Now we enter a world that better resembles the Post Walrasian model. With strategic interaction lurking around the corner, the possibility arises that the macroeconomic equilibrium will not be unique. Solow (1998) explains this possibility by arguing that suppliers with a degree of market power focus on quantity expectations. Prices are (partly) under their own control and are therefore not of prime importance. But quantities are a key variable, which can lead to strategic complementarities across wide areas of the economy (Cooper and John 1988). This concept indicates that greater output or employment in one sector of the economy, increases the marginal profitability of output or employment in another sector in the economy. This gives rise to reaction functions that slope in the same direction and lay the foundation for self-fulfilling equilibria which are anything but unique. In other words, strategic complementarity is a likely source of multiple equilibria and the circle model is an appropriate microfoundation for this kind of behaviour.

But there is more. Entry is a risky business with a real possibility of irreversible loss. Suppose that increasing returns to scale play a role. Then a new firm must achieve a non-trivial size in order to have any hope of success. This means that a substantial, lumpy initial investment may be required to establish a potentially viable firm. The new firms may therefore have a substantial effect on capacity, generating a multiplier process. It may also be connected with that other typical Keynesian aspect, animal spirits. It seems likely that entry will occur when animal spirits (optimism, aggressiveness) are favourable. Otherwise many potential entrants will refrain from investing. Additions to capacity can thus be seen in relationship to the state of long term expectations. It is clear, then, that the circle model can be used to support the construction of a macroeconomic theory with typical Keynesian features, such as the presumption that animal spirits drive investment.

CONCLUSION

This chapter has indicated that even within the neoclassical paradigm developments arise with important disequilibrium features. These developments may be used to underpin standard general equilibrium analysis, as Fisher (1983) tried to achieve. It may also lead to an approach which depicts the economy in a continual state of change, which has nothing to do with a stable general equilibrium. It is here that these developments border on the conclusions of more radical groups in economics like Post Keynesians and evolutionary theorists.

However, there is one aspect which still sharply separates these groups. This is the complexity of the formal models used in disequilibrium analysis.

The approaches discussed in this section invariable employ state-of-the-art mathematical tools, generating highly technical models. Colander (2006) complains about this high degree of technicality, stating that it pushes the vision behind these theories out of sight. Increasingly, teachers and students need all their energy to learn and resolve technical issues, which leaves little time for talking about vision. But see what alternative he is promoting. Post Walrasian Macroeconomics poses challenging questions, but it only makes theory even more difficult and more technical. Surely, the debate on the fundamentals or vision of economics will not prosper on this soil. To get a meaningful discussion about the advantages and disadvantages of cross-fertilization in disequilibrium analysis, the role of mathematical modeling needs to be curtailed to a considerable extent. The least one should require is an obligatory course on the history of economic thought and applied economic policy in the economic curriculum to give future generations a sense of what economic theory is all about.

NOTES

1. We have seen that Walras discussed the possibility of multiple equilibria in his partial analyses. His theory of price adjustment addressed the issue of stability in the general equilibrium setting. I have explained this theory in Chapter 9.
2. See Samuelson (1983, 270ff).
3. This condition means that a rise in the price of any one good increases the demand for every other, including income effects.
4. By the end of the 1950s Hahn proved that the assumption of gross substitutes is equivalent to the condition of the alternation of the principal minors. See Hahn (1958).
5. Scarf (1960) provided the first counterexample, which showed that the optimism of Arrow, Block and Hurwicz was unfounded. I shall further leave the tatonnement literature for what it is. For an excellent review, the reader is referred to Ingrao and Israel (1990). See also the reconstruction of the theory of stability by Weintraub (1991) and the review of the literature in Schinkel (2001).
6. The notion of an orderly market in Hahn's construction of the non-tatonnement process means that after trade one cannot have simultaneously excess demand and excess supply for the same commodity.
7. There are two additional reasons to prefer the Hahn process in this context. The first one is that it allows a role for money as an unit of exchange. Secondly, it provides a natural way to include typical aspects of market trading like locational advantages of sellers and information asymmetries in one's model of disequilibrium price adjustment. See Fisher (1983, 47–48).
8. Schinkel (2001, 177) raises the question why one should want prices to converge to the outcomes of competitive equilibrium. He calls the disequilibrium story with a competitive

ending the 'Holy Grail' of economic theory. The reason for this is that the economic conditions which facilitate disequilibrium trading are logically incompatible with competitive equilibrium. In his view, there is a trade-off between stability and static efficiency (ibid., 213). Schinkel is probably right, but he too easily sacrifices something which Fisher values very highly, the link between economic analysis and welfare theory. Without efficiency, the two Pareto theorems do not apply. As a result, economics loses what Fisher (1983, 9) called 'the single most important set of ideas' that economists have to convey to lay people. I suspect that this is the reason why Fisher stubbornly continued his quest for the Holy Grail.

9. Fisher refers to Schumpeter's notion of entrepreneurship as an example of this kind of disequilibrating forces. According to Schumpeter, entrepreneurs introduce innovations into the system such as new technologies, new raw materials, new markets or new forms of organization. The effect of these innovations is that they upset the current market order governed by the equality of supply and demand. Like Schumpeter, Fisher argued that it cannot be true that an economy in which new opportunities constantly arise will converge to equilibrium.

10. If the economy is hit by a continuous stream of such shocks, it will be impossible to discern a tendency of any kind.

11. It is remarkable that Fisher focused on the exclusion of unexpected optimistic expectations, while pessimistic expectations would have the same disruptive effect. In this sense, Schinkel's condition of no statistical surprise is more general and includes both positive and negative surprises.

12. Fisher (1983) argued that the assumption of no favourable surprise is sufficient to prove global stability of economic equilibrium.

13. It is evident that we are speaking here about a case of rational expectations. See Fisher (1983, 215). Concerning the model of Schinkel (2001), the question arises whether people actually learn in a Bayesian fashion. In his own words, 'this may be quite questionable' (ibid., 215). But at least his model opens up the possibility to investigate the price adjustment process under different learning rules.

14. Of course, there are other defects that, however, I shall leave aside. The most prominent of these is the inability to say anything about the speed of convergence. Fisher considered this one of the two core issues underpinning the need for a proper disequilibrium analysis. Another important issue is the role of firms. The models of Fisher (1983) and Schinkel (2001) assume a fixed number of firms. But a crucial feature of disequilibrium in particular markets is the entry and exit of firms.

15. It was later shown that Brouwer's fixed point theorem and the theorem asserting the existence of Walrasian general economic equilibrium are equivalent. This equivalence gives an interesting mathematical twist to the existence proof in GE-analysis, namely that this proof will also serve as a demonstration of the fixed point theorem itself. 'As profound as economists may be, it is unlikely that they would have demonstrated one of the more sophisticated mathematical theorems of the twentieth century as a casual by-product of their concern with the general equilibrium model' (Scarf 1973, 12).

16. The word 'understanding' here is vague. van der Hoog (2005, 32–22) tries to explicate it by developing a methodological perspective on numerical estimation and simulation. In his view, simulations can serve as counter-examples in a world in which universal statements are hard to prove by methods of deduction. He even calls for the re-entrance of 'inductive methodology' in economic science, given that theory may be updated when a simulation 'proves' that a certain analytical approach is a dead alley. The reader should note that Van der Hoog is exclusively concerned with the problem of veracity in a logical sense. The correspondence between theory and empirical reality does not enter his purview. Further, it should be noted that his methodological defense is based on an unproved assumption, namely that a computational model is seen as a true representation of the formal mathematical model. When this assumption does not hold, many of his lessons fall to pieces.
17. Given that the disequilibrium process finally leads to equilibrium, we need to assume that agents can only exchange commodities indirectly, that is via the money unit as a medium of exchange in market transactions. This is the quintessence of the cash-in-advance constraint. In Chapter 11 I have argued that it is very difficult to model the role of money in general equilibrium any other way. One option is to give it a search-theoretic foundation.
18. Of course, in a more general analysis of this problem production should play a role. In van der Hoog (2005) this role is ignored.
19. Schinkel (2001, 85) sees this remark as evidence of an optimistic attitude towards the possibility of socialist calculation. But I shall argue further on that this was certainly not the case.
20. CPB is an independent public institute with a central role in the economic policy making process of the Dutch government. It produces the macroeconomic forecasts that are used by the government to guide decisions on the yearly fiscal budget. In addition it makes economic analyses to ex ante assess the effects of targeted policies and acts as a strategic 'thing tank' for long term policy issues in a broad range of subjects.
21. For an excellent example, see de Mooij (2006).
22. As Don and Verbruggen (2006, 33) put it: 'CPB's strength lies not so much in the development of models, but more in the responsible use of these instruments . . . When using models, it is crucial to bear in mind the limitations and weaknesses of the model, in order to prevent misleading outcomes.'
23. It has to be stressed that in recent years the CPB has steadily shifted its attention from the quantitative modeling work towards more qualitative microeconomic and institutional research.
24. Of course, there is a whole set of questions related to this objective, such as the scientific reward scheme in economics, which is said to favor the acquisition of expertise in mathematical economics and econometric research. See Klamer and Colander (1990).
25. Knight (1921), Morgenstern (1935), Keynes (1936) and Hayek (1937 and 1945) are well-known examples of early theoretical applications with knowledge in a leading role.

26. In Akerlof's market for lemons it is quality uncertainty which explains why trade may not take place. See Akerlof (1970, 491).
27. Stiglitz noted that there had been some attempts in general equilibrium analysis to recognize the importance of problems of information. But the attempt to modify the abstract theory of general equilibrium to incorporate problems of information imperfections proved, in the end, less fruitful than the alternative approach of beginning with highly simplified models for concrete cases. See Stiglitz (2002, 469 n15).
28. With identical workers, if one firm offers a higher price, his competitors will follow suit. Hence, to explain the (higher) efficiency wages, there has to be an opportunity cost, which is the difference between the current wage and the benefit workers receive when they are unemployed.
29. In this case, the anomaly is that the theory of monopoly assumes that the monopolist offers the same price to all customers, without explaining why he does not differentiate his price. After all, the standard theories of monopoly assumed perfect information, which implied that they would have an incentive and the ability to price differentiate perfectly.
30. Recent reviews of the literature on the search-theoretic models of the labour market are van der Berg (1999), Mortensen and Pissaridis (1999), Eckstein and van den Berg (2003) and Rogerson, Shimer and Wright (2005).
31. The point is that what one ends up with (job or employee) is at least partially a matter of luck, which means similar workers may earn different wages. See Rogerson, Shimer and Wright (2005, 960).
32. The procedure for determining the wage is as follows. It is assumed that each possible match has a surplus defined as the excess gain over continued search. According to the generalized Nash solution to this bargaining game, a fixed fraction of the surplus goes to the worker in the form of a wage. In equilibrium, only matches with positive surpluses are realized. See van der Berg (1999, 300) and Rogerson, Shimer and Wright (2005, 968–969).
33. This outcome can be explained as follows. In general, an unemployed worker's optimal search strategy is characterized by a reservation wage which is an increasing function of his unemployment benefits level. Assuming identical workers, it is sub-optimal for firms to offer a wage that is higher than the common reservation wage. Thus, the equilibrium wage offer distribution is concentrated at this reservation wage and this common wage must be equal to the lowest wage that is acceptable to the unemployed, that is, their unemployment benefits level. In this set up, the question arises why workers should search at all. Every wage offer they encounter during their sequential search process is the same. In this partial model with identical workers and identical firms, there is no wage dispersion and all wage offers are always acceptable. See van den Berg (1999, 284–285).
34. There are other issues related to equilibrium search models that I shall ignore. One of these issues is the critique on the partial framework of equilibrium search models (Rothschild 1973). Using an endogenous wage offer distribution is one way to overcome this objection, as we have seen above. Another solution is to interpret equilibrium search as a signal extraction problem, as Rogerson, Shimer and Wright (2005, 967) argue. For

example, one can imagine workers looking for wage offers like fishermen looking for the most promising lake to fish in. Then the wage offer distribution is the distribution of fish across lakes, which can logically be taken as fixed. According to Rogerson, Shimer and Wright, this shows that search theory can be reformulated as a theory about the behaviour of a multiple market system in equilibrium, without changing its essence.

35. The existence of path-dependency and hysteresis is related to the fact that information imperfections are not a static magnitude. In many cases, markets create information problems, for example in an attempt to exploit market power. See Stiglitz (2002, 470). This is an important aspect to stress, because phenomena related to information problems like price dispersion are often seen as the failure of markets to fully arbitrage price differences. But in many cases, these price differences are in fact created by the market, which has important consequences for economic policy.

36. Knowing the structural parameters, we should be able to draw up a closed form solution of the set of structural equations. This gives us the data needed to compute the behaviour of the system over time and to solve the issues related to path-dependence, stability of equilibrium and even the speed of convergence to equilibrium.

37. There is, of course, the point that Fisher himself did not want to reject the assumption of a convergence towards competitive equilibrium, because this tendency implied that the two welfare theorems of neoclassical analysis could be saved. See above.

38. Kirman (2006) adds a footnote to this definition, which says that Colander interprets the Walrasian GE model in a specific sense. Colander deals with what Kirman calls the informal interpretation of the GE model, which assumes that the economy is made up of agents bargaining their way to equilibrium. In this case, for general equilibrium to emerge agents need to possess perfect foresight et cetera. But this is not the case in the Arrow**Fout! Bladwijzer niet gedefinieerd.**-Debreu formulation of GE theory, which assumes the existence of a central planner who processes all this information. Individual agents then only need to know the current price vector, which is a much less demanding assumption. Of course, the disadvantage of the central planner model is that is wholly incapable of addressing situations other than equilibrium.

39. The potential impact of learning comes to the fore when we move to a world where the individuals have limited knowledge and calculating capacities. A well-known example is the sunspot equilibrium, which emerges when agents believe in the 'wrong' model of the economy, but by behaving accordingly they establish a state that corresponds to this image. See Kirman (2006).

40. It is this kind of institutions which may provide individuals with an anchor when making their economic decisions in an uncertain environment. See the discussion earlier in Chapter 13 (Post Keynesians) and Chapter 15 (evolutionary economics).

41. Indeed, Mehrling refers to Minsky as a precursor.

17. Economics With or Without Equilibrium?

THE NEED FOR DISEQUILIBRIUM ANALYSIS

I used the term 'Economics without equilibrium' for theories which do not a priori assume equilibrium and take the issue of explaining coordination failures seriously. It turns out that this label is really a misnomer. We have seen that even the harshest critics of equilibrium analysis fail to develop a theoretical alternative without applying some kind of equilibrium concept. Economics without equilibrium does not exist and neither should we worry about this. I have demonstrated that equilibrium methods generate many valuable insights both in theory and in applied analysis like equilibrium search theory of the labour market. Disequilibrium dynamics aims to explain how the economy functions over time and it is here that the equilibrium concept may play a useful role in controlling potentially disruptive forces. Providing this sense of order in a field of dynamic analysis is the main role which the equilibrium concept plays in the more radical schools of thought like Post Keynesian, Austrian and Evolutionary Economics, which consider combatting neoclassical analysis as a *raison d'être*.

All this should not hide that there are limits to how far one may penetrate into the field of disequilibrium economics with the tools of equilibrium analysis. We have seen in Chapter 16 what it takes to develop a proper disequilibrium foundation for general equilibrium analysis. Sixty years of theory development has been insufficient to develop a satisfactory theoretical explanation of the highly intuitive notion that equilibrium is a stable position of the multi market economy. One must either adopt strong assumptions like the condition of 'no favourable surprise' or accept the likelihood of multiple equilibria, which may or may not possess local stability. This is as good as 'anything goes'. I have also argued that this end result may not be undesirable as long as the disequilibrium model generates dynamics which is interesting for its own sake.

The equilibrium stronghold may become straining in cases where theorists want to retain equilibrium as a foundation for welfare analysis. The economics of information is an example of the tension that emerges when theorists feel the need to explore explicit dynamic effects (for example including evolutionary aspects) but also aim to conduct formal welfare analysis as a means to rank the effects of different policy schemes. In the end, one of these aims will prove unattainable. One either retains the possibility of formal welfare analysis, which requires specific equilibrium assumptions and so constrains the scope for disequilibrium analysis. Or one relaxes these constraining assumptions and increases the scope for disequilibrium analysis, but then loses formal welfare analysis as a tool for evaluating policy proposals.

My investigation of the different schools of economic thought has shown that abandoning formal neoclassical welfare analysis does not mean that applied economic analysis is impossible or meaningless. Key elements of virtually all alternative approaches to disequilibrium analysis concern the dynamics of learning, dealing with uncertainty, institutional analysis and the exploration of evolutionary changes. These are topics that provide the stepping stones of a joint analysis of disequilibrium dynamics among competing paradigms in economics. I am convinced that cross fertilization of this kind will enrich our knowledge of disequilibrium events in economics. To mention just one example, we have seen that institutions may provide a focal point for the analysis of non-price coordination processes. Without an equilibrium condition imposing order 'from the outside', disequilibrium changes are likely to result in chaotic behaviour. Institutions play an important role in preventing such uncontrollable movement from occurring. They are in a significant way the equilibrating fabric of the economic system and this role is recognized in every school of economic thought. What is more logical than to explore what lessons different economic traditions offer in this field? Neoclassical economics of information may benefit from the Austrian analysis of market processes in terms of entrepreneurial alertness. In turn the Austrians may benefit from the economics of information, which shows how information may be created in the market. This is an important source of novelty, the bread and butter of the Austrian entrepreneur. Post Keynesian economics may help Post Walrasians to explain why institutions like nominal contracts have a stabilizing effect on economic changes. In turn Post Walrasian analysis may show the Post Keynesians how such lessons can be formalized in a theory of nominal rigidities.

One general lesson which emerges from this broad development in disequilibrium analysis is that the age-old view that the supply and demand mechanism secures market equilibrium, feeding the image of the invisible hand benefitting us all, is long overdue. This is probably the lesson that some Austrians find hardest to accept, but that others in their tradition have already recognized as an important principle. This is probably also the most important opportunity cost of retaining equilibrium theory. As Stiglitz (2004,

146) reports, the simplifying assumptions needed for 'clear' welfare analysis may give us a false sense of how well markets work. 'When the simplifying assumptions are dropped, it becomes apparent that the invisible hand is partly visible because it is simply not there: resource allocations will not, in general, be constrained Pareto efficient.' Stiglitz adds that it is extremely hard for the government to implement Pareto improvements due the demanding requirements on the information needed for such improvements. 'Thus, while a half century ago, some may have marvelled at the wonders of the market, believing that somehow we had the best of all possible worlds, today we are cognizant of the limitations of our world – but are unsure how, or in fact whether, it can improved upon.'

This observation may elicit two possible reactions. The first is to ignore the discomforting news that the invisible hand will not solve all our troubles. This is the choice equilibrium theorists make. The second option is to accept the reality that it is difficult to support policy proposals that may actually improve the economic well-being of mankind. At least the formal approach of neoclassical welfare analysis does not allow us to prove this potential for improvement in an unambiguous manner. My lesson has been that a less formal disequilibrium approach may offer a viable alternative. But this alternative will not be grand unifying theory on a par with general equilibrium analysis. The preferred approach is likely to be multifarious, leaning on different economic traditions and combining the insights of several scientific disciplines, and tailored to the question at hand. Disequilibrium analysis relies on knowledge that is specific and historically located, which means that we may be able to improve or replace the invisible hand after all. I find this a prospect that is well worth exploring and which deserves more attention from the economics profession at large.

WITH OF WITHOUT EQUILIBRIUM?

This book started with the observation that the concept of equilibrium has a long history in economics. As an afterthought, I shall return to some of the questions which started this inquiry in Chapter 1. What does economic equilibrium mean? What explains the persistence of the equilibrium concept? Why does it cause controversy between the different schools of economics?

These questions are interrelated. This book has shown that the popularity of the equilibrium concept, defined as an explanatory principle used to explain the working of decentralized coordination, is certainly not due to its success as a scientific tool. In particular, it demonstrates that Schumpeter in his seminal *History of Economic Analysis* (1954) has given us a false image of economics. Schumpeter's book has one overriding message and that is that the historical development of economic analysis underlines the steady growth of knowledge in economics. Reviewing the lessons of this book, my observation would be: What growth? Certainly, our theories have improved a great deal in various fields of economics, improving its consistency to great extent. In addition, the theoretical section of the economics department has been joined by an empirical counterpart which is the envy of many other social sciences. Nonetheless, we have left some huge gaps in our knowledge base. One of them is economic equilibrium.

Recall the discussion of the origin of equilibrium economics in Chapter 4. There, I cited Blaug who once said that the starting point for economics was the mystery which fascinated Adam Smith as much as it does the modern economist, namely the sense of order in the economic universe. This order refers to the relative harmonious way in which profit-seeking individuals conduct their exchange transactions with equally self-minding trading partners. Has equilibrium theory solved this mystery? I do not think so. We have a highly advanced theory, called Walrasian general equilibrium theory, which offers a sophisticated mathematical description of the problem and proves that, indeed, under specific conditions this dreamland may exist. How this solution comes about, we cannot prove in a rigorous manner, but of course there are many ad hoc ideas to fill in the blanks. This raises the question why we do not consider Walrasian general equilibrium analysis the final solution to Smith's mysterious invisible hand.

The reason why the quest continues, in both Walrasian and non-Walrasian corners of economics, is the lack of vision in Walrasian general equilibrium theory. In Chapter 2 I have defined vision as Schumpeter's notion of a pre-analytic knowledge, structuring a field of scientific study even before inquiry has begun. Schumpeter argued that the progress of scientific inquiry would sooner or later remove such ideological overtones from its tool kit. In the case of Walrasian general equilibrium theory, I would argue that this is indeed what has occurred, only the rooting out of ideology succeeded a bit too well. I believe that vision plays a crucial role in scientific discourse, not only as a pre-analytic guide for study, but also in more mature sciences for the interpretation and communication of results. In Walrasian general equilibrium analysis, this function has been lost due to its excessive mathematical formalism. The mathematics has become so complex that the step from mathematics to economics can no longer be made.

Is this bad? Other sciences have reveled in excessive mathematics as well and some of them seem to be thriving. The reason why I think that excessive formalism in economics is bad is that it has a tendency to conceal the problem underlying the theory. What knowledge have we gained when we solve the difficult formulas of Walrasian general equilibrium theory? A tool to Pareto optimize the economy, so the text book answer runs, referring to the two Welfare theorems that are linked to Walrasian general equilibrium theory. But these theorems operate under such strict (static) conditions that it is an illusion to think that they have any bearing on reality (Blaug 2007). This leaves Walrasian general equilibrium theory without compass, because what does it say about the mysterious coordination problem? It seems to suggest a laisser faire approach to policy, due to its emphasis on perfect competiton. But a small change in the problem setting of Walrasian general equilibrium is able to overturn this conclusion. Take the example of Akerlof and Yellen (1985b) who just slightly relax the condition of strict maximization and get results that are Pareto optimal to the fully rational GE model. This change of the equilibrium result has implications for policy, because the near rational GE model leaves scope, and in fact advises, active government involvement.

How does one discriminate between such theories that are almost identical, but for one small detail, the parameter *ß* which says that a fraction of the population fails to maximize? Lacking decisive empirical tests, most economists probably use something like intuition or vision. I do not think this is particularly bad or damaging to our science. I support Keynes's claim that 'economics is a science of thinking in terms of models joined to the art of choosing models which are relevant to the contemporary world'. GE theorists are very skillful mathematicians, but they have lost the art of understanding which model is relevant to the contemporary world. They are developing a model which originated in 1874 and seem to forget that the world underlying this model is changing rapidly. If after 135 years of theory development, Walrasian general equilibrium theory still offers no base to jump from theory to policy prescriptions, I contend that this theory has utterly failed as a solution to the coordination puzzle.

Does non-Walrasian theory fare any better? I have discussed several alternative schools in economics, which are certainly more 'visionary' than the Walrasian approach, but also do not generate impressive results. We have seen that where the economy is 'visualized' as a process rather than an end-state equilibrium, difficult questions emerge which have not been satisfactory solved by any of the alternative, non-Walrasian schools. Also, without the straightjacket of mathematical rigour, we notice a downside of the ideological impetus to science. Visions tend to collide and are thereby the fuel of many scientific quarrels. This explains the combative reputation of economic schools that principally eschew mathematics as a tool of inquiry, such as the Austrians. Apparently, the artists have a stronger penchant for disagreement and altercation than Walrasian general equilibrium theorists.

On the other hand, the disappointing results of these process-oriented alternatives to Walrasian general equilibrium also provide us with an answer to the question why the equilibrium concept is so long lived: Equilibrium is indispensable. Virtually all challengers to the Walrasian doctrine and its equilibrium concept, at one time or another, introduce their own variant of the equilibrium concept. They are forced to do so due to the sheer complexity of the economic world. What better way to study this world than by freezing it for a second. This is the essence of any equilibrium concept. Just assume that data remain fixed for a while; that forces balance; that potentially disrupting forces on average cancel out; that exchange proceeds at equilibrium prices, albeit temporarily; that prices tend towards a cost of production level; that competition pushes profits to a uniform rate; that capital reproduces at a constant rate; that evolution proceeds along a stable strategy; that the future is correctly foreseen; that there occur no unfavorable surprises, et cetera. Process theories often become end-state equilibrium economics in disguise, due to the adoption of such simplifying assumptions. These short cuts are not worrisome, as long as their function is recognized and their employment does not push the need for a more process-oriented approach to economic theory out of sight.

References

Akerlof, G.A. (1970), 'The Market for Lemons: Qualitative Uncertainty and the Market Mechanism', *Quarterly Journal of Economics*, **84** (3), 488–500.

Akerlof, G.A. (2002), 'Behavioral Macroeconomics and Macroeconomic Behavior', *American Economic Review*, **92** (3), 411–33.

Akerlof, G.A. and J.A. Yellen (1985a), 'A near rational model of the business cycle with price and wage inertia', *Quarterly Journal of Economics*, **100** (supplement), 823–38.

Akerlof, G.A. and J.A. Yellen (1985b), 'Can Small Deviations from Rationality Make Significant Differences to Economic Equilibria?', *American Economic Review*, **75** (Sep.), 708–20.

Akhtar, M.A. (1975), 'The 'classical dichotomy' in Ricardian economics', *History of Political Economy*, **7** (3), 299–311.

Alchian, A.A. (1950), 'Uncertainty, Evolution and Economic Theory', *Journal of Political Economy*, **58**, 211–21.

Allais, M. (1990), 'My conception of economic science', *Methodus*, **2** (1), 5–7.

Allen, R.G.D. (1967), *Macro Economic Theory: A Mathematical Treatment*, London: Macmillan.

Alter, M. (1990), *Carl Menger and the Origins of Austrian Economics*, Boulder, CO: Westfield Press.

Andvig, J.C. (1991), 'Verbalism and definitions in interwar theoretical macroeconomics', *History of Political Economy*, **23** (3), 431–55.

Anspach, R. (1972), 'The implications of the Theory of Moral Sentiments for Adam Smith's economic thought', *History of Political Economy*, **4** (1), 176–206.

Arrow, K.J. (1959), 'Toward a Theory of Price Adjustment', in M. Abramowitz (ed.), *The Allocation of Economic Resources*, Stanford, CA: Stanford University Press, pp. 55–63.

Arrow, K.J. (2000), 'Increasing returns: historiographic issues and path dependence', *European Journal of the History of Economic Thought*, **7** (2), 171–80.

Arrow, K.J., Block, H.D. and L. Hurwicz (1959), 'On the Stability of the Competitive Equilibrium, II', *Econometrica*, **27** (1), 82–109.

Asimakopulos, A. (1991), *Keynes's General Theory and Accumulation*, Cambridge, UK: Cambridge University Press.

Asimakopulos, A. (1992), 'The Nature and Role of Equilibrium in Keynes's General Theory', in M. Sebastiani (ed.), *The Notion of Equilibrium in Keynesian Theory*, London: Macmillan, pp. 1–12.

Backhouse, R.E. (1991), 'The neo Walrasian research programme in macroeconomics', in N.B. de Marchi and M. Blaug (eds), *Appraising Modern Economics: Studies in the Methodology of Scientific Research Programmes*, Aldershot UK and Brookfield, USA: Edward Elgar, pp. 403–426.

Backhouse, R.E. (1993), 'Lakatosian perspectives on general equilibrium analysis', *Economics and Philosophy*, **9** (2), 271–82.

Backhouse, R.E. (2004), 'History and equilibrium: A partial defense of equilibrium economics', *Journal of Economic Methodology*, **11** (3), 291–305.

Backhouse, R.E. (2006), 'Equilibrium and problem-solving in economics', in Mosini, V. (ed.), *Equilibium in Economics: Scope and Limits*, London: Routledge, pp. 150–65.

Baird, C.W. (1987), 'The Economics of Time and Ignorance: a review', *Review of Austrian Economics*, **1** (1), 189–206.

Barens, I. (1989), 'From the 'banana parable' to the principle of effective demand: some reflections on the origin, development and structure of Keynes's General Theory', in D.A. Walker (ed.), *Twentieth-Century Economic Thought*, Aldershot, UK and Brookfield, USA: Edward Elgar, pp. 111–32.

Barna, T. (1975), 'Quesnay's Tableau in modern guise', *Economic Journal*, **85** (Sep.), 485–96.

Barna, T. (1976), 'Quesnay's model of economic development', *European Economic Review*, **8** (4), 315–38.

Barro, R.J. and H.I. Grossman (1971), 'A General Disequilibrium Model of Income and Employment', *American Economic Review*, **61** (1), 82–93.

Barro, R.J. and X. Sala i Martin (1995), *Economic Growth*, New York: McGraw Hill.

Bast, J.H. (1935), *Vauban en Boisguillebert, hun beteekenis voor de economie in verleden en heden*, Groningen: J.B. Wolters.

Bast, J.H. (1966), 'Boisguilbert et le mercantilisme' in Institut National D'Études Démographiques (INED), *Pierre de Boisguilbert ou la Naissance de l'Économie Politique*, 2 vols., Paris, pp. 27–40.

Baumol, W.J. (1977), 'Say's (at least) eight laws, or what Say and James Mill may really have meant', *Economica*, **44** (May), 145–62.

Baumol, W.J. (1999), 'Retrospectives: Say's law', *Journal of Economic Perspectives*, **13** (1), 195–204.

Baumol, W.J. and Becker, G.S. (1952[1960]), 'The classical monetary theory: the outcome of the discussion', in W.R. Allen and J.J. Spengler (eds), *Essays in Economic Theory*, New York: McGraw-Hill.

Billoret, J.-L. (1989), 'Le circuit et l'équilibre de Boisguilbert dans le courant de l'analyse économique', in J. Hecht (ed.), *Boisguilbert parmi nous; actes du colloque international de Rouen (22-23 Mai 1975)*, Paris: L'Institut National D'Études Démographiques (INED), pp. 59–82.

Binmore, K. and L. Samuelson (1994), 'An Economist's Perspective on the Evolution of Norms', *Journal of Institutional and Theoretical Economics*, **150** (1), 45–71.

Birner, J. (1999), 'The Place of the Ricardo Effect in Hayek's Economic Research Programme', *Revue d'Économique Politique*, **109** (6), 803–16.

Birner, J. and R.W. van Zijp (eds) (1994), *Hayek: Co-ordination and Evolution*, London: Routledge.

Bittermann, H.J. (1940), 'Adam Smith's empiricism and the law of nature', *Journal of Political Economy*, **48** (4) and (5), 487–520 and 703–34.

Black, R.D.C. (1972), 'W.S. Jevons and the Foundation of Modern Economics', *History of Political Economy*, **4** (Fall), 98–112.

Blanchard, O. and S. Fischer (1989), *Lectures on Macroeconomics*, Cambridge, MA: MIT Press.

Blaug, M. (1958), *Ricardian Economics, a Historical Study*, Westport: Greenwood Press.

Blaug, M. (1975a), 'Kuhn versus Lakatos, of paradigms versus research programmes in the history of economics', *History of Political Economy*, reprinted in M. Blaug (1986), *Economic History and the History of Economics*, Hemel Hempstead: Harvester Wheatsheaf, pp. 233–64.

Blaug, M. (1975b), *The Cambridge Revolution: Success or Failure?*, second edition, London: The Institute of Economic Affairs.

Blaug, M. (1980), *The Methodology of Economics*, Cambridge, UK: Cambridge University Press.

Blaug, M. (1985), *Economic Theory in Retrospect*, third edition, Cambridge, UK: Cambridge University Press.

Blaug, M. (1991a), 'Second Thoughts on the Keynesian Revolution', *History of Political Economy*, **23** (2), 171–92.

Blaug, M. (1991b), 'Afterword' in N.B. De Marchi and M. Blaug (eds) (1991), *Appraising Modern Economics: Studies in the Methodology of Scientific Research Programmes*, Aldershot, UK and Brookfield, USA: Edward Elgar, pp. 499–512.

Blaug, M. (1992), *The Methodology of Economics, or How Economists Explain*, second edition, Cambridge, UK: Cambridge University Press.

Blaug, M. (1995), 'Why is the quantity theory of money the oldest surviving theory in economics?', in M. Blaug et al., *The Quantity Theory of Money:*

From Locke to Keynes and Friedman, Aldershot, UK and Brookfield, USA: Edward Elgar, pp. 27–49.

Blaug, M. (1997), 'Competition as an end-state and competition as a process', in *Not Only an Economist: Recent Essays*, Cheltenham, UK and Lyme, USA: Edward Elgar, pp. 66–86.

Blaug, M. (2001), 'Is Competition Such a Good Thing? Static Efficiency versus Dynamic Efficiency', *Review of Industrial Organization*, **19** (1), 37–48.

Blaug, M. (2003), 'The Formalist Revolution of the 1950s', in W.J. Samuels, J.E., Biddle and J.B. Davis (eds), *A Companion to the History of Economic Thought*, Oxford, UK: Blackwell, pp. 395–410.

Blaug, M. (2007), 'The fundamental theorems of modern welfare economics, historically contemplated', *History of Political Economy*, **39** (2), 185–207.

Blaug, M. (2008), 'The trade-off between rigour and relevance: Sraffian Economics as a case in point', *History of Policital Economy*, **41** (2), 219–47.

Bleaney, M.F. (1976), *Underconsumption Theories: a History and Critical Analysis*, New York: International Publishers.

Bliss, C.J. (1975), *Capital Theory and the Distribution of Income*, Amsterdam: North Holland.

Boettke, P.J., Horwitz, S. and D.L. Prychitko (1994), 'Beyond equilibrium economics: reflection on the uniqueness of the Austrian tradition' in P.J. Boettke and D.L. Prychitko (eds), *The Market Process: Essays in Contemporary Austrian Economics*, Aldershot, UK and Brookfield, USA: Edward Elgar, pp. 62–79.

Böhm-Bawerk, E. von (1921a), *Kapital und Kapitalzins. Zweite Abteilung: Positive Theorie des Kapitales*, Erster Band, fourth edition, Jena: Gustav Fischer.

Böhm-Bawerk, E. von (1921b), *Kapital und Kapitalzins. Zweite Abteilung: Positive Theorie des Kapitales*, Zweiter Band: Exkurse, fourth edition, Jena: Gustav Fischer.

Boisguilbert, P. (1695[1966]), *Le Détail de la France*, in Institut National D'Études Démographiques (INED), *Pierre de Boisguilbert ou la Naissance de l'Économie Politique*, 2 vols., Paris, pp. 581–663.

Boisguilbert, P. (1705[1966]), *Factum de la France*, manuscrit inédit, in Institut National D'Études Démographiques (INED), *Pierre de Boisguilbert ou la Naissance de l'Économie Politique*, 2 vols., Paris, pp. 741–98.

Boisguilbert, P. (1707a[1966]), *Traité de la nature, culture, commerce et intérêt des grains*, in Institut National D'Études Démographiques (INED), *Pierre de Boisguilbert ou la Naissance de l'Économie Politique*, 2 vols., Paris, pp. 827–78.

Boisguilbert, P. (1707b[1966]), *Factum de la France*, in Institut National D'Études Démographiques (INED), *Pierre de Boisguilbert ou la Naissance de l'Économie Politique*, 2 vols., Paris, pp. 879–956.

Boisguilbert, P. (1707c[1966]), *Dissertation de la nature des richesses, de l'argent et des tributs*, in Institut National D'Études Démographiques (INED), *Pierre de Boisguilbert ou la Naissance de l'Économie Politique*, 2 vols., Paris, pp. 973–1012.

Boland, L.A. (1986), *Methodology for a New Microeconomics: the Critical Foundations*, Boston, MA: Allen & Unwin.

Boland, L.A. (1987), 'On the relevance of neo-Walrasian economic theory: a review', *History of Political Economy*, **19** (4), 659–666.

Boland, L.A. (1992), *The Principles of Economics: Some Lies My Teachers Told Me*, London: Routledge.

Bowley, M. (1963), 'Some seventeenth century contributions to the theory of value', *Economica* N.S., **30** (May), 122–39.

Bowley, M. (1973), *Studies in the History of Economic Theory Before 1870*, London: Macmillan.

Brakman, S. and B.J. Heijdra (2004), 'Introduction' in S. Brakman and B.J. Heijdra (eds), *The Monopolistic Competition Revolution in Retrospect*, Cambridge, UK: Cambridge University Press, pp. 1–45.

Brandis, R. (1989), 'Time concepts in the history of economic thought: the case of the stationary state', in D.A. Walker (ed.), *Classical and Neoclassical Economic Thought*, Aldershot, UK and Brookfield, USA: Edward Elgar, pp. 71–81.

Brewer, A. (1988), 'Cantillon and the land theory of value', *History of Political Economy*, **20** (1), 1–14.

Brown, D.J. (1991), 'Equilibrium Analysis with Non Convex Technologies', in W. Hildenbrand and H. Sonnenschein (eds), *Handbook of Mathematical Economics*, vol. IV, Amsterdam: North Holland, pp. 1963–95.

Brown, V. (1994), *Adam Smith's Discourse: Canonicity, Commerce and Consience*, London: Routledge.

Buchanan, J. and V. Vanberg (1991), 'The market as a creative process', *Economics and Philosophy*, **7** (2), 167–86.

Bürgenmeier, B. (1994), 'The misperception of Walras', *American Economic Review*, **84** (1), 342–52.

Caldwell, B. (1982), *Beyond Positivism: Economic Methodology in the Twentieth Century*, London: Unwin Hyman.

Caldwell, B. (1988), 'Hayek's Transformation', *History of Political Economy*, **20** (4), 513–41.

Caminati, M. (1981), 'The theory of interest in the classical economists', *Metro-economica*, **33** (1-2-3), 79–104.

Campbell, T.D. (1971), *Adam Smith's Science of Morals*, London: George Allen & Unwin.

Canard, N.F. (1801), *Principes d'Economie Politique*, Paris: F. Buisson.

Cantillon, R. (1755[1931]), Essai sur la Nature du Commerce en Général, transl. H. Higgs, New York: Kelley, 1964.

Caravale, G. (1992), 'Keynes and the Concept of Equilibrium', in M. Sebastiani (ed.), *The Notion of Equilibrium in the Keynesian Theory*, London: Macmillan, pp. 74–98.

Caravale, G. (1997), 'The notion of equilibrium in economic theory', in G. Caravale (ed.), *Equilibrium and Economic Theory*, London: Routledge, pp. 11–35.

Cassel, G. (1927), *Theoretische Sozialökonomie*, fourth edition, Leipzig: A. Deichertsche.

Chalk, A.F. (1951), 'Natural law and the rise of economic individualism in England', *Journal of Political Economy*, **59** (4), 332–47.

Choksy, G.D. (1992), 'Previously undocumented macroeconomics from the 1680s: the analytical arguments and policy recommendations of Sir Dudley North and Roger North', *History of Political Economy*, **24** (2), 515–32.

Choksy, G.D. (1995), 'The bifurcated economics of Sir Dudley North and Roger North: one holistic analytical engine', *History of Political Economy*, **27** (3), 477–92.

Clark, C.M.A. (1987), 'Equilibrium, Market Process and Historical Time', *Journal of Post Keynesian Economics*, **10** (2), 270–81.

Clark, C.M.A. (1992), *Economic Theory and Natural Philosophy*, Aldershot, UK and Brookfield, USA: Edward Elgar.

Clower, R.W. (1965), 'The Keynesian counter-revolution: a theoretical appraisal' in F. Hahn and F. Brechling (eds), *The Theory of the Interest Rate*, London: Macmillan, pp. 103–25.

Clower, R.W. (1995), 'Axiomatics in Economics', *Southern Economic Journal*, **62** (2), 307–19.

Clower, R.W. (1998), 'Three centuries of demand and supply' *Journal of the History of Economic Thought*, **20** (4), 397–410.

Coats, A.W. (1969) , 'Is there a 'structure of scientific revolutions' in economics?' *Kyklos*, **22** (2), 289–96.

Coddington, A. (1983), *Keynesian economics: the search for first principles*, London: George Allen & Unwin.

Cohen, A.J. (1993), 'Does Joan Robinson's Critique of Equilibrium Entail Theoretical Nihilism?' in G. Mongiovi and C. Ruhl (eds), *Macroeconomic Theory: Diversity and Convergence*, Aldershot, UK and Brookfield, USA: Edward Elgar, pp. 222–39.

Cohen, A.J. and G.C. Harcourt (2003), 'Whatever Happened to the Cambridge Capital Controversies?', *Journal of Economic Perspectives*, **17** (1), 199–214.

Colander, D. (2006), 'Post Walrasian Macroeconomics: Some Historic Links' in D. Colander (ed.), *Post Walrasian Macroeconomics: Beyond the Dynamic Stochastic General Equilibrium Model*, Cambridge, UK: Cambridge University Press, pp. 46–69.

Colonna, M. (1990), 'Hayek on money and equilibrium', *Contributions to Political Economy*, **9** (1), 43–68.

Comte, A. (1975), *Auguste Comte and Positivism: the Essential Writings*, G. Lenzer (ed.), New York: Harper & Row.

Cooper, R. and A. John (1988), 'Coordinating Coordination Failures in Keynesian Models', *Quarterly Journal of Economics*, **103** (3), 441–63.

Cottrell, A. (1994), 'Post Keynesian Monetary Economics: A critical survey', *Cambridge Journal of Economics*, **18** (6), 587–605.

Cournot, A.A. (1838), *Researches into the Mathematical Principles of the Theory of Wealth*, transl. N.T. Bacon, New York: Macmillan, 1927.

Cowan, R. and M.J. Rizzo (1996), 'The Genetic Causal Tradition and Modern Economic Theory', *Kyklos*, **49** (3), 273–317.

Cowen, T. and R. Fink (1985), 'Inconsistent equilibrium constructs: the evenly rotating economy of Mises and Rothbard', *American Economic Review*, **75** (4), 866–9.

Daal, J. van and A. Jolink (1993), *The Equilibrium Economics of Leon Walras*, London: Routledge.

Damme, E. van (1994), 'Evolutionary Game Theory', *European Economic Review*, **38** (3-4), 847–58.

Davidson, P. (1991), *Controversies in Post Keynesian Economics*, Aldershot, UK and Brookfield, USA: Edward Elgar.

Davis, J.R. (1990), 'Adam Smith on the Providential Reconciliation of Individual and Social Interests: Is Man Led by an Invisible Hand or Misled by a Sleight of Hand?', *History of Political Economy*, **22** (2), 341–52.

Debreu, G. (1959), *Theory of Value: An Axiomatic Analysis of Economic Equilibrium*, New Haven: Yale University Press.

Debreu, G. (1991), 'The mathematization of economic theory', *American Economic Review*, **81** (1), 1–7.

Desai, M. (1994), 'Equilibrium, expectations and knowledge', in J. Birner and R.W. van Zijp (eds), *Hayek: Coordination and Evolution*, London: Routledge, pp. 25–50.

Diamond, A.M. (1988), 'The empirical progressiveness of the general equilibrium research program', *History of Political Economy*, **20** (1), 119–35.

Diamond, P.A. (1994), *On Time: Lectures on Models of Equilibrium*, Cambridge, UK: Cambridge University Press.

Dimand, R.W. (1989), 'The reception of Keynes's Treatise on Money: a Review of the Reviews', in D.A. Walker (ed.), *Perspectives in the History of Economic Thought*, vol. II, Aldershot, UK and Brookfield, USA: Edward Elgar, pp. 87–96.

Dixit, A.K. (2004), 'Some reflections on theories and applications of monopolistic competition' in S. Brakman and B.J. Heijdra (eds), *The Monopolistic Competition Revolution in Retrospect*, Cambridge, UK: Cambridge University Press, pp. 123–33.

Dixit, A. and J. Stiglitz (1977), 'Monopolistic competition and optimum product diversity' in *American Economic Review*, **67** (3), 297–308.

Dixon, W. (2008), 'Ricardo: Economic Thought and Social Order', *Journal of the History of Economic Thought*, **30** (2), 235–53.

Domar, E.D. (1946), 'Capital Expansion, Rate of Growth, and Employment', *Econometrica*, **14** (2), 137–47.

Dome, T. (1989), 'A Theoretical Analysis of Sismondi's Tableau Economique', *Metro-economica*, **40** (2), 119–34.

Don, H. and J. Verbruggen (2006), 'Models and methods for economic policy: 60 years of evolution at CPB', *CPB Discussion Paper* no. 55, The Hague.

Dow, S.C. (1996), *The Methodology of Macroeconomic Thought*, second edition, Cheltenham, UK and Brookfield, USA: Edward Elgar.

Dupuit, J. (1844), *De l'Utilité et de sa mesure*, in M. de Bernardi (ed.) (1934), Torino: La Riforma Sociale, 97–162.

Dupuit, J. (1849), *De l'Influence des Péages sur l'Utilité des Voies de Communication*, Paris: Guilaumin.

Dyke Roberts, H. van (1935), *Boisguilbert, Economist of the Reign of Louis XIV*, New York: Columbia University Press.

Eagly, R.V. (1969), 'A physiocratic model of dynamic equilibrium', *Journal of Political Economy*, **77** (1), 66–84.

Eatwell, J. and M. Milgate (1983), *Keynes's economics and the theory of value and distribution*, London: Duckworth.

Ebeling, R. (1997), 'Money, economic fluctuations, expectations and period analysis: the Austrian and Swedish economists in the interwar period', in W. Keizer, B. Tieben and R.W. van Zijp (eds), *Austrian Economics in Debate*, London: Routledge, pp. 42–74.

Eckstein, Z. and G.J. van den Berg (2007), 'Empirical labor search: A survey', *Journal of Econometrics*, **136** (2), 531–64.

Edgeworth, F.Y. (1881), *Mathematical Physics*, London: Kegan Paul.

Ees, H. van and H. Garretsen (1990), 'The right answers to the wrong question? An assessment of the microfoundations debate', in *De Economist*, **138** (2), 123–145.

Eichner, A.S. and J.A. Kregel (1975), 'An Essay on Post Keynesian Theory: A New Paradigm in Economics', *Journal of Economic Literature*, **13** (4), 1293–314.

Ekelund, R.B. and R.F. Hébert (1997), *A History of Economic Theory and Method*, third edition, New York: McGraw-Hill.

Ekelund, R.B. and R.F. Hébert (2002), 'Retrospectives: The Origins of Neoclassical Microeconomics', *Journal of Economic Perspectives*, **16** (3), 197–215.

Eltis, W. (1975a), 'François Quesnay: a reinterpretation I: the Tableau Economique', *Oxford Economic Papers*, **27** (2), 167–200.

Eltis, W. (1975b), 'François Quesnay: a reinterpretation II: the theory of economic growth', *Oxford Economic Papers*, **27** (3), 327–51.

Eltis, W. (1995), 'John Locke: the quantity theory of money and the establishment of a sound currency', in M. Blaug et al., *The Quantity Theory of Money: From Locke to Keynes and Friedman*, Aldershot, UK and Brookfield, USA: Edward Elgar, pp. 4–26.

Eltis, W. (1996), 'The Grand Tableau of François Quesnay's Economics', *European Journal of the History of Economic Thought*, **3** (1), 21–43.

Endres, A.M. (1995), 'Carl Menger's theory of price formation reconsidered', *History of Political Economy*, **27** (2), 261–87.

Endres, A.M. (1996), 'Some Microfoundations of Austrian Economics: Böhm Bawerk's Version', *European Journal of the History of Economic Thought*, **3** (1), 87–109.

Ertürk, K. (1996), 'On the Keynesian notion of equilibrium and dynamics', *Cambridge Journal of Economics*, **20**, 371–86.

Evensky, J. (1987), 'The two voices of Adam Smith: moral philosopher and social critic', *History of Political Economy*, **19** (3), 447–68.

Evensky J (1998), 'Adam Smith's moral philosophy: the role of religion and its relationship to philosophy and ethics in the evolution of society', *History of Political Economy*, **30** (1), 17–42.

Fetter, F.W. (1969), 'The rise and decline of Ricardian economics', *History of Political Economy*, **1** (1), 67–84.

Fisher, I. (1911), *The Purchasing Power of Money: Its Determination and Relation to Credit, Interest and Crises*, New York: A.M. Kelley.

Fisher, I. (1930), *The Theory of Interest: as Determined by Impatience to Spend Income and Opportunity to Invest it*, New York: Macmillan.

Fisher, F.M. (1971), 'Aggregate Production Functions and the Explanation of Wages: A Simulation Experiment', *Review of Economics and Statistics*, **53** (4), 305–25.

Fisher, F.M. (1983), *Disequilibrium Foundations of Equilibrium Economics*, Cambridge, UK: Cambridge University Press.

Fitzgibbons, A. (1995), *Adam Smith's System of Liberty, Wealth and Virtue: The Moral and Political Foundation of The Wealth of Nations*, Oxford, UK: Clarendon.

Forget, E.L. (1990), 'John Stuart Mill's Business Cycle', *History of Political Economy*, **22** (4), 629–42.

Fox-Genovese, E. (1976), *The Origins of Physiocracy: Economic Revolution and Social Order in Eighteenth Century France*, Ithaca: Cornell University Press.

Freeman, A. and G. Carchedi (1996), *Marx and Non-equilibrium Economics*, Cheltenham, UK and Brookfield, USA: Edward Elgar.

Friedman, M. (1953), *Essays in Positive Economics*, Chicago, IL: University of Chicago Press.

Garegnani, P. (1970), 'Heterogeneous Capital, the Production Function and the Theory of Distribution', *Review of Economic Studies*, **37** (3), 407–36.

Garegnani, P. (1976), 'On a change in the notion of equilibrium in recent work on value and distribution', in J. Eatwell and M. Milgate (eds.) (1983), Keynes's Economics and the Theory of Value and Distribution, London: Duckworth, pp. 129–45.

Garegnani, P. (1983), 'A reply to Joan Robinson', in J. Eatwell and M. Milgate (eds.) (1983), Keynes's Economics and the Theory of Value and Distribution, London: Duckworth, pp. 72–8.

Garretsen, H. (1991), *Beyond the Invisible Hand: How to Extend Keynes's Analysis of the Coordination Problem?*, Ph.D. thesis, University of Groningen.

Garrison, R.W. (1995), 'Equilibrium and Entrepreneurship', in R. Koppl, P.J. Boettke and M.J. Rizzo (eds), *Advances in Austrian Economics*, **2** (A), Stamford, CT: JAI Press, pp. 67–78.

Gay, P. (1966), *The Englightenment, an Interpretation, Vol.I: The Rise of Modern Paganism*, New York: W.W. Norton & Company.

Gay, P. (1969), *The Englightenment, an Interpretation, Vol.II: The Science of Freedom*, New York: W.W. Norton & Company.

Georgescu Roegen, N. (1983), 'Gossen: his life and work in historical perspective', in H. Gossen, *The Laws of Human Relations*, Cambridge, MA: MIT Press.

Gerson, L.P. (1990), *God and Greek Philosophy. Studies in the Early History of Natural Theology*, London: Routledge.

Gibbons, R. (1992), *A Primer in Game Theory*, Hemel Hempstead: Harvester Wheatsheaf.

Giocoli, N. (2003), *Modeling Rational Agents: From Interwar Economics to Early Modern Game Theory*, Cheltenham, UK and Brookfield, USA: Edward Elgar.

Gordon, R.J. (1990), 'What is New Keynesian Economics?', *Journal of Economic Literature*, **28** (3), 1115–71.

Gossen, H.H. (1854), *Entwickelung der Gesetze des Menschlichen Verkehrs und der daraus fließenden Regeln für menschliches Handeln*, Braunschweig: Friedrich Vieweg.

Grandmont, J.M. (1983), *Money and value: a reconsideration of classical and neoclassical monetary theories*, Cambridge, UK: Cambridge University Press.

Grattan-Guinness, I. (2006), 'Equilibrium in mechanics and then in economics, 1860–1920', in V. Mosini (ed.), *Equilibium in Economics: Scope and Limits*, London: Routledge, pp. 19–44.

Groenewegen, P. (1970), 'A reappraisal of Turgot's theory of value, exchange and price determination', *History of Political Economy*, **2** (1), 177–96.

Groenewegen, P. (1971), 'A reinterpretation of Turgot's theory of capital and interest', *Economic Journal*, **81** (June), 327–40.

Groenewegen, P. (1983), 'Turgot's place in the history of economic thought: a bicentenary estimate', *History of Political Economy*, **15** (4), 585–616.

Groenewegen, P. (1987), 'The international foundations of classical political economy in the eighteenth century: an alternative perspective', in S. Todd Lowry (ed.), *Pre Classical Economic Thought*, Boston, MA.: Kluwer, pp. 211–20.

Grossman, S.J. and J.E. Stiglitz (1976), 'Information and Competitive Price Systems', *American Economic Review*, **66** (2), 246–53.

Grubel, H.G. (1961), 'Ricardo and Thornton on the transfer mechanism', *Quarterly Journal of Economics*, **75** (2), 292–301.

Guggenheim, T. (1989), *Preclassical Monetary Theories*, London: Pinter.

Gunning, J.P. (1989), 'Mises on the evenly rotating economy', *Review of Austrian Economics*, **3** (1), 123–35.

Gunning, J.P. (1997), 'The theory of entrepreneurship in Austrian economics', in W. Keizer, B. Tieben and R.W. van Zijp (eds), *Austrian Economics in Debate*, London: Routledge, pp. 172-91.

Hahn, F.H. (1958), 'Gross Substitutes and the Dynamic Stability of General Equilibrium', *Econometrica*, **26** (1), 169–70.

Hahn, F.H. (1961), 'Review of Theory of Value', *Journal of Political Economy*, **69**, 204.

Hahn, F.H. (1965), 'On Some Problems of Proving the Existence of an Equilibrium in a Monetary Economy', in F.H. Hahn and F.P.R. Brechling (eds), *Theory of Interest Rates*, London: Macmillan, pp. 128–32.

Hahn, F.H. (1973), *On the Notion of Equilibrium in Economics*, Cambridge, UK: Cambridge University Press.

Hahn, F.H. (1975), 'Revival of Political Economy: The Wrong Issues and the Wrong Argument', *Economic Record*, **51** (Sept.), 360–4.

Hahn, F.H. (1981), F.H., 'General Equilibrium Theory', in D. Bell and I. Kristol (eds), *The Crisis in Economic Theory*, New York: Basic Books.

Hahn, F.H. (1982), 'The Neo Ricardians', *Cambridge Journal of Economics*, **6** (4), 353–74.

Hahn, F.H. (1984), *Equilibrium and Macroeconomics*, Oxford, UK: Basil Blackwell.

Hall, R.L. and C.J. Hitch (1939), 'Price theory and business behaviour', *Oxford Economic Papers*, **2** (May), 12–45.

Hamilton, E.J. (1969), 'The Political Economy of France at the Time of John Law', *History of Political Economy*, **1** (1), 123–49.

Hamouda, O.F. and B.B. Price (1997), 'The justice of the just price', *European Journal of the History of Economic Thought*, **4** (2), 191–216.

Han, Z. and B. Schefold (2006), 'An empirical investigation of paradoxes: reswitching and reverse capital deepening in capital theory', *Cambridge Journal of Economics*, **30** (5), 737–65.

Hands, D.W. (1984), 'What Economics is Not: an Economist's Response to Rosenberg', *Philosophy of Science*, **51** (3), 495–503.

Hands, D.W. (1985a), 'Second thoughts on Lakatos', *History of Political Economy*, **17** (1), 1–16.

Hands, D.W. (1985b), 'The structuralist view of economic theories: a review essay. The case of general equilibrium in particular', *Economics and Philosophy*, **1** (2), 303–35.

Hansson, B.A. (1982), *The Stockholm School and the Development of Dynamic Method*, London: Croom Helm.

Harcourt, G.C. (1972), *Some Cambridge Controversies in the Theory of Capital*, Cambridge, UK: Cambridge University Press.

Harcourt, G.C. (1985), 'Post Keynesian Theory: Quite Wrong and/or Nothing New' in P. Arestis and T. Skouras (eds), *Post Keynesian Theory A Challenge to Neo Classical Economics*, Sussex: Wheatsheaf, pp. 125–45.

Harcourt, G.C. and P. Kerr (2003), 'Keynes and the Cambridge School', in W.J. Samuels, J.E. Biddle and J.B. Davis (eds), *A Companion to the History of Economic Thought*, Oxford, UK: Blackwell, pp. 343–59.

Hardach, K. (1980), *Political Economy of Germany in the Twentieth Century*, Berkeley, CA: University of California Press.

Hargreaves Heap, S.P. (1992), *The New Keynesian Macroeconomics*, Aldershot, UK and Brookfield, USA: Edward Elgar.

Harrod. R.F. (1936), *The Trade Cycle: An Essay*, London: Macmillan.

Harrod, R.F. (1939), 'An Essay in Dynamic Theory', *Economic Journal*, **49** (March), 14–33.

Harrod, R.F. (1948), *Towards a Dynamic Economics*, London: Macmillan.

Harrod, R.F. (1970), 'Harrod after twenty one years: a comment', *Economic Journal*, **74** (December), 737–41.

Hausman, D.M. (1981a), *Capital, Interest and Prices: an Essay in the Philosophy of Science*, New York: Columbia University Press.

Hausman, D.M (1981b), 'Are General Equilibrium Theories Explanatory?' in J. Pitt (ed.), *Philosophy in Economics*, Dordrecht: Reidel, pp. 17–32.

Hausman, D.M (1981c), 'John Stuart Mill's Philosophy of Economics', *Philosophy of Science*, **48** (3), 363–85.

Hausman, D.M (1990), 'Supply and demand explanations and their Ceteris Paribus clauses', *Review of Political Economy*, **2** (2), 168–86.

Hausman, D.M. (1992), *The Inexact and Separate Science of Economics*, Cambridge, UK: Cambridge University Press.

Hayek, F.A. (1926), 'Some remarks on the problem of imputation', in R. McCloughry (ed) (1984), *Money, Capital and Fluctuations*, London: Routledge & Kegan Paul, pp. 33–54.

Hayek, F.A. (1928), 'Intertemporal price equilibrium and movements in the value of money', in R. McCloughry (ed.) (1984), *Money, Capital and Fluctuations*, London: Routledge & Kegan Paul, pp. 71–117.

Hayek, F.A. (1931a), *Prices and Production*, second edition, London: Routledge & Kegan Paul, 1935.

Hayek, F.A. (1931b), 'Reflections on the 'Pure Theory of Money' of Mr. J.M. Keynes (I)', in J.C. Wood, and R.N. Woods (eds), *Friedrich A. Hayek: Critical Assessments*, vol. I, London: Routledge.

Hayek, F.A. (1933a), *Monetary Theory and the Trade Cycle*, New York: Kelley.

Hayek, F.A. (1933b), 'Neutral Money', in R. McCloughry (ed.) (1984), *Money, Capital and Fluctuations*, London: Routledge & Kegan Paul, pp. 159–62.

Hayek, F.A. (1937), 'Economics and knowledge', *Economica*, N.S. **4**, 33–54.

Hayek, F.A. (1939), 'Price expectations, monetary disturbances and malinvestments' in F.A. Hayek (1975), *Profits, Interest and Investment*, New York: Kelley, pp. 135–56.

Hayek, F.A. (1941), *The Pure Theory of Capital*, London: Macmillan.

Hayek, F.A. (1944), *The Road to Serfdom*, London: Routledge, 1991.

Hayek, F.A. (1945), 'The use of knowledge in society', *American Economic Review*, **35** (4), 519–30.

Hayek, F.A. (1952), *The Sensory Order: An Inquiry into the Foundations of Theoretical Psychology*, Chicago, IL: University of Chicago Press.

Hayek, F.A. (1967a), 'The Theory of Complex Phenomena', in F.A. Hayek (1967), *Studies in Philosophy, Politics and Economics*, London: Routledge & Kegan Paul, pp. 22–42.
Hayek, F.A. (1967b), 'The Result of Human Action but not of Human Design', in F.A. Hayek (1967), *Studies in Philosophy, Politics and Economics*, London: Routledge & Kegan Paul, pp. 96–105.
Hayek, F.A. (1967c), 'Notes on the Evolution of Systems of Rules of Conduct', in F.A. Hayek (1967), *Studies in Philosophy, Politics and Economics*, London: Routledge & Kegan Paul, pp. 66–81.
Hayek, F.A. (1976), *Denationalization of Money: An Analysis of the Theory and Practice of Concurrent Currencies*, London: Institute of Economic Affairs.
Hayek (1978), 'Competition as a discovery procedure', in F.A. Hayek (1978), *New Studies in Philosophy, Politics, Economics and the History of Ideas*, London: Routledge & Kegan Paul, pp. 179–90.
Hayek, F.A. (1979), 'Toward a Free Market Monetary System', *Journal of Libertarian Studies*, **3** (1), 1–8.
Hayek, F.A. (1988), *The Fatal Conceit: The Errors of Socialism*, London: Routledge.
Heath, E. (1995), 'The commerce of sympathy: Adam Smith on the emergence of morals', *Journal of the History of Philosophy*, **33** (3), 447–66.
Hébert, R.F. (1987), 'In search of economic order: French predecessors of Adam Smith' in S. Todd Lowry (ed.), *Pre Classical Economic Thought*, Boston: Kluwer, pp. 185–210.
Heilbroner, R.L. (1982), 'The socialization of the individual in Adam Smith', *History of Political Economy*, **14** (3), 427–39.
Heijdra, B.J., and A.D. Lowenberg (1988), 'The neoclassical economic research program: some Lakatosian and other considerations', *Australian Economic Papers*, **27** (Dec.), 272–84.
Heilbroner, R. (1990), 'Analysis and Vision in the History of Modern Economic Thought', *Journal of Economic Literature*, **28** (3), 1097–114.
Heiner, R.H. (1983), 'The origin of predictable behaviour', *American Economic Review*, **73** (4), 560–95.
Hellwig, M. (1993), 'The challenge of monetary theory', *European Economic Review*, **37** (2), 215–42.
Herlitz, L. (1996), 'From spending and reproduction to circuit flow and equilibrium: the two conceptions of Tableau Économique', *European Journal of the History of Economic Thought*, **3** (1), 1–20.
Hicks, J.R. (1936), 'The General Theory: A First Impression', in J.R. Hicks (1982), *Money, Interest and Wages*, Oxford: Basil Blackwell, pp. 83–99.

Hicks, J.R. (1937), 'Mr. Keynes and the Classics', in J.R. Hicks (1982), *Money, Interest and Wages*, Oxford: Basil Blackwell, pp. 100–15.

Hicks, J.R. (1939), *Value and Capital*, second edition, Oxford: Clarendon.

Hicks, J.R. (1950), *A Contribution to the Theory of the Trade Cycle*, Oxford: Clarendon.

Hicks, J.R. (1956), 'Methods of dynamic analysis', in J.R. Hicks (1982), *Money, Interest and Wages*, Oxford: Basil Blackwell, pp. 217–35.

Hicks, J.R. (1965), *Capital and Growth*, Oxford: Clarendon.

Hicks, J.R. (1967a), 'A Note on the Treatise', *Critical Essays in Monetary Theory*, Oxford: Clarendon, pp. 189–202.

Hicks, J.R. (1967b), 'The Hayek story', *Critical Essays in Monetary Theory*, Oxford: Clarendon, pp. 203–15.

High, J. (1990), *Maximizing, Action and Market Adjustment*, München: Philosophia Verlag.

Hirshleifer, J. "The expanding domain of economics", *American Economic Review*, **75** (6), 53–68.

Hodgson, G. (1985), 'Persuasion, expectations and the limits to Keynes', in T. Lawson and H. Pesaran (eds), *Keynes' Economics: Methodological Issues*, London: Routledge, pp. 10–35.

Hodgson, G.M. (1988), *Economics and Institutions, A Manifesto for a Modern Institutional Economics*, Cambridge: Polity Press.

Hodgson, G. (1993), *Economics and Evolution: Bringing Life Back into Economics*, Cambridge: Polity Press.

Hodgson, G.M. (1998), 'The Approach of Institutional Economics', *Journal of Economic Literature*, **36** (1), 166–92.

Hodgson, G.M. (1999), *Evolution and Institutions: On Evolutionary Economics and the Evolution of Economics*, Cheltenham, UK and Brookfield, USA: Edward Elgar.

Hollander, S. (1977), 'Ricardo and the Corn Laws: a revision', *History of Political Economy*, **9** (1), 1–47.

Hollander, S. (1979), *The Economics of David Ricardo*, Toronto: Toronto University Press.

Hollander, S. (1985), *The Economics of J.S. Mill*, 2 vols., Toronto: Toronto University Press.

Hollander, S. (1987), *Classical Economics*, Toronto: Toronto University Press.

Hoogduin, L.H. (1991), *Some Aspects of Uncertainty and the Theory of a Monetary Economy*, PhD. Thesis, Groningen.

Hoover, K.D. (1995), 'Why does methodology matter for economists', *Economic Journal*, **105** (May), pp. 715–734.

Hume, D. (1752), *Writings on Economics*, E. Rotwein (ed.), Edinburgh and London: Nelson.

Huntington, S.P. (1996), *The Clash of Civilizations and the Remaking of World Order*, New York: Simon & Schuster.

Hutchison, T.W. (1953), *A Review of Economic Doctrines, 1870–1929*, Oxford: Clarendon.

Huussen, G.M. (1985), *Economisch Evenwicht: Een Vakwijsgerig-methodologisch Onderzoek naar de Betekenis en Funktie van het Evenwichtsbegrip in de Economie*, Ph.D. thesis, Amsterdam: VU Universiteitspers.

Ingrao, B. and G. Israel (1990), *The Invisible Hand: Economic Equilibrium in the History of Science*, Cambridge, MA.: MIT Press.

Irwin, D.A. (1996), *Against the Tide: An Intellectual History of Free Trade*, Princeton: Princeton University Press.

Isnard, A.N. (1781), *Traité des Richesses*, Lausanne: François Grasset.

Jaffé, W. (ed.) (1965), *Correspondence of Léon Walras and Related Papers*, 3 vols., Amsterdam: North Holland.

Jaffé, W. (1969), 'A.N. Isnard, Progenitor of the Walrasian General Equilibrium Model', *History of Political Economy*, **1** (1), 19–43.

Jaffé, W. (1974), 'The Birth of Leon Walras's Elements', in D.A. Walker (1983), *William Jaffé's Essays on Walras*, Cambridge, UK: Cambridge University Press, pp. 78–92.

Jaffé, W. (1976), 'Menger, Jevons and Walras De-homogenized', *Economic Inquiry*, **14** (4), 511–24.

Jaffé, W.(1977), 'The normative bias of the Walrasian model: Walras versus Gossen', *Quarterly Journal of Economics*, **91** (3), 371–87.

Jaffé, W. (1980), 'Walras's Economics as Others See It', *Journal of Economic Literature*, **18** (2), 528–49.

Jaffé, W. (1981), 'Another look at Léon Walras's theory of tâtonnement', *History of Political Economy*, **18** (2), 313–36.

Janssen, M.C.W. (1990), *Micro and Macro in Economics: an Inquiry into their Relation*, Groningen: Wolters Noordhoff.

Janssen, M.C.W. (1991), 'Comment on R. Backhouse' in M. Blaug and N. de Marchi (eds), *Appraising Modern Economics: Studies in the Methodology of Scientific Research Programmes*, Aldershot, UK and Brookfield, USA: Edward Elgar, pp. 427–32.

Jevons, W.S. (1877[1958]), *The Principles of Science: a Treatise on Logic and Scientific Method*, New York: Dover.

Jevons, W.S. (1879), *The Theory of Political Economy*, second edition, New York: Kelley.

Jolink, A. (1991), *Liberté, Egalité, Rareté: The Evolutionary Economics of Léon Walras*, Amsterdam: Thesis/Tinbergen Institute.

Kahneman, D. (2003), 'A Psychological Perspective on Economics', *American Economic Review, Papers and Proceedings*, **93** (May), 162–68.

Kaldor, N. (1942), 'Professor Hayek and the Concertina Effect', in J.C. Wood and R.N. Woods (eds) (1991), *Friedrich A. Hayek: Critical Assessments*, vol. 2, London: Routledge, pp. 1–25.

Kaldor, N. (1956), 'Alternative theories of distribution', *Review of Economic Studies*, **23** (2), 83–100.

Kaldor, N. (1957), 'A model of economic growth', *Economic Journal*, **67** (September), 591–624.

Kaldor, N. (1972), 'The irrelevance of equilibrium economics', *Economic Journal*, **82** (December), 1237–52.

Keesing, F.A.G. (1939), *Het Evenwichtsbegrip in de Economische Literatuur*, Purmerend: J. Muusses.

Keizer, W. (1994), 'Hayek's critique of socialism', in J. Birner and R.W. van Zijp (eds), *Hayek, Coordination and Evolution*, London: Routledge, pp. 207–31.

Keizer, W. (1997), 'Schumpeter's Walrasian Stand in the Socialist Calculation Debate', in W. Keizer, B. Tieben and R.W. van Zijp (eds) (1997), *Austrian Economics in Debate*, London: Routledge, pp. 75–94.

Keynes, J.M. (1923), *A Tract on Monetary Reform*, London: Macmillan.

Keynes, J.M. (1930), *A Treatise on Money*, 2 vols., in D. Moggridge (ed.) (1971), *The Collected Writings of John Maynard Keynes*, vols. V and VI, London: Macmillan.

Keynes, J.M. (1933), 'Thomas Robert Malthus' *Essays in Biography*, D. Moggridge (ed.) (1972), *The Collected Writings of John Maynard Keynes*, vol. X, London: Macmillan.

Keynes, J.M. (1936), *General Theory of Employment, Interest and Money*, D. Moggridge (ed.) (1973), *The Collected Writings of John Maynard Keynes*, vol. VII, London: Macmillan.

Keynes, J.M. (1937), 'The General Theory of Employment', in D. Moggridge (ed.) (1973), *The Collected Writings of John Maynard Keynes*, vol. XIV, pp. 109–123.

Keynes, J.M., (1973), *The General Theory and After: Preparation*, in D. Moggridge (ed.), *The Collected Writings of John Maynard Keynes*, vol. XIII, London: Macmillan.

Keynes, J.M., (1979), *The General Theory and After: a Supplement*, in D. Moggridge (ed.), *The Collected Writings of John Maynard Keynes*, vol. XXIX, London: Macmillan.

Kim, K. (1988), *Equilibrium Business Cycle Theory in Historical Perspective*, Cambridge: Cambridge University Press.

Kindleberger, C.P. (1978), *Manias, Panics, and Crashes: A History of Financial Crises*, third edition, New York: John Wiley & Sons.

King, J.E. (2003), *A History of Post Keynesian Economics since 1936*, Cheltenham, UK and Brookfield, USA: Edward Elgar.

Kirman, A. (2006), 'Foreword' in D. Colander (ed.), *Post Walrasian Macroeconomics*, Cambridge, UK: Cambridge University Press, pp. xiii–xxi.

Kirzner, I.M. (1973), *Competition and Entrepreneurship*, Chicago, IL: Chicago University Press.

Kirzner, I.M. (1976), 'Equilibrium versus market process', in E.G. Dolan, *The Foundations of Modern Austrian Economics*, Kansas City: Sheed & Ward, pp. 115–25.

Kirzner, I.M. (1978), 'The entrepreneurial role in Menger's system', *Atlantic Economic Journal*, **6** (3), 31–45.

Kirzner, I.M. (1979), *Perception, Opportunity and Profit: Studies in the Theory of Entrepreneurship*, Chicago, IL: Chicago University Press.

Kirzner, I.M. (1988), 'The economic calculation debate: lessons for Austrians', *Review of Austrian Economics*, **2**, 1–18.

Kirzner, I.M. (1990), 'Commentary' to S. Boehm, 'The Austrian tradition: Schumpeter and Mises', in K. Hennings and W. Samuels (eds), *Neoclassical Economic Theory, 1870 to 1930*, Dordrecht: Kluwer, pp. 242-49.

Kirzner, I.M. (1992), *The Meaning of Market Process*, London: Routledge.

Kirzner, I.M. (1994a), 'Introduction', *Classics in Austrian Economics*, vol. I, London: Pickering & Chatto.

Kirzner, I.M. (1994b), 'On the economics of time and ignorance', in P.J. Boettke and D.L. Prychitko (eds), *The Market Process: Essays in Contemporary Austrian Economics*, Aldershot, UK and Brookfield, USA: Edward Elgar, pp. 38–44.

Kirzner, I.M. (1997a), 'Entrepreneurial Discovery and the Competitive Market Process: An Austrian Approach', *Journal of Economic Literature*, **35** (1), 60–85.

Kirzner, I.M. (1997b), *How Markets Work: Disequilibrium, Entrepreneurship and Discovery*, London: Institute of Economic Affairs.

Kirzner, I.M. (1999), 'Creativity and/or Alertness: A Reconsideration of the Schumpeterian Entrepreneur', *Review of Austrian Economics*, **11** (1), 5–17.

Kiyotaki, N. and R. Wright (1989), 'On Money as a Medium of Exchange', *Journal of Political Economy*, **97** (4), 927–54.

Klamer, A. and D. Colander (1990), *The Making of an Economist*, Boulder: Westview Press.

Klant, J.J. (1972), *Spelregels voor economen: De logische structuur van economische theorieën*, Leiden: Stenfert Kroese.

Klant, J.J. (1985), 'The slippery transition', in T. Lawson and H. Pesaran (eds), *Keynes' Economics: Methodological Issues*, London: Routledge, pp. 80–98.

Klant, J.J. (1994), *The Nature of Economic Thought: Essays in Economic Methodology*, Aldershot, UK and Brookfield, USA: Edward Elgar.

Klausinger, H.J. (1990), Equilibrium methodology as seen from a Hayekian prespective, *Journal of History of Economic Thought*, **12** (1), 61–75.

Klausinger, H.J. (2008), 'Hayek's monetary and capital theories: puzzles and controversies', mimeo.

Kleer, R.A. (1993), 'Adam Smith on the Morality of the Pursuit of Fortune', *Economics and Philosophy*, **9** (2), 289–95.

Kleer, R.A. (1995), 'Final causes in Adam Smith's Theory of Moral Sentiments', *Journal of the History of Philosophy*, **33** (2), 275–301.

Kleer, R.A. (2003), 'The 1696 Recoinage', *The Literary Encyclopedia*, http://www.litencyc.com.

Knight, F.H. (1921), *Risk, Uncertainty and Profit*, Boston: Houghton.

Kohn, M. (1986), 'Monetary analysis, the equilibrium method, and Keynes' General Theory', *Journal of Political Economy*, **94** (6), 1191–224.

Koopmans, J.G. (1933), 'Zum Problem des Neutralen Geldes', in F.A. Hayek (ed.), *Beiträge zur Geldtheorie*, Vienna: Julius Springer.

Koopmans, T.C. (1957), *Three Essays on the State of Economic Science*, New York: McGraw Hill.

Koppl, R. (1992), 'Invisible-hand explanations and neoclassical economics: toward a post marginalist economics', *Journal of Institutional and Theoretical Economics*, **148** (2), 292–313.

Koppl, R. (1995), 'The Walras Paradox', *Eastern Economic Journal*, **21** (1), 43–55.

Kornai, J. (1971), *Anti-Equilibrium: on Economic Systems Theory and the Tasks of Research*, Amsterdam: North-Holland.

Kregel, J.A. (1973), *The Reconstruction of Political Economy: an Introduction to Post Keynesian Economics*, London: Macmillan.

Kregel, J.A. (1976), 'Economic modelling in the face of uncertainty', *Economic Journal*, **86** (June), 209–25.

Kregel, J.A. (1995), 'Neoclassical price theory, institutions, and the evolution of securities market organisations', *Economic Journal*, **105** (March), 459–70.

Kresge, S. and L. Wenar (1994), *Hayek on Hayek: An Autobiographical Dialogue*, London: Routledge.

Kubota, A. (1966), 'La théorie des prix proportionnels et de l'équilibre chez Boisguilbert', in Institut National D'Études Démographiques (INED), *Pierre de Boisguilbert ou la Naissance de l'Économie Politique*, 2 vols., Paris, pp. 71–84.

Kurz, H.D. and N. Salvadori (1995), *Theory of Production: A Long Period Analysis*, Cambridge, UK: Cambridge University Press.

Kydland, F.E. and E.C. Prescott (1982), 'Time to Build and Aggregate Fluctuations', *Econometrica*, **50** (6), 1345–70.

Lachmann, L.M. (1940), 'A reconsideration of the Austrian theory of industrial fluctuations', *Economica*, **7** (May), 179–96.

Lachmann, L.M. (1943), 'The role of expectations in economics as a social science', *Economica*, **10** (Feb.), 12–23.

Lachmann, L.M. (1945), 'A note on the elasticity of expectations', *Economica*, **12** (Nov.), 248–53.

Lachmann, L.M. (1947), 'Complementarity and substitution in the theory of capital', *Economica*, **14** (May), 108–19.

Lachmann, L.M. (1956), *Capital and its Structure*, Kansas City: Sheed Andrews and McMeel.

Lachmann, L.M. (1971), *The Legacy of Max Weber*, Berkeley: The Glendessary Press.

Lachmann, L.M. (1976a), 'From Mises to Shackle: an essay on Austrian economics and the kaleidic society', *Journal of Economic Literature*, **14** (1), 54–62.

Lachmann, L.M. (1976b), 'On the Central Concept of Austrian Economics: Market Process', in E.G. Dolan, *The Foundations of Modern Austrian Economics*, Kansas City: Sheed & Ward, pp. 126–32.

Lachmann, L.M. (1977), *Capital, Expectations, and the Market Process: Essays on the Theory of the Market Economy*, W.E. Grinder (ed.), Kansas City: Sheed Andrews and McMeel.

Lachmann, L.M. (1986), *The Market as an Economic Process*, Oxford: Blackwell.

Laidler, D. (1991), *The Golden Age of the Quantity Theory: The Development of Neoclassical Monetary Economics: 1870–1914*, Hemel Hempstead: Philip Allan.

Laidler, D. (1999), *Fabricating the Keynesian Revolution: Studies of the Inter-war Literature on Money, the Cycle, and Unemployment*, New York and Cambridge: Cambridge University Press.

Lakatos, I. (1970), 'History of Science and its Rational Reconstructions', *PSA: Proceedings of the Biennial Meeting of the Philosophy of Science Association*, 91–136.

Lakatos, I. (1976), *Proofs and Refuations, the Logic of Mathematical Discovery*, Cambridge, UK: Cambridge University Press.

Lambert, P. (1956), 'The law of markets prior to J.B. Say and the Say-Malthus debate', *International Economic Papers*, **1**, 7–22.

Lange, O. (1936), 'On the Economic Theory of Socialism', in B.E. Lippincott (ed.) (1964), *On the Economic Theory of Socialism*, New York: McGraw Hill.

Langlois, R.N. (1986), 'The new institutional economics: an introductory essay' in R.N. Langlois (ed.), *Economics as a Process*, Cambridge, UK: Cambridge University Press, pp. 1–25.

Langlois, R.N. (1994), 'The market process: An evolutionary view', in P.J. Boettke and D.L. Prychitko (eds.), *The Market Process: Essays in Contemporary Austrian Economics*, Aldershot, UK and Brookfield, USA: Edward Elgar, pp. 29–37.

Latsis, S.J. (1976), 'A research programme in economics', in S.J. Latsis (ed.), *Method and Appraisal in Economics*, Cambridge, UK: Cambridge University Press, pp. 1–41.

Lavoie, D. (1985), *Rivalry and Central Planning: The Socialist Calculation Debate Reconsidered*, Cambridge, UK: Cambridge University Press.

Lavoie, D. (1990), 'Introduction to F.A. Hayek's Theory of Cultural Evolution: Market and Cultural Processes as Spontaneous Orders', *Cultural Dynamics*, **3** (1), 1–11.

Lawson, T. (1985), 'Uncertainty and Economic Analysis', *Economic Journal*, **95** (Dec.), 909–27.

Lawson, T. (1997), *Economics and Reality*, London: Routledge.

Lawson, T. (2003), *Reorienting Economics*, London: Routledge.

Lawson, T. (2005), 'The (confused) state of equilibrium analysis in modern economics: an explanation', *Journal of Post Keynesian Economics*, **27** (3), 423–44.

Lawson, T. (2006), 'Tensions in modern economics. The case of equilibrium analysis', in V. Mosini (ed.), *Equilibium in Economics: Scope and Limits*, London: Routledge, pp. 133–49.

Leijonhufvud, A. (1968), *On Keynesian Economics and the Economics of Keynes*, London: Oxford University Press.

Leijonhufvud, A. (1981), 'The Wicksell Connection', in *Information and Coordination*, Oxford, UK: Oxford University Press.

Le Mercier de la Rivière, P.P. (1767[1910]), *L'Ordre Naturel et Essentiel des Sociétés Politiques*, Paris: Paul Geuthner.

Leontief, W. (1971), 'Theoretical Assumptions and Nonobserved Facts', *American Economic Review*, **61** (1), 1–7.

Lester, R.A. (1946), 'Shortcomings of marginal analysis for wage employment analysis', *American Economic Review*, **36** (1), 63–82.

Letwin, William (1963), *The Origins of Scientific Economics: English Economic Thought 1660–1776*, Westport, CT: Greenwood.

Lewin, P. (1997), 'Hayekian equilibrium and change', *Journal of Economic Methodology*, **4** (2), 245–66.

Lindahl, E. (1929), 'The place of capital in the theory of price', in E. Lindahl (1939), *Studies in the Theory of Money and Capital*, New York: Augustus M. Kelley, pp. 271–350.

Lindahl, E. (1939), *Studies in the Theory of Money and Capital*, New York: Augustus M. Kelley.

Lindgren, J.R. (1969), 'Adam Smith's Theory of Inquiry', *Journal of Political Economy*, **77** (6), 897–915.

Lindgren, J.R. (1973), *The Social Philosophy of Adam Smith*, The Hague: Martinus Nijhoff.

Littlechild, S. (1979), 'Comment: Radical Subjectivism or Radical Subversion?' in M.J. Rizzo (ed.), *Time, Uncertainty and Disequilibrium*, Lexington, MA: LexingtonBooks, pp. 32–48.

Loasby, B.J. (1991), *Equilibrium and Evolution*, Manchester: Manchester University Press.

Loasby, B.J. (1999), *Knowledge, Institutions and Evolution in Economics*, London: Routledge.

Locke, J. (1691), *Some Considerations on the Consequences of the Lowering of Interest and the Raising of the Value of Money*, London: Awnsham and John Churchill.

Lovejoy, A.O. (1936), *The Great Chain of Being, a study of the history of an idea*, New York: Harper Torchbook, 1960.

Lowry, S.T. (1969), 'Aristotle's mathematical analysis of exchange', *History of Political Economy*, **1** (1), 44–66.

Lowry, S.T. (1974), 'The archaeology of the circulation concept in economic theory', *Journal of the History of Ideas*, **35** (3), 429–44.

Lowry, S.T. (1979), 'Recent literature on ancient Greek economic thought' *Journal of Economic Literature*, **17** (1), 65–86.

Lucas, R. (1975), 'An Equilibrium Model of the Business Cycle', *Journal of Political Economy*, **83** (6), 1113–44.

Lundberg, E. (1930), 'On the concept of economic equilibrium', *Structural Change and Economic Dynamics*, **7** (3), 361–90.

Lundberg, E. (1937), *Studies in the Theory of Economic Expansion*, New York: Kelley & Millman, 1955.

Macfie, A.L. (1959), 'Adam Smith's Moral Sentiments as a foundation for his Wealth of Nations', *Oxford Economic Papers*, **11** (3), pp. 209–228, reprinted in J.C. Wood (ed.) (1984), *Adam Smith: Critical Assessments*, vol. II, London: Croom Helm, pp. 87–104.

Macfie, A.L. (1961), 'Adam Smith's Theory of Moral Sentiments', *Scottish Journal of Political Economy*, **8** (1), pp. 12–27, reprinted in J.C. Wood (ed.) (1984), *Adam Smith: Critical Assessments*, vol. I, London: Croom Helm, pp. 297–309.

Macfie, A.L. (1967), 'The moral justification of free enterprise. A lay sermon on an Adam Smith text', *Scottish Journal of Political Economy*, **14** (Feb), pp. 1–11, reprinted in J.C. Wood (ed.) (1984), *Adam Smith: Critical Assessments*, vol. I, London: Croom Helm, pp. 343–50.

Macfie, A.L. (1971), 'The invisible hand of Jupiter', *Journal of the History of Ideas*, **32** (4), 595–99.

Machlup, F. (1958), 'Equilibrium and Disequilibrium: Misplaced Concreteness and Disguised Politics', *Economic Journal*, **68** (March), 1–24.

Machlup, F. (1959), 'Statics and Dynamics: Kaleidoscopic Words', in F. Machlup (1963) *Semantic Issues in Economic Methodology*, Englewood Cliffs: Prentice-Hall, pp. 9–42.

MacLennan, B. (1972), 'Jevons's philosophy of science', *The Manchester School*, **40** (1), 53–71.

Mailath, G.J. (1998), 'Do People Play Nash Equilibrium? Lessons From Evolutionary Game Theory', *Journal of Economic Literature*, **36** (3), 1347–74.

Mäki, U. (1996), 'Two portraits of economics', *Journal of Economic Methodology*, **3** (1), 1–38.

Mäki, U. (2008), 'Method and appraisal in economics: 1976–2006', *Journal of Economic Methodology*, **15** (4), 409–23.

Malinvaud, E. (1972), *Lectures on Microeconomic Theory*, Amsterdam: North-Holland.

Malinvaud, E. (1977), *The Theory of Unemployment Reconsidered*, second edition, Oxford: Basil Blackwell.

Mankiw, N.G. and D. Romer (1991), *New Keynesian Economics*, 2 vols., Cambridge, MA: MIT Press.

Marchi, N.B. de (1970), 'The empirical content and longevity of Ricardian economics', *Economica*, **37** (August), 257–76.

Marchi, N.B. de and M. Blaug (eds) (1991), *Appraising Modern Economics: Studies in the Methodology of Scientific Research Programmes*, Aldershot, UK and Brookfield, USA: Edward Elgar.

Marshall, A. (1898), 'Mechanical and Biological Analogies in Economics', in A.C. Pigou (ed.) (1925), *Memorials of Alfred Marshall*, London: Macmillan, pp. 312–318.

Marshall, A. (1920), *Principles of Economics*, 8th edition, London: Macmillan.

Marx, K. (1997a), *Capital*, vol. II, *Karl Marx Friedrich Engels Collected Works*, **36**, New York: International Publishers.

Marx, K. (1997b), *Capital*, vol. III, *Karl Marx Friedrich Engels Collected Works*, **37**, New York: International Publishers.

Mayer, H. (1932), 'Der Erkenntniswert der funktionellen Preistheorien', in H. Mayer (ed.), *Die Wirtschaftstheorie der Gegenwart*, **2**, Wien: Springer, pp. 147–239.

Mayer, T. (1993), *Truth versus Precision in Economics*, Aldershot, UK and Brookfield, USA: Edward Elgar.

Maynard Smith, J. (1982), *Evolution and the Theory of Games*, Cambridge, UK: Cambridge University Press.

McCloskey, D.N. (1983), 'The rhetoric of economics', *Journal of Economic Literature*, **21** (2), 481–517.

McCloskey, D.N. (1985), *The Rhetoric of Economics*, Brighton: Harvester Wheatsheaf.

McCloskey, D.N. (1994), *Knowledge and Persuasion in Economics*, Cambridge, UK: Cambridge University Press.

McCloskey, D.N. (1997), *The Vices of Economists: The Virtues of the Bourgeoisie*, Amsterdam: University of Amsterdam Press.

McCormick, B.J. (1992), *Hayek and the Keynesian Avalanche*, Hemel Hempstead: Harvester Wheatsheaf.

McDonald, S.L. (1954), 'Boisguillebert; neglected precursor of aggregate demand theorists', *Quarterly Journal of Economics*, **68** (3), 401–14.

Meek, R.L. (1963), 'Physiocracy and the early theories of under-consumption' in *The Economics of Physiocracy*, Cambridge, MA: Harvard University Press, pp. 313–44.

Meek, R.L. (1967a), 'The Scottish contribution to Marxist sociology' in *Economics and Ideology and Other Essays*, London: Chapman & Hall, pp. 34–50.

Meek, R.L. (1967b), 'The Decline of Ricardian Economics in England', in *Economics and Ideology and Other Essays*, London: Chapman & Hall, pp. 51–74.

Meek, R.L. (1973), *Studies in the Labour Theory of Value*, London: Laurence and Wishart.

Mehrling, P. (2006), 'The problem of time in the DSGE model and the Post Walrasian alternative' in D. Colander (ed.), *Post Walrasian Macroeconomics*, Cambridge, UK: Cambridge University Press, pp. 70–79.

Ménard, C. (1990), 'The Lausanne Tradition: Walras and Pareto', in K. Henning and W. Samuels (eds), *Neoclassical Economic Theory, 1870 to 1930*, Boston, MA: Kluwer, pp. 95–136.

Menger, C. (1871), *Principles of Economics*, Grove City: Libertarian Press, 1994.

Menger, C. (1883[1985]), *Investigations into the Method of the Social Sciences: with Special Reference to Economics*, New York: New York University Press.

Milford, K. (1990), 'Menger's methodology', in B.J. Caldwell (ed.), *Carl Menger and his Legacy in Economics*, Durham and London: Duke University Press, pp. 215–40.

Milgate, M. (1987), 'Economic Equilibrium', in J. Eatwell, M. Milgate and P. Newman (eds), *The New Palgrave: A Dictionary of Economics*, London: Macmillan.

Mill, J.S. (1909), *Principles of Political Economy*, Sir William Ashley (ed.), Clifton: Kelley.

Mill, J.S. (1974), *A System of Logic*, in J.M. Robson (ed.), *Collected Works of John Stuart Mill*, vols. 7 and 8, London: Routledge and Kegan Paul.

Mirabeau, Victor de Riquetti marquis de (1760), *L'Ami des Hommes, ou Traité de la Population*, 4 vols., 6th edition, Hambourg: Chrétien Hérold.

Mirowski, P. (1982), 'Adam Smith, empiricism and the rate of profit in eighteenth century England', *History of Political Economy*, **14** (2), 178–98.

Mirowski, P. (1989), *More Heat than Light: Economics as Social Physics, Physics as Nature's Economics*, Cambridge, UK: Cambridge University Press.

Mirowski, P. and P. Cook (1990), 'Walras's "Economics and Mechanics": Translation, Commentary and Context' in W.J. Samuels (ed.), *Economics as Discourse: Analysis of the Language of Economists*, Boston, MA: Kluwer, pp. 189–224.

Mises, L. (1920), 'Economic calculation in the socialist commonwealth', in F.A. Hayek (ed.) (1933), *Collectivist Economic Planning*, (translated by S. Adler), Clifton: Kelley.

Mises, L. (1924), *Theorie des Geldes und der Umlaufsmittel*, second edition, Leipzig: Duncker & Humblot.

Mises, L. (1936), *Socialism: an Economic and Sociological Analysis*, new edition, London: Jonathan Cape.

Mises, L. (1949), *Human Action*, London: William Hodge.

Molinier, J. (1959), *Les Métamorphoses d'une Théorie Économique: Le Revue National chez Boisuilbert, Quesnay et J.-B. Say*, Paris: Armand Colin.

Mongiovi, G. (2002), 'Vulgar economy in Marxian garb: a critique of Temporal Single System Marxism', *Review of Radical Political Economics*, **34** (4), 393–416.

Monroe, A.E. (1923), *Monetary Theory Before Adam Smith*, New York: A.M. Kelley, 1966.

Mooij, R.A. de (2006), *Reinventing the Welfare State*, The Hague: CPB.

Morgan, M.S. (1990), *The History of Econometric Ideas*, Cambridge, UK: Cambridge University Press.

Morgenstern, O. (1935), 'Vollkommene Voraussicht und wirtschaftliches Gleichgewicht', *Zeitschrift für Nationalökonomie*, **6** (3), 337–57.

Morishima, M. (1977), *Walras's Economics: a Pure Theory of Capital and Money*, Cambridge, UK: Cambridge University Press.

Morishima, M. (1991), 'General Equilibrium Theory in the Twenty-First Century', *Economic Journal*, **101** (Jan.), 69–74

Morrow, G.R. (1927), 'Adam Smith: Moralist and Philosopher', *Journal of Political Economy*, **35** (3), pp. 321–342, reprinted in J.C. Wood (ed.) (1984), *Adam Smith: Critical Assessments*, vol. I, London: Croom Helm, pp. 168–81.

Mortensen, D.T. and C.A. Pissarides (1999), 'New Developments in Models of Search in the Labor Market', in O. Ashenfelter and D. Card (eds), *Handbook of Labor Economics*, Amsterdam: North Holland, pp. 2567–627.

Mosini, V. (ed.) (2006), *Equilibium in Economics: Scope and Limits*, London: Routledge.

Moss, L.S. (1978), 'Carl Menger's Theory of Exchange', *Atlantic Economic Journal*, **6** (3), 17–30.

Moss, L.S. (1997), 'Austrian economics and the abandonment of the classic thought experiment', in W. Keizer, B. Tieben and R.W. van Zijp (eds), Austrian Economics in Debate, London: Routledge, pp. 151–71.

Moss, L.S. and K.I. Vaughn (1986), 'Hayek's Ricardo Effect: A Second Look', *History of Political Economy*, **18** (4), pp. 545–565, reprinted in J.C. Wood and R.N. Woods (eds) (1991), *Friedrich A. Hayek: Critical Assessments*, vol. 2, London: Routledge, pp. 156–76.

Mosselmans, B. (1999), *From Classical to Neoclassical: The Economic Thought of William Stanley Jevons (1835–1882) and its Relation to his Ethics, Logic and Aesthetics*, Ph.D. thesis, Brussels.

Mosselmans, B. (2000), 'The Omitted Mathematics of Hans von Mangoldt', *Journal of Economic Studies*, **27** (4/5), 382–93.

Murphy, A.E. (1986), *Richard Cantillon: Entrepreneur and Economist*, Oxford: Clarendon.

Myers, M.L. (1972), 'Philosophical Anticipations of Laissez Faire', *History of Political Economy*, **4** (Spring), 163–75.

Myers, M.L. (1976), 'Adam Smith's concept of equilibrium', *Journal of Economic Issues*, **10** (3), 560–75.

Myers, M.L. (1983), *The Soul of Modern Economic Man: Ideas of Self Interest, Thomas Hobbes to Adam Smith*, Chicago, IL: University of Chicago Press.

Myerson, R.B. (1999), 'Nash Equilibrium and the history of economic theory', *Journal of Economic Literature*, **37** (3), 1067–82.

Myrdal, G. (1939), *Monetary Equilibrium*, New York: Augustus M. Kelley.

Nagel, E. (1961), *The Structure of Science: Problems in the Logic of Scientific Explanation*, London: Routledge & Kegan Paul.

Negishi, T. (1989), *History of Economic Theory*, Amsterdam: North Holland.

Nell, E.J. (1967), 'Theories of Growth and Theories of Value', *Economic Development and Cultural Change*, **16** (1), 15–26.

Nelson, R.R. (1995), 'Recent Evolutionary Theorizing About Economic Change', *Journal of Economic Literature*, **33** (1), 48–90.

Nelson, R.R. and S.G. Winter (1982), *An Evolutionary Theory of Economic Change*, Cambridge, MA: Belknap Press of Harvard University Press.

Nelson, R.R. and S.G. Winter (2002), 'Evolutionary Theorizing in Economics', *Journal of Economic Perspectives*, **16** (2), 23–46.

Nieli, R. (1986), 'Spheres of Intimacy and the Adam Smith Problem', *Journal of the History of Ideas*, **47** (4), 611–24.

North, Sir Dudley (1691), 'Discourses Upon Trade', in Jacob H. Hollander (ed.) (1907), *A Reprint of Economic Tracts*, Baltimore, MD: John Hopkins Press.

Nozick, R. (1994), 'Invisible Hand Explanations', *American Economic Review*, **84** (2), 314–8.

O'Driscoll, G.P. (1977a), *Economics as a Coordination Problem: The Contributions of Friedrich A. Hayek*, Kansas City: Sheed Andrews & McMeel.

O'Driscoll, G.P. (1977b), 'Spontaneous order and the coordination of economic activities', *Journal of Libertarian Studies*, **1** (2), 137–51.

O'Driscoll, G.P. and M.J. Rizzo (1996), *The Economics of Time and Ignorance*, 2nd edition, London: Routledge.

Oncken, A. (1886), *Die Maxime 'Laissez faire et laissez passer': ihr Ursprung, ihr Werden*, Bern: K.J. Wyss.

Oncken, A. (1897), 'The Consistency of Adam Smith', *Economic Journal*, **7** (September), pp. 443–450, reprinted in J.C. Wood (ed.) (1984), *Adam Smith: Critical Assessments*, vol. I, London: Croom Helm, pp. 1–6.

Oswald, D.J. (1995), 'Metaphysical beliefs and the foundations of Smithian political economy', *History of Political Economy*, **27** (3), 449–76.

Pack, S.J. (1995), 'Theological (and Hence Economic) Implications of Adam Smith's "Principles which Lead and Direct Philosophical Enquiries"', *History of Political Economy*, **27** (2), 289–307.

Pasinetti, L. (1960), 'A mathematical formulation of the Ricardian system', *Review of Economic Studies*, **27** (2), 78–98.

Pasinetti, L.L. (1969), 'Switches of technique and the "rate of return" in capital theory', *Economic Journal*, **79** (September), 508–31.

Pasinetti, L.L. (2000), 'Critique of the Neoclassical Theory of Growth and Distribution', *Banca Nazionale del Lavoro Quarterly Review*, **53** (No. 215), 383–431.

Patinkin, D. (1956), *Money, Interest and Prices*, Evanston Ill.: Row, Petersen and Company.

Patinkin, D. (1976), *Keynes's Monetary Thought: A Study of Its Development*, Durham: Duke University Press.

Patinkin, D. (1982), *Anticipations of the General Theory? And Other Essays on Keynes*, Oxford: Blackwell.

Patinkin, D. (1992), 'A Note on Keynes's Use of the Term Equilibrium in the General Theory', in M. Sebastiani (ed.), *The Notion of Equilibrium in Keynesian Theory*, London: Macmillan, pp. 13–17.

Patinkin, D. (1993), 'On the Chronology of the General Theory', *Economic Journal*, **103** (May), 647–63.

Peach, T. (1988), 'David Ricardo: a review of some interpretative issues' in W.O. Thweatt (ed.), *Classical Political Economy*, Dordrecht: Kluwer, pp. 103–31.

Peach, T. (2007), 'Ricardo as a "Classical Economist": The "New View" Reexamined, *History of Political Economy*, **39** (2), 293–306.

Peart, Sandra J. (1993), 'W.S. Jevons's Methodology of Economics: some implications of the procedures for "inductive quantification"', *History of Political Economy*, **25** (3), 435–60.

Perrot, Jean Claude (1992a), 'Équilibre économique et déterminisme au XVIIIe siècle', in *Une Histoire Intellectuelle de l'Économie Politique; XVIIe XVIIIe siècle*, Paris: Éditions de l'École des Hautes Études en Sciences Sociales, pp. 237–55.

Perrot, Jean Claude (1992b), 'La main invisible et le Dieu caché' in *Une Histoire Intellectuelle de l'Économie Politique; XVIIe XVIIIe siècle*, Paris: Éditions de l'École des Hautes Études en Sciences Sociales, pp. 333–54.

Petsoulas, C. (2001), *Hayek's Liberalism and its Origins: His Idea of Spontaneous Order and the Scottish Enlightenment*, London: Routledge.

Petty, W. (1690), *Political Arithmetick*, London: Robert Clavel.

Peyton Young, H. (1998), *Individual Strategy and Social Structure: An Evolutionary Theory of Institutions*, Princeton, NJ: Princeton University Press.

Phelps, E.S. (1969), 'The New Macroeconomics in Inflation and Employment Theory', *American Economic Review*, **59** (2), 147–60.

Popper, K.R. (1963), *Conjectures and Refutations: the Growth of Scientific Knowledge*, New York: Harper Torchbooks.

Quesnay, F. (1756), 'Fermiers', article paru dans le tome VI de l'Encyclopédie, in F. Quesnay (1888), *Oeuvres Économiques et Philosophiques*, Aalen: Scientia, pp. 159–92.

Quesnay, F. (1757), 'Grains', article paru dans le tome VII de l'Encyclopédie, in F. Quesnay (1888), *Oeuvres Économiques et Philosophiques*, Aalen: Scientia, pp. 193–249.

Quesnay, F. (1758), *Tableau Économique*, in M. Kuczynski and R.L. Meek (eds), *Quesnay's Tableau Économique*, London: Macmillan.

Quesnay, F. (1764), *Philosophie Rurale, ou Économie Générale et Politique de Agriculture*, Aalen: Scientia.

Quesnay, F. (1765), 'Le Droit Naturel', in Institut National D'Études Démographiques (INED) (1958), *Quesnay et la physiocratie*, 2 vols., Paris, pp. 729–42.

Quesnay, F. (1766), 'Analyse du Tableau Économique', in F. Quesnay (1888), *Oeuvres Économiques et Philosophiques*, Aalen: Scientia, pp. 305–28.

Rankin, S. (1980), 'Supply and demand in Ricardian price theory: a reinterpretation', *Oxford Economic Papers*, **32**, 241–62.

Raphael, D.D. (1975), 'The impartial spectator', in A.S. Skinner and T. Wilson (eds), *Essays on Adam Smith*, Oxford, UK: Clarendon, pp. 83–99.

Raphael, D.D. and A.L. Macfie (1976), 'Introduction', *Glasgow Edition of the Works and Correspondence of Adam Smith, vol. I, Theory of Moral Sentiments*, Indianapolis: Liberty Fund, pp. 1–52.

Rashid, S. (1977), 'Malthus' model of general gluts', *History of Political Economy*, **9** (3), 366–83.

Redman, D.A. (1993), 'Adam Smith and Isaac Newton', *Scottish Journal of Political Economy*, **40** (2), 210–30.

Reid, G. (1987), 'Disequilibrium and increasing returns in Adam Smith's analysis of growth and accumulation', *History of Political Economy*, **19** (1), 87–107.

Reisman, D.A. (1971), 'Henry Thornton and classical monetary economics', *Oxford Economic Papers*, **23** (1), 70–89.

Remenyi, J.V. (1979), 'Core Demi Core Interaction: Toward a General Theory of Disciplinary and Subdisciplinary Growth', *History of Political Economy*, **11** (1), 30–63.

Reuten, G. (2004), '"Zirkel vicieux" or Trend Fall? The Course of the Profit Rate in Marx's Capital III', *History of Political Economy*, **36** (1), 163–86.

Ricardo, D. (1951–1955), *The Works and Correspondence of David Ricardo*, P. Sraffa (ed.), 11 vols., London: Cambridge University Press.

Rizzo, M.J. (1979), *Time, Uncertainty and Disequilibrium: Exploration of Austrian Themes*, Lexington, MA.: Lexington.

Rizzo, M.J. (1996), 'Introduction: Time and Ignorance After Ten Years' in G.P. O'Driscoll and M.J. Rizzo (1996), *The Economics of Time and Ignorance*, 2nd edition, London: Routledge, pp. xiii–xxxiii.

Robbins, L.C. (1930), 'On a Certain Ambiguity in the Conception of Stationary Equilibrium', *Economic Journal*, **40** (June), 194–214.

Robbins, L.C. (1932), *An Essay on the Nature & Significance of Economic Science*, 2nd edition, London: Macmillan.

Robbins, L.C. (1971), *Autobiography of an Economist*, London: Macmillan.

Robinson, J. (1933), 'The Theory of Money and the Analysis of Output', *Review of Economic Studies*, **1** (1), 22–6.
Robinson, J. (1954), 'The production function and the theory of capital', *Review of Economic Studies*, **21** (2), 81–106.
Robinson, J. (1956), *The Accumulation of Capital*, London: Macmillan.
Robinson, J. (1962a), *Essays in the Theory of Economic Growth*, London: Macmillan.
Robinson, J. (1962b), *Economic Philosophy*, London: C.A. Watts & Co.
Robinson, J. (1974), 'History versus Equilibrium', *Indian Economic Journal*, **21** (3), 202–13.
Rogers, C. (1989), *Money, Interest and Capital: a Study in the Foundations of Monetary Theory*, Cambridge: Cambridge University Press.
Rogerson, R., Shimer, R. and R. Wright (2005), 'Search Theoretic Models of the Labor Market: A Survey', *Journal of Economic Literature*, **43** (4), 959–88.
Romer, D. (1986), 'A Simple General Equilibrium Version of the Baumol Tobin Model', *Quarterly Journal of Economics*, **101** (4), 663–86.
Romer, D. (1996), *Advanced Macroeconomics*, New York: McGraw Hill.
Romer, P.M. (1986), 'Increasing Returns and Long run Growth', *Journal of Political Economy*, **94** (5), 1002–37.
Rosenberg, A. (1983), 'If Economics Isn't Science, What Is It?', *Philosophical Forum*, **14** (3/4), 296–314.
Rosenberg, A. (1986), 'What Rosenberg's Philosophy of Economics Is Not,' *Philosophy of Science*, **53** (1), 127–32.
Rosenberg, A. (1992), *Economics: Mathematical Politics or Science of Diminishing Returns*, Chicago: University of Chicago Press.
Rosenberg, A. (1994), 'Does evolutionary theory give comfort or inspiration to economics?' in P. Mirowski (ed.), *Natural Images in Economic Thought: Market Read in Tooth and Claw*, Cambridge: Cambridge University Press, pp. 384–407.
Rosner, P. (1994), 'Is Hayek's Theory of Business Cycles an Austrian Theory?', in J. Birner and R.W. van Zijp (eds) (1994), *Hayek: Co-ordination and Evolution*, London: Routledge, pp. 51–66.
Rothbard, M.N. (1970), *Man, Economy and State*, Los Angeles: Nash Publishing.
Rothbard, M.N. (1985), 'Professor Hébert on entrepreneurship', *Journal of Libertarian Studies*, **7** (2), 281–86.
Rothbard, M.N. (1987), 'Breaking out of the Walrasian box: the cases of Schumpeter and Hansen', *Review of Austrian Economics*, **1** (1), 97–108.
Rothbard, M.N. (1995), *Economic Thought Before Adam Smith: an Austrian Perspective on the History of Economic Thought*, vol. I, Aldershot, UK and Brookfield, USA: Edward Elgar.

Rothschild, M. (1973), 'Models of Market Organization with Imperfect Information: A Survey', *Journal of Political Economy*, **81** (6), 1283–1308.

Rothschild, M. and J.E. Stiglitz (1976), 'Equilibrium in Competitive Insurance Markets: An Essay on the Economics of Imperfect Information', *Quarterly Journal of Economics*, **90** (4), 629–49.

Salop, S.C. and J.E. Stiglitz (1982), 'The Theory of Sales: A Simple model of Equilibrium Price Dispersion with Identical Agents', *American Economic Review*, **72** (5), 1121–30.

Samuelson, L. (2002), 'Evolution and Game Theory', *Journal of Economic Perspectives*, **16** (2), 47–66.

Samuelson, P.A. (1947), *Foundations of Economic Analysis*, enlarged edition, Cambridge, MA: Harvard University Press.

Samuelson, P.A. (1962), 'Parable and Realism in Capital Theory: The Surrogate Production Function', *Review of Economic Studies*, **29** (3), 193–206.

Samuelson, P.A. (1966), 'A Summing Up', *Quarterly Journal of Economics*, **80** (4), 568–83.

Saviotti, P.P. (ed.) (2003), *Applied Evolutionary Economics: New Empirical Methods and Simulation Techniques*, Cheltenham, UK and Brookfield, USA: Edward Elgar.

Say, J.B. (1821), *Letters to Mr. Malthus*, New York: Kelley.

Say, J.B. (1880), *A Treatise on Political Economy*, New York: Kelley.

Scarf, H.E. (1960), 'Some Examples of Global Instability of the Competitive Equilibrium', *International Economic Review*, **1**, 157–72.

Scarf, H.E. (1973), *The Computation of Economic Equilibria*, New Haven: Yale University Press.

Scarf, H.E. (1984), 'The computation of equilibrium prices' in H.E. Scarf and J.J. Shoven (eds), *Applied General Equilibrium Analysis*, Cambridge, UK: Cambridge University Press, pp. 1–50.

Scarf, H.E. (1987), 'Computation of general equilibria' in J. Eatwell, M. Milgate and P. Newman (eds), *The New Palgrave: General Equilibrium*, London: Macmillan, pp. 84–96.

Schabas, M. (1990), *A World Ruled by Number: William Stanley Jevons and the Rise of Mathematical Economics*, Princeton: Princeton University Press.

Schinkel, M.P. (2001), *Disequilibrium Theory: Reflections Towards a Revival of Learning*, Ph.D thesis, University of Maastricht.

Schmidt, Ch. (1990), 'Game theory and economics: an historical survey', *Revue d'Économique Politique*, **100** (5), 589–618.

Schoorl, E. (1980), *Jean-Baptiste Say: Hoofdstukken uit zijn leven en economisch denken*, Ph.D. Thesis, University of Amsterdam.

Schumpeter, J.A. (1942), *Capitalism, Socialism and Democracy*, New York: Harper & Row.

Schumpeter, J.A. (1949), 'Science and Ideology', *American Economic Review*, **39** (2), 346–59.

Schumpeter, J.A. (1954), *History of Economic Analysis*, London: Allen & Unwin.

Sebastiani, M., (ed.) (1992), *The Notion of Equilibrium in the Keynesian Theory*, London: Macmillan.

Selgin, G.A. and L.H. White (1994), 'How Would the Invisible Hand Handle Money?', *Journal of Economic Literature*, **32** (4), 1718–49.

Shackle, G.L.S. (1967), *The Years of High Theory: Invention and Tradition in Economic Thought 1926–1939*, Cambridge, UK: Cambridge University Press.

Shackle, G.L.S. (1972), *Epistemics & Economics: A Critique of Economic Doctrines*, Cambridge, UK: Cambridge University Press.

Shapiro, C. and J.E. Stiglitz (1984), 'Equilibrium Unemployment as a Worker Discipline Device', *American Economic Review*, **74** (3), 433–44.

Sheffrin, S. (1983), *Rational Expectations*, Cambridge, UK: Cambridge University Press.

Shoven, J.B. and J. Whalley (1984), 'Applied General Equilibrium Models of Taxation and International Trade: An Introduction and Survey', *Journal of Economic Literature*, **22** (3), 1007–51.

Simonde de Sismondi, J.C.L. (1991), *New Principles of Political Economy*, translated and annotated by R. Hyse, New Brunswick: Transaction Publishers.

Siven, C.H. (1997), 'Capital theory and equilibrium method in Wicksell's cumulative process', *History of Political Economy*, **29** (2), 201–17.

Skaggs, N.T. (1994), 'The Place of J.S. Mill in the Development of British Monetary Orthodoxy', *History of Political Economy*, **26** (4), 539–67.

Skaggs, N.T. (1995), 'Henry Thornton and the development of classical monetary economics', *Canadian Journal of Economics*, **28** (4b), 1212–27.

Skidelsky, R., (1992), *John Maynard Keynes: The Economist as Savior 1920–1937*, London: Penguin Books.

Skinner, A.S. (1965), 'Economics and History: The Scottish Enlightenment', *Scottish Journal of Political Economy*, **12** (1), 1–22.

Skinner, A.S. (1967), 'Say's law: origins and content', *Economica N.S.*, **34** (May), 153–66.

Skinner, A.S. (1970), 'Introduction' in A. Smith, *Wealth of Nations*, London: Penguin, pp. 11–97.

Skinner, A.S. (1972), 'Adam Smith: Philosophy and Science', *Scottish Journal of Political Economy*, **29** (3), pp. 307–319, reprinted in J.C Wood (ed.) (1984), *Adam Smith: Criticial Assessments*, vol. I, London: Croom Helm, pp. 460–77.

Smale, S. (1976), 'Dynamics in General Equilibrium Theory', *American Economic Review, Papers and Proceedings*, **66** (2), 288–94.

Smale, S. (1987), 'Global Analysis in Economic Theory, in J. Eatwell, M. Milgate and P. Newman (eds), *The New Palgrave: General Equilibrium*, London: Macmillan, pp. 162–6.

Smith, A. (1759[1976]), *Theory of Moral Sentiments*, in D.D. Raphael and A.L. Macfie (eds) (1976), *The Glasgow Edition of the Works and Correspondence of Adam Smith*, vol. I, Indianapolis: Liberty Fund.

Smith, A. (1795a[1980]), *The Principles which Lead and Direct Philosophical Enquiries; Illustrated by the History of Astronomy*, W.P.D. Wightman and J.C. Bryce (eds) (1980), *The Glasgow Edition of the Works and Correspondence of Adam Smith*, vol. III, Indianapolis: Liberty Fund.

Smith, A. (1795b[1980]), *The Principles which Lead and Direct Philosophical Enquiries; Illustrated by the History of Ancient Physics*, W.P.D. Wightman and J.C. Bryce (eds) (1980), *The Glasgow Edition of the Works and Correspondence of Adam Smith*, vol. III, Indianapolis: Liberty Fund, 1982.

Smith, A. (1937), *An Inquiry into the Nature and Causes of the Wealth of Nations*, E. Cannan (ed.), New York: Modern Library.

Sober, E. (1983), 'Equilibrium explanations', *Philosophical Studies*, **43** (2), 201–10.

Solow, R.M. (1956), 'A contribution to the theory of economic growth', *Quarterly Journal of Economics*, **70** (1), 65–94.

Solow, R.M. (1957), 'Technical Change and the Aggregate Production Function', *Review of Economics and Statistics*, **39** (3), 312–20.

Solow, R.M. (1963), *Capital Theory and the Rate of Return*, Amsterdam: North Holland.

Solow, R.M. (1988), 'Growth Theory and After', *American Economic Review*, **78** (3), 307–17.

Solow, R.M. (1998), *Monopolistic Competition and Macroeconomic Theory*, Cambridge, UK: Cambridge University Press.

Sowell, T. (1972a), *Say's Law: an Historical Analysis*, Princeton: Princeton University Press.

Sowell, T. (1972b), 'Sismondi: a neglected pioneer', *History of Political Economy*, **4** (1), 62–88.

Sowell, T. (1974), *Classical Economics Reconsidered*, Princeton: Princeton University Press.

Spence, A.M. (1973), 'Job Market Signaling', *Quarterly Journal of Economics*, **87** (3), 355–74.

Spence, A.M. (1974), *Market Signaling: Informational Transfer in Hiring and Related Screening Processes*, Cambridge, MA: Harvard University Press.

Spengler, J.J. (1945), 'The Physiocrats and Say's law of markets', *Journal of Political Economy*, **53** (3), reprinted in J.J. Spengler and W.R. Allen (eds) (1960), *Essays in Economic Thought: from Aristotle to Marshall*, Chicago, IL: McNally, pp. 161–213.

Spengler, J.J. (1954), 'Richard Cantillon: First of the Moderns', *Journal of Political Economy*, **62** (4), 281–95 and 406–24.

Spengler, J.J. (1968), 'Exogenous and Endogenous Influences in the Formation of Post-1870 Economic Thought: a Sociology of Knowlegde Approach', in V. Eagly (ed.), *Events, Ideology and Economic Theory: the Determinants of Progress in the Development of Economic Analysis*, Detroit: Wayne State University Press, pp. 159–187 and 191–204.

Spengler, J.J. (1984), 'Boisguilbert's economic views vis à vis those of contemporary réformateurs', *History of Political Economy*, **16** (1), 69–88.

Spiegel, H.W. (1971), *The Growth of Economic Thought*, 2nd edition, Durham: Duke University Press.

Spiegel, H.W. (1975), 'A Note on the Equilibrium Concept in the History of Economics', *Économie Appliquée*, **28**, 609–17.

Sraffa, P. (1960), *Production of Commodities by Means of Commodities: Prelude to a Critique of Economic Theory*, Cambridge, UK: Cambridge University Press.

Steuart, J. (1767), *An Inquiry into the Principles of Political Oeconomy*, in R.L. Meek (ed.) (1973), *Precursors of Adam Smith 1750–1775*, London: J.M. Dent & Sons, pp. 147–72.

Steedman, I. (1997), 'Jevons's Theory of Political Economy and the "marginalist revolution"', *European Journal of the History of Economic Thought*, **4** (1), 43–64.

Stewart, D. (1793[1980]), *Account of the Life and Writings of Adam Smith, LL.D.*, in W.P.D. Wightman and J.C. Bryce (eds) (1980), *The Glasgow Edition of the Works and Correspondence of Adam Smith*, vol. III, Indianapolis: Liberty Fund.

Stigler, G.J. (1958), 'Ricardo and the 93 Per Cent Labor Theory of Value', *American Economic Review*, **48** (3), 357–67.

Stigltiz, J.E. (2002), 'Information and the Change in the Paradigm in Economics', *American Economic Review*, **92** (3), 460–501.

Stiglitz, J.E. (2004), 'Reflections on the state of the theory of monopolistic competition', in S. Brakman and B.J. Heijdra (eds), *The Monopolistic Competition Revolution in Retrospect*, Cambridge, UK: Cambridge University Press, pp. 134–48.

Stirati, A. (1995). 'Smith's legacy and the definitions of the natural wage in Ricardo', *Journal of the History of Economic Thought*, **17** (1), 106–32.

Streissler, E.W. (1972), 'To what extent was the Austrian school marginalist?', *History of Political Economy*, **4** (2), 426–41.

Streissler, E.W. (1990a), 'The influence of German Economics on the work of the Menger and Marshall', in B.J. Caldwell (ed.), *Carl Menger and his Legacy in Economics*, annual supplement to vol. 22 of *History of Political Economy*, Durham: Duke University Press, pp. 31–68.

Streissler, E.W. (1990b), 'Menger, Böhm Bawerk and Wieser: the origins of the Austrian school', in K. Hennings and W. Samuels (eds), *Neoclassical Economic Theory, 1870–1930*, Dordrecht: Kluwer.

Swan, T.W. (1956), 'Economic Growth and Capital Accumulation', *Economic Record*, **32** (2), 334–61.

Teulings, C.N. and J. Hartog (1998), *Corporatism or Competition? Labour Contracts, Institutions and Wage Structures in International Comparison*, Cambridge, UK: Cambridge University Press.

Thomson, H.F. (1965), 'Adam Smith's philosophy of science', *Quarterly Journal of Economics*, **79** (2), 212–33.

Thornton, H. (1802), *An Enquiry into the Nature and Effects of the Paper Credit of Great Britain*, F.A. Hayek (ed.) (1939), London: Allen and Unwin.

Tieben, B. (1997), 'Misunderstandings and other coordination failures in the Hayek–Keynes controversy', in W. Keizer, B. Tieben and R.W. van Zijp (eds), *Austrian Economics in Debate*, London: Routledge, pp. 95–126.

Tieben, B. and W. Keizer (1997), 'Introduction: Austrian Economics in Debate', in W. Keizer, B. Tieben and R.W. van Zijp (eds), *Austrian Economics in Debate*, London: Routledge, pp. 1–21.

Trautwein, H.M. (1996), 'Money, Equilibrium, and the Business Cycle: Hayek's Wicksellian Dichotomy', *History of Political Economy*, **28** (1), 27–55.

Trejos, A. and R. Wright (1995), 'Search, Bargaining, Money, and Prices', *Journal of Political Economy*, **103** (1), 118–41.

Turgot, A.R.J. (1766), *Réflexions sur la formation et la distribution des richesses*, in E. Daire (ed.), *Oeuvres de Turgot*, Paris: Guillaumin.

Turgot, A.R.J. (1769), *Valeurs et monnaies*, in E. Daire (ed.), *Oeuvres de Turgot*, Paris: Guillaumin.

Vanberg, V.J. (1986), 'Spontaneous market order and social rules: a critical examination of F.A. Hayek's theory of cultural evolution', *Economics and Philosophy*, **2** (1), 75–100.

Vanberg, V.J. (1994), *Rules and Choice in Economics*, London: Routledge.

Van den Berg, G.J. (1999), 'Empirical Inference with Equilibrium Search Models of the Labour Market', *Economic Journal*, **109** (June), 283–306.

Van der Hoog, S. (2005), *Microeconomic Disequilibrium Dynamics*, Amsterdam: Thela Thesis.

Varian, H.R. (1992), *Microeconomic Analysis*, 3rd edition, New York: Norton.

Vaughn, K.I. (1980), *John Locke: Economist and Social Scientist*, London: Athlone.

Vaughn, K.I. (1992), 'The problem of order in Austrian economics: Kirzner versus Lachmann', *Review of Political Economy*, **4** (3), 251–74.

Vaughn, K.I. (1994), *Austrian Economics in America: the Migration of a Tradition*, Cambridge, UK: Cambridge University Press.

Vega-Redondo, F. (1996), *Evolution, Games and Economic Behaviour*, Oxford, UK: Oxford University Press.

Verburg, R.M. (1991), *The Two Faces of Interest: The Problem of Order and the Origins of Political Economy and Sociology as Distinctive Fields of Inquiry in the Scottish Enlightenment*, Ph.D thesis, Rotterdam: Tinbergen Institute.

Vickers, D. (1959), *Studies in the Theory of Money, 1690–1776*, Philadelphia: Chilton Company.

Viner, J. (1927), 'Adam Smith and Laissez Faire', *Journal of Political Economy*, **35** (April), pp. 198–232, reprinted in J.J. Spengler and W.R. Allen (eds) (1960), *Essays in Economic Thought: from Aristotle to Marshall*, Chicago: McNally, pp. 305–29.

Visser, H. (1971), 'Neutraal geld: een overzicht', *De Economist*, **119** (4), 393–439.

Visser, H. (2002), 'Neutrality of money', in B. Snowdon and H.R. Vane (eds), *An Encyclopedia of Macroeconomics*, Cheltenham, UK and Brookfield, USA: Edward Elgar, pp. 526–33.

Vromen, J.J. (1995), *Economic Evolution: An Enquiry into the Foundations of New Institutional Economics*, London: Routledge.

Vromen, J.J. (2004), 'Taking evolution seriously. What difference does it make for economics?' in J.B. Davis, A. Marciano and J. Runde (eds), *The Elgar Companion to Economics and Philosophy*, Cheltenham, UK and Brookfield, USA: Edward Elgar.

Wald, A. (1936), 'Über einige Gleichungssysteme der mathematischen Ökonomie', *Zeitschrift für Nationalökonomie*, **7** (5), 637–70.

Walker, D.A. (1983), *William Jaffé's Essays on Walras*, Cambridge: Cambridge University Press.

Walker, D. (1984), 'Is Walras's theory of general equilibrium a normative science?', *History of Political Economy*, **16** (3), 445–69.

Walker, D.A. (1987), 'Walras's theories of tatonnement', *Journal of Political Economy*, **95** (4), 758–74.

Walker, D.A. (1988), 'Iteration in Walras's theory of tatonnement', *De Economist*, **136** (3), 299–316.

Walras, L. (1909), 'Economique et Mécanique', reprinted in *Métro-economica*, **12** (1), 3–13.

Walras, L. (1954), *Elements of Pure Economics, or the Theory of Social Wealth*, translated by W. Jaffé, Homewood, Ill.: R.D. Irwin.

Walsh, V. and H. Gram (1980), *Classical and Neoclassical Theories of General Equilibrium: Historical Origins and Mathematical Structure*, Oxford: Oxford University Press.

Weintraub, E.R. (1979), *Microfoundations: the Compatibility of Microeconomics and Macroeconomics*, Cambridge: Cambridge University Press.

Weintraub, E.R. (1985a), 'Appraising General Equilibrium Analysis', *Economics and Philosophy*, **1** (1), 23–38.

Weintraub, E.R. (1985b), *General Equilibrium Analysis*, Ann Arbor: University of Michigan Press.

Weintraub, E.R. (1988), 'The Neo-Walrasian Program is Empirically Progressive', in N. de Marchi (ed.), *The Popperian Legacy in Economics*, Cambridge, UK: Cambridge University Press, pp. 213–227.

Weintraub, E.R. (1991), *Stabilizing Dynamics: Constructing Economic Knowledge*, Cambridge: Cambridge University Press.

Weintraub, E.R. (2002), *How Economics Became a Mathematical Science*, Durham: Duke University Press.

Wetenschappelijke Raad voor het Regeringsbeleid (2007), *Identificatie met Nederland*, rapport no. 79, Amsterdam: Amsterdam University Press.

White, L.H. (1984), *Free Banking in Britain: Theory, Experience, and Debate, 1800–1845*, Cambridge: Cambridge University Press.

White, M.V. (1989), 'Why are there no supply and demand curves in Jevons?', *History of Political Economy*, **21** (3), 425–56.

Wicksell, K. (1898), *Geldzins und Güterpreise*, Aalen: Scientia Verlag.

Wicksell, K. (1935), *Lectures on Political Economy*, 2 vols., London: Routledge & Kegan Paul.

Wieser, F. von (1893), *Natural Value*, New York: Augustus M. Kelley.

Wieser, F. von (1927), *Social Economics*, New York: Augustus M. Kelley.

Williamson, J.G. (1971), *Karl Helfferich 1872–1924, Economist, Financier, Politician*, New Jersey: Princeton University Press.

Wilson, T. (1940), 'Capital theory and the trade cycle', *Review of Economic Studies*, **7** (3), 169–79.

Witt, U. (1989), 'The evolution of economic institutions as a propagation process', *Public Choice*, **62**, 155–172, reprinted in U. Witt (2003), *The Evolving Economy, Essays on the Evolutionary Approach to Economics*, Cheltenham, UK and Brookfield, USA: Edward Elgar.

Witt, U. (1994), 'The theory of societal evolution: Hayek's unfinished legacy', in J. Birner and R.W. van Zijp (eds) (1994), *Hayek: Co-ordination and Evolution*, London: Routledge, pp. 178–89.

Witt, U. (1997), 'Self organization and economics: What is new?', *Structural Change and Economic Dynamics*, **8**, pp. 489–507, reprinted in U. Witt (2003), *The Evolving Economy, Essays on the Evolutionary Approach to Economics*, Cheltenham, UK and Brookfield, USA: Edward Elgar.

Worland, S.T. (1976), 'Mechanistic analogy and Smith on exchange', *Review of Social Economy*, **34** (3), pp. 245–257, in J.C. Wood (ed.) (1984), *Adam Smith: Critical Assessments*, vol. I, London: Croom Helm, pp. 601–11.

Wright, R. (2005), 'Introduction' to 'Models of Monetary Economies II: The Next Generation', *International Economic Review*, **46** (2), 305–16.

Yeager, L.B. (1997), 'Austrian themes in a reconstructed macroeconomics', in W. Keizer, B. Tieben and R.W. van Zijp (eds) (1997), *Austrian Economics in Debate*, London: Routledge, pp. 22–41.

Young, J.T. (1986), 'The impartial spectator and natural jurisprudence: an interpretation of Adam Smith's theory of the natural price', *History of Political Economy*, **18** (3), 365–82.

Zappia, C. (1997), 'Private information, contractual arrangements and Hayek's knowledge problem', in W. Keizer, B. Tieben and R.W. van Zijp (eds) (1997), *Austrian Economics in Debate*, London: Routledge, pp. 264–84.

Zappia, C. (2001), 'Equilibrium and disequilibrium dynamics in the 1930s', *Journal of the History of Economic Thought*, **23** (1), 55–75.

Zijp, R.W. van (1992), *Austrian and New Classical Business Cycle Theories*, Amsterdam: Thesis Publishers.

Zijp, R.W. van (1995), 'Lachmann and the wilderness: on Lachmann's radical subjectivism', *European Journal of the History of Economic Thought*, **2** (2), 412–33.

Index